IN SEARCH OF WESTERN OREGON

In Search of Western Oregon

by

Ralph Friedman

All photos by author unless otherwise noted.

The CAXTON PRINTERS, Ltd.
Caldwell, Idaho
1990

Library of Congress Cataloging-in-Publication Data

Friedman, Ralph.
  In search of western Oregon / by Ralph Friedman.
      p.   cm.
  Includes index.
  ISBN 0-87004-332-3 : $14.95
  1. Oregon--Description and travel--1981- --Guide-books.
2. Automobile travel--Oregon--Guide-books.   3. Oregon--
Description and travel--1981- --Views.   I. Title.
F874.3.F68   1990
917.9504'43--dc20   90-43035
                                                          CIP

Lithographed and Bound in the United States of America by
The Caxton Printers, Ltd.
Caldwell, Idaho 83605
149586

To Phoebe and Kya

Table of Contents

List of Illustrations

Page

Page

Page

Page

List of Abbreviations

m	mile or miles
E	east or eastern
W	west or western
S	south or southern
N	north or northern
L	left
R	right
O	Oregon (road designation)
US	United States or federal road designation
CB	covered bridge
SP	state park
CP	county park
FS	US Forest Service
BLM	US Bureau of Land Management
CG	campground
PA	picnic area
BL	boat landing
BR	boat ramp
DS	dumping station
FHP	facilities for handicapped persons
DLC	donation land claim
HS	high school
PS	public school
PO	post office
PM	postmaster
Rec	recreation (al)
Res	reservoir
RR	railroad
RY	railway
pop	population
inc	incorporated
est	established
Mtn	mountain
Jct	junction
station	service station
*	off the main road
**	off prime secondary road from main road

Other abbreviations are readily identifiable.

A Personal Word

If not for the memory of my beloved wife I would have dedicated this book to Tom McCall, who understood precisely what I was trying to do. "You're interpreting Oregon," he once told me. Another time, he said: "You're showing Oregonians the real Oregon." Impressed, he remarked: "You're doing the work of fifty people."

Had cancer not dragged my wife to its dark and hideous lair, this book would have been completed at least three years earlier. Her taking brought on waves of trauma that I am sure need no further explanation. To keep the travel portion of the book current I made repeated trips throughout Western Oregon, covering some of the same ground nine or ten times.

Actually, this book covers more than Western Oregon. It extends from the Pacific to US 97 (and bits east of it), thus also treating parts of Central Oregon.

Why did I not cover the entire state? The question is sure to be asked and deserves an answer. Basically, employing the format I have chosen for this book, a text on overall Oregon would have been too large and too expensive for my liking.

For the "finding of places" composition of this book I have retained the style which, says booksellers, made Oregon for the Curious so successful — best-selling travel guide ever written on the state. (It has been estimated to have been read by about a million people.)

But this offering is more. Where Oregon for the Curious is basically an "action" book, this will prove valuable to people who cannot step out of the house to see the state. It is strong on history, literature, mythology, folklore, anecdotal material and personal profiles, all oriented to specific places and to the state as a whole. It ought to find a niche in educational institutions, from grade schools to universities, and will be, I hope, a sturdy and friendly guide to at least the western portion of the state.

For the traveler, this book has eliminated the obsolescent places in Oregon for the Curious and added hundreds of newfound places. The material on the flora and fauna of the section is stronger and there is much more on geology, clamming, beachcombing and fishing.

There is something else here which I think is a first in any book of this kind. Repeatedly I have shown what was in many towns and hamlets in the year 1915 as contrasted to the contemporary setting.

I chose the year 1915 for two reasons. Firstly, I regarded it as the most definitive juncture – or breaking point – between the horse age and the automobile age. Secondly, the data on that year is accurate and plentiful.

Thus, travelers with a bit of imagination can envision what the towns and hamlets looked like before the automobile was the only way to go.

Some readers may wonder why there are so many cemeteries in this book. I have found that cemeteries comprise excellent resource material for an understanding of the history, demography, religion and life of the peoples of the various localities. There is in the location of the burial ground and writ upon the gravestones a record of whence and when came the people, their spiritual expressions, and their urgent words to those on this side of the mystic river.

I could caution travelers obsessed with reaching all the off-the-beaten-path ("curious") places in the book to be realistic in their planning. Two of my friends, determined to pinpoint and photograph every place between Portland and Eugene listed in Oregon for the Curious, estimated it would take them three days. (By all places, of course, they meant those sites peripherally east and west of Oregon 99E.) I suggested it would require them five days. All of us were wrong. It took my friends eight days to complete the trip, and some places they did not photograph because they were running too far behind schedule.

If the couple began the same venture with this book in hand, rest assured their journey would be at least twice as time-consuming.

This book can be used at any point within its confines. Simply turn to the voluminous index, locate your position (by the last town passed, if nothing else), and carry on from there.

Tom McCall once asked me, "Have you ever been lost?" "No," I replied, "but I sure as hell have been misdirected."

This book will not misdirect you. Following the text, there is little chance of your being lost, even in the most far-flung outreaches of the area.

This book is not concerned with where to bed down because such places change, because it is assumed that in tourist spheres (such as the Coast), facilities are abundant, because you are never more than an hour or so from a commercial accommodation, and because, if you have an RV or carry a sleeping bag, there is a campground close at hand wherever you are. (Consult the index.)

Except where accommodation and food facilities possess keen tourist interest and are open to tourist viewing, they are not included here. Prices are not listed because, in general, they are unstable.

The vast majority of travel guides list mileage on a cumulative basis. Using this book it will soon become obvious why mileage here is point-to-point. The odometer therefore becomes a key instrument in your travels.

It will soon be evident to you that mileage variations arise. An odometer as utilized is an imprecise and inconsistent instrument. How you drive is even more critical in the recording of mileage. For proof, start from home to work or to the supermarket three days in a row (or in the space of a week), each time noting the exact mileage – and by exact I mean to the tenth of the mile. If you travel more than five miles each round trip, the chances are very slender that you will have a series of identical readings. But, with an ounce of patience, this book will get you to every place listed.

As with *Oregon for the Curious,* this book — except for tours, which are very easy to follow – has been arranged in the simplest, yet most precise form possible, by section and road. Areas off the main roads are indented and are preceded by an asterisk (*). When the specific indented section ends, you are back on the key road. In addition, phrase guides have been inserted at many returns to the main road, to guard against confusion.

It goes without saying, though it is noted in the text, that the privacy of persons and places be respected. A farmer in Linn County said it best: "I like folks taking pictures of my barn from the road but I'm not happy about their opening my gate and going into the barn without asking me."

This book is my deepest legacy to Oregon. I hope that the energies which I poured into its research for almost a decade will reflect enough fire to charge up the spirits of the adventurous and warm the souls of the imaginative and poetic.

As for Tom McCall, I think of him wherever I travel, and somehow, out of sentiment, perhaps, I keep telling myself that he is saying, "Well done, Ralph."

IN SEARCH OF WESTERN OREGON

The Oregon Coast — US 101

Astoria calls itself Oregon's oldest city and is joined in that claim by the official *Oregon Blue Book.* The more zealous of the Astorians also insist that their city is the "Williamsburg of the West." But for the majority of people, living in fear that still another economic calamity may befall the city and render them closer to hard times, history is for those who have the luxury to afford it.

Still, the past will not go away, nor should it, and Astoria has plenty of the past. Unfortunately, relatively little has been written of the Native Americans (henceforth to be designated as Indians) who inhabited the NW corner of Oregon for millennia before the Yankees arrived. Indian history for most writers begins with Concomly, the one-eyed Chinook chieftain who was a contemporary of the first land-based traders.

The first European Americans (henceforth to be designated as Americans) to see what became Astoria arrived May 11, 1792 on the fully-rigged windjammer *Columbia Rediviva,* commanded by the one-eyed Revolutionary War hero, Robert Gray. Gray's 5th officer, John Boit, thought the place would be fine to set up a trading post but Gray was not impressed. Although his was the first vessel to enter the "Great River of the West," he showed little enthusiasm for exploring the Columbia and not much patience for doing in-depth business here. After a short buying spree, Gray's crew came away with salmon purchased at "two for a board Nail" and furs gotten in exchange for "Copper and Cloth." Then Gray moved on, northward, toward Vancouver Island, where the big marketing was supposed to be.

There is sufficient evidence that in the next decade some ships on the west Pacific trade route paused at or near Astoria to barter with the Indians. But after Gray left a period of 13 years elapsed before the next Yankees arrived. They included a young Indian mother and her babe, a black man, and a wife-beating French-Canadian, and they traveled as the Lewis and Clark party.

It is likely that at one point or another some members of the party trod where the business district is now located but the fort they built to spend the winter of 1805–06 was 7 m. SW of the city.

What history-minded Astorians consider to be the birth of the community came in April 1811, when John Jacob Astor's ship, the *Tonquin,* arrived to set up a trading post. Two of Astor's partners, Duncan McDougal and David Stuart, wanted to have a good look at the lower Columbia but the skipper of the *Tonquin,* the insufferable Capt. Jonathan Thorn, was itching to land his cargo, and the compromise site was a landmark called Point George. A post was built and named Fort Astoria, for the man who financed the undertaking.

Astor's maritime contingent was joined the following February by the overland, hard-hit, emaciated Wilson Price Hunt party. Added to its problems was the cruelty-induced madness of John Day, a Virginia backwoodsman, who, stripped of all his garb by Indians in winter, almost starved and froze, whichever would have come first. In compensation, John Day is remembered in Oregon by 2 rivers, a valley, a town, and fossil beds.

The War of 1812 finished Astor's Pacific Fur Company as far as the Oregon Country was concerned. Representatives of the rival North West Company, headquartered in Montreal, convinced the frightened Americans that British warships would soon arrive and take the post by force. Wouldn't it be more prudent and profitable, they argued, for Astor's people to sell the post while they could? The Astorians caved in though there was no sign of a gunship — one arrived about 8 weeks later — and on Oct. 23, 1813 the bargain was sealed and Fort Astoria was on its way to becoming Fort George.

The British held Astoria under the name of Fort George until 1818, when it was given back to the US. But the North West Company continued to maintain the post until 1821, when the Norwesters joined forces with Hudson's Bay Co. Dr. John McLoughlin, an HBC man, grew increasingly disillusioned with the location, which he felt too isolated for large-scale operations, and in 1824 moved the business upstream to what is now Vancouver, Wash., where he established Fort Vancouver. He left behind a lookout station and minor trading post but these faded away and by the time the first emigrants arrived in 1844, there was no trace of Fort George.

Clatsop County was est. June 22, 1844 but Astoria is 18th among Oregon cities in rank of incorporation (1876). The first PO in the American Far West opened in Astoria in March 1847 and 2 years later the first American Customs House in the W was founded.

Once it became recognized as the trading center of the lower Columbia, Astoria thrived. In 1850 its population was already 250, a large number for that period. With the building of the first salmon cannery on the Columbia in 1866, Astoria entered a long span of prominent fish processing; in time, salmon canning became Astoria's chief industry. Then came a formidable fishing fleet, more canneries, sawmills, flouring mills, an ever increase in residents. In 1911, when Astoria observed its Centennial, it was the 2d largest city in Oregon.

In 1920 Astoria numbered 14,027 inhabitants and was still the state's most populous city behind Portland. Two years later disaster struck. In 1922, December 9 was only 2 hours old when fire erupted on the waterfront. In the next 35 hours, before the conflagration was brought under control, the entire business district had been wiped out; 32 city blocks — 40 acres of buildings — had been reduced to ashes. Astoria rebuilt but its population diminished. By 1940 its inhabitants had fallen in number to less than 10,500 and the figure has since hovered between 10,000 and 11,000.

For long Astoria (at least some of it) profited handsomely from lumber, fishing, and canning. But these economic bases are gone or have seriously been weakened. The depletion of timber closed the mills; the depletion of salmon crippled the fleet and dealt a harsh blow to commercial canning. (For more on this, see "The Glorious Fisherman" in author's *A Touch of Oregon*.)

For some years Astoria was one of the most cosmopolitan cities in the state, with sizeable populations of Chinese, Swedes, and Finns. The Finns were the dominant ethnic force and their cultural presence was everywhere, with their steam baths, choral and folk dance groups, cafes, meeting halls, stores and daily newspaper. Street signs were posted in Finnish as well as English, probably the only city in Oregon to be bilingual in this respect.

In the first or second decade of this century there arose a story in Astoria that is now part of Oregon folklore and tells better than anything else how Finnish Astoria was.

A 16 year old girl from Finland, who had traveled to the US to live with her grandparents in Astoria, arrived unmet at the RR station. Failing to see her grandparents and unable to speak English, she slumped down on the wooden platform of the depot and began to sob. Seeing her anguish, a Chinese passerby paused to ask what was wrong. Tearfully, she told him. "Where do your grandparents live?" he asked. She took from the pocket of her dress a slip of paper and gave it to the man. "I know where this house is at," he said. "I will take you there." And he picked up her suitcase.

As they walked, the girl asked, "How is it that you speak Finnish?" "In Astoria," the Chinese good samaritan replied, "if you do not speak Finnish you had better move elsewhere."

According to Julia Ruuttila, former resident of Astoria and labor historian, the Chinese were brought to Astoria in the 1880s to break a gillnetters strike. They had not been told of the situation and were harshly punished for their unwitting scabbing. Those who did not perish at the hands of the furious fishermen or fled to a safer clime became menials, advancing to small businessmen.

Astoria winters can be depressing but contemporary tolerance to them is certainly an improvement over 1813. On December 24 of that year, Alexander Henry, Jr. noted in his journal: "The almost incessant rain we have had is truly unpleasant, and I fear will have a bad effect on our men, who are now building a house for themselves; they are daily exposed to the inclemency of the weather, wet to the skin, tramping through mud and water all day, and at night without other shelter than bars covered with mats, which must be very damp. Even in the garret of our storehouses, which is perfectly tight and stanch, things become moldy and will rot. During the rainy season there is no moving out of doors, except in mud and water. If you step on a stone or billet of wood, ten to one you measure your length on the ground; everything is slippery with green moss, even stockades and buildings are becoming incrusted."

Early city Astoria had a hard time adjusting to the age of growth and speed, particularly the latter. In 1880, when the city was bursting with a pop. of 2,803, life on the streets was endangered by the recklessness with which some people rode horses. After numerous complaints by those scared half out of their wits by the hot riders, the city council set a speed limit for beasts of burden at 6 miles an hour on unsupported streets and 4 miles an hour on roads built on pilings.

When bicycles became the vogue they also posed a problem, creating traffic hazards. Acting decisively to correct the situation, the Oregon legislature passed a law stating that cyclists should stop whenever they approached within 100 yards of a team, dismount, and remain standing until the horses had passed. The *Daily Astorian* didn't think the law went far enough. Its editorial of July 13, 1866 reads: "This law . . . should be amended so as to compel the bicyclist to take off his hat and remain uncovered while the driver of the team is passing."

Much of Astoria's history is emblazoned on a 525-ft. spiral frieze of the 125-ft.-high **Astoria Column** atop Coxcomb Hill, 1.2 m. up 16th St. from Marine Dr. Inside the tube a circular stairway of 166 steps climbs to a viewpoint platform. The vistas encompass sea, rivers, forests, hills, towns, and farms on both sides of the Columbia.

At 14th and Madison, near Column, **Pioneer Cemetery,** with markers back to early 1850s.

On or off Marine Dr., which is both US 101 and US 30:

Columbia River Maritime Museum, 1792 Marine Dr., one of the truly great maritime museums of the nation. Skillfully crafted, dramatically arranged — Astoria's brightest jewel.

Behind museum, as part of it, *Lightship Columbia,* last lightship active on Pacific Coast.

Pier 11, off 11th St.: mall of zesty shops with picture windows in restaurant inviting diners to watch ships passing by and under graceful curve of Columbia River Bridge.

Suomi Hall, 244 Marine Dr., kind of Finnish hall that was popular in early years of this century.

Josephsons's Smokehouse, 106 Marine Dr., built 1898. Board and batten construction used in the building. Across street is **Union Steam Baths,** so popular with Finnish workers in decades past.

Downtown has **Liberty Theatre** (12th and Commercial), child of the 1930s, and the former **John Jacob Astor Hotel** (14th and Commercial), tallest structure in town and once the great hostelry of the North Oregon Coast.

Astoria is a cornucopia of 19th century buildings, mostly homes. A walking tour, no more than 1.5 m. in length of route, covers almost all these sights. Begin at the **Flavel Mansion** (1883), 441 Eighth St. Bldg., long a museum, has been restored as elegant Victorian home. It was designed by a San Francisco architect for Capt. George C. Flavel, sea captain, bar pilot and shipping magnate, and his wife, Mary Lydia Christina Boelling, who wed the captain when she was not quite 14. Across street is old **Clatsop County Jail,** built between 1904–07. It served as jail 1914–1976, one of longest continuously operated in W US.

Boelling Residence (1863), 765 Exchange; 788 Franklin Ave. (1884); 544

Astoria Column

Phoebe L. Friedman

Eighth St. (1885); 828 Franklin (1885); 818 Grand (1885); 960 Franklin (1888); 989 Franklin (1870, home of Dewitt Clinton Ireland, early newspaper publisher); 687 12th St. (1895); 591 12th (1895); 1229 Franklin (1870); 1243 Franklin (1875), with outstanding decorative porch in true Victorian mode; 1278 Franklin (1898); 1294 Franklin (1892); 1337 Franklin (1854), oldest house in Astoria and one of oldest in Oregon. West portion built by Capt. Hiram Brown, river pilot in Adairville (East Astoria) in 1854 and barged down river to then Columbia backwater at 12th and Franklin, from where it was drawn on log rollers by oxen to this site. Rollers remained as footing and barged portion was attached to E part already built. In 1964 house was authentically restored.

1370 Franklin (1892); 1388 Franklin (1862); 1393 Franklin (1879); 1410 Franklin (1869); 636 14th (1895); 1546 Franklin (1870); 1555 Franklin (1885), Grace Episcopal Church, oldest church bldg. in Astoria in continuous use. Belfry has 2 bells, and there is some folklore associated with that fact. The original was brought around the Horn from church in Philadelphia. It pealed purely until, in last century, its notes were impaired by crack in the metal. The bell had to be recast. James Lovel, the artisan, had enough metal left over for an additional bell.

1583 Franklin (1868); 637 16th, original rectory of Grace Episcopal Church, first occupied in 1883; corner, 16th and Franklin, N wing of Trinity Lutheran

Lightship *Columbia*   *Courtesy Columbia River Maritime Museum*

Representation of Ft. Astoria   *Phoebe L. Friedman*

Church, built 1885, was home of unwilling participant in one of Astoria's most famous murder cases. On Sept. 14, 1913, after granting a divorce to a woman, Judge Frank J. Taylor was shot by her husband while walking along Commercial St. There was more excitement when the assailant was hanged.

1681 Franklin (1870); 690 17th (1883), interesting example of elaborate Victorian architecture; 1711 Grand (1890); 1687 Grand (1880), home of John Henry Dix Gray, son of missionary W. H. Gray, who came to the Oregon Country in 1836 with Dr. Marcus Whitman. J. H. D. supposedly 2d white child born W of Upper Missouri.

1661 Grand (1882); 1643 Grand (1893); 1607 Grand (1882); 1588 Grand (1897); 1573 Grand (1885); 1465 Grand , St. Mary's Catholic Church. First edifice constructed 1874; present bldg., 1903. As late as 1941, bell tower was landmark for ships which entered Columbia River.

836 15th (1883); 698 15th (1865), originally built on corner of 14th and Franklin, moved here 1895; 627 15th (1880); 15th and Exchange, representation of Fort Astoria, where Astoria began in 1811. Here was McTavish gravemarker, oldest in state, now in Clatsop County Historical Society Museum. Donald McTavish was head of Fort George (Fort Astoria) when he drowned in 1814. He had brought with him from England a Portsmouth barmaid, flaxen-haired, blue-eyed and curvaceous, the first white woman on the lower Columbia. Jane Barnes was to become not only a matter of romantic dispute between McTavish and one of his aides, the much younger Alexander Henry, Jr. (who also drowned on the same day and at the same place), but was to be the object of friction with the Chinooks, some of whom plotted to kidnap her after she imperiously rejected the suit of the chief's son. (For more on the juicy tale, see "Stone, Wind and Fire" in author's *This Side of Oregon*.)

1543 Exchange (1880), front portion of Chalet Apartments was once part of the former Col. James Taylor mansion; back portion is former home of locally prominent brewer. Taylor mansion was in its prime regarded as one of Astoria's fanciest homes. 1585 Exchange (1885), elegant home with carved walnut staircase and 3 marble fireplaces. One of the owners was cannery boss John Devlins, whose workers had to protect themselves from being shanghaied by runners from sailing ships by carrying revolvers as they went to and from work. Legend has it that men were "recruited" from farms, woods, and villages by strongarm thugs and delivered to sea captains for a fee.

1618 Exchange, former city hall, now **Clatsop County Historical Society Museum.** Among treasures here: intricately carved woodwork of Sing Lee, who came to Astoria from his Kwantung village in 1912. His artistry was long in hall of Hip Sing Society, last remaining organization of Astoria's once populous Chinatown, abounding 6th and Bond and torn down for parking lot. Sing Lee lived 42 years in tumble-down shack near Miles Crossing, passing away at 85. Old city hall also once housed town library, was USO HQ during WWII, and was original home of Columbia River Maritime Museum.

Other old homes in Astoria: 469 Bond (1863), built completely of Port Orford cedar, home of John Hobson, member of first wagon train to come to Oregon, in 1843.

4495 Leif Erickson Dr. (1890); Benjamin Young Home, 3652 Duane Ave.

Benjamin Young House, Astoria   *Phoebe L. Friedman*

Contemporary scene at Ft. Clatsop *Courtesy State of Oregon*

(1888), magnificent house with grounds and carriage house maintained in original style; 682 34th (1890), large and impressive.

The W part of Astoria includes the 2 last-named houses and Historical marker at 34th and Leif Erickson Dr. Here stood the first US Customs office on Pacific Coast, established April 3, 1849. Historical marker at 37th and Leif Erickson Dr., opposite road from Bumble Bee cold storage plant. Here military road entered Astoria.

Uniontown (aka Finn Town), entered from 45th and Leif Erickson Dr. Once occupied almost entirely by Finns and working class in character, this true "flat part" of Astoria seems a village unto itself.

From downtown Astoria: *1.2 m.,* turnoff for West Mooring Basin, home of fishing fleet.

Jct., Columbia River Bridge. The graceful 4.m-long span, built as the world's largest truss bridge, curves across the broad river to Washington state.

0.4 m., jct., US 101 Business — 0 202.

    * Take L — Business US 101-0 202. *1.4 m.,* jct., 0 202, at N end of bridge across **Youngs Bay.** (For 0 202 see *Cross-Coast Range Roads.*) William Clark called Youngs Bay "Meriwether's Bay" for Capt. Lewis. The explorers had by now come some 433 m. along the Oregon shore since Oct. 18, 1805, the day they first touched what is now the state. From here the party ascended the Netul River, later changed to the Lewis and Clark River, for *2 m.* to the "first point of highland on the Western bank." '2.4 m., drawbridge over Lewis and Clark River. 1.3., jct., **Fort Clatsop National Memorial.** (Historical marker at jct.) 0.8 m., Visitor Center, Fort Clatsop, Visitor Center combines entertainment and education to dramatize stay of the explorers. A short trail leads to a replica of Fort Clatsop, the designs and measurements taken from the field book of Capt. Clark. The Lewis and Clark party occupied the fort, which they built, from Dec. 7, 1805 to March 23, 1806. of the 106 days spent here, it rained 94 days, almost 8 out of every 9 days. Inside the stockade young men, dressed as the elk-skin Corps of Discovery, demonstrate aspects of fort life. Another trail leads to Canoe Landing, the boating point for the party. For an account of the Lewis and Clark expedition at Ft. Clatsop, see "The First (Christmas) in Oregon" in author's *This Side of Oregon*.

Only 2 members of the expedition ever saw the Far West again. One was Sacagawea's babe, Jean Baptiste Charbonneau, better known to Corps of Discovery buffs as Pomp. After a vivid career as a mountain man, the European-educated Charbonneau came to the Mother Lode of the Sierra Nevada. In 1866 he left his job as hotel clerk in Auburn, Calif., to trek to Montana Territory, for reasons inexplicable. Along the way he came down with flu and died at Inskip's Station, near Jordan Valley, in SE Oregon and is buried there. The other party member to set foot on Pacific land was Alexander Willard, blacksmith, gunsmith, saltmaker and hunter in the expedition. In 1852, at the age of 72, he drove an oxteam across the plains to Franklin, CA. There, after a little blacksmithing, he spun out his years rocking on the porch of his frame house and regaling anyone who cared to listen about his days with Lewis and Clark. He passed away in 1865. There is no evidence that Jean Baptiste Charbonneau and Alexander Hamilton Willard, no more than 50 m. apart for 13 years, ever knew of each other's presence.

Most of the Lewis and Clark party died young. But one man, Patrick Gass, the last survivor, lived to the ripe old age of 99. In the War of 1812, at 41, he lost an eye at the battle of Lundy's Lane; at 60 he married and to make up for lost time, he and his wife rapidly produced 7 children. At 87 he gave up tippling to convert to the Campbellite faith and was baptized in the Ohio River. The event drew hundreds, who came to see the old boozer cleansed of sin. He was 90 when he made an inspirational and instructive Fourth of July speech to Union soldiers departing for the front. He died in 1870, one year after the completion of the transcontinental RR. One wonders what he thought when he heard tell about people being able to ride the train all the way to the Pacific Ocean. It was time for Paddy Gass to move on.

Fort Clatsop was not built to be permanent and even if Lewis and Clark had durability in mind the fort was left to the mercy of the elements and the needs of the Indians, who had small sentiment for the houses of white foreigners. Less than 10 years after Lewis and Clark departed, little was left of

Fort Clatsop. On Dec. 13, 1813, Alexander Henry, Jr. trekked into the forest and wrote:

"We walked up to see the old American winter quarters of Captains Lewis and Clark in 1805–06, which are in total ruins, the wood having been cut down and destroyed by the Indians; but the remains are still visible. In the fort are already grown up shoots of willows 25 feet high. The situation is the most pleasant I have seen hereabouts, and by far the most eligible, both as to security from the natives and for hunting. The place is deeply shaded with spruce, pine, sapin, etc.; the woods seemed gloomy and dark, the beams of the sun being prevented from reaching the ground through so thick a foliage. Having examined this spot, we returned to our horses, which are left in care of the Indians; there being no grass near the fort, we allow them to graze on the salt marsh along the bay and river."

    * Return to US 101 — Business. Turn L. *2 m.*, jct, Warrenton — Hammond. *0.5 m.*, US 101. From jct., US 101 — US 101 Business — 0 202. (On US 101.) *2.3 m.*, jct., Warrenton — Hammond.

    * *1.2 m.*, **Skipanon River,** home of Warrenton charter fleet. *0.2 m.*, jct., downtown Warrenton — Hammond — Fort Stevens. (Downtown Warrenton S to US 101 *1.4 m.*)

Warrenton was named for Daniel Knight Warren, the big landowner here in the late 19th and early 20th centuries. He platted the town and financed the bldg. of a dike 2.5 m. long on Skipanon river. His labor costs weren't enormous; the Chinese laborers he hired worked cheap, having few options. Dike turned Warrenton into fishing town and eventually it became charter boat center for salmon fishing at mouth of Columbia. Warrenton has less than 3,000 pop. but city hall seems equipped to serve 10,000. Campbell House, seedy bachelor house put up by 2 brothers in 1894, glooms corner of SW 1st and Alder.

    * At jct., turn square R. *0.3 m.*, on L, largely obscured, **Warren Mansion,** former home of Warrenton founder. Originally, stairs led down to Skipanon River wharf, now filled in as boat basin. Back of house is supposed largest Hooker willow in state, surrounded by other willows, Hooker and Scouler. Distinguishable when catkins present.

    * Return to jct. Turn R for Hammond — Fort Stevens. *1.8 m.*, 14th St. Turn R. *0.2 m.*, site of completely gone town of Flavel. Stately hotel erected here 1898; after one glorious social season the last waltz was danced. *0.1. m.,* Tansy Point, on Columbia.

    * Return to Hammond — Fort Stevens Road. Turn R. *1.1 m.*, Hammond. Inc. 1899 as New Astoria; changed to **Hammond** in 1915 since big wheel A. B. Hammond had most of public bldgs. named for him. At an election voters opted to go the whole hog. A wit explained the town: "We save money by keeping the sidewalks rolled up." Former Coast Guard station, now occupied by US gvt. marine labs, has flair of sea. Next to it is complex of condo-

miniums looking across river to Astoria. Affluent condos in 600-pop. Hammond! The world moves.

  *0.4 m., jct., Fort Stevens — Fort Stevens SP. Straight. 0.2 m., entrance to **Fort Stevens.** 0.7 m., Visitor Center, with full information on fort, est. 1864, terminated as military post 1947. At close of WWII, all guns and mounts were taken from emplacements and used for scrap material to help alleviate the shortage of iron for civilian use.

Return to entrance. Turn R. 0.2 m., Fort Stevens compound and parade ground, occupied and used by civilians. Turn L onto Russell Dr. 0.1 m., forks. Take R, Russell Dr. 0.1 m., straight, Dead End Road. 0.4 m., Fort Stevens Cemetery. Gravestones go back to 1875.

Return to Ft. Stevens — Fort Stevens SP jct. Turn R. 0.7 m., jct., Battery Russell. Turn R. 0.1 m., turn L for Battery Russell. Best-kept and most popular of the "big gun" emplacements. On June 21, 1942, Battery Russell became the first — and only — military object on the US continental mainland to be attacked by the Japanese, from submarine. An account of that happening is described by Marshall Hanft in the his excellent narrative, *The Cape Forts*, published by the Oregon Historical Society:

"One of several incoming enemy projectiles exploded about three hundred yards in front of Battery Russell, but with no important damage. The installation was in its turn on standby status. Jack Wood of The Dalles, Oregon, duty officer in charge, and his executive officer were in quarters below the battery commander's station playing cribbage when they heard the sound of firing. Wood quickly ran upstairs to the command station where he sighted on muzzle flashes far out at sea, and he soon determined his range to the target, an apparent submarine, was beyond that of his guns."

Return 0.1 m. to road. Turn L. 0.2 m., turn L for beach and Lake Coffenbury. 1.2 m., turn R for beach. 0.4 m., ocean beach and remains of *Peter Iredale*, British bark stranded on beach during heavy storms in autumn, 1906. Each year sees less of the old boy. Return to Lake Coffenbury Rd. Turn R. 0.3 m., Lake Coffenbury. Return to Battery Russell Rd. Turn L. 3.7 m., South Jetty. Here begins the Oregon Coast Trail.

If only one book can be taken along it should be the pocket size *A Hiker's Guide to the Oregon Coast Trail*, written by David E. M. Bucy and Mary C. McCauley and published by the Oregon State Parks and Recreation Branch. Among cautionary tips for hiking the coast are these:

"Never turn your back on the ocean; a sudden, large wave is not uncommon."

"Be careful of logs and driftwood. A heavy, stable log can be hurled many feet by an incoming tide."

"Make camp well above the high tide line."

"Don't build campfires in driftwood. Strong winds can turn a small campfire into a huge beach fire."

"Be alert for vehicles. Parts of the Oregon Coast are open to motorized traffic."

In early spring, and again in early winter, armed with binoculars, California gray whales may be seen. The Hatfield Marine Science Center at Newport offers these suggestions to make whale-watching successful:

"When and Where: Coastal headlands with good elevation that jut out into the ocean are the best . . . Early morning hours when the sea has fewer whitecaps makes sightseeing easier. Choose a calm ocean and an overcast day to avoid glare for best results.

"What to look for: Scan the horizon for the 'blow' (vapor and water blown in the air to up to 12 feet when the whale exhales) . . . Once you locate a blow, stay with it. Where you see one, you'll see others. Usually, only a small portion of the whale's head and back show during a blow."

The normal diving sequence for gray whales is: shallow dive, 1-2 min.; deep dive, 5-8 min.; shallow dive, 1-2 min., all within a distance of 300-400 yds. Just before the deep dive the tail flukes are sometimes seen.

Observations recorded by the Hatfield Marine Science Center over a period of several years indicate that the heaviest flow of CA Gray Whales is in late Dec., when about 30 whales an hour pass a given point. In March, northbound for the Bering Sea, the rate is 8 to 12 whales per hour, with the contingents consisting of males and calfless females. There is little movement in April. The migration is observed again in May, with an average of 4 whales an hour, chiefly females with calves. Because of the calves the whales come "extraordinarily close" to shore; at other times they are generally about 2 m. from land.

About 100 whales do not go N beyond the Oregon Coast, so whales are observable along the coast all year, an added bonus for charter boats.

South Jetty is rich with flora: Seashore Lupine, Seaside Tansy, Coast Strawberry, Yellow Sand-verbena, Beach Morning Glory, Beach Pea, Sand Mat, Gray Beach Pea, and American Sea Rocket. On the beach S, glass floats are occasionally found. More numerous are sand dollars, agate, jasper, petrified wood, and Oregon jade.

Pink shrimp — *Pandalas jordani* — appear at and near South Jetty in abundance. The largest shrimp ground between Alaska and San Diego is between the Columbia River and Yaquina Head.

In this area heronries also appear, found in trees such as spruce, red alder, hemlock, and oak. During early Feb. the herons start arriving at the heronries though they don't get around to laying eggs until the end of the month.

* Return to Fort Stevens SP — Seaside Road. Turn R. *0.3 m.*, entrance to Fort Stevens SP camping area. FHP. *1.5 m.*, road splits here into lower and upper branches. At split, turn R. *0.1 m.*, historical landmark. Here, on June 21, 1942, states marker, a 5.5" shell exploded, one of 17 fired at Columbia River harbor defense installation by Japanese submarine I-25 — first time US mainland shelled by hostile forces since War of 1812.

Return to split in roads. Take L, or lower road. 0.4 m., **Ocean View Cemetery.** Among pioneers buried here is Bethenia Owens-Adair. She lies in rear center of cemetery.

Bethenia Owens-Adair, first woman graduate physician on Pacific Coast, was born in Missouri in 1840 and came with her family to Oregon in the Great Migration of 1843 that included Jesse Applegate, who later encouraged her to study medicine. Married at 14 and a mother at 16, she left her husband at 18 ("because he whipped my baby unmercifully, and struck and choked me, — and I was never born to be struck by mortal man!"), and at 19 obtained a divorce and restoration of her maiden name of Owens. It was a daring thing to do in 1859. By then she had returned to her parents' home and, scarcely able to read or write, she commenced school, going to class after completing daybreak-starting chores. A year later she taught a 3-month course, having 16 students who paid her $2 a month. Three of her pupils were more advanced than she but "I took their books home with me at night, and with the help of my brother-in-law, I managed to prepare the lessons beforehand, and they never suspected my incompetency." All her life she was a prodigious learner.

After teaching school in Oregon and Washington, she moved to Roseburg, where she opened a millinery and dressmaking establishment. (While

Grave of Bethenia Owens-Adair   *Phoebe L. Friedman*

operating her business, she put her son and only child into university and later paid his way thru medical school.) In Roseburg, she took to nursing and received the support of several prominent men. In 1870, she "found myself seated in the California stage, beginning my long journey across the continent." Her trip ended in Philadelphia where she enrolled in the Eclectic School of Medicine, the only woman in her class. She moved to Portland to practice medicine in 1878 but in 1880 went E again and obtained a medical degree from the U of Michigan. At the age of 44 she married for the 2d time, to Col. John Adair, whose fanciful schemes came near ruining her hard-earned savings and her health; at 47 she gave birth to daughter, who died 3 days later. Hungry for children, she took into her home her grandson (after the death of her son's wife), whom she and her husband made their heir-in-law, and a girl she delivered of a mother who begged the doctor to take the child. She left practice in 1905 and died in 1926 near Warrenton. During her medical days, she attracted attention by advocating sterilization of habitual criminals, the feeble-minded and other so-called defectives. Her views were put into law by state legislature but overturned by the courts. A forceful person, with positions on almost everything, she early aligned herself with the pioneer band of Oregon suffragists. *0.4 m.,,* US 101.

* At split in roads — above — R, or upper road; *0.7 m.,* stone marking site of **Smith Mission,** est. 1840 by Solomon Howard and Celiast (Helen) Smith. (See Clatsop Pioneer Cemetery, below.) *0.9 m.,* turn R. *0.2 m.,* US 101.

US 101 at Warrenton Jct.:

0.5 m., jct.: W, Warrenton; E, Fort Clatsop Nat. Mem.

0.5 m., jct., Fort Stevens SP.

* *0.8 m.,* Crab Pot Restaurant. N of here was hamlet of Lexington. *0.1 m.,* Main Avenue. Turn L. *0.2 m.,* Ridge Road. Turn R onto Ridge Rd. *0.4 m.,* **Ocean View Cemetery.** (See above) Return 0.4 m. to upper road. Turn L. *0.1 m.,* historical marker locally known as **Submarine Monument.** (See above) Return 0.1 m. to upper road. Take sharp R. *0.7 m.,* Smith Mission. (See above) *0.9 m.,* turn R. *0.2 m.,* US 101.

1.9 m., Columbia Beach Road.

* *0.2 m.,* turn L. *0.9 m.,* on R, **Smith Mission** marker. (See above) *0.7 m.,* jct. L, *0.1 m.,* **Submarine Monument.** (See above) R from jct.: *0.4 m.,* **Ocean View Cemetery.** (See above) Straight from jct.: *1.5 m.,* **Fort Stevens SP CG** (See above for Ft. Stevens).

0.3. m., jct., **Camp Rilea,** National Guard encampment, and **Clatsop Plains Community Church,** also known as Clatsop Plains Pioneer Church and Gray Memorial Chapel. Bldg. on site of Presbyterian Church erected 1850 as outgrowth of Presbyterian Society org. 1846, first Presbyterian church W of Upper Missouri. Congregation included William H. Gray, pioneer missionary, compatriot of Marcus Whitman, and author of probably the most controversial history of Oregon.

Back of church is **Clatsop Pioneer Cemetery,** est. 1846. Buried here are Solomon Howard Smith and his wife, Helen, born Celiast, princess-daughter of Coboway, Chief of the Clatsops. The Smiths are correctly noted on a plaque as Oregon's first school teachers. Smith, who came to Oregon with Nathaniel Wyeth in 1832, did his teaching at Ft. Vancouver (1833–34) and at French Prairie (1835–37), with his wife assisting. In 1840 he took up a land claim on Clatsop Plains and that year herded the first cattle to the Oregon Coast. The next year he brought horses to Clatsop Plains by boat, from St. Helens, and started the first Columbia River ferry , lashing canoes together. An early partisan for Americanization of the Oregon Country, he was a participant at Champoeg on that eventful day of May 2, 1843. Having studied medicine in Vermont, the New Hampshireman practiced it in Oregon. In the versatile style of the pioneers he was also a sawmill operator, dairyman, storekeeper, farmer, and, at the age of 65, state senator. The last survivor of the first American settlers in Oregon, he had done much, but he was proudest of his wife, whom he married in 1833 and who bore their 7 children. To him she was, as to others who knew her, a wise, strong and beautiful woman. (For more, see "The Untypical Smiths" in author's *Tracking Down Oregon.)*

2 m., jct., Cullaby Lake.

*0.2 m., turn R. 0.7 m., **Cullaby Lake CP,** inland joy. In park is Carnahan Cabin, homesteader's log palace moved from original site, deep in woods, and now museum.

3.2 m., jct., Del Rey Beach

*0.9 m., thru wild fields of bursting Scotch broom, **Del Rey Beach,** little-known, narrow scythe of foreshore with powerful ocean and coastal vistas. Day use SP.

1 m., jct., Gearhart Golf Course.

*0.4 m. N of here was site of **Clatsop City,** inc. as "Town of Clatsop." It included nearly all of Clatsop Plains, being bounded by present Gearhart on S, ocean on W, Skipanon River and Warrenton on N, and RR line on E. Clatsop City had city hall, PO, RR station, saloon, some houses. In 1917 it was absorbed by Gearhart. Not a twig of old Clatsop City remains. 1.1 m., past lush golf course and opulent condos, Gearhart city center.

0.8 m., Gearhart Jct.

*0.4 m., **Gearhart** city center. Gearhart began in the usual modest manner. In 1849 its identifiable pop. consisted of 2 adults, 4 children, 2 calves and 2 mares brought across the plains. Philip Gearhart and his family worked their farm in dubious isolation until some other folks came along and wanted their piece of the good earth near the sea. In 1913 a group of entrepreneurs, seeking gold at the foot of the rainbow, formed the Gearhart Park Co. and raised $300,000 "to establish and maintain a beach resort." And that's how Gearhart lost its identity as a farming community.

0.9 m., Seaside Jct. (1.4 m., Seaside city center.)

1.4 m., jct., **Seaside** city center. *(0.4 m.,* downtown Seaside.)

In 1871 transportation tycoon Ben Holladay, riding the crest of his fortune and fame, est. a high-class resort hotel and called it Seaside House. By then almost everyone alive, Indians as well as whites, had forgotten — most whites never knew — of a Clatsop Indian village here, *Ne-co-tat* by name.

Holladay, who couldn't tie his shoelaces without flair, put on quite a show here. He surrounded his hotel with beautiful horses, barns, race track, tame deer, and caged wild animals. A flag flown from atop the hotel was saluted by the cannons of Holladay's coastal steamers as they passed Seaside House. Woe to the employment of the captain who forgot to honor the king!

For the guests there was everything, including fresh fish daily from a trap in the Necanicum River. Nothing was too good for the affluent.

Seaside never lost the Holladay touch, though there were times when it seemed ready to completely plunge into a Coney Island carnival. In 1920, 23 years after Holladay's death, Seaside built its famous Promenade. Old Ben would have been proud. The Promenade extended, as it still does, about 1.5 m. along Seaside's ocean front and is one of the most popular walking and cycling routes on the coast.

Those who remember Seaside as a hurdy-gurdy cotton candy and rock and roll town will be surprised how things have change. Gone is the frizzled carnival ambience; in its place is a crispness of smart shops and laid back respectability. Some things don't change: Seaside is still the most popular resort town, with the most populated beach, from which people actually enter the ocean for swimming. **Salt Cairn,** on Lewis and Clark Ave., between Beach Dr. and end of street, is supposed site of crude plant built by members of the Lewis and Clark party to obtain salt by boiling sea water. Across house at 2471 Ocean Vista — *1.7 m.* from Broadway and Holladay (downtown) — are graves of four Portuguese fishermen found on beach April 25, 1865. Marker reads: Known only to God.

Events that keep Seaside in the news include the presence or absence of the Miss Oregon Pageant and the 26-m. Marathon run. The Necanicum River, which winds thru town, has good reputation for cutthroat trout in late summer, salmon in autumn, and steelhead in winter. Along the beaches, surf fishing is popular; those more daring head down to the cove area to drop lines off rocks. The cove area S of town also draws surfers. One of Oregon's finest razor clam beaches, particularly on outgoing minus tides, is at Seaside. The area was once home to a large Indian population. Archaeologists from Smithsonian Institution excavated an Indian long house carbon dated to 3,500 years old.

For those who have time and enjoy hiking, a delightful way to reach Cannon Beach from Seaside is to hoof the 12 m. along the Oregon Coast Trail, via Tillamook Head and Indian Beach. The trek slithers thru rain forest, looks down from steep cliffs 1,000 ft. to the sea, and darts in and out of rushes of wildflowers. (Take Edgewood St. at S of Seaside to parking lot at end of road.)

3.8 m., jct., US 26. On E are exquisite gardens of **Crab Broiler.**

Lewis and Clark Salt Cairn, Seaside   *Courtesy State of Oregon*

2.8 m., Viewpoint.

Now US 101 has found itself on the long haul down to the California line, between the Coast Range and the Pacific Ocean. Few people ponder the Coast Range as they drive US 101, but it should be noted. It is, geologically, a mixture of volcanics and sediments, uplifted and partly folded, in a gentle sort of way, although parts of it are craggy and much of it not the place to get lost. Put another way, it is low and rolling, with a mean elev. of less than 2,000 ft. and occasional peaks up to 4,000 ft. Its W foothills leave but a narrow margin of coast plain — actually, less than 25 m. in average width. At some places, precipitous promontories jut out into the ocean and roads have had to be cut out of cliffs. Many streams rise in this range and flow W into bays and estuaries or directly into the Pacific. Two S rivers, the Umpqua and the Rogue, penetrate the Coast Range from the W slope of the Cascades, more than 100 m. inland. Some of the streams were once picturesquely active with steamboat commerce for a distance of up to 20 m.; today, river craft go up a few streams as much as 30 m.

Rainfall on the Coast Range averages 72" annually, the climate is made mild by the closeness of the Pacific, and luxuriant vegetation, green the year round, affords natural grassland for farming, particularly dairying, along the lower valleys.

The first cars had to use the beaches and couldn't be driven when the tide was in. Or, when there wasn't beach, they had to squash thru marshland. It took a full day for the early cars to travel from Astoria to Seaside.

Not until 1914 was the first coast highway project undertaken, and that was in Clatsop County. Two miles of bituminous section were laid near Seaside and a short section of concrete pavement was placed near Astoria. Work didn't start on some parts of the coast highway until 1925. The 396.5 m. highway was completely hard-surfaced in 1932 at a cost of nearly $21 million, about what it costs to build 21 miles in some parts of the state now. In 1935, five major bridges were completed, at an additional cost of $6 million. Even into the 1950s, much of the coast highway was narrow, winding and troublesome to drive. It has been widened and straightened, but it is still not a freeway and should not be approached as such. In winter, parts of the highway, especially in the N, are sometimes under water.

0.4 m., jct., Cannon Beach Loop.

    * *0.4 m.,* turn R for Ecola SP. *1 m.,* turn R for **Indian Beach.** *1.5 m.,* on narrow, twisty road, Indian Beach parking lot. Incredible vistas of offshore rocks swept up in churning tides. Below parking area, the stony beach cove is a shamble of logs, looking like big dead fish. For sunbathers and beachcombers the span of white sand is a plus; for surfers, Indian Beach is one of the coastal favorites. Near parking lot is PA and Tillamook Nat. Rec. Trail, North Headland —6 m. Only for the fit — but what a feeling of kinship with the forest, and what oceanic views! Return to Indian Beach Jct. Turn R. *0.2 m.* **Ecola SP** parking lot. Sweeping grass slopes are rustled by sea winds from

View from Ecola State Park

S, W & N. From several points there are powerful views of Tillamook Rock Light House, active from 1881 to 1957, when the US placed it on the auction block. The base of the structure is 88 ft. above mean sea level and the light's focal plane was an additional 48 ft. more. From the first, supplying the lighthouse and taking people on and off required steel nerves and steel cables held fast between the lighthouse and anchored ships. Almost daily the sea scooped giant handfuls of its water across both rock and lighthouse. Storms brought terror, with the enraged sea catapulting rocks thru windows and even the lighthouse lens. Ecola SP has PA, fishing, FHP.

  * Return to Cannon Beach Loop. Turn R. *0.3 m.,* Ecola Creek, as far down the coast as the Lewis and Clark party ventured. Early in Jan., 1806, Capt. Wm. Clark and about a dozen of his men reached a Tillamook settlement of 5 cabins. Clark had come in response to a report by 2 of his saltmakers at present Seaside that Indians were cutting up a whale, whose skeleton measured 105 ft. Hungry for an addition to their generally monotonous and meager fare, the party made haste for the coast. After much pleading, Sacagawea was permitted to come along. Clark found logic in her argument that she had come so far and deserved to see the big water and the big fish. Clark named the creek Ecola, Indian for whale. (White settlers later changed the name to Elk Creek.) After haggling with the Indians, Clark managed to purchase 300 lbs. of blubber and a few gallons of oil Always ready to look on the bright side, Clark noted in his field book that Providence had been "more kind to us than he was to Jonah, having sent this monster to be swallowed by us instead of swallowing us as Jonah's did."

Cannon of *Shark*, near Cannon Beach

*0.2 m., **Cannon Beach,** named for a washed-ashore cannon from the US Sloop of War, *Shark,* shipwrecked in 1846. From a hamlet shrouded in misty obscurity, Cannon Beach bloomed into a vibrant village of artists and artisans. But its most renowned feature is Haystack Rock, which the chamber of commerce calls "the third largest monolith in the world." During low tides, the pools around the rock are aswarm with jellyfish, small crabs, starfish, sea anemones and other marine specimens swept in by the tides. (Do not attempt to climb the rock!) Just S of 235-ft.-high Haystack are two rock pinnacles called The Needles. Each summer the Sand Castle Contest draws thousands here. Others are attracted by plays at the Coaster Theater.

1.9 m., **Tolovana Park,** redolent with affluence. Oddly, it was named for a communication post way up in Alaska. Tolovana Wayside, facing sea, has FHP. 0.9 m., US 101.

From N entrance to Cannon Beach (on US 101):

0.1 m., on W, **Escola Historical Marker,** telling of a detachment of the Lewis and Clark party come to beach to buy whale blubber.

1.1 m., Cannon Beach Jct. 1 m., Tolovana Park Jct. 1 m., S end, Beach Loop Road.

0.2 m., Viewpoint. There are many such on the Coast and the traveler not bent for hell or something as urgent would do well to pause at as many as possible. Beaoh is a flash (or flask) to fill the soul with nectar of sea wonder.

0.8 m., **Arcadia Beach SP,** a rustic, grassy turnoff peering down at a broad, silent, smooth-sanded beach walled at N end by rock outthrust of continental wall. PA, beach access, fishing.

1.2 m., **Hug Point SP.** Hug Point was a literal description: the road hugged the point where the hill met the sea. Today the rough, crude, brine-worn bend seems archaic, almost primitive beyond belief, but when the well-cemented sandstone was cut and blasted out of the hill it marked a great advance in coastal travel. (See "A Closeness to Hug Point" in author's *Tracking Down Oregon.)* SP has waterfalls, PA, caves, ocean beach, fishing. Two-tiered rock due W of entrance to beach resembles a mind's image microcosm of Alcatraz.

0.7 m., on E, **Cannon Beach Historical Marker.** Near marker is cannon from US Shark, wrecked while trying to leave Columbia River Sept. 10, 1846. This small iron cannon drifted down to the beach, giving the name of the area and the town, Cannon Beach.

To E is 3058-ft. Onion Peak. The Nature Conservancy describes it as a "massive basalt prominence arising abruptly from the surrounding sedimentary rocks of the northern Coast Range, and supports one of Oregon's outstanding rare plant assemblages." The 40 acre preserve is not open to the public. Peak was named for wild onions growing there.

0.7 m., **Arch Cape,** country store village named for the arch in the offshore configuration. A single store on the Coast does not necessarily mean a thinness of pop. in area. There could be, as seen around Arch Cape, many homes, most of

Hug Point   *Phoebe L. Friedman*

recent vintage and above-average price. US 101 tunnels under the cape and a
hiking trail treks across it.

0.3 m. — from Arch Cape PO — Arch Cape — Mill Road.

    * *0.4 m.,* on L, gate. Beyond gate a trail — old logging road — leads 3.7 m.
to top of 2,775-ft. Angora Peak. Climb is stiff but from top one can see far N &
S along coast and all the way E to Cascade Mtns.

0.1 m., bridge across Arch Cape Creek. Slow down and look oceanward. Or
park on Arch Cape-Mill Creek Rd. and walk to bridge. View is great: sudden
sensation of rock and sea worth remembering.

2.2 m., turnoff to Cove Beach and Falcon Cove.

    * Along the coast are numerous turnoffs to small beaches, practically pri-
vate, and coves which, for all public knowledge, could be secret. The chief
users are the people whose homes sweep down the winding lanes to the briny
deep. Still, if you are adventurous, do not be deterred by the small highway
indicators which almost blushingly point to roads of figleaf modesty. *0.4 m.,*
forks. Take R. *0.3 m.,* Tide Ave. turn L. *0.2 m.,* on R, Falcon Head. Rural
settlement of Falcon Head extends *1 m.,* developer's dream at idyllic location by sea.

1.8 m., **Oswald West SP.** Parking for PA. Oswald West is generally regarded as Oregon's greatest governor, though he served only one term. Perhaps his most monumental achievement was playing a key role in preserving the Oregon foreshore for the public.

0.1 m., **Oswald West SP** — parking area on E side of highway.

0.1 m., Oswald West SP — overnight parking area. Os West despised comfort on a silver platter and fashioning nature to satisfy the spoiled character of "civilization." To get into this park you have to load your gear on a wooden wheelbarrow and push it down to the CG, which is rugged and deep in the woods. Trails lead to the pristine CG and Short Sand Beach thru a bewildering carnage of forest. At points the giant, twisted, broken, bent, glowering spruce and cedars look like an arboreal gotterdammerung or like battered and bleeding monsters shattered in battle, their dripping wounds crying for revenge in the darkling rain forest. Three headlands boldly thrust into the sea at Oswald West SP: at the N end, 900-ft-high Arch Cape; in the center, Cape Falcon; in the S, Neahkahnie Mtn. Between Neahkahnie Mtn. and Cape Falcon, Short Sand Beach rests on the lap of Smuggler's Cove. A trail from Short Sand Beach slithers *1.2 m.* to Cape Falcon thru shiny rain forest.

Now the road climbs up the shelf of Neahkahnie Mtn., the mighty ocean open and endless. The mtn., rising 1,631 ft. above the water, is a most impressive sight for many miles S and N, and even traveling the shelf (whose maximum height is 602 ft.) one has the feeling of being far higher. Obviously, such a rise and such a name has to inspire conjecture and folklore. The facts, alas, are these: no one really knows how or why the mtn. got its name or what the name means, and as for the tales of buried treasure from wrecked Spanish galleons, intense exploration has revealed not a clue. The Tillamook Indians called Neahkahnie Mtn. "The Place of the Fire Spirit" and showed it reverence.

About 20 million years ago, during Miocene time, when this part of the Coast Range was still below water, a pile of basalt erupted and became a volcanic island several miles offshore. This was Neahkahnie Mtn. before even the algae thought of tourism.

From Oswald West SP CG entrance:

1.2 m., 0.3 m., 0.1 m., 0.2 m., marked Viewpoints on Neahkahnie Mt.

* From the E side of US 101, part of the Oregon Coast Trail switchbacks 1,000 ft. to the top of Neahkahnie Mtn. — *2.5 m.* — and then drops *1.8 m.* to US 101. Along the route are elk trails, Wilson's Warblers, American Goldfinches, woodpeckers, and a host of vegetation, including Canada Thistle, Chickweed, Foxglove, Indian Paintbrush, Seaside Tansy, Tiger Lilies, Wild Hollyhock, Wild Irish, Wild Onion, Yarrow, and Thimbleberry thickets. The view from the top of Neahkahnie is one of heartswell and heartbreak — from fertile farmland to massacred slopes. The Nehalem River estuary and Nehalem sand spit seem close at hand and on a clear day it is no great trick to see 50 m. out to sea.

0.8 m., turnoff to Neahkahnie Beach.

* *0.8 m.,* **Neahkahnie Beach,** at base of mtn. An isolated patch of beach that epitomizes the Oregon Coast gloom on a windy, rainy day. But the view N, of Neahkahnie Mtn.'s ocean face, has the chill of beauty to it.

0.3 m, Manzanita Jct.

* *0.4 m.,* downtown **Manzanita.** The town was designed as a resort community and although it has year-round pop. of about 500, it is still known for its summer comers. *0.2 m.,* Manzanita Beach, which some of the locals say is 7 m. long, forgetting the claims of adjoining settlements. Off the beach near Manzanita, at the bottom of the sea, lies a pattern of ballast rock, the only remains of a shipwreck that, declare geologists, happened before 1820. In October the menopausel wind haunts the nocturnal sand and one is reminded of a line of poetry by Paul Verlaine: "Les sanglots longs des violons de l'automne." (The long sobs of the violins of autumn.)

0.7 m., jct., Nehalem Bay SP.

* *1.8 m.,* **Nehalem Bay SP CG.** (Complete SP, including horse trails.) *1.3 m.,* Nehalem Bay SP boat ramp. Here the wind does not blow, it trumpets. Returning to US 101, view of Neahkahnie Mtn. is one of sheer magnificence.

1.1 m., **Nehalem.** First PO about 1870 but it jumped around and at one time was called Onion Peak. Since 1884, however, PO has been in present Nehalem town. Just below burg the Nehalem River, which courses thru all 4 of Oregon's NW counties, enters the sea. Nehalem in 1915 was institutionally fatter than it is today, with three lodges, Grange, Angling club, Commercial Club, weekly paper. Riches were expected from undeveloped coal deposits but they did not materialize. Pop. then was 250; in 1940, 245; in 1985, 280. Such growth leaves

Neahkahnie Mountain as seen from Neahkahnie Beach

Nehalem still yawning. In the 1920s and 1930s Nehalem had the appearance of a closed-in New England fishing village. In the 1970s antique shops began to open in the weary, windy bldgs. The entire town looks like an antique which is put to rest for the night at 5 p.m. About the nicest thing that can be said of Nehalem is its view of Neahkahnie Mtn. — at sunset a Japanese painting. View particularly exquisite from old Nehalem River bridge.

    1.3 m., jct., 0 53.

      * *1 m.,* **Nehalem Bay Winery,** in old cheese factory. What was village of Mohler — store, tavern. *0.2 m.,* Miami River Jct. Continue straight.

      This is the route the locals sometimes take to get to Portland via US 26. It begins with lush pockets of meadowland, plunges into the wan remains of a rain forest, winds about at a dizzying pace, staggers between chopped down forests, then straightens out to breeze to US 26. From Miami River Jct.: *4.3 m.,* on R, turnoff to **God's Valley,** which is what somebody thought of this

Nehalem
River

cove in the woods. *5.7 m.,* **Nehalem Fish Hatchery,** on N Fork of Nehalem River. *7.1 m.,* Hamlet Jct. Turn E.

* Few outsiders have been to **Hamlet.** There is little reason for going there. The community — called Hamlet because its pragmatic Finnish founders knew it was only that — never had a store, PO, church or village center. *3.7 m.,* on R, Hill Rd. *(0.5 m.,* path on L to cemetery, 50 yds. thru brush. Here in old-fashioned iron fenced plots lie the families of the founders, each family tight together.) *0.1 m.* — on Hamlet Rd. from Hill Rd. — on L, old schoolhouse, now community hall. Next *2.2 m.,* until main road runs out, Hamlet, all of the spread out houses back of road. (For early days here, see "The Small Drama of Hamlet" in author's *Tracking Down Oregon.)*

* Return to 0 53. Turn R. *0.7 m.,* Necanicum, on US 26.

* From Miami River Jct.: Turn R. *1 m.,* turn onto Foss Rd. for Nehalem River drive. Although the road accompanies the stream much of the way, the Nehalem is too often obscured by brush and trees for most of its passage — but what is seen, at road level or canyon deep, is exhilarating. (See "A Sprite Called River" in author's *Tracking Down Oregon.)* Unlike 0 53, this county pike has long stretches without habitation and is more difficult to negotiate. *7 m.,* on L, Nehalem Falls Park, where the river handsprings over rocks in a jubilant demonstration of its freedom. *6.9 m.,* **Salmonberry.** Nothing here but a house or two, Salmonberry Creek entering the Nehalem, and RR tracks which long ago carried passenger trains bound for the coast. (Little more than logs going E now.) *7.7 m.,* Spruce Run CP, on the Nehalem, Wooded, open spaces. Neat. *5.3 m.,* US 26. (W, 0.3 m., Elsie)

From Jct. 0 53 on US 101:

0.1 m., **Wheeler,** best-known for its hospital, now regional medical facility. Between RR tracks and Nehalem Bay there was, early in the century, another "town", at least a PO, called Hoevet. Masculine spirit of the town is to be found early morning at the local cafe, where loggers, fishers and truckers gather to swap tales before going out to earn their daily bread. Told by a visitor, "I wonder what people do here," a long-time resident, staring down the one-minute-walk business section, replied, "I wonder." But something must keep the 300 people here, in the once-gusty fish-packing town. In 1940 there were three fish-packing houses along waterfront. Wheeler is N terminus of summer RR excursions originating in Tillamook.

Now US 101 winds around Nehalem Bay before facing the ocean, and there is the feeling here of the Maine Coast, a dance of pastels. Between Wheeler and Rockaway Beach US 101 is thinly sprinkled by the homes of working folk, most of whom are islands unto themselves, and yet the homes lend a gentleness to the highway so that, on a foggy, eerie night, each home becomes a friend, a way station of succor. An old Irish folk song comes to mind: "Where you live and where I live are places far apart/The little houses by the road lie closer to my heart."

5.6 m., jct., **Manhattan Beach Wayside.**

* *0.2 m.,* Wayside parking area. FHP. 100 yd. trail to beach.

1.5 m., **Lake Lytle.** On an early gray-shrouded spring or fall morning the boat of a fisher seems fixed, as though in a photograph. Back of the cafe a family of raccoons dwells in the brush, coming out, plump and cautious, for whatever is tossed them.

0.5 m., **Rockaway Beach,** an unglamorous town whose steady growth is attributable to retired seniors who find the town meets all their needs. (Rockaway Beach Wayside is parking area for outside beach users.) But there is beauty here for those who look. A vignette of Rockaway Beach, written in 1966 by the author, reflects a scene still true, except for the human and animal element:

"The restless wind bestirs the sea between the last gasp of Neahkahnie Mountain and the mist of Cape Meares.

"In the western sky the great globe sun trembles above the horizon, ensheathed by a dazzling rim of fire, flashes streamers of gold filtering on the terraced wave. One swirls through a gap in an offshore rock that from this firmament is a Roman arch of antiquity.

"My dog follows me along the beach, not knowing why I tarry so long in the chill and rising wind. She circles me, looking up, her eyes studying mine. How can I tell her that a sunset can be as beautiful as a bone?

"We follow the tide as it retreats toward the sun. In its wake it leaves a thousand veins, the motley borders of lakes, rivers, and estuaries. Hush of sandlap flows into the murmur of the tide which rises in the ocean's breast as a chant.

"The smooth sand bequeathed by the withdrawing elements of the deep is splashed gold on yellow-brown, and where the last has been uncovered therein is the sun mirrored, in the moistness of the renaissance foreshore.

"Hung between a valley of flames and a blue burnished sky, the solar monarch extends its lavishness north and west but Neahkahnie, gossamer in the subtle shadows, stand craggier in silhouette.

"As though it has seen enough of the world for one day, the sun sinks into the sea until it is but a red wreath. Then that too is gone. And where the sun departed, there is a redpink roof, a lavish ephemeral cenotaph to a dot of eternity.

"Now the magic of eventide is at work. The golden sands that touched the sea are bronze and copper soaked in wine.

"The eye lifts slowly, absently, to the western sky, south of where the sun went down, lifts slowly there, for no reason at all, and meets the moon, so wan and inappropriate. Beneath the pale lunar peninsula pools of pomegranate swirl and boil, flecked by violets that shimmer in the stiffening breeze. Yet the wind is but a minor voice, overpowered by the full-throated oratorio of the deep.

"Wine-colored twilight washes down the western slope from the cerise rim and cloaks the waterway world of the fresh, moist breeze.

"Now the wine gives way to plum and plum to hazes of amber. A woman, arms akimbo, descends from twilight to dusk as she silently crosses the beach toward the rasp of the tide.

"My little dog sits motionless now, resigned to her fate. She has chosen her way of life and what one cannot comprehend or change one must abide.

"The eyelight at Cape Meares twitches and turns. Below Neahkahnie a string of bluishgreen and yelloworange lights flicker like fireflies on parade.

"Beneath the brightening moon the waves run silver in a bed of gunmetal blue to the accompaniment of a hundred thousand drums. Now the moon belongs. I turn toward our cabin, my dog at my side, tail wagging. We are going home. Night was fallen."

St. Marys By the Sea (Catholic Church) at S Third, overlooking beach, is kind of church New England coastfolks built to keep vigil over their fishers.

Old Growth Cedar Swamp, 47-acre tract managed by The Nature Conservancy, is last known land form of its type, yet much of the NW coastline was once covered with red cedar swamp and spruce-hemlock forests. A ring count of a Sitka spruce snag revealed the oldest known tree of that species in Coast Range. (Turn E on S 6th Ave. 3 blocks, on Beacon, turn R. At end of street dim trail leads into swamp.)

0.5 m. — from S 6th Rockaway — **Twin Rocks.** Cluster of homes, with PO named for two large offshore rocks. Years ago, most such settlements were summer-oriented; now many residents are year-round.

2 m., **Barview.** In 1915 this village was summer retreat and site of Tillamook Bay Life Saving Station. Named for bar at entrance to Tillamook Bay. Little more than peek along road now.

Jct., **Barview Jetty CP.**

  * *0.1 m.,* CP at N jetty of Tillamook Bay. Some pros say here is best deep-
  sea jetty fishing on coast.

0.6 m., one of the small-framed, sudden-gasp cameos along coast, tree growing out of rock in bay.

0.4 m., Viewpoint, **Tillamook Bay.**

There is more to see of Tillamook Bay than the water and shoreline. This is particularly true in autumn and winter. Then, ducks, geese and sea birds which are not common spring and summer callers settle here — and in other sheltered bays, such as Netarts and Yaquina — to rest and feed. Conspicuous from Sept. thru Nov. is one of the oddest of our winged friends, the California Brown Pelican. With a wing spread of 5 ft. at full growth, the pelican resembles a dive bomber as it wheels and plunges for its food. A formation of pelicans zooming just inches above the water or gliding out of a cloudbank is a gripping sight. A note of recognition: the head and neck of the adult is pure white: of the younger bird, dark brown.

Early in the 1970s the California Brown Pelican was placed on the endangered species list, its reproductive capacity wiped out by DDT, which was ingested thru fish food. In 1970 only one chick was produced from several hundred nests on the islands off California. Since DDT was banned in 1974, pelican pop. had gradually increased.

Another winter resident in Tillamook and other coastal bays is the Great Egret, sometimes called the Common or American Egret. For identity: it is pure white with yellow bill, has black feet and legs, reaches length of 3 1/2 ft. at maturity.

Clamming is popular in all four bays of Tillamook County, including this one. Along Tillamook Bay there are beds of Blue, Cockle, Quahog, Littleneck, Softshell, and Razor clams.

Tillamook Bay was first called Quicksand Bay by John Meares, the British sea captain, sailing his trading vessel, *Nootka,* along the coast. His explorations hereabouts are included in his 1790 book, *Voyage to the Northwest Coast of America.*

0.7 m., **Garibaldi** — at pier & boat basin. Named by admirer of Giuseppe Garibaldi, famed 19th century revolutionary. When the mill closed a lot of people thought the town would go under, but somehow it survived, though wounded. Coast Guard Station on E side of US 101 is pretty picture. Pier, *0.4 m.* W of US 101, has boat moorage (always a gusty scene), fish plant and seafood cafes. During whaling migrations, in Dec. & Jan. and again in spring, boats are available for close-up viewing. **Lumberman's Memorial Park,** *0.2 m.* beyond pier, on W side 3d St., has 1926 steam engine, tintype coach car (converted into local museum), caboose.

Sandpipers on the Oregon beach   *Phoebe L. Friedman*

A tree near Garibaldi   *Phoebe L. Friedman*

0.8 m., Miami River Jct.
    * This pike darts in and out of "secret valleys," each a contributor to the dairy industry of Tillamook County. *11.7 m.,* jct. Turn R onto Foss Rd. L, *1 m., 0 53.7 m.,* Nehalem Falls Park. *6.9 m.,* Salmonberry. *7.7 m.,,* Spruce Run CP. *5.3 m.,* US 26. (See earlier, US 101, 0 53 and Foss Road; also, US 26, 0 53 and Spruce Run CP roads.)
    1.3 m., on W, **Captain Robert Gray historical marker.** In mid-August 1788, almost 4 years before he entered the Columbia River, Capt. Gray crossed the bar and anchored his ship, *Lady Washington,* inside Tillamook Bay and dispatched a party of seamen to find and bring back fresh fruits and game for the scurvy-weakened crew and to take on water and wood. Indians on shore initially greeted the sailors with gifts of berries and boiled crabs but a misunderstanding developed. A dispute flared when the cutlass of Gray's cabin servant, a young Black named Marcus Lopius (Lopez), who was hired on at Cape Verde, was taken. In his attempt to recover his sword, Lopius was seized by the infuriated Indians. The ship's party tried to rescue the young man and what followed, from the crew's point of view, was told by Robert Haswell, mate of the *Lady Washington:* "The first thing which presented itself to our view was a very large group of the natives among the midst of which was the poor black with the thief by the colour loudly calling for assistance saying he had caught the thief, when we were ob-

served by the main boddy of the Natives to haistily approach them they instantly drenched their knives and spears with savage fuery in the body of the unfortunate youth. He quited his hold and stumbled but arose again and stagered toward us but having a flight of arrows thrown into his back and he fell within fifteen yards of me and instantly expiered while they mangled his lifeless corse." Gray's party fled for their lives and the *Lady Washington* was hastily put out to sea. Haswell named the place Murderer's Harbor. Marcus Lopius was the first person killed under an American flag in the Oregon Country. The date of his death was Aug. 16, 1788. How close the marker is to the site of the conflict is anybody's guess.

Near the marker there once stood the village of Hobsonville, a snappy lumber and cannery burg big enough to boast a hotel. It also had a creamery and was a stop on the Tillamook Bay and Pacific Railway and Navigation Co. railroad. In the late 1930s the walls of the empty mills were overtaken by the bay. Eventually the townsite was overgrown with alders.

0.3 m., Tillamook Bay viewpoint.

1 m., jct., **Bay City,** a neat, quiet village that keeps its distance from the highway. **United Methodist Church** (5th & D), built 1893, 5 years after founding of town, is oldest church in Tillamook County.

Lumberman's Memorial Park, Garibaldi

1 m., jct., Kilchis River Road.

    * Named for a Tillamook chief of lore, the Kilchis is a silky, sweet, smooth river flowing thru pungent dairyland, with Norman Rockwell houses and barns. There are "dream spots" in Oregon where the weary traveler sighs, "I'd like to settle here." This is one of them. *5.4 m.,* **Kilchis River Rec. Area** entrance. *0.5 m.,* Kilchis River Park, invigorating, peaceful CG.

    1.6 m., on E, **Tillamook Cheese Factory,** the county's bit of industrial Disneyland. One of most visited places in Oregon. On grounds of factory is *Morning Star II,* replica of *Morning Star I,* built in Tillamook County 1854–55. The replica was launched at Garibaldi July 26, 1959 and for many years was at home in Garibaldi boat basin.

    0.9 m., on W, Goodspeed Rd.

        * *1.4 m.,* **Rain River Preserve,** 141 acres of fresh and saltwater marshland and frontage on Trask and Wilson rivers in Tillamook Bay estuary. Managed by The Nature Conservancy as wildlife refuge.

    0.3 m., on E, **Blue Heron Cheese Factory.** Another processing tour.

    0.9 m., downtown **Tillamook. Pioneer Museum** has finest wildlife exhibits in state, art of the late, enormously talented, deeply concerned Alex Walker. Oldest and most architecturally exciting houses in town are on 1st St., between Courthouse and RR bridge, *0.4 m.* For its modest pop. — less than 5,000 — Tillamook seems much larger. That is because it is a true market town, without serious competition for many miles in any direction. Still, it has grown slowly, little more than 50% since 1915. But then it had more newspapers, lodges and hospitals, and was the terminus of a RR and twice-daily motor train transportation to Mohler.

    When Tillamook's main stem was alive with loggers, fishermen and dairymen, each group could be identified by its occupational boots. The loggers wore caulked boots (sharp spikes attached to the soles) which could tear up a good hardwood floor and prompted stores to post signs, "No caulked boots allowed." Dairymen wore knee boots, used to wade through marshes to herd their cows. Fishermen had on hip boots. There is very little such boot-wearing today. Loggers are few, dairymen remove their boots before coming to town, fishermen are less colorfully garbed. In 1989, in an effort to attract more tourists, Tillamook initiated a summer RR excursion to Wheeler.

    Tillamook is a fishing center. Five rivers flow into Tillamook Bay, including the Wilson, Trask, and Tillamook. Fishers come to these rivers for spring and fall chinook, winter steelhead, and summer steelhead.

    Jct., 0 6. (See *Cross-Coast Range Roads.*)

    Jct., Three Capes Rd.

        * Turn W onto 3d. *1.8 m.,* jct. (L, short cut to Netarts and Cape Lookout SP.) Take R — Three Capes Scenic Route. *5.1 m.,* marker indicating site of **Bay Ocean Park.** There were a goodly number of towns throughout Oregon that have completely disappeared; Bay Ocean Park may have been the

largest. Founded in 1906 by a real estate broker from Kansas City who envisioned an Oregon version of Atlantic City here, the town grew swiftly. The first person to purchase a lot, in 1907, was also the last to leave, in 1952. On June 22, 1912, Bay Ocean Park had its grand commercial opening. The business district contained a store, PO, 3-story hotel (with automatic fire sprinklers), bowling alley, tin shop, bakery. Nearby was natatorium, with 50 x 160 ft. pool. Town had 4 miles of pavement, its own electric lighting, water and telephone systems, harbor, ferry boat, narrow gauge RR. By 1914, 600 bldg. lots had been sold. By 1915, it had a large natural park, tennis court and golf links, as well as a PS, Commercial Club, Methodist Church. Meanwhile the bay was at work, the water cutting away at the banks. The natatorium was the first to go, in 1932. By 1949 more than 20 homes had fallen into the deep. Three years later the tides ripped thru the land and made Bay Ocean Park an island. In an attempt to save the village, a breakwater was built in 1956 and the peninsula reestablished. But the village was doomed, with home after home devoured by the arm of the sea or dismantled and moved away. On Feb. 15, 1960 the last house (deserted) tumbled into the bay — and that was all she wrote for Bay Ocean Park.

Driftwood beach near Cape Meares

0.2 m., jct., (Straight: *0.7 m.,* driftwood beach. Fantastic driftwood sculpturing. Ghost fort by the sea. One of most unusual spectral bits of beach on Oregon Coast. Return *0.7 m.* to 3 Capes Scenic Rte. jct. Turn R)

Turn L at jct. to driftwood beach. *0.2 m.,* entrance to **Cape Meares SP.** *(0.6 m.,* SP parking lot.) Trail leads to unoccupied Cape Meares Light House, restored structure with photo mural display. Another trail, into woods, bends to **"Octopus Tree,"** giant Sitka spruce with massive trunk that branches like candelabra at base. Brief walk beyond this massif leads to outreach of Cape Meares, named for colorful British sea adventurer and maritime entrepreneur, John Meares, who came this way in 1788. In one of those not too uncommon situations of confusion, Meares called present Cape Meares, Cape Lookout. This 700 ft. rocky headland, looking almost as wild and beautiful today as it did when only Indians dwelled in these parts, was unseen to European eyes until sighted in 1775 by Bruno Heceta, Spanish explorer. John Meares, who arrived 3 years later, found the bay (Tillamook) shut off by a sand barrier and called it Quicksand Bay. A variety of bird life uses this habitat of ocean shore, estuary and freshwater lake (Cape Meares Lake). Migrat-

Octopus Tree, Cape Meares   *Phoebe L. Friedman*

ing whales observed from cape in Dec. and Jan. and again in early spring. Seabirds nest offshore on Three Arch Rocks during spring and summer. *2.5 m., jct.* Turn R. *0.2 m.,* **Oceanside,** a breeze-filtered hamlet facing out to **Three Arch Rocks Nat. Wildlife Refuge.** During nesting season, rocks are inhabited by swarms of murres, gulls, cormorants, puffins, petrels and guillemots and have become one of the largest "bird cities" on continent. Rocks also permanent home of large herd of Steller sea lions. **Oceanside Beach Wayside is parking area.** Town boasts "one of the finest bathing beaches on the Oregon Coast, with no crab holes, assuring you of the utmost safety in surf bathing." Also: "Excellent Rock and surf fishing, scenery that will thrill the camera fan, agate and driftwood hunting, and at low tides you may explore ocean caves and natural marine gardens. You will enjoy smooth sandy beaches, the tunnel, sand dunes, more sun, less wind." End of commercial — except that the tunnel is gone.

* Return *0.2 m.* to jct. Curve R. *2.1 m.,* **Netarts,** modest village of family cottage type. Prefix *ne* is common among Indians names of NW Coast and there is an ethnological theory that *ne* means place, or location, such as the place of *tarts,* whatever *tarts* means in Indian. In contemporary society "netarts" could mean the place of a special kind of bakery or, well . . . *0.4 m.,* turn R. *0.1 m.,* **Netarts Bay Rec. Area.** BL & marina. *1.3 m.,* jct. Turn R. *3.9 m.,* entrance to **Cape Lookout SP.** CG, PA, fishing, DS, FHP, Located in typical coastal rain forest — Sitka spruce, western hemlock and western red cedar most common, with red alder along clearings. Undergrowth of area is thick tangle of salal, box blueberry, salmonberry, and Pacific waxmyrtle. Sword fern, skunk cabbage and wildflowers such as lily-of-the-valley and trillium make up the ground cover of the moist, shady forest. To S., cape is intriguing to those with geological bent. Volcanic in origin, its basalt cliffs have withstood the onslaughts of wind and water for more than 20 million years. Cliffs on S are much higher and steeper than those on N, which are indented with several coves. N of CG a *4 m.* sand spit and dunes parts Netarts Bay from ocean. Netarts estuary is habitat for many of the park's 154 species of birds. From parking lot at far reach of SP, easy trail to gold-burnished beach. From parking lot, *8 m.* easy trail to lip of Cape Lookout. But read on: there is another way to get there.

1.1 m., **Anderson's View Point.** Splendid vista of Cape Meares, Three Arch Rocks, and sea. 1.6 m., parking area at top of cape for Cape Lookout trails. (To end of cape, *2.5 m.;* to day use area, *2.5 m.;* to beach, *2 m.*) Most popular trail is to cape's end. Trail weaves thru towering trees, including virgin Sitka spruce, with no undergrowth but blanket of sword fern; beneath mammoth trees toppled by wind; into moist and shadowy glens where wildflowers are massed; along cliffs plunging 500 ft. into Pacific; looks out S along coast; touches plaque where B-17 crashed in 1943; points the eye to a sea bird rookery, with flocks of California murres in nesting season. The doleful

Murre Colony on Cape Lookout   *Courtesy Alex Walker*

sounds heard along upper trail are those of a warning buoy *0.5 m.* NW of
cape; buoy, too, comes into view. Trail's end provides views of migrating
whales in Dec. and Jan., March and May as well as seals and sea lions on
offshore rocks all year and migrations of shore and sea birds in spring and fall.

Between Cape Lookout SP parking area for trails and Cape Kiwanda there
are stretches of road atypical for this section of the Oregon Coast: thick banks
of wild shrubbery, tall beach grass and dune ridges, and past overlooks, beach
and camping and picnic grounds. The scene shifts from gloomy moors of
19th-century British novelists to barnyards out of Iowa.

* 3.3 m., turn R onto Woods Rd. *1 m.* **Sandlake.** Store. In 1915, place had
more people than in 1990. (Turn W for Sand Beach Park. *2.7 m.,* **Sand Beach
Park,** FS CG on tidal basin off Pacific called Sand Lake. Dunes area to N is
Dunebuggy Heaven and is great for motor bikes equipped to handle sand.)
4.2 m., **Tierra Del Mar,** a growing toss of houses. *2.7 m.,* **Cape Kiwanda,** an
exercise in calendar art; sculptured headland flanking a merry cove, gleaming beach, and (another) Haystack Rock. Day use SP. This cape is one of the
few place in the world where boats are launched into the open surf from
sandy beach. During appropriate season, hundreds of commercial and sports

fishers take off from here each morning, sometimes westering 50 m. from shore in pursuit of salmon. Since the 1920s, the unique sport of dory fishing has been popular here. Dory fleet has grown to more than 1,000 boats and is celebrated at the dory derby, usually held in early June. The N side of cape is a literal jumping-off point for hang gliders, who indulge themselves all seasons but winter. Those with skill and luck ride an air current hundreds of feet before touching beach. To S, beach rolls 4 m. along day-use **Robert Straub** (formerly Nestucca Spit) **SP** to mouth of Nestucca River, regarded by fishers as one of the finest streams in state and second only to the Rogue for fighting steelhead. No part of the coast is — to date — as unspoiled as Nestucca Spit, a "sand wall" for Nestucca Bay. Dunes topped by waves of beach grass roll back from the water to heights of 40 ft. in narrow part of spit; in widest part, a higher, naked "traveling dune" is pushed back and forth by capricious winds. Winter hikers find Japanese glass floats, sand dollars and odd bits of driftwood. *1.1 m.*, **Pacific City,** shopping village of area. Store bldg. was once

Haystack Rock is background for dory landing at Cape Kiwanda

Courtesy State of Oregon

stagecoach inn and later, reputedly, hideout for rum runner. Turn S. *2.8 m.,* US 101.

From Tillamook, on US 101:

Leaving Tillamook , the land of trees, cheese and ocean breeze, US 101 leaves the water and pokes thru dairy country, small towns, and rather unimaginative settings. Here it is not all marine in flavor and seems far removed from the ambience of the littoral. But if you like cows and barns and the odor of clover, you're home.

2.4 m., jct., Industrial Park.

    * *1.1 m.,* turn R. onto Blimp Blvd. *0.6 m.,* hangers which housed Naval dirigibles during WWII.

2.4 m., Rest Area.

2.3 m., turnoff E to **Munson Creek CP.**

    * *1.1 m.,* turn into park. *0.5 m.,* parking. The park is a darkling mass of moss-hung firs, maples, cedars, spruce and hemlock. Sunlight filters in as though it were holy water meted out to the anointed. A shadow sleeps on until new light or dark dissolves it. The next shadow rests on the same bed of cones or couch of ferns. Look up and down and all around you. Here is the forest primeval as it was a century ago, as much of the northern coast was 100 years — and much more — back. If you look sharply you may see the red-legged frog, a native to the damp forested areas of W Oregon. A trail cuts *0.5 m.* thru the mossy, dark, magnificently sombre forest to **Munson Creek Falls,** at 319 ft. highest in Coast Range. (For more, see "A Rising of Spirit at Munson Falls" in author's *Tracking Down Oregon.*)

3.9 m., Sandlake Jct.

    * *4.4 m.,* Three Capes Scenic Route. Turn L for Sandlake and Pacific City; straight for Cape Lookout SP and Oceanside.

3.5 m., Beaver-Nestucca River Access Rd. (See *Cross-Coast Range Roads.*) In Oregon, there are Beaverton, Beaver Marsh, Beaver Landing, Beaver Hill, Beaver Creek, and, here, just plain old **Beaver,** all of them honoring the state animal, the American Beaver (*Castor canadensis*), and all in W Oregon, which ought to make the ghosts of Central Oregon trapper frown. Anyway, if there was a beaver colony here, it would probably outnumber the humans in Beaver. In 1915 village had about same number of people but it also had cheese factory, sawmill, Co-operative Loganberry Assn. and two lodges. Now it's TV.

2.6 m., on E, wayside. A place to park, a toss of grace, the shade of trees, a table to picnic on.

1.1 m., **Nestucca River Bridge.** Below sings the Nestucca on its way to the sea. There always seems to be a fisher in the water or on a bank.

0.8 m., **Hebo.** In 1915, Hebo had creamery and shingle mill, which is more than it has today. Hebo was named after nearby 3,153 ft. Mt. Hebo, which derived its designation, according to the authoritative *Oregon Geographic Names,* from a pioneer Heave Ho, "because from their position, the mountain seemed to have

Munson Creek Falls

been heaved up above the surroundings." As anyone who takes the road to Mt. Hebo (see *0 22*) will readily ascertain, the description seems sound.

Jct., 0 22. (See *Cross-Coast Range Roads.*) (*0.2 m on 0 22*, turnoff to Hebo Lake.)

2.4 m., **Cloverdale.** One glance at the rural environs and it isn't difficult to see how the village got its name. Started as cheese town, Cloverdale is still cheesy, but not as dairy vital as it was a few decades ago. It was bigger in 1915, when it had a bank and several lodges. US 101 here is a narrow street curling its way thru a fatigued, weatherbeaten town that looks like a shaggy cocker spaniel sitting in a mud puddle. Spire of St. Joseph's Catholic Church can be seen from many parts of the valley.

2.4 m., jct., **Woods.**

County rd. to Woods, 4.8 m., passes thru sweet, rolling land and touches some of the most photogenic barns on Oregon Coast. From Woods, county rd. continues *4 m.* to Cape Kiwanda.

0.5 m., jct., **Pacific City.**

1 m., jct., Little Nestucca River Road.

 * A nice, unhurried way to get to the valley — or the coast in reverse — by bypassing part of state roads 0 22 & 0 18. *1.3 m.,* Little Nestucca River, a rippling sapphire, narrow enough to be intimate. The first of six bridges across the Little Nestucca on this short road. *0.4 m.,* Meda Loop Jct. (At this jct., turn R. Nothing left of hamlet, started in 1887. Some barns and houses along Meda Loop go back to turn of century— and earlier, perhaps to 1875. *2.1 m.,* forks. Take L fork. *0.9 m.,* US 101.) Straight from Meda Loop Jct.: *1.4 m.,* Little Nestucca CP. PA. Small gouged-out shade spot. River across road. As road continues E, Little Nestucca grows wider and swifter. *3.2 m.,* jct., 0 22. (For 0 22, See *Cross-Coast Range Roads.*)

0.5 m., Little Nestucca River Bridge. At whatever point one looks, this stream refreshes the soul.

1.m., **Oretown.** The cheese factories and salmon cannery of yore are grey with dust. Town was named not for any minerals but as abbreviation of Oregon town; original suggestion was Ore Town. Except for church, Grange hall and hint of houses, a deserted village could not be more deserted.

0.7 m., on W, Winema Jct.

 * *0.6 m.,* **Winema,** Christian camp with public access to relatively little-used beach.

3.8 m., **Neskowin,** affluent resort community on the increase. **Neskowin Beach Wayside (FHP)** provides parking for beach walks. Most famous landmark is Proposal Rock. Legend has it that a sea captain took his sweetheart to this rocky island to propose. There is no record of her response. For all we know, he may still be waiting for her answer somewhere on the great sea of time. S of rock is "**Sunken Forest,**" plot of stumps indicating presence of forest here. Stumps visible according to movement of sand and tide.

1 m., **Scenic Forest Drive.**

 * Drive thru coastal woods, part of Siuslaw National Forest know as Cascade Head Experimental Forest. Foresters say it contains finest example of Sitka spruce-western hemlock forest that originated after 1846 fire. Also contains pure red alder forests. Research conducted here in forest management. *4.3 m.,* Neskowin Creek FS CG, close to the sea yet deep in the trees. *5.6 m.,* jct., 0 18, at Otis.

2.3 m., jct., Cascade Head Rd.

 * Road twists thru **Cascade Head Experimental Forest** with stirring views of hills, dales, coast and marching woods. Far more beauty on this pike than along most of US 101. *2.5 m.,* jct. R to N View Point. *0.7 m.,* N View Point. Marvelous panorama of ocean and Coast Range, and often the viewers are alone since relatively few people come here.

 * At jct., fork toward Nature Conservancy Trail: *0.4 m.,* Spruce-Hemlock Forest Community, arboreal concept. *0.4 m.,* start of Nature Conservancy

Proposal Rock, Neskowin

Sunken Forest, Neskowin   *Courtesy Oregon State*

N Trail. *(0.7 m.,* from trailhead, summit viewpoint; *1.5 m.* from trailhead, cover overlook. Trail affords ocean views, grasslands and Pacific forest.) *0.9 m.,* start of Harts Cove Trail *(3 m.).* In 1969 part of Cascade Head, a 1400-ft. promontory jutting out into the sea, was purchased by The Nature Conservancy as a natural area. This includes high meadows, rainforest groupings with coniferous trees up to 200 ft. in height, and steep rocky cliffs down which waterfalls fling themselves into the rushing sea. The Nature Conservancy notes of its Cascade Head Preserve: "A portion of the preserve serves as important ungrazed coastal grassland along a narrow strip fronting the Pacific Ocean. The rare plant, *Silene douglasii var. oraria,* which occurs in only two other locations in the world (also on the Oregon Coast) is located on the preserve."

2.7 m., jct., on W, Three Rocks Rd.

* *2.3 m.,* turn R. *0.3 m.,* turnoff for Sitka Center for Art and Ecology. *0.1 m.,* on R, entrance to Cascade Natural Area. *0.1 m.,* jct. Take L. *0.2 m.,* end of road, where Salmon River curves to enter Pacific.

There is a legend here. The first white settlers were told by the local Indians of a sailing ship that was wrecked long, long ago, and of strange men who boated ashore with treasure chests which they buried before disappearing into the timber. The settlers began to dig around and uncovered several

Mouth of Salmon River at Cascade Head   *Phoebe L. Friedman*

Highway marker on US 101

pieces of a wrecked ship and in a shell mound found the skeletons of two non-Indians. One, goes the legend, was a black man 8 ft. tall.

Jct. On E, Scenic Drive.

* *0.7 m.,* take R. *0.3 m.,* merger with Scenic Forest Dr. (See above) *0.4 m.,* 0 18.

1.3 m., jct., 0 18 — to McMinnville and 0 99 W. (See *Cross-Coast Range Roads.*)

1 m., jct., **East Devil's Lake Rd.**

* *0. 5 m.,* postcard pretty lake, centerpiece of 10 m. loop drive. Relatively shallow, warm lake, adorned by three fine parks, is popular with swimmers, waterskiers, fishers (trout, catfish, bass), and hydroplaners (world speedboat records have been set at races here on 4th of July and last week in Sept.) According to Indian legend, there lived in this placid pond a monster who on occasion rose up to attack humans. *0.2 m.,* forks. Take R. *0.6 m.,* US 101 at Devil's Lake Golf Course.

0.5 m., **Neotsu.** PO is only business in town — except maybe golf course across road.

0.2 m., **45th Parallel Marker.** Halfway point on coast between Equator and North Pole.

0.8 m., jct.

* Turn sharp W for Road's End Beach Wayside. *0.9 m.,* Wayside parking. Sand, tide and solitude on a crisp morning. PA. Great view of Cascade Head. At entrance to Wayside is Oregon historical marker: "Phil Sheridan

Road. Built when Sheridan was on police patrol at Ft. Yamhill. It facilitated necessary travel via the old elk trail (Salmon River), Ocean Beach, and the Siletz Indian Agency."

0.1 m., on W, **Lincoln City Information Center,** N beginning of Lincoln City, made up of five small, once-independent towns. Lincoln City today is stretched out like taffy, with skipping-across-the-pavement hopscotch mercantile clusters, so by the time you think you're out of Lincoln City, you find yourself in another part of it. Lincoln City trumpets to the world of its "20 Miracle Miles." But it has been more Coney Island than anything else, though in recent years it has been trying to clean up its act. Still, it remains about as true to the spirit of the Oregon Coast as Iago was to Othello. Among the gimmicks, the Lincoln City promoters have conjured up to hustle tourist business is Dolly the Trolley, which can be rented in the evening for $50 an hour. "Out of the days of yesteryear, comes a method of transportation unique in the Northwest called the Dolly the Trolley, a modern vehicle, patterned after an old fashioned trolley car, that serves as a transit system for local residents and a memorable experience for visitors to Lincoln City, Oregon." So it is writ.

0.3 m., on E, **Lacey's Doll & Antique Museum.**

0.6 m., N 22d St.

E *0.1 m.,* **Abraham Lincoln Memorial,** 14-ft. bronze statue, "Lincoln on the Prairie." The lank lawyer, deep in the saddle, is engulfed in his book as his horse nibbles on grass along the way. Statue was originally in city park, refreshed by the green of life. But commercialism is King in Lincoln City and statue was moved to side of busy street, where Lincoln is treated to a steady stream of car pollution. In its new location, the statue looks very much out of place and almost ugly.

0.2 m., N 21st St. Turnoff to public beach access.

0.6 m., on E, Devil's Lake SP.

* *0.1 m.,* **Devil's Lake SP.** CG. FHP. Fishing and lake swimming almost in heart of Lincoln City. Anglers find catfish weighing up to 20 lbs., as well as rainbows more than 2 ft. long and large bass.

0.3 m., **D River Wayside.** Beach access. FHP. Locals point to Guinness as proof that D River, which runs 440 ft. from Devil's Lake to Pacific, is world's shortest river. The experienced traveler learns two things: first, question the natives, then question what they tell you.

Just about at site of Wayside, at beach, is where the first white vacationers on the Oregon Coast camped in 1837. Early missionaries, Jason Lee and Cyrus Shepard, guided by Joe Gervais, the canny old settler of French Prairie, came with their brides, Anna Maria Pittman and Susan Downing, to honeymoon on the whispering sands. Legend records that, in the week the ardent missionaries were here, they cured themselves of malaria and evangelized the Salmon River Indians. Neither the malaria nor the Indians could have been serious.

0.7. m., jct., East Devil's Lake Rd.

   * *1 m.,* East Devil's Lake SP. PA, BR, FHP.

2.6 m., **Schooner Creek Bridge,** open window to Siletz Bay. In winter of 1972–73, severe erosion came close to playing havoc on Siletz Spit. A house under construction was destroyed and other houses were saved only by prompt placement of riprap, large rocks laid at the base of the property to ward off wave erosion. There was dread concern that Siletz Split might breach, as Bayocean Spit had 20 years earlier. Bayocean Spit's erosion was caused by building of jetty at entrance to Tillamook Bay. The situation here is different. In the words of Paul D. Komar and C. Cary Rea in *The Ore Bin* (Aug. 1976), "No jetties are present at the Siletz Bay inlet. Instead, the erosion is associated with rip currents, strong

Mouth of D River   *Phoebe L. Friedman*

narrow currents that flow across the surf zone and out beyond the breakers. Rip currents erode embayments on the beach, at times cutting back into the dunes on which houses were built." But some people do not learn and demand to build anywhere.

1.5 m., Drift Creek Road.

* *1.5 m.,* forks. Take R. *0.5 m.,* on L, **Drift Creek CB,** considered oldest CB in Oregon. Built in 1914 at cost of less than $2,000, CB was constructed of cedar shingle roof, wooden flooring and flared batten-board siding of Douglas fir. Long in disuse, it is for pedestrians only.

0.9 m., jct., 0 229 — **Kernville.** The town began as a cannery in 1896 on N shore of Siletz River, about 2 m. E of US 101. It was never much and is less today, a tavern. **Siletz River,** which empties into S end of Siletz Bay, is popular salmon stream, especially for chinooks in Aug. and Sept.; silvers in Oct. and Nov. The Siletz has another distinction; it is known as the crookedest river in Oregon. Though it is 125 m. in length, its headwaters rise only 14 m. from its mouth.

* 0 229. From US 101 the river of the Siletz is accompanied by the road to town of Siletz. It is a dreamy, lovely stream, though trailer villages near its lower reaches have marred its beauty. Yet, even so, there is a rare stillness here, with the tranquility seldom disturbed. There is no definite information as to the origin or meaning of Siletz. All that is really known is that the Indians were the southernmost of the Salishan linguistic family, and the river

Drift Creek Bridge

and town preserve the name. The Luckiamute Calapooya called the Siletz *Tsa Shnadsh amin* but there is no translation for that name, and it would not go as well on a map as Siletz. *1 m.,* approximate original site of town of **Kernville,** with sawmill, PO, store. *0.5 m.,* across river, site of house built for movie, *Sometimes a Great Notion. 0.4 m.,* approximate site of salmon cannery started by Kern brothers in 1896. *0.1 m.,* on R, historical marker tells of Indian legend of Coyote: "To insure himself of a constant supply of salmon, Coyote attempted to dam the river here and was partly successful. In the fall, especially, large chinook salmon wait here for the first rains before ascending to upriver spawning beds." *15.7 m.,* **A. W. "Jack" Morgan Park,** Lincoln County greensward on N bank of Siletz. *6.2 m.,* **Siletz,** known as Agency HQ of Siletz Indian Reservation. Est. 1855 by Federal directive, it initially covered almost 1.4 million acres. Under pressure of white expansion, acreage had been pared to 47,000 only 37 years later. Example: In 1866, a 20 m. section, including Yaquina Bay, was removed from center of reserve for exclusive use to white settlement. First Indians, vanquished of Rogue River Wars, brought here. They included all Oregon Athapascan tribes except the Umpqua; the Kusan and Yakonan tribes; some of the Salishan peoples of Oregon; and a few of the Kalapooian peoples: in time, all became know as Siletz. The placing together of several antagonistic tribes was responsible for bloodshed and strange rituals. Legend has it that Indian braves felled in intertribal warfare were sometimes buried with a $20 gold piece in one hand and a knife in the other — equipped to pay or fight their way to the happy hunting ground. Hunger and disease took a far heavier toll than fighting. By 1887 only 550 members of the reservation were alive. Still, with all the miseries, there developed a rich intermingling of Indian culture and about the turn of the century, Indians here joined fad of other reservations by forming a coronet band. Eventually agency was moved to Salem and in 1925 closed and reservation terminated. Five decades later a drive for reservation status was on in earnest and culminated in success, but with only a handful of acres. For 10 years, from its erection in 1856 to its abandonment, Siletz Blockhouse here was home of bored soldiers, with little more to do than menial labor but gripe and gamble. No trace of fortification exists.

** Jct., **Logsden** and **Nashville.**

The road from Siletz to Logsden and Nashville and then over to Summit and down to Kings Valley roughly approximates in reverse the thorny trail cut across the Coast Range by Phil Sheridan when he was stationed at Ft. Hoskins, from July of 1856 to May of 1857. After the sharply-graded trace was completed, Sheridan sought to demonstrate its practical value, so, as he reminisced in his *Memoirs,* "I started a Government wagon over it loaded with fifteen hundred pounds of freight drawn by six yoke of oxen, and escorted by a small detachment of soldiers." At the base of a steep hill, the oxen balked and would not move, despite the severe whip lashings laid on by the soldiers.

Then, wrote Sheridan, "Following as a last resort an example I heard of on a former occasion, that brought into use the rough language of the country, I induced the oxen to move with alacrity, and the wagon and contents were speedily carried to the summit. The whole truth was at once revealed; the oxen had been broken and trained by a man who, when they were in a pinch, had encouraged them by his frontier vocabulary, and they would not realize what was expected of them under extraordinary conditions until they heard familiar and possible urgent phrases." Sheridan took the wagon to Siletz Blockhouse, all right, but concluded wryly, "as it was not brought back, even in all the time I was stationed in that country [until Sept., 1861], I think comment on the success of my road is unnecessary."

** *0.3 m.,* E of 223, on N, **Government Hill marker,** telling of reservation. (*0.1 m.* up this road, **Paul Washington Cemetery,** named after PFC in Co. G., 361st Inf., 91st Division, who at age 26 was killed Sept. 1918 in WWI. Indian cemetery contains graves of Charles DePoe, after whom Depoe Bay was probably named; the Catfish family; Chas. Shellhead; Joseph Adams, a graduate of Carlisle; Norman Strong, born at Siletz in 1864; and scores of others. Across street is office of Confederated Tribes of the Siletz, in handsome, airy bldg.)

** *1.8 m.,* on S, **Riverside Cemetery;** many Indians also here. Tombstones in rear date back to 1886. *2.8 m.,* Sams Creek Rd. On S was CB, put up 1922 at length of 100 ft. Gone now. *2.9 m.,* **Logsden,** named after elderly Indian who lived on Siletz Reservation. Store. Logsden is typical of the meagre settlements along the roads N of US 20. Many of the people here are urban expatriates who have opted for the slow-paced cooperative life, where keeping up with the Joneses is redundant, since everyone assumes the status of a homespun Jones. People here have learned a sort of neighborhood sufficiency, which their predecessors a century ago knit for themselves. Between these sparse rural settlements are tomahawked hills, ladle-scooped valleys, dales that come out of Grandma Moses, and, at their bases, fine farms and prosperous-looking farmhouses.

** *0.2 m.,* jct., **Moonshine Park.** (Take L. 3.5 m., bend L. *0.4 m.,* Moonshine CP on Siletz River. Attractive, roomy, better than some SPs. CG, PA.)

5.4 m., **Siletz River Fish Hatchery.** *5.1 m.,* start of lovely little valley cupped by folds of hills. *4.6 m.,* **Nashville,** named for town's most prominent citizen, Wallis Nash, well educated Englishman who visited Oregon in 1877 and returned for good in 1879. He was a founder of Oregon Pacific RR and Oregon Agricultural College (now Oregon State University), a businessman, lawyer, farmer, journalist, staunch advocate of the Workmen's Compensation Law, and author, best known for *Oregon, There and Back in 1877; Two Years in Oregon;* and *A Lawyer's Life on Two Continents.* He died at Nashville in 1926, at age 89. The town never was much; in 1915 it had pop. of 15 and hasn't improved substantially on that, though residences are mushrooming in its environs. If there weren't a marker, you wouldn't know you were in town.

** Jct., Eddyville Rd.

*** The Yaquina River is frequently met; so are RR crossings — five in all. The tracks laze along the roads like a carefree boy gone fishing. By fifth crossing, when freight train is running, car riders and train crews come to feel they know each other. 5.2 m., **Nortons,** formerly RR station. PO est. 1895; long gone, with everything else. 6.7 m., US 20.

** From jct., Eddyville Rd. 2.5 m., **Summit.** For all its vacancy, it's hard to believe that village once had HS, church, Grange & MWA Lodge. That was in 1915, when pop. was 55. Summit Community center, in old church, moved here by volunteers on 4/11/78 from hill 0.3 m. S.

** 0.3 m., jct. (To L, Hoskins. 2.2 m., jct. Turn R. 6.2 m., over low-saddled hills and past trooping woods and corsucant meadows, with nary another car on road, Hoskins-Luckiamute River Rd. Turn R. 0.1 m., **Hoskins.** Tavern. 1.6 m., 0 223.)

** (To R, **Blodgett.** 0.6 m., on L, **Summit Cemetery** (1899). Thru the weeds and the dandelions to the land where the dead dreamers lie. 4.2 m., twisting thru alders and friends, US 20 — Blodgett.)

* S on 0 229 from Siletz town center:

0.1 m., on E, **Hee Hee Illahee CP.** PA. BL on Siletz River. 6.7 m., on W, historical marker. Approximate site of US Army depot for Siletz Reservation. 0.7 m., US 20.

From turnoff to Kernville — 0 229 on US 101: 1 m., Immomen Rd.

* 1 m., on N. **Mossy Creek Pottery.** 0.2 m., on N, **Alder House II,** glass blowing studio. Demonstrations. There are many potteries and glass blowers along coast, but this is such a benign road it ought to be befriended.

0.4 m., **Salishan,** the brightest jewel of Oregon hostelries. If you have to ask what the rates are you shouldn't ask. But you can stroll about, observing the Japanese walks, the elegance of the landscape, and the magnificent art collection. Here is a rare example of where human construction can actually enhance the environment.

0.2 m., jct., **Gleneden Beach.**

* 0.9 m., Gleneden Beach, small, roadstrip village too young for legends.

0.9 m., jct., Gleneden Beach SP.

* Gleneden Beach Wayside, PA overlooking the broad Pacific. FHP.

1.8 m., **Lincoln Beach,** community so strung out it ought to be called Stringtown. Young, PO est. 1933.

0.6 m., jct., **Fogarty Creek SP.**

* 0.2 m., SP parking lot. Delightful park with lots of grass, picnic tables, trees, rustic bridges across creek. FHP. Hard-surfaced paths to ocean beach. Creek sleepwalking across beach invites wading. Wind protection for sun bathing provided by N and S bluffs.

0.4 m., highway view of Fogarty Creek SP beach. Sheltered creek trickling into sea below seagrass bluffs splits swath of well-trod beach, creating cheerful, photogenic scene. On 1st Sat. after Labor Day, beach is scene of annual Depoe Bay Indian-style Salmon Bake.

0.9 m., **Boiler Bay SP.** PA with unbroken view of ocean adjoining bay named for boiler that was last remains of small freighter lost here 1910. Low tide reveals sight of boiler. Here, crashing against 40 ft. high natural seawall, the Pacific can be mighty scary. Tidal pools aswarm with mussels, hermit crabs, sea urchins, orange starfish and anemones.

1.3 m., **Depoe Bay.** This most geographically exciting town on the Oregon seaboard, whose rockbound bay and colorful harbor, with its amphitheater setting, tingles with flair, is so crowded on a summer Sunday you may have to park a mile away from the center of the one-street (US 101) business section. Locals claim the 6-acre harbor is smallest navigable harbor in world. Geologists reckon it took little Depoe Creek 14 million years to saw thru the ornery basalt to create the inlet. People come here for charter boat fishing and to shop the picturesque stores, but mostly for the scenery. Next to the secluded cove the most popular sight is **Spouting Horn,** a gap in the rock thru which the tide races upward in a geyser of spray, viewed from the sidewalk on W side of US 101. Nearby plaque memorializes two local fishers of the trolling fleet who perished Oct. 4, 1936 on rescue mission. Depoe Bay SP here is PA, viewing site and gift shop. Aquarium, near cove, has wide variety of sealife exhibits and one of the best shell shops in Pacific NW. Origin of town's name obscure: derived either from cove, a haven or "depot", or named after Charley DePoe, Siletz Indian who caught fancy of whites with his charm and kindness.

2 m., **Whale Cove,** restaurant as hamlet. Nearby are caves cut in sandstone formations.

Rocky Creek SP. Wayside (PA) in plot of meadow and stunted trees. Excellent views of ocean and scalloped seawall. N of park, trail falls to S side of cove named for whale that washed up here and was promptly butchered by whale-steak-loving Indians early in 20th century.

Along this part of the coast, whale watching by residents is a way of life. Some of finest viewing areas are along the seawall at Depoe Bay but Boiler Bay, Whale Cove and Rocky Creek also draw the faithful. The "insiders" make swift for the rocky headlands before the "tourists" crowd them.

0.3 m., jct., Otter Crest Loop.

* *1.6 m.,* unmarked turnoff for dazzling picture of **Otter Crest** and **Cape Foulweather.** *0.4 m.,* Otter Crest Viewpoint on Cape Foulweather.

The following, somewhat condensed article, penned by the author, appeared in the May 19, 1984 edition of Medford *Mail Tribune:*

"What do you see from Otter Crest Viewpoint?

"The rugged coast of Oregon sinuating through the farthest reach of the Pacific?

Cape Foulweather and Otter Crest

"The shallow rocks half-a-mile offshore on which gray sea lions and seals dwell? Sea otters once lived here, before hunters slaughtered the herds.

"The seabird rookery on the larger offshore rocks?

"I see a ghost ship captained by James Cook.

"On a nasty March day in 1788, Cook named the headland on which the viewpoint is perched Cape Foulweather.

"He was 49, one year away from a quibbling death which would not minimize his stature as the foremost navigator of the century.

"So there he sways, near the helmsman, glimpsing the eerie land through rents in the swirling fog and whispering to himself as he prepares to note his thoughts. 'Think I'll call this Cape Foulweather. That occurs to me as a likely designation.'

"James Cook, the Yorkshire farm laborer's son who taught himself astronomy and trigonometry, who could chart without a chronometer, who produced charts of the Labrador and Newfoundland coasts that were used for more than 100 years, whose ingenuity conquered the decimation of scurvy.

"There was a mariner, this British seadog. He roamed through the vast Pacific, was the first white man to find the Hawaiian Islands, circumnavigated the South Pole, mapped the long coast of eastern Australia and the entire coast of New Zealand's two islands, and sailed through Bering Strait to the northern tip of Alaska, proving once and for all that the Northwest Passage was not a navigable route for sailing ships.

"Despite some shortcomings, one of which did him in, Cook could rise to the heights of universal excellence. A Maori chief said of him: 'A noble man cannot be lost in a crowd.' And La Perouse, the French mariner who was

Cook's chief rival in Pacific exploration, summed up the Englishman's achievements in one classical sentence. Chance, declared La Perouse, might enable the most ignorant man to discover islands, but it belonged only to great men to leave nothing more to be done regarding the coasts they had found.

"Cook's fabled life came swiftly to an end in 1779, at the age of 50, on the island of Hawaii. A misunderstanding over a small stolen boat arose with a group of the islanders and Cook momentarily lost his renowned poise. At the water's edge, facing the ocean he loved, he was suddenly clubbed and stabbed.

"There is some doubt as to the precise location of his grave but that matters not to me. I know his spirit is at sea, and every time I come to Otter Crest Viewpoint on Cape Foulweather, I hear a March wind swish the sails of his *Resolution,* and through the fog of time my eyes perceive a ghost ship that will not die."

Devil's Punch Bowl   *Courtesy State of Oregon*

* Otter Crest Viewpoint provides excellent platform for watching migrating whales.

* At Otter Crest Viewpoint, forks. L, *0.2 m.*, US 101. R fork: *0.2 m.*, turn R. *1.3 m.*, **Devil's Punch Bowl SP** (PA, FHP) at town of Otter Rock. *0.1 m.*, parking for tourist business section of Otter Rock and Devil's Punch Bowl, the latter a wave-worn bowl-shaped rock where incoming tides pour thru openings in the deep, round cauldron to boil up, then retreat in satanic fury. Trails lead thru Marine Gardens and to beach. Return to Otter Crest Loop. Turn R. *0.4 m.*, jct., US 101.

From N end of Otter Crest Loop, on US 101:

1.5 m., turnoff for Otter Crest Viewpoint.

* *0.2 m.*, **Otter Crest Viewpoint.** *1.1 m.*, Otter Rock Jct. Turnoff W for Devil's Punch Bowl SP. *0.5 m*, S end of Otter Crest Loop.

1.1 m., jct., **Beverly Beach SP.**

* *0.1 m.*, SP. CG, PA, FHP. Group tent facilities, club camping, special CG area for hikers-bikers. Camping in heavily vegetated area drained by Spencer Creek. Broad, sandy beach great for casual strolling or vigorous hiking. Finds of Miocene marine fossils, including bones of whales and sea lions, have been made in cliffs here.

1.5 m., Moolack Beach parking area. Short walk down to smooth sands.

2 m., Lighthouse Rd.

* *1.1 m.*, **Yaquina Head Light Station,** no longer manually operated. Still a sight, though, is the 96 ft. tower, highest of all Coast lighthouses. Built by mistake, the designated site being Otter Crest. Original lenses, manufactured in 1868, still there. To R of tower, cliffs plunge to rocky caves tumultuous with wild agitation of lunging waves. Offshore from lighthouse is **National Wildlife Refuge** — massive dark and green-stained cliffs cleaved from mainland by ruthless sea. Cacophony of scoldings, complaints and calls from flight wheel of cormorants, murres, herring gulls, cliff swallows and pigeon guillemots. Harbor seals rest on rocks all year. Guided field tours to head offered thru Hatfield Marine Science Center, near Newport. Best time to see nesting seabirds on offshore rocks is May thru Aug. Good platform for watching migrating whales.

0.1 m., **Agate Beach,** noted for beach deposits of agate, especially those of water and moss. The late, great composer Ernest Bloch lived here and is memorialized by plaque off W side of US 101 near Lighthouse Rd.

0.6 m., on W, turnoff to **Agate Beach Wayside.**

* *0.7 m.*, Wayside. Driftwood piled up as though felled from sea forest. Good view of Yaquina Head Light Station. PA, FHP.

2.1 m., jct., US 20. (For US 20, see *Cross-Coast Range Roads.*)

0.3 m., downtown **Newport.** Once the social lion of the Central Oregon Coast, Newport today is a tourist town for all classes, the largest city between Astoria and North Bend, and the hub of the central coastal rocky beach. Along

Yaquina Head Lighthouse   *Phoebe L. Friedman*

View from Yaquina Head Lighthouse   *Phoebe L. Friedman*

Bloch Memorial at Agate Beach   *Phoebe L. Friedman*

these beaches are found a rich variety of seashore life, including limpets, mussels, clams, sea slugs, snails, chitons, sculpins, sea lettuce, surf grass, squirts, barnacles, sea palm, sea urchins, sea cucumbers, sea stars, sea anemones, sponges and crabs. (Newport calls itself "Dungeness Crab Capital of the World."

Then, too, are seen the jellyfish: the *Velella velella*, the *Aurella*, the *Cyanea*, and others, blue and purple and ribboned on the beach. The *Velella velella* is more commonly known as the "purple sailor" or "by-the-wind sailor" and is told by its triangular sail lined diagonally along its length. The *Aurella* is moon jelly to the beach walkers and is identified by its clear, flat mass. The *Cyanea*, lion's mane to lay folk, is recognized by its yellow or orange mass and more often than not has tentacles attached. All the jellyfish have poison cells, the *Cyanea* being the most poisonous to their prey. It is generally not dangerous to touch the jellyfish after it has shored, but it is strongly advisable not to finger one's eyes or mouth after touching.

There is also the "brain corral," a gray, round, rock-like mass dotted with oval holes, most of them rather small, that houses a colony of black-bodied worms that scientists calls *Dodacaceria fistulicola*.

And there are the microscopic single-celled sea plants called *phytoplankton* by marine biologists and "plant wanderers" in common usage. There are billions of them along the shores of the central coast and when they reproduce, and they reproduce phenomenally, they create a typical spring and summer sight of foaming bubbles which boil up where the sea meets land.

Anyone who has walked the continent's lip of this area has seen bull kelp, also known as bull whips, commonplace names for *Nereocystis luetkeana*. Washed ashore, the brown alga conveys the imagery of bull whips to some and to others appears as onionheaded snakes which, when entwined with each other, look like a heap of sleeping rattlers. Culinary connoisseurs of the coast use the bull kelp to make a marine delicacy called seaweed pickles.

Newport is as well known for its sport as for its commercial fishing. Deep sea boats on the prowl for salmon make regular or chartered trips from May thru Sept. Aug. brings swarms of fishers to Yaquina Bay and River, their hopes high for chinooks and silvers. Still, Newport is a serious commercial fishing town and watching the fishers take off in the morning one is reminded of some lines from Virgil's *Aeneid,* "When we could trust the sea and the winds provided/Calm waters, when the gentle South wind sighed/and called us to the deep, my comrades crowded/Down to the beach and launched our fleet of ships."

Places of interest on and just off US 101:

Lincoln County Historical Museum, in log bldg., back of Information Center at 555 SW Coast Hwy.; near museum stands white frame 1895 **Burrows House,** for 23 years boardinghouse and for almost five decades a mortuary, now Victorian-style museum with period furniture.

In 1856 Phil Sheridan built a fort at, say local historians, where US 101 meets US 20. No trace of it remains. Another opinion is that the blockhouse was built on S shore of Yaquina Bay, and from this conjecture stems a legend. Before the blockhouse was erected, Sheridan encountered strong objections from the Indians, who argued that ancient tradition forbade them from removing the hundreds of burial canoes on the desired ground. After numerous conferences, the Indians agreed the canoes could be moved, but not by them. So, at high tide, Sheridan's soldiers launched the strangest flotilla ever seen in these parts. As the Indians mournfully watched from a bluff, the canoes, bearing the dead, drifted slowly out toward the sunset.

On the Oregon Coast, the legends rise and fall and, emptied of substance, drift in circles.

A more recent legend is that of sharks. Ever since, some years ago, a small salmon shark was killed by a razor clam digger in the surf near Newport, there has been talk of sharks off Newport's waters. In reality, the sharks have more to fear than have humans. Of the 12 species of sharks reported as being in Oregon waters, the really dangerous sharks, the white and the blue, rarely visit coastal Oregon. The sevengill and sleeper sharks can also get mean but they, too, are seen more in hallucination than in fact. Best advice: If you see a shark off Newport or anywhere else, give it the ocean.

The real charm of Newport is down at **Bay Front,** where the town's history began. First white settler arrived in 1855; few years later village was started. In 1866 — two years before PO was opened — swank Ocean House overlooking bay was built by Dr. J. R. Bayley. Named after super-fancy hotel in Newport,

R.I., Ocean House was first bldg. in Newport. It was acquired by US Coast Guard in 1935, who still occupy the site (Ocean House gone decades ago). On July 4, 1866, first celebration of Independence Day in then Benton County was held, with about 400 whites and 300 Indians attending. After the patriotic services were concluded, persons who held land claims along bay met and voted to call their town Newport and spoke of the tiny settlement as the "germ of the San Francisco of Oregon." It didn't quite make the grade but Bay Front came as close to being a Barbary Coast as any Oregon coast town could.

Bay Front is an iridescent buttery stew of sea food restaurants, pubs, wharfside bldgs., **Underseas Gardens** (the finest underwater marine life show on the Coast), and fishing boats nodding at rest, like plow horses after a hard day's pulling. Sunset at Yaquina Bay, when the fishing fleet rides at anchor, is a color symphony of vivid orange, yellow, red and saffron, muted by a subtle range of pastels. The lacey, patrician Yaquina Bay Bridge, focused on from Bay Front, is a photographer's dream.

One of the finest drives in W Oregon, trailing first **Yaquina Bay** and then Yaquina River begins at Bay Front. The route commences with moorages and fishing boats, shifts into marshes and tidal flats occupied by diverse families of seabirds and starring great blue herons.

0.3 m. — from Underseas Garden — on L, giant waterwheel advertising inn. *4.1 m.,* site of **Yaquina City,** just a fishing supply point now but in 1880s boom town, with docks, warehouses, shops, hotels, bank and sizeable pop. In 1887, 144 ships cleared harbor. Town was port of entry for Yaquina Bay. Early medic, Dr. N. M. Davis, est. drug store 1882, became first pres. of Oregon Pharmaceutical Assn. Oregon Pacific RR, ambitious enterprise of volatile promoter T.E. Hogg, reached here 1885, first RR in Oregon to touch salt water. RR station, shops, roundhouse built. Travelers at Newport took steamer for 3 m. ride across bay to Yaquina City, then boarded 7 a.m. Oregon Pacific for 3 1/2 hours ride along "The Yaquina Route" to Corvallis. Going W from Corvallis, train left 1 p.m., arrived Yaquina City 4:30 p.m., travelers got to Newport hotel in time for supper. OP ran into financial difficulties, was purchased by lumberman A.B. Hammond, renamed Corvallis & Eastern RR Co. (For more, see *Stations West* by Edwin D. Culp.)

1 m., purported site of **Oysterville.** Native oysters discovered here 1861; first mdse. store on Yaquina Bay opened 1864. Fish cannery came later. Oysterville thrived in 1860s, then declined; disappeared early this century. To add to confusion, its PO name was Winant.

2.8 m., Oregon Oyster Co., here since 1907. (Retail sales) *2.3 m.,* **Craigie Point.** Marker here to James Craigie, native of Scotland, came to US 1834 at age 21. Employed by Hudson's Bay Co. Married Mary Ann, daughter of Bannock chief, 1845. After knocking around West, moved 1866 to Yaquina Bay. Wife died within year and buried on hilltop near home. Craigie passed away 1895, is only Hudson's Bay man to be buried in Lincoln County (Eureka Cemetery at Newport). *0.7 m.,* approximate site of 1852 homestead of George Luther Boone, great-grandson of Daniel. Returning from Calif. gold mines in 1851, he wintered at Myrtle Point where he met, wooed, married 13-year-old Mourning Ann Young. Riding double on horseback they reached here, built stalwart home, raised 12 children.

2.8 m., **Toledo,** at Business US 20. Turn R. *0.4 m.,* at 1st stop light, turn R. Follow along industrial area. Backcountry road keeps pace with Yaquina River. There always seems to be a stillness of peace here. *1.6 m.,* forks. Take L. *0.5 m.,* forks. Take L. *8.3 m.,* **Elk City,** one of the earliest, if not first, white settlements in Lincoln County.

George A. Waggoner in his *Stories of Old Oregon* described the origin of Elk City:

"Excitement ran high. A graveyard was started, and soon became a popular resort. The only man buried there within the first three months who did not have a bullet hole in him was a poor minister, who being a non-combatant, was unfit for honorable fight and was knocked in the head with a whiskey bottle, and buried in the potter's field, unwept, unhonored, and unsung."

Elk City developed because it was head of navigation on Yaquina River and for years was overland terminus of stage and mail route. From here, W-

Yaquina Bay Bridge, Newport, with Coast Guard facility in foreground   *Courtesy State of Oregon*

bound travelers left stage coaches to take boats down Yaquina River to Yaquina Bay. In 1866 Corvallis and Yaquina Bay Wagon Co. built warehouse.
Two years later, place platted and named Newton. Name changed to present in 1888 because of large number of elk in vicinity. Elk City flourished
during heyday of Oregon Pacific RR; as RR declined, so did Elk City. In 1915
it had two sawmills, Grange, PS, pop. 150; state almanac stated: "Temperature has never been above 90 degrees nor below zero since 1865." By 1940
town was down to 43 persons. In 1981, 120 m. wind caved in 100 ft. long CB
over Yaquina built 1922. Elk City Country Store in operation since 1866. Elk
City CP. CG, rest rooms.

 ** (N from Elk City: 5 m., US 20.)

 * E of Elk City a wayward pike flirts with Big Elk Creek, fine fishing
stream, to Harlan. At times the road tightly narrows; keep far R then, in
deference to charging logging trucks. Otherwise, few vehicles met; homes
and stump ranches pop up at odd intervals. 5.2 m., pretty vale, in V-shape.
Green field beyond calendar photo barbed wire fence has virgin charm. 4 m.,
forks. Approximate site of **Salado.** PO est. 1891; 1915 saw sawmill and PS.
Not a twig remains. (4 m. S of Salado, **Glen:** in 1915 had PS. Nothing now.)
Take L fork at Salado site. 10.3m., **Big Elk CG,** used chiefly by astute fishers
and campers. 0.5 m., Grant Creek Dr., narrow lane that is secret bit of
Oregon, with small vales pillowed again leafy hills, sort of gentle miniature of
Wallowa Valley — or parts of Switzerland. Drive up couple of m. for look-
ing. It may take that far to find a turn-around. 1.1 m — from jct., Grant Rd. —
Harlan. House was store that closed 1971. PO est. 1890, closed 1970. In 1915
Harlan had PS and pop. 200. There is no longer a town as such, as is the case
throughout many W Oregon areas. When outland people speak of a town,
they mean the rural areas; thus, "town" may consist of everyone for miles
around, with the common tie often being church, store, community hall or
Grange. (5 m. E of Harlan there was from 1900-1903 the PO of Wesley, but
don't try to find it. Asking the locals won't help, few have been here more
than few years. So goes it in these and many other parts.)

 ** From Harlan N: 7.9 m., US 20.

On US 101 from Information Center, Newport:

 0.4 m., turnoff for **Yaquina Bay SP.** PA. Old Yaquina Bay Lighthouse, constructed 1871 and 2d oldest light station in Oregon, first being at Cape Blanco,
built 1870. Lighthouse was earliest aid to navigation standing within range of first
recorded landfall made from ship to shore of Pacific NW — by Capt. James
Cook, March 3, 1778. Station functioned only three years because light could not
be seen by ships approaching from N because of protruding headlands; discontinued with construction of more efficient station at Yaquina Head. Place was
unique in that light tower and lightkeeper's quarters (family of 14 lived here) were
built as single structure. Only other Oregon lighthouse built this way, at Adams
Point, burned 1912. Lighting apparatus consisted of simple whale oil lamp and

Frensnel lens. Lighthouse, oldest existing bldg. in Newport, now authentically furnished and open as museum.

Just to S of turnoff to Yaquina Bay SP is N end of Yaquina Bay Bridge, cantilever structure completed 1938. Deck of bridge high enough, at 138 ft. above channel, for ocean-going craft to pass under. Surely one of the most graceful and photogenic bridges in state.

0.5 m. — across Yaquina Bay Bridge — turnoff for Mark O. Hatfield Marine Science Center of Oregon State University.

> ** 0.3 m.,* **Zig-Zag Zoo,** free outdoor museum. Mind-boggling collection of things from sea, land, and, for all its exuberant zaniness, sky. *0.5 m.,* **Hatfield Marine Science Center.** Museum and aquarium designed to sensitize visitors to awareness of beauty and frailty of ocean. Educational programs best on coast.

Between the US 101 jct. and Yachats the littoral is a narrow, slightly elevated coastal plain, with the bedrock generally sedimentary. Students of geology have no difficulty pointing out the Pleistocene marine terrace levels and, of course, the sand dunes which give the plain the contours of a rolling topography. In this area the coast is defined by lengthy stretches of sandy beaches resting against low sea cliffs except by lava flows at Yachats and a sill at Seal Rock, both basalt formations. But the coast in this area is not completely homogenous; streams cutting into it have carved out small valleys and ravines.

0.2 m. — from jct., **Hatfield Marine Science Center** — South Beach, mundane hwy. strip.

1.1 m., turnoff W to South Beach SP.

> ** 0.3 m.,* **South Beach SP.** CG, PA, FHP, hiker-biker camping area. Long clean beach that seems to find the Pacific more genial than most places do.

3.9 m., on W, **Lost Creek SP.** Drifting beach ruffled by Pacific landward blows is feast for eyes from parking area.

1.5 m., on W, sandy turnout to sprawling beach. Park and walk — no vehicles on beach.

0.3 m., on W, **Ona Beach SP.** Harmonious coastal plain here disturbed by alluvial plain of Beaver Creek. BR on E side of 101 — at Beaver Creek. PA. Fishers and waders tingled by splashing salt water.

1.5 m., **Seal Gulch,** rude, crude, hayseed, tongue-in-cheek "frontier" amusement park built by chainsaw sculptor.

0.3 m., **Seal Rock,** put-on collection of bldgs. dominated by realtors and gift shops.

0.2 m., on W, **Seal Rock SP.** PA. Here was terminus of Corvallis and Yaquina Bay Wagon Road, privately owned toll road begun 1863; first road connecting Williamette Valley to Oregon Coast. Townsite of Seal Rock platted 1877 and large hotel (Seal Rock Resort) built. When RR from Corvallis reached Yaquina City, vacationers took boat to beach and came down beach by buggy. But resort was never a great success; too hard for people to reach.

Seal Rocks

For the geologically curious, the outer reef of the beach at Seal Rock SP is basalt; reef exposed on beach is resistant layer of Yaquina formation dipping seaward beneath the basalt. Outstanding attraction of SP is **Elephant Rock,** which *The Ore Bin* described as "an elongate knob of columnar jointed basalt ... a remnant of a sill emplaced between layers of the Yaquina Formation." You have only to look at the formation from the right perspective— looking S — to understand why it was thus named. S of Elephant Rock the smaller rocks appear as petrified wood and lava slags. N of Elephant Rock is a flotilla of other offshore rocks of various sizes, looking as though a mad giant had used a gargantuan cleaver to hack off a cliff, chip it into bits, and with a roar that shook the firs, pines, cedars, hemlocks and spruces on the slope back of him, flung the pieces into the brine where, magically, they settled into a rather even line. Actually, the rocks and offshore ledge of partially submerged basaltic rock were created by underground lava flow 14 million years ago — give or take a few hundred decades.

0.4 m., turnout, with grand view of littoral. *0.1 m.,* another such informal turnout. *1.8 m.,* on W, **Driftwood Beach Wayside SP**. PA. (Oddly, there is much more driftwood at many other parcels of beach.) Fringing beach are plants common to area — rhododendron, huckleberry, salal and yellow verbena. Indians considered the root of the trailing yellow verbena a luxury. Wayside approximate location of Bayview PO (1901).

2.8 m., and across 3-span cantilever Alsea Bay Bridge, with clearance of 70 ft., **Waldport,** at Jct., 0 34. (For 0 34, see *Cross-Coast Range Roads*.) Here coastal plain is disturbed by estuary of Alsea River. Settled in 1880s, Waldport grew up on clam and crab fishing and packing. It grew slowly, with pop. of 300 in 1915 and 367 in 1940. After WWII came tourism on a big scale and by 1990 Waldport had about 1,300 people and was still growing.

In early autumn of 1975 Waldport briefly became national news because of mysterious exodus from area of some persons following "another life in space" talk given at the Bayshore Inn by man and woman known only as "The Two." On S shore of Alsea Bay, Indian name corrupted by whites conventionally careless in pronunciation, Waldport is a fisher town. But real beauty is N of bay. Cross bridge and take first turn W. Here are beaches wild, dunes that scream back to the wind, gorgeous sunsets. But "civilization" is intruding rapaciously and tomorrow the glory may be in a scrapbook. Actually, there was a tiny village here. PO (1874–1919) started as Drift Creek, changed to Collins, then to Waldport, back to Collins, then to Lutgens, then to Stanford, back to Lutgens, finally to Nice, for salmon packer Henry Nice, who had cannery here. In 1915, PS.

Between Waldport and Yachats the only road for years was the beach. It was not uncommon for inexperienced drivers to mire their vehicles in the sand and, sometimes, to see them lashed by the incoming tide. Today, along US 101, road is lined with beach houses, unnamed beach communities, and motels.

0.3 m., on W, **William P. Keady Wayside.** Good view of Alsea Bay. *0.9 m.,* on W, **Governor Patterson SP.** PA, FHP. Landscaped artistry juxtaposing unfettered beach. *2.2 m.,* on W, **Beachside SP.** CG, PA, fishing. What will impress many are the gorgeous shrubs. Camping in scented garden. *1.3 m.,* **Tillicum Beach FS CG.** There is an arboreal fairyland ambience here, where every camp-site seems a private Shangri-la.

3.2 m., on W. **Smelt Sands Beach Access SP.** Trail leads to beach, which is no more than outcrop of burnished and mossy rocks. Geologically, as explained in *The Ore Bin,* "conglomerates consisting of large basalt boulders overlies basalt along the shore . . . These boulders were eroded from the basalt and rounded into their present shape by wave action."

0.6 m., **Yachats** (Ya-hots), Indian name; various interpretations. One: "At the foot of the mountain." Another, referring to the river, "Small mouth with a big voice." PO est. 1887 with name of Ocean View; named changed to present 1916. Town semi-isolated until 1914 when wagon road blasted around Cape Perpetua. In 1930 hwy. opened N to Waldport and **Yachats** linked to entire coast and rest of state. Though largely diminished, agates, petrified wood, blood stones and flowered jaspers are taken from gravel of Yachats Bay. Yachats Community Church has unusual agate windows on S side. Little Log Church-By-The Sea, dedicated 1932, purchased 1968 by Lincoln County Historical Society for use as Yachats Museum. Ocean Drive is sight-seeing road of Pacific. Due W of District Water Office bldg. is trace of stage road that ran along beach. Town popular resort for salmon fishers; surf fishing and clam digging also attract visitors. **Yachats SP,** bordering Yachats River as it enters sea, is on sheer bluff hurtling to rocky scablands creviced by minute pools. Rock formations here are remnants of Pleistocene wave-cut bench. Geologists say "exhumed" bench slowly being re-moved by present wave actions, with erosion cutting trenches along frontiers. At short sand beach, fishers thrash into surf to net smelt that come to spawn on small beaches such as this one. PA.

0.1 m. — from Information Center — on E, Yachats River Rd.

    * This pike winds without rancor alongside glossy stream fed by snowmelt and sunray. Where the road rises, it looks out to vales and dells that bespeak an earlier time, when we were seeing Nellie home. *7.1 m.,* across cement bridge, "T". (R along S fork of Yachats.) Take L, to N Fork of Yachats. *1.5 m.,* **N Fork of Yachats Bridge.** Built 1938 at cost of 1,500; at 42 ft. it is one of the shortest CBs in state, is supported by hand-split pilings. Other end of bridge leads into farm.

0.3 m., on W, immediately after crossing Yachats River Bridge, **Yachats Ocean Wayside.** At L of staircase to beach is remnant of shell heap, perhaps hundreds of years old. Indians gathered about their fires and tossed emptied shells of clams, crabs, and oysters. To deodorize stink of decomposition, sand & earth were from time to time thrown on the heap and formed a "cement" to "glue" the contents. Mound is vestige of "skookum chuck" feasts which were source of delight for Indians.

1.8 m., turnout. Majestic view of Pacific and its coastline insinuating S to N. Yachats looks like toy village jutting toward sea.

0.4 m., **Devils Churn Viewpoint.** Follow gently sloped *0.5 m.* Trail of the Restless Waters to Devils Churn, deep-wrought fissure where sea rushes in like wounded whale and spouts furiously. Volcanic action created fracture in earth's surface and eons of water erosion have done the rest. As intriguing as is Devils Churn are sights along and off trail — profuse coastal vegetation, many-splendored coastline, tidepools etched in rocky shelf.

0.1 m., E for **Cape Perpetua.** On March 12, 1778, Capt. James Cook wrote in his journal: "The coast seemed almost everywhere straight, without any opening or inlet; and it appeared to terminate in a kind of white sandy beach; though some on board thought that appearance was owing to the snow. Each extreme of the land that was now before us, seemed to short out into a point. The Northern one was the same which we had first seen on the 7th." He named the cape after St. Perpetua, who was martyred for professing her faith on 3/7/203 in Carthage. Cook knew well the pantheon of saints.

    * Jct. — off US 101. To R, *0.2 m.,* **Cape Perpetua FS CG.** (From CG, *1.5 m.,* trail to viewpoint.) To L, *0.7 m.,* forks. Take L. *1 m.,* top of 800 ft. high aerie of Cape Perpetua. On Trail of the Whispering Spruce, vistas extend

Netting for silver smelt near Yachats   *Courtesy State of Oregon*

from Cape Foulweather to Cape Blanco — distance of 150 m. But often as not there is fog.

0.2 m., on E, Cape Perpetua Visitors Center.

* 0.2 m. Films and dioramas introduce interested to "living museum" that is Oregon Coast. Trails from Center lead to Cape Creek (lush coastal forest and fern-lined stream); Cook's Chasm (spouting horns, rock fishing, ancient shell mounds); Cape and Good Fortune Coves; Devils Churn; "Trail of the 'Riggin' Slinger" and 1 1/4 m. slow hike thru forest.

0.2 m., turnout. There is no precise count of seaward turnouts along coast because (1) there would be argument on what constitutes a turnout and (2) more are added, formally and informally, every year. Each has its own touch of magic. 0.4 m., gravel turnout. Heavy use may have it paved. 0.2 m., wayside. Parking area off road, with trail inviting curious to beach and scarred rocks that look like lava slags. View S representative of green and ochre sinuating shoreline in area.

0.3 m., turnoff E on FS Rd. 1050.

* Riding shoulder-high above Cummins Creek, road is lined by firs, alders, hemlocks and friends. Pleasant excursion thru unpeopled woods. 0.5 m. from start, old roadbed skids downhill to creek. 3.7 m. from start, road ends.

0.1 m., **Neptune SP.** PA. Beach trail to primitive, rocky shoreline. At Cook's Chasm, on N, sea charges in on bull-throated roars of vengeance; in retreat, leaves pullulating foam. Trees stunted and bent by banshee winds shrink against slopes scrubbed by evergreen huckleberry. Surf fishing from rocks for rock fish, perch and greenling.

60 yds., on E, black and white concrete barrier poles. Beyond is **Cummins Creek** roadless area.

* Near barrier, trail forks. R fork levels after short, sharp climb and heads into stand of old Sitka spruce. In 0.3 m., trail starts to fade. Novices should turn back. Others, continuing, push their way into spruce-Douglas fir transition zone, followed by reign of Western hemlock, which, further on, changes to forest of Western hemlock and Douglas fir.

* L fork, 50 yds. to creek and takeoff point for stream hikers who use creek bottom and banks to make their way. From early spring to first bite of autumn, stream banks are profuse with columbine, foxglove, candy-flowers, monkey flowers and host of wildflower companions. Waving down upon banks are lichen of portly big leaf maples and baton branches of orchestrated alders, metronomes to wind and water. Along stream some fallen Sitka spruce are more than 7 ft. in diameter and up to 165 ft. high. For an intimacy with nature, Cummins Creek is a lovely rendezvous.

0.8 m., **Strawberry Hill Parking Area.** Big attraction here is colony of Harbor seals on offshore rocks 100 ft. across channel, seen at low tide all year. Sea lions frequent area; gulls and cormorants common. There are also soul-stirring views of choppy seawall N and S. Here before you, in the words of T. S. Eliot, is "the menace and caress of wave that breaks on water."

0.7 m., wayside. A thin green bluff is overlook to pebbly strip called beach and illimitable deep beyond. *0.3 m..* casual turnout that seems to catch ocean in candid camera shot. *1.2 m.,* **Stone Field Beach SP.** Fishing. Small beach beyond broken "field" of stone. There was tiny settlement, Samaria, here in first part of century. Just to R, seagulls sometimes mass in the hundreds.

1.2 m., turnout. A sort of spying on the sea from unconventional point of view. *1.1 m.,* **Ocean Beach.** Wayside with PA. *0.2 m.,* turnout for beach looking. *0.1 m.,* on E, turnoff for **Rock Creek FS CG.**

> ** 0.3 m.,* CG. One of the nice and rarely mentioned joys of FS CGs is that the caretakers are volunteers, retired couples generally, who are delightful, warm, witty folks with knack for making campers feel at home.

1 m. on W, **Muriel O. Ponsler Memorial State Wayside.** Trail to beach is favorite for young kite-fliers and waders. PA, fishing.

0.7 m., **Carl G. Washburne Memorial SP.** On W, turnoff to parking for beach access. On E, CG. Park includes walk-in tent sites. Park, load gear on wheelbarrow at trailhead, and advance 200 feet to set up tents. PA, swimming, fishing, showers.

The rolling westward hills do not look like sand dunes but they are. They have

Heceta Head Lighthouse   *Courtesy State of Oregon*

been stabilized and covered by shore pine, Sitka spruce, small fir, cedar, hemlock and other species, with an understory of evergreen huckleberry, rhododendron, salal, manzanita and other plants.

2.3 m., **Devil's Elbow SP.** PA, FHP, fishing, beach. Most striking sight here is, to N, **Heceta** (Heh-see-ta) **Head lighthouse,** which has guided mariners since 1894 and stands on 520 ft. high promontory named for Spanish explorer Bruno Heceta, who came this way 1775. (Heceta House, next to lighthouse, built 1893. In 1915 there was community of 50 pop. called Heceta, with PS.) The spongy beach seems part of the elements: hear the sea voices, feel the silent fog touch your hands before you see it. **Devil's Elbow Tunnel,** within the SP, is 600 ft. bore thru a far flank of Coast Range. US 101 swings around cliff far above Pacific, flashing sharp pictorial slides of sea and land.

0.5 m. — from entrance to Devil's Elbow SP — turnout. Fine view of Heceta Head Lighthouse. *0.3 m.,* turnout. Best view of Heceta Head Lighthouse. *0.3 m.,* commercial **Sea Lion Caves,** huge marine cavern inhabited by varying number of huge Steller sea lions. Reputed to be only mainland sea lion home in world.

1.3 m., turnout. Long view of sandy beach to S. *0.3 m.,* turnout. *0.1 m.,* turnout. The vistas are so dazzling a lot of turnouts are needed. And summer tourist traffic is thick. From top of hill, far-reaching exposure of weaving coast line and sandy foreshore. From here to next mile are several turnouts, closely spaced, that provide feast of viewing.

2.1 m., from top of hill, turnoff to **Alder Dune FS CG.**

* 0.3 m., typical, well-cared-for, woodsy, salubrious FS CG.

0.3 m., on W, Buck Lake, pond-like, contained on W by sand dune mesa. *0.9 m.,* on E, Sutton Lake boat site. *0.6 m.,* turnoff E for **Darlingtonia Wayside.**

* 0.1 m., nature walk thru unique "gardens" of coastal vegetation. Big attraction here — bog clusters of the carnivorous, fly-catching pitcher plants *Darlingtonia californica* commonly known as the cobra-lily and cobra-orchid, because they look like cobras poised to strike. Insects that crawl into the hood-like leaves are trapped and devoured. Plants need these minerals as their small root systems cannot supply them with necessary nutrition. This unusual plant has an unusual range — sea level to 6,000 ft. PA. Return to turnoff road and turn R. *1 m.,* first view of **Mercer Lake.** With Capri flavor, 359 acre lake is ringed by affluent houses that seem to live in world of their own. Indians called this former stream valley *Kow-y-ich,* "The place of the lake." Whites named it in 1880s for gvmt. surveyor George Mercer. Brushy shoreline makes angling difficult but boaters find trout from early spring to midsummer. Largemouth bass and yellow perch of ample size also fished. *2.1 m.,* public BR on Mercer Lake. Once on shore of lake, hamlet of Mercer. PO 1904. In 1915, pop. 36, PS.

0.2 m., turnoff to **Sutton FS CG.**

* 0.8 m., entrance to CG. In many another state such wooded, recreation-rich CG would be a flaming banner. Oregonians take such CGs for granted.

Heceta Head Lighthouse

Courtesy US Forest Service

Heceta Head lightkeeper's house

Courtesy US Forest Service

Darlingtonia Wayside

Courtesy State of Oregon

1.4 m., PA. From picnic parking area, narrow path thru thickets of Oregon grape and salal and trees whose head and shoulders are swept back by stormy seawinds. Constantly the drone of the ocean's churn accompanies path. W of the path vast expanses of sand, persistently remolding, sweep in waves and troughs to chain of low black hills which shield sand from sea.

0.4 m., **Indian Forest** (commercial). Set in plot of coastal woods are replicas of representative Indian dwellings, including Mandan earth lodge, Plains tipi, Hupa cedar plank house and birch-bark wigwam. Gift shop carries exquisitely -crafted jewelry made by SW Indians.

1.4 m., on E., jct., **Heceta Beach.**

    * *2 m.,* "T". Turn R. *0.3 m.,* Heceta Beach CP. 50 yd. trail to cozy little beach dwarfed by king-size, grandiose motel. Rates are compatible.

0.6 m., first sight of regional sand dunes off US 101 from N. Sand dunes occupy about 140 of the 310 m. of Oregon coast and only S of Port Orford are they not a common landform. They vary from small patches of 100 to 300 ft. to stretches that seem to go on forever; the longest strip of dunes extends more than 50 m. There are places in the prime sand dune region where the area is less than 0.5 m. wide but most of it is more than 2 m. wide and at Florence a maximum of 3 m. in width is reached. Geologically, the dunes aren't that old, formed within the last 10 or 15 millenia, since the end of the Ice Age.

1 m., turnoff to beach.

    * *0.9 m.,* "T". Turn L. *1.2 m.,* entrance to **Harbor Vista CP.** *(0.1 m.,* CG and vistas of N jetty and ocean.) *1.1 m.,* N Jetty.

1.2 m., **Florence** — Jct., 0 126. (For 0 126 see *Cross-Coast Range Roads.)*

Like a number of other Oregon towns, Florence has spawned suburbs which threaten to submerge it. There is no downtown in spun-out Florence; the center of town, explained the local librarian, is the Safeway store, because that's where the majority of people shop. Not only is there no downtown grid, there are no sidewalks of length in the main business district, which flanks the hwy. Window shopping is almost impossible. To get to the other side of the street is to cross four lane US 101. Practically all shopping, therefore, is by car.

Town has been replaced by community, which is defined here as persons bound together by common, localized cultural, service and shopping ties. Where people share cultural activities, where they buy and what services they have joined, not necessarily the same in all instances, constitutes a community. Thus, much that is outside the political boundaries of Florence is part of the Florence community.

Contrary to popular assumption, town was not named for a woman but, most likely, for A. B. Florence, a pro-slavery state senator from Lane County who was in the legislature during the crucial decision year of 1860. A Siuslaw River-mouth fishing town and trading post for farmers of the narrow Siuslaw Valley, town is best known for its showy Rhododendron Festival, held latter part of May. In spring and early summer, rhododendrons run riot over hills and lowlands. Sand dunes rise to heights of 100 ft. between Florence and the ocean. It is eerie to walk the streets at dawn or at twilight and look up to see the ghostly dunes, just beyond your fingertips, looming in the mind thrice as high as they actually are.

Most interesting part of Florence is "**Old Town**," on waterfront. Here is where city began and where it was rooted until bridge was built across river in 1930s. Slowly, then, commerce moved to hwy. and pioneer area dimmed in importance. It was a dank has-been when resurrection began in 1970s. Today "Old Town" is district of seafood restaurants, taverns, boutiques, gift shops, and other retail businesses targeted at tourists. Bridgewater Restaurant was Kyle Bldg. when constructed 1901. It housed town's PO thru 1913 and general store until 1961. Upstairs has been scene of town hall, political and lodge meetings, Fourth of July celebrations and was also dance hall and roller skating rink. Of several houses on Maple St., best known is **Johnson House** (1892), now Bed and Breakfast facility. RR depot at Mapleton in 1913 is now mdse. store on waterfront.

Turn W off US 101 onto Rhododendron Dr., almost in center of Florence. *4.1 m.,* turn L for **Harbor Vista Park.** *0.1 m.,* CG of Lane CP. *1.1 m.,* N Jetty — stirring view of Siuslaw River rushing into sea. On a foggy morning, with the wind chill, fog horns droning warnings of peril, the stream disappeared under waddy layers of gray, and frowning fishers jigging to keep warm, scene is existential, as though the world had narrowed to a last band of doomed survivors. Work on N Jetty began 1892, completed 1917, length of 4200 ft.

A backcountry drive of rural loveliness begins 1 m. E of US 101 intersection, on 0 126. Road goes along N Fork of Siuslaw; it starts as held fast to stream but in few miles changes character and turns into small cattle vales.

From turnoff on 0 126:

　　* *1 m.,* Munsel Lake Rd. (*1.2 m.,* BL on 110 acre, 71 ft. max. depth, Huck Finn lake.) Return to N Fork Rd. Turn N. *1.8 m.,* on R, turnout for "fishing hole" on N Fork. Restrooms. *8 m.,* original site of **Minerva**, PO named for wife of early settler James E. Bay. *0.9 m.,* 2d site of Minerva, at bridge and jct. Here was store, gas pump, house, United Evangelical Church, Grange, PS. All gone. And here for about six decades stood 105-ft.-length Meadows CB. Some of the locals are still spitfire mad because it was torn down. From bridge site, "Mapleton Loop" continues 8 m. E to 0 36, goes S 3 m. to Mapleton, and turns W on 0 126 to return to Florence. Along way from Mapleton, it passes nature preserve Cox Island. (To reach Cox Island from Florence, there is BL at end of Harbor St.) (For Cox Island, see *Cross-Coast Range Roads, 126.*) On US 101, from jct., 0 126.

0.6 m., Siuslaw River Bridge. *0.4 m.,* S end, Siuslaw River Bridge. *0.2 m.,* turnoff to S Jetty Dune — Beach Access.

　　* *0.6 m.,* entering **S Jetty Rec. Area.** *0.4 m.,* Siuslaw Vista Rd. Turn R. *0.1 m.,* parking lot. 80 yds. to viewpoint — wide expanse of sand dunes, their ghostly trees fringing ridges of woods, and of rivers and mountains and ocean. Return to S Jetty Rd. Turn R. *0.5 m.,* Green Pasture Staging Area, for off-

road vehicles. Return to S Jetty Rd. Turn L. *0.7 m.,* parking area. 200 yds. uphill and downhill sandy trail thru beachgrass, lupine and wild strawberries to beach. *1 m.,* ditto. *0.6 m.,* ditto. *0.2 m.,* **Siuslaw Goose Marsh.** From Dec. thru April, whistling swans rule the roost here. Canada geese and ducks of many species call this winter home from Nov. thru March. Hawks are year-round boarders. *0.5 m.,* S Jetty, where Siuslaw River enters sea. Popular here is crabbing at high tide off fishing dock. Locals call the Siuslaw the most productive searun cutthroat trout fishery in any Oregon estuary, perhaps in the world. Bottom fish such as flounder, sea bass, perch and salmon in season caught off either S or N Jetty. Where Siuslaw enters Pacific stood village of Acme. In 1915 it had pop. 100, two sawmills, Pres. church, PS, Woodmen and Royal Neighbors lodge hall.

0.1 m., entering **Oregon Dunes National Rec. Area,** the most extensive sand dunes area of Oregon's "Sahara by the Sea." The sand basically is derived from the sandstone bedrock of the Coast Range that is continually being eroded by the moistness. Winter floods carry the grinded material to the sea and the sand is washed onto the beaches and blown inland by W winds. Constantly moving, the sand is massed into wave-shaped formations, with dunes upward of 300 ft. The

Oregon Dunes National Recreation Area   *Courtesy US Forest Service*

general movement of the dunes is NE and rate of advance is about 6 ft. per year. Beach grass, scotch broom and shore pine have been planted to stabilize the dunes where river channels and hwys. might be endangered. Dune treasure seekers, scouring the area from the forest to the sea, find sandblasted wood, driftwood, Japanese glass fishing floats, agates, sea shells and old bottles. Best time for looking is between Nov. and April. That is also best time to see true beauty of wind sculpturing. Twisted, grotesque and ghostly trees, remnants of forests, are gravemarkers of past. They stand, as lonely as a crumbling barn that is a last survivor of an abandoned town, entwined by beach grass or in the full capture of the pitiless sand. Some of the trees, not yet completely denuded, seem to spring from a passage of Lafcadio Hearn's *Chila:* they "all bend away from the sea; and, even of bright, hot days when the wind sleeps, there is something grotesquely pathetic in their look of agonized terror." They seem "like fleeting women with streaming garments and windblown hair, — bowing grievously and thrusting out arms desperately . . . to save themselves from falling."

Extending for the next 41 m. and 1 to 3 m. inland, the Oregon Dunes Nat. Rec. Area ought to be seen slowly, carefully, with eyes focused for detail. Look for prostrate evergreen shrub that may form mats, hairy manzanita, European beach grass, false lily-of-the-valley, coast monkey flower, rhododendron, scotch broom, seashore lupine, tree lupine, evergreen huckleberry, trailing blackberry, salmonberry, wild strawberry, Western red cedar, Western waxmyrtle, red alder, Scouler's willow, shorepine, Sitka spruce, Douglas fir, Western hemlock.

Waxmyrtle is special to conservationist Cecelia Ostrow, who wrote: "A dark, glossy shrub, it has the presence of belladonna or jimson weed. It protects tender marshes of the dunes by not growing thick walls around them. It does not like people, and you must make peace with the waxmyrtle if you are ever to feel at home in the dunes. I don't know this from lore, I know it from getting lost in the marshes, trying to get to the beach through the dunes, and meeting the waxmyrtle face to face."

Birds, mammals and amphibians are so numerous of species, with each piece of the dunes having its own, that it must at times appear that Noah's ark had unloaded here. (Do not at all be surprised to note deer prints on the dunes.)

Looking W, the sand dunes can mesmerize and distort perceptions. Suddenly, atop a ridge, a band of Bedouins enters the horizon, and behind them trails a camel. But as suddenly they disappear, and then it becomes obvious that robes of fog, slipping from behind a bent tree, have created the image.

So many people set out on foot across the dunes that the Nat. Rec. Area issued a brochure. In part it reads:

"Try to plan your hike to walk with the wind. If possible, use two vehicles and park one near your destination point to minimize confronting the wind. However, if you have to return to the same spot, start your hike into the wind; this will test your determination and leave you with reserve to better enjoy your day. Winds are generally out of the northwest during the summer and southwest the rest of the time. Early morning hours are best for hiking because the winds usually don't start until 10 or 11 a.m. Winds are usually less forceful in the deflation plain or directly behind the foredune.

"A tide book is recommended for knowledge of high tide periods. Crossing Siltcoos, Tahkenitch, and Threemile Creeks can be difficult and dangerous during high tides or periods of heavy runoff.

"Hikers should carry drinking water. Use purifying tablets or boil the water if you intend to use any surface water.

"The best area of backcountry activity is in the north dunes between the Siltcoos and Umpqua Rivers. The heaviest use by hikers is in the area between Honeyman State Park and the ocean."

0.5 m., on W, **Siuslaw Pioneer Museum** in old Lutheran Church. *0.3 m.,* business district of Glenada. It had more going for it in 1915.

1.2 m., on W, **Honeyman SP,** one of the most popular and best-equipped parks in state system. CG, PA, DS, showers, fishing, FHP, excellent swimming area, sand dunes; indeed the entire park area is in an ancient sand dune formation, low and undulating. A park brochure gives details:

"The ever-shifting sands are almost free of growing vegetation and very unstable. The dunes still are being built up by the ocean winds and are ever crowding inward. Inch by inch they progress, first covering the herbs, grasses and shrubs at the foot of the interior slopes, finally enveloping the tops of tall trees. Some of the visible ones are dead, others are still living, awaiting their inevitable submergence by the relentless, smothering winds, whose steep inland slopes are susceptible to the slightest disturbance of their surface. A wisp of wind, a cone from a tree top, or a timorous mouse crossing their lower slopes cause the unstable sands to ravel from base to top."

Honeyman SP is also noted for its rushes of rhododendrons, which turn every day of their existence into a floral parade.

* *0.1 m.,* **Cleawox Lake,** name Indian in origin but meaning unknown. Across water is dune, intriguing photo. *Atlas of Oregon Lakes* says: "More than half of the Western shore is bordered by actively advancing sand dunes that have overpassed the earlier masses responsible for the lake's impoundment. These dunes are estimated to be moving northward at 15 to 20 feet per year . . ."

On E: road to Canary and Ada.

* *0.3.,* **Woahink Lake,** part of Honeyman SP. At 820 acres it is almost 10 times the size of Cleawox Lake and, on the whole, is more attractive. Bottom of Woahink, at 74 ft., is 36 ft. below sea level. *4.3 m.,* remains of Canary, never much to start with. *3.2 m.,* Siltcoos Station Rd. Turn R onto it. *1.4 m.,* start of Siltcoos Lake on this road. *3.4 m.,* road narrows as Douglas County is entered and winds like cautious deer thru old growth firs. *0.2 m.,* forks. Take R. *0.2 m.,* Ada, on Siltcoos Lake, largest on Oregon Coast, with surface area of 3,164 acres. Lake is deceptively shallow, 82 percent of it less than 15 ft.

Sand dunes above Cleawox Lake, Honeyman State Park *Courtesy State of Oregon*

deep. Freshwater marshes bordering lake — Miller Arm, Fiddle Creek, Maple Creek — are rich in natural vegetation, particularly canary grass and tule. Butterfly, Reed, and Jernigan Islands are seasonal waystops for large numbers of birds, including American ospreys and bald eagles. Formerly spelled Tsiltcoos, guessed at being name of local Indian chief. One of top warm water fishing lakes in PNW and one of premier recreation-use lakes on state coast. Caught here have been bass weighing over 9 lbs., salmon, steelhead, cutthroat trout, perch, crappies, bluegill and catfish. Ada, settled about 1890, has store, resort on lake. Return to forks. Take R. Narrow road twists along lake. *1.6 m.,* reentering Lane County, and road improved. *2.2 m.,* forks. Take L. *2.1 m.,* Siltcoos Station Rd. Continue straight. *3.2 m.,* Canary Store, abandoned. *4.6 m.,* US 101.

1.2 m., Sand Dunes Frontier. *0.6 m.,* Woahink Lake. On W., Lakeshore Myrtlewood Factory, gallery of sculptured rare wood. *0.8* North Beach Area.

* *0.1 m.,* turn R. *0.3 m.,* Siltcoos Lake. Commercial BL.

0.8 m., **Tyee CG Jct.** Boating and fishing on Siltcoos River and Lake.

* CG at jct. *0.2 m.,* **Westlake,** also known as Dunes City. PO has long been known as Westlake, burg is inc. as Dunes City. Like everywhere in

This was Canary   *Phoebe L. Friedman*

Oregon, local politics here can get pretty frenetic and store is used for cau-
cuses, debates, deals and gossip. Body of water here is marked West Lake
but it is really W part of Siltcoos Lake. Public BR.
1.3 m., on W, Dune Beach Jct.
    * *0.6 m.,* **Lodgepole CG.** *0.3 m.,* **Lagoon CG** and **Waxmyrtle CG.** *0.1
m.,* on R., **Chief Tsiltcoos Trail.** *1 m.,* thru leaf-floored woods of true and
typical coastal vegetation, to beach. *0.3 m.,* **Driftwood II CG.** *0.4 m.,* end of
road. *(0.3 m.,* up and down sand dunes to glistening beach. Sand dunes buggies hop around here like goats.) On E, Siltcoos Lake Area.
    * *2 m.,* **Siltcoos Lake.**
0.7 m., **Carter Lake CG** Boating in the golden shadows of the dunes. *0.4 m.,*
East Carter CG. *1.5 m.,* turnoff W to Oregon Dunes Overlook.
    * *0.3 m.,* overviews of dunes and coastal forest facing down the ocean.
Trail leads 0.2 m. to dunes and 1 m. to beach. Upper platform is one of best in
Dunes area for all-inclusive scenery.
2 m., on W, turnoff to **Tahkenitch Lake Dam.**

* *0.1 m.,* dam. Cross dam on foot, climb down ladder at other side, take rough trail to dunes, then hike free-wheeling to beach, *1.5 m.,* dam. Trail is passable only when dry, is rugged in its ascent, persons not in good physical condition should not chance it.

0.4 m., on E, BR of **Tahkenitch Lake.** A natural lake of 1,674 acres, Tahkenitch has very long shoreline, 25.5 m., due to its "many arms," which Tahkenitch means in Indian. Boat fishers — the shore is too brushy for shore sport — come for yellow perch, bluegill, catfish, rainbow and cutthroat trout, silver salmon and steelhead in winter, and, uncommon to most lakes, both smallmouth and bigmouth bass.

In 1922 five moose, transported from Alaska's Kenai Peninsula, were brought to the shore of Tahkenitch Lake, first known moose in W Oregon. From the start, ill-luck dogged the scheme to establish sizeable moose herd here. One of the moose broke a leg twice (the same one) and each time was fitted with plaster of paris cast. Then, too, the wilderness of spirit attributed to Alaska moose seemed absent in Oregon. A moose with a boarding house tongue made himself a steady, though not always welcome, caller at a ranch, where he consumed large quantities of corn, carrots, skimmed milk, rolled oats, grain hay, and maple and willow foliage. There were good moments, too: several of the antlered beasts achieved a high attendance record at the Ada school house, where the children became quite fond of them. After the herd had increased to 9,however, farmers in the area began to complain that the moose were committing numerous depredations, including breaking thru strong fences to reach gardens and orchards and that the moose were now so vicious that the farmers were afraid to let their wives and children walk the public roads. Others countered that the moose had, instead, become semi-domesticated and could be approached without fear. But one by one, thru one means or another, including being hit by a train or shot because they had allegedly become pests, the moose were destroyed. The final chapter in the tale of the last moose was told in an article in the Dec. 16, 1939 issue of *The Oregonian:* "In his loneliness the bull moose was always, as a cattleman would say, on the prod. He called across Tahkenitch, across Siltcoos, and never an answer was bawled back to him. So far as he knew, he was the last moose in the world. To drive him away from their clearings, people peppered the lonely bull with birdshot, increasing his irritability, and eventually somebody fired a charge of birdshot in his face, blinding him. And blindly he wandered, stumbling into the timber again, to be trapped between two great fallen logs." He was found there by a game warden, who lifted his weapon and put an end to the final fallen dream of a great notion. (A full account of the moose at Tahkenitch Lake was told by Ron Shay in Feb. 1976 issue of *Oregon Wildlife.*)

Near BR: Indian remains of a village that existed about 7000 years ago were found here; pits have been covered without trace of digging.

0.2 m., on E, FS CG. *0.3 m.,* on W, **Tahkenitch FS CG.** Tahkenitch Dunes Trail winds *0.8 m.* thru old-growth woods to dunes, then it's another 1 m. to beach. From start of trail, *2.8 m.* to Three Mile Lake, orphaned between dunes.

0.6 m., **Elbow Lake,** which looks like a sleepy lagoon. At sunset it could be taken for watercolor painting. *3.3 m.,* Douglas County Rd. 247.

> * *4 m.* on bouncy trace to feral beach, part of which looks like used timber lot.

1.8 m., **Gardiner.** "Gardiner," said an elderly local woman whose family roots in the town go back to the community's early days, "is another of those Oregon sea towns that was started as a result of a shipwreck."

In this case a Boston merchant named Gardiner sought to cash in on territorial commerce by having his sailing ship, *Bostonian,* ply the Umpqua River for trade. But the vessel, as with so many others, was smashed up at the mouth of the stream. The date was Oct. 1, 1850. Fortunately, most of the cargo was saved and hauled to N shore of the Umpqua. So began Gardiner City, later Gardiner. The following year it was named HQ of the Umpqua customs district and PO was est.

By 1854 the town was important enough to be visited by J. Ross Browne, confidential agent of the Treasury Dept. and an astute observer and gifted writer.

Tahkenitch Campground, Oregon Dunes National Recreation Area   *Courtesy US Forest Service*

He found the "town" consisting of only 2 houses. One was the home and office of Addison C. Gibbs, Collector of the Port, who came to the Umpqua from Calif. in 1850 and laid out Gardiner. Subsequently, he was elected to the Territorial legislature in 1852 and chosen governor of the state in 1862, after fighting in the Rogue River Indian War and practicing law in Portland, both ferocious occupations. A strong supporter of Abraham Lincoln, he raised an Oregon regiment for the Union in 1864. Later he was Oregon US Attorney. He died in London in 1886 and by legislative act was brought to Portland for burial in Riverview Cemetery.

The other structure Browne saw was a small warehouse chiefly occupied by a large iron safe for the deposit of public funds. But there was not a cent in the safe since there were no direct imports and never had been. Because of a tricky sandbar the harbor was simply too difficult to reach.

Close to the entrance of the river was another "town," without name. Of the 3 houses there, 2 were empty. Two more farmhouses stood opposite Gardiner and they, with the other hovels, comprised the entire settlement of the Port of Umpqua Bay. Beyond this dismal scene there was nothing but 25 m. of unscraped mountains and wild forests all the way to Scottsburg.

Like almost every town in Oregon, Gardiner was victimized by fire. A conflagration in 1880 destroyed all but a few of the homes. Those pre-fire houses still standing include one at 485 First St. (1865 — oldest in town), one on SE corner of First and Plateau (1876), and, a question mark, one at 537 Front (1880 and perhaps for some time occupied by Wilson Jewett.) Jewett was manager of surviving mill and most important man in town. He told his workers they could have all the lumber they needed to build their houses, which is why Gardiner had such nice, white painted houses and pretty picket fences, giving it title, "The White City." Jewett planted a poplar tree to celebrate birth of his son. He liked the tree so much he planted the main street with poplars. Trees were cut down when state put hwy. thru town. In 1908 Jewett built a house at SE corner of Linden Lane (also called Jewett Lane). Painstakingly landscaped, it still looks like baronial small-town mansion. Next to it, on S, is handsome house of same period occupied by Jewett's son. (When lady of Wilson Jewett house was asked in 1985 how many rooms were in mansion she replied charmingly, "I don't count them, I just clean them.") Block-long Linden Lane, a bucolic moment slipping into US 101, is lined with turn-of-century mill houses. House at 643 Front was once brewery. **Gardiner Cemetery,** on old 101, across from mill HQ, has gravestones dating back to 1872.

In 1915 Gardiner was much bigger and more active than it is now. It was home to boats which daily plied Smith and Umpqua rivers and it had daily stage to Siuslaw Harbor, Coos Bay and Drain. It was business and transportation center of western Douglas County. Town possessed sawmill, cannery, tannery, had HS, PS, 3 churches, 2 lodges, Commercial Club, weekly newspaper, pop. above 400.

1.4 m., **Smith River,** honoring Jedediah Smith, one of the truly legendary mountain men and co-founder of Rocky Mountain Fur Co. Always on move, he was first white to cross Sierra Nevada and first to travel up Pacific Coast from Mexican province of Calif. to Columbia. In mid-July 1828, while camped just W of here on N bank of Umpqua, into which Smith empties at this point, Jedediah's party was attacked by Indians, who hauled away all the furs group had accumulated. Happily for Smith, he and 2 other men were away from camp. Only 1 of the 17 men in camp escaped with his life and he eventually reached Ft. Vancouver, a day before Smith did. (The survivor claimed the assault was unprovoked; the Indians insisted the whites had leveled guns at them.) Thru intervention of Dr. John McLoughlin, who dispatched some of his Hudson's Bay Co. veterans down to the Umpqua, Smith got his furs back. He promptly sold them, at no discount, to McLoughlin.

In spring 1829 Smith left Oregon. The next year he led a hunt into the Blackfoot country, working the Judith River tributary of the Missouri, in what is now Montana. But the Blackfeet stood in his way, menacing his passage, and trapping was no longer profitable. So Smith, weary of 8 long and hard years in the wilderness, purchased a Missouri farm and a town house in St. Louis and intended to go into business as a merchant with his brother. But, needing more capital, he determined upon one last trade journey, and led a caravan bound for Santa Fe. On the Cimarron crossing, always dangerous, Smith was killed by Comanche warriors. He was 32. One of the greatest of all American land explorers, he had seen more of the W US than any other man and, in the eyes of studious historians, had even more of a genius for geographic detail than possessed by Lewis and Clark.

Jct., Smith River Rd. (See *Cross-Coast Range Roads, Smith River Road.*)

0.3 m., Umpqua River Bridge. The Umpqua is the largest river flowing into the ocean between the Columbia and San Francisco Bay. It is regionally famous for its striped bass, which were introduced to the Pacific Coast in 1879, at San Francisco Bay, and some years later found their way to Oregon rivers. Original 132 striped bass dropped into SF Bay came from Navesink River, New Jersey; first recorded landings of striped bass in Umpqua River were 1934.

0.5 m., **Reedsport** — Jct., 0 38. (For 0 38, see *Cross-Country Range Roads.*) Platted in 1900 and PO est. 1902, Reedsport grew slowly. In 1915 it had pop. of only 100, with salmon cannery and creamery. Nine years later Reedsport gained international fame when one of its own, Robin Reed, won Olympic gold medal in wrestling at Paris. (He later was editor of *Port Umpqua Courier.*) By 1940 Reedsport had grown to pop. of almost 1,200, but it still looked shabby. *Oregon: End of the Trail* commented: "Much of Reedsport was filled in from earth cut from the sandy clay banks of the hills behind the town. Most of the population lives in the dozen or so two-story houses and hotels, and is composed of transient dwellers. There is little residential section, the majority of the dwellings being scattered over the town's edges." But as lumber, fishing and tourism prospered, Reedsport settled into the mold of a typical coastal town, becoming a community rather than an indigenous city. "Downtown," the original business section, is on 0 38. The other part of "town" is strung along US 101. On SW corner of Jct. 0 38 is HQ of Oregon Dunes Nat. Rec. Area, with graphic displays that need to be looked at for better understanding of dunes area.

4.3 m., from jct., 0 38, Winchester Bay Jct.

    * *0.2 m.,* Beach Blvd. in **Winchester Bay,** called Salmon Harbor by locals, to bring in trade for its charter boats and ocean fishing. Winchester Bay has not only traditionally been the 4th-ranked commercial fishing port in the state (led by Astoria, Coos Bay and Newport) but trumpets that it is the state's foremost sports fishing harbor. In summer, silvers and chinooks are caught by trolling (mostly herring). Gulls wheel low over the bobbing rows of boats in the sheltered basin; the wind spices the blown spray with the aroma of salmon, and ducks carry on as though they owned the place. Motels here deliciously located.

    Turn L onto Beach Blvd. *0.1 m.,* Salmon Harbor Dr. Turn R. *0.2 m.,* on L, Windy Cove CP. On R, **Jack Unger Memorial Wayside:** an impression of helmsman at wheel and beneath it dedication to men and women of Winchester Bay who lost their lives at sea while fishing for a living. *0.3 m.,* on R, **Childrens Fort Park.** Across Umpqua River from this park stood Ft. Umpqua, built 1856 to fight the redskins. But by then the so-called Rogue River Indian War had ended and the troopers soon became bored. In 1862 they were out on hunting trip when paymaster arrived. His report to HQ was not favorable and the command, concluding that there weren't enough Indians around to warrant a military post, withdrew the Yankee protectors. Later, some brainless brasshat decided that, in case Indians reappeared, they ought to be confronted with show of force; therefore, reactivate Ft. Umpqua. But just as the new troops were about to leave San Francisco, wiser heads prevailed.

    At the site of the fort there came, like a camp follower, a village, if in flattery one would so call it, and designated itself Umpqua City. In spring of 1864, Cpl. Royal Bensell, quartered at Ft. Yamhill, came this way out of curiosity and, being literary-minded, observed in his journal: "Stopt at Umpqua City consisting of a small grocery store and a large untenanted Hotel. Here originally stood Fort Umpqua and among these bleak sand hills Jo' Drew established an Ind. Agency. The remains of the garrison can be seen ready for shipment to Scotsberg, Government having left no one to take charge of the property at the time of its vacation. The Officers Quarters were expensive buildings. Some conservatories still stand, monuments of useless extravagance." The blockhouse and the barracks were hauled to Gardiner, where they went the way of all old, unused wood. What happened to the shipment to Scottsburg is a mystery. By the summer of 1868 the last soul had departed from Umpqua City. *The Oregonian* predicted that the town site would "soon be covered with a mountain of sand." It was right.

    * *0.4 m.,* Umpqua River jetties. *0.1 m.,*, forks. Take L. *0.6 m.,* **Umpqua River Lighthouse,** opened 1857. Four years later, destroyed by flood. Re-

built, it has been at same site since 1892. Height — 67 ft. Visibility — 18-20 m. 1.8 million candle power. *0.1 m.,* **Umpqua Lighthouse SP.** PA, fishing, boating. Trail thru tall trees to small, ruby-like Lake Marie. *0.2 m.,* CG of Umpqua Lighthouse SP. (Brochure of Oregon Dunes Nat. Rec. Area states: "The area commonly called 'Umpqua Dunes' extends from the Umpqua Lighthouse . . . to Tenmile Creek. These are the biggest and widest dunes in the entire area.") Sand dunes in area S of lighthouse claimed to be highest in US. Long, wide view of ocean-rim scablands and driftwood beaches have macabre look. Come in spring, at the efflorescence of rhododendrons, and you will want to return.

     * *0.3 m.,* jct. L, *0.1 m.,* US 101. R, *0.4 m.,* US 101.

From Winchester Bay Jct.:

1 m., Umpqua Lighthouse SP Jct.

     * SP and Lake Marie. (See immediately above.)

0.5 m., **Winchester Bay Viewpoint.** Beyond maze of coastal shrubbery the sea changes color and pattern: slate blue in its recline and lacteous in churn; trig in orderliness and, when aroused, it waves a froth of gyres. Seashore life here reflects marine richness of rocky beaches of Central Oregon Coast: sponges, sea anemones, isopods and amphipods, barnacles, crabs, limpets, clams, mussels, chitons, snails, nudibranchs, sea stars, sea urchins, sea cucumbers, sea squirts, sculpins, seaweeds, and more. Those who know this area well say it is wisest to explore at the lowest tide levels during the hour or two before the tide turns; that holes and crevices in rocks can be fruitful in the quest; and that the keen observers look under rocks but do not try to tear animals away from their clinging places.

4.2 m., turnoff to **William Tugman SP,** named for gutsy newspaper editor who stood up to mccarthyism and its assaults upon Bill of Rights. CG, PA, FHP, swimming, fishing, paved BR to Eel Lake.

0.6 m., jct., Lakeside — Tenmile Lakes Rec. Area.

     * *1.2 m.,* **Lakeside,** where N and S Tenmile lakes are linked by channel. Burgeoning community of those who have settled down to enjoy the (still, but diminishing) sizeable and uncluttered recreationland. Shoreline for both lakes comprises 179 m., few of it reached by road. Nobody really knows how lake got its name; legend is that it was inspired by directions of "old Indian" who, whenever asked how far it was to any place, invariably replied, "Ten mile." Tenmile Lake CP here. PA. Good fishing for rainbow and cutthroat trout and especially bluegill, bass and catfish. Since 1925, changed from famous trout and salmon fishery to perhaps best bass lake in Oregon.

0.3 m., turnoff to **North Eel Creek FS CG.** 200 yds. on Umpqua Dunes Trail to vast dunes scenic area; *2 m.* to beach.

0.4 m., turnoff to **South Eel Creek FS CG.**

     * Turn R at first road to R. *0.3 m.,* South Eel CG. Another way to dunes. *1 m.,* on R, **Spinreel FS CG,** in Oregon Dunes. Road practically runs into dunes.

Umpqua Lighthouse

1.5 m., turnoff for Spinreel FS CG. Fine place for dunes buggy riding. *1.4 m.,* **Clear Lake,** a winding between fjord-like formations in the mossy woods.

0.8 m., turnoff for **Saunders Lake CP.**

* *0.5 m.,* park. PA, BR, fishing for cutthroat, rainbow trout, yellow perch. Most of shoreline of this 52-acre lake privately owned.

0.7 m., turnoff to Saunders Lake.

* *0.6 m.,* open view of **Saunders Lake,** moody scene when fog drips from mossy boughs above shores.

2.1 m., **Hauser,** originally called North Slough, probably because of far reaches of cranberry bogs and inlets where wild geese and ducks fed. Just small clutter of bldgs. on E side of road but the dunes, close at hand — or foot — are very impressive.

S of here, at various points, dunes are close to W side of US 101.

0.3 m., Myrtlewood Chalet (factory and store), coming in from N, first of prominent Myrtlewood establishments in Coos Bay area. There are an increasing number of myrtlewood plants and gift shops in this part of coast because the beautifully-grained myrtle trees grow predominantly in Coos and Curry counties and are said to grow nowhere else in world except in Holy Land. The biblical-

Myrtle trees, Coos County   *Courtesy State of Oregon*

minded sometimes quote of Isaiah 55:13 to prove their special place on Earth: "Instead of the thorn shall come up the cypress; instead of the brier shall come the myrtle; and it shall be to the Lord for a memorial, for an everlasting sign which shall not be cut off." There are some who believe the myrtle has been overexploited and that the state ought to up its holding of myrtle groves.

The first Anglo to find the Oregon myrtle or single it out for attention was David Douglas, Scottish botanist. The Indians, who didn't have souvenir shops, ate the seeds of the tree and from its bark concocted a pleasant tea.

Coloring varies from sober, satin gray to outrageously multi-colored grains of yellow, red and brown, with grain containing a multitude of burls and shapes. Apart from the above, there are several ways to tell a myrtle: its odor is like the bay and , like the bay, the myrtle has glossy leaves. Finally, it has a symmetrical, closely branched crown.

It takes at least a century for the myrtle, which has been called America's most beautiful hardwood, to grow to commercial size. In the myrtlewood factories, skilled craftspeople use their hands, handsaws and lathes to turn the finely textured wood into roughs of gift items. After several months of drying, roughs are returned to the lathes, where they are turned, sanded and polished. Finally, several coats of polyurethane are applied. Then the products are ready to be displayed and sold. Tours, which outline the complete process, are available in most factories.

3.4 m., turnoff W for Horsfall Dunes and Beach.

Oregon Dunes from Horsfall Road

* *0.9 m.,* **Horsfall Staging Area.** CG. (L, 0.4 m., road ends at foothill of sand dunes.) *0.2 m.,* turn L. *0.1 m.,* road into dunes for off-road vehicles only. *1.0 m.,* **Bluebill FS CG.** The shorepine forests of stabilized dunes and deflation plain are home to 74 species of songbirds. Look close and speak low and you may see gray fox, Pacific shrew, raccoon, chickaree, California quail and red-tailed hawk. Depending on the water level of the marshes, life teems here, particularly between Sept. and May, when 49 species of water, shore and wading birds join such aquatic mammals as muskrat and beaver to thrive on this natural unspoiled habitat. And there is more. Between forest and marsh the grass, rush and sedge plant community, comprising a complex ecosystem, is habitat to 92 wildlife species; among most common: meadowlark, marsh harrier, Townsend vole, Pacific treefrog. A 1.2 m. boardwalk trail loops around Bluebill Lake — trail begins on E side of CG near space No. 11, which is marsh in summer. Children and dogs find trail attractive. *0.8 m.,* beach area; ocean (driftwood beach) just few yds. off.

0.2 m., leaving Oregon dunes. *0.5 m.,* N end of McCullough Bridge, at 1 m. across Coos Bay Channel, longest of Oregon's coastal spans.

At S end of bridge is **Simpson Park,** small but containing large specimens of Port Orford cedar. Park named for Capt. A.M. Simpson, founder of North Bend, long a shipping and lumber tycoon and supposedly prototype of novelist Peter B. Kyne's Cappy Ricks. Located at park is Coos County Historical Museum, its mind-boggling collection ranging from pioneer manuscripts to Locomotive No. 104, logging RR engine built 1922.

0.7 m., Virginia Ave., downtown **North Bend.** In block between Virginia Ave. and Little Theatre on the Bay (old Liberty Theater) are bldgs. dating from turn of century.

At Virginia Ave., follow *0.5 m.* to **Pony Village,** most architecturally surprising mart in state. Continue *0.3 m.* to Broadway. Turn L. *0.2 m.,* at 2112 Broadway, largest buckthorn cascara in state is in corner of back yard.

From Virginia Ave., North Bend: *2.8 m.,* Commercial St., downtown **Coos Bay.**

For 90 years the town was known as Marshfield. Late in 1944 electorate voted to change name. Most populated city on Oregon Coast, Coos Bay lays claim to being world's largest forest products shipping port, to have largest bay and best natural harbor between Columbia River and San Francisco, and to be center of striped bass fishing in Oregon. Traditionally imbued with working class spirit, town and county consistently vote Democratic, even if rest of state (except for Multnomah County) goes other way. Relying as heavily as it does on lumber, every jolt to the wood products industry rocks Coos Bay and its sister cities. Then despair, escapism, anger, abuse and self-destruction move into fill the voids of stability. Then the more thoughtful speak in contemporary words the spirit William Blake expressed in poetry 2 centuries ago: "And did these feet in ancient time/ Walk upon England's mountains green?/ And was the holy lamb of God/

On England's pleasant pastures seen?/ And did the countenance divine/ Shine forth upon our clouded hills?/ And was Jerusalem builded here/ Among these dark Satanic mills?

"Bring me my bow of burning gold!/ Bring me my arrows of desire!/ Bring me my spear! O Clouds, unfold!/ Bring me my chariot of fire!/ I will not cease from mental fight,/ Nor shall my sword sleep in my hand,/ Till we have built Jerusalem/ In England's green and pleasant land."

On waterfront, at Bayshore and Fir, is 5 cornered bldg. of **Marshfield Sun Printing Museum,** built 1891. Publication ceased 1944. Downtown mall is chic and spruce, except when times are hard and locals wonder which store will go out next. **Coos Art Museum,** in old PO bldg., at S 2d and Anderson, has much to admire. **Egyptian Theater,** 229 S. Broadway, opened 11/19/1925. Said the man who owned facility on its 50th birthday: "A theater built in the 1920s was not just a building. There was a motif, a feeling, art work." And art work is what made the Egyptian special in Coos Bay. Two hefty statues of seated pharaohs look down upon lobby patrons. Doorways into the showhouse suggest portals leading into Valley of the Nile tombs. An artist from Los Angeles was brought up to paint ceiling borders in Egyptian motif. Except for power outages, Egyptian has stayed open and it has survived far longer than most pharaohs did. House of Myrtlewood, 1125 S First, is leader in its field.

Walking tour of downtown homes includes following: **Norton House** (1898), 491 N. Second; **Bennett House** (1893), 202 N Second; **Nels Rassmussen House** (1893), 276 Birch; **Andrew Nasburg House** (1873), 687 N Third; **Siglin House** (1891), 474 Park; **Dr. Horsfall House** (1900), 1007 S Second. Other places worth seeing in Coos Bay: **Old City Hall,** Fourth and Central; **IOOF Cemetery,** Seventh and Ingersoll; **Mingus Park,** N 10th.

There are several appealing trips out of Coos Bay and about Coos County. The county is much more geographically diverse than a casual glance at a map would indicate. Within its 1,627 sq. m. are elevations ranging from 4,319 ft. on Mt. Bolivar in the SE corner to sea level along 44 m. of coastline. The varied land and water forms provide haven for host of pelagic birds, waterfowl, shorebirds and passerines. No less than 264 species of birds are common in Coos County and another 47 species have been sighted often enough to appear in the field checklist issued by the state. It is important not to regard these trips out of Coos Bay as destination journeys but, rather, to experience them as a continuing series of impressions flowing out of Nature. The first of these trips comprises visits to 2 unique parks.

  * *1.3 m.,* on US 101, from Commercial St., Eastside-Allegany Jct. *1.1 m.,* Eastside Jct. (For Eastside, see *Cross-Coast Range Roads, Coos Bay Wagon Road.*) Turn R toward Allegany. Road now follows S fork of Coos River and then Millicoma River, with some rustic stream attractions for the photographic eye. *2.5 m.,* drawbridge. *3.6 m.,* Public BL. *2.5 m.,* **Rooke-Higgins CP.** CG, PA, fishing, BR. *3.7 m.,* Allegany School. *0.5 m.,* **Allegany.** PO est.

1893. In 1915 town was favorite summer camping place for Coos Bay residents, who generally got there by steamer. Today, store. *4.2 m.,* **Millicoma Myrtle Grove Park,** on Millicoma River. Small PA. Surrounded and smothered by trees you feel you are a hundred miles from anywhere — or nowhere. The solitude seems to be holding a sign reading "No Trespassing." *2 m.,* **Nesika CP.** PA. *3.7 m.,* **Golden and Silver Falls SP.** From little wooden bridge at parking area, falls are about 1 m. apart, and a trail leads to each. Golden Falls plunges over lip of cliff almost 300 ft., swirls and froths in the imprisonment of moss-covered boulders, then wrenches itself free to rush to the Millicoma River. Silver Falls, at end of old logging road, cascades in a bridal veil of 150 ft., the sheen mist lacing shrubs and wildflowers, which bob their heads like tiny mermaids. Look for the coast monkeyflower, peeping out of the ever-washed niches of the mossy rocks. Oddly, though waters of falls are clear and cool, there is no pump or faucet in park. Bring your own water or drink from pools.

For one of the most joyous coastal scenic trips, turn W on Commercial Ave., in Coos Bay, from US 101.

* **Empire,** now part of Coos Bay. Started in 1853 as Empire City, because it was to be center of great gold mining and commercial empire, town was first seat of Coos County and customs port for S district of Oregon. PO est. 1858, name changed to Empire 1894. Town was shipping port for low grade coal mined to S. Emergence of Marshfield, later Coos Bay, diminished importance of Empire and place is now more integral a part of Coos Bay than it is a suburb.

4.5 m., **Charleston,** fishing village that seems to comprise elements of Maine coast, Cannery Row, and Oregon harbor. Smack of salt air is heavy and wind spices blown spray with portents of good fortune. Those who hold devotion to poet William Vaughn Moody may here be reminded of a verse from his "Gloucester Moors":

"Over the shelf of the sandy cove/ Beach-peas blossom late./ By copse and cliff the swallows rove/ Each calling to his mate./ Seaward the sea-gulls go,/ And the land-birds all are here:/ The green-gold flash was a vireo,/ And yonder flame where marsh-flags grow/ Was a scarlet tanager."

Charleston was settled at mouth of South Slough in 1853 and grew lamely. In 1940 its outstanding feature was Coast Guard Station, by mouth of Coos Bay. In recent years town has gained even greater recognition as one of state's largest commercial fishery centers, packing tuna, salmon, other fish, shrimp and crab. Located here is **University of Oregon Institute of Marine Biology,** near **S Slough Estuarine Sanctuary,** 3,800 acres of upland forest and 600 acres of tidal land, including extensive undisturbed tideflats. S Slough is first estuary on W Coast to be set aside in its natural state for study and appreciation. Slough provides habitat for many Pacific birds and includes

Silver Falls, Golden and Silver Falls State Park

Phoebe L. Friedman

large great blue heron rookery. At least 22 commercially important species of fish and shellfish are found in estuary. Sanctuary occupies S half of S Slough.

Although S Slough is regarded as wilderness area by most people, much of it has been logged 2 or 3 times, and practically all areas have been logged at least once. Log trains roll along the estuary and here and there are still some, though faint, traces of abandoned homesteads. One of the islands of S Slough even had a saloon, with proprietor storing wine in nearby cave.

* *0.7 m.*, jct., state parks. Take SPs road. *0.2 m.*, jct., Seven Devils Road. Straight for SPs. *1.5 m.*, turnoff R for **Bastendorff CP.** (*0.2 m.*, CG, PA on Bastendorff Beach, at foot of Cape Arago. **Cape Arago Lighthouse** perches on promontory above beach. Overlook of beach and ocean is impacting. **Childrens Park** has small scale replica of pioneer stockade. Near here, less than *0.2 m.* from ocean, is 10 acre **Bastendorff Bog,** owned by The Nature Conservancy, which gives it this description: "This bog hosts *Lilium ocidentale,* a plant restricted to a few coastal *sphagnum* bogs and wetlands along the southern Oregon and extreme northern California coasts. The bog also contains *Darlingtonia Californica* (california pitcher plant) and *Xerophyllum tenax* (beargrass), a species usually restricted to the mountains. The preserve is dominated by shrubs such as *Rhododendron macrophyllum, Myrica californica, Gaultheria shallon* and *Vaccinium spp.*")

* *0.8 m.*, turnoff R on No Trespass Lane to Cape Arago Lighthouse. (*0.3 m.*, parking area for view of LH. Permission required to travel lane. Phone LH station.)

0.5 m., **Sunset Bay SP.** CG, PA, FHP, fishing, showers. The lowing sun transmutes the wind-shorn and wave-battered cliffs and offshore rocks into, oddly, a touch of Polynesia — or is it Alaska? Sunset Bay, within the park's boundary, is small cove protected by high sandstone bluff on N and S. Because of its narrow opening to sea the bay is excellent for swimming — but only on incoming tides.

1.2 m., **Shore Acres SP.** PA, FHP. Park was once estate famed for botanical gardens, with flowering trees, shrubs and plants brought from many parts of the world by fast-sailing clipper ships and schooners. Luxurious gardens — and princely, remote mansion — now belong to state. But most compelling reason for coming here is the imagery of continental rim. S and N the coastal bluffs appear as desert formations, with miniature sand dunes plastered into whorls on some of the rocks. To S, chain of rocks, perhaps *0.5 m.* out from land, appears at dusk, or in spongy web of fog, as displaced bit of Maine coast. And the eye returns to the cliff and the massive openings, fantasized as tunnel entrances gouged by metallic giants and hollowed by fire-breathing serpents.

1.1 m., **Simpson Reef.** At sundown the scene westward look like a fragment from the lost continent of Atlantis. Bring out field glasses for spotting

Cape Arago Lighthouse   *Courtesy State of Oregon*

sea lions on Simpson Reef and Shell Island. For most persons, the compelling
drama here is the changing sea — the constant interacting forces of struggle.

0.4 m., **Cape Arago SP.** PA, fishing, trail to beach. In summer of 1977
scholars from Ore. and Calif. met here to confirm their findings that the S
cove of Cape Arago was the northernmost point Sir Francis Drake reached
on the N American continent, more than halfway in his plan to sail around
the world. In June 1579 Drake's *Golden Hind* dropped anchor briefly in a
"bad bay." Marker commemorating Drake's anchorage is at edge of bluff
overlooking S Cove. The next European mariner to sight the cape was Capt.
Cook, on March 12, 1788. He named it after saint of the day, Gregory. On
July 4, 1828, Jedediah Smith camped here. About 1850 name of cape changed
to honor Dominique Francois Jean Arago, French geographer, physicist,
astronomer, politician. Arago has another distinction. At 3 p.m., Monday,

Aug. 19, 1839, at the Institut de France in Paris, Prof. Arago announced to the packed assemblage in the lecture hall the birth of photography, its parents being Louis Jacques Mande Daguerre. (See *Masters of Early Travel Photography*.)

Oregon's largest scallop is found on beach at Cape Arago (and Shore Acres) in greater numbers than elsewhere. The shells, to quote authority Jim White, "have the characteristic flaring ears at the hinge and may be bright yellow, orange, or beige colored. Some look like miniature Shell Oil Company emblems. When the rock scallop grows [from size of dime] to about the size of a quarter, it picks out a rock or other solid surface and cements its shell to its home spot. The bright yellow or orange . . . slowly fades and the new growth is a camouflage brown . . . Soon the growing scallop looks just like a rock . . . When the dead shells are washed upon the beach, they appear gray and riddled with holes, almost like a dead sponge."

* From SP jct. near Charleston there is another fascinating journey, a back road to Bandon that reaches the scene of once hectic gold activity.

4.2 m., on L, Estuary Study Trail. (500 yds., S Slough Interpretive Center.) *2.1 m.,* on R, Seven Devils Rd. — narrow, rough, not for trailers. Keep straight. *4.5 m.,* jct., Whiskey Run Beach. (Straight, *2 m.,* US 101.) R for Whiskey Run Beach. *2.5 m.,* jct., Seven Devils Rd. — Whiskey Run Beach. Turn R for Seven Devils Wayside. *1.6 m.,* **Seven Devils Wayside.** PA, just few steps to beach. Masses of Scotch broom give way to long, smooth and often deserted beaches.

Return to Whiskey Run Beach Jct. Turn R. *1.4 m.,* **Whiskey Run Beach;** 3d most important platinum-bearing gold placers mined in Oregon was here and along other beaches in Coos and Curry counties. (See US 199 for more important discoveries of genre.) Original gold find here 1852.

Creek dribbling into ocean here was named Whiskey Run because of heavy drinking or because creek suggested firewater to some thirsty prospector.

At its zenith, during Coos County Gold Rush of 1853–55, Whiskey Run, or **Randolph,** as place was later formally named, had largest pop. of any gold camp on coast and even rivaled prestigious Jacksonville. After gold fever began to dwindle, Randolph was moved to mouth of Coquille River. Later, after gold fever had completely subsided, Randolph was moved again, inland.

Whiskey Run was renamed Randolph by couple of early gold rush comers, evidently Southerners, in devotion to an earlier congressmen from Roanoke, Virginia, whom history best remembers for his having fluttered Philadelphia in 1803 with the happy announcement that he had fathered a child out of wedlock. He also duelled with Henry Clay and popularized the term "doughface," applied to Northern congressmen who voted with Southern slave-holding interests.

John Randolph was described by a contemporary as "one of the most sarcastic men that ever lived" and gave this account to prove his point: One time a young man attempted to make Randolph's acquaintance. He obtained an introduction, and among the first remarks said: "I passed by your house lately, Mr. Randolph." "I hope you always will," was the short reply.

The bite of John Randolph passed to the tongue and teeth of the Whiskey Run argonauts; if tartness carried the price of gold a thousand fortunes would have been made. Out of the sharp give and take arose a flock of legends, including one of "lost gold."

In the 1850s two miners who had made a rich strike buried a 5 gallon can of gold dust beneath a tree and went off for supplies. During their absence a forest fire swept the mining district, leaving thousands of black-charred snags and stumps without any mark to identify the site of the cache. There is no record of the gold ever having been found. But, then again, maybe the legend is only that.

Insights of the 3 towns of Randolph were penned by Florence Angelelo of Portland in 1978:

"My grandparents were married at the Black Sand mines in 1876 and my mother died in Randolph many years ago. In the early 1880s my grandfather owned and operated a hotel and saloon at Randolph complete with a Chinese cook.

"My grandfather told me he purchased whiskey in ten gallon barrels. He would empty half into another barrel, tack a plug of tobacco to the bottom inside the barrel, add a can of cayenne pepper and finish it off with *good* spring water. Twenty gallons for ten. Unfortunately, cut proof notwithstanding, he was his own best customer and he gave up the hotel business and went to steamboating on the Coquille. Being a man of small stature and a large capacity for bourbon, he was known to miss the river occasionally with his boat. However, he did earn his captain's papers and retire from the river with a certain amount of dignity and respect.

"There was off-and-on mining at Whiskey Run for many years. During the 1930s a mine was opened up with outside investors, only to close as had all the others, but without any profit. Whiskey Run left a scar on me received from a fall on a broken bottle. A whiskey bottle, what else?

"The 'true' town of Randolph disappeared under a pile of dirt when the hill came down in a landslide and covered most of it."

Modern day prospectors still come to the beach, hoping their metal detectors will bring them riches. But there is more here than the possible flecks of gold. Whiskey Run and the beaches N of it — Merchant's, Agate and Sacci — contain not only agates, agatized myrtlewood and jasper but are rich in clams. And Pacific vistas are superb.

(For story on Whiskey Run Beach, see "The Seasons of Randolph" in author's *Tracking Down Oregon*.)

* Return to jct. at Seven Devils Rd. Turn R. *2.8 m.,* US 101. *1.9 m.,* turnoff to Bullards Beach SP. *3.4 m.,* Bandon.

From Commercial St., Coos Bay:

0.9 m., House of Myrtlewood, long prominent in the trade. *0.4 m.,* Eastside-Allegany Jct. (See trips to Millicoma Park and Golden and Silver Falls SP, above, and *Cross-Coast Range Roads, Coos Bay Wagon Road.*)

2.3 m., turnoff to public BL. *2.5 m.,* jct., 0 42. (See *Cross-Coast Range Roads, 0 42.) 12.4 m.,* Randolph Jct.

* Turn E. *1 m.,* **Randolph,** 3d site of town. Nothing here now but a few pleasant homes and a look at the unenchanting Coquille River.

* Turn W. *0.5 m.,* turn R. *1.9 m.,* turn L. *1.4 m.,* Whiskey Run Beach. *0.7 m.,* jct., Seven Devils Rd.

* *4.8 m.,* Whiskey Run Beach.

2 m., turnoff to **Bullards Beach SP.**

* CG, PA, BL, FHP, fishing. *2.6 m.* from registration gate to **Coquille River Lighthouse,** out of commission since 1963, at mouth of Coquille. Old photos in 1896 lighthouse tell story of place. Located here was 2d site of Randolph, born as Whiskey Run. (SP has horse camp, where visitors can camp near their horses.)

0.8 m., Prosper Jct.

* Turn E. *0.9 m.,* turn L. *0.9 m.,* **Prosper,** on Coquille, with its own yacht club. Blue roofs were painted by yacht club members, who wanted to give place distinctive air.

Coquille River Lighthouse, before renovation   *Phoebe L. Friedman*

* Turn W. *2.9 m.*, Bandon Beach.

1.4 m., jct., 0 42-S. (See *Cross-Coast Range Roads, 0 42-S.*)

1 m., downtown **Bandon.** Bandon is really something for a town of about only 2,500. For starters, it calls itself "Cranberry Capitol of Oregon." Large bogs N and S of town produce from their thick, maroon, close-to-earth vines the berries which at harvest time in early autumn are inspiration for Bandon Cranberry Festival. Shop in Old Town (downtown) makes and sells more than 25 varieties of cranberry candy.

Bandon also heralds itself as "Storm Watching Capitol of the World" (no lack of modesty in this town) and prides itself upon the wicked bar at mouth of Coquille. Brochure reads: "Bar swells may reach great heights with the changing tides, aided by currents and freshets of the river creating a navigator's nightmare."

Bandon also fancies itself as an up-and-coming seaport, because ocean-going barges haul lumber from mills upstream on Coquille. it also boasts that it is one of Oregon's 10 biggest commercial fishing ports and a shipper of tuna, salmon, snappers, halibut and shrimp.

It is impossible to convince anyone in Bandon that the Coquille is not the finest fishing stream in Oregon. In truth, a lot of sport fishers do favor the river, particularly those who aim for steelhead and cutthroat. Shad, salmon and striped bass are

Beach scene below Bandon   *Courtesy State of Oregon*

also proclaimed in local publicity. Near the Pacific, crabs are numerous; on the tidal flats, clams are pursued.

For bird watching, Bandon folk swear there is no more inviting area than the wetlands N of town, where sky-darkening flocks of migratory birds settle down for a while to feed and rest.

Oregon's second largest cheese factory is here. Closed for financial reasons, it was reopened in 1988 as community effort. Through observation windows weekday morning visitors watch flavored cheddar cheese made.

Scientific-minded of Bandon are quick to tell guests that area around town along sea is rife with silicoflagellates, bizarre planktonic plant micro-fossils.

What else does Bandon inflate its chest about? "Oregon's largest metaphysical bookshop"; sternwheeler *Bold Duck* for rides up Coquille; art galleries, myrtlewood shops, Coquille River Museum in old Coast Guard Station; and shops of Old Town, along Coquille, where former city hall and jail are now smart mercantile ventures.

Town burned down twice, once in 1914, again in 1936, when conflagration wiped out all but 16 of more than 500 houses. Flames were so fierce humidity in seacoast village dropped to 12 percent. But Bandon rebuilt and is bigger, better-looking and cockier than ever.

Bandon is town that will whirl into celebration at turn of the breeze. Example: In 1985, when rather nondescript veterans hall was completed, main street of Old Town was roped off for festivities. So many American flags were displayed that an awakened Rip Van Winkle might have thought it was either end of WW II or total destruction of nuclear weapons.

For drive along Beach Loop, start at Old Town:

* *0.3 m.*, forks. Take L uphill. *1.6 m.*, **Face Rock Viewpoint.** Offshore rocks, which can evoke fanciful images, may to students of Greek mythology look like sea serpents, sirens and weird demi-gods of the deep arisen to snatch at an invisible Homer. To anthropologist, Face Rock may look like brow of Neanderthal. Viewpoint is best site along Loop for cameos of nesting shorebirds on offshore rocks. *1.7 m.*, **Bandon Beach SP.** PA, FHP, fishing. Tides lash against sand given moral support by marshgrass. *0.5 m.*, Bandon Beach SP. *0.2 m.*, Bandon Beach SP. Beach access. *1.1 m.*, US 101.

From 11th St., Bandon, on US 101:

3 m., S end of Beach Loop. *0.5 m.*, turnoff to Bradley Lake. Public BL. *2.2 m.*, Oregon Myrtlewood Factory. *0.3 m.*, Zumwalt's Myrtlewood. *0.6 m.*, Pacific Myrtlewood. *0.5 m.*, **West Coast Game Park,** which calls itself "largest animal petting park in the West." Deer, sheep and goats eat out of hands. Wide variety of domestic and exotic animals, too many, probably, for size of area. Most species are penned, as in zoo, but in far more confined and less conducive quarters. Conclusion: delightful and sad.

6 m., **Langlois,** one of many downhill towns along S Coast. Named for 1854 settler. In 1915 was center of 5 cheese factories, had 2 sawmills, weekly paper, 3

Floras Lake

Phoebe L. Friedman

lodges, 2 cooperage plants which built tubs for preserving fish, had pop. 150. By 1940 pop. increased to 250. Now only store.

Langlois is N settlement of Curry County, whose shore, wrote Ernest H. Lund, "is the most continuously rugged segment of the Oregon Coast . . . Numerous state parks, waysides, and lookout points . . . afford magnificent views of the ocean, the rocks, and the scenery.

"Curry County lies at the western margin of the Klamath Mountains province, a region composed of some of the oldest rocks in Oregon. Tremendous forces within the earth's crust have made mountains out of rocks that were once sedimentary and volcanic materials on the sea floor. Metamorphic recrystallization and intense folding, faulting, and shearing have altered these rocks to varying degrees. In general, the more ancient the rocks, the more severely they are disrupted and altered."

Travelers will see for themselves that Curry is the least commercialized of the coastal counties and without doubt possesses the most beautiful and exciting shoreline. It also has, all things considered, the most temperate climate along the coast, yet remains the least-populated. It seems a natural for fleeing metropolites and retired, yet its growth is painfully slow and, lacking a year-round strong economic base, is quickly jolted by downturns in fishing and logging. Why hasn't Curry County been invaded for residence by other Oregonians and Californians? Too isolated, access too difficult, say the analytical locals.

1.1 m., turnoff W. for Floras Lake.

　　＊ 1.1 m., turn R. *1.5 m.,* Boice-Cope Rd. Turn R. *0.3 m.,* on L, Boice-Cope CP. CG. BR on **Floras Lake;** fishing for salmon, trout, catfish, yellow perch, largemouth bass and carp. Among first whites here were miners seeking gold

but they didn't strike it a tenth as rich as promoters who built city on Floras Lake. Grandiose plan was to construct canal from lake to sea and make Pacific City, or Lakeport — town had one name and then another — great shipping port. Push started in 1908 and thousands of lots were sold, with price jumping from $12.50 to $300 each. Wharves were built, sidewalks laid, houses rushed to completion and business district opened, topped by 3-story hotel. For a while city was largest in Curry County and the upstart Floras Lake *Banner* ran wild with purple predictions. Then came the cold discovery: lake would empty into Pacific if canal was built without complicated and expensive locks. About that time the citizens began asking each other what would be economic base of city. None, they agreed, and the exodus began. On Nov. 6, 1909 hotel clerk scrawled final entry in register: "Not a damn sole." It should have been town's epitaph but some sturdy folks rooted down and on first summer day of 1910 Lakeport PO was opened. Closed 5 years later. Not a stick of town remains; site retaken by forest. (For more, see "Villa Francia of Floras Lake" in author's *This Side of Oregon*.)

1.5 m., **Denmark,** founded by Danes. Another downer. In 1915: sawmill, cheese factory, creamery, PS. Now, store. Geologists say place is S end of fossil-bearing sandstone bed which starts at Coquille River.

5.1 m., **Sixes,** named for river. Name, corruption of a Chinook jargon word which is itself in question, may mean salutation (Klahowya Sikhs), friend (which may have had same connotation as salutation), or "people of the far north country." Name Sixes was applied by miners who came in 1850s to pan black sands near mouth of river for gold. Store.

Turnoff to Sixes River Rec. Site:

    * *4.2 m.,* **Edson Creek CP,** distinguished by grove of giant myrtle trees at entrance. Wild blackberries grow in profusion, ripening in late summer. *7.1 m.,* **Sixes River Rec. Site.** CG on whispering Sixes. Experienced fishers know stream for its salmon, steelhead, cutthroat trout.

0.9 m., Cape Blanco Jct.

    * Road has the same contours it had when built many decades ago. It still staggers thru rhododendron and azalea thickets and over lupine-covered hillocks. *4.4 m.,* on L, site of long-gone Cape Blanco Catholic Church. The 1940 *Oregon: End of the Trail* described it as "now in ruins; bats clinging to the altar and the glass in the pointed window frames is shattered." *0.6 m.,* jct., Cape Blanco SP. Turn L. *0.3 m.,* **Cape Blanco SP,** called "most Westerly park on the continental US." SP on ranch once owned by Patrick and Jane Hughes, 1860 settlers, parish founders and builders of Cape Blanco Catholic Church. Both were buried in church cemetery, now lie in Portland. Restored 1898 **Hughes House,** now operated as a museum during summer months by Curry County Historical Society, was jewel of 1880 acre ranch, which was a dairy and livestock operation 1860–1970. SP has CG, PA, FHP, hiker-biker camp area, DS, showers. Trail leads to unusual black sand beach, 200 ft.

Hughes House, Cape Blanco   *Courtesy Patrick Masterson*

below camp. A 2 m. walk S on beach to mouth of Elk River from July to Oct. is sometimes rewarded with sight of rare brown pelicans feeding. Cape offers unobstructed view of migrating gray whales in Dec. and Jan., again in spring. Return to SP jct. Turn L. *0.5 m.,* **Cape Blanco Lighthouse,** oldest and loftiest lighthouse structure in Oregon and state's most W rampart. Opened Dec. 20, 1870, light has been shining nightly since, throwing out beam 22 m. from 245 ft. elevation. In addition to light, a radio beam reaches up to 250 m.

Before road was built, lighthouse was reached only by clumping over washboard trace in buckboards, buggies and wagons. But a relative lot of people came, an average of 200 per year. Among keepers to welcome them was James Langlois, of Langlois town fame, who was lighthouse keeper for 42 years. An early feminist, he employed two women as his assistants. But the govt., not as progressive, ordered them discharged.

Cape so named because of its chalky appearance (*blanco* is white in Spanish) by Martin d'Aguilar, who captained a ship separated by bad weather from the small flotilla of exploration headed by Sebastian Viscaino in 1603. (Actually, the "white cliffs" are composed of fossilized sea shells.) Yankee mariners changed the name to Port Orford but eventually, about a century ago, it made its way back to navigation charts as Cape Blanco. Waters around cape can become savagely turbulent; several vessels have been wrecked in immediate vicinity, prompting cape to be known as "Port of No Return."

Standing on the cape, one gets the feeling of being on a ship plowing its way thru the deep six. Nowhere else on the Oregon Coast is this feeling so intense.

1.2 m., jct., Elk River Rd.

* The Elk is almost legendary among fishers for its chinook, steelhead, cutthroat and coho salmon. *6.8 m.,* **Elk River Salmon Hatchery,** only one of its kind on the S Oregon Coast, and sited between the stream and stands of lofty Douglas fir. *2.9 m.,* forks. R for McGribble FS CG. *2.1 m.,* turn R. *0.9 m.,* **McGribble FS CG.** Tall firs and Port Orford cedar look down on moist vale licked by cool waters of Bald Mtn. Creek. Good fishing and hiking in this primitive area. Return to Elk River Rd. Turn R. *6.7 m.,* **Panther Creek FS CG,** at confluence of Panther Creek and Elk River. *1.3 m.,* **Butler Bar FS CG,** in glorious stand of Douglas fir. None of the CGs have formal trailer space. All are sited in woods ablaze with wildflowers and thick with shrubs and ferns. Especially lovely is the dogwood, which brightens every corner it touches.

3 m., **Port Orford,** most W inc. city in contiguous US, first white settlement in Curry County, first county seat. Name given April 24, 1792 by Capt. George Vancouver in honor of his "much respected friend," George, Earl of Orford. Actually, Vancouver was then looking at Cape Blanco, but eventually the name crept S a few m. and Cape Orford became Port Orford.

Town's history really began in early June 1851 when Capt. William Tichenor, New Jersey native, brought his small sailing vessel, *Sea Gull,* here to land nine men and supplies on large rock at S end of present town — **Battle Rock.** Tichenor's purpose was very simple: to get rich by setting up supply depot so that freight could be hauled from San Francisco, unloaded at the nearest feasible coastal point, then packtrained overland to gold camps. He had sailed up and down the Oregon Coast and had determined exactly where to est. his base of operations.

No sooner had *Sea Gull* departed, on June 9, when Tichenor's nine were attacked by resident Indians, Coquilles, who resented white intrusion. Fortunately for the palefaces, Tichenor had the foresight to equip them with a 4 lb. cannon. Without it, Battle Rock might be called Massacre Rock. You know the story: when the whites won, it was a victory; when Indians won, it was a massacre. When Coquilles relaxed their vigilance, whites fled to settlements N.

Tichenor returned on July 14 with 67 armed men under command of James S. Gamble and proceeded to build two blockhouses "inside of heavy logs." Tichenor had recruited and the 67 from the streets of San Francisco, which "were thronged with idlers who were destitute and willing to go anywhere as long as their wants were supplied." Before the month was over, "it was found necessary," wrote Tichenor, "to send 14 of the most desperate and insubordinate of the crew back to the city." Later, Tichenor laid out and named Port Orford. By then hamlet was site of 10-acre Fort Orford, US army post with somewhat less than glorious history.

Greatest boom in Port Orford's history was 1854–55. Discovery of gold swamped village with miners. Five hotels were hastily erected; in addition, there were five stores, twice as many saloons, two butcher shops, bowling alley, sprinkle of individual dwellings. There wasn't enough room in hotels to accommodate all gold seekers and soon arose along beach a string of tents.

Port Orford ran high on voltage of gold fever. Every hour brought rumors of new discoveries. It did not seem to the hopeful that the gold would ever run out. This may have been key factor in way gold was separated from sand, losing much gold. After day of digging and panning, miners put pans of sand into ovens to dry, then blew away the black sand, leaving gold dust. It was a careless and costly operation.

With typical arrogance of get-rich-quick invaders, miners regarded all Indians as nothing better than to be used for target shooting. Onslaughts upon the Indians were numerous and grisly and went unpunished by authorities. In 1854, following cowardly attack upon Indian village at mouth of Chetco, Joel Palmer, superintendent of Indian Affairs in Oregon, reported to Washington in frustration: "Arrests are evidently useless as no act of a white man against an Indian, however atrocious, can be followed by conviction."

Fighting for their homeland, Indians could be ferocious, too, and afflicted heavy casualties upon whites before they were subdued.

Battle Rock, Port Orford

"Though the red man was savage and cruel," wrote regional historian Orvil Dodge, "he learned much of it from the white man."

Chief John lamented that the land had belonged to his people ever since the tall Port Orford cedars were small. Whites, in same spirit of clearing the land, cut down both Indians and trees.

PO est. 1855; following year Curry County govt. organized and operated here in home of settler (though town not inc. until 1935). In 1856 many miners failed and Port Orford was virtually emptied. Orvil Dodge described the scene: "Weird, silent, ghost-like stood the five hotels, the saloons and stores; homes for the birds, store houses for the wood rats, sport for the north wind that played at hide and seek through the broken windows and open doorways, broken fences, deserted farm yards, roofless dwellings . . ." The historian Bancroft dismissed the settlement in one curt sentence: "Port Orford is a little hamlet on the wrong side of the mountain with no reason on earth for being there." But two years later a resurgence of mining had sufficiently revived the hamlet to raise $800 to build a jail.

Devastating forest fire of 1868, which burned or badly damaged most of cedar near Port Orford, almost leveled town, and from then on it was slow process of starting all over again.

Thru the years Port Orford saw many famous personages, quite a few of whom stopped at the hearth-warming, long-gone hotel operated by Louis Knapp, whose nightly light in the window (before lighthouse was built) warned mariners of rocky coast ahead. Town can also boast one of the best of Oregon poets, the gifted Minnie Myrtle Dyer, whose tragic marriage to Joaquin Miller was publicized up and down the state by the abandoned woman. (For more on town's fascinating history and characters, see "Tichenor and Associates Present Port Orford" in author's *Tracking Down Oregon*.)

In 1970 Port Orford was site of marine life experiment; 29 sea otters were flown here from Alaska's Amchitka Island and released in Cape Blanco area. In 1971 more sea otters followed. Few years later sea otter pop. began to decline and very few of these playful animals have been seen since.

Built on a bluff overlooking lovely, deep-water bay S of promontory known as "The Heads," Port Orford is neat both in dictionary and contemporary use of the adjective. Strolling about this pleasant town of little more than 1,000, one is reminded of four lines of poetry by Elinor Wylie: "This is the city where the spring/ Blooms in the sky before its hour/ In sunsets fleeter than a wing/ And sweeter than a flower."

Port Orford is in bird watching area known well to Audobonists. From the rocky islands offshore to the crest of the Coast Range, more than 300 species of birds have been identified. They include black-footed albatrosses, sooty shearwaters, fulmars, common loons, Western grebes, American coots, brown pelicans, cormorants, harlequin ducks, great blue herons, common egrets, peregrine

Sketch of Fort Orford 1851–1856   *Courtesy Patrick Masterson*

falcons, sanderlings, Western sandpipers, black-bellied plovers, dunlins, dowitchers and red-necked phalaropes.

Local partisans claim that their tidepools contain "some of the richest and most diverse environments in the world. As the tide moves out, layer after layer of different yet connected environments unfold. Unfamiliar organisms with unfamiliar names inhabit these places between the tides. Goose Barnacles, Whelks, Limpets, Anemones, and Sea Urchins are just a sample of the creatures to be found."

At 906 N Washington stands 1892 **Lindberg House,** home of at least five generations of family; Victorian gothic style with Queen Anne tower. Other interesting structures: Austere, hipped roof **White House** (1905), 504 N. Washington; Victorian gothic style **Masterson House** (1898) with imbricated shingling patterns, 611 N Jackson; **Nygren House** (1888), 921 N. Jackson; **Long House** (1892), 9th and Jefferson.

Wm. Tichenor built two blockhouses; one was at Fort Point, S end of Jackson; other was at 18th and Jackson. For grave of Tichenor, turn W off US 101, Oregon St., onto 9th St. *0.1 m.,* turn L at forks. *0.3 m.,* take R fork of rough trace *0.2 m.* to Tichenor Cemetery. Knoll affords splendid overlook of freshwater Garrison Lake and, just beyond, wild and boundless Pacific. Return to paved road. Turn R. *0.4 m.,* **Port Orford Heads Wayside.** PA, trails. Best place for whale watching. Keeper's house part of former Coast Guard facility here.

For Paradise Point SP, turn W onto Paradise Point Rd. Just beach and view of Orford Reef. For Buffington Park, one of nicest city parks on S coast, with dock on lake for fishing, swimming, PA, hiking trails, horse arena, turn W onto 12th — *0.2 m.* Continue *0.4 m.* to **Garrison Lake.** Public BL, waterskiing.

At S end of downtown, uphill *0.1 m.* from curve, site of Fort Orford, 1851-56, most W fort of US Army. Compound consisted of 15 bldgs., main ones protected by plank wall and earthen glacis. After closing, most bldgs. moved to Ft. Umpqua.

Battle Rock is point of historical interest, no more, no less. Climbing to and on rock, keep tight rein on small children and pets.

From downtown Port Orford:

1.2 m., Cemetery Loop Rd.

> * *0.6 m.,* **Pioneer Cemetery** (1852). Buried here are many of Port Orford's early comers, including Louis Knapp.

4.3 m. — with US 101 swinging around Rocky Point, clam digger's paradise — Humbug Mtn. Trail. Parking. *0.3 m.,* jct., Humbug Mtn. SP. CG, PA, DS, fishing, showers.

> * (Near entrance to SP, R turn onto mtn. road that winds *4 m.* to McGribble FS CG.) *0.3 m.,* **Humbug Mtn. SP CG.** Humbug was once known as Sugar Loaf Peak and later as Tichenor's Humbug because an exploring party he sent out got lost and mistook this landmark for another, 180 degrees from

Humbug Mountain beach

Rain forest, Prehistoric Gardens　　　　　　　　　　*Courtesy State of Oregon*

where they were supposed to go! (See story in author's *Tracking Down Oregon*.)

Past alders, myrtles and maples and trout stream, it is only *0.5 m.* from CG HQ to sand beach, where awaits wealth of aesthetic pleasures, ephemeral and material. Whales, sea lions and otters provide — when seen and heard — sights and sounds most pleasurable to the hearts of those who believe these creatures have as much right as we to inhabit this frail, precious star which is the only home most — or any — of us will ever know. Japanese glass floats come in every shade of blue and green, orange, yellow, smoke, white and pink, and sometimes there is that special one — purple, a spindle of glass thru the center, sand blasted, and with distinctive markings. Best time to go hunting for glass floats is late Dec. thru early May. Finds also include driftwood in every conceivable form, Oregon "jade", jasper, petrified wood, agate, marine fossils, rare shells, beeswax, bamboo and bottles. And undoubtedly there is more. The serious beachcomber carries plastic basket, rock hammer and small garden rake.

Several trails from CG HQ. Most challenging and rewarding is hike to top of Humbug Mtn. — *0.2 m.* to trail from CG HQ and *3 m.* to 1,756 ft. peak, highest on S Oregon coast. When wind is strong atop Humbug Mtn. it does not require much imagination to believe that mtn. is a ship moving out to sea.

0.8 m., turnoff for Humbug Mtn. SP PA.

Now the road scoots between the green walls of Brush Creek Canyon, deepest gorge in these parts, and close to shore passes 568-ft.-high basaltic cone called Lookout Rock.

5.5 m., on W, **Prehistoric Gardens,** "recreation" in rain forest of "lost world" of life-sized replicas of dinosaurs and other prehistoric animals that roamed the earth a good many millions of years ago. If you'd like a parrot-beaked Psittacosaurus in your life, this is the place. A walk thru luxuriant ferns and huge moss-covered trees is fine lesson in elementary paleontology.

1.8 m., **Sisters Rocks,** of scenic and historic interest. Three rocks, two on land and one on nearby island, had the profiles of sisters to early settlers. At cove S of rocks stood village of Frankport, with shipping port on island of offshore rock. Port was connected to mainland by bridge and wooden railway. Hides and tanbark among principal products; as late as 1950s port was shipping lumber. Gone, all of it. Sisters Rocks at N end of belt of Otter Formation, that extends unevenly S to Whalehead Cove. Formation is comprised of subtle melange of volcanic rock, sandstone, conglomerate and mudstone, folded and sheared. Geologist Ernest H. Lund wrote that "the whole assemblage has been aptly referred to as chaotic."

2.8 m., viewpoint. In any other state, viewpoints such as this would be celebrated; in Curry County they are a dime a dozen.

1.9 m., Ophir Jct.

    * *0.5 m.,* **Ophir,** probably named for the rich black beach sands to W. On Euchre Creek, with Euchre said to be probable corruption of Tututni word *Ykichetunne,* meaning "people at the mouth of a river." Store. S of Ophir the road runs over sandy hills bright in spring with raging lupine and blazing yellow verbena. It follows Cedar Creek and Squaw Creek and dips thru Squaw Valley *8.2 m.* to S bank of Rogue River.

2.1 m., Rest Area. After being gorged by so much beauty it may be time to rest.

1.9 m., jct., Nesika Beach.

    * *0.4 m.,* **Nesika Beach,** beachside community whose residents would like to keep their slice of heaven a secret. Store.

1.3 m., **Geisel Monument SP.** Picnic area in grove of Douglas fir, maple, Port Orford cedar, alder, pine. Monument here to John Geisel and his three young sons, John, Henry and Andrew, slain by Indians Feb. 22, 1856. There is no monument to the 19 Indians killed in ambush near this spot by vengeful whites as the unarmed Indians were being marched to a Reservation.

    * Somewhat caliginous trail from park to Nesika Beach Preserve, which abuts N boundary of park. Preserve is owned by The Nature Conservancy which gives this description: "Ecological transition between the California

redwoods and the Sitka spruce/western hemlock forests of the Oregon Coast, Neskia Beach, with its Sitka spruce/grand fir forests contains a plant community with no other known example. The old growth coastal fronting forest is bounded on both north and south by undisturbed grassland bluffs. Nelson's thistle (*Cirsium acanthodontum*) and black crowberry (*Empetrum nigrum*) grow at the site."

2.1 *m.*, **Otter Point SP.** Wayside with trail to beach. *2 m.*, turnoff W to mouth of Rogue River.

* *1.5 m.* road winds along bit of river and ends up at US 101.

Geisel Monument

0.8 m., **Rogue River Viewpoint.** *0.3 m.,* Wedderburn Jct., turnoff for business district of mini-town on N bank of Rouge. Although Wedderburn is presently regarded as appendage of Gold Beach, it wasn't always so. In 1915, it had largest salmon packing plant in state outside Columbia River district, large sawmill, shingle mill, cold storage plant, ice plant, electric lighting plant, PS.

* *0.5 m.,* N jetty, at mouth of Rogue. *1.2 m.,* on R, site of Miners Fort, now cow pasture. In 1856, at moment of urgency and fear, during heightened period of Indian armed militancy, hastily built stockade, surrounded by moat, was refuge of miners and settlers. Fort abandoned when Indians suppressed.

Turnoff L for boat trips up Rogue River.

* *0.4 m.,* boat docks for much-ballyhooed "white water" excursions. Most popular are 64 m. round-trips to Agness. Two lodges serve lunch, board overniters. More exciting is 104 m. round-trip to Paradise Bar. Mail to Agness still carried by boat when boats are running; at other times, by truck.

0.3 m., Jerry's Flat Rd., turnoff for Agness & Grants Pass on Rogue River Rd. (See *Cross-Coast Range Roads, Rogue River Road.)*

0.6 m., **Gold Beach,** first called Ellensburg, then Sebastopol. Name since 1890 is reflection of gold fever on beaches at mouth of Rogue. Initially isolated, ferry on Rogue in 1857 was first land breakthru. Not until 33 years later was wagon road built to connect town with points N and S. In 1922, Roosevelt Highway (US 101) was completed with opening of Rogue River Bridge.

Town began as wild as most W gold camps. County seat since 1859, first courthouse was in log cabin saloon. Flood of 1861 swept beach "placer mines" into sea and miners departed or turned to commercial salmon fishing. In 1924, Gold Beach was only unincorporated county seat in US; finally inc. 1945.

For years town was home to the *Mary D. Hume,* built on Rogue River in 1880 and "The Last Steam Powered Arctic Whaler Still Afloat," crowed local blurbs. But — loaded on a craft for transfer, vessel toppled off and sank to bottom of river. Farewell, Mary.

As colorful as 90. ft. long *Mary D. Hume* was its builder, R.D. Hume, who named Wedderburn for his ancestral home in Scotland. For quarter of century, until his demise in 1908, Hume was big man of Curry County. He owned huge sections of riverfront and oceanfront land, a large ranch, substantial timber holdings, sawmill, salmon cannery, commercial fishing boats, ocean freighters, boat works, weekly newspaper, profitable store and private race track. When word came that the *Mary D. Hume* was off the river, R.D. Hume would rush out with a large sign, make an appraisal of bar conditions, and hold up the side of the sign that was applicable. One side read, "O.K. to come in"; the other side, "Not O.K." He would have fitted neatly into TV's "Dallas."

Sea lions and seals follow major fish runs into Rogue River estuary from spring until fall, with peak months April–July. Sea mammals seen best from N and S jetties.

Sophisticated fishers call the Rogue one of the great streams of the W, if not the nation. Season begins in early April, when hefty-size spring chinook come up river. Run lasts until mid-June and with chinook are cutthroat. In Aug., summer steelhead run is usually over, but with autumn rains come fall chinook. Then Nov.–March, winter steelhead is the prey.

On both sides of mouth of Rogue anglers catch perch, sea bass, ling cod. Port docks home to commercial and sports fishing boats.

From stoplight, Gold Beach:

0.3 m., **Curry County Museum,** a "scrapbook" of pioneer times. *0.9 m., jct.,* Hunter Creek.

  * *0.5 m.,* Hunter Creek, rural area clustered around store. Ambience here is of Gold Beach being 50 m. away.

0.3 m., turnout at foot of **Kissing Rock,** named for suggestiveness of formation rather than for its convenience as local lovers lane, which it also is. Below it, with easy access, inviting beach.

4.2 m., on W, **Cape Sebastian Marker.** Cape was named by Spanish sea captain Sebastian Viscaino on Jan. 20, 1603 in honor of saint of day, San Sebastian. Sighting a high white bluff, Vizcaino marked the latitude to be 42d parallel. His instruments may have been off; exact reading is N latitude 42°19' 40"; or he may have been focusing on another feature of the coast. His journey, wrote historian Gordon B. Dodds, ended "Spain's last thrust toward the Oregon Country for 171 years, and she then settled to a conscious policy of neglect concerning the Pacific Northwest."

0.1 m., turnoff for **Cape Sebastian SP.** (No water or restrooms.)

  * *0.2 m.,* turn R. *0.1 m.,* viewpoint. Return to SP road. *0.3 m.,* viewpoint. The cape seems to explode from the sea to height of 715 ft., providing awesome vista: S 50 m. to Point St. George; N more than 40 m. to Cape Blanco, with twists of rugged seawall panoramically clear. Trails lead to best views and one trail winds *1.8 m.* to floor of continent. Trails are not difficult; an easy one leads across open grassy plateau from parking area to brow of cape. But cliffs are precipitous; watch kids and pets. Roller coaster road is fitting prelude to far viewpoint; not recommended for house trailers.

Easing down S slope of cape, US 101 swings past Hunters Cove and Hunters Island. *1.7 m.,* almost sea level viewpoint. Jumble of gigantic offshore rocks, including one with outlines of sheer-cliffed island. On foggy day they appear as monsters risen from the deep. Or, to another mind, they strike image of whales skimming toward shore.

0.9 m., viewpoint. Another observation of these incredible rock formations, which geologists call sea stacks. The one straight ahead suggests the horns of a rhinoceros hung above a grotto. Geologists explain such formations with the preciseness of a recipe for a cherry pie. Both are necessarily dry. The tropes of literature are better applied to what the eye sees and cannot in detail fathom. At low tide razor clams are found in tidepools surrounding the closest rocks.

0.6 m., on E, turnoff to Pistol River.

   * *0.3 m.,* turn L for cemetery *(0.2 m.) 1.3 m.,* **Pistol River.** Store. River and town got name from 1853 incident, when one James Mace lost his shooting iron in stream. Out of such small events is posterity born. Before whites arrived and did their thing, Indian village near mouth of river was doing fine. It even had pretty name — *Chetl-Essentan.* Fierce battle was fought here June 17, 1856, with the Yankees smashing the Chetcos. The volunteers who assailed the Indians always put in damage claims to the federal govt. For this battle, one of the volunteers demanded $500 for loss of wagon load of apples. At one time, Pistol River had a cheese factory; after its abandonment it became tintype of nostalgia.

   * Old US 101 ran thru Pistol River and S to Brookings thru thick woods and past isolated farms. It is still there, a county road now, and if you want to know how horrid driving was before construction of present hwy., try the old road. Endless curves and climbs and descents. Still, the road is now not without advantages. It holds scarcely any traffic and overlooks of the ocean are better from this road than from the popular one hugging the coast.

   * From Pistol River: *0.5 m.,* forks. Straight. *7.7 m.,* on L, a house all that is left of **Carpenterville,** at 1,715 ft. elev. peak of the road. On a clear day, say the few residents of this pike, Calif.'s Mt. Shasta can be seen. On a very clear day. Settled late, 1921, Carpenterville probably never had more than 35 pop. but it did have PO, PS, sawmill, and when it was on *the* road it also had a store and tourist cabins. *13.5 m.,* US 101. (There are some interesting touches along the Pistol River–Carpenterville road. At one house, where a traveler had paused to ask directions, a llama suddenly appeared and thrust his or her snout into open rear window of the car. Having satisfied himself or herself that the situation was normal, llama nobly sauntered off.)

From Pistol River Jct.:

1 m., **Pistol River Battle Historical Marker,** commemorating battle, March 1856 of last so-called Rogue River Indian Wars. Company of 34 "minute men" (volunteers) holed up in makeshift log fortification, were charged by angry force of Pistol River and Rogue River Indians. The battle, which involved hand-to-hand fighting, lasted several days, until whites were rescued by contingent of regular troops. Too bad there is not another marker alongside this one to tell the Indian story.

0.3 m., turnoff to **Pistol River SP.** PA. Because its shore is walled by sea cliffs, little of Curry County coast is conducive to dune formation. Largest of the county's dunes, rising 100 ft. or so above beach, is just S of mouth of Pistol River, where dunes area begins; extends 2 m. along beach to Crook Point. Here is the SP, popular for horseback riding, dune sliding and beachcombing. Dunes are flowered by fragrant native yellow lupine, planted by State Hwy. Dept. for stabilizing dunes. For this, dept. won national award. When the lupines blossom in early summer, the air is so redolent that its sweetness permeates every car that comes up or down the road.

2.8 m., past the headland of Crook Point, **Mack Arch,** a 325-ft.-high offshore monolith that is part of Mack Reef, which is composed of Otter Point conglomerates and basalts. From S side of Crook Point there is a smashing view of arch clear down to Cape Ferrelo.

1 m., start of 9 m. of viewpoints. You can spend a day glutting yourself at every viewpoint. If it's foggy you can spend hours at one viewpoint waiting for clearing.

1.6 m., **Arch Rock Viewpoint.** Another aperture along the road to feast the senses upon the fairyland of the Curry County coast. (Actually, there is little habitation or travel in the county that is not on the coast.)

0.2 m., turnoff for Arch Rock Point of **Samuel H. Boardman SP.** A number of viewpoints, separate park areas, PAs. FHPs, opportunities and services comprise the 11 m. length of the park, named for the father of Oregon's excellent state parks system. He became its first supt. in 1929 and from then until he retired, in 1950, he led in est. 181 elements of the SP system. (Town of Boardman, in E Oregon, named for him.)

* 0.2 m., parking area. Arch Rock is more than a great arched rock; clumps of trees grow out of the tops of rocks; broken shells of cliffs are boiling pots for waves; the bulky, green-thorned face of the seawall is a mash of eternity. Caution is advised in driving thru park. Deer, mountain goats and other wild animals, as well as stray sheep, can come up unexpectedly onto the highway and create disastrous hazards.

0.3 m., **Spruce Island Viewpoint,** rocky isle topped by spruce. 0.8 m., **Natural Bridge Viewpoint.** Above the natural bridge, which spans current appearing as river, is huge island rock erupting from roof of grotto. Stream flows past cove, thru arch of bridge, past smaller cove, thru another arch, and returns to the ocean. Geologists say the "bowl" behind the natural bridges was formed by collapse of roof rock of intersecting sea caves; bridges are what is left of the cave roofs.

0.7 m., viewpoint. This is singled out among the unnamed viewpoints because of its photographic interest: a headland facing a scatter of rocks that are wrinkled pebbles compared to the sea massifs directly N. 1.1 m., **Thomas Creek Bridge,** at 345 ft. above canyon bottom, Oregon's highest bridge. 0.2 m., bridge viewpoint, at S end of bridge.

* 450 yds. to grassy viewpoint; base of **Thomas Creek Bridge** to one side; at other, long rock resembling reclining dragon.

0.7 m., **Indian Sands Viewpoint,** abundant sight of forest plunging to the sea. Trail flanked by toadstools of brilliant orange and yellow polka-dots descends to where trees and wildflowers are halted by rocks, sand and thundering waves.

0.7 m., turnoff to Whalehead Beach, part of Boardman SP system.

* 0.2 m., **Whalehead Beach.** Offshore rock formation resembles spouting whale.

Natural Bridge, Curry County   *Courtesy State of Oregon*

0.5 m., **Whalehead Trail Viewpoint.** View from above. *1.5 m.*, turnoff for House Rock Viewpoint.

    * 0.2 m., monument on crest honors Samuel H. Boardman. Beyond monument a wavy roll of native shrubs caterpillars to the brow of hills which slide down to the sea.

0.7 m., **Cape Ferrelo Viewpoint,** named for Bartolme Ferrelo, who sailed up the Calif. coast in 1543 but probably not far enough to see this cape It was named for him by an American in 1869. Top of cape is flat surface 250 ft. above sea level. That's not very high but it is the first prominent headland mariners observe as they sail N along Oregon Coast. A touch of Scotland: sweet-smelling thistled hills softly rolling down to a mauve-toned beach.

0.6 m., turnoff for **Lone Ranch Beach.**

    * 0.3 m., parking. This point is, asserts a plaque, "approximately the center of two miles of spectacular ocean coast line." A curve of beach between two minor headlands; stacks of driftwood; clusters of offshore boulders. As name suggests, there was once remote ranch here.

Just S of Lone Ranch Beach is as rugged a shoreline as is found in Curry County.

Whalehead Beach   *Phoebe L. Friedman*

Harris Beach State Park

1.2 m., **Rainbow Rock Viewpoint.** On a sunny day the minerals in the bare face of the rock throw off a dazzle of hues. *1 m.,* jct., Carpenterville Rd. *1 m.,* turnoff to **Harris Beach SP.**

     * SP, open all year. Complete facilities, including FHP. *0.3 m.,* CG; thick shrubs and firs provide privacy for each campsite. *0.3 m.,* PA, at shorefront. **Goat Island,** 21 acres and 184 ft. high, is Oregon's largest coastal island; now bird refuge. Vistas from **Harris Butte,** near registration booth, encompass 24 m. of curving coastline, from Point St. George in Calif., around Pelican Bay, and N to Cape Ferrelo.

1.5 m., **Brookings,** which probably enjoys most temperate climate of any city in Oregon. About 90 percent of all Easter lilies grown in US come from this area (S Curry County and N part of adjacent Del Norte County — in Calif.), so town calls itself "Easter Lily Capital of the World." Brookings is one of top 10 commercial fishing ports in Oregon, with leading catches being salmon, tuna, crab, shrimp and rock fish. City lies at mouth of Chetco, best-known salmon and steelhead stream S of Rogue River. Fishing off jetty at mouth of Chetco does not require license. Charter boats operate out of port during summer and fall.

On Sept. 9, 1942, Brookings broke into national news when an incendiary bomb was dropped on forest E of town by Japanese pilot flying seaplane that had been stored in waterproof deck hangar of sub. In 1962, the Brookings–Harbor Jaycees sponsored return of the pilot, Nobuo Fujita, to be its guest at annual Azalea Festival. He came, brought his family, and presented city his family ancestral samurai sword. It now resides in Brookings City Hall.

Brookings boasts that it is the only community in Oregon to have two SPs within its city limits — Harris and Loeb.

0.6 m. — from town center — jct., Azalea SP, Loeb SP, North Bank Rd.

     * *0.1 m.,* forks. L, *0.2 m.,* **Azalea SP,** 26 acre natural park abounding with wild azaleas. (Most activities of Azalea Festival, held last weekend in May, are staged here.) Spring pushes up wild strawberry blossoms, purple and red violets, and wild cherry and crabapple blooms, partitioned by bushes of five varieties of native azaleas, some hundreds of years old. Swarms of butterflies, bees and hummingbirds feed on the plants; fir and spruce house finch, robin, jay and killdeer colonies. Eat off hand-hewn myrtlewood tables, each weighing more than 200 lbs. PA, trail, FHP.

     * At forks, turn R onto North Bank Rd. *7.6 m.,* **Loeb SP;** 320 acres, much of it in virgin myrtle. CG, PA, fishing, swimming in Chetco River. (Trail *0.9 m.* from SP entrance to redwood grove,many of the trees already stalwarts when Columbus came to New World.) *5.7 m.,* **Little Redwood FS CG,** on Little Redwood Creek. Tall Douglas firs, wildflowers, berries, fishing, swimming, hiking — but no redwoods. *2.7 m.,* on FS Rd. 1376, FS Rd. 1909. Follow this FS road. *15 m.* to Vulcan Lake Trailhead and entrance to Kalmiopsis Wilderness.

The 180,000 acre **Kalmiopsis Wilderness** includes some of the most rug-

**Vulcan Peak from Little Vulcan Lake,
Kalmiopsis Wilderness**

Courtesy Merle Pugh

Vulcan Lake, Kalmiopsis Wilderness

Courtesy Merle Pugh

ged and inaccessible country in the Siskiyou National Forest as well as the headwater basin of the Chetco River and a portion of the Illinois River Canyon. There are six rds. to it from US 101 and five from US 199 but no road enters the Wilderness. Within it are about 20 trails, ranging in length from 1.4 m. to 30 m. Many of the trails in use now were once miners' routes and many of the miners' camps are now used by hikers. Mining activity of past is evident in abandoned artifacts: tools and utensils, and here and there an old cabin foundation, and ditches, dug by hand by Chinese laborers to carry water for hydraulic mining.

The USFS calls Kalmiopsis Wilderness and its environs the most interesting botanical region in the NW US. Fourteen species of conifers and nine species of broadleaf trees thrive in the Wilderness, along with odd cousins of the lily family, darlingtonia, getnians, and several species of orchids. But what really makes the Wilderness unique is the presence of the Kalmiopsis *leachiana,* for which the area was named. It is one of the rarest shrubs in the world; a mono-typic genus, meaning the only one of its group; the oldest member of the Heath family; and a relic of the pre-Ice Age. The small shrub, looking like a miniature rhododendron, was discovered in Gold Basin, in the E part of the Wilderness, about 2.2 m. due W of 5098 ft. Pearsoll Peak, in 1930 by Lilla Irvine Leach of Portland, hence the *leachiana.*

Ever since their marriage in 1913, Lilla, who started the botany dept. at Eugene HS after her graduation from UO in 1908, and John R., a Portland pharmacist, had spent off-work time exploring woods, mountains and just about everywhere else outdoors looking for rare plants. Even after her husband's death in 1972 at age 90, Mrs. Leach maintained a lively interest in botany. She passed away in 1980 at age 93. The Leach home is now part of the Portland city park system.

Because of its rarity no part of the plant may be collected without special written permit, and unless you convince the skeptical FS you have a strong scientific need, you won't get a permit. Which is as it should be.

The Wilderness is not meant for Sunday morning strollers. In general, the terrain is difficult, clean water is scarce (come prepared), poison oak is almost everywhere, wood ticks are plentiful, wasps and yellow jackets are liberally scattered about, rattlesnakes are not uncommon. (Hikers are discouraged from taking dogs along.)

A FS guide to this area advises: "Anyone traveling through the Kalmiopsis should expect to be completely self-sufficient, since visitation is low and help may be delayed in case of emergency."

Why, with all its drawbacks, do people continue to come, in growing numbers, to Kalmiopsis Wilderness? Perhaps for the plants, perhaps for the area's grotesque beauty, more likely because it is far off the beaten path and hiking this wilderness is looked upon by those who made it as a badge of valor.

Most visited places are Babyfoot Lake and Vulcan Lake, both easy to reach, small and scenic. As a result, they have been abused and campers are urged to go elsewhere. FS also prefers people to avoid Boulder Creek Camp and Slide Creek Camp, each close to trailhead and both along the Chetco River. They, too, have suffered from overuse.

From jct., Azalea SP, Loeb SP, North Bank Rd.:

Vulcan Lake, Kalmiopsis Wilderness   *Courtesy US Forest Service*

0.3 m., jct., South Bank Rd.

   * E, *6 m.* on county rd. to FS Rd. 1205. *12 m.* on FS rd. to **Wheeler Creek Research Natural Area.** *0.5 m.,* trail to marker siting Japanese incendiary bomb dropped Sept. 9, 1942.

0.4 m., Harbor Jct.

   * *0.2 m.,* **Harbor.** Although now virtual suburb of Brookings, Harbor PO est. 1894, 19 years before Brookings PO opened. Actually, town was once site of Chetco PO, started up 1863. At mouth of Chetco, Harbor is sport and commercial fishing port. Fields of commercially grown daffodil bulbs spread out from town.

2 m., on E, **Chetco Valley Museum,** in oldest standing house (1857) in area. Serene setting; rich in pioneer lore.

1.7 m., Winchuck Rd.

   * *8.5 m.,* for most part following **Winchuck River,** which locals say is one of few pure streams in Oregon, meaning you can drink from it without fear, **Winchuck FS CG.** (*2 m.* N, Fourth of July Creek enters E Fork of Winchuck. Other picturesquely-named streams in general area: Little Emily, Horse, Bear.)

0.5 m., Winchuck River. Here stood hamlet of **Chetco.** It had PS and was on stage line to Grants Pass via Crescent City, Calif.

The noun Chetco comes from a small Indian tribe which lived along the lower river of the same name. (Earlier white spellings had it as Chetko or Chitko.) Like many small and not so small tribes which were visible when the Yankees descended upon Oregon, the Chetcos are now extinct. Last survivor was a woman named Lucky Dick, who passed away in early January, 1940, at Harbor.

0.4 m., Calif. state line. (*17 m.,* jct., US 199 to Grants Pass. See *Cross-Coast Range Roads.*)

Cross-Coast Range Roads

US 30 — Astoria to Portland

US 30, the Lincoln Highway of yore, is the oldest, most historic and most populated road between the Oregon Coast and the Great Heartland.

Along this way came the Indians of the lower Columbia, Lewis and Clark, the William Price Hunt Party, the colorful characters of Ft. Astoria and Ft. George, captains and privates of Hudson's Bay Co., missionaries and soldiers, settlers of the Clatsop Plains, merchant princes and derelicts.

They came by canoe, bark, sidewheeler, sternwheeler, and any other craft that its owners and pilots thought could make it up or down the river. They journeyed on, by or in horseback, muleback, buggy, prairie schooner, buckwagon, train, Stanley Steamer, Model T and anything else that would carry the pilgrims to the sea or back.

The road at points affords grand views of the Columbia; for grander views take the turnoffs, to Brownsmead and Clifton, Fanny's Bottom and Columbia City, and others.

This is not the fastest road between Portland and the Pacific; too many towns slow the traveler. But if one is afraid of being stuck on a road after dark with no facilities available for many miles, US 30 is a paragon of comfort.

Like so many other roads across the Coast Range, US 30 has been widened and straightened. Fortunately, it has lost most of its numerous crooks and curves and is now as easy to drive as any other pike. Furthermore, despite everything modern times has done to it, US 30 has retained much of its historic flavor. Here nostalgia is making one of its last stands.

From 12th and Commercial — Astoria.

0.3 m., **Maritime Museum.** *0.9 m.,* Historical Marker, US Customs House. (First US customs office in American W located here.) *1.9 m.,* Tongue Point Jct.

    * *0.7 m.,* **Tongue Point.** Discovered (by whites) and named by British in 1792. On Nov. 25,1805, the Lewis and Clark Party landed on "a beautiful shore of pebbles of various colors." Lewis named the site "Fort William," after Clark's given name. But the British designation survived.

1.7 m., on N, **John Day Park.** BL. *0.9 m.,* **John Day River,** named for the mentally disturbed Virginian backwoodsman. A problem at Ft. Astoria, Day was sent back to St. Louis in the early summer of 1812 in the party led by Robert Stuart. Before they had really embarked upon their voyage Stuart wrote: "evident symptoms of mental derangement made their appearance in John Day one of my Hunters who for a day or two previous seemed as if restless and unwell but now uttered the most incoherent absurd and unconnected sentences . . . it was the opinion of all the Gentlemen that it would be highly imprudent to suffer him to proceed any farther for in a moment when not sufficiently watched he might embroil us with the natives, who on all occasions he reviled by the appellations Rascal, Robber &c &c &c—" Day had good reasons for his appellations; indeed, if that was all he said he was very mild in his opinions. He had been robbed and beaten by Indians, who had stripped him of all his clothes and left him to starve; that was only a year before and the effects of his traumatic experience were still deep within Day. He was returned by Stuart's men to Ft. Astoria, where he recovered and went on to resume his outdoor life. Pioneers carved a road thru the forest from this river to Astoria. It is now site of boat colony.

1.2 m., Fernhill Jct.

    * SW corner, old **Community Hall.** *0.4 m.,* on R, gorgeous country home elegantly landscaped. Across road is holly orchard. *0.1 m.,* site of old **Fernhill School,** later used as fire station, then abandoned. Children now bused to Astoria. *0.2 m.,* on R, house built in 1870s; was pioneer **Fernhill PO.** In early days mail came by boat from Astoria and farmers would ride horseback here to pick up their mail.

1.2 m., on N, Burnside Jct.

    * *1.1 m.,* **Burnside,** named for 1855 DLC settler. Now rural neighborhood with nothing to show of old Burnside.

1.1 m., E turnoff to Burnside. *0.9 m.,* Svensen Jct.

    * **Wickiup Grange,** store, station, cafe. Svensen had more in 1915.

3.7 m., **Knappa,** lively hwy. stop. There is a Lewis and Clark footnote here, as the explorers trudged W. On Nov. 26, 1805, beleaguered by rain and bogs on the N shore of the Columbia, the party voted to move across the river, on the far side of Cathlamet Point, which the captains called Point Samuel. Moving westward, the party called upon an Indian village named *Tle-las-qua,* near present Knappa, then moved on, camping for the night under a high hill about 8 *m.* W, between Svensen and Tongue Point.

    * Turn N for Blind Slough and Brownsmead. *0.1 m.,* turn R. *0.3 m.,* on L, **Prairie Cemetery,** est. 1878. Most interesting is gravemarker in form of totem pole. *0.6 m.,* Brownsmead Jct. Straight, *0.2 m.,* forks. Take R, cross wooden bridge. *0.2 m.,* **Knappa dock.** Uncrowded, open view of Columbia. Return to Brownsmead Rd. Turn L. *0.2 m.,* on L, sculpted wooden bald eagle looking down on sign which reads: "This land dedicated to/ The song of birds/ The sound of wings/ To all of Natures/ Creatures for the joy/ Their presence brings/ No hunting — Bob Ziak." Robert Ziak, combat veteran of South Pacific during WW II, opened 250 acres of his 400 acre farm for the use of waterfowl and other birds that are at home in water-oriented environment. Visitors welcome but no fishing permitted and, of course, respect the land and its occupants. *1.5 m.,* Olsen-Sprogis Rd. Turn L. *0.3 m.,* **Blind Slough.** There was a PO and tiny hamlet here once: PO 1910–1924. And a logging camp.

    In 1912, Whitney Co. at Blind Slough installed baths and single steel bunks with mattresses, an innovation described as revolutionary in the lumber busi-

Totem pole gravemarker in cemetery at Knappa

ness but long overdue as far as the loggers were concerned. An old timer recalled decades ago: "These were the talk of the country. Loggers tried to get on there just to satisfy their curiosity. Such a luxury as a bath was too much to believe . . ." Body lice and bedbugs were an accepted part of a logger's life and steel bunks were no place for bugs. With adversity comes the humor of absurdity. Hundreds of jokes about lice circulated thru the camps. Typical was the tale that during the day the men would kill lice by turning their shirts around from inside to outside, thereby walking the critters to death.

The RR bridge at Blind Slough is wheeled manually into place by resident bridge tender when trains are due. At other times, bridge is swung aside to let water traffic pass.

Return to Brownsmead Rd. Turn L. *1.1 m.*, Barendse Rd. Turn L. *0.7 m.*, turn L. *0.6 m.*, **Brownsmead.** Community is the child of diking reclamation; named for W. G. Brown, engineer who directed project and the old English word for meadow. (From old store across road from Grange hall, take Rudat

Railroad bridge at Blind Slough

Rd. *0.1 m.*, on L, barn was Brownsmead School. *0.5 m.*, Gertulla Rd. Turn R. *0.1 m.*, on R, barn with "cow" on weather vane.)

Return *0.6 m.* to Barendse Rd. Continue straight. *1 m.*, turn L onto Aldrich Point Rd. *2.4 m.*, thru rich dairy country and long canopied lanes of thick foliage that in autumn is a shower of russet leaves, **Aldrich Point,** small BL on Columbia. On a warm afternoon following rain, the hills across the river seem to be shaking off their wetness and the rising vapor foams into silvery plumes that float along the rims.

Take any road S back to US 30.

From Knappa and Brownsmead Jct., on US 30:

2.6 m., Brownsmead Jct.

  * *4.8 m.*, thru bucolic landscape, **Brownsmead.** Corn grows high here, though no one has brought in an elephant to measure. Corn Festival is a real hoedown.

1.2 m., entrance to what was Gnat Creek Forest Park. Facilities removed but the woods are still there. *1 m.*, **Gnat Creek Fish Hatchery.** Since 1960, hatchery has been raising summer and winter steelhead for release into Columbia River tributaries. Over 155,000 summer and 420,000 winter steelhead, averaging 60 to 90 thousand lbs. of fish, are released annually from this hatchery.

1.6 m., Clifton-Bradwood Jct.

  * L, or N: *2.6 m.*, jct. To the R, *0.6 m.*, is where stood **Bradwood,** named synthetically for Bradley-Woodward Lumber Co., Inc. as company town 1930. At its peak the plant, then operated by Columbia-Hudson Lumber Co., employed more than 150 workers and had an annual production of $30 million. It provided a $75,000 monthly payroll, 2d largest in Clatsop County. Early in June, 1963 company decided it could no longer afford to continue; lumber market too depressed. A spokesman for the auctioneer said: "The equipment, land, buildings, homes, general store and docks as well as the saw and planing mills and machine shops will be sold at auction. It probably will take us all day but when the sun sets, everything will be gone." At that time, Bradwood had 36 homes and had been termed a "ghost town" for the past 4 months. The occupants then could have quoted Horace: "The day approaches, when we must/ Be crumbling bones and windy dust." The gavel fell at 10 a.m. on June 25, 1963. By sundown the auctioneer had been proven right. Bradwood's plant had been one of few which rode out the Great Depression and the economic downturns which follows. *The Oregonian* stated that "Bradwood is one of more than 200 lumber 'ghost' towns which have shut down because of the lumber market." Twenty years after the auction, the few remaining bldgs. were leveled and a gate put across the road, denying entrance to Bradwood.

Continue *1.2 m.,* to **Clifton,** the most picturesque ghost town on the S shore of the lower Columbia. There was a time, not too long ago, when the site of Clifton could be pinpointed by the abandoned houses which half-slid into the river, enveloped in an atmosphere of isolation and fishing village requiems. But now the watery houses are gone, leaving only the few structures still on land to tell of Clifton.

The last of Bradwood

The town is a good case history of what was. The problem is where what was. Looking about, it seems nigh impossible that there could have been so much here. There doesn't seem enough room.

As early as 1874 Clifton had a PO and was a stray gillnet outpost until a cannery was built about 1890. Greek, Yugoslav and Italian fishermen supplied the gleaming products of the river for Chinese workers to can. About 1906 the cannery closed and the Chinese departed, leaving behind their bunkhouses on the slope above the road. (No trace of them now.) The fishers stayed on, the Greeks occupying the upper end of town, the Yugoslavs the middle, and the Italians the lower end.

In its prime, Clifton had two saloons, one of which had a skating rink/ dance hall upstairs; two stores, one of which held the PO; and a one room schoolhouse. Never inc., village had no city hall, jail, fire dept. or street lamps. When dance hall caught fire in 1921, the town watched it burn to the ground. People carried lanterns at night as they walked along the RR tracks, which was the "main street."

The road linking Clifton to US 30 was not built until 1937. People "went out" by boating to Cathlamet, Wash., across the Columbia, or taking the train to Portland or Astoria. At one time, there were four passenger trains daily — two E-bound, two W-bound.

In the early part of the century five logging camps stood within a 3 m. area of Clifton. After the camps folded the gyppos moved in. In 1930 all logging stopped; there was no more to cut.

Clifton declined because fish runs were depleted and seasons shortened. One store closed in 1950; it is now a strew of splinters, as is the church; the other store, selling its last groceries in 1960, became an office for the caretaker of Clifton, owned by Bumble Bee. As people moved out, their houses were dismantled for lumber and only a few people are alive who remember Clifton in its glory.

The town was going downhill when electricity finally arrived, in 1958. Today, a freight train chugs thru Clifton every other day and on a rare day about a dozen persons fish out of the dock — but they live elsewhere.

R, or S, from Bradwood-Clifton Jct.

* Only 4-wheel drives or sturdy pickups should attempt this far-out trip. *1.8 m.,* forks. Take L. *1.2 m.,* forks. Take L. *0.4 m.,* forks. Take R. *1.1 m.,* remains of shingle mill. Park at end of fence and take on foot "road" ahead. *500 yds.,* end of trace. "Trail" downhill to precipice overlooking **Gnat Creek Falls,** which plunges an awesome distance in untamed fury. One of the least seen, most spectacular and most dangerous of all Oregon falls. Acrophobiacs stay away; keep children and pets away; tie a rope to the daredevil poised on the lip of the cliff. Sensational — but is it worth the risk? You're on your own. *0.7 m.,* Coast Range Summit here — 656 ft. *0.1 m.,* jct., **Bradley State Wayside.**

    * *0.1 m.,* **Clatsop Crest,** for a grand view of the smoggy Columbia. Just below crest is **Puget Island,** a long, flat, green-weaving pattern in the river. Though close to Oregon shore, island lies within state of Wash. Named in 1792 by Lt. William R. Broughton of British Navy for Lt. Peter Puget, after whom Puget Sound was also named. To L, or W of Puget Island, is Tenasillahe Island, part of Oregon. Name composed of two Chinook jargon words, meaning "little land."

2 m., Wauna-Taylorville Jct.

    * N, *1 m.,* Wauna, smoky lumber company complex. Hills of sawdust resemble sand dunes. In the mythology of Columbia River Indians, Wauna is a representation of the stream. The map Wauna does not reflect this romanticism.

    * S, *1 m.,* **Taylorville.** Only few houses at former sawmill town.

2.1 m., at W edge of **Westport, Plympton Creek Bridge.** In Sept. Chinook salmon migrate to spawning grounds above bridge,which provides excellent viewpoint.

Westport is the lowest point on the Columbia for (relatively) good salmon fishing. Although there was fine salmon fishing in the upper Columbia tributaries, the most renowned salmon streams and bays are those which empty directly into the Pacific.

The first whites to visit the lower Columbia found the Chinook Indians of the area well-fed from the giant salmon which abounded in the river, so the salmon

View from Clatsop Crest   *Courtesy Oregon State*

were called Chinook. In other Pacific waters the specie is also known as Tyee salmon, spring salmon, king salmon and quinnat salmon. Ichthyologists solve the name problem by calling the salmon *Oncorhynchus tschawytscha*. (Average weight is between 15 and 25 lbs.) *Oncorhynchus kisutch* is the coho or silver salmon, the smaller brother of the Chinook and only slightly less than the Chinook as a sport fish. (Average weight is about 8 lbs.) It runs in the fall and early winter. Some fishers refer to the steelhead as a salmon but, though it is more closely related to the Atlantic salmon than to the five Pacific species, in reality it is a sea-going rainbow trout. (Other PNW salmon are pink, sockeye and chum.)

The life of the salmon is perilous. Few survive to return to their spawning grounds, generally in the creeks and rivers high in the mountains. Within nine months to two years of birth the salmon find their way to the sea, there to live on marine life until maturity, which could be in their 3d, 4th or 5th year. Then they begin the long, hard journey back, as much as 1000 miles from the sea, to their native streams to spawn and die. (Their course is severely hindered by dams and dam effects.) Once in fresh water homeward bound, the salmon rarely feed, but will attack anything that gets in the way. Because salmon will lunge at whatever flashes in the water, the most popular lure is a spinner or wobbler.

For the Indians of the PNW, salmon was sacred, being the main food supply, which they did not want contaminated. When Alexander MacKenzie completed his crossing of the continent in 1793 at Bella Coola, B.C., the Indians confiscated his iron kettle because, they explained, the alien odor would scare the salmon into fleeing the river. When MacKenzie was ready to leave the Indians strenuously objected to his placing venison in his canoe, arguing that the smell would send the fish scurrying from the river and bring starvation to the tribe.

The PNW Indians, who called themselves "The Salmon People," in the same spirit that the Plains Indians thought of themselves as "The Buffalo People," were animistic and spoke to and of the salmon as though the fish were people. Each tribe had its own ritual of the "First Salmon Ceremony" as celebrated by the Kwakiutl:

"O Supernatural Ones, O Swimmers, I thank you that you are willing to come to us. / Don't let your coming be bad, for you come to be food for us. / I beg you to protect me and the one who takes mercy on me, that we may not die without cause, Swimmers."

But then, far from the spawning grounds, came the prayer killers, and the salmon runs depressingly declined. Then the fishers on the Columbia turned to angling for the great fossil fish of the ancient river, the white sturgeon, the flesh of one sufficient for a winter's larder. (Only sturgeon between 40 and 72 inches are legal catches.)

For the true, garden-variety amateur, there is the tasty, herring-size smelt, the fast food of the Columbia. Its volume is uncertain but whatever the numbers, whatever the joy or disappointment, smelt watchers stand at the ready to grab their long handled dipnets and run to the streams where, in boat or on bank, they fill their pails with smelt. (No license needed.) The populist catch beings in Dec., when the smelt pour into the lower reaches of the Columbia. From Dec. until April the smelt fill the tributaries of the Columbia and if the run is heavy the harvest is fruitful.

In June, the Columbia shad cruise past Westport and out to nab them come both commercial and sport fishers. Trout and whitefish are also sought for seizure and upstream, beyond where the Columbia is first dammed, swims in jeopardy the walleye, whose partisans contend that it is the most delicious of all fish food. But tell that to the salmon lover!

Westport was named for John West, known as Captain West to the townsfolk. He was an energetic, innovative Scotsman who settled here in 1850 and in 1856 built a small sawmill, followed by other enterprises, which made West the big industrialist of the area. The first cargo of lumber to be shipped to a foreign port left form Westport in 1868.

In 1915, Westport had a pop. of 300, more than it could boast seven decades later. But it has remained a casual town where the genial tavern is the social center.

0.4 m. past footbridge to former inn, ferry landing. Passage to the other side of the Columbia and from there bridge to Cathlamet, Wash. Breezy ride and pastel river touches.

0.3 m., turnoff R to West Tunnel (on road that was formerly part of US 30.)

0.2 m., **West Tunnel.** (0.1 m., US 30.) Before John West died, in 1887, he had a tunnel dug that is the only one of its kind known anywhere, and remains the last visible relic of the old Bull Team logging operations in the Pacific NW. To S of here was Hungry Hollow Logging Camp and West wanted its logs for his and other mills in area. But bringing the logs to water meant hauling them around the hill, and that way was too far and too expensive. So West had a hole bored thru the hill. Ox teams then pulled the logs down the skid road to Westport Slough, to the N, and from there the logs were towed to sawmills. In 1907 the oxen gave way to a steam engine after a RR was built thru the enlarged tunnel. With the depletion of logs on the hill on S, about 1915, RR operations halted, the tracks were taken up, and the tunnel fell into disuse. On a hot day the tunnel is a cool grotto, whatever else might be said of its condition.

2.2 m., **Woodson,** named for Woods Landing (on Westport Slough), which got its name from a Mr. Woods, who hauled logs to the slough. Store, few houses.

2 m., Marshland Jct.

* Old town was on both sides of hwy. but all that remains of village, settled in early 1860s as Skunk Cabbage Flat, is on L side: *0.1 m.,* white frame house put up about 1875. Country to core is broad-shouldered Grange hall.

4.3 m., jct., 0 47.

* *11.8 m.,* **Mist.** The road spins like a top. Few houses and no stores on this hilly, green-bordered asphalt thread. (See *0 47 N,* following *US 30.*)

West Tunnel   *Phoebe L. Friedman*

0.3 m., main intersection, Nehalem St., **Clatskanie,** from Indian *Tlats-kani,* hunting ground in Nehalem Valley. It was whites who named a stream Tlastkanie and then corrupted it to Clatskanie and Klaskanine. *Oregon: End of the Road* states that town was first named Bryantsville, after 1852 settler E. G. Bryant, and name changed to Clatskanie in 1870. In 1915, town had cooperative fruit and vegetable cannery and eight lodges. Lodge halls have given way to TV for fraternity and entertainment.

Turn R onto Nehalem St. *0.3 m.,* turn R on 7th. One block, turn R on Tichenor. At 620 Tichenor, oldest and most intriguing house in town. Built between 1898 and 1900 for lumberman Thomas J. Flippin, who said, "A man's home is his castle and so I built mine to look like one." Which is why **Flippin House** is better known as "The Castle," or "The Palace." A National Historic Site, it has been restored to and furnished in manner near as possible to original state. Now operated by Clatskanie Senior Citizens, who conduct tours thru house, a jewel of Americana, for modest fee.

Return to Nehalem St. and US 30.

* Cross US 30 and continue straight on Nehalem thru downtown Clatskanie to W 5th St., *0.2 m.* At end of Nehalem St. (W 5th) is white frame three-story bldg., **Benson House,** that was last word in local opulence when completed 1903. It had crystal chandeliers, marble kitchen counter tops, pool table deluxe, five bedrooms, four baths. Owner was famed lumber baron Simon Benson, who built house for his son, Amos, who managed his father's

45,000 acres of choice timber land in the Clatskanie area. Simon Benson was builder of Portland's Benson Hotel, benefactor of Portland's Benson HS, donor of downtown Portland's copper drinking fountains and sponsor of the old Columbia River Hwy. Benson SP is named for him.

* (At W 5th St., turn R. *0.4 m.*, turn L onto Haven Acres Rd. *0.1 m.*, Wood Lane. Turn R. *0.1 m.*, **Bryant Cemetery.** Stones date back to 1859.)

* At W 5th St., turn L onto Mayger Rd. *3 m.*, Mayger Jct. Turn L for Mayger. *0.4 m.*, Rutters Rd. In "V" of jct., and growing on edge of Rutters Rd., is largest Pacific Dogwood in state. Across road at diagonal is old Quincy PS. Set back off L side of Mayger Rd., opposite school, is eye-catching white house circa 1890.

* *0.7 m.*, **Quincy.** Store. Place was never much. Settled 1882 by farmers from Quincy, Ill. Pop. was 40 in 1915; town had two churches, two schools. That was the high water mark.

** At Quincy, turn L on Hermo Rd. *1.5 m.* (*0.3 m.* beyond bridge), turn L onto Collins Rd. *1.5 m.*, turn R onto dike road. *1.7 m.*, turnaround. Turn L. *0.1 m.*, dead end. Here or near here, and for the sake of accuracy to say "in this vicinity," is **Fanny's Bottom,** and somewhere near here was first American trading post in Oregon.

In late May, 1810, an old sailing ship, the *Albatross,* owned by Winship Brothers of Boston, which had hopes of est. a commercial empire in the NW, entered the Columbia and followed the torturous N channel about 45 m. upstream. On the fertile S bank, which the shipmaster, Nathan Winship, called Oak Point, the crew built a two-story log fort amidst white oak, ash, cottonwood and alder trees, and planted the first garden in Oregon. But high water and the unfriendly disposition of the Chinooks forced Winship to leave before he really got started and the Indians had another year to themselves before the whites came for good and settled at Astoria, from where they reached out to all of Oregon. Lewis and Clark years earlier had named this place Fanny's Bottom, in honor of Clark's favorite sister, Frances. Given the chance to do it over again, in view of contemporary Americanese, they would probably eschew the redundant name.

Fanny's Bottom is at a "bottleneck" of the Columbia, the narrowest point on the lower Columbia, and about the turn of century was called "Seining Grounds." Narrowness of stream made it ideal for seiners. Horses would pull in the nets and haul them to fish-drying sheds. Here was also a bunkhouse for the fishers and shed workers as well as several homes.

* From Quincy toward Mayger:

1.5 m., Port Townsend Jct. (*1.2 m.*, once Columbia River port, now utility facility.) *2.1 m.*, Mayger Jct. Turn L. *0.2 m.*, the creakiness that was once snappy **Mayger.** About 1915 it had pop. 350. Best place to take photo of wharf is from beach to R of dock. Be extremely careful about walking on saggy planks. Better still, stay off them. (For fuller account of lower Columbia ghost towns on Oregon side, see "Ghost Towns of the Lower Columbia" in author's *Tracking Down Oregon*.)

Return to forks. Take L. *0.7 m.*, **Mayger–Downing Community Church and Cemetery**. A lovely rural church, portrait of solace. Names on gravestones point to settlement of area by German-born. *6.3 m.*, Alston. Store. Turn L. *0.3 m.*, US 30.

From Clatskanie, on US 30:

6.8 m., Delena Jct.

   * *0.1 m.*, **Delena**. Rather late-settled burg on Beaver Creek and logging RRs. 1922 abandoned school tells it all.

1.6 m., on L, Alston-Mayger Rd. (See preceding for Mayger.)

   * On R, at Alston-Mayger Jct., road to Apiary. *1.5 m.*, turn R. *5.7 m.*, **Apiary**, just rural neighborhood now. PO (1889–1924) honored activity of first postmaster, a beekeeper. *0.5 m.*, Fern Hill. Jct. Straight. *0.8 m.*, Meissner Rd. Straight on Apiary Rd. *12.1 m.*, 0 47. Turn S. *0.9 m.*, Big Eddy CP. *3.2 m.*, Pittsburg. *5.1 m.*, Vernonia. (See *0 47*.)

2.2 m., on R, turnoff to Hudson Park.

   * *0.3 m.*, **Woodbine and Green Mountain Cemeteries**, side by side, with no fence between. Older graves are in Woodbine Cemetery. *0.5 m.*, "T." Straight. *0.2 m.*, **Hudson–Parcher CP**, quiet retreat on Beaver Creek. CG. "Town" of Hudson, with PO 1892–1913, stood here.

0.4 m., Mt. St. Helens viewpoint. *0.4 m.*, another such lookout, also facing the Columbia and Longview, Wash. If your eyes and nostrils are clear, the view can be rewarding. *0.6 m.*, turnoff for Longview. *0.6 m.*, on R, 1884 House, so named because it was built in 1884 by sawmill owner George F. Mack and his wife, supposedly first white woman born in Columbia County. for their family of nine and as boarding house for sailors who came into then thriving port of Rainier.

0.1 m., on R, road to **Fern Hill**.

   * Turn R to B St. *0.2 m.*, turn L onto Fern Hill Rd. *4 m.*, Lentz Rd. (Turn L. *0.1 m.*, grocery in 1914, two level, two room — cafeteria basement — Fern Hill School bldg.) Straight on Fern Hill Rd. from Lentz Rd. *3.4 m.*, on L, Apiary Cemetery Rd. (0.1 m., Apiary Cemetery — 1893.) *0.5 m.*, Fern Hill and Apiary Rds. (R, *0.5 m.*, Apiary.) [To return to US 30, *5.7 m.*, from Apiary, old US 30, *1.5 m.*, US 30.] *0.8 m.*, from Fern Hill and Apiary Rds., Meissner Rd. *16.2 m.*, Pittsburg. *5.1 m.*, Vernonia.

(See *0 47*.)

0.2 m., main intersection, **Rainier**. Founded 1851 as Eminence by Charles E. Fox, name changed to Fox's Landing, then to Rainier, for visible Mt. Rainier, which was named in 1792 for Rear-Admiral Peter Rainier of British Navy by explorer George Vancouver. Rainier has about same pop. it had in 1915.

Turn L at main intersection. *0.1 m.*, old business section, on Columbia. RR line here and so is old US 30. All early river towns were built close to water and hwy. ran thru every downtown it could find.

Store in Fern Hill School

0.2 m., E 5th St. Turn R. *0.2 m.,* E. St. Turn L. *0.7 m.,* follow E St. past Middle School uphill to **Knights of Pythias Cemetery,**where early makers and shakers make and shake no more.

3.6 m., Prescott Rd.

  * Turn L. *0.5 m.,* across RR tracks, formerly small town started early in century. Just a small toss of undistinguished houses now.

0.9 m., Trojan Nuclear Plant. From a distance its steam configuration conjures up image of omniscient nuclear specter that gives nightmares.

1.3 m., on R, Neer Rd.

  * *0.8 m.,* site of **Neer City,** est. 1883, or at least one of the purported sites. Another is supposed to be on the river, where boats took on cordwood cut by small colony of woodcutters. A man standing between two scraggly bldgs. said: "What you see is what was there." *0.2 m.,* turn R, uphill. *0.1 m.,* **Neer City Cemetery.** A lady leaning over a grave marker remarked: "It's the right proper quiet place to be dead."

0.4 m., on R, Nicolai Rd.

  * *4.7 m.,* forks. Keep on Nicolai Rd. Beyond this point are sweeping views of meadows and mountains and turn-of-century farmsteads. *1.9 m.,* on R, **Shiloh Basin Community Church.** Plaquestone honors Lee R. Marvin, founding pastor, who served the church 44 years. *0.1 m.,* Tide Creek Rd. (To L is 1902 Shiloh Basin Cemetery.) Turn R onto Tide Creek Rd. *1.3 m.,* on R,

story book log house built about 1900. *1.5 m.,* Meissner Rd. Turn R. *5.7 m.,* Meissner Rd. and Apiary Rd. *16.2 m.,* Pittsburg. *5.1 m.,* Vernonia. (See 0 47.)

0.1 m., **Goble.** Store. Settled 1853, area once had big dreams. Before RR bridge between Vancouver, Wash. and Portland was built, Goble — with the town down by the river — was landing of Northern Pacific RR from Kalama, Wash. Goble in 1915 had PS, church, three lodges and 172 people — lot more than it has today.

0.4 m., Jaquish Rd. Here or near here stood long-gone Reuben. PO 1890 –1923. PS in 1915.

4.1 m., on R, yawning lily pond that comes as surprise. There ought to be a turnout here for enjoyment of this odd and lovely silkscreen vision. Alas, by now it may be gone.

0.6 m., on L, **Deer Island Historical Marker.**

0.3 m., **Deer Island,** named after island in river. Meriwether Lewis, who had a happy propensity for Indian names, called the island Elalah, a Chinook Indian word for deer, though note was also taken of the rich grass on the island, which provided a sanctuary for wild life. The elkskin explorers first stopped here downstream on Nov. 5, 1805. On March 28, 1806, homeward bound, the party made another appearance and had their fill of venison. Lewis observed that the island ponds afforded "refuge to great numbers of geese, ducks, large swan, sandhill cranes, a few canvas-backed ducks, and particularly the duckinmallard, the most abundant of all." But he was most impressed with the "extreme voracity of the vultures," who "had devoured in the space of a few hours, four of the deer killed this morning; and one of our men declared, that they had besides dragged a large buck about thirty yards, skinned it, and broke the back-bone." Later travelers observed more mosquitos than deer. In 1915 town of Deer Island had two lodges and US 30 was the same as the main street, which is sleepy land now.

Canaan Rd., Deer Island.

* *4.2 m.,* Canaan School, now barn-like dwelling. Store opposite is modern rural crossroads grocery. *2.5 m.,* Canaan Rd. becomes Meissner Rd. and soon plunges into hemlock and fir with occasional cedar, followed by thick stands of alder. *1.1 m.,* "T" with Tide Creek Rd. Straight on Meissner. *5.7 m.,* Apiary Rd. Jct. *16.2 m.,* Pittsburg.

5.1 m., Vernonia. (See 0 47.)

1.6 m., on L, **Kinder Cemetery** (1892). The dead lie so near the RR tracks that the song of the wheels may have become a psalm.

1.8 m., **Columbia City,** at I St.

* Turn L for Caples House. *0.2 m.,* at First St., **Caples House** (1870). Built by Dr. Charles Green Caples, pioneer doctor-dentist-oculist-whatever, on land grant taken by his father in 1840s. Structure, almost all original, has been turned into fascinating museum. Dr. Caples, sitting on his porch at turn of century, could watch daily passenger boats to Astoria and Portland. From little park across street, vision is clear for freighters plying Columbia now.

1.7 m., on R, Pittsburg Rd.

* *2.2 m.,* **Yankton Cemetery** (1888) and early Yankton Baptist Church (1903). *0.3 m.,* Yankton store. For obvious reasons, originally called Maineville and Yankeetown, Yankton PO est. 1894. *0.2 m.,* forks. Bend L and immediately turn onto Kappler. *0.7 m.,* Kappler–Cater Rd. Turn onto Cater. *0.1 m.,* take L, uphill on Cater. *1 m.,* Stone Rd. Straight. *3.5 m.,* at Spitzenberg, Pittsburg Rd. (See *Pittsburg-Vernonia Rd.,* following.)

0.5 m., **St. Helens,** main intersection, Columbia Blvd. Town founded 1847 by H. M. Knighton, who named it Plymouth Rock because of large rock on riverbank. (In 1834 Nathaniel Wyeth called the temporary post he built here Wyeth's Rock.) Lt. Theodore Talbot of U. S. Army called the two-house village New Plymouth in 1849. Three months later Knighton noted on a legal paper, "Plymouth and now called Kaseneau," the latter in flattering reference to a nearby Indian chief. But when PO was est. by Knighton, it was Plymouth again. Then Knighton signed papers "Casenau now called St. Helens." The folks at Washington, D.C. forgot the finals "s" and for a while the town was Saint Helen. Saint Helens was named for the mountain, which was so-named by the great name bestower, George Vancouver, to honor Baron Saint Helens (Alleyne Fitzherbert), who as British ambassador to Spain in 1790–1794 negotiated the Nootka Treaty, so advantageous to British commerce in the PNW. House Knighton built in 1847, with lumber shipped around the Horn from Bath, Maine — talk of bringing coals to Newcastle! — stands at 155 S 4th, but greatly changed.

Turn L onto Columbia Blvd. *1.3 m.,* turn R onto S 1st. *0.2 m.,* **Courthouse Square,** with sleepy look of Andy Hardy movie. Columbia County Courthouse holds county historical museum. Old part of town, facing courthouse, is blend of plain past and breezy present. Grand views of Columbia and Mt. St. Helens from rear of courthouse.

Site of RR station at St. Helens was once PO of Houlton, which was originally Milton City. When PO was est., in 1890, there was by then a PO in Umatilla County named Milton, so postmaster named office for his home town of Houlton, Maine. In 1946 Houlton PO became a station of St. Helens PO. But do not neglect Milton City, lost in the shadows of history. In 1850 it was 5th largest urban center in Oregon, with 141 households. Only Oregon City, Portland, Salem and Astoria were bigger, and Milton City had grand dreams of challenging Portland as a river town.

Columbia Blvd., main intersection.

* Turn R onto Columbia Blvd. *0.3 m.,* Columbia Blvd. becomes Bachelor Flat Rd. at stop sign. *0.6 m.,* four-way stop sign. Turn onto Sykes Rd. *1.5 m.,* forks. Keep L. *0.1 m.,* Sykes becomes Kappler. *0.8 m.,* Kappler becomes Cater. (Turn onto Kappler.) *0.7 m.,* turn R. *0.2 m.,* Yankton store. *0.3 m.,* Yankton Cemetery (1888) and old-time Yankton Baptist Church. Return to where Kappler becomes Cater. Straight on Cater. *0.1 m.,* forks. Take L,

uphill on Cater Rd. *1 m.,* Stone Rd. Straight. *3.5 m.,* Spitzenberg, named for early farmer, on Pittsburg Rd. (See Pittsburg–Vernonia Rd., following.)

3.1 m., Church Rd., **Warren.**

    * Turn L. Cross RR tracks. Aged Eagle Lodge bldg. seems as old as Warren (PO est. 1885). Turn L. *0.7 m.,* **Bayview Cemetery** (1874).

    * Turn R onto Church Rd. *0.1 m.,* Bethany Lutheran Church and Cemetery (1908). *1.2 m.,* Hazen Rd. Turn R. *0.5 m.,* St. Helens Golf Course. *0.3 m.,* Stone Rd. Turn L. *2 m.,* Cater Rd. Turn L. *3.5 m.,* Spitzenberg at Pittsburg Rd. (See Pittsburg–Vernonia Rd., following.)

0.3 m., on R, turnoff to **Dahlberg Farm.** 1890 water tower. Next to it, windmill put up 1926. In rear, two barns constructed 1926.

4.1 m., Pittsburg–Vernonia Jct.

    * *5.8 m.,* site of **Spitzenberg,** former logging camp. *0.5 m.,* on R, 1913 schoolhouse now residence. This was part of Chapman District, collection of logging camps. *0.7 m.,* on L. turnoff to Grange hall and church. (*0.2 m.,* Chapman Grange, built in early bleak Depression year. *0.1 m.,* **Chapman Community Church,** with PA and "Enchanted Forest" trail system) Return to Pittsburg–Vernonia Rd. Turn toward 0 47. Now the road twists and twists thru a green labyrinth, with quick openings, revealing flashes of farms and dwellings rich and poor. *7.7 m.,* on L, **Scaponia Rec. Area,** on Jim George Creek, which old timers insist was the N fork of the Nehalem before BLM est. park, which is one of real beauties of area. *5.3 m.,* 0 47. Turn L. *0.3 m.,* Pittsburg. *5.1 m.,* Vernonia. (See 0 47.)

0.4 m., **Scappoose,** descriptive from Indian "gravelly plain." Scappoose had very likely been a key lower Columbia trading mart before Lt. Broughton of the Royal Navy came by this way in 1792. He was shown copper swords and iron battle axes, which the Indians said came from other Indians far, far to the E. The Indian pop. here was decimated by infectious diseases, previously unknown to them, by white seamen. First white settler was an American sailor who deserted from the brig *Owyhee,* the disease-carrying ship, which had been trading in the area, in 1829. PO est. 1872.

From main intersection — road to airport.

Turn L. *0.3 m.,* turn L onto Airport Rd. *1.2 m.,* Honeymen Rd. Turn R. *1.5 m.,* Freeman Rd. Turn L. *0.4 m.,* 54176 Freeman Rd. Behind old trailer house back of modern house, grave of Thomas McKay, well-known early trader and trapper. Old timers claim McKay actually lies in unmarked grave about 200 yds. SE.

Next to police station, Scappoose City Hall, built 1902, was originally home of James Grant Watt, who helped inc. town and served as its first mayor.

0.6 m., on R, **Thomas McKay Historical Marker.** McKay, half-Indian stepson of John McLoughlin, arrived in Astoria at age 14, grew up in the service of Hudson's Bay Co., had as first wife daughter of Chinook chief Concomly, turned farmer at Scappoose, died 1849 at age 52.

1 m., on R, Fairview Cemetery. *0.2 m.,* on R, Dutch Canyon Rd.

* Turn R. *0.3 m.,* **Fairview Cemetery** (1871). On a grey day markers seem imbued with sadness of Gray's country churchyard.

0.7 m., Watson Rd.

* *0.8 m.,* forks. Take L. *1.2 m.,* gate entrance to **Vedanta Retreat,** for Buddhists. Octagonal bldg. with white onion dome, set against pine tree background, overlooks Columbia. For visitation, contact Vedanta Society in Portland or phone from house downhill across road.

4.8 m., **Logie Trail.**

* *4.4 m.,* Skyline Blvd. Sharp uphill, twisty, with not a house along steepening part. Historically, trail named for James Logie, overseer of Hudson's Bay Co. farm on Sauvie Island, ran from the island to Tualatin Valley. Present contours do not neatly fit the past.

1 m., on R, Cornelius Pass Rd.

* *3.5 m.,* forks. Take L. *3.6 m.,* West Union. (W *0.8 m.,* historic **West Union Baptist Church and Cemetery.)** *1 m.,* turnoff to US 26. (Straight, *0.3 m.,* pioneer **Imbrie House.)**

0.6 m., Burlington. Started as suburban village on the electric United Railways. Substitute hwy. for tracks and Burlington hasn't changed much.

1.8 m., Sauvie Island Bridge.

2.6 m., **Linnton.** Town laid out by 1843 comers Peter Hardeman Burnett and Morton Matthew McCarver soon after arrival here. They envisioned wealth thru selling lots but their land speculation failed, the other overlanders being

Old gas pump on road from Scappoose to Pittsburgh

equally as poor. Burnett, never modest, proclaimed that Linnton would become the great port of commerce for the Oregon Country. But when his real estate business did not sweeten, Burnett moved W, to take up farming near Hillsboro. Eager to be known he became a power in local politics. Within a year he was chosen to serve on the nine-member legislative committee of the Provisional govt. The following year he was made judge of the Supreme Court. In 1848 Burnett was elected to the legislature of the new Territorial govt. and pledged that he had hitched his future to the rising star of Oregon. He would have gone further; Pres. Polk appointed him Supreme Court Justice. But that was the year gold was discovered in Calif. and by the time Polk's decree reached Oregon Burnett was long gone. Two years later, in 1850, he was elected Calif.'s first governor. He never returned to Oregon. McCarver, of whom more in the writings on Oregon City, also went to Calif., where he achieved some notoriety as a staunch racist. (So was Burnett.)

In 1915 Linnton, named for ardent pro-expansionist Sen. Lewis Fields Linn of Missouri, had its own bank, PS, church, private owned water works system and "sea-going vessels docked here, taking on large cargoes to foreign ports." A 1940 guide of Oregon described Linnton as "an important industrial district of the city [Portland]; large lumber shipments leave from its wharves." The impression of Linnton today is that of a shabby, dreary outpost of Portland, where the people who live in the hills above the store and tavern rarely come into Linnton.

1.1 m., turnoff to **St. Johns Bridge,** without doubt the most expressive and graceful in the Portland area.

7 m., downtown **Portland,** 5th and Morrison.

0 47 — Clatskanie To US 26

From Clatskanie, US 30:

The road to Mist whips around like a dog chasing its tail, with scarcely a house or meadow in sight.

11.4 m., **Mist Cemetery** (1899). Near it a pinched-face schoolhouse empty for years sulks in the shadows.

0.4 m., **Mist Store.** Back in 1915 Mist had PS, shingle mill, PO (est. 1888), Grange, Swedish Lutheran Church. All it has now is the store, probably older than the town, a few dwellings, and the accurately descriptive name. Store is social center, cafe, beauty parlor, gift shop and political platform. Sometimes it is even a grocery.

0.1 m., jct., 0 202.

From Mist S the curves are gentler by far than the twists up from Clatskanie. And the country is more tamed, and there is more traffic. Each year witnesses a diminishing of the deep-trenched rural atmosphere,with houses more affluent, more businesses along the road, stump farms kneaded into pastures and gardens.

   3 m., on R, 1888 **Peterson House,** "country museum" of Nehalem Valley artifacts. *0.8 m.,* on L, Natal Grange hall and pioneer schoolhouse. *3.6 m.,* Apiary-Rainier Jct. (See US 30.) *1 m.,* **Big Eddy CP,** fishing and camping haven on Nehalem River. *3 m.,* St. Helens-Scappoose Jct.

   * 5.2 m., on R, **Scaponia Rec. Site,** stream clearing in the forest. *14.4 m.,* US 20, Scappoose.

   0.3 m., **Pittsburg.** There is no sign of sawmill and gristmill built 1879 by early settler Peter Brous, nor of PO which operated form 1879 to 1908. Just parking lot for state trucks and cafe.

   4.4 m., on L **Columbia County Historical Society Museum.** Located in 1922 office bldg. of long deceased Oregon American Lumber Co., which locals say was largest electrically operated mill under cover in the world. Its closing in 1957 threatened to make a ghost town of Vernonia. A school teacher called the devastated town, "A slice of Appalachia." But it survived.

   0.4 m., in **Vernonia,** State St. — Keasey Jct.

   * Turn R. 0. 8 m., on L, **Pioneer Cemetery.** When the old timers of Vernonia talk about "going up on the hill" they mean being buried here. There is a frontier nuance to the land conversing with the road; not many strangers come this way, and those who do approach with respect. *8.8 m.,* Keasey, est. 1890 and short decades ago a large and bustling lumber camp, with typical bunkhouses, cookshack, shops, RR tracks — the works. There was also PO & PS here. Today there is not a stitch of what was. Even the few houses aren't for real; they were trucked in here after Keasey was cleared out.

1888 Peterson House, between Pittsburgh and Mist

House at Keasey that was once a post office

0.2 m., Adams St., Vernonia. **Transportation Park.** RR steam locomotive here is relic of Keasey days.

0.1 m., downtown Vernonia. In its raw and early days the town was called a "hole in the woods," and there is the feeling now that if the forests rise again the

Vernonia Hotel, the only public lodging in an area of more than fifteen hundred square miles

Railroad trestle on road to Vernonia   *Phoebe L. Friedman*

will, in revenge, smother the town whose ancestors massacred the woods. The hills which engulf the village seem to look down upon it in sorrow — but life goes on and even here, in the bypass of a hinterland, neighbors on back streets often do not know each other. Alienation binds Vernonia to New York.

Counter in city hall came from 1st bank in town. Vernonia Hotel, which has been around long enough for even the old timers to forget when it was built, is the kind of small town, wooden, earthy hostelry common to logging towns in the 1920s and '30s. Other wooden structures which harken back to a happier time, when Vernonia was bustling mill town, are: Vernonia First Evangelical Church, State and A; Vernonia Grange, Washington and North; IOOF Hall, Grant and North. (For history and spirit of Vernonia, see "The Spencers of Vernonia" in author's *This Side of Oregon.*)

2.8 m., Timber Jct. *(10.3 m., US 26.)*

0.6 m., on R, typical W Oregon Xmas tree farm.

0.1 m., geodetic house, touch of Buckmaster Fuller in burly rural landscape. Throughout Oregon, wherever one goes, modernistic touches in design appear to spring up out of nowhere. Chief influence comes from city people, professionals who bring their sophistication to their islands of paradise.

5.2 m., high RR trestle, kind prominent in W Oregon in heyday of RR logging. Over this trestle came trains bound to and from Vernonia; when mill closed, RR became excursion line for passengers, who were treated to fresh strawberries at Banks and fried chicken at Vernonia. But in 1969 the last excursion train of the Banks–Vernonia (or Vernonia, South Park and Sunset Steam RR) chugged into Vernonia, and one more Oregon chapter was closed.

6 m., US 26.

O 202—Astoria to Mist, 0 47

O 202 is the least-known and least-traveled Cross-Coast Range road in N Oregon. It is used almost completely by localized traffic. Which is a shame, because O 202 is a clean-air, charming pike with no hangups or strains. From the ocean to the valley it is a longer route than others because it does not reach all the way. But for scenic interest it has its own rewards and, on a crowded summer day (especially Friday or Sunday) for the other roads, US 202 is a tonic for an edgy disposition.

From Astoria by way of Youngs River Loop:

1.5 m., from city center of Astoria, jct., US 101, Business US 101. Stay on Business US 101.

1.4 m., O 202, at N end of bridge across Youngs Bay. *1.4 m.,* jct., on L, Youngs River Loop.

The country road winds easily, as though built for a Sunday drive, thru bottomland pastures of cows and barns.

7.2 m., or R **Youngs River Falls.** "Stairs" lead down to Youngs River and, turning R, to base of falls. The falls, up to 50 ft. in descent, are always impressive; in spring the cataract is so powerful as to send spray hurling about 100 yds.

In 1978 Clatsop County historian Russell Dark advanced this information on the falls:

"R. M. Brayne began construction of a dam across Youngs river above the falls

Youngs River Falls   *Phoebe L. Friedman*

in 1886. In July, 1887, he began installation of pulp grinding machinery below the falls, having leased the falls for a ten year period from a homesteader, J. Hans Oliverson. Some of the grinding stones were barged down the river from Camas, Wash., where an earlier pulp mill had burned.

"The first bales of pulp were barged to Astoria on Dec. 4, 1887, and shipped to San Francisco aboard the steamer GEORGE W. ELDER.

"FALLS PULP CO. was incorporated Oct. 19, 1887, by R. M. Brayne. R. F. Elbon and C. R. Donoher. Rising cost of shipping pulp caused the firm to lose money and the plant was auctioned by the sheriff for debts on Nov. 26, 1891. Purchaser was H. W. Pierce of San Francisco. He went out of business when the plant burned.

"My committee has dug up 12 of the grinding stones at the mill site. They weigh 1200 pounds each."

3.3 m., jct. Turn L. 0.6 m., O 202, which is entered just E of **Olney Store.** (Olney is one of the few places in Oregon named for a judge; more towns have been named for scoundrels than for judges, though undoubtedly some people were both.) But Cyrus Olney, pioneer, was also a legislator and, more important, a resident of Astoria. The hamlet of Olney did not enhance his reputation, never more than one store at a time. In 1915 pop. was 50, and that was the sky.

(To return to Astoria, turn L at junction and pass Olney Store W.)

From start of O 202:

4.5 m., on N, **Greenwood Cemetery** (1891). 5 m., Olney Store. 0.1 m., jct., Youngs River Loop. (For Youngs River Falls, turn S.)

2.1 m., **Klaskanine River Salmon Hatchery.** Young coho and Chinook salmon seen all year. In late May, chub and suckers spawn in large numbers below hatchery dam.

12.9 m., on S, **Fishhawk Falls.** (Parking cutout across road.) Here, 20 m. from the Pacific, as the crow flies, and where Fishhawk Creek cascades down a 75 ft. cliff, is divide point between the coastal hemlock and spruce rain forests to the W and drier Douglas fir belt to the E.

0.1 m., on S, **Lee Worden CP.** Trail leads to base of Fishhawk Falls.

1.9 m., elk viewpoint. 1 m., **Jewell Meadows Wildlife Area HQ.** From early winter into early spring the great prairie is alive with elk. Bring binoculars for best viewing — and stay on road. 0.2 m., elk feeding ground viewpoint.

1.1 m., Beneke Creek Rd.

* Turn N onto Beneke Creek Rd. for drive that steals thru forest primeval, without a house in sight for miles, and views of mountains that swim in mists rising from cavernous sinks. The silent road begins in sweet arboreal innocence, then plunges into the woods and turns the traveler around in a dizzying pace, as though trying to shake the intruder from the trail. One constant to remember: at every fork, keep R. 3 m., "Y". Take R. 1.2 m., "Y". Hang a R. 0.3 m., "Y". Keep R. 0.1 m., "Y". R. Here Squaw Ridge and Crawford Ridge seem to become one. Now the road snakes to the height of this terrain

Elk feeding ground, Jewell

and from the top there is the most unusual view of Saddle Mtn. seen from anywhere. The world to the E is a sea of clouds and mtns. and it takes a fine eye to sort them out. *3 m., O 202.*

0.1 m., Elsie Jct.

    * 50 yds. on R, Rip Van Winklish vine-covered falling down house; gorgeous when matted in fall colors. *0.1 m.,* on R, big leaf maple that in autumn is candelabra dipped in giant paint pot. Tree is 35' in circumference; 101' high; and has average crown spread of 90'. Local children have played on its lower boughs for many years. *0.3 m.,* on R, Jewell School, covering grades K thru 12, in idyllic setting, the jewel of Jewell. Road swings back and forth as it chases the Nehalem River S. *3.8 m.,* approximate site of Grand Rapids PO (1892–1897). *1.6 m.,* site of Vinemaple, PO 1891–1902. *0.5 m.,* on L, **Nehalem Valley Community Church,** charming rural house of worship. *2.7 m.,* US 26.

0.1 m., **Jewell.** Settled in 1874 and named for postmaster general then, Jewell grew slowly but steadily. In 1915, it had PS and Grange, garage and poolhall. What happened then? A 70 year resident explained: "They logged it over and the town went out." Mammoth graves of felled trees are everywhere. "Downtown" is only a tavern. Folks drive more than 60 round-trip m. for supermarket shopping.

0.3 m., Crawford Ridge Rd., where O 202 is reentered upon completion of Beneke Creek Rd. trip.

0.3 m., Nehalem River. This stream is crossed several times on O 202 and is always a delight.

Old house near Jewell

9 m., on N, **Emanuel Episcopal Church,** a country Lord's house from another era that seems to beckon to the lonely and the lost.

2.3 m., **Birkenfeld.** At one time almost every middle-aged native of NW Oregon knew at least one Birkenfeld, some undoubtedly descendants of German-born Anton Birkenfeld, who put down roots in the Nehalem Valley in 1886 and 24 years later started this community. Most of the old timers are gone, their places taken by metropolitan expatriates. As in many other villages, the store, the tavern and the church bind the folds together. Still, the way things are, Birkenfeld seems targeted to be another housing tract.

0.9 m., on N. Fishhawk Rd.

* 0.1 m., turn R on Fishhawk Cem. Rd. 0.8 m., Fishhawk Cemetery, serene hilltop burial ground. Return to Fishhawk Rd. Turn R. 3.5 m., Fishhawk Lake, private gem for householders around lake. Everywhere in Oregon there seem to be exclusive enclaves for those who can afford them. This is one.

1.9 m., **Nehalem River.** 1.2 m., on S, 1905 house considered old timer for Nehalem Valley. 1.2 m., jct., 0 47. **Mist Store,** in original location, bldg. constructed 1871, is one of oldest general stores in Oregon. Inside, it lacks the eclectic stock of former years, say in the 1930s, when it was also the PO, and the pungency of the frontier-like clientele, but outside is still photogenic.

US 26 — Seaside Jct. to Portland

US 26, the Sunset Highway, is the shortest, most direct and most popular road between the coast and Portland. It is more a boulevard than a trans-mountain road, has few on-road points of interest, and is taken for time rather than scenery. The road was probably more interesting in its original form, when it was called the Wolf Creek Highway. Still, as the jump off for the old and the obscure, US 26 is a most intriguing pike.

From Seaside Jct. (US 101) to Portland:

2 m., — from Seaside-Cannon Beach Jct. — on N, **Klootchy Creek Park.** Giant firs and spruces tower as hoary monsters of a dim age. Mammoth trees, with twined roots above ground, seem to belong in an ancient arboreal museum. World's largest Sitka spruce is *0.1 m.* into park, on R. A sign reads that its circumference is 52' 6''; height, 216'; crown spread, 93'. Those measurements were made some time ago, so the tree is probably taller and wider now. Its birth was probably in the 13th century.

7.4 m., **Necanicum.** Started in the 1890s as Ahlers and then changed to Push, PO became Necanicum after adjacent river, in 1907. Stream called Clatsop in 1806 by Wm. Clark of Lewis and Clark party and much later in century was named for pioneering homesteader William Latty. But Indian name has survived thru several spellings and several interpretations, none of which was explained to the palefaces by the Indians. In 1915, Necanicum had pop. of 50 and PO. Today, store, cafe, but place is bound to spread.

Jct., O 53.

* On O 53: *0.7 m.,* Hamlet Jct. Turn L. *3.7 m.,* Hill Rd. (R on Hill Rd.: *0.5 m.,* 75 yds. below crest of hill, trail on L leads 50 yds. into woods to Hamlet Cemetery. (Pioneer of Hamlet lie in fenced family plots.) Return to Hamlet Rd. Turn R. *0.1 m.,* on L, old **Hamlet School,** now community hall. *1.4 m.,* approximate center of where old Hamlet stood. Hamlet never had store, PO or church; it was, as it is now, merely a community. But there is a significant difference between the settlement of the founding Finns and today's ambience. In old Hamlet, there was the sense of an extended family; each person in the handful of families knew all the others. Today, with suburban-like houses sprouting on the slopes and the early houses decaying into doom, and with practically every house sporting a TV saucer and the inhabitants dug into the trenches of the tube, many folks here don't really know each other. *0.8 m.,* end of Hamlet community. (For Hamlet of past, see "The Small Drama of Hamlet" in author's *Tracking Down Oregon.)*

* Return to O 53. Turn L, or S. The first stretch of O 53 is a grim and choppy sea of logged-off woods. Later the way opens into a lovely valley at foot of Coast Range. In democratic style the road swings blithely past stump ranches and prosperous-looking farms without slowing for either. *7.1 m.,* on W, turnoff to **Nehalem Fish Hatchery.** (*0.2 m.,* hatchery, on N Fork of

**World's
Largest**

Circumference: 52'-6"
Height: 216'
Crown Spread: 93'

CrownZellerbach

Klootchy Creek Park

Courtesy State of Oregon

Nehalem River. About 600,000 cohos and 200,000 steelhead, raised here, are released annually.) *5 m., jct., N Fork Rd.* — Nehalem. (Straight: *0.2 m.,* on L, site of former Aldervale Cheese Factory, opened 1920s, closed circa 1958. There were many such small cheese factories in Tillamook County, each claiming to produce "the finest cheese in the county," but they all closed to join cooperative in Tillamook. *4.9 m., US 101–Nehalem.*)

* From jct. at N Fork Rd., S on O 53:

0.7 m., on L, turnoff to **Gods Valley.** (*7 m.,* Gods Valley, small pleasant vale in logging area. No one knows origin of name; probably given by the same earthy fellow who, after a sip of cool water on hot afternoon, enthused, "Now, that's God's nectar!") *4.3 m.,* jct. (L, *1 m.,* road to **Spruce Run CP.** *11.7 m.,* on Foley Creek Rd., US 101.) *0.3 m.,* **Mohler.** Once on US 101, town was famous for its cheese factory "that, like others of the region," reported *Oregon: End of the Trail* in 1940, "is identified by its yellow paint. Many people of Swiss birth or descent operate dairies in the vicinity. They are particularly fond of playing the accordion and yodeling during their leisure hours." In 1915, Mohler had pop. 25, large cheese factory, Grange, private water works system, and had service twice daily to Tillamook on the motor train over the tracks of the Pacific Railway and Navigation Co. Cheese factory is now winery and whatever accordion playing and yodeling is heard these days generally comes over TV. *1 m.,* US 101. (S, *1 m.,* Wheeler.)

From Jct., O 53 on US 26:

0.8 m., turnoff to Saddle Mountain SP.

     * *7 m,* **Saddle Mtn. SP.** The 3,283 ft. peak, with its explosive volcanic

From the top of Saddle Mountain   *Courtesy State of Oregon*

features and uneven crest, was known in Clatsop legend as *Swallalahoost* or *Swol-la-la- chast*. Accounts vary as to the meaning of the Indian name; most fanciful is that of eagle, or Thunder Bird. One version of the legend is that a great chief, after being slain by his foes, took on the shape of an eagle, or Thunder Bird, and from his perch on the peak created thunder and lightning. Another version of the legend is that the Thunder Bird was a she that lived in two caves in the volcanic cliffs and "laid the eggs that rolled down the mountain side and hatched into tribes of men." From the end of the 4 m. trail, at the top, the eye meets its reward in views of the mouth of the Columbia, beaches and breakers, and the spines of the Coast Range. Some hikers, as reckless as they are irresponsible, take short cuts by sliding down slopes instead of adhering to trails. This not only invites danger but scars the slopes.

7.5 m., on S, **Camp 18,** logging museum containing equipment generally used in 1930s. It seems odd that in W Oregon, with such a rich lumber history, there are so few living remembrances of the past. This is the best of its kind in area.

1.7., **Elsie,** which began life as Mishawaka in 1876 and has been Elsie since 1892, is largest US 26 stop between the coast and Portland. In 1915, Elsie had PS, long gone. Restaurant-tavern has well-displayed memorabilia of early logging.

0.3 m., turnoff S to Spruce Run CP and lower Nehalem River.

* The Nehalem is a sweetheart of a river wherever it is and no more joyous than in these parts. (For an upclose portrait, see "A Sprite Called River" in author's *This Side of Oregon*.) The Nehalem is especially interesting in spring, when it whets the ambitions of river runners. It puts on a marvelous show then, constantly switching moods and actions, as though to say, "If you don't keep your eyes on me every minute you'll miss something great." 5.3 m., **Spruce Run CP,** on the Nehalem. One of the finest CPs in state and equal in attractiveness to many SPs. 1.9 m., on W, remains of bridge or long-loading dock; there isn't agreement. 5.8 m., **Salmonberry,** at confluence of Salmonberry Creek and Nehalem. In spring, one of prettiest places in NW Oregon. RR tracks at Salmonberry (which is otherwise a wide, unmarked place on road) attest to its once being a stop on the route from Portland to the coast, and vice versa. (There was small RR station here once.) Trails lead to river; it is favorite for fishers.

* 6.9 m., on W, **Nehalem Falls Park.** (0.1 m., parking for 0.1 m. trail to riffling Nehalem Falls.)

Beyond park, road enters charming little pungent valley, with small farm cameos coming one after the other, as though a camera rapidly clicking. (6.8 m., site of former CP. Still a good place to pull off the road and look at the Nehalem, now to E, and have pedestrian lunch.

0.2 m., jct., Foley Creek — O 53. (L on Foley Creek Rd., which in its lower stage follows the syrupy Miami River. 11.7 m., US 101. N, 0.8 m., Garibaldi.) R at jct.: 1 m., O 53. L, 0.3 m., Mohler and winery. 1 m., US 101. S, 1 m., Wheeler.

On US 26, at jct., Spruce Run Park:

0.7 m., Lower Nehalem Rd.

* 0.4 m., Spruce Run Rd. (5 m., Spruce Run CP.)

1.4 m., on S, Luukinen Rd.

* 0.4 m., on R, World Peace University. Woodsy campus with several outdoor basketball courts.

0.2 m., Jewell Jct.

* 0.1 m., "T". (L, 1 m., on Dead End Rd., with pleasurable overlooks and water level views of Nehalem River. Houses on E side of rd. suggest that this is the "country club set" of the area.) Turn R. 2.6 m., on R, **Nehalem Valley Community Church.** 0.5 m., site of Vinemaple (PO 1892–1897). 1.6 m., site of **Grand Rapids** (PO 1892–1897). 3.8 m., Jewell School, grades K thru 12, with preschool facility. 0.3 m., on L, awesome broadleaf maple. In autumn, when it is a pillar of fire, it is worth traveling half-a-day to see. 0.1 m., on L, disintegrating house that in October is smothered by fall colors, as though this forlorn beggar is given the love missing the rest of the year. 50 yds., O 202. (E 0.1 m., "downtown" **Jewell** — tavern.)

5 m., Coast Range Summit — 1,642 ft., highest Oregon state hwy. summit of Coast Range.

1.8 m., on N, turnoff to Rest Area.

* 0.1 m., Rest Area. Across bridge is start of approximate 2 m. Forest Trail. Place was formerly Sunset Wayside Nature Study Area. A pleasant walk and a text for the curious.

9 m., Vernonia-Timber Jct.

* N to Vernonia: The road steals thru a calm, second-growth, chimney smoke vale of few pretties, reminiscent of Maine. 8.4 m., on W, Currier and Ives-looking house with octagonal window. 1.8 m., forks. Continue straight. 2 m., Vernonia. (For Vernonia, see O 47 N.)

* S to Timber: 3 m., **Timber.** Tavern. Timber was so named because of thick forests hereabouts. In 1915, it had pop. 75, saw and shingle mill, PS, and was focal point on Pacific Railway & Navigation Co. During heavy logging of steam engine days, according to long-time railroader Clayton Brothers, Timber had round house and was helper station en route to Tillamook. Extra locomotive was put on to make steep climb up to Cochran. (From W end, with train full of timber, as many as six engines were needed to make the climb to the summit.) 2.3 m., thru stump ranch terrain, Reeher's Park, primitive CG widely used by "dirt bike" riding families. 4.4 m., thru true forest land, forks. Take L. 0.1 m., fork. Take L. 0.1 m., site of Cochran. Although Cochran continues on official state map, only RR water tank here, and old timers say that's about all there ever really was. 0.3 m., on R, Cochran Pond, hideaway angling delight.

* From Timber S to O 6: 6.2 m., "If you like woods," said a local, "you'll like this road."

7.7 m., jct., O 47 N.

* *6 m.,* high RR trestle. *5.2 m.,* geodetic house. *0.1 m.,* typical W Oregon Xmas tree farm. *3.4 m.,* Vernonia. *16.9 m.,* **Mist.** *11.8 m.,* **Clatskanie,** on US 30. (See *O47N* for details.)

0.4 m., Buxton Jct.

* *0.9 m.,* **Buxton.** First settler, James Steel, received land grant in 1871 from Pres. Grant. But Steel didn't have the patience to deal with his forested property, so he sold it to a fellow named Pfanner, who upped the price to $120 and found buyer in Henry T. Buxton, son of 1841 pioneer. In 1886, two years after Henry T. settled here, PO was opened in his log cabin and Buxton was on its way. At one time, Hannon's mercantile store was biggest around for many miles and the 40 room Elk Horn Hotel had few vacancies. In 1915, town had pop. 200, saw and shingle mill, HS and PS, two churches, was on line of Pacific Railway & Navigation Co. Buxton's pop. isn't more now. Elk Horn Hotel, Hannon's store and mill are gone. Entire business district consists of small country store. At forks, in front of church, go R. This uphill scenery was, said a woman who lived on its lower slope, "so pretty you could taste it." The hills that kept rising with the road could take a cynic's breath away. But no more. The woods have been slashed and ravaged as though in mad revenge for something Nature did to humanity. *7.7 m,* on R, road scything E. *0.7 m.,* on L, **Jeppesen Place,** pioneer homestead with weather-rubbed barn. When Jeppesen Family came here about turn of century they stocked up six months of supply of groceries and other necessities in fall, because snows shut them in until late spring. *0.4 m.,* Bacona. Settled in the 1890s, **Bacona** (named for early Bacon family) grew into settlement that in 1915 reached pop. of 70. It was an primitive and isolated a settlement as existed in W Oregon; in winter the only way to get in and out was by sleigh. (For story on early Bacona and Jeppesens, see "Baptism at Bacona" in author's *Tracking Down Oregon.*) Only a house stands where there was a village called Bacona.

* Return to jct., *0.7 m.,* below Jeppesen place. Turn L. *4.9 m.,* site of **Snooseville,** a burg whose name never appeared on any map nor in any dictionary of Oregon names. When mill burned down in 1940s hamlet practically evacuated. Only few houses continued to be occupied. Some of these later torn down.

At Snooseville, Fern Flat Rd. (*1 m.* up it, on R, Little Bend (BLM) Rec. Area on E Dairy Creek.) *2.3 m.,* Meacham Rd. (R, *0.1 m.,* Meacham Crossing, on E Dairy Creek. Site of pioneer sawmill.) *0.9 m.,* on R, **Big Canyon Ranch.** Thru ranch to BLM-managed Big Canyon, wilderness area open to visitors. *3.5 m.,* on R, red Mountaindale School, built 1885, closed 1954. *0.8 m.,* Mountaindale Store, all that remains of community that in 1915 had two sawmills. Store built on other side of road in 1885; stood there three years, then moved to present location. Just above it is abandoned blacksmithing barn. Jct. Turn L. *2 m.*, US 26.

At Buxton turnoff, on US 26:

* Turn R. *0.2 m.*, forks. R uphill. *0.3 m.*, **Buxton Cemetery** (1890). The beauty of this pastoral scene is marred by timber-felled slope, the carnage revolting to the neutral eye, and the quiet torn from its moorings by the scream of dirt motor bikes.

1.7 m., **Manning,** small hwy. strip settlement. In 1915, it was busier, with three sawmills. All that remains of old Manning, on L, is Grange hall.

Turnoff R for Hayward:

* This road once embodied the best of Washington County's graceful past, but the frontier cabins, moss-covered barns, secretive hermit homes and windmills have all been removed. But for the moment the nuance of tranquility remains. *4.8 m.*, Hayward Rd. becomes Cedar Canyon Rd. *0.1 m.*, turn R onto trace that is first lane this side of farm house, also on R. *30 yds.*, take tire trace another *30 yds.* to **Hayward Cemetery.** Wild snapdragons engulf gravestones of settlement founders. Below cemetery stood community of Hayward; PO 1891–1904. *1.1 m.*, dazzling view of Tualatin Valley. *2 m.*, turn R. *0.1 m.*, O 6, Wilson River Hwy. Turn L. *1.1 m.*, Cedar Canyon Rd. Turn R. *0.4 m.*, Strohmayer Rd. Turn L. *1.4 m.*, Greenville Roy Rd. (Straight: *0.3 m.*, site of **Kansas City,** that was never a city and isn't anything now. Relics of past include community hall and school; both have been on last legs for ages. Turn R on Clapshaw Rd. *1 m.*, forks. R *0.6 m.*, to winery, Tualatin Vineyards. L on Clapshaw Rd: *1.4 m.*, on L, **Hillside School,** now museum, 19th century place of learning that looks more like 19th century country school than any other in W Oregon. For full story, see "A Heap of Schoolboy Memories at Hillside," in author's *This Side of Oregon.* Next to school is **Hillside Church,** put up 1900, *0.1 m.*, **Hillside Cemetery,** est. 1887.)

* At Greenville Roy Rd.: Turn L at jct. *1.5 m.*, on R, early **Greenville School,** now used as storage shed. One of the oldest bldgs. in Washington County that was school. To L of it is barn which held horses on which children rode to school. *0.2 m.*, site of old **Greenville,** which had PO from 1871 to 1907, when PO was moved to Banks. Turn L. Carport on S of first house was site of PO. (Turn R at corner: *5 m.*, Forest Grove.) *1.1 m.*, turnoff for Portland. (Portland, *25 m.*) *0.2 m.*, O 6. *0.8 m.*, North Plains Jct.; curve L. *2.5 m.*, US 26.

US 26 at Hayward Jct.:

1.6 m., Banks Jct. — O 47 S.

* *1.8 m.* (in Banks), Banks Rd. (Turn onto Banks Rd. *0.9 m.*, on R. **Union Point Cemetery** [1860], on smooth hilltop with open views of undulating countryside. *5 m.*, North Plains.) *0.4 m.*, downtown **Banks,** which looks just like a small, slow-pokey town should. Started rather late, in 1902, Banks grew

only from 350 to 515 between 1915 and 1980. If you can get lost in Banks you should not be let out of the house. *0.5 m.,* on R, Marek residence, home of master artisan and mechanic, whose self-built or rebuilt cannons and vintage cars are housed in back. Be certain to first inquire.

For O 47 S, see section immediately following.

From Banks Jct., on US 26:

3.8 m., jct., O 6. *0.5 m.,* Mountaindale Jct.

   * *1.6 m.,* **Mountaindale.** (See earlier, this section.) Jct., Roy.

   * *1.2 m.,* turn L onto Roy Rd. *0.8 m.,* **Roy.** Started as RR station, Roy never got up head of steam. Brick and stucco St. Francis Catholic Church one of prettiest around.

1.3 m., jct., Dersham Rd.

   * *0.2 m.,* turn R. *0.1 m.,* forks. Take R. *0.3 m.,* on L, **Harrison Cemetery** (1856).

1.8 m., jct., North Plains.

   * *0.2 m.,* turn L. *0.5 m.,* turn L. *0.4 m.,* village of **North Plains.** Since early white settlement this area has been known as North Plains, to distinguish it from rest of Tualatin Valley, so town name came by way naturally. Some years ago North Plains broke into media attention because an amiable, non-descript footloose hound who liked to hang around tavern was collared with name Hitler. Whoever inflicted that cruel appellation on this gentle creature had neither brains nor humor. *0.2 m.,* Old West Union Rd. *(0.1 m.,* on L, **Village Blacksmith Shop,** oldest of its kind in state. Now private museum, in original condition. Operated nearly 75 years by Charles Walter, who died 1964 at age 94. Shop was surrounded by other businesses and homes of Glencoe, which had PO from 1871–1904. When village ran down it was "moved" to North Plains.)

   * At exit of North Plains Jct. turn R for Old Scots Church. *1.3 m.,* Old Scotch Church Rd. Turn L. *0.6 m.,* on L, **Tualatin Plains Presbyterian Church,** known for decades as "Old Scotch Church" and more recently as "Old Scots Church." Buried here is Joe Meek, hard luck mountain man, "gentlemen" farmer, outrageous liar and delightful folk hero. (For more, see "The Not So Meek Joe" in author's *Tracking Down Oregon.)*

3.7 m., Helvetia Rd.

   * *0.2 m.,* turn L for Helvetia. *2.4 m.,* **Helvetia,** named by Swiss settlers in honor of their country. Nothing here but church, cemetery and tavern, the last named being famous for its hamburgers. (Returning toward US 26, *1.5 m.,* West Union Jct. Turn L. *0.7 m.,* **West Union Baptist Church,** oldest of its kind W of upper Missouri, built 1853. In adjacent cemetery grave markers date back to 1860s and include names of some illustrious Oregonians. *0.9 m.,* West Union. Turn R. *1 m.,* US 26.)

1.1 m., Cornelius Pass Rd.

   * *0.3 m.,* Turn R. *0.2 m.,* on R, **Imbrie House,** built 1862–66. Six genera-

tions of Imbries lived here. In recent years house has been restaurant and roadhouse-brewery. *1.7 m.*, 231st Ave. Turn L onto it. *0.3 m.*, Alder St. Turn L. *0.1 m.*, site of **Orenco,** acronym of Oregon Nursing Community. In 1915, within decade after its founding, Orenco had pop. 30, was home of one of the largest nurseries in US, had HS and PS, Farmer's Co-operative Marketing Assn. and Civic Improvement League and was on Forest Grove division of Oregon Electric railway. Only abandoned store testifies that here a town stood. *1.8 m.*, on L, Washington County Fair Grounds, in midst of formerly rich agricultural area that has been turned over to hi-tech industries, including Japanese-owned. An environmentalist said grimly: "Well, when there isn't enough land to produce food we can eat computers."

   * From (Cornelius Pass) overpass turnoffs: L to West Union. *1 m.*, **West Union.** Turn L. *0.9 m.*, on R, **West Union Baptist Church.** *0.7 m.*, Helvetia Rd. Turn R. *1.5 m.*, **Helvetia.**
From Cornelius Pass Rd.:
6 *m.*, **Bearverton** exit. *0.9 m.*, jct., O 219 — to Tigard.
8 *m.*, downtown Portland.

O 47S — US 26 to 0 99W (near McMinnville)
The beauty of this road is chiefly in the imagery the land and its distant vistas will evoke in the poetic. To the E ruffle the whorled fields and family farm orchards that remind one from Abraham Lincoln's country of the Illinois prairie. Westward, beyond pastoral scenes of sheer delight, the hirsute hills curl from the far edge of the saucered plain and arch misty green and haze blue into the foam-waves of the Coast Range. On a summer day the sun drips golden shadows on the feathered slopes and in evening the moon is a brassy gong hung on an invisible peak or a jack-o-lantern rolled into a saddle of the cordillera. Then shards of the wind, splintered by the foothill woods, come lancing into the meadows, gathering capes of dust around them, until they stub their jagged edges in a marshy ravine and fall flat, the last ripple of breeze bending the grass under a drowsy-eyed cow.
   From jct., 0 47N and US 26, on US 26:
0.4 m., Buxton turnoff. *1.7 m.*, Manning. (On S, Hayward turnoff.) *1.6 m.*, jct., 0 47S—Banks.
   1.8 m., Banks Rd., in Banks. (*0.9 m.* up Banks Rd., Union Point Cemetery.) *0.4 m.*, downtown Banks. *0.6 m.*, jct., 0 6. *0.3 m.*, on L, Wilkesboro Rd.
   * *1 m.*, on L, Aerts Rd., site of Wilkesboro, first settled 1845; town platted 1912; PO est. 1916. In 1915 pop. 50, 2 churches, lodge, Farmers' Alliance, RR depot. Later, grocery, meat market, blacksmith shop, brickyard. Nothing now but old timers know where streets were laid out. *1 m.*, turn R onto Roy Rd. *0.8 m.*, former village built around RR station and PO in early 1900s.

Attractive St. Francis Catholic Church draws parishioners from all corners of the prairie. Only creaky store bldg. indicates where mercantile Roy stood. 1 m., Kansas City Jct. Here stood Greenville, which had PO from 1871 to 1907.

* Turn R. *0.2 m.*, on L, former **Greenville School,** built 1870s and now storage shed. *1.5 m.*, turn L. *0.2 m,* **Kansas City,** which never was a city. No identification markers because as soon as one is put up some rogue pilfers it. Turn R onto Clapshaw Rd. *1 m.*, forks. Take R. *0.6 m.*, Tualatin Vineyards, winery. *0.2 m.*, Old Clapshaw Rd. The lane, narrow and winding thru thick foliage, resembles what roads must have been like 125 years ago. *1 m.*, historic **Hillside School.** *0.1 m.*, **Hillside Cemetery** (1887). Across road from burial ground, pioneer Hillside church.

From Kansas City Jct., on 0 47:

3.2 m., Verboort Jct.

* *2 m.*, **Verboort,** regionally known for its autumn sausage festival.

1 m., on L, **Davidson Century Farm.** Apple tree in front of house planted by Orus Brown, son of Tabitha Brown, in 1848; house built 1863 by Alvin Clark Brown.

0.6 m., turn R. *0.1 m.*, turn L. *0.1 m.*, **Pacific University.** Old College Hall (in mid-campus), built in short weeks in 1850 to house Tualatin Academy, predecessor of PU, is oldest college bldg. still in use W of Missouri River. PU had its genesis in missionary school started in 1841 by Vermont-born independent Congregationalist Rev. Harvey L. Clark, who was also participant in celebrated 1843 Champoeg meeting and chaplain of first provisional legislature. Clark's earliest charges were Indian and part-Indian youth. In 1847 he was joined at West Tualatin, now Forest Grove, by Tabitha Moffat Brown, to whom he gave haven after her gruelling trip to Oregon. Mrs. Brown's suggestion that she would like to settle "in a comfortable house and receive all children and be a mother to them" was instantly taken up by Clark, who turned over to her his log schoolhouse. It became the first orphanage in the Oregon Country and went on to become Tualatin Academy (1848) and, in 1854, Pacific University. In 1912 the academy was discontinued.

Although Clark was the driving force behind the growth of Tualatin Academy into Pacific U, Tabitha Moffat "Grandma" Brown remains most intimately associated with PU, despite her having very little to do with the college as a college.

There were few pioneers more remarkable than Tabitha Brown. At the age of 66, and 29 years a widow, she crossed the plains in 1846 on the notorious Scott-Applegate Trail, with her son Orus, wagon train pilot, and her elder, feebling brother-in-law Capt. John Brown. They and others had been induced by Jesse Applegate at Ft. Hall (Idaho) to take the "southern cutoff" to the Willamette Valley. Tabitha Brown wrote later of that "rascally fellow" who claimed to know it all: "He robbed us of what he could by lying and left us to the depredations of Indians and wild beasts and to starvation."

In one agonizing sentence the small, frail woman (she did not weigh more than

100 lbs) summed up a hellish stretch of Nevada: "We had sixty miles of desert without grass or water, mountains to climb, cattle giving out, wagons breaking, emigrants sick and dying, hostile Indians to guard against by night and day, if we would save ourselves and our horses and cattle from being arrowed and stole."

In a letter she penned after completion of her journey, she recalled: "Worse than alone in a savage wilderness, without food, without fire, cold and shivering, wolves fighting and howling all around me. The darkness of night forbade the stars to shine upon me; all was solitary as death." Somehow she survived, reached the Willamette Valley with a single coin, worth a few cents, with which she bought material, started sewing, and made her way up to the Tualatin Plains and the home of Rev. Harvey Clark. Both Clark and Mrs. Brown passed away in the spring of 1858, he on March 24 and she 6 weeks later, on May 4. (For more on Tabitha Brown, see "The Courage of Grandma Brown" in author's *A Touch of Oregon*.)

Two other pioneer women associated with the school were Mary Richardson Walker and Myra Fairbanks Eells, who crossed the plains in 1838 as missionary wives. Always perceptive and sometimes caustic, Mary Walker wrote of her traveling companions as they assembled at Independence, Mo. to begin their long journey: "We have a strange company of missionaries. Scarcely one who is not intolerable on some account." Both the Eells and Walker families, after serving in E Wash., moved to Tualatin Plains in 1848–49. Here Rev. Cushing Eells taught for 2 years at Tualatin Academy, founded in 1848 thru efforts of the congregational Assn. in which both families were active.

Among great Americans who comforted and sustained PU in various ways were Samuel F. B. Morse, Edward Everett Hale, Henry Ward Beecher and Rufus Choate. First graduating class consisted solely of Harvey W. Scott, longtime editor of the Portland *Oregonian*, historian, and brother of Abigail Scott Duniway.

Across street from W rim of campus (on 0 47) is **United Church of Christ Congregational,** with magnificent stained glass window above altar, 4th church of same denomination since 1845 at this site. Also on W side of 0 47 are **Valley Art Center,** devoted in main to creations of W Oregon potters; **Walker Hall,** home of Rev. Sidney Harper Marsh, first PU president, who continued in that office until 1879 (25 years); and **Knight Hall,** occupied by Marsh's widow after his death.

Knight Hall has reputation for being "haunted," though no one knows why or the origin of the legend. In the spring of 1979 two student journalists described an overnight experience in Knight Hall in the *Pacific Index*. It was the usual "hair-raising" adventure: creaking footsteps in an empty hallway, lights going on by themselves, a whisper by an invisible female, and a piano playing in front of the investigative eyes without anyone touching the keys.

Outstanding old homes in Forest Grove include: **Ben Cornelius** (1873), 2314 19th, large 2 story built in late classical revival style. Cornelius came to Oregon in

1845 as a member of the ill-fated Stephen Meek Party, better known as the "Lost Emigrant Party." He was the father of Thomas R., after whom town of Cornelius was named. Also: **Himes House** (1859), saltbox residence at 1604 Birch, and **Roe House** (1872), 2126 17th.

0.1 m., from PU campus at Valley Art Center, downtown Forest Grove and 0 8.

0.2 m., 0 47 turns S.

    * Going W — *0.4 m.,* forks. Straight on 0 8. *0.3 m.,* on L, Forest View Cemetery (1874). Return to 0 8. Turn W. *0.9 m.,* on N, turn onto Thatcher-Kansas City Rd. *0.1 m.,* turn L onto Watercrest Rd. *0.5 m.,* **Mountain View Memorial Gardens** (1860). Here lie Rev. Harvey Clark; Orus Brown, son of Tabitha Brown; and Belle Cooke, Oregon author. Apart from the historic graves there is from here an inspiring view of the Tualatin Valley.

Return to jct., 0 8 and 0 47. Turn S onto 0 47.

2.1 m., Dilley. This would be a ghost town if there was a ghost around. In 1915 there was a village here of 150 people, privately owned electric lighting and water works system, Methodist Episcopal Church and United Artisan lodge. Just grade school now.

0.3 m., Old T(ualatin) V(alley) Hwy.

    * *2.2 m.,* Scoggins store. *2.5 m.,* turn L for Scoggins Dam, in heart of **Scoggins Valley Park.** *(0.2 m.* to dam; drive around 1153-acre Henry Hagg Lake, starting from dam, includes view of elk pasture.) *0.1 m.,* turn L for Viewpoint and Interpretive Trail. *0.2 m.,* PA. *0.6 m.,* turnoff to BR (0.2 m.) Despite lake being a flutter of small sailboats, looking like promenading swans, it is surprising how few people in Portland Metropolitan Area know of this man-made lake. In 1967 the Oregon Dept. of Geology and Mineral Industries collected shark remains in this area: 22 vertebrae, 1 anterior tooth, and a few patches of calcified cartilage. The remains, of course, were not of recent vintage.

0.9 m. turnoff to Cherry Grove.

    * *0.4 m.,* forks. Turn L. 25 yds., "T". Turn L onto Patton Rd *5.1 m.,* **Cherry Grove.** The derivation of the name of this spread-out village was in 1974 given by L. A. Lovegren, who came here in 1910, in a letter to his children: "My father [August Lovegren] wanted a name that had something to do with fruit. He thought of Appleton, but there was another place in Oregon by that name. In talking with a cousin of mine, she suggested Cherry Grove, which is the name of the township (out in the farming country -not even a village) where her home was — and still is. My father liked the name so that is the name. My cousin's home is in Goodhue County, Minnesota." PO 1912–1959. Between 1915 and 1990 Cherry Grove grew at rates of less than 4 people a year, so it can't be all bad. Turn from SW 1st onto Bruce. *0.4 m.,* path to remains of **Cherry Grove Dam,** built 1913. L. A. Lovegren, who was the resident engineer, wrote, "The dam was built to produce a lake for recreation, and as a millpond, with the latter the main reason, though a small-

Remains of Cherry Creek Dam   *Phoebe L. Friedman*

er lake area would have sufficed for this. Early in 1914 there came a big flood
and the boom holding what logs there were in the lake broke and the logs
partially blocked the spillway so the dam was overtopped. However, the dam
itself was not breached, but the south end was against a hill, and the water
broke through there where there was only an earth fill, with a thin core of
concrete." Only slabs of concrete now indicate where the dam blocked the
Tualatin River. There is a medieval mood to the huge, dank, tree-shrouded
rampart thick with undergrown foliage. Return to SW 1st. Turn L. *0.4 m.*,
turn L. *0.8 m.*, on R, Nixon House, collection of rural antiques. *0.1 m.*, turn L.
Park car. Walk to **Little Lee Falls.** Take river path 80 yds. to opening.
Token cascade of Tualatin River. Across river is largest yew tree in state. *1.7
m.*, 65 ft. **Lee Falls,** tumbling down a chute off a rock platform that is beach
for beer-drinking sunbathers.

    0.8 m., from Cherry Grove turnoff — Gaston-Laurelwood Jct.

    * For **Laurelwood,** turn E. *0.9 m.*, jct. Turn R. *1.3 m.*, forks. At corner is
abandoned Hill School, another of those has-beens which dot the Oregon
countryside, though their numbers are swift disappearing. Turn L. *0.6 m.*,
turnoff R on gravel lane. *0.1 m.*, **Hill Cemetery** (1850). Return to Laurelwood Rd. Turn L *1.5 m.*, former Laurelwood Adventist Academy, opened
1903, closed 1985. Academy, shut down for economic reasons, was heart and
soul of village and when it departed a great vacancy came to stay. *1.6 m.*, jct.,
Bald Peak Rd. (R, *2 m.*, **Bald Peak SP.**) (For more on back road to Laurel and
Tigard see *0 219 N*, following.)

Gaston named for 1862 Oregon arrival Joseph Gaston. He tried to make the big time by going into the RR business and was part of a bitter war with Ben Holladay for contract to build RR up Willamette Valley and to Calif. The sharper and rougher Holladay won and Gaston settled for putting thru a narrow gauge line from Dayton to Sheridan. A lawyer and journalist, he ran as a Populist Party candidate for justice of the Supreme Court and was defeated. After he was done with law and business he wrote the 3-volume *Portland, Its History and Builders* and the more solid 4-volume *Centennial History of Oregon,* which in essence left out as much as it said. More a mover than a shaker, Gaston labored at Jacksonville, Salem, Portland, Hood River and Alkali Lake, where he involved himself with soda borax mines, but he did live for some time in this area, where he tried farming on land that had formerly been part of Wapato Lake.

Though Gaston of 1990 had 155 more people than the 400 pop. of 1915, Gaston of 1915 had much more industry and greater activity. Beyond the onion fields the foothills seem to be breakers holding back the push of seaweed waves, and high in the E rises Bald Peak. House at 312 Park is said to date back between 1860 and 1870. House at 314 Park, with steep hipped roof, may be child of 1880s. House at 315 Park, more gussied up, is another town elder. Bates House, 2nd and Oak, built 1890. **Congregational Church** put up 1875, same year church bldg. at 209 Church, formerly Evangelical, was constructed.

0.3 m., on 0 47, Olson Rd.

* *3 m.,* Elk Cove Wineries.

1.9 m., **Wapato.** PO est. 1853 as Wapatoo and had an on-and-off life until death in 1883. All that is now is country store hanging on for survival.

0.4 m., turnoff E to **Dewey.**

* *1.4 m.,* turn R. *1.2 m.,* Dewey Rd. Turn L. *0.1 m.,* Lakeview School turned into duplex. It was called Lakeview because it faced Wapato Lake before lake was drained for onion farms. Across road, near oak tree, say locals, was where Dewey PO stood. PO est. 1898; named in honor of Adm. George Dewey, whose Yankee tars whipped a demoralized Spanish fleet at Manila Bay. But as Dewey's star dimmed, so did Dewey PO, and in 1904 was closed. Still, as late as 1915 village had Farmers Grange and Civic Improvement Club.

2.6 m., **Cove Orchard.** Another 1 store burg — and nothing else. Back of store a seedy derelict of a once-proud school bldg. and a wagon-day church too tired to blink its sleepy eyes.

2.9 m., Pike Rd., in Yamhill.

* Turn W. Keep on Pike Rd. *0.1 m.,* forks. Take L. *3.7 m.,* turn R onto cemetery rd. *0.3 m.,* turn L for **IOOF and Pike Cemetery** (1854), steeped in nostalgia. (For story of Pike Cemetery and of pioneer Hines grave-marker, see "A Peacefulness At Pike" in author's *Tracking Down Oregon.*) One of most memorable and touching tombstones in state is here, that of Katherine Heath Perkins, born in Mass. May 31, 1920, died in Portland Sept. 25, 1979.

Business section of Wapato

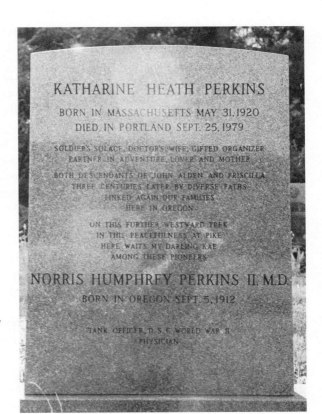

Gravemarker at Pike Cemetery

She was "Soldier's solace, Doctor's wife, gifted organizer, partner in adventure, lover and mother." Both she and her husband, Norris Humphrey Perkins II, M.D., were "descendants of John Alden and Priscilla. Three centuries later by diverse paths linked again our families here in Oregon. On this further westward trek in this peacefulness at Pike here awaits my darling Kae among these pioneers." On the back of the marker are these heart-rendering lines: "May all who ever laughed with Kae/ And shared her dancing eyes/ Celebrate with me thanksgiving/ For memories of her love and life."

If one would adopt the format of Edgar Lee Masters in his *Spoon River Anthology*, this is what Katherine Heath Perkins might say of the inscription on her tombstone: "Dear husband, I understand. This knoll beneath the wave of gentle hills is more fitting of our westward course of history than a cemetery between subdivisions of the city. Here we have come full circle across the continent from the rough and clean woods and fields of Priscilla and John. I await you here, to begin the privacy of our adventure anew. Dear husband, I thank you. I always liked wild roses better."

Five generations of Perkins lie here, with the grass curling around their graves and roses wild on thickets and Scotch broom glowing at the edges.

* Return to Pike Rd. Turn R. *0.9 m.*, **Pike.** Settled by Missourians from Pike Country, named for Zebulon M. Pike, who is also honored by Pike's Peak. Hamlet was never much, and less now, just a couple or so houses. *2.8 m.*, **Menafee Park,** on Turner Creek, with delightful little footbridge and bit of Eden at edge of wilderness. Once many deer and elk roamed here, but the deer have all but been eliminated and the elk are swiftly being slaughtered. The few, thinly-spread families here are more afraid of hunters, particularly spotlighters, who illegally hunt at night by shining lights at the game, thus "freezing" them, than they are of wild animals. Unfortunately, game wardens, who are scarce, generally work daylight hours. Beyond Menafee Park the land is almost uninhabited by humans and the road is sometimes so rough it seems to be sponsored by a tow truck company. (For primitive road to Tillamook, see *Cross-Coast Range Roads, Old Toll Road, Tillamook-Yamhill.*)

Return to Pike. Continue E *2 m.* Turn R toward Fairdale. *5.1 m.*, forks. Turn R onto old State Rd. *4.1 m.*, Fairdale. About 1915 there was here PS, Farmers Grange and mineral spring. Nothing now but small marker. The beauty of the drive from Pike to Fairdale is the undulating characteristics of the Coast Range foothills, the lively streams that hide under the banks of the roads, the rawness yet of some of the land, the green fields, and the feeling of being quite far from the placid towns along 0 47. *0.3 m.*, jct. *1 m.*, **Flying M Ranch,** popular W Oregon guest ranch.

From Yamhill to Fairdale:

* *8.9 m.*, on Fairdale Rd., site of long gone Fairdale, appropriately named by its founders. *0.3 m.*, jct. *1 m.*, Flying M Ranch.

0.4 m., from Pike Rd., **Yamhill,** one of those slow-paced, freckle-faced, casual Yamhill Valley towns whose residents swear they have the best of all things: elbow room; closeness to Portland, the mountains and the coast; unhurried life and good neighbors; ever-changing landscapes and clean air; and a slice of the state that keeps the riches of the past as it saunters into the present. With such a cornucopia of attractions, one wonders why Yamhill has grown so slowly — from 520 pop. in 1915 to 660 in 1990. But no one in town is complaining. Actually, Yamhill had more social and fraternal institutions in 1915 than it has today but who needs them when there are so many TV channels? Among several picturesque 19th century gingerbread houses in Yamhill is the calendar art one, with mansard roof, at W end of 3d St. This was home of prominent childrens book writer Beverly Cleary; here she wrote the popular *Emily's Runaway Imagination.* Laughlin House, across street from Yamhill Elementary School, smacks of faded opulence. United Methodist Church, 1 block S, is striking compartmentalization of old and new

In Yamhill, jct., 0 240:

* *0.1 m.,* on S, Carpenter Gothic Victorian house built 1879 (across street from Yamhill Grade School). *1.7 m.,* Dewey Jct. (to N, Dewey — *5 m.) 0.5 m.,* on S, 19th century rural home of kind that once dotted Yamhill Valley in profusion. *3.3 m.,* jct. (To S, Lafayette, *6.2.,* Carlton, *5.7 m.) 0.7 m.,* Gaston

House at west end of Third St., Yamhill

Jct. (N, 9.6 m., Gaston. At jct., ancient, hoary schoolhouse ages ago boarded up.) 1.7 m., on N, **Ewing Young Marker,** in center of land claim of one of true giants of Oregon pioneers.

Tennessee born, Ewing Young learned the cabinet making trade, then set out for the SW, where he was an intimate of all the great mountain men of the region, including Kit Carson. From Tennessee he carried with him a two volume set of Shakespeare that he read by a thousand campfires. In 1843 he arrived in Oregon with Hall Jackson Kelley, the weak-eyed, sniffling Boston schoolteacher who spent most of his life passionately promoting the Oregon Country. The small party included the 3rd Black man to come to Oregon, the 2nd by land, the 1st to settle. His name was Winslow Anderson and he is best remembered, perhaps, for his role in the "Cockstock Affair," a point of provenance for efforts to exclude Blacks from Oregon soil. (See "Holmes v. Ford: A Chapter in Ebony" in author's *This Side of Oregon*.) Arriving at Ft. Vancouver, the party was erroneously accused by Dr. John McLoughlin of being horse thieves. Kelley was shipped home by way of the Sandwich (Hawaiian) Islands and Young was declared *persona non grata*. Angry, Young took revenge by setting up a still to make whiskey but before he started producing spirits he bowed to the petitioning of Jason Lee's hastily organized temperance society. By 1835 Young had crops growing in the rich soil of the Chehalem Valley, practically all of which he came to own. He also built a gristmill, a sawmill, opened a store, and started other businesses. In 1837 the black-bearded, powerfully-built, iron-willed Young led the first long cattle drive in the nation — from the San Francisco Bay area to the lower Willamette Valley. The drive ranks as one of the epic events in Oregon history and would have been a complete failure without Young's grim determination. It was initiated and largely financed by a secret agent of the US, its purpose being to break the economic monopoly of Hudson's Bay Co. and to Americanize the Oregon Country, but Dr. John McLoughlin, the wily "White-Headed Eagle," invested heavily in the enterprise. (For more on the dramatic undertaking, see "The Great Cattle Drive" in author's *Tales Out of Oregon*.)

In 1837 the articles of incorporation for the cattle company he was instrumental in organizing were the first to be drawn up in Oregon. The following year he built the first sawmill in the valley, on Clackamas Creek near its confluence with the Willamette. It was washed away in 1840.

Young died suddenly, perhaps from pneumonia, on Feb. 15, 1841, leaving no will or known legal heirs. A meeting was called to probate his will. Almost all his belongings were sold, the two volume edition of Shakespeare being purchased by C. M. Walker for $3.50. When his estate was settled it netted $3734.26, which was lent out. Three years later this money was collected and paid into the treasury of the provisional gvmt., which pledged itself to refund the money to Young's heirs or creditors whenever they would appear. (Years later a relative of Young showed up and profited handsomely from the accident of birth.) Of the estate money, $1500 was used to build a jail at Oregon City, the first in the American Far West.

Three-quarters of a century after Young's death the *Oregon Journal* described the event at this estate sale as "The Primary Meeting of the State of Oregon," and added, "His death might well be called the response for organization of the provisional government in Oregon." What is certain is that the political session which followed the estate sale was a strong step forward in the Americanization of Oregon.

Five years after Young's death, an oak was planted in the soil of his grave. Today the Young Oak, as it is known, is a tall and far-spreading tree. No road leads to it from 0 240. From the marker it stands *0.3 m.* to the N, the L of 2 thick, round-topped oaks. (For more, see "A Mighty Oak for Ewing Young" in author's *This Side of Oregon.*)

1.4 m., Sunnycrest Jct. *(1.1 m.,* Sunnycrest, rural suburb of Newberg.) *2.5 m.,* past several interesting structures on R (see O 99W), jct., O 99W, Newberg.

From jct., 0 240, on 0 47:

1.5 m., on E, **Zimmerman Century Farm barn,** build 1869 without single nail. As with many pioneer barns, floor was used in early days for threshing wheat by horses. (Elsewhere, people used their legs for pulping grapes into wine.)

0.2 m., on E, turnoff for **Yamhill-Carlton Pioneer Memorial Cemetery.**

   *** 0.4 m.,* cemetery. Markers date back to 1860s. From this hillock there is a bountiful vista of hills to the W. Soft-sloped mound in foreground across 0 47 is **Alec's Butte,** deeply buried in Oregon legend. Here 1811 arrival Alec (Alexander) Carson, solitary trapper for several years, was killed circa 1814 by Indians and his flesh devoured by wolves. Other trappers, finding his bones, buried them, but his grave has not since then been found.

2 m., **Carlton,** originally called Carl Town, after pioneer Carl family, with PO est. 1874, same year Oregon Central RR built station here. In 1915 town had nearby 2 of best-known livestock farms in state, 3 large nurseries, and was terminus of Carlton & Coast logging RR. Between 1915 and 1990 pop. increased average of less than 9 persons per year, but this overall statistic is misleading. Lumber industry flourished and town swelled until 1933 Tillamook Burn, which destroyed thousands of acres and brought disaster to many businesses. A 2nd forest fire spelled the end of all mills but one, and that one left Carlton in 1957. Since then Carlton's economy has been kept from going under by locals farmers and by folks who work in cities as far away as Salem and Portland. There is a brick bldg. charm to Main St. that sets it off into another age and mood. First Baptist Church, on W Main, with belfry tower and stained glass windows, has solid rural mien of its parishioners. Home on corner of W Main and N Scott has gingerbread and long, narrow windows of late 19th century architecture. House at 741 W Main

Alec's Butte as seen from Yamhill-Carlton Cemetery

started as Methodist Church circa 1900 on land claim of Peter Smith, who came overland at age 50, died at 71, and whose grave is few feet from house.

    * For glimpses of backcountry Carlton, take Meadow Lake Rd. *2.5 m.* to McBride Cemetery Rd. Turn R. *0.4 m.*, entrance to **McBride Cemetery** (1857). Continue straight. *1 m.*, on L, **Bunn House,** built 1860 — or before.
(For Meadow Lake Rd. to US 101, see *Cross-Coast Range Roads, Nestucca River Access Rd.*)

    From Carlton there is a direct road to Newberg, with some indirect interest.

    * *1.4 m.*, turn R, on Mineral Springs Rd., toward Lafayette. *1.1 m.*, turn L onto Bailis Rd. *0.6 m.*, on L, **Youngberg Farm.** (Obtain permission from owner to trek to small burial ground in middle of wheat field.) Here lies Absalom J. Hembree, a Tennessean who hoofed it to Oregon in 1843 at age 30, got himself a DLC here and moved into politics and commerce. He was a sheriff of Yamhill County, a provisional legislator, a director of the Portland and Valley Plank Rd. Co., a Territorial legislator, and president of Pacific Telegraph Co. Then he turned soldier and became Capt. Hembree of Co. E of the 1st Rgt. Sent to fight the Yakima Indians, his military career ended on its 179th day. Near Toppenish, Wash., he set out with 9 others to capture Indian horses. Instead, the Yakimas ambushed the detail and shot Hembree. As his horse ran off he called to his men, "Don't leave me, boys," but his men were riding hell bent to save their own skins. Reinforcements returned Hembree's body to camp, where it was placed on a litter strapped to 2 mules and carried to The Dalles. The steamer *Columbia Belle* brought the corpse to Portland and it was taken to his farm, part of the journey being by canoe on the Yamhill river. On April 20, 9 days after he was slain, he was buried on his farm. It was a grand funeral. The Masons gave him full honors, a brass band played loudly, a company of Volunteers stood at attention and fired off a last salute to their fallen comrade, and between 700 and 1000 people, from all parts of the valley, gathered to honor their hero. Some of the mourners may have thought he should have stayed on his farm; 42 was too old for hard fighting. But others might have replied that no man was too old to kill Indians.

* Return to Mineral Springs Rd. Turn L. *2.2 m.,* on L, Chateau Benoit Winery. *0.8 m.,* on L, **Masonic Lafayette Cemetery** (1855). Beware of poison ivy. *0.8 m.,* on L, Golden West Bird Farm — exotic birds. *0.1 m.,* 0 99W. N, *0.4 m.,* Lafayette.

* From Mineral Springs Rd. turnoff on Carlton-Newberg Rd.:

4.3 m., jct., 0 240. Keep R. *0.8 m.,* on R, abandoned Valley View School. Wild foliage has arisen to screen it from road, as though Death was protecting its own. *1.7 m.,* on N, Ewing Young Marker. *1.4 m.,* Sunnycrest Rd. (*1 m.,* Sunnycrest.) *2.5 m.,* Newberg at 0 99W.

From Carlton, on 0 47:

4.5 m., jct., 0 99W.

O 6 — O 8, Tillamook to Portland

As well known as the Wilson River Highway as its numerical designation, 0 6 is the most direct road between the Tillamook area and metropolitan Portland. It is not a direct road, liaising with either US 26 or 0 8 to complete its journey to the inland valley. A free-styled road with little settlement burdening it, 0 6 can be as crowded as other main thoroughfares on summer weekends. In winter and early spring it seems to be a magnet for rain; certainly it is the floodingest of all roads across the Coast Range.

From downtown Tillamook:

2.5 m., Trask River Jct. (See *Old Toll Road, Tillamook — Yamhill,* following.) *14.9 m.,* to N, **Keening Creek Forest Park.** (*0.5 m.,* spread-out PA and CG in primitive area.) *4.9 m.,* to N, **Jones Creek Forest Park,** deep in the timber. *1 m.,* **Lee's Camp.** Only store, started in 1930s, but important to travelers as landmark and focal point for area's residents. "You wouldn't know so many people live around here but they just pop out of the woods," said the storekeeper. *4.2 m.,* on N, **Elk Creek Forest Camp,** where Elk Creek enters Wilson River.

* *0.4 m.,* start of CG. From here, moderate to difficult 2-m. trail extends from elev. 817 to 3,226 ft. across King Mtn.; difficult 3-m. trail crosses King Mtn. and Elk Mtn.; 6-m. jaunt via logging road and trail to King Mtn. is suitable for hikers and horse riders (along way is "Coast Range rock garden" with rare plants such as the smooth *douglasia* and the fringed *synthyris*) and

an easy 9 m. trail, also suitable for horseriding, that passes University Falls and ends up at Camp Brown. This trail follows old Wilson River Wagon Road, opened 1933 as way from Tillamook to Gales Creek. The big timber along this route was somehow missed by the 3 devastating Tillamook fires.

4.8 m., **Tillamook Burn Historical Marker.** This point was swept by all 3 fires which ravaged large expanses of trees. The first was in 1933, which burned 240,000 acres and destroyed 12 billion board ft. of Oregon's finest timber, enough to build more than a million modern 5-room houses. This fire broke out on August 14 and was held in relative check for 10 days, 40,000 acres being consumed. Then — let the *Forest Log* of the Oregon State Dept. of Forestry tell the story:

"But with the coming of daylight on the morning of Aug. 24, the picture changed. Dust rose in clouds from the summer fallow in the valley carried by a new surge of east wind. Humidity again dropped. Foresters knew the threat and ordered fire fighters away from the west side of the fire.

"Over a 15-mile front, the Tillamook fire broke out with a fury. Massive thunderheads of smoke boiled and surged to a height of 40,000 feet, spreading out to darken coastal cities.

"The fire rolled up through the forest of the Coast Range with a frightening force, uprooting trees, twisting them off and cracking cliffs with the terrific heat.

"A choking, blinding smoke settled in the valleys until cars had to creep along in a cloud denser than any fog that ever rolled in from the Pacific Ocean. Charred needles of trees, ashes and cinders fell in the streets of Tillamook. The debris fell to a depth where it had to be scooped up in shovels.

"By late evening the east wind had died down and a fog rolled in from the Pacific Ocean. But the 40,000 acres of that morning had grown to 240,000 acres just 20 hours later."

In 1939 the woods were struck by another holocaust, which covered about 190,000 acres, much of it within the original burn. And in 1945 a third fire consumed 180,000 acres of timber.

After many legal complications, planting began in late Nov., 1949. In 1973 the former burn was dedicated as Tillamook State Forest. Fifty years after the first fire the first commercial thinning timber sale was sold in the TSF. It was then recognized that the Tillamook Burn had, for all practical purposes, been reforested.

0.2 m., Coast Range Summit — 1586 ft.

Jct., Rogers — Camp Brown.

* Entrance to **Rogers Camp,** wayside that is starting point for motorcycle trails. Turn R. **Rogers Memorial Forest.** 2.6 m., thru thrice-savaged woods, **Camp Brown,** PA and CG basically for motorcyclists.

2.5 m., **Gales Creek Forest Park.** (1 m. to shaded campsites.)

2.5 m., turnoff N to **Oregon Electric Railway Museum,** formerly Trolley Park.

* One of the best family fun places in Portland Metropolitan Area. Com-

plete electric 1910 style trolley system with shops, car barn, depot and all types of trolley cars, including double-decker from Blackpool, England, SF cable car, open car from Sydney, Australia, and old time Portland car. Fishing, swimming, picnicking in and on Gales Creek. Overnight camping in park reached only by vintage trolley cars. There is a legend that the first Tillamook fire started here, on a very hot day, when friction of heavy logging chain pulled across another heavy chain set off the sparks that erupted into flames. More natural than trolley facility is rough dirtlane, chuckhole, thorny community huddled against trees.

0.1 m., **John W. Blodgett Arboretum,** cool retreat and forest textbook owned by Pacific U. *1.1 m.,* jct. (Timber, *6.2 m.;* Vernonia, *21.4 m.*) *0.5 m.,* Glenwood Store, W wing of aptly-named spread-out hamlet that is older than it seems; PO est. 1886. *0.3 m.,* on L, rude plank private bridge across Gales Creek. *0.9 m.,* on L, picturesque private foot bridge across Gales Creek. *1.7 m.,* jct., O 8. (For O 8, see at end of O 6.)

On O 6 from O 8 jct.:

6.8 m., jct., O 47 — Banks. (See O 47, preceding. *2.6 m.,* jct., US 26. (See *Cross-Coast Range Roads, US 26,* preceding.)

O 8 from jct., O 6:

1.7 m., on L, **Balm Grove.** Here were held the country dances of yore. Dance hall, on creek, burned down decades ago.

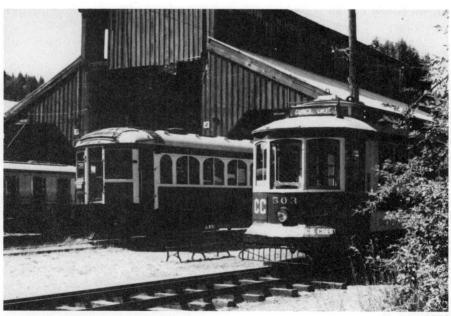

Oregon Electric Railway Museum, Glenwood   *Courtesy OEHS*

0.3 m., on L, Clapshaw Hill Rd.

* *0.9 m.,* brow of hill — and suddenly the valley magically opens. *0.3 m.,* on R, **Hillside Cemetery.** Buried here under one stone are Edward and Fanny Faul, who gave land for Hillside School. The inscription on the Edward Faul side of marker reads, "We will meet again." On other side, under name of Fanny Faul, are etched the words, "Reunion after many a lonely year." He died in 1895; she in 1909. She had waited 14 years. *0.1 m.,* Hillside Church and historic **Hillside School.** (See *Trips Out of Portland, West Tour B.*)*0.2 m.,* turn L onto Old Clapshaw Hill Rd. *1 m.,* forks. Take Seavy Rd. *0.3 m.,* turn L for Tualatin Vineyards. *0.3 m.,* winery. The view from here evokes image of fruit bowl: the hills comprise the rim and the rich vale is the fruit. Return to turnoff to vineyards. Turn L. *1.6 m.,* Kansas City.

0.7 m., **Gales Creek,** named for versatile pioneer Joseph Gale — trapper, shipbuilder, sailor, farmer, founding father, and much more. He came to Oregon with Ewing Young in 1834 and settled in this area but moved across state when chimney smoke of new neighbors came too close. He was then 50 but still the mountain man in spirit. In Baker County he trapped, farmed, married a Nez Perce woman named Eliza, fathered 5 children, died on his farm at age 81. First school built 1859, present bldg. modern. Gales Creek Church built before turn of century; is typical of rural churches that have added modern wings to original centerpiece. House across O 8 from store was built 1860s but completely remodeled.

1.7 m., on L, Shafer Vineyard Cellars. *2.1 m.,* turn R onto Stringtown Rd. *(0.2 m.,* on L, site of millrace which directed water from Gales Creek to produce power for local sawmills.)

2.2 m., on L, Thatcher Rd. (Turnoff to Kansas City.) (See *Trips Out of Portland, West Tour B.*)

0.7 m., turn R onto Ritchie Rd., at E end of Forest Grove HS. *(0.3 m.,* on R, **Forest View Cemetery,** est. 1846.)

0.2 m., jct., O 47S. *0.3 m.,* jct., O 47N — downtown **Forest Grove.** City is seat of Pacific U and calls itself "Balladtown" for annual Barber Shop Quartet happening, which jams streets of otherwise low-keyed city. In 1915 Forest Grove was almost as big as Hillsboro and 6 times larger than Beaverton. (It also had concrete sidewalks, which Beaverton did not.) In 1990 Forest Grove was about one-third the size of Beaverton and Hillsboro, but more liveable. (For more on Pacific U and Forest Grove, see O 47S, preceding.)

1.2 m., Oak St., turnoff L for Porter Grove and Verboort. (See *Trips Out of Portland, West Tour B.*)

0.2 m., turnoff S to McMinnville. *1.2 m.,* **Cornelius,** at 10th Ave. Town named for 1845 pioneer T. R. Cornelius, who became Col. Cornelius fighting Indians. In 1915 Cornelius actually had more pop. than Beaverton; in 1990 it was only one-sixth the size.

2.6 m., the 1-way branches of O 8 enfold **Hillsboro Pioneer Cemetery** (1862), where lie the white roots and limbs of the area.

0.8 m., **Hillsboro** — jct., O 219N. Seat of Washington County, burgeoning Hillsboro is now plagued by spillover of urban problems. Settled by whites around 1845, place was first called East Tualatin Plain, then Columbia and Columbus. In 1850 name changed to Hillsborough, honoring early comer David Hill, one of the May 2, 1843 "Men of Champoeg" and in 1847 chosen to represent the district of Twality in the provisional legislature. In 1855 town officially became Hillsboro. Celebrated early in century for hops, Hillsboro is better known today as hi-tech center.

0.8 m., Cornelius Pass Rd. Drivers of commercial vehicles Portland-bound often turn N here to US 26, Sunset Hwy., because that road is easier to travel than O 8.

0.7 m., Farmington Jct. *(5 m.,* Farmington.) *3.5 m.,* Jct., Orenco — West Union. *0.3 m.,* on S, most conspicuous and best-known landmark along O 8, giant rabbit facing road in front of Harvey Marine. First rabbit placed here circa 1960; present rabbit is 24' 3 1/2" in height.

Here, too, for whatever it is worth, is ambiguous village of **Reedville,** scarcely suggesting solid affluence of Columbia River transportation tycoon and mercantalist Simeon G. Reed, after whom place was named, because he had blooded stock farm here before there was a town. (PO est. 1877.) More in line with Reed's grandeur of style is Portland's Reed College, founded upon wealth of his property after death of his widow, Amanda Wood Reed.

0.2 m., 209th Ave.

   * Turn R. *0.5 m.,* turn L onto Kinnaman. *0.1 m.,* on R, **Masters House,** built 1853.

1.2 m., **Aloha.** Place is so confusingly spread out one doesn't know where to say hello or goodbye. Founded 1912, Aloha was called "suburban" early on. People who move from Portland to places like Aloha to escape urban living find that, in their plastic middle class warrens, they have jumped from the lukewarm frying pan to the very hot fire.

3 m., downtown **Beaverton.** *0.4 m.,* jct., O 217S — to Tigard and O 99W. *0.4 m.,* jct., O 219N — to US 26. *1.3 m.,* West Slope, a rather recent bedroom in the Portland mansion. *1.7 m.,* turnoff to Sylvan.

   * *0.2 m.,* turn L onto Skyline Blvd. (Do not turn R onto prior Scholls Ferry Rd.) 1 block, turn R onto SW 58th. 1 block, turn L at Metropolitan Baptist Church. *0.1 m.,* turn onto roadway of church. In rear of church is **Jones Cemetery,** aka Sylvan and Zion. Cemetery est. 1854 but oldest gravestone is 1863. Most prominent person buried here is Nathan B. Jones, 1847 pioneer who founded Zion Town (or at least gave the area that name) and platted lots under name of Zion in 1892–93. By then, however, PO of Sylvan opened (1890); closed 1906. Postal authorities had turned down name of Zion; too much confusing duplication. Jones, a hermit who would today be called an eccentric old hippie, splash-painted the outside of his house with psychedelic colors and confided to those who would listen that his great aim in life was to make Zion Town the political and cultural capital of Oregon. But on Jan. 25, 1894, he was fatally beaten in robbery attempt.

4 m., Portland city center.

Old Toll Road — Tillamook to Yamhill

The roughest of Cross-Coast Range Roads, this one is little-known even by locals and is seldom used. It is not improbable to drive the entire Old Toll Road without meeting another vehicle or seeing, as the only signs of "civilization," the ugly tire slashes of motorbikes and the occasional print of a logging truck.

From Tillamook, on O 6:

2.5 m., turn S onto Trask River Rd. 0.3 m., **Fairview. Fairview School** and **Foursquare Church** occupy same bldg., one of few places in state where church and school combine to share space. School put up in 1920s. 0.5 m., on R, **Obrist House,** erected late 1870s or early 1880s. 0.9 m., Trask River Jct. Turn L. Road now accompanies **Trask River,** named for Elbridge Trask, who first came to Oregon in 1834, returned in 1842, and lived in Tillamook County from 1852 until his death in 1863. For next 10 m. road looks up to joyous scenes of the Coast Range, full-bodied in green undulation and such a welcome sight after seeing so much of NW Oregon hills butchered, as though self-doomed humanity had sought to mutilate nature before blowing up the planet. Along this road are ecstatic touches of Switzerland — the hills, the stream, the redolent meadows, the neat farmhouses, the fat-bellied barns, the lazying cows. 10.4 m., **Trask River Forest Park,** at confluence of N and S forks of Trask River. CG 0.9 m., Trask River Store and PG at small settlement.

Backtrack 0.2 m. for Old Toll Rd., on R. This passage, especially in the W half, is not for the tenderfoot unaccustomed to atrocious mountain pikes. Once pavement is left, near Trask Store, the horrors begin. With deft driving, count on averaging 7 m. per hour the first 2 hours. After that the road becomes a speedway, where the heady motorist can push the pedal down to 20 m. an hour at stretches. On this road, where only feverish motorcyclists and cool-nerved log drivers feel at home, the Coast Range in all its primitive nakedness is seen better than anywhere else in NW Oregon. For those who think the Coast Range is the gentlest and simplest of Oregon mtn. chains, come here. The range is seen as a convolution of intricate links, with hills falling away and exploding to higher hills. Deer burst from thickets to stare at the newcomers before plunging into safe greenery. When the sun is blazing upon the valley floor, this road is in twilight. Not a habitation is seen for 23 m., which at times can seem to be a hundred. 23.8 m. from start, near Trask Store, Toll Rd. escapes from the cage of timber at the Flying M Ranch — Fairdale jct. (R, 1.3 m/. Flying M Ranch, guest ranch.) Straight: 9.2 m., O 47 — Yamhill.

O 219N — *Hillsboro to Newberg*

From O 8, Hillsboro.
3.9 m., Burkhalter Rd.
   * Turn L. *0.4 m.*, "T". Turn R. *0.2 m.*, on R. Oak Knoll Winery. *0.4 m.*, on L, **Lewis Cemetery** (1847), one of oldest burial grounds in state.
1.6 m., Farmington Jct.
   * *1.3 m.*, turn L. (*0.6 m.*, on R, early Farmington School, which in abandonment looks like shabby, deserted scarecrow.) Return to Farmington Rd. Turn L. *0.9 m.*, **Farmington.** Tavern. (PO 1884–1904.) *1.4 m.*, on S, yellow house that suggests it was one of valley's elite when built 1880s or 1890s. *1.8 m.*, Hazeldale. Store. *2.5 m.*, on N, 16575 Farmington Rd., red house with windmill and water tower. Attractive turn-of-century mansion. *2.4 m.*, Beaverton.
1.1 m., Laurel Jct.
   * Turn R. *1.4 m.*, **Laurel Valley Store,** probably built around 1910, with modern horse and buggy folksiness. It is hard to imagine that a town once stood here: In 1915 Laurel had pop. 150, 2 sawmills, 2 churches, HS and PS.
   * Straight, *0.6 m.*, on R, **Mt. Olive Cemetery** — 1878. Return to Laurel Valley Store. Turn L. *3 m.*, jct., Bald Peak — Laurelwood Rds.
   * Angle L onto Bald Peak Rd. The roller coaster pike is as exhilarating as the flashes of farmsteads and hills that fall away into gossamer images. *2.1 m.*, **Bald Peak SP.** PA, scads of grass, woods to tramp, and, of course, the viewpoint. Bald Peak (1,629 ft.) would be only a pimple in the Cascades but local elevation and topography give it a commanding position in these low hills. The result: dazzling vistas of the valleys and troughs below.
   * Return to Bald Peak-Laurelwood Rds. jct. Turn L onto Laurelwood Rd. Caution is advised here, for the road is steep as it twists down a burry spur of the Chehalem Hills. *1.7 m.*, and seemingly longer, bldgs. of former **Laurelwood Adventist Academy,** opened 1903, closed 1985. School song boasted: "Laurelwood's the greatest place/ On this old earth's battered face;/ Nestled close among the hills,/ Midst Laurel shade and rippling rills;/ Far from noisy care and strife/ Here we live a sheltered life . . . " The last line could be said again. *1.5 m.*, forks. At corner is educational relic, old Hill School. Turn R. *0.6 m.*, turnoff R on gravel lane. (*0.1 m.*, **Hill Cemetery** — 1860.) Return to Laurelwood Rd. *1.3 m.*, Gaston Rd. Turn L *0.9 m.*, O 47. (*0.4 m.*, to S, Gaston.)
From O 219N at Laurel Jct.:
2.2 m., jct., Laurel-Laurelwood. Road goes to same places as listed above.
0.9 m., Kelvin Grove Stock Farm. Largest number of llamas in W Oregon here, along with other exotic animals. Phone for permission to visit ranch.
1.5 m., jct., O 210.

* (L, *0.7 m.*, Scholls Store. For more on area, see O 99W, Tigard, Bull Mtn. Rd.)

Turn R onto O 219N at jct., O 210.)

1. m., **Mountainside Cemetery** (1886). Total community effort, as reflected in statement of principles written May 30, 1902 by pioneer W. W. Jaquith: "There is hardly anything that reflects the character of a community as does the condition of the neighborhood cemetery. If the fence is all broken and rotted down, the ground covered with brush and successive layers of weeds and grass with a general air of neglect and don't care about it, we rightly can conclude that there is something the matter with the business management and the moral sense of that community. 'Dead and Forgotten' is an epitaph which could rightly be written over the gate of many a country cemetery."

0.1 m., walnut dryer, the kind of which there were once more in the valley.

0.3 m., Jaquith Rd.

* Turn R. *1.4 m.*, turn R for Mulhausen Vineyards — Chehalem Mtn. Winery.

3.3 m., Chehalem Mtn. Summit — 1,272 ft.

50 yds., turnoff R for Bald Peak SP.

* *3.1 m.*, jct. Straight. *2.9 m.*, **Bald Peak SP.**

1.5 m., another turnoff to **Bald Peak SP.** It connects to prior road to SP.

1.5 m., Springbrook Rd.

* Turn L. *2.3 m.*, jct. On opposite corner, **Uplands Farm,** built 1889 on 1852 DLC. Impressive. Photogenic. Turn R. *2.3 m.*, O 99W.

2.3 m., **Newberg.** Turn L on O 99W. *0.7 m.*, O 219, S-bound. (See O 99W, *Newberg*, for continuation of O 219.)

Nestucca River Access Road — Beaver to Carlton

This was once known as Meadow Lake Road but lake was drained some time ago. Practically limited to fishers and campers, there is not a station or store for almost 50 miles. Much of the way this lonely, very scenic pike looks down upon the Nestucca, a stream that seems to revel in its solitude. Well, perhaps it is not so much alone, for trees bend low over it to keep watch and grasses gather at every bend to herald salutation and wildflowers pop out of bogs to swish their yellow and pink and scarlet banners at the river, which responds with silvery sprays.

6.9 m., **Blaine.** Appropriately, PO (and town) named in 1892 for James G. Blaine, a Republican who almost made it to the presidency and who was later dubiously honored by the mythical James G. Blaine Society, dedicated to keeping the rest of the world out of Oregon. The outsiders sure haven't come to Blaine, whose old schoolhouse is going board by board. The burg seem as empty as a windbag's promise. It takes a bit of pondering to accept the fact that 150 people lived here in 1915.

7.8 m., **Rocky Bend FS CG,** small piece of paradise on island of shadow. *2.8 m.,* **Alder Glen Rec. Site.** *(0.1 m.* upstream, on opposite side, shy and modest waterfall which some irreverent wag named "Tom Thumb.") *2.5 m.,* those who know area say bald eagles frequent and nest here. Look at a distance. *0.6 m.,* **Elk Bend Rec. Site.** *3.3 m.,* **Fan Creek Rec. Site.** *2.8 m.,* **Dovre Rec. Site.** *2.2 m.,* on N, or L, road to pike and Yamhill. *(0.1 m.* W of bridge over Nestucca.)

    * This is a very rough unpaved road, not meant for the impatient or for cars with weak shocks. Isolated, the met vehicle is rare. For compensation: subtle waterfalls gliding off the rocky side; now and then a bayou-like pool; rich views of the Coast Range, including strange-shaped hills, one that, when sails of clouds are tacked to its firs, looks like a hermaphrodite brig; and the feeling that here you are really alone. The road grinds thru the Tillamook Burn for *26.6 m.* — 26 m. without human habitation — to Menafee Park, small PA at Turner Creek. *2.8 m.,* site of former village of **Pike.** *0.9 m.,* turnoff L to **Pike Cemetery** *(0.2 m.).* For the pastoral romanticist this unspoiled, pioneer burial ground is pure delight — the slope flowing into a meadow, rising to a mounded plateau, and lapping against the upland woods. (See O *47S,* preceding.) *4 m.,* O *47S,* at Yamhill.

From turnoff to Menafee Park and Yamhill:

0.1 m., bridge above deep rocky canyon thru which Nestucca River charges. *3.9 m.,* **McGuire Dam and Res.** *0.8 m.,* first view of Yamhill Valley. The sudden and expansive vista is as throbbing as the drive thru the woods; the sense at night is of being released by darkness to a world of light. Now the road comes tumbling into the valley, which slides into a hundred undulating patterns. There are farms with seemingly acres of wooden white fences, a hill which looks like a giant salmon covered with parsley, lawns where tulips and geraniums run to the road to greet visitors, as though they were friendly dogs, and Jersey cows who turn to look at milky clouds floating across the lea. *4.5 m.,* turnoff N, or L, to **McMinnville City Water and Light Park.** *(0.6 m.,* turn L for PA. *0.1 m.,* PA. Lovely park alongside creek and at foot of gusty falls. 200 yds. uphill to pretty lake.) *2.6 m.,* on N, or L, turnoff for Flying M Ranch. *(4.5 m.,* Fairdale Jct. Turn L. *1 m.,* **Flying M Ranch,** dude spread at contoured cove of Coast Range.) *6.8 m.,* O *47S* — Carlton.

0 22W — Hebo to Salem

Unlike 0 18, with which it partially shares pavement to the Willamette Valley, 0 22 W is leafy, winding, neighborly and uncrowded. It seems more of a farm road than a through pike and as such is preferable to travel on a hectic summer day.

From Hebo — US 101:

0.2 m., turnoff to Hebo Lake.

    * *4.8 m.,* **Hebo Lake FS CG,** at deep green pond in maw of forest. *1.1 m.,* compound of Mt. Hebo Air Force Station. *2.2 m.,* jct. To R on dirt road,

Hebo CG *(2 m.)* North Lake *(3 m.)*, South Lake *(4 m.)*. Straight, at top of 3,153-ft.-high Mt. Hebo, Mt. Hebo Radar Station. Vistas from road to summit are stirring — folds of green, green hills engulfing swaths of meadows, and yonder here and there a dollhouse on a farm.

1.2 m., **Cedar Creek Fish Hatchery.** Cutthroat trout, chinook salmon and steelhead reared here. Large brood trout held all year. Spawning salmon and steelhead viewed in Cedar Creek Sept. to late March.

3 m., **Castle Rock FS CG.** *6.2 m.,* Little Nestucca River Jct. *(9.4 m., US 101.)* *3.2 m.,* Coast Range Summit — 672 ft.

8.1 m., site of **Grand Ronde Indian Agency,** where Catholic Church now stands, on NW corner. Indians from several W Oregon tribes were placed on reservation; 1867 census showed Indian count to be 1064. In 1908 supt. of reservation transferred to Siletz and 2 agencies combined. After Grand Ronde Reservation terminated, land divided among remaining Indians and some land still farmed by descendants of Indians and, in cases of intermarriage (not infrequent) interracial settlers. In 1915 there were about 300 Indians and 60 whites still on reservation land. Community then had Catholic and German Methodist churches, Commercial Club and 18-piece Indian band. A new trading post was est. to S (on O 18) and is Grand Ronde of today.

2.3 m., turn L onto dead end Old Fort Rd. *0.2 m.,* on R, barn-like house that local legend holds was built by Phil Sheridan in 1856. (An article in the 8-29-15 issue of *The Oregonian* was headed: "Phil Sheridan's Oregon Home at Grand Ronde Agency is Razed." The article stated: "Sheridan's home is being torn down this week to make room for a modern farm house. Where the fort stood is now a grain field, but the hill is still known as the fort hill.") Uphill to L (when facing house) is presumed site of Ft. Yamhill, est. 1856 and evacuated 10 years later. The fort, garrisoned by a small contingent of Calif. volunteers, consisted of an officers' quarters, barracks, hospital, laundress' quarters, bakery, stable, granary, guard house and store house unevenly spaced around a central parade ground of 1,300 sq. ft. with blockhouse and flag staff in center. There was also a sutler's store and PO, est. 1861 by Benjamin Simpson, father of famed poet Samuel Simpson, and called Grand Ronde because PO, like fort, was on Grand Ronde Indian Reservation. In 1894 this PO was moved to Grand Ronde Agency. A year later a new PO, Butler, was opened at former fort site, to serve immediate area. It was closed in 1911. After Ft. Yamhill was abandoned, blockhouse was moved to Grand Ronde Agency and used as jail. In 1911, after some fast sleight-of-hand politics, blockhouse was carted to Dayton.

Several officers of prominence had at least some casual connection with Ft. Yamhill. The most famous was Phil Sheridan, who as a lieutenant was stationed at the fort on and off from 4-25-1856 to 9-1-1861. Itching to be called to action in the Civil War, Sheridan eagerly waited from week to week for the day when the post's courier was expected back from Portland. "I would go out early in the morning to a commanding point above the post, from which I could see a long distance down the road as it ran through the valley of the Yamhill," he wrote, "and there I would watch with anxiety for his coming, longing for good news." When finally Sheridan was summoned to action he quickly packed his necessities, mounted his horse, gathered his men around him, and called, "I am going into this war to win a captain's spur, or die with my boots on. Goodbye, boys, I may never see you again." He died with his boots off as a 4 star general.

    0.7 m., jct., 0 18. *0.8 m.,* Valley Junction, another brief hwy. strip. Fort Hill Rd.

      * Turn L, or N. *0.2 m.,* turn L onto Hill Rd. 677. *0.4 m.,* forks at house. Take L, up cow pasture. *0.1 m.,* forks. Walk up hill *0.2 m.* to reservoir. Walk *250 yds.* to L, thru woods, to brow of hill overlooking shelf. Below is supposed site of Ft. Yamhill.

    3 m., Willamina-Sheridan exit.

      * *2.3 m.,* **Willamina,** drawing its name from creek honoring first white woman to cross it on horseback, Willamina Maley, later Willamina Williams. An overland emigrant of 1845 she was never a resident of this area. Settled in the 1850s, Willamina grew as a brick and tile factory, sawmill, and veneer plant town, but growth has been slow, especially after state hwy. was removed to S.

      * From downtown, go W *0.3 m.* to Branson St. Turn sharp, uphill *0.1 m.,* on R, **Willamina Cemetery,** with graves harkening back to 1850s. From downtown, turn off Main St. R onto Willamina Creek Dr. *2.3 m.,* turn L. *0.1 m.,* picturesque 1903 Fendall School. Return to Willamina Creek Rd. Turn L. *2.2 m.,* on L, **Blackwell Park,** tranquil dab of greenery on Willamina Creek. PG. *0.7 m.,* Buck Hollow Rd. Turn R. *0.2 m.,* on R, **Buck Hollow Cemetery,** gravestones dating back to 1866. *1.3 m.,* Rock Creek Rd. Turn L. *1.1 m.,* on L, **Highland Cemetery** (1865).

      * E from Willamina: *3.3 m.,* Rock Creek Rd. Turn N onto it. *1.5 m.,* entrance to former Jesuit Novitiate and Delphian (Scientologist) school, now federal prison. View of valley is best in area. Return to Willamina-Sheridan Rd. Turn L, or E. *1.4 m.,* turn N off W Main onto Lincoln. Follow Lincoln around school; it becomes Evans. *0.8 m.* from W Main, **Masonic Cemetery,** gnarled burial ground on hillock. Return to W Main. Turn E. *0.1 m.,* main intersection, **Sheridan,** on S fork of Yamhill River and named for Phil Sheridan, whose memory is celebrated in summer horsey doings, Phil Sheridan Days. Town is ultra-sensitive to lumber economy and has melancholy look of depressed Appalachia when economy is pinched. Somehow it has never risen above its bootstraps. In 1850s, even before PO was est. (1866), Sheridan Academy, a satellite of Willamette U, was chartered by M. E. Church but school did not open until 1880. Six years later it closed, with the announcement that "patronage is insufficient to justify its opening." Gussied-up former RR station is about as pretty as any in state and is former bank branch. Only a few 19th century homes remain in Sheridan. Typical is one at 236

Water, put together with square nails and windows with pegs. *1.5 m.* —from main intersection of Sheridan — 0 18. (Backtrack on 0 18 for 0 22.)

From Willamina-Sheridan Exit on 0 22:

0.4 m., 0 22 leaves 0 18 and rolls on toward Salem.

4.1 m., on R, Gooseneck Creek Rd. White house on corner was residence of famed opera singer Ernestine Schumann-Heink. House, originally located on Mill Creek Rd., was moved to present site in 1940s, say local oldtimers. Schumann-Heink, in Oregon, fell in love with this part of state and, according to *Oregon: End of the Trail,* "came to live for a time to rest after a strenuous concert tour abroad."

0.1 m., on L, **Buell** — just a small store. In 1915 Buell had PS, M.E. Church, W.O.W. Lodge.

* At store, make R turn. *0.4 m.,* on L, **Buell CP.** There, Buell Grange hall. Across road, old Buell School, sleeping away in nature's rest home.

0.5 m., on R, Mill Creek Dr.

* *0.2 m.,* on R, site of **Cruikshank Farm,** where Madame Schumann-Heink lived in Oregon. House later moved to Gooseneck Creek Rd. *2 m.,* **Mill Creek CP,** small green wayside in cluster of firs. *0.3 m.,* **Mill Creek Rec. Site,** BLM hideaway for privacy-seeking wayfarers.

0.3 m., on L, or N, largest white oak in state — guarded by poison oak.

1.8 m., Beck Rd.

* L, *0.2 m.,* **Singing Winds,** goat dairy.

1.6 m., Ballston Jct. *(5.8 m.,* Ballston. See 0 18, below.)

1.2 m., approximate site, say local historians, of Jesse Applegate's cabin, where first articles of the Oregon unofficial gvt. were revised. In this vicinity the 3 Applegate brothers — Jesse, Lindsay and Charles — laid out their sq. m. claim.

1.7 m. on R, or S, Salt Creek Rd.

* Turn S. *1.7 m.,* on R, Salt Creek Baptist Church. *0.2 m.,* on L, turnoff to **Salt Creek Cemetery** *(0.3 m.)* Markers back to 1847.

0.6 m., Perrydale Jct. *(5.5 m.,* Perrydale. See 0 18 below.)

0.9 m., jct., 0 223. (See 0 223 immediately following 0 22.)

1.5 m., on N, information boards, **Baskett Slough Wildlife Refuge** — literally for the birds. Canada geese and ducks concentrate here up to 6 weeks in mid-spring.

1.4 m., turnoff to Dallas.

0.4 m., jct., 099W — Rickreall. (See *The Great Heartland,* 0 99W.)

3.8 m., on L, or N, **Brunk House.** One of oldest and showiest pioneer homes in Willamette Valley, lovingly restored by Polk County Historical Society.

0.4 m., jct., 0 51. (See following.)

1.5 m., **Holman SP.** PA. In this immediate area, on N bank of Willamette River, stood pioneer village of **Cincinnati,** PO est. 1851; name changed 1856 to Eola. It was one of many villages which aspired to be territorial capital of Oregon. Not a stick or stone remains. Area is still known as Eola but Cincinnati seems more fitting because it reminded the namer of Cincinnati, Ohio. And so it still does, for the broad Willamette can beckon a homesick soul to memory of the free-flowing Ohio, though the Willamette is cleaner now. But around 1850 the Ohio may have been pretty clean. The great suffragist, Abigail Duniway, taught school at Cincinnati when she was 18.

2.1 m., jct., 0 221. (See *0 221,* following.)

2.3 m., downtown Salem.

0 223 — 0 22 to US 20

If the state roads of the "Sunday Drive" still exist, one of them is surely 0 223. Light of traffic, it is neither a prime commercial road nor a link between sea and valley. Only one community along 0 223 can without blushing be called a town; the other gatherings of people, always sparse in number, are scarcely noticed. There aren't great thrills along 0 223; no explosive tourist attractions, nothing of Brobdingnagian proportion. But, as a traveler observe, "Everything is real." It is a road where people live as they please and where old barns can weep without feeling embarrassed and no hovel cringes when a Cadillac struts by (though this not a Cadillac road). The pleasant, malleable hills dance in the sun and throw their hemlock hair back in the rain, the cows are in eternal portrait, the sheep are certain that all that is wanted of them is their fleece, dogs bark in surprise that others know of their secreted world. 0 223 ought to be denumeraled and renamed "The Road of the Sunday Drive," whatever day Sunday falls upon.

From 0 22, *3.3 m.* W of 0 99W:

0.5 m., on R, **Polk Station,** RR stop of yore. House at SW corner built 1875; was schoolhouse for many years. What was store and PO form utility room of brown house on NE corner.

　　* E on Fir Villa Rd. *0.8 m.,* **Harland Ranch.** Turn L for ranch house. On farm is **Fast Cemetery,** which supposedly holds 36 bodies — but few markers remain. There are many such small burial plots thruout state and this one is typical. Inquire at house for permission to visit cemetery.

0.8 m., on R, **Brown Cemetery.** Markers go back to 1860s. Empty, shattered vault is trash bin — and the dead weep.

1.5 m., Ellendale Ave., in Dallas.

　　* Turn W onto Ellendale. *1.5 m.,* on R, **Bottle Ranch.** Everything decorative here made of bottles — chapel, wishing well, Xmas tree, etc. Work of a single couple, who collected bottles from roadsides in their area. *0.8 m.,* Reuben Boise Rd. (Turn R. *0.5 m.,* Ellendale Winery, cheerfully operated. Tasting room is art exhibit of paintings by co-owner.) Return to Ellendale Rd. Turn R. *0.3 m.,* approximate site of **Ellendale,** pioneer settlement (1845). First grist mill in Polk County here, at creek. Among prominent names associated with village: James A. O'Neil, James W. Nesmith, Reuben P. Boise. Settlement underwent various name changes: O'Neil's Mills,

Pumping Station Bridge

Bottle Ranch

Phoebe L. Friedman

Nesmiths, Hudson, finally Ellendale. In 1860 woolen mill opened here —
but that was Last Hurrah for Ellendale. Nothing to indicate past. At approximate site of Ellendale, forks. Take R, Robb Mill Rd. *50 yds.,* forks. Take L,
Martin Rd. *1.8 m.,* to L, lane, blocked by mounds of earth. About *60 yds.* up
lane, **Pumping Station CB,** built 1915–16 at length of 84 ft. Narrowest of
Oregons CBs, it is also the ugly duckling of all the state's roofed spans and the
most vandalized, probably because of its secretiveness. (Very few people
know how to get to it; it cannot be seen from road and it is utterly un-
protected.) Fires have been built on board floor and pieces of the CB have
been removed for burning. Bridge is over Rickreall Creek, water source for
city of Dallas.

0.7 m. — from Ellendale Rd. — **Polk County Court House,** the attractive
part built 1889–1900 of local sandstone and covered with ivy — or Virginia
Creeper. On grounds is mill stone from grist mill on Rock Creek built 1850s.

On SE corner of county complex stands old oak ignominiously used for masked
vigilante hanging in 1887. None of the lynchers, about 30 in number, punished.
Victim was Oscar Kelty, who had fatally shot his wife. Some years after the

The Hanging Tree, Dallas   *Phoebe L. Friedman*

lynching the limb from which Kelty was strung up was blown down in a storm, as though the wind wanted to destroy the mark of shame. But the tree later became the gallows of legal public executions. The local paper has a copy of invitation sent out in 1900 by sheriff to those he favored to watch spectacle of a condemned man have his neck broken by a rope. (For more, see "The Hanging Tree" in author's *This Side of Oregon.*)

Town of **Dallas** — named for George M. Dallas, vice president of US in administration of James K. Polk — grew up around La Creole Academy, which opened in second half of 1850s as non-sectarian, coeducational school. In 1900 La Creole Academy merged with Lafayette Seminary, founded 1889 by Evangelical Church. Out of this merger came **Dallas College.**

The Dallas College basketball team, known as "The Oregons," was first team of state cagers to gain national recognition. According to an historical account, "The Oregons" journeyed to Brooklyn, NY to play a local hotshot team. Exhausted by the long train ride, Dallas College lost, 21 to 19.

In Dec., 1908, "The Oregons" began a basketball tour that took them thru 22 states and 58 games in less than 3 months. They traveled almost 10,000 m. and won 49 contests. The most memorable game was on Jan. 20, 1909, in Buffalo, NY, where "The Oregons" met the Buffalo Germans, who were riding a 111-game winning streak. The game was tied at 20-20 when the Germans scored just before the game ended.

La Creole Academy and Dallas College closed 1914 — lack of funds.

In 1915 Dallas was on the Salem, Falls City & Western RR, had 4 sawmills, tannery, flour and feed mill, creamery, planing mill, wagon factory, 25 hop kilns, 10 fruit driers, iron foundry and RR machine shop, right well for a town of 2500. Surviving is the tannery, **Muir & McDonald** (1863), 505 SW Levens St., oldest operating business in Polk County and oldest of 5 tanneries in US using the slow vegetable process for the tooling strap and saddle leather. In late 1980 company was inducted into National Register of Historic Places.

The main street of Dallas, dominated by 2 story brick bldgs. holding small shops and stores, is fascinating tintype of earlier Oregon; could have been a movie set for an Andy Hardy film. Old houses are plentiful: representative are houses at 717 and 848 Levens. Oldest house in central Dallas is **Lovelady Hotel** (1870), at 990 Shelton. Victorian beauty. Some locals say small house at 1678 Miller was originally cabin built 1844 by David and America Grant. If so, you can't tell it now.

1.3 m., — from county courthouse — **Dallas Cemetery,** with graves of some people prominent in county's history, including Col. Cornelius Gilliam, who led volunteer army in Cayuse War efforts. Returning to Willamette Valley for supplies he was accidentally killed by discharge of his gun. Died 3/24/1848, at age 50. Gilliam County was named for him.

4.6 m., jct., Falls City.

* *0.9 m.,* on L, cemetery, with gravestones dated back to turn of century.

Near here was approximate site of Syracuse (PO 1885). *3.1 m.*, **Falls City,** founded 1889. It was bigger and livelier in 1915; today, an oozy main street waiting for someone or thing to awaken it. Footbridge to Little Luckiamute Riverbank park behind city hall. Picnic tables on HS lawn. City park, *0.5 m.* NW of town center, has towering trees, tables, rest room. (Turn L at entrance to park and road leads *2.5 m.* to **Socialist Valley,** named in early 1900s for group of socialists who resided here. Even at height of so-called mccarthyism, no one suggested the name be changed. Across bridge, at W end of business street, turn R. *0.1 m.,* 30-ft. falls which gives town its name. In summer, HS lads hurl themselves from high rocks into the creek. An Oregon bit of Acapulco — and dangerous. A scribe wrote: "From the rock bluff of the falls, the little town looks almost as if it were sketched by a 19th century book illustrator." Almost.

Return to road. This is the way now to what was Valsetz. It is a lonely, shadowy pike, hemmed in by the forest, brutal in winter. *8.1 m.,* on L, small falls. Drinking water. *8.3 m.,* site of **Valsetz.** Until it was leveled in 1984, Valsetz was a company town of about 300. When the mill's profits slipped the workers lost their jobs and the families were given their walking papers. Valsetz was the terminus of the Valley & Siletz RR, from which it derived its name. It proved to be the terminus of a lot of long-range plans. One of the state's rainiest spots, Valsetz also knew the terrors of winter storms and ice. Power outages and impossible road conditions could isolate the town from the world but Valsetz folk took the worst in stride, and being forced to move from their homes was anguishing to many.

The great attraction beyond what was Valsetz is **Valley of the Giants** but gated Valsetz bars the old way. Turn L and drive *3 m.* around pond to rejoin old way. From here, *4.1 m.,* turn R, uphill. *0.2 m.,* forks. Take L. *2.1 m.,* on L, small falls on N Fork of Siletz. *1 m.,* more small falls on N Fork of Siletz. *0.7 m.,* Johnson Falls, on N Fork of Siletz. *0.8 m.,* forks. Keep straight. *0.2 m.,* Boulder Creek Bridge and Warneke Rd. Keep straight. *0.2 m.,* N Fork of Siletz timber bridge. *1.1 m.,* Jct., turn onto Carter Creek Rd. *0.5 m.,* on R, gouged out parking area for Valley of the Giants. Trail begins on rear side of large log at R end of parking area. *0.8 m.,* path leads to N Fork of Siletz River, crossed by walking across giant log, made safe by cable for hand support, and then into magnificent forest. The BLM Valley of the Giants is actually on a hillside and the uphill travel is not to be taken lightly by asthmatics and cardiacs. The long trail from the opposite side of the stream winds around and over debris common to blown-down trees in virgin forests. Valley of the Giants contains at least a dozen Douglas firs over 25 ft. in circumference and 2 more than 30 ft. The champion of these woods, "Big Guy," 35', 6" in circumference and 230 ft. tall, was toppled by the 11/13/81 windstorm. (That storm also felled the world's largest black cottonwood tree, near Unionvale, in Yamhill County.) Studies indicate that this 47-acre stand originated about 1615 A.D.

On 0 223, from Falls City Jct.:

The hills between here and Kings Valley are plump and soft and lovable. And at stretches there seems to be one tree farm after another.

0.5 m., mail box on E, in front of house. Park here, if permission of owner is obtained, and walk *165 yds.* S off road, to avoid oncoming traffic, and turn uphill, bending L. *100 yds.,* **Hart Cemetery,** on DLC. Buried here are Thomas Hart, who died 1874 at age 86, 6 children in one family who perished between Nov. 1874 and Dec. 1875, and James A. O'Neil, one of the more colorful of Oregon's pioneers. Born 1800, O'Neil came to Oregon in 1834 with Nathaniel Wyeth and took up land claim on Willamette River, near what became Wheatland, being first settler in that area. O'Neil was a member of Ewing Young's stock drive in 1837, an early campaigner for Americanization of the Oregon country, builder of the first grist mill in Polk County, a judge of Yamhill County, and builder of first mercantile establishment at Buena Vista. He died in Sept. 1874. (For more, see "Two Instead of One" in author's *This Side of Oregon.*)

0.5 m., jct.

* To E: *2.5 m.,* Airlie Jct. (Airlie, *9 m.*) *5 m.,* Monmouth, solid farm scene all the way, thru land that seems to have been rolled by hand.

* To W: *1.4 m.,* on R, Bridgeport School. There stood here in this area more than century ago a casual community along Little Luckiamute River than had PO, est. 1854, named Bridge Port, later changed to Bridgeport. PO went out of business 20 years later but name of area and of school survived. In Oregon, at least, school is often last survivor of town name. *3.1 m.,* Falls City. *1 m.,* jct. (R, *4 m.,* Falls City.)

Valley of the Giants

  * To L: *3.3 m.*, Elkins Rd., site of old **Lewisville.** (School, which had been turned into sheep barn before being torn down, was to N at bottom of hill, where farm pond is now, on W.) James O'Neil died on a farm near Lewisville and was buried on his property. When farm was sold his remains were transferred to farm of his friend, Thomas Hart. Named for early settler, Lewisville was for decades gentle farming hamlet. In 1915 it had, in addition to school, 2 churches, blacksmith shop, cluster of homes. Nothing now. *1 m.,* site of tiny village of Maple Grove, which briefly flourished about 1903–04. *2 m.,* **Airlie,** in land at ease with nature. Named for the Scottish Earl of Airlie, town was S terminus of narrow gauge line of Oregonian Railway Co., Ltd., of which Earl was president. Later, tracks acquired by SP RR but no rails now. In 1915 Airlie was a right lively burg, with HS and PS, Grange, several lodges, church, businesses, pop. 100. All gone. (*0.3 m.,* turn into tall grass. *0.1 m.,* park at abandoned barn. *0.2 m.,* walk uphill thru thick Canadian thistle, blackberries and high grass, **Williams Cemetery,** enclosed, wind-ravaged plot, with markers to 1868.)
  5.9 m., Airlie Jct.
  0.6 m., **Pedee,** named for nearby Pedee Creek by Col. Cornelius Gilliam, native of N Carolina, for Carolina's Pedee River. In 1915, Pedee had pop. 75, which is a lot more than live in non-town now. Actually, there are 2 parts to

Tumbled gravestone of James A. O'Neil   *Phoebe L. Friedman*

Pedee, which is pronounced here as Pee-dee. The parts are 1 m. apart, with farms between. The N part contains a store; the S part the old "town center."

0.4 m., Ira Hooker Rd.

    * E, *0.1 m.,* **Taylor Cemetery.** Grave of James Taylor, born 1794, died 1858, and graves of 5 other members of family, including child who passed away in 1857 at age two.

0.9 m., Pedee Creek Rd.

    * Turn W. *0.6 m.,* on L, former structure of **Ft. Hoskins,** moved here around turn of century. Legend has it that Phil Sheridan occupied this house and from it reviewed his troops. House probably built circa 1856.

0.5 m., **Pedee Elementary School,** old-fashioned country school near "church-in-the-dell" kind house of worship.

0.3 m., turnoff W.

    0.2 m.,* 2 cemeteries: **Edwards Pioneer, on S (1859); **Pedee,** on N, of more recent vintage. Spirited view of encircling hills from cemetery knoll, with profusion of Scotch broom in foreground.

Return to 0 223.

    * Turn R onto Burbank Rd. *2 m.,* **Ritner Creek Park.** PA. Trails thru fulsome woods along peaceful Ritner Creek.

1.4 m., **Ritner Creek CB,** built in 1926 at length of 75 ft. and last of CBs on state hwys., until 1976. Slated for destruction it was saved by efforts of Pedee school-children and other aroused county citizens. Moved to E side of road, CB is now a tourist stop and adjoins Minnie Ritner Ruiter Wayside. Trails lead to Ritner Creek.

2.1 m., **Kings Valley,** at store. In 1915 this place had school, church, 2 lodges, 2 sawmills, flour mill, pop. 120. Now, if there wasn't an entrance marker you wouldn't know you were in town.

0.2 m., on W, **Chambers House,** built by Rowland Chambers, who came to Oregon with "Blue Bucket Mine" wagon train in 1845, built flour mill 1853, est. PO 1855.

0.2 m., on E, **Kings Valley Community Center,** built as schoolhouse 1877, was for years a church, for years empty. House behind it is as old.

1.3 m., on W, turnoff to **Kings Valley Cemetery.**

    * *0.3 m.,* cemetery. Weedy burial ground holds remains of Nahum King, 1845 pioneer after whom Kings Valley was named, and Rowland Chambers.

0.2 m., Hoskins Jct.

    * *0.6 m.,* on R, mailbox. On L, about *100 yds.* back, **Watson House,** first plastered house in Benton County, or W Oregon, or Oregon — take your pick. Built 1852, oldest house in area. James Watson had the lumber sawed nearby and dressed by hand; all doors and windows were hand made. Part of house was plastered. House cost Watson $2,400 in gold in addition to labor of 3 members of family for 6 months.

    * *1 m.,* **Hoskins.** On hill above tavern, appropriately named "The Fort"

Historic marker at Kings Valley

COMMEMORATING
THE SETTLEMENT OF
KINGS VALLEY
BY THE ROWLAND CHAMBERS &
NAHAM KING FAMILIES
IN 1846

Phoebe L. Friedman

stood Ft. Hoskins (1856–65.) For some years Hoskins was RR town, yards and roundhouse of Siletz & Valley RR. Community arose and CB built across Luckiamute. CB gone, yards gone, roundhouse gone. *0.1 m.* E of tavern, also on N side of road, large white house on hill is said by oldtimers to have been hospital of Ft. Hoskins, has been residence for many decades.

   * *0.1 m.,* bridge. Turn L. Cross bridge. Straight. *8.7 m.,* across low, cuddly hills that glow with joy, Summit, which seems to sit confused between the Yaquina River watershed and Willamette Valley. Couple of pup tents would just about double size of place. (See *US 101, 0 229.*)

   * For look at shimmering backcountry, make sharp L turn at end of bridge (near Hoskins). *5 m.,* return to 0 223, *3 m.* N of US 20.

1.3 m., on W, pioneer house with look of patrician affluence.

4.7 m., Toledo-Newport turnoff, cutoff to US 20 and Coast.

   * *0.8 m.,* US 20.

At turnoff is **Marys River,** originally named River de Souris, or Mouse River, by early fur traders. Name officially changed to Marys River in late 1846, though there is confusion as to which Mary was honored. Anyway, it's a pretty stream, as pretty as the Mary of Robert Burns who sleeps in the hush of another caring stream.

0.5 m., Wren turnoff.

   * *0.1 m.,* **Wren.** Shabby looking tavern, Wren Community Church and former PO bldg., tiny structure not recommended for claustrophobiacs. *0.1 m.,* Harris Rd. (Straight: *0.5 m.,* US 20.) R on Harris Rd.: *2.5 m.,* **Harris CB,**

Harris Covered Bridge   *Phoebe L. Friedman*

across Marys River, built 1936, 75 ft. in length. At or near CB was tiny village of Harris, or Elam, on Corvallis & Eastern RR, then SP. PS. Beyond CB a typical old-fashioned backwash farm road winds seemingly in all directions until it reaches the hwy. Thickets are plentiful, farms are scarce. Many people at Wren have never taken this road; only the lost traveler gets here. *4.8 m.,* "T". Turn R. *0.5 m.,* "T". Turn R. *0.1 m.,* at Blodgett Community Church, turn L. *0.1 m., US 20*

0.2 m. — on 0 223 at Wren Jct. — US 20.

0 51 — 0 22 to US 20

0 51, which bends with the Willamette River to Independence and then keeps within respectable distance of the stream, was one of those farm-to-market roads common in the Willamette Valley and now has become a suburban pike, a spoke of the wheel of which Salem is the hub.

Farms along this road are a microcosm of a general agricultural pattern of the state — certainly of W Oregon. Farmers in economic trouble seek to stay afloat by renting or selling some of their land.

This is no road for leisurely motoring. Cars come up and down it at breakneck speed and to slow at a curve is to court mayhem. Still, there are good things to see along 0 51 and down its tributaries there is a feeling of being far, very far, from Salem or any other city. That's when Oregon takes on new meaning of the old.

From jct., 0 22W:

3.1 m., jct. Rickreall *(4.8 m.,)* Dallas *(9.2 m.)*

3.2 m., **Independence,** one of the many self-styled "End of the Oregon Trail" towns. It was actually that in 1959, Oregon's statehood centennial, when an Oregon wagon train completed the long haul from Independence, Mo.

Independence is one of the oldest towns in the state, being settled in 1845; PO est. 1852. It grew slowly but solidly and by 1915 was on the West Side branch of the SPRR, terminus of the Independence & Monmouth Interurban line, and had daily steamboat service to Portland. It was also one of the most important hop centers of the US. During hop picking season families from all parts of the NW descended upon Independence for yard work and pop. zoomed from census 1,800 to more than 5,000, exceeding the town's present pop., since hops are now machine-picked.

In 1915 Independence had a sawmill, creamery, flouring mill and 2 weekly papers, which it doesn't have today. Absence of dynamic business district clearly shows that most people do not do their major shopping here.

Exterior mural at Taylor's, Independence

Independence is one of those towns which at first glance appears rather prosaic and provincial. But TV has sophisticated and universalized all Oregon towns and, as for dullness, look around a bit and feel the enchantment grow.

Downtown, one street wide and a couple of streets long, is anchored by the **J. S. Cooper Block** (1895), built by a man who supposedly made his money in Calif. mining. The tower was used to keep an eye on the Willamette River. When a steamer was observed rounding the bend of the Willamette, the cry went out, "Steamboat's a-coming!" and the townsfolk hastening to the landing. **Opera House,** circa 1875, at 268 Main.

Taylor's Store has turn-of-the-century flavor, with soda fountain and a wall lined with collectible Coca Cola trays, each with a different illustration. Bank bldg. on corner of Main and Monmouth was built 1870. Behind it is enclosed covered wagon that made centennial trek from Independence, Mo. City park, a block off Main St., has PA and concrete BR with large parking area. In summer the Willamette here is alive with water sports.

The old houses of Oregon towns are generally near the business section and Independence falls into this pattern. Monmouth St. is lined with 19th century homes: representative are houses at 275 (1861); 461 (1880), most gingerbread in town; 411 (1892); 386 "Out of the Blue" (1880).

Library, at 3rd and Monmouth, built as church in 1914. Behind it is **Independence Womens Club,** org. 1914, earlier built as church.

Across street from library is circa 1900 bldg. which has gone thru several denominations. **Brinker Hoff House,** 116 S. Second, most pretentious in Independence, is early 20th century mark of conspicuous consumption. **Independence Elementary School,** S 4th and C, constructed of red bricks in 1925, has Philadelphia Independence Hall look. **Hermitage Museum,** 3rd and B, built 1888 as first Baptist Church, is one of premier small town museums in state, containing, among other things, organ used when the First Baptist Church opened; Doctor's Room (old instruments and books); farm equipment, including early wagon; pioneer apparel; and rustic schoolhouse.

There is a noteworthy consistency about Independence: In 1890 it had 7 taverns and about 100 years later the number was the same.

0 51 ends at Independence but a network of roads lead S, to Buena Vista and US 20. Along these paved channels of farm heartland are found some of the interesting little corners that make this part of Oregon so endearing.

(From Main and Monmouth, W 2.4 m., 99W.)

0.5 m., from Main and Monmouth, jct.

*E, Roberts, former station on Oregon Electric RR, 6.8 m.; Salem, 11.7 m. 1 m., jct., Corvallis Rd.

* Straight, 1.8 m., **Hilltop Cemetery** (1872).

At jct., Corvallis Rd., take L. The road touches affluent farms, the kind associated with bank calendars. Today on the calendar, tomorrow in the hands of the bank.

Buena Vista ferry　　　　　　　　　　　　　　*Courtesy State of Oregon*

3 m., forks. Turn R. *2.4 m.,* on R, eye-warming turn-of-century farmhouse overseeing road. *0.7 m.,* jct. Turn L. *0.1 m.,* turn L on gravel road for cemetery. *0.4 m.,* **Buena Vista Cemetery,** with markers back to 1848. One of the most impressive burial grounds in state, stirring in its patient solemnity, neat simplicity, weathered wisdom and hymnal currents of the wind. View from hillock is splendid panorama of Oregon Farm Gothic.

Return to paved road. Straight on Riverview St.

0.1 m., turn L onto Willamette Ferry St. *0.1 m.,* turn R. *0.1 m., turn L into* **Buena Vista Park,** CP at bend of Willamette. Return *0.2 m.* to jct. Turn R. *0.1 m.,* ferry to W side of Willamette; S-most ferry in Oregon

Return to Riverview St. Turn L. *0.1 m.,* site of **Buena Vista,** settled 1847. By 1850 village had ferry across river, became river landing, boasted fine warehouse; then town was platted. By 1915 Buena Vista had pop. 121, 3 lodges, 2 churches, HS and PS, welcomed steamboats daily. But by 1940 Buena Vista had so completely declined that it was not even mentioned in the official state guide. All that remains of the town's great days are the **Community Methodist Church** (1868) and the seldom-used **IOOF Hall** (1905). Apart from well-equipped rural fire dept., there is little else here.

0.1 m., turn L onto Buena Vista Rd. *0.4 m.*, forks. Take L. *3.9 m.*, Springhill Rd. Turn R. *0.8 m.*, Independence Hwy. Turn L. *0.9 m.*, Camp Adair Rd. Turn R. *1.4 m.*, **E. E. Wilson State Pheasant Farm.** This was part of Camp Adair, which WW II troops called "Swamp Adair." Camp HQ were close by; parts of camp still stand but it is doubtful if most who soldiered here would recall any.

Return to Independence Hwy. Turn R. *1 m.*, NW Palestine Rd. Turn L. *1.1 m.*, Oak Grove Dr. Straight. *0.1 m.*, **North Palestine Memorial Church and Cemetery.** Church, built 1882, no longer in use as such. Delightful pastoral scene. Coming here you can say you have been to Palestine, because there was a rural community here by that name.

0.7 m., jct. Turn R. *1.7 m.*, jct., NW Grove Dr. *0.1 m.*, turn L. *2.3 m.*, US 20. Turn L. *0.6 m.*, downtown Albany.

0 18 — Otis Jct. to 0 99W (McMinnville)

0 18 comes tearing off US 101 as though bound for hell or glory and it does not ease up until it has run out of wind, at 0 99W. Because it is generally a straight, low road it is often crowded in summer, especially between Friday afternoons and Sunday nights. The attractions on and off 0 18 are more numerous than most travelers would suppose, which is why the best time to make this road for off-beat purposes is in the middle of the week, when travel is lighter.

From US 101, N exit:

0.4 m., merger with S exit off US 101.

1.1 m., **Otis,** wayside village that is another of those Oregon nets for the wandering. A retired NY policeman, seeking his rainbow place to settle down for the rest of his life, drove W until he came to Otis. "This is it," he said. And that's how most of the other town partisans feel.

Jct., **Scenic Drive Exp. Forest.** (See US 101.)

*Turn N. *0.3 m.*, turn E onto North Bank Rd. (Straight to Scenic Drive Exp. Forest.) *0.6 m.*, on N Bank Rd., **Salmon River Fish Hatchery;** coho and chinook salmon — viewing all year. *3.5 m.*, 0 18 at **Rose Lodge.** (This is really the nicest way to get from Otis to Rose Lodge, being free of the thunderbolt traffic and skirting excellently landscaped homes.)

4 m., **Rose Lodge PO.** Locals claim the village is 10 m. long and nobody knows where is the center. Between parts of the village are rushes of coppices, waving their rain-stained hands to cry, "We're part of Rose Lodge, too." Place named by first PM for roses she grew in front of her PO home. In 1915 hamlet had 2 sawmills and cheese factory — a lot more than it has now.

At PO, turnoff to N Bank Rd. (See above.)

3.3 m., entering Van Duzer Corridor, green hall of nature. On a scorching summer day, not commonplace here, the woods appear candent but in the foggy pall of rainy winter they are caliginous.

Palestine, Oregon

    1.1 m., **Van Duzer SP.** PA on banks of Salmon River, so named for plenitude of salmon streaming in from sea — but no more. (Hiker/Biker camping.)

    4.7 m., leaving Van Duzer Corridor. *1.4 m.,* reentering Van Duzer Corridor. *3.1 m.,* releaving Van Duzer Corridor.

    2.4 m., **Grand Ronde,** another hwy. strip with facilities for food and gas. This is not where original town stood. Across road from Bonanza Restaurant is lovely little park, open to strolling but not picnicking. Windmill, water wheel, wooden bridges, covered wagon, old tractor, farm wagons — touch of Ruralia.

    Turn N onto Grand Ronde Rd. 0.1 m., turn L. *0.1 m.,* RR station, built 1923, long inoperative but one of last small town RR stations left in state. *0.6* m., office of Confederated Tribes of Grand Ronde. In late 1983 Indians regained tribal status, for which they had been trying since 1975. Just N of office is Indian cemetery, which Indians say was founded 1850s but stones bear more recent dates. 0.8 m., jct., 0 22. On NW corner, where Catholic Church stands, was site of Grand Ronde Indian Agency, HQ of Reservation. (See 0 22, preceding.)

    *Turn R, or E. 2.3 m., turn L onto Old Fort Rd. (Dead End Rd.) for site of Ft. Yamhill. (See 0 22, preceding.)

1.2 m., to N, on hill, 3 storied old house with wide veranda facing calendar art red barn. 0.7 m., jct., 0 22.

    *Turn R. 0.7 m., Old Fort Rd. (Dead End Rd.)

0.2 m., site of **Ft. Yamhill.** (See 0 22, preceding.)

0.8 m., Valley Junction, one more briefy hwy. strip. Fort Hill Rd. (See 0 22, preceding.)

3 m., Willamina-Sheridan exit. (For Willamina and Sheridan, see 0 22, preceding.)

0.4 m., 0 22 — Salem Jct. 0.7 m., turnoff. (0.5 m., 0 22.) 2.6 m., **Mill Creek.** Exposure of mudstone and silt stone along Mill Creek is known to geologists as the Yamhill Formation, defined in *The Ore Bin* of Nov. 1973 as the "sequence of marine sedimentary rocks that overlies the Siletz River Volcanic Series."

0.2 m., Harmon-Buell Rd.

    *Turn S. 0.1 m., **Stuart Grenfell CP.** PA. 0.1 m., on R, picture postcard

Former Grand Ronde Railroad Station   *Phoebe L. Friedman*

house with early 20th century gingerbread. *1.2 m.,* **Union Baptist Church and Cemetery** (1861). *3 m.,* **Buell.** Store. At store, make flat turn. *0.4 m.,* on L, Buell CP. Contiguous to it, mackinaw-feel Grange hall. Across road stands early 20th century Buell School, converted into residence. *0.3 m.,* jct., 0 22.

   **Straight, Mill Creek Rd. (See 0 22, preceding.)

   ***E from 0 22 jct.: *0.4 m.,* on L, at narrow land, giant white oak locally claimed to be largest of species on Pacific Coast, expanding state Forestry assertion that it is largest in Oregon. As though to protect its vulnerability from marauders, tree is protected by a fan of poison oak.

On 0 18 — going E from Buell Jct.:
1.9 m., Sheridan Exit.

   *Sheridan-Ballston Jct.

   *Toward Ballston: road rambles thru broad green fields lying at the pillows of low hills. *1.5 m.,* turn R onto gravel road. *2 m.,* over roller coaster hills, **Pleasant Hill Pioneer Cemetery.** Markers go back to early 1860s on wind-swept hilltop burial ground.

   Return to Sheridan-Ballston Rd. Turn R, or S. *4.8 m.,* **Ballston.** Founded as Ballsville in 1878 by narrow gauge RR backer Isaac Ball and changed to Ballston in 1880. In 1915, Ballston had pop. 104, PS, 2 churches, 3 lodges — today, tiny crossroads store. Back of store, in Ballston CP, is **Ballston School,** erected 1855 on site *0.5 m.* SW of here, as Lawn Arbor School, with lumber from Elias Buell's mill on Mill Creek, brick from local area, and square nails. Pulled by oxen on rollers to present site in 1874. Used as school until 1880s. School donated to Polk County and now local museum. Sheltered by family of oaks, school ought to be prized subject for sensitive photographers. Turn L at store. *0.1 m.,* turn L onto Weber Rd., which becomes Mae Yokum Rd. *0.3 m.,* turn R onto tire trace. *0.2 m.,* **Ballston Cemetery,** in high grass. Here lie in a row 6 members of the Ball family, ages 3 to 27, who died between 1858 and 1860. (From Ballston: Buell, *10 m.;* Dallas, *14 m.*)

   *N from Sheridan-Ballston Jct.: *0.7 m.,* Sheridan. (See *0 22,* preceding.)

On 0 18, going E:
0.7 m., **Western Deer Park and Arboretum,** nice microcosm of W Oregon fauna and flora.

1.3 m., Gopher Valley Rd.

   *Turn N onto road. *4.3 m.,* approximate site of Gopher, PO of short life span — 1899–1905. *1.2 m.,* turn L *0.3 m.,* **Deer Creek CP,** little-used, pleasant PA with the good grass feeling for footsteps. Return to Gopher Valley Rd. Turn L. *0.2 m.,* on L, abandoned fire house, looking like Rip Van Winkle's barn. *0.6 m.,* turn L. *2.8 m.,* Dead End Rd. Take it. *0.5 m.,* forks. Take L. Walk *350 yds.* to crude forks. Take L. *50 yds.,* former **Beaverdam School,** early 20th century learning house. (Later used as feeding station.) Why a schoolhouse in this tangle of woods, seemingly so isolated? Because about the 2nd decade of the 1900s there was a lumber camp nearby and the land was also populated by homesteaders. The small farmers couldn't make it and moved out; the logging camp ran out of timber.

From Gopher Valley Jct., on *0 18:*

0.9 m., Ballston-Perrydale Jct.

    0.8 m., Ballston Jct. To R, *2.4 m.,* Ballston. (See *0 18,* earlier.)

    *Straight from above jct. (toward Perrydale): *2.8 m.,* Amity Jct. *0.9 m.,* South Yamhill Bridge. Below it, riverbank in summer is veritable beach. *1 m.,* Broadmead Rd. Jct. To L, *2.3 m.,* Amity, 99W. Return to Broadmead Rd. R to Perrydale. *3.1 m.,* turn L toward Perrydale on Broadmead Rd. *2.2 m.,* forks. Take L, for Perrydale. *0.4 m.,* **Perrydale,** founded 1870. In 1915 village had flour mill and warehouse, store, HS, 2 churches, pop. 100. Today — just school, church, 2 homes of elegant 19th century status. (Straight: *2.2 m.,* McCoy.) Return to Broadmead Rd. and turn N. *1.3 m.,* on E, stately white house of yore with gingerbread richness. *0.8 m.,* white patrician house of long ago yesteryear. *0.2 m.,* Ballston Jct. Turn R. *2.4 m.,* "T". *0.8 m.,* 0 18. This land S of 0 18 — the land that envelops Buell, Ballston, Perrydale and Amity — is as flat-bellied as a ballet dancer, as pungent as a cow barn, as productive as a queen bee.

1 m., on N, red bldg. was Bellevue School.

0.4 m., **Bellevue.** Store, art gallery. In 1915 village had 3 churches.

Muddy Valley Rd.

    * *0.2 m.,* turn L onto paved road. *0.3 m.* —or just past 8th telephone pole from corner — turn R onto dim grassy trace. *0.4 m.,* **Yoakum** (aka Bellevue) **Cemetery** (1858).

Amity Jct.

    * *200 ft.,* turn R onto gravel road. *0.6 m.,* just before small bridge, gate on R. *70 yds.* beyond gate, thru tall grass, **Deer Creek Cemetery** (1858), typical backcountry burial ground, broken, weathered and deserted. Return to Amity Rd. Turn R. *1.5 m.,* on W, gingerbread house of 19th century vintage. *1.5 m.,* S Yamhill River. Summer beach below. *1 m.,* Broadmead Rd. (For ways to Amity and Perrydale, see above, 0 18.)

0.7 m., on S, calendar farmhouse with water tower.

0.8 m., on N, turnoff for Glacial Erratic.

    * *0.8 m.* up county rd. to footpath on L. *0.5 m.,* uphill trail to **Glacial Erratic Rock.** Rafted from far up Columbia River by iceberg at twilight of Ice Age. Erratics are so called because they are unrelated to local rocks. Bonus of climb is vast gob of scenery — plains and mountains — from knoll.

0.5 m., on N, **Glacial Erratic Marker.** *2.5 m.,* on S, Currier and Ives farmhouse with water tower. *0.9 m.,* jct., Muddy Valley Rd.

    * Forks. Take L. *1.8 m.,* "Y". Turn L. *50 yds.,* turn R, up lane to knoll, site of **South Yamhill Baptist Church,** 3rd Baptist congregation organized W of Upper Missouri, 1846. First church erected 1850. Back of site is one of oldest

Erratic Rock

and least-known historic cemeteries in state; hoary gravestones go back to 1850s. Return to road below knoll. Turn R. *0.4 m.,* turn R on dirt lane to **McCabe United Methodist Church,** on hillock commanding overpowering view of valley. Built 1886, church has original pews and is heated by round iron stove, genuine antique. Except for electric light, church is as it was 14 years before 20th century.

1.7 m., Bypass, 0 18.

  * *2 m.,* McMinnville Jct. *1.8 m.,* on E, **Eagles Hall,** built as schoolhouse in 1913. *0.1 m.,* **Evergreen Airlines,** persistently rumored (and denied) to be CIA front. *0.8 m.,* jct. (Amity, *9 m.;* Salem, *23 m.*) *1.3 m.,* jct. L, Lafayette; R, Amity, Hopewell. *1.3 m.,* jct., 0 221. *1.5 m.,* jct., 0 99W.

0.7 m. — from bypass, 0 18 — jct., 99W — McMinnville.

US 20 — Newport to Albany (I-5)

A low-pass road with no town big enough to slow traffic until Philomath is reached, US 20 is popular year-round. It is an easy road to drive and rather prosaic, except at places where it seems to slow down to say hello to cows, trees, dogs and houses.

From US 101, at Newport:

0.3 m., Eads St.

  * Turn N. *0.1 m.,* turn R onto 3rd. *0.6 m.,* turn L for **Eureka Cemetery.** *0.1 m.,* cemetery, on hill. Clear view of town and ocean. When cemetery was est. in 1889, plot cost $5. In 1985 plot cost $200. Buried here is James Craigie

(1813–1895), only Hudson's Bay Co. employee to settle (along Yaquina River) and die in Lincoln County.

0.2 m., turnoff S to Bay Front. (See *US 101, Newport,* preceding.)

5.2 m., jct., Toledo.

　　* *1.4 m.,* downtown **Toledo.** Town named 1868 for Ohio city for which, according to legend, son of pioneer settler was homesick. Neither of the communities have much charm; both are strongly working class. Indeed, Toledo, Oregon, is a model of class hierarchy. In this hilly mill town the workers live at the low levels, the small shopkeepers and sub-middle management above them, and the affluent at the top. And the homes reflect the local elevation levels. In 1918 the US gvmt. built the world's largest spruce sawmill to make WW I airplanes. Toledo is still a mill town, a long way off from Newport in style and character.

　　* For **Toledo Cemetery** (*1 m.*), take A St. off US 20-Business, to 11th. Turn R to Arcadia and follow to cemetery. A hillside burial plot where sleep the merchants without their wares, the earth breakers without their plows, the mill workers with silenced hands, the day-at-a-time realists with a handful of eternity. Markers to 1877.

0.1 m., jct., Siletz — 229:

　　* *7.5 m.,* Siletz. (See *US 101 — Kernville-O 229,* preceding.)

1.8 m., jct., Toledo.

　　* S, *0.9 m.,* jct. Straight. *1.3 m.,* downtown Toledo.

2.7 m., Coast Range Summit — 337 ft.

3 m., Elk City Jct.

　　* *2 m.,* approximate site of Pioneer, 19th century hamlet long non-existent. *0.7 m.,* site of Pioneer City. PO opened 7/2/1868; closed 39 days later. *2.1 m.,* Elk City. (See *US 101-Newport,* preceding.)

1.3 m., on S, Thornton Creek Rd. An 84 ft. length CB, built 1924, once stood here.

1.2 m., on S, **Chitwood CB,** 96 ft. in length, built 1930. At S end of bridge, Chitwood, product of Corvallis & Eastern RR, built early 1880s. In 1915 it had pop. 50, PS, Adventist Church. Today it could just about pass for ghost town.

6.2 m., jct., Nashville.

　　* *6.7 m.,* Nortons. *5.2 m.,* Nashville. (See *US 101-Kernville — O 229* preceding.)

0.3 m., **Eddyville.** PO started 1888 as Little Elk, being near mouth of creek by that name. Town is generally cooler than Willamette Valley and warmer than coast. In 1915 Eddyville had pop. 20; by 1940 town had grown to 41; hasn't advanced much since. The old stores are boarded up or have been turned into homes; the emigrants of the 20th century have moved in at confluence of Little Elk Creek and Yaquina River. Town seems good place to fish and raise kids. Bright marks in otherwise drab ambience are schools, whose enrollment is about four times pop. of town. Back of schools is rare weeping fir.

Chitwood Bridge   *Phoebe L. Friedman*

(* Backtrack *0.9 m.* to house on S. Park there and walk *80 yds.* thru tall grass to **Eddy Cemetery;** markers to 1875.)

From Eddyville, on US 20:

7 *m.,* Cline Hill Summit — 770 ft. *1.1 m.,* **Ellmaker SP.** PA, FHP. *0.7 m.,* **Burnt Woods,** which owes its name to forest fires in area. If you're looking for a town, settle for store.

    * To S: *7.9 m.,* Harlan. (See *US 101-Newport,* preceding.)

6.4 *m.,* **Blodgett,** on Marys River. Est. 1888 as Emrick. In 1915 town had pop. 33; by 1940 it had dwindled to 12 but had sawmill (now gone). Today — store.

    * N, *5.1 m.,* Summit. (See *US 101-Kernville, 0 229,* preceding.)

1.2 *m.,* on R, lane that is driveway of brick red colored house. (Lane is 50 yds. W of paved Davis Rd.)

    * *0.2 m.,* **Blodgett Cemetery.** Seven generations of Blodgetts lie here — most in a straight line, the others clustered close by. Earliest born: Grandma Susan Bar, 1792; earliest death, 5-year-old Maria Blodgett, 1862.

4.2 *m.,* jct., O 223. (See following *Cross-Coast Range Roads, O 22.*)

4.3 *m.,* jct., O 34. (See *O 34,* following.)

0.7 *m.,* **Philomath,** founded as a school, its name a combination of two Greek words meaning love of learning. In 1849 George W. Bethers, DLC pioneer farming *1.5 m.* SW of Corvallis, wrote to Dayton, Ohio, to ask the Church of the United Brethren to send a preacher to serve the Marys River settlements. Four years later, and after a journey of five months, two preachers arrived, one leading 96 people and 16 wagons.

In 1865 a group of church members met at the Maple Grove School (near where S 13th crosses Marys River) to talk about building a HS or institution of higher learning. Subsequently, a total of $17,500 was offered to the United Brethren with the stipulation that UB cooperate in building a literary institution under the moral influence of Christianity. UB accepted the terms and land was purchased for the college and for est. of a town. A clause in the sale of each town lot forbade grog shops, gambling saloons or theaters ever to be located or allowed upon the premises covered by the deeds.

On Nov. 22, 1865, Articles of Incorporation were drawn up for Philomath College. Two years later the main bldg. was completed. (Wings were added in 1905 and 1907.) In 1867, too, a bell was purchased for $250.

Gradually the college expanded. In 1877 a dormitory was built. Fees were modest: in 1899 rooms rented for 25 cents a week, two students to a room. Meals were $1.75 per week. Students staying with local families did as well: $2 a week for room and board in 1910. A 2-room bldg., originally for music classes, was built 1897–99 and gymnasium constructed 1902–03.

However, all was not always rosy. In 1889 there was a split in the United Brethren. A conservative faction est. a separate school, College of Philomath, on hill above Philomath College. But C of P folded in 1912 and its bldg., a 2-story frame structure, was purchased by Philomath College to house the Conservatory of Music.

In 1929 Philomath College closed. Three factors doomed it: financial mismanagement; the rise of tax-supported schools, particularly Oregon Agricultural College (now OSU) at Corvallis; and the onset of the Great Depression. During its 62 years, the college had enrolled over 6,000 students; more than 1,200 became teachers.

After 1929, church services, which had always been held at the college, continued in the main bldg. until 1968, marking a century of continuous use. By then United Brethren had merged with the Evangelical Association, becoming the Evangelical United Brethren; the EUB then merged with the Methodist denomination to form the United Methodists. In 1969 the congregation voted not to restore the old main bldg. but to build a new structure. So, for the first time in more than 100 years, what had been Philomath College was left vacant. In 1978 Benton County voters approved a levy to operate a county museum in the old bldg. Restoration of the first floor was completed in 1980, of the second floor in 1983, and now the entire bldg. has been restored.

What remains to be presently seen? The main bldg. of Philomath College is the **Benton County Museum.** College of Philomath, at 10th and Pioneer, is apt. house. President's residence is a bungalow at 1544 Main St.

Benton County Museum is professionally managed and its displays skillfully arranged. Among the displays are a photographic record of Philomath College, attesting to its full and varied life. Visitors are surprised to note that PC had a vigorous athletic program, including basketball teams for women as well as men, a highly developed system of intellectual organizations and, within its strict moral bounds, a social program.

Studying the faces of the students, one is struck by their purity and purpose. There is strength in the handsome faces of the women and a sense of determination in the eyes of the men. Men and women fanned out to teach in every corner of Oregon, bringing to one-room country schoolhouses and more modern town schools a love for learning acquired in this small college in this small town. Philomath College left a mark of integrity upon the state that to this day is not really appreciated.

In 1981 Philomath made national news when Tami Maida, daughter of an OSU doctoral candidate from British Columbia, made the HS freshman team as quarterback. The town was back on the front pages of the sports sections in Oregon papers when the HS girls basketball team went undefeated in winning in 1987, its second consecutive Class AA state championship. Its star, Trisha Stevens, a unanimous selection for all-state honors and voted the most valuable player of the tournament, was perhaps the greatest female basketball player ever developed in Oregon. A veritable scoring machine, she could score more points than the entire output of the opposing team.

5.4 m., jct., O 99W.

0.7 m., downtown Corvallis. (For Corvallis, see *The Great Heartland, O 99W*.) 2.9 m., on S, Pilkington Rd.

* *0.2 m.*, on R, **Woodcock House,** built 1873 at NW corner, 5th and Jackson, Corvallis; moved here about century later.

2.5 m., Lewisburg-Granger Rd.

* Turn N. *2.3 m.*, site of **Lewisburg,** founded on his DLC by 1845 pioneer and Oregon constitutional convention delegate Haman C. Lewis. Town was one of many "small stops" on stations placed every 5 to 10 m. along West Side Division of SPRR. In 1915 town had H and graded PS, church, store, State Game Farm stocked with thousands of wild birds, and Grange (Mountain View). Only Grange hall, built 1910, survives. (*0.1 m.*, 99 W.)

0.6 m., turnoff N to Buena Vista (*10 m.*) *1.2 m.*, on S, **Hyak Park,** green spot on the Willamette. 2.7 m., on N, Spring Hill (or Springhill) Rd.

* *2.3 m.*, Oak Grove. Turn R. *0.1 m.*, NW Oak Grove Dr. (Palestine, *3 m.*) Straight. *1.7 m.*, NW Palestine Dr. *0.6 m.*, Springhill Rd. Turn L. *2.6 m.*, Independence Hwy. Turn for Buena Vista. *2.2 m.*, Suver Rd. Straight. *1.9 m.*, Prather Dr. Turn R. *1.2 m.*, Main St. Turn R. *0.1 m.*, **Buena Vista.** (Ferry across Willamette River.) Return *0.1 m.* to jct. Turn for Independence. *3.2 m.*, Buena Vista Rd. Turn R. *2.6 m.*, Corvallis Rd. Turn R. *1.5 m.*, Independence. (See O 51, preceding.)

0.3 m., Willamette River. 0.2 m., downtown Albany. 0.5 m., O 99E — I-5.

O 34 — Waldport to Lebanon

A road of many moods, O 34 is an absolute delight in its W part, where it is tandem with the smiling, generous Alsea River. In this section of O 34, the road is lined with boat landings and rural clusters of developments. Leaving the plain of the Alsea, O 34 turns erratic and absent-minded, traveling like a man with one leg shorter than the other wobbling home after a tippled night. Finally, O 34, reaching the valley bottom, shakes off its cobwebs and lunges straight ahead. E of the town of Alsea O 34 passes thru basalts which were part of the Pacific Ocean floor some time ago — 50 to 60 million years, to be exact.

2.4 m. on S. **W. B. Nelson SP,** on Eckman Lake, blue-ruffled slough fringing the green hems of gently contoured hills. PA, fishing.

4.8 m., Alsea River ripples under O 34 at Happy Valley, commercial CG.

3 m., **Tidewater.** Store. Town so-called because of location near head of tide on Alsea River. Salt water mingles with fresh at estuary. Yet the romantic will see another picture: the Alsea flowing mistily between apple trees, rushes of corn, tawny slopes, pilings, and back porches of solidly built wooden homes.

0.2 m., on S, turnoff to Alsea Riviera.

* *0.4 m.,* Alsea Riviera, one street development of single-family houses — the way a lot of folks fancy they'd like to live.

0.1 m., on S, turnoff to Little Switzerland.

* *0.6 m.,* **Little Switzerland,** gorgeous green setting that reminds one briefly of a lower alpine scene from "The Sound of Music." Across the river and above a vale the wooded hills rise in waves, as on a musical scale, and at the crest the leafy crowns of a line of erect trees shimmer in the breeze. The only sound in this idyllic scene is the occasional putt-putt of an outboard motor.

6.4 m., **Mike Bauer FS.** PA. *1.2 m.,* **Blackberry FS CG,** on Alsea. Popular with shore anglers. *1.8 m.,* FS BL. Marker here reads: "The Alsea River and its tributaries provide spawning beds for chinook, salmon, coho or silver salmon, steelhead and cutthroat trout. These fish migrate between fresh and salt water, and depend on unsalted gravel beds for spawning grounds."

2.4 m., on S, Five Rivers Rd.

* Lilting drive to backcountry CB and across wild, rugged mountain country to O 36. Roads are unmarked or badly marked and in the maze of logging roads, bewilderment comes easily. Few vehicles are met; you're on your own. But, with a little patience, trip can be rewarding experience.

* *3.2 m.,* Lobster Valley Jct. (L, Five Rivers Jct. *2.9 m.,* jct. Turn L *3.7 m.,* **Lobster Valley.** Site of PO of Box, est. 1897; now almost completely obliterated in memory. Box so-named because mail put in box along road and carried to Alsea by anyone going to town. Incoming mail also put into box and settlers passing by picked up their letters. Lobster Valley Rd. charac-

terized by occasional small farms pocketed between flow of second-growth timber encasing the twisty pike. 8.7 m., turn L. 0.9 m., Alsea.)

 * At Lobster Valley Jct., keep straight. 6 m., on R, **Fisher CB,** across Five Rivers, so-named because of five creeks — Alder, Buck, Cherry, Couger and Crab — that make up stream. Old time residents say 72-ft.-long bridge was built 1927 of lumber floated 7 m. downstream from Paris Ranch, first sawmill in valley. (Official Oregon CB map says Fisher CB erected 1925; *Roofs Over Rivers — A Guide to Oregon's Covered Bridges* puts construction date at 1919.) Nothing remains of Fisher Village, started 1892. Store now dwelling. Grange hall torn down, school empty and unused. 6.8 m., with occasional stump ranch farmhouses along road, site of PO of **Paris.** Named for home-steader George E. Parris; postal authorities removed an "r." Paris School stood below uphill house on L of road.

Paris is the last dwelling on this trip for almost 15 m., that can seem like 50 to the uninitiated. From Paris: 4.8 m., forks. Take L. 0.2 m., great panorama of maw of Coast Range. 0.7 m., another splendid overlook. From here the Coast Range has more body, contours and segments than when seen at most other viewpoints. 0.4 m., jct., Deadwood Creek. (Straight, 16 m., O 36.) Turn L onto Deadwood Rd. This pike has many false turnoffs and dead ends, so follow directions closely. 1.2 m., forks. Straight. 1.7 m., forks. Straight. 1 m., forks. Take L. 1.6 m., forks. Take R. 0.6 m., forks. Take L. 1.8 m., forks. Take R. 0.6 m., on L, bridge leading to **Alpha Community,** vegetarian commune with typical collective elitism. Living room of main community house was PO (est. 1890) of Alpha, named for daughter of first postmaster.

On grounds of present commune was Alpha School, long gone. 2 m., forks. Straight. 0.4 m., turn L onto grassy trace. 0.2 m., **Deadwood CB.** Built 1932 at cost of $4,814, span has length of 105 ft. Return to Deadwood Creek Rd. Turn L. 0.4 m., on L, house that was country school in 1900. (Directly to N of house is Nature Trail that slithers thru virgin woods 5 m. to Windy Peak. Among ob-served denizens of this forest, a bear.) 4.8 m., O 36.

From Five Rivers Jct., on O 34:

6.7 m., turnoff for **Alsea River Salmon Hatchery.**

 * 2.4 m., hatchery. Far more captivating than the hatchery is triangular-shaped valley rolling down from three-hatted hills and the scenery along narrow, fidgety road. **Fall Creek,** on L, with its mossy air and thick-leafed alder canopy, looks like a bayou lifted out of Louisiana. At other places its delicate stone island configurations and flower arrangements seem taken from Japan. At mouth of Fall Creek — near hatchery jct. — stood PO of Angora (1899–1907), named for goats in area.

4.7 m., **Missouri Bend Recreation Area.**

 * 0.2 m., BLM CG on Alsea. First white occupants of this part of Alsea Valley were Missourians.

1.9 m., Salmonberry Rd.

* S, *0.4 m.,* **Salmonberry CP,** wide spot off farm road on Alsea River. PA, FHP.

Now O 34 is streaming thru low hills which have their own beauty, no lesser to the heart than taller hills.

1.6 m., **Campbell CP.** PA, BL. *3.6 m.,* on S, Hayden Rd.

* *0.1 m.,* **Hayden CB,** 91-ft.-long, built 1918 over Alsea River. Spacious, tastefully designed white house just beyond bridge built 1883.

0.2 m., **Mill Creek CP.** PA, BL, FHP. *0.6 m.,* on N, Cemetery Rd.

0.6 m., on N, Cemetery Rd.

* *0.2 m.,* **Alsea Cemetery,** on hilltop. Markers back to 1875.

0.8 m., **Alsea,** biggest town between Waldport and Philomath, is charming one street, one story "downtown" with store, food, gas. Whites started settling in 1852 but never in great numbers. In 1915 town had three lodges, Grange, Farmers Union, pop. 150. With timber cut and small farmers leaving, pop. declined to 100 in 1940, has remained more or less constant. Asked why folks stay, longtime resident replied, "Because we keep our nose clean."

Jct., Alsea Park — Alpine — Monroe.

* Turn S. Jct. (To R: *8.7 m.,* Lobster Valley. Turn R. *3.7 m.,* jct. Turn R. *6 m.,* Five Rivers. Straight. *2.9 m.,* Fisher Jct. See *Five Rivers Rd.,* this section, above.)

* To L: *1.8 m.,* jct. Take L. The houses thin out and suddenly the country seems wild and disorderly, so far a scene from the cohesion and neatness of O

Deadwood Bridge

34. The only farms observed here appear to be a hundred miles from the state road. *6.2 m.,* **Hubert K. McBee Memorial Park.** CG deep in darkling woods and little used. *0.7 m.,* turnoff to Alsea Falls Rec. Area. PA. Trail leads to **Alsea Falls** on S Fork of Alsea. The small cascades have so little splash that persons sitting behind them do not get drenched. On hot days, swimmers and waders invade the pools. *0.3 m.,* **Alsea Falls Rec. Site CG.** The road E is lined on both sides shoulder to shoulder with trees, as though to screen off whatever is behind them. Then the road, after a slow climb, comes spinning down into the valley like a top out of control. *7.1 m.,* site of **Glenbrook,** once branch line terminus of RR; PO 1898–1905. *1.2 m.,* turnoff to Alpine Winery *(1.2 m.). 1.5 m.,* turnoff N to **Alpine Cemetery** (1851). *0.2 m.,* **Alpine.** Backwater village emerging from scene short years ago when it looked like it had been pillaged by the Huns. Things were brighter in 1915, when town had HS, two lodges, was RR stop, and had pop. 300. (N, *2.4 m.,* Bellfountain; W, *3.6 m.,* O 99W.)

At Alsea, on O 34:

1.7 m., turnoff to **Clemens CP** *(0.1 m.),* beautiful bit of woods by fun-paddling N fork of Alsea River. PA, FHP. *0.6 m.,* turnoff N to **Alsea River Fish Hatchery** *(0.5 m.) 4.8 m.,* Coast Range summit — 1,231 ft. *0.1 m.,* turnoff N to Marys Peak.

Hayden Bridge   *Phoebe L. Friedman*

9.5 m., parking area of **Marys Peak,** at 4,097 ft. highest point in Coast Range. Indians called the mtn. *Chintimini;* various interpretations. From crest, Pacific Ocean is visible; so are Cascades. But most impressive panoramas are of topographical scenes, seaweed hills, villages, farms, mills, waves and weaves of forests. Flora enthusiasts will exult in the wildflower glories of Marys Peak. With the melt of snowbanks come glacier lilies, white anemones, the effusive bloom of the sythris, masses of purple and yellow violets, and the most delicate and photogenic of all, the fawn lily. Beneath alpine first tiny fungi peek out from the forest duff and in the shadows of weather stumps and strewn logs mushrooms reach maturity. PA. Trails. Road to parking area curvy but paved and lined with trees. Lookouts along way.

0.5 m., here O 34 abruptly starts to corkscrew down into the valley and twists for *2.1 m. 6.2 m.*, from end of winding piece of road, jct., US 20. *0.7 m.*, downtown Philomath. (See *US 20*, preceding.) *5.4 m.*, jct., O 99W. *0.7 m.*, downtown Corvallis. (See *The Great Heartland*, O 99W, following.)

From Van Buren and 3rd: *0.1 m.*, Willamette River Bridge.

1.1 m., on R, or S, Peoria-Harrisburg Jct.

* Turn S onto Peoria Rd. *0.8 m.*, on R, house (circa 1880) has austere look of 19th century self-confidence bourgeois affluence.

* *3.4 m.*, Church Rd. Turn E onto it. *1.3 m.*, **Oakville.** Community of Oakville as a commercial entity (PO 1878–1902) is no more and neither are most of the beautiful white oaks for which village was named. On SE corner stands **Oakville-Willamette United Presbyterian Church,** oldest of its denomination W of Missouri, reputedly first psalm-singing congregation in Oregon, probably best-known rural church in mid-Willamette Valley. Organized 1850, present church bldg. erected 1878–79. Basement added 1932. Steeple rebuilt 1962. Parsonage was early schoolhouse. Turn R at church onto Oakville Rd. *0.2 m.*, on L, house built somewhere between 1860 and 1878. Just below it is Oakville School, looking older than its 1923 construction year. (*1.7 m.*, Peoria Rd.)

* N onto Oakville Rd. from church. *0.6 m.*, turnoff L for **Oakville Cemetery** (*0.2 m.*) Site of founding of church. Markers back to 1850. Inscription on grave marker of Jane T. Purdy, wife of Andrew Purdy, dead Sept. 9, 1859 at age 19, reads: "There is nothing sweeter on earth than the heart of a woman in which piety dwells." We can see Jane thru the curtain of time: slender, lean-cheeked, soft-eyed, brave, a good neighbor, a sturdy wife, more worried about how Andrew will get along than in her fate. And somehow she seems dressed in white. Not far from Jane lies Dr. W. B. Mealey, whose marker tells the story of an eminent pioneer: "Born in Pennsylvania in 1809. Came to Oregon in 1845. First school built on his land. Donated land for the cemetery. Member of first legislature. Helped draft constitution of Oregon. Assisted in organizing United Presbyterian Church."

Oakville-Willamette United Presbyterian Church

Grave in Oakville Cemetery

* Return to Peoria Rd. at Church Rd. Turn S onto Peoria Rd.

0.7 m., first view of Willamette River on this road. *0.4 m.,* Oakville Rd. *0.4 m.,* on W, attractive old-fashioned house on Century Farm. *1.5 m.,* Brattain Dr.

* Turn E onto Brattain Dr. *1.3 m.,* on W side of bridge, and on L, *0.7 m.* foot path to **Brattain Cemetery** (1854). Old headstones tilt drowsily in the high weeds. *0.1 m.* past trailhead to Brattain Cemetery, and on R (ask permission of farm owner), farm lane leading *0.4 m.* to top of low slope. To L, thru thick undergrowth, hungry thorns and guillotine limbs, *40 yds.* to **Coon-Miller Cemetery,** small cluster of weathered grave markers (oldest is 1853) of pioneer families.

* Return to Peoria Rd. Turn S. *1.1 m.,* Fayetville Rd. Turn E onto it. *2.4 m.,* **Fayetville.** Once prominent station on Oregon Electric RR. Only one of the several large warehouses of the great wheat shipping days remains. Hamlet had store, blacksmith shop, gas pump — all gone. (Shedd, *2.6 m.,*)

* Return to Peoria Rd. Turn S. *0.2 m.,* Peoria Park, popular BL on Willamette.

0.4 m., **Peoria.** Store. In the 1870s there were four grain warehouses on the Willamette here, with capacity of 60,000 bushels of wheat, and Peoria was thriving river town. But coming of RR to the E — Shedd, Halsey and Fayetville — doomed Peoria as a hub of commerce. Still, in 1915 it could afford three Methodist churches (Episcopal, South and Free). Today hamlet is little more than a suburb of Corvallis, but church, *0.1 m.,* on R, has — though faded — the grace and puritanism of a strait-laced river town, and Peoria was that. Former Methodist Church is now Fundamentalist house of worship. All throughout Oregon, especially in rural areas, in small towns, and in poorer sections of cities, conservative, fundamentalist churches have replaced traditional churches. The symbolism is clear.

3.1 m., Pine Grove Rd. Turn W onto it. *0.3 m.,* **Pine Grove Cemetery** (1853) and chapel (services no longer held there). Cemetery has homey, patient air about it, as though the residents don't know when the newcomers will arrive but are ready to receive them anytime.

* Return to Peoria Rd. Turn S. First house on L, *50 yds.,* has oldest part built 1880s. *1.3 m.,* on W, Irish Bend Rd. A 5.3 m. loop brings the traveler back to Peoria Rd. (At jct., E, *6.2 m.,* Halsey.)

* From Irish Bend Rd.: *1.9 m.,* **Lake Creek.** Grange hall has that wood-stove, howdy look that is the style of most middle-aged Grange halls. *3.3 m.,* on E, attractive 1898 home. *2.9 m.,* O 99E. *0.3 m.,* downtown Harrisburg. On O 34, at Peoria-Harrisburg Jct.:

1.9 m., on N, Riverside Dr.

* *0.6 m.,* on L, **Orleans Chapel,** formerly Orleans Grange. On R. Orleans Cemetery, with grave markers back to 1853. Orleans was est. about 1850 and was once thriving little community. It was the upstream end of the 1851 run for the pioneer steamboat *Multnomah.* Town destroyed by great flood of

Pine Grove Marker

1861, which altered river course; cemetery remains because it was laid out on high ground.

2.4 m., Albany Jct. (Albany, 6.1 m.) 0.1 m., Calapooia River. 2.1 m., O 99E. (To S, Tangent, 1.3 m.) 1.9 m., on S, Tangent turnoff. (Tangent, 2.8 m.) 0.6 m., turnoff to I-5.

0.7 m., on S, Seven Mile Lane.

   * Turn R, or S. 3.5 m., Shedd Jct. (Shedd, 7 m.) 1.2 m., "T". Take L. 0.8 m., forks. (Straight, 1.1 m., **Plainview Mennonite Church,** last institution of Plainview. In 1915 settlement was station on E Side line of SPRR, had HS, PS, United Brethren Church, store. 9 m. on, Sodaville.)

   * At last forks, take R, onto Seven Mile Lane. 0.7 m., on W, Morgan Dr. (5 m., Shedd.) House on SW corner of Morgan Dr. and Seven Mile Lane has the secure look of the successful plowman.

   * 0.2 m., on E, Ward Butte. 0.7 m., on W, Saddle Butte.

Everywhere you look along this road there are mounds and domes and hillocks that seem to foam up from a deep green sea and then fall away, to rise again on other lunges of the restless deep, so that there is no sense of the land being frozen but in movement, sometimes swift and sometimes slow, and always moving in an undulating contour. Of this land, *Oregon: End of the Trail* said laconically: "The prairie-like expanses are dotted at intervals by

Seed burning clouds as seen from Seven Mile Lane

dome-like barriers. Formed by volcanic upthrusts, it is believed that at one time they formed islands in the waters that formerly filled this valley. Their upper strata abound with marine fossils, including the tusks and teeth of mammoths and mastodons. In the surrounding foothills petrified rock is frequently exposed by the weathering of crumbling volcanic tuff."

   * *1.3 m.*, forks. Take L. *0.1 m.*, on E — 100 yds. off road but quite visible from it — turn-of-century balconied house, shaded by maples, that is classical rural beauty.

   * *0.4 m.*, turnoff W for **Pleasant Butte Baptist Cemetery** (*0.5 m.*). Gravestones go back to 1860. The solitude on this hill is of being on an island where you can see other islands and passing ships but you are unseen — as though the cemetery is alive and the dead are out there. Only the wind seems to visit here, but it does not keep vigil; there is no point waiting for that which never was.

   * *2.5 m.*, Brownsville.

On O 34, at Seven Mile Lane:

2 m., turnoff N to Goltra Rd.

   * *3.2 m.*, on L, **Fairview Mennonite Church and School.** This is Mennonite country and the Mennonites, industrious and good-neighborly, have dotted the mid-Willamette Valley with their institutions. *0.1 m.*, "T". Turn L. *0.4 m.*, forks. Turn R onto Spicer Rd. *0.2 m.*, on R, remodeled old country school now "Conservatory for Music Education."

1.2 m., on N, Red Bridge Rd.

   * *1.1 m.*, turn R onto Gore Dr. Tallman School, which was on R (SE corner), burned down. Due E about 100 yds. was house (long gone) in which Frederic Homer Balch, author of *Bridge of the Gods*, was born. *1 m.*, turn L onto Tallman Rd. *0.2 m.*, just before RR tracks, turn L. *0.1 m.*, at rutted "Y"

Old house near Sand Ridge Cemetery   **Petersons Butte from Sand Ridge Cemetery**

in patch of raggedy grass, was RR station that was center of **Tallman,** local shipping point with grain elevator, store, PS and Baptist Church.
1.7 m., on S, Denny School Rd.

  * *0.9 m.,* on R, old **Denny School.** Printed marker on school reads: "Chinese pheasants were introduced to Oregon in 1882. Judge Owen Denny sent the birds to his brother John from China. John released 28 birds on Petersons Butte. John Denny donated school site in 1877." Mural on outside wall shows two pheasants. Judge Denny was US Consul at Tientsin when he sent the Chinese, or ring-necked, pheasants to his farmer brother. (On a link to more graphic history, Owen Denny's wife was Gertrude Hall, a survivor — and presumably the last — of the Whitman Massacre.) According to local lore, the first batch of pheasants were eaten by sailors of ship which carried them. Whether fact or fancy, it is fact that pheasants did arrive at the Denny farm in 1882. Again, according to local lore, they were liberated from the slopes of Petersons Butte, straight S of the school. There is a tale here that the birds which stayed on the butte perished; those that flew into the valley survived. At any rate, land here was known for years as Denny Pheasant Farm.

  * Turn R at school onto Sand Ridge Rd. *0.5 m.* (across mail box whose address is 32800 Sand Ridge Rd.), supposed home of John Denny. Originally, according to local lore, it was sited just back of school and had two stories instead of the one story now. *1.5 m.,* "T". Turn L, following Sand Ridge Rd. *0.7 m.,* on R, late 1880s home. TV antenna gives it mingled look of old and new. *0.1 m.,* Glaser Dr. (It's pronounced "Glasser" in these parts.) Keep straight. *0.2 m.,* on L, turnoff to **Sand Ridge Cemetery** *(0.3 m.).* In 1855 this land was selected as site of seat of Linn County. But nothing was built and in 1858 cemetery was opened. Backdropping the burial ground is Petersons Butte.

0.9 m., on L, **Sand Ridge School.** Back of it is "Little Red Schoolhouse," original school now used as kindergarten and library. Teachers here, as through-out Oregon, think nothing of driving 40 or 50 or 60 round trip m. a day to do their chores.

On O 34, from Denny School Rd.:

2.5 m., jct., US 20, at Lebanon. (For Lebanon, see *Trans-Cascade Roads, US 20.*)

O 36 — *Florence to O 99 (near Junction City)*

This is the slow road from Florence to the upper Willamette Valley because of its wanderings. Still, because it is lightly traveled and is such a folksy pike, it has some advantages over the heavier-used, straighter, more impersonal O 126 to the S.

O 36 takes off from O 126 at Mapleton, *14.5 m.* W of Florence.

From jct., O 126:

0.6 m., Public BL on Siuslaw River. PA. *1.4 m.,* on E, site of **Seaton;** early hotel (stagecoach stop) stood here. PO est. 1885, moved to present site of Mapleton 1889; named changed to Mapleton 1896.

1.3 m., **Brickerville.** Store. Jct., N Fork Rd. (W, Minerva. See *US 101, Florence,* preceding.)

2.5 m., **Tide Wayside** (CP) on Siuslaw River. *2.5 m.,* **Swisshome.** Mill, store. Named by Swiss family Zwidler. PO est. 1902. Never big, Swisshome had pop. 30 in 1915, 50 in 1940, no bigger in 1980s. At confluence of Siuslaw River and Lake Creek. Siuslaw, which fur trapper John Work called "Yangawa" when he came this way in 1834, begins to bend S and passes the baton for the E journey to Lake Creek, an inconstant runnel.

2.4 m., Indiola Public BL. PA. *0.1 m.,* Indian Creek Rd.

    * *5.4 m.,* jct. Turn R. Indian Creek flows smoothly in shadow and to the W the ridge of hills ripples in the play of wind. *5.3 m.,* on R, turnoff onto narrow lane that crosses creek on wooden bridge. Just W of creek is site of Taylor homestead where PO of Reed was est. 1900. In 1905 PO moved to house E of bridge and uphill. In 1915 about 100 people lived within a few m. of Reed. The canyons around were then alive with mills; not a single one remains. Everywhere in W Oregon there are vacant places where lumber mills once hummed.

1.7 m., turnoff to Five Rivers (16 m.) (See *O 34,* preceding.) *0.7 m.,* **Deadwood.** Store. Place gets its name not because of violence but because Deadwood Creek was so-called for dead timber snags on banks, sad product of bad Coast Range fires. In 1915 hamlet was considerably bigger; had state fish hatchery, PS, Pres. Church. pop. 80, prominent for nearby-grown clover, kale, rutabagas.

0.3 m., Deadwood Creek Rd.

    * Excellent backcountry pike zipping between low wooded hills typical of Coast Range. *4.8 m.,* on R, 1900 country school remodeled into arty house.

Just beyond, to R, Nature Trail, slither in the darkling woods. *0.4 m.*, to R, turnoff to **Deadwood Creek CB** (*0.2 m.*) *0.4 m.*, forks. Straight. *2 m.*, on R, across bridge, Alpha Community, on site of former hamlet of Alpha. (See O *34, Five Rivers Jct.*, preceding.)

4.4 m., Nelson Mtn. Rd.

   * *0.1 m.*, **Lake Creek CB.** Built 1928 at cost of $3,155; length, 105 ft.

0.6 m., **Greenleaf.** One of smallest POs in state. "We dare not get too much mail because the shack couldn't hold it," quipped a local. Hamlet started in early 1880s; in 1915 had PS, Pres. Church, store, pop. 40; has lost ground since.

8.4 m., **Triangle Lake County BL.** PA. Formed by fault across Lake Creek, Triangle Lake is square m. in area. Fine homes look down upon it and the flotilla of sailboats. The prime local aquatic playground for Eugene before completion of Fern Ridge Dam, Triangle Lake is still popular and still breezy.

2.2 m., on N, round barn, an eyestopper in ruralia. *2 m.*, **Blachly.** Store, PO, three large solidly built houses of yesteryear. In 1940 town had pop. of only 12 but it had Grange, church and HS, which is more than there is today. Store is informal social center in pocket-size vale.

1.9 m., Horton Rd.

   * A rural working class road that looks a lot more like a mining country pike of W Virginia than the middle class properties just a few m. E. *2 m.*, **James-**

Round barn at Triangle Lake

town, huddle of houses of washline kind. *1.7 m.,* **Horton.** Store. In 1915 Horton had PS, two churches, two lodges.

3.8 m., **Low Pass.** Store, cafe. Throughout W Oregon the traveler comes across place names not found on official state map or the excellent *Oregon Geographic Names.* Low Pass is one of these.

2.5 m., Hall Rd. There stood here several decades ago the settlement of **Burp Hollow,** a gusty, swinging crossroad cauldron of fun. Not a bar glass remains.

0.3 m., **Alderwood SP Wayside,** heavily timbered tract along Long Tom River. PA. Since vandals keep pilfering signs, best way to recognize wayside is picnic tables seen from road — unless they, too, are taken.

1 m., Noti Jct.

    * *6.9 m.,* thru well-kept farms and beginning of rural suburbia, O 126. (*0.9 m.,* Noti.)

3.3 m., Lawrence Rd. — Elmira Jct.

    * *3.7 m.,* Clear Lake Blvd. Straight. *0.3 m.,* **Richardson Park,** glistening greensward fanned by breezes of lake water. *1 m.,* Fern Ridge Dam. Beyond it, **Fern Ridge Reservoir,** human-made lake that has become center of middle class residential commuters from Eugene. Return to flashing lights at intersection. Turn L. *3.8 m.,* Elmira, O 126.

1.2 m., Goldson Rd.

    * Turn N. *0.3 m.,* site of **Goldson.** PO est. 1891, gone long ago.

2.6 m., Territorial Rd.

    * *1 m.,* on E, **Franklin Cemetery** (1891). Asleep forever here are Daniel Smith (1818–1909) and other white pioneers of area. *0.7 m.,* on W, two lovely country churches (Bethany built 1897). Across road, hall of Franklin Grange. *0.2 m.,* **Franklin** store. Hamlet sits on W side of old Territorial Rd., 1848–1865. In 1852 Daniel Smith settled here on DLC. In 1855, Franklin PO est. In 1857, R. V. Howard opened store here. In 1891 Smith laid out townsite and filed plat for Smithfield. But Franklin continued to appear on 1900 postal map. In 1909 US Geological Survey called town Smithfield. Confusion became so rampant that Lane County commissioners in 1934 voted to set up road signs bearing both names. For years the perplexed called the village Franklin-Smithfield. But now it's Franklin and most recent residents do not know of Daniel Smith. Franklin store was once schoolhouse and Grange hall, moved here 1914. *2.9 m.,* Lawrence Rd. (See *Lawrence Rd.-Elmira Jct.,* above.)

1.5 m., jct., Territorial Hwy.

    * Cutoff for O 99W. *9 m.,* Monroe.

0.2 m., **Cheshire.** Store. Pleasant bedroom of Eugene and environs.

Jct., Applegate Trail.

    * *2.7 m.,* Territorial Rd. at Franklin.

2 m., Alvadore Jct.

    * *5.5 m.,* **Alvadore.** Store, garage, PO, fire station. Rural W Oregon is

liberally spotted with fire stations, all of them with fine equipment and serviced by volunteers. Some of these stations have more modern, bigger rigs than some towns. At this station, community bingo games are held. Village was once stop on Portland, Eugene and Eastern RY but in 1936 track torn up. (*12 m., Eugene.*)

2 m., O 99. (N, *2 m.,* Junction City.)

O 126 — Florence to Eugene (I-5)

The main thoroughfare between the Coast and the upper Willamette Valley, O 216 is more heavily traveled than a glance at the map would suggest. With few towns en route, it is an "open road," with little twisting and little climbing.

1 m., jct., N Fork of Siuslaw. Although the Siuslaw is in summer an attractive and innocent stream, it can be a mauler in winter and early spring. (For N Fork Rd., see *US 101, Florence,* preceding.)

0.4 m., on S, historical marker stating that main village of Siuslaw Indian tribe was located W of marker, near N fork of Siuslaw. In July, 1826 a Hudson's Bay Co. exploring party comprised the first whites to cross river bar and camp in this area.

O 126 moves along the Siuslaw River, which drains this narrow valley. Before there were roads along the stream, much of the transportation was by row boat or one-cylinder marine engine craft called "one lungers."

0.4 m., on R, excellent view of early 1900s, 2-story house on 187-acre **Cox Island,** estuarine reserve owned by The Nature Conservancy. House, favorite of painters and photographers, was Ken Kesey's model for the Stamper home in *Sometimes A Great Notion.* Tom McCall termed the island "the last extensive immature salt marsh on the Southern Oregon Coast and most productive high salt marshes on the entire Oregon-Washington coasts." Nearly untouched, island is haven for 80 species of birds, including snowy egret, peregrine falcon, hawks, ospreys and ducks, and reputedly contains best clamming beach on S Coast. Its W tip is near mouth of Siuslaw River and island is reachable by boat.

0.2 m., site of place called **Acme.** Evidently it overrated self.

1 m., **Cushman.** Store, RR swing bridge across Siuslaw. *Oregon: End of the Trail,* official state guide pub. 1940, stated of Cushman: "Ocean boats are often at its docks. The hills above the rich adjacent farm lands produce much valuable Port Orford cedar." Neither assertion is current.

Beyond Cushman the setting is pastoral, with small farms spread along S bank of river.

4.9 m., bend of river. The Siuslaw, rolling glassily, curves toward a hill which for a moment seems to block the river. When the morning sun streams down the greenness of the hill the river catches fire. Here hymn singers may recall the lyric words: "Yes, we'll gather by the river,/ The beautiful, the beautiful river,/ Gather with the saints by the river,/ That flows by the throne of God."

6.1 m., W part of **Mapleton,** traditionally head of deep-water navigation on Siuslaw River, has been around since 1880s. In 1915 it had pop. 200, was terminus of completed portion of Willamette Pacific RR. W part of town has lumber mill, NF Ranger Station, PO. 0.2 m., E of W part of town, turnoff to IOOF Cemetery (0.1 m.); markers to 1880. 0.3 m., from cemetery road, E part of Mapleton, block of off-road small shops.

Jct., O 36. (See *Cross-Coast Range Roads, O 36,* preceding.)

0.1 m., at E end of bridge, turnoff S for site of former hamlet.

    * 4.8 m., turn R onto Bernhardt Creek Dr. 0.2 m., site of **Point Terrace.** PO 1890; in 1915, PS, Pres. Church. Today, zero.

3 m., on S, **Archie Knowles FS CG.** PA. RV delight on banks of Knowles Creek. Fishing reportedly good. 1.1 m., turnoff to Hood Creek PA.

    * 1.5 m., PA on Hood Creek. The quiet seems to grow with the grass.

    * 5.8 m., **Linslaw CP,** on bubbly runnel.

    * 2.3 m., jct., Siuslaw River Rd. — Whittaker Creek Rec. Area.

    * Highly recommended for get-away-from-it-all driving. Little thru traffic. Vastness of forest. 1.6 m., turnoff to **Whittaker Creek BLM Rec. Area.** (0.1 m., BR; 0.1 m., CG, PA.) At turnoff to Rec. Area: 6.9 m., forks. Take R. 1.7 m., "Y".

    R fork, known as West Fork Rd.: This leads to Smith River Rd. and, going W, to Coast. Not a habitation to be seen in this unending mass of forest. This is all BLM land, with fine network of roads, none of which is adequately marked. Here you have to go by compass, the sun, or the lay of the land. It is a good place to go to be alone, and some people do, and they look with surprise upon others who do the same, each family thinking it has found for itself a precious niche of unknown land.

    6.4 m., forks. Take L. 3.8 m., forks. Straight. 0.5 m., forks. Straight. 8.9 m., Smith River Rd. (32.3 m., US 101.)

    * L fork at "Y": This fork, Siuslaw River Access Rd., is almost completely unpopulated, winding thru clear cutting and timber stands. Clearly, this pike belongs to loggers. 6.4 m., **Clay Creek BLM Rec. Site.** CG, PA. 9 m., jct., South Sisters Rd., continuation of original Smith River Rd. (See *Smith River Rd.,* following.)

6.2 m., Walton. Store. Never much more.

6.1 m., on N. **Farmer Hale House,** on hill.

    * 0.1 m., former site of **Hale,** PO 1886–1907. In 1915 *Oregon Almanac* noted: "Lumbering is chief industry" and that Hale had a graded PS. Oldest of the old-timers remembered that at turn of century Hale had stagecoach inn on road from Eugene to Mapleton.

2.2 m., Triangle Lake Jct.

    * 6.8 m., thru placid farmland, O 36.

0.8 m., **Noti.** Here, according to *Oregon Geographic Names,* a white settler double-crossed an Indian on a "riding and tying" journey from the coast to Eugene, forcing the Indian to walk from here to their destination while the sneaky white man rode. Betrayed, the Indian exclaimed, "Him no tie!" and so the name. And so the legend. A quick look on the wrong side and Noti is missed. Still, Noti marks the outer arc of the Eugene bedroom area.

Turnoff to Vaughn.

* *4.1 m.,* **Vaughn,** a mill in the meadows. *2 m.,* forks. Straight. *3.9 m.,* Crow.

5 m., **Elmira** — Veneta Jct. A growing suburb of Eugene, traffic in Elmira has metropolitan quality to it on weekday afternoons. Once called Duckworth, thriving little hamlet on Long Tom Creek, Elmira is bigger now than it was in 1915 but it is less tight knit and a lot more sophisticated.

* Turn L onto Warthen Rd. *1.3 m.,* turn R onto Sheffler Rd. *1.3 m.,* turn onto Burgundy Lane. *0.3 m.,* Forgeron Vineyard. Winery.

0.9 m., Eugene Jct.

* Straight. *0.4 m.,* **Veneta** city center. A fast-growing suburb of Eugene, Veneta's pop. is 20-fold that of 1915.

For a brief moment, in the early 1950s, Veneta came into greater attention than it ever dreamed it would. The happening began when a student at the U of Oregon received a general mailing letter from a firm back E inviting him to send for a product information kit. A pre-stamped return card was enclosed and this fired the student's imagination. He had been to Veneta a few weeks earlier and found it to be a dismal little place. "I'll put Veneta on the map," or words to that effect, he vowed. Gathering throw-away letters from others at his student housing project, he filled the cards with exotic names and addresses, giving to Veneta an Admiral Nimitz Terrace, Douglas MacArthur Meadows, Queen Victoria Blvd., Victor Hugo Esplanade, and the like. Soon other students were not only bringing the initiator cards collected from garbage cans outside small town POs but doing their own imaginative bit. It is not known how many product information kits descended upon Veneta but the postmaster must have wondered where the system had broken down. (Unless, of course, the company got wise soon.) At any rate, so goes the legend.

* Jct., Territorial Hwy.

4.6 m., **Crow,** named not for bird but for Andy Crow, first postmaster. In 1915 Crow had pop. 50, Baptist Church, three lodges. Today it is suburban-rural outpost of Eugene. **Applegate Pioneer Museum** in circa 1900 Pine Grove School moved here from deeper hinterland. **Gates Cemetery** est. 1850.

* *1 m.,* Eugene Jct. (Eugene, *16 m.*)

* *0.3 m.,* jct., Wolf Creek Rd.

** Wolf Creek Rd. begins in a quiet, orderly way, passing thru informal communities, then plunges over a hill to spin down to S Sisters Rd. *0.2 m.,* Coyote Creek Rd. *(0.1 m.,* on R, **Crow Farm,** calendar art, Grant Wood farmhouse of abundant proportions. *0.4 m.,* **Coyote Creek CB,** built 1922 with span of 60 ft.) *6 m.,* site of **Panther.** PO 1894–1909. In 1915, pop. 50, PS. *5.6 m.,* S Sisters Rd. (See *Smith River Rd.,* following.)

　** Territorial Rd.: *0.6 m.,* Battle Creek Rd. (Turn R. *0.1 m.,* CB across Coyote Creek.) *3.4 m.,* turnoff to Hinman Vineyards. *(0.5 m.,* winery.) *0.4 m.,* on R, **Hadley House,** built late 1870s or early 1880s. Was PO of Hadleyville, 1890–1903. *8.9 m.,* Siuslaw River Rd. Lorane. (See *Smith River Rd.,* following.)

　E on O 126 from Eugene Jct.:

3 m., turnoff N for Perkins Peninsula Park of **Fern Ridge Lake.** Lake, a reservoir, is favored by many species of birds for year-round habitation. From Dec. to April Canada geese and ducks cover the waters. When they depart the ospreys arrive and stay until Sept. In this area the reddish-hued Madrone trees are not common but neither are they rare. They are transition belt trees, growing where the moist valley climate meets the more arid climate to the S. When the trees shed their outer bark they appear to be mortally wounded, bleeding as the skin peels off in strips, but the process is natural, a cycle of regeneration.

4.2 m., Greenhill Rd. — Crow Jct.

　* *9.1 m.,* Crow.

6.2 m., downtown Eugene.

Smith River Road — Gardiner to Cottage Grove

　Although this pike is popularly known as the Smith River Road, it follows the river only in part and after leaving the Smith has other names.

　Smith River reflects the strange personality of the legendary Jedediah Smith, after whom the stream was named. In the W it is serene, glassy, poolish, reflecting patience and wisdom. In the E along the road it is stone-bottomed, rocky, tough and feisty. Smith's nature was likewise charged with turns of personality.

　In the W, gleaming green vales, well stocked with cattle, fall away from the river and roll on in neat saucers to the rising woods. As the road whirls E, the vales shrink and the cattle diminish in number. There comes a time then when the grass runs out and the riversides are captured by brush and trees.

　Along this road there stand the ranch houses, in stubborn and severe solitude, some of them as far back of the pavement as they can be, and a few of the ranchers strongly indicating in one way or another that the less they are bothered by strangers the higher they regard the human race.

　Along the river are many self-made CGs by RVers. Generally, spots hold no more than one or two vehicles.

　N and S of Smith River Rd. are networks of nameless, unnumbered roads flung hither and yon, perhaps known only to their makers, bewildering and madden-

Along Smith River Road

ing, and reminding one of the Greek myth in which Zeus condemns Ixion to Hades, there to revolve on a perpetually rolling wheel.

8.7 m., — from US 101 — **Noel Ranch BL.** *10 m.,* on N, site of **Sulphur Springs.** Former cold water mineral spa. PO 1878–1920. In 1915 Sulphur Springs had Catholic and ME churches, PS, pop. 30. Transportation was chiefly by boat.

4.5 m., footbridge across stream. *2.8 m.,* another footbridge across Smith. *0.1 m.,* **Smith River Falls.** Pleasant. *0.4 m.,* footpath to smaller falls. *0.1 m.,* **Smith River Falls Rec. Site.** CG, PA.

3.7 m., **Vincent Creek Rec. Site and Guard Station.** CG, PA.

Forks. R, *15 m.,* O 38. Keep L on Smith River Rd.

2 m., jct., West Fork Smith River Rd. (*29.8 m.,* O 126.) (See O 126, preceding.)

4.6 m., marker of **Oxbow Burn,** 8/20/66, Oregon's fourth worst fire; destroyed 43,000 acres. A thousand men fought the holocaust. Entire area subsequently reseeded and now another crop of timber is growing.

4.7 m., on N, **Twin Sisters CG.** PA. *0.1 m.,* jct., Weatherly Creek Rd.

　　* *20.8 m.,* O 38. Smith River turns S near this road and the two meander S together.

The road E becomes the S Sisters Rd. Take that.

15.5 m., jct., Siuslaw River Rd.

　　* *25.6 m.,* O 126. (See O 126, preceding.)

1.3 m., site of **Alma,** one of very few empty places in W Oregon that looks as though a hamlet may have been here. PO est. 1888. In 1915 Alma had PS and pop. 35, which may indicate a store was also here.

1.4 m., obliterated site of **Mound.** PO 1892–1910. In 1915, PS here.

Jct., Wolf Creek Rd. — Territorial Hwy.

  * *17.7 m.*, Veneta. (See *O 126, Veneta,* preceding.)

Pike now becomes Siuslaw River Rd.

8.8 m., jct., Siuslaw Falls Rd.

  * *0.5 m.*, PA overlooking ripples of Siuslaw River.

0.2 m., Lane CP. PA.

8.8 m., **Lorane,** drowsy two-store village that has become a sunporch of Eugene. PO est. 1887. **Lorane Christian Church,** on hill, built 1889. Near it is elderly hall of **Lorane Lodge,** IOOF. Grange hall, over brow of hill, is as homey as they come. In 1915 town had more.

Jct. N. Territorial Hwy.

  * *19.2 m.*, Veneta, on O 126. (See *O 126, Veneta,* preceding.)

Jct. S.

  * *1 m.*, on R, old **IOOF Cemetery.** *1.5 m.*, site of **Mountain House Hotel,** or Cartwright House (1853). Was PO, stagecoach inn, telegraph station. One of first messages received was of President Lincoln's assassination. Destruction of this house was little noticed and not protested. Why the state did not intervene to preserve this historic landmark is a good question until one begins to realize that, on the whole, Oregon has done a miserable job in historic preservation. *13.3 m.*, Drain, O 99. Jct. E.

12.5 m., Cottage Grove, O 99.

O 38 — Reedsport to Drain, O 99
O 138 — Elkton to Roseburg

From US 101:

0.4 m., business section, **Reedsport.** *0.2 m.*, turnoff to Public BL.

Singing along with the proud, historic Umpqua River, O 38 is a delight to drive when it isn't congested, as it often isn't. Look to the stream, visualize a vessel plodding its way a century and a half ago, and, in the words of Walt Whitman, hear "The boatman singing what belongs to him in his boat, the deckhand singing on the steamboat deck."

8.7 m., **Umpqua Wayside SP,** on river. PA, fishing, boating. Here, on Aug. 6, 1850, the first schooner to go up the Umpqua, the *Samuel Roberts,* on her maiden voyage to Scottsburg, ran aground on the bar. While waiting thru the night for the tide to float the vessel free, the crew fell to on the brandy. When the captain caught on to the tippling he threw the keg into the river, but by then there were some drunken sailors around and the name of Brandy Bar was born, and to this day has persisted.

The highway now acts as matchmaker between the gentle river and the sweet meadows, then abandons grass for wavy trees and humble hills. On this road, to quote Emily Dickinson, the cars "lap the miles and lick the valleys up."

3.9 m., Loon Lake Jct.

    * The road cavorts uphill thru **Elliott State Forest.** *5.1 m.,* forks. Take R. *1.8 m.,* start of **Loon Lake Rec. Area.** Forks. (R, *0.1 m.,* Loon Lake CG. *0.1 m.,* Loon Lake PA. Lake is best seen in early spring or mid-autumn, when few people, if any, are at the shore. Then, though loons are rare, the cry of a loon seems to come from the water. A young man from Los Angeles, deeply moved, whispered, "This place is swollen with peace.") Straight: *0.1 m.,* beneath the bridge a creek charges between huge boulders and scolds its way thru minor but impressive chasm. *0.9 m.,* **East Shore Rec. Area.** Road glides around the lake, exposing the jewel in all its fragments. *3.8 m.,* forks. Straight. *0.3 m.,* **Ash Valley School,** where village of Ash stood. Name comes from the many ash trees in the narrow valley. In 1915 Ash had cheese factory and sawmill. Now the old-timers debate where the PO stood. The one-room schoolhouse, with grades 1-8, seems out of tune with the time of busing. But folks here insist on their independence and there have been some furious battles about composition of school board. Anyone who does not think that rural village politics can be feverish simply has not lived in a little burg.

    On O 38, from Loon Lake Jct.:

    2.5 m., **Scottsburg Park PA.** BL on Umpqua River. *0.9 m.,* at E end of bridge, turnoff to Scottsburg West Rd.

Loon Lake

* Make sharp L turn downhill. For a glimpse of the good life, drive this narrow lane which winds along Umpqua. Houses on this dreamy pike are practically on bank of stream, most idyllic setting. Yet in mid-19th century this road was Lower Scottsburg and was lined with docks.

A house on this road was the home of Gladys Workman, author of best-selling *Only When I Laugh*, pub 1959. In 1985 a neighbor and friend of Mrs. Workman recalled: "At the time the book came out there were some pretty unhappy locals here; it really wasn't too flattering to some people. Most of them are now gone, so the valley has forgiven Gladys. The book signing party was held in Emma Hedden's store. We were all decked out in really fancy pioneer costumes. Today it sounds dumb, but in '59 it was really a great idea." Emma Hedden was the last female descendant of mercantile pioneer Cyrus Hedden, one of the nine men Capt. William Tichenor had brought aboard his *Sea Gull* to Battle Rock, Port Orford. (See *US 101, Port Orford*.) A century and a quarter after Cyrus Hedden opened his store in Scottsburg, and in the third bldg. that carried the Hedden name, Emma Hedden was phasing the store out. Thus closed, in the words of a local historian, "the oldest commercial establishment in Oregon under one management."

0.3 m., **Scottsburg,** at its zenith one of the busiest, most colorful towns in Oregon Country. Founded 1850 by Levi Scott, co-opener with the Applegates of the S Rd. into Oregon in 1846, Scottsburg quickly prospered because of its location as head of navigation on the Umpqua and for almost two years was the big city of S Oregon. It is hard to believe, looking at the sleeping hollow now, that ships from San Francisco docked here, disgorging supplies for the S mines; that the dirt streets were aswarm with strings of pack mules, hustling merchants, gamblers, saloonkeepers, salesmen, fortune hunters and sailors out to better their luck; that *The Umpqua Gazette,* published here, was the first newspaper in all of S Oregon; that one of the roomers at the fancy hotel owned by Daniel Lyons, the blind minstrel, was Joe Hooker, later to become a Civil War general. Scottsburg began to fade with the founding of Crescent City, Calif., which provided easier access to the gold camps, and stage routes from other cities, but Scottsburg's streets were still lined with stores, hotels and saloons. The Umpqua flooded heavily in 1861, completely wiping out Lower Scottsburg and doing heavy damage to Upper Town. One of the few businesses to survive was that owned by Cyrus Hedden.

0.2 m., on R, **Scottsburg Historical Center,** in early school, is really community hall. Here stood the "city square" of yore.

0.3 m., on R, **Indian Rock.** Ponderous rock which from O 38 looks only a fraction of real size. You have to scramble down the often slick slope to see the significance of what probably was for centuries an Indian CG. Indian writings on rock — and Indian artifacts have been dug up. River side of rock overhang shelter for settlers during first winter.

1.7 m., turnoff to PA on Vincent Creek.

15 m., PA at Smith River Rd.

0.4 m., Wells Creek, rural shopping mart, with store the center of cultural activities.

0.7 m., turnoff N to **Scottsburg Cemetery.**

   * *0.2 m.,* cemetery. Old markers abound, going back to 1861.

4.9 m., BL on Umpqua. *5.6 m.,* on S. Bunch Bar. Parking area and steep trail to river.

6 m., **Elkton,** center of first area in Douglas County to be settled by whites. As early as 1828 a party of Hudson's Bay Co. trappers came thru here. In 1832 the wily Dr. John McLoughlin, who headed the W division of HBC from his HQ at Ft. Vancouver, ordered a trading post to be est. in this expanse. The famous trapper, Michel La Framboise, and his equally well-known partner, John McLeod, built stockade on low plain across Umpqua River from present Elkton and called it Ft. Umpqua. Jean Baptiste Gagnier, who managed post, is regarded as first (white) resident farmer and merchant in Douglas County. Basically, the trading post, whose chief mission was to collect furs, consisted of a large warehouse of hewn slabs, barn and some homes in stockaded area. Inside the outer walls cattle grazed and vegetable plots were tended. The Gold rush and the splurge of DLCs following US control of the region made existence of Ft. Umpqua untenable and in 1853 the already abandoned post was leased to American settler W. W. Chapman. In 1856 HBC lost title to land. There is no trace of the fort; trees cover the site.

Elkton was platted and PO est. 1851. When Scottsburg was in its prime, supplies to mines passed thru Elkton. Pack trains and freight wagons made a line a mile long, waiting to cross the river. Although this prosperity declined with opening of coast ports, Elkton continued to grow. But flood in 1890 did havoc to bldgs. along W bank of Elk Creek, fire in 1915 destroyed more of the town, and conflagrations between 1920 and 1950 further whittled down the business district. In 1878 Elkton had pop. 350; by 1915 pop. had declined to 150; has since remained at that plateau. Oddly, town not inc. until 1948.

Church at 2nd and B, built 1903, has look of stern patrician. **Elkton Masonic Hall,** on 1st, put up 1916, has false front affectation of earlier period. Much of town's 20th century history associated with hall. Stage was used for school plays, graduation ceremonies, Xmas programs, elections, literary meetings and pie socials. Vaudeville was brought here by travelling troupes. Silent movies were shown regularly. The "talkies" were introduced here. In this hall desperate farmers and workers gathered to hear of the Townsend Plan, a panacea of the Great Depression. Roller skating was a regular happening of the 1930s and 1940s. When Xmas flood of 1964 made homeless the riverbank dwellers, hall was opened to house them.

Other historic structures: **R. O. Thomas Storefront** (1916), on SE corner of 1st and O 38; **Robinson House** (1895), SE corner of Main and O 38; **Tyson House** (1895), 2nd and River Dr.; **Finley House** (1900), 3rd N of River Dr.

0.3 m., jct., O 138.

     * *0.1 m.*, Azalea Dr. (*0.4 m.*, L to Elkton Cemetery — headstones back to 1880s.)

     *0.2 m., turnoff O 138 onto Mehl Creek Rd. This is the back-back road to the Umpqua Valley, stealing thru woods and hills as though it were eluding a posse bent on its hanging. It moves so quickly and furtively away from directions that keeping up with it becomes a problem of major magnitude. (Few people in Elkton seem to have been on this road.) But it has its consolation in solitude and fume-free air.

     * On Mehl Creek Rd.: *3.7 m.*, forks. Take L. Road follows Umpqua and is lonelier than river. *5.3 m.*, "T". Turn L onto Douglas County Rd. 57. At times the woods seem endless, and there are places along this road where there is a swift and sudden cleft in the foliage, opening to such delightful emerald vistas that the impulse is to exclaim, "How green is this valley!" And where the grass is alive there are sheep, so that after a while the vales become chambers of Sheep Heaven. *0.8 m.*, O 138. Turn R onto it. *0.9 m.*, **Kellogg Grange,** all that is left of what was Kellogg, which in 1915 had pop. 50, PS, Grange. *4.3 m.*, BL on Umpqua. *1.9 m.*, Bullock Rd. (R across bridge. Turn R. *0.4 m.*, **Tyee Rec. Site,** BLM CG and PA overlooking Umpqua.) Straight: *0.2 m.*, Tyee Store. *0.2 m.*, Tyee Rd. Turn R onto it. *8 m.*, **Mack Brown CP.** PA on Umpqua. *4 m.*, Umpqua Jct. (Straight, *7.6 m.*, with brief flirtation with Calapooya Creek, I-5 and Sutherlin.) Turn R. *0.1 m.*, **Umpqua.** Store. There was more in 1915: schools, churches, Grange, pop. 120. Turn R. *0.3 m.*, Garden Valley Rd. Turn L. Road quickly turns "civilized," with many more homes, and farms, and more sheep. *11 m.*, on R, turn onto Old Garden Valley Rd. (*1.6 m.*, turn. *0.3 m.*, **River Forks CP.** PA where S and N forks of Umpqua join.) Return to road. Turn R. *1 m.*, turn R on Curry Rd. (*1.7 m.*, turn R. *0.7 m.*, **Singleton CP.** PA. Refreshing grassy grounds on Umpqua — but posted warnings of what not to do reads like a Salem manifesto.) Return to road. Turn R. *3.2 m.*, Roseburg.

     ** From Umpqua store, on backcountry road to Winston:

     In the spring, especially, this is an exhilarating pike, rich with treats for the senses and lavish with the small wonders of Douglas County: the coffee table picture book hills; the undulating farms; the slopes dipping as graceful as the bowing of a swan; the kept-up houses, maintained as though rich relatives were coming to supper; the fat and fleecy sheep. *0.3 m.*, turnoff for Roseburg. (See road just described.) Straight. *0.3 m.*, Henry Winery. *0.8 m.*, Melqua Rd. Turn onto it. *1.2 m.*, **Coles Valley Cemetery** (1854). *1 m.*, on R, Burma Shave sequence rhyming signs — perhaps last in Oregon. *3.2 m.*, on L, Cleveland Cemetery (1877). *0.4 m.*, forks. Take L. *4.2 m.*, **Melrose,** formerly Hogan. In 1915 Melrose had pop. 100 and schools. Store only now; still, Melrose is compass point in this landscape; folks refer to it as though it anchors the valley. (L, Roseburg, *6 m.*) Turn R. *1.9 m.*, "T". Turn L. *4.8 m.*,

Lookingglass. Legend has it that an 1846 traveler thru valley was so struck by light reflection of tall grass that he compared phenomenon to a mirror. In 1915 town had pop. 200, with facilities proper for community of that size. Now, only store. In 1970s storeowner drew national attention for his "urban" antics: parking meter, manhole cover, airmail box high on a telephone pole, etc. But when he went off to seminary in Indiana he took his imagination with him. *0.7 m.,* turn L. *2.3 m.,* forks. Take R. *2.4 m.,* Dillard Rd. Straight. *1.4 m.,* Winston. *0.2 m.,* O 42–O 99.

   * O 138 — from O 38:
   * *0.3 m.,* Mehl Creek Rd. (See earlier, O 38.)
   * *0.1 m.,* on R, **Ft. Umpqua Historical Marker;** site of early Hudson's Bay Co. post. *6.8 m.,* Kellogg Grange. *4.3 m.,* BL on Umpqua. *1.9 m.,* on R, Bullock Rd. (Turn R. *0.2 m.,* across bridge, turn R. *0.4 m.,* Tyee Rec. Site. BLM CG and PA on Umpqua.) *0.2 m.,* Tyee Store. *0.2 m.,* Tyee Rd. The road now wends its way thru a fruitful land blessed with original pastel touches. Sheep on the far hillsides look like apple blossoms fallen on a green sea. From Elkton — on O 38:

0.3 m., jct., O 138. *7.4 m.,* on R, privately-owned CB *0.1 m.,* off O 38 on dirt road. *6.7 m.,* Drain. (See *The Great Heartland,* O 99.)

Coos Bay Wagon Road — Eastside to Roseburg

Military wagon roads were one of those commonplace deceptions Americans have practiced upon themselves since the founding of the Republic.

Give something a patriotic name, no matter how much it smelled of porkbarrel legislation, and there was a better chance of Congress forking out the money for it. The pundit who observed that the natural tendency for crooks and scoundrels was to wrap themselves in the flag could have added that behind many a cry for military expenditure was a smiling profiteer.

Though few "military roads" were really built for military purposes and a good number were less than excellently designed and as much laid out by political and commercial clout as by geographic expediency, and despite most of these pikes having been superseded by more practical routes, some "military roads" were essential for their time. A case in point is the Coos Bay Wagon Road..

It was built in 1873 to meet an urgent need for a fast pike between the Umpqua Valley and the Coast. Before it was built the only way of travel was to Scottsburg by land, then by boat down the Umpqua River to Gardiner, and finally to tightrope the sandy beaches, between high tides, to the Coos Bay settlements. It was a long and trying journey.

There wasn't much time or money, in this case, to construct a fine thoroughfare, so the engineers followed a rough-hewn trail that had been hacked out by a Coos County pioneer.

The road today is partly paved and partly graveled, but it continues to follow the same course and is as narrow and winding as it has been for more than a century. And that's the beauty of it, taking an uncrowded voyage back in time.

Right from the first the military wagon road was open to coach travel and the US Mail. It took stagecoach passengers a full 24 hours to make the trip between Coos Bay and Roseburg in 1873 and in 1910 it still took 24 hours.

In 1873 the fare was $5 per person; by 1910 the tariff had almost doubled. In the early years, six passengers were all that could fit into a stage; later, larger coaches were introduced. It generally took five drivers and 42 head of horses to complete a one-way run; at places eight horses pulled the stage. Initially, Concord coaches were used in the summer; at other seasons passengers could be expected to ride in large wagons, to whose sides they were strapped by canvas rope.

Comfort was not one of the line's strong points. Dry weather brought irritating clouds of dust and rain turned the pike into a churn of mud. Sleep was never easy, being imperiled by the specter of a possible mishap. Every time a wheel slipped or a horse balked or a curve was taken too sharply the nodding passengers were jerked awake in fright and those who hadn't dozed off trembled and paled.

The road started at Isthmus Inlet, just E of US 101, but to simplify, it starts here at Eastside. (To reach Eastside: *1.3 m.,* S on US 101 from Commercial St., Coos Bay to Eastside-Allegany Jct. *1.1 m.,* Eastside Jct.)

From Eastside Jct., at Eastside and D St., Eastside:

1 m., Bridge Jct. Straight on Ross Inlet Rd. *2.7 m.,* jct. (Here the road from Isthmus Inlet is met.) Turn L. *4.6 m.,* turn L. *0.2 m.,* **Sumner.** In 1915, town had pop. 100. Today, only store, but in the glistening green meadows between Eastside and Sumner the land is well settled.

Beyond Sumner the farms and houses slip away quickly, and the road loses itself in absent-mindedness and hallucination. Logging trucks make it no place to relax.

8 m., **Fairview.** PO 1873–1913. Busy crossroads store, delightfully located PS.

Jct. To R: *8.4 m.,* O 42, Coquille.

Jct. To L:

    * *2.7 m.,* on R, **Homestead Tavern,** with all the illusion of RR depot. Stained glass window is owner's pride. *1.2 m.,* on L, eye-stopping mansion in these parts. *0.2 m.,* **La Verne CP.** CG, PA, swimming.

3 m., jct. Burnt Mtn. — Park Creek Rec. Site.

    * *8 m.,* forks. Angle R across bridge. *2.5 m.,* **Park Creek Rec. Area,** true wilderness ambience, with few people during weekdays.

1.5 m., McKinley Jct. Straight. *0.6 m.,* **McKinley.** PO named in 1897 for Pres. Wm. McKinley. It is said some people around here are so nostalgic about past they write in McKinley's name at presidential elections. Nothing remains of village but old store, garage and gas station, abandoned and fit for dusty antique sale.

0.6 m., **Cherry Creek CP.** Lovely PA. *1.7 m.,* jct. Straight. *0.5 m.,* **Frona CP.** PA. *1.2 m.,* on L, mammoth 2-1/2 story wooden house; looks like old style hunting lodge. Built as stagecoach stop but coaches quit running before house completed.

0.4 m., **Dora.** PO est. 1874; out long ago. In its prime Dora had a United Brethren Academy, Grange, PS. Only a small store hangs on.

Probably the most authentic feel of the old military wagon road is the 6 m. stretch between Dora and Sitkum. Here you know, absolutely, that if you close your eyes hard and think deep into time before you, a Concord stage is sure to come by.

Just before Sitkum the road shakes off the confines of the E fork of Coquille to burst into a vista of Brewster Valley, its grass lustrous and its buttercups dazzling.

Sitkum, Chinook jargon word for half, was est. as stage stop in 1872, to anticipate trade of wagon road. PO followed next year. All stages pulled up at Halfway House, which was combination eating place, tavern, overnight rooming house, PO and telegraph station. Here, while the drivers changed and a fresh relay of horses took over, passengers had their longest pause and their fullest meal. In 1975 an aged man recalled that in 1910 he paid about $1.50 for the meal, which was a feast the day he was at Sitkum. He remembered: "The lady had prepared a great big platter of chicken and when she saw that there weren't as many passengers as she had expected she told us to eat it all up. So I was gorged."

The lady was Belle Laird, sole survivor of the pioneer John Alva Harry family, 1852 Oregon comers. In 1857, when she was 17, newly-wed Chloe Amelia Cook Harry and her husband, 23, moved to his land claim on the Coquille River. A chronicler of this area wrote: "They made this trip on horseback and, months afterward, small bits of her dress could be seen where they caught on the wild rose thorns along the narrow trail over Sugar Loaf Mountain." A year after J. A. Harry

Dora   *Phoebe L. Friedman*

passed away, in 1874, the widow became the bride of James Laird. A news report of the time stated: "They were married in Roseburg and the day they started for Douglas County, Mr. Laird's team ran away and piled the wagon and its two occupants in the creek."

Chloe Amelia Laird breathed her last in 1924, having outlived her second husband by 15 years. Her first — and last — illness began when she contracted the flu the winter before. Until then she had never required the services of a physician. She had come into the vale of the E Fork of the Coquille with only Indian trails to follow; at her death she had been the oldest pioneer of Coos County.

Chloe's daughter, Belle, married her step-brother, also named J. D. Laird. The Myrtle Point *Herald* wrote of her in 1949, 4 years after her husband's earthly departure. "For many years she and her daughters cooked twice daily meals for the stage passengers over the old Coos Bay wagon road and passengers on those stages looked forward eagerly to the dinner hour at her home. Her light-bread biscuits won for her an honored spot in the archives of pioneer culinary."

At 83, still doing her own housework and caring for the Sitkum PO, she was known as "Mother of Brewster Valley." She is even now spoken of so vividly by the old timers that new residents to Beaver Creek think she must still be alive.

Halfway House burned down long ago. Not a trace of it remains. The rest of the town folded.

5.9 m., — from Dora — on R, former 2-room **Sitkum School,** now dwelling. On grounds are former teacher's residence, also dwelling now, and old gym. *0.1 m.,* site of what was **Sitkum.**

Jct., Maria Jackson SP.

   * *1 m.,* SP. PA. Picture book forest. No water.

Now comes the "wildest" part of the road, vacant of habitation, little-traveled, shrouded by pecking woods, met counterpoint by the E Fork of Coquille, sprinting and hurdling on to the far-off sea. *4.6 m.* from Sitkum the stream splashes down a boulder-filled narrow canyon in frenzied cascades.

9.5 m., on S, trail angles down to **Douglas CP.** *0.7 m.,* **Iverson Memorial Park.** PA. *1.8 m.,* Tenmile Jct.

   * *2.3 m.,* Bjelland Vineyard and Winery. *1.5 m.,* Girardet Winery. *0.7 m.,* O 42, at Tenmile.

0.1 m., on L, large 2-story house with two covered porches. This stagecoach stop was the center of **Reston** and is its sole survivor. The *Oregon Almanac* of 1915 wrote of Reston: "On line of Coos Bay (Brewster Canyon) stage road, which is one of the most beautiful scenic highways in Southern Oregon." Reston then had pop. 30.

From this point on the road, sleek and swift, dips into the Umpqua Valley. Farms and rural residences grow increasingly numerous. The stagecoach is now on its last leg. Hold tight and relax.

8.3 m., **Lookingglass,** by now a suburb of Roseburg. When first seen by whites the green, green grass reflected the rays of the sun so purely that 1846 pioneer Hoy Flournoy, for whom valley was named, was struck by the metaphor of a mirror.

Turn L at store. *0.3 m.,* turn R. *8.2 m.,* city center, **Roseburg.** Home for the horses: oats and rest.

O 42 — *Coos Bay Jct. to Winston, O 99*

This is the high road between the Pacific littoral and the Umpqua Valley. Frugally sprinkled with tiny settlements, O 42 is a flyer but those who want to savor the riches of the country will move at a more restrained pace. Along the Middle Fork of Coquille River O 42 is particularly appealing, the insouciant stream flowing between chiaroscuro hills.

O 42 begins off US 101, *6.1 m.* S of Commercial St., Coos Bay.

4.9 m., site of **Coaledo.** It is not generally known that low grade coal was once mined in the area S of Coos Bay and that the coal was shipped to ports on the Pacific Coast. Coaledo, one of the mining towns, was so-named because of finding of a vein, or lead, of coal. PO est. 1875. When coal ran out people did too. So there is today just a hwy. marker that means nothing to almost all travelers. Some geologists believe there is still plenty of coal to be mined in these parts but the coal mining towns have been long gone.

1.8 m., jct., North Bank Rd. (Bandon, *14 m.;* Charleston, *18 m.)* Off this road is the site of **Beaver Hill,** another former mining community.

4.1 m., on L, The Myrtle Burl, producing handcrafted giftware since 1907.

0.3 m., turnoff to Fairview.

  * A glimpse into the cozy backcountry and its has-been village. *7.8 m.,* L for Fairview Cemetery. *(0.4 m.,* cemetery, est. 1884.) *0.6 m.,* Fairview, at jct. of Coos Bay Wagon Rd. Store. Straight: *2.7 m.,* **Homestead Tavern.** From short distance looks like train station. May be only tavern in state with stained-glass window. Folks who patronize here will not only give you time of day but all day to chat. *1.2 m.,* turn-of-century house whose architecture is more akin to Willamette Valley. Original settler was member of Donner Party before it split up, the ill-fated group going on to Calif. and disaster. *0.2 m.,* **La Verne CP.** CG, PA, swimming.

0.7 m., **Coquille,** Indian name with indeterminate meaning. Seat of Coos County, which provides town some economic sustenance when times get hard. Like other mill towns, a whisper that the local mill will close sends the community into shivers. Unfortunately the whisper is too often truth. With closing of mill comes exodus of workers, shutting down of shops, general deterioration of business district, and the searing, back-burner effects of child abuse, wife abuse, alcoholism, emotional breakdown and, as the last tragic consequence, suicide.

Coquille's **Sawdust Theatre** is one of best and best-known grassroots stage groups in state. Started 1966, the Sawdusters have traditionally from Memorial

Day to Labor Day been performing old-fashioned melodramas — such as "The Curse of the Devil's Eye (or Five Fast Friends Foil a Fiend)" — and olios, in addition to plays using familiar place names and spoofs of local politicians. All Sawdusters are town people and all quite talented.

Street uphill from Safeway store is "fanciest" part of town, has many old and distinguished-looking residences. They include **Maune House** (1888), 1st and Dean; house caddy-corner (1888); late 19th century house at 1st and Elliott; Judge Harlocker House (1891), Collier and Main; and the residence most splendid of all, **Bonney House** (1901), Collier and Main, estate-like mansion flanked by rows of majestic myrtlewoods.

2.2 m., on R, **Coquille Valley Art Center.** *3.1 m.,* Fairview Jct. (For Fairview and environs, see *Coos Bay Wagon Road,* preceding and above, this section.) *0.7 m.,* Norway Jct.

   * *0.1 m.,* **Norway.** Settled by Norwegians in 1870s, PO has hopped around like skier out of control. In 1915 village had pop. 125, creamery, private electric lighting plant, PS. Almost all gone.

1.9 m., Arago Jct.

   * *0.7 m.,* turn R. *0.1 m.,* turn L. BR. Return to Arago Rd. Turn R. *0.1 m.,* "T". Turn R. Serene lane, pastoral to the core. *4 m.,* turn R. *1.1 m.,* **Arago,** in its early days called Halls Prairie. In 1915 town had shingle mill, cheese factory, two churches, PS. School bldgs. still stand, but they are empty. Arago now is small colony clustered around typical country store.

0.8 m., Gravelford Jct.

   * *8.1 m.,* **Gravelford** — two houses. PO 1878–1934. Looking at the vacancy of land it is difficult to realize that in 1915 Gravelford could boast of two cheese factories, two churches, Adventist Academy, PS. The "old-timers" here arrived after Gravelford had left.

   (** At Gravelford, turn L. *0.5 m.,* **Bennett CP.** CG. Park kept in natural condition, with old-growth lumber.)

0.1 m., **Myrtle Point.** Founded as Meyersville in 1861 and renamed Otis in 1866, town has had present name since 1872. Name, of course, is tribute to myrtle trees, which once were abundant hereabouts and are still in good number. Tallest of these trees in town is at 7th and Harris, in front of **Endicott House,** 708 Harris.

Best preserved older town in Coos County, Myrtle Point looks pretty much as it did several decades ago. Reflecting the past are: **Presbyterian Church** (1890), Railroad and Maple; **Bank of Myrtle Point** (1895), now dept. store at 333 Spruce; pioneer **Benson Home,** 604 7th; **Guerin Hotel** (1897), 312 5th; **Volkmars Hotel** (1889), 324 Spruce; **Machado Bldg.** (1896), 302 2nd; **Huling and Lund Hardware** (1890), 323 Spruce; **A. H. Black Bldg.** (1894), 531 Spruce. Homes dating from late 19th century seem more commonplace than oddities in Myrtle Point.

Coos County Logging Museum is graphic text of timber industry of county at work level. Display area divided into depts. found in well-equipped early day logging camp.

American Legion Hall has to many viewers look of Russian Orthodox Church architecture. But it was designed by 1853 arrival, brickyard owner Samuel Giles, who sought to emulate, on modest scale, Mormon Tabernacle in Salt Lake City, which he had seen, and its phenomenal acoustical properties. The framing system was described in a 1966 article by Charles McCracken, local resident born 1882. He and Thomas Dickson, also of Myrtle Point, and born 1871, helped build the original LDS structure: "The ribs or staves, continuous from floor to cupola, are laminated of three 1 x 4's nailed up in forms to the proper curvature. Set to sixteen inches on center at the floor, the ribs form a solid wall in the upper part of the ceiling. The sheathing was sprung around the ribs for a smooth surface." The design of Giles, however, was not quite right, and when the Reorganized Church of Latter Day Saints was formally dedicated in 1910 a serious flaw was discovered. False ceilings installed later toned down the acoustical chaos but never brought about tonal clarity. Mormons held services there until late 1927, when bldg. was purchased by recently organized Four Square Gospel Church, which boldly declared it would occupy premises until end of world, expected within decade by congregation's leader, the dynamic Mrs. A. T. Train, who installed the first false ceiling. In early 1940s local American Legion post bought structure and put in permanent ceiling, as well as resurfacing bldg. with composition shingles to match color of original cedar shingles, long weathered.

2.6 m., **Hoffman Wayside.** (PA reached by trail.)

0.3 m., Powers Jct.

   * *2.5 m.,* **Broadbent.** Store. Started to house cheese factory (no longer there) in second decade of 20th century, town could never become more than an adjunct of Powers. Hermann House, Dement Creek and Broadbent Roads, built 1861. *5 m.,* **Albert H. Power Memorial Park,** named for tycoon-philanthropist of area. *2.3 m.,* Gaylord. Nothing but a name. *0.5 m.,* **Coquille Myrtle Grove SP.** PA, fishing on S fork Coquille River. *7.1 m.,* **Powers CP.** CG. *1.1 m.,* **Powers,** named for A. H. Powers in 1914. Town was outfitting jumpoff for Johnson Creek and Salmon Creek gold mining area before it became noted for lumber. **Pioneer Museum** is 2-story, hand-hewn, log-slab house built 1872 by David Wagner and his son, John, who came to S Fork of Coquille River with about 80 other people from North Carolina. Nine children of the John Wagner family were born and raised in this house, which is furnished with household items of the period. Powers House is example of hinterland affluence.

   * Beyond Powers the road runs wild and free, with scarcely a homestead along the way. Passing thru these woods, where sunlight battles furiously with the twilight of thick foliage, one would expect to find deer bounding out of the shadows, and sometimes they do, and bear crashing thru the brush, which, alas, doesn't happen. *6.1 m.,* **Elk Creek Falls,** 75-ft. drop over rock bluff; from road it appears as a rumble over boulders. *2.6 m.,* **Myrtle Grove FS CG.** *5.7 m.,* **Daphne Grove FS CG,** on S Fork of Coquille. Now the

road is only a whisper away from the stream. *2.2 m.,* jct. (Eden Valley, *15 m.;* at *38 m.* there is jct., with upper road arching 15 m. to Glendale and lower road curving *7 m.* S to Grave Creek and another jct. At this point the road S goes down *7.3 m.* past old Almeda gold mine and Almeda Bar Rec. Area, to Galice. At Grave Creek Jct. road E splits at *8.9 m.,* with upper road following Wolf Creek *6.1 m.* to Wolf Creek and lower road continuing along Grave Creek *6.2 m.* to I-5, above Sunny Valley. Although most prospector cabins along these roads have burned down or otherwise been obliterated, a few in shadows survive, wretched souls on their last legs, their survival doomed by time, weather and vandalism. It goes without saying that those taking this network of back roads start full on gas, carry a good spare, come with food.) From Eden Valley Jct., straight: *8.3 m.,* Foster Creek. *8.1 m.,* Agness Jct. W for US 101. (See *Rogue River Road,* following.)

From Powers Jct., on O 42:

7.1 m., Bridge Jct.

* *4.4 m.,* forks. Take R. *4.3 m.,* on R, white house that is last echo of **Bancroft,** settled 1891. In 1951 it had sawmill, grist mill, Christian Church, PS.

0.1 m., turnoff to Bridge.

* *0.2 m.,* **Bridge.** Store, tavern, station. Settled in early 1880s and named for bridge over Middle Fork of Coquille. In 1915 Bridge was much larger than it is now, with creamery, sawmill, grist mill, school, Christian Church. Places such as Bridge have survived not as marketing centers but as supplemental providers to community rural residents.

3.8 m., approximate site of **Enchanted Prairie.** PO est. 1871. Pioneer legend had it that Indians buried their dead in foothill cavity nearby. PO name changed to Angora in 1883, closed 1894. Five years later another Angora PO, this one in Lincoln County, opened. It closed in 1907, leaving behind Angora School, which was sole evidence of place in 1915. Otherwise, goats have done well in Oregon.

2.8 m., on N. **Sandy Creek** Bridge, built 1921 with length of 60 ft. and inoperable, due to road realignment.

0.4 m., turnoff to Remote.

* *0.1 m.,* **Remote.** Store. When settled in late 1880s village seemed away out from anywhere, hence name. Pointing to myrtlewood trees across road, storekeeper says: "These are the last people see going east and first they see going west." House next door built 1883 or 1884. Legend says it was stagecoach stop, but these days legend has it that every old 2-story house was stagecoach stop. Some mossy old orchards sleep on, shaking off rain and wind to slumber deep, though sometimes tremulously, like an aged dog, and they seem to take on apples like the laming dog takes on dandruff.

8.4 m., on L, **Bear Creek Rec. Area.** *7.3 m.,* **Camas Valley.** So profuse grew the pale blue-flowered camas plants here before white settlement that the first Yankees coming into the valley, in 1848, mistook the fields of blossoms for a lake.

Indians came to this vale to pick the nourishing sweet-fleshed bulbs of the Camassia. If any Indians came these days to pick whatever "Lakamass" grows they'd probably be arrested for trespassing. Indians cooked the starchy, edible bulbs in earth-covered pits over burning hot stones, then pressed them into cakes resembling cheese, to dry and store for winter larder. Whites took a leaf from the Indians, mashing the roots into pulp and making tasty pies by cooking them pumpkin-style. Sawmill town of 1915 has changed and low-grade coal deposits are too uneconomical to mine. Like many small towns, Camas Valley prides itself on community spirit. "We rally round our own," said a storekeeper. Camas Valley is largest settlement between Myrtle Point and Winston, which may not be saying much, but, as same storekeeper put it, "You toot your own horn whenever you can."

2.8 m., Rest Area. 5.1 m., turnoff for Ben Irving Reservoir.

* 1.2 m., forks. Take R. 0.9 m., forks. Take L. 1.4 m., rather unappealing little lake. Day use only.

0.4 m., **Tenmile.** Store (with typical PO inside) has old logging tools and photos of old time logging on walls. Area settled by whites in 1852 and town got its name because it was supposed to be 10 m. from some locale — stories differ.

0.2 m., Reston Rd.

* 0.7 m., Girardet Winery. 1.5 m., Bjelland Vineyard and Winery. 2.3 m., forks. Take R. 0.1 m., on L, 2-story house with large, covered porches. Genuine stage stop on road from Roseburg to Coos Bay. But the sawmills and PS are gone.

7.5 m., **Brockway,** originally called Civil Bend, a sarcasm aimed at the boisterous goings-on at the horse races here. The only betting now is lottery tickets at the lone store. (See *The Great Heartland, O 99, Winston.*)

1.4 m., Civil Bend Ave., Winston.

* 1.3 m., **Civil Bend Cemetery** (1882).

At W and E ends of Winston are roads leading to Lookingglass:

* From E end: 4.1 m., forks. Turn L. 2.2 m., turn R. 0.8 m., **Lookingglass Store.** In 1915 town had about four times as many folks, but rural environs are becoming densely spotted with houses. (For more on Lookingglass, see *Cross-Coast Range Roads, O 138 and Coos Bay Wagon Rd.,* preceding.)

0.2 m., — from Winston city hall — jct., O 99.

O 42S — Bandon to Coquille

From US 101, at N end of Bandon:

0.4 m., on L, **Knights of Pythias Cemetery.** 0.3 m., turnoff to **Bandon Fish Hatchery.**

* 0.3 m., hatchery, raising steelhead and pre-smelt salmon, the latter 200 fish to lb. when released.

0.9 m., Prosper Jct.

1.8 m., **Prosper.** PO 1893–1928. In 1915 town had pop. 500, two salmon canneries, two saw and shingle mills; and passenger boats went thrice daily on Coquille River to Bandon and Coquille. Today Prosper isn't on map, but this is where town stood.

1.5 m., turnoff L for **Judah Parker Park.**

* *1.3 m.*, park, small, grassy plot with picnic tables.

7.7 m., Public BL.

0.3 m., **Riverton,** nothing place going nowhere. In 1915 it had pop. 200 and coal mined hereabouts was shipped by steamers to Calif. ports. Town had HS and PS. The Coquille continues to roll on, as though nothing has happened.

6.2 m., Coquille. (See O 42, above.)

Rogue River Road
Gold Beach to Grants Pass

This, without doubt, is the most adventuresome long road between the Coast and the Great Heartland. It is a pike almost vacant of communities, and never out of wondering what is around the bend. Beginning on a tranquil note, its large middle section is wilderness, and then it recedes to bucolic tranquility, ending as it started, in a flurry of traffic. Although the road accompanies the Rogue River at the E and W bookends of the pike, it sees very little of the scenic waterway, that part to be traveled on foot, with CGs frequent in the E portion.

The road begins its E questing at Jerry's Flat Rd., on the S end of the Rogue River Bridge and just N of Gold Beach, on US 101.

5.9 m. — from busy US 101 — Huntley CG. *2.8 m.*, **Lobster Creek FS PA.** *0.1 m.*, forks. Take R. *4.4 m.*, **Quosatana FS CG.** *(0.3 m.*, CG on Rogue River.) *13.5 m.*, Cougar Lane, the major W commercial stop on the pike: store, station, cafe, motels, trailer park. *1.1 m.*, across Shasta Costa Creek, jct. (L, *2 m.*, forks. Turn sharp L onto Agness-Illahe Rd. *3.1 m.*, **Agness.** Store. School, with one of smallest enrollments in state. PO est. 1897. Mail comes by boat in summer, motor vehicle in winter. In 1915 Agness had pop. 60, sawmill, PS, Commercial Club. Only PS remains. Village pop. smaller now but Agness "community" numbers between 80 and 100. Great place to get away from it. Agness is terminal for Rogue River tour boats starting downstream at Wedderburn. Near store are two rustic lodges, which provide lunch for boat travelers and rooms for over-nighters.)

* From Agness Jct., road goes straight N to Powers and O 42, near Myrtle Point. *33 m.*, Powers; from Powers, *18.5 m.*, O 42. (See O 42, Powers Jct., preceding.)

From Shasta Costa Creek Jct., moving E:

One gets the feeling on this stretch of road of ghosts, terror and sheer delight. The prospectors who beat the bush in the highly mineralized rough terrain have been gone so long that even their shadows of posterity no longer imprint the earth. Yet one senses they are out there, squatting along a wan creek, crackling branches to the beat of the wind, following a sliding rock as they plod down a hillside. The road rises higher, ever higher, then higher still; in May there are yet globs of snow along the road and the sides of the upper hills look like white breastplates. Far and away this road is the highest and steepest crossing of the Coast Range, and for its size just about the loneliest. Even in mid-spring it is possible, at least on a weekday, to drive the length of the wilderness without meeting another car. For some distances the road is so narrow and so pressed against the edge of the canyons as to freeze acrophobiacs who make the mistake of looking down. Where the hillsides fall off into great bowls of chasms the vistas are almost overpowering: below, the depths of the lost and the damned; across the chasms, bull-horned peaks snorting their independence. One awakens here to an Oregon still not mortally mauled, and the shades of twilight are drawn so quietly that the heart hears every note of silence.

36.6 m., past the site of **Bear Camp** and over the 4,973-ft. summit, jct.

* L, *0.3 m.,* **Galice.** Store, BR. Town named after French doctor who came here in 1852, discovered placer gold, and supposedly buried nearby. In 1915 village had pop. 300, two sawmills, PS. Gone. But some interesting river characters gather at lunch counter of store. One told a journalist who tried to buy a ball point pen: "Come on down to my shack. I'm only a quarter of a mile down the river. I'll give you whiskey, breakfast, and lot of pens." (For

Galice Creek Marker off Rogue River Road   *Phoebe L. Friedman*

story of most legendary character along Rogue, see "Hathaway Jones" in author's *This Side of Oregon*.)

Near jct.: **Galice Creek Historical Marker.** It reads: "Old mining camp and scene of battle of Rogue River Indian War of 1855–56. Gold discovered here in 1852."

0.4 m., **Carpenter Island BLM Rec. Site,** on Rogue. *3.3 m.,* **Rainbow BLM Rec. Site,** on Rogue. *0.6 m.,* **Indian Mary CP.** Marker reads: "Smallest Indian Reservation ever created. Granted to Indian Mary by the U.S. Government in 1894 in recognition of gratitude to her father, Umpqua Joe, who gave the alarm which saved the white settlers of this area from a planned massacre." CG, PA, swimming, boating; one of best-maintained CPs in state.

1.6 m., **Hellgate Overlook,** looking down on narrowest, steepest canyon of the Rogue. *0.6 m.,* Hog Creek BL.

5 m., **Merlin,** supposedly named for birds known locally as pigeon hawks. Apple tree here became prominent because it was planted at site of Haines farm, where Haines family was wiped out by Indians in 1855. Merlin today is bustling suburb of Grants Pass. *3.5 m.,* Merlin Exit, I-5. (*4.3 m.,* downtown Grants Pass.)

Hellgate   *Phoebe L. Friedman*

Driftboat in Mule Creek Canyon of Rogue River

Courtesy US Forest Service

US 199

Jct., US 101 to Grants Pass

US 199 enters Oregon from Calif., so that residents of Brookings (and other communities in the area) must drive more than 50 m. thru Calif. before coming back to Oregon. Still, there is consolation, though perhaps small to those who make the trip often; the grandest scenery of US 199 is in Calif., where majestic redwood forests flank the road. It would be a crime against the aesthetics of the soul for the traveler not in a hurry to pass by these cathedral woods without at least taking a short stroll into them and looking, for more than a glance, up, up, up to the noble crests that soar to the sky. In each redwood there is a Sistine Chapel.

US 199 has other distinctions. It is the most varied of all CCR roads, has far more on its tributaries, and, save for US 30, is paramount in history. One could take a full fortnight travelling US 199 and its offshoots and at the end conclude that the explorations were quite incomplete.

1.5 m. — from state line and *0.3 m.* E of Redwood Hwy. — was place called **Deering,** which had PO 1902–08 and PS in 1915. Nothing now.

3.6 m., **O'Brien,** one of those hamlets in the Illinois Valley that gained media attention for marijuana growing. Raids are not uncommon and it is not unusual for a stranger to be asked, "Are you a federal agent?", as though one who answered in the affirmative could expect to be around long. A local wisecracked: "Around here the main industries are growing pot and welfare kids." Asked if he was in the marijuana trade — another foolish question — he replied with a grin, "A few of us have to stay legal." The Illinois Valley also gained a reputation of sorts for its bands of survivalists. But acceptance of the "Nuclear Winter" thesis has changed attitudes, and at the entrance to "counter-culture" colonies are signs proclaiming "Nuclear Free Zone."

0.8 m., Waldo Rd.

  * *3.1 m.,* marker giving brief history of **Waldo,** flourishing business and mining center in the late 1850s. Entire area here was called Sailors Diggins, because gold was found in locality by seamen who, so the legend goes, deserted their ship at Crescent City in the gold frenzy of the 1850s. Reputedly, they took a lot of gold from the placer strips. In 1856 Waldo became the first territorial seat for Josephine County. By then the town and its environs boasted pop. of between 3,000 and 5,000 "citizens," meaning white adult males and an indeterminate number of Chinese, probably 2,000 or 3,000, who were denied citizenship, but who probably took out a lot more gold from the placers than did the seafarers. In its prime Waldo was a metropolis of the mining area, with several stores, even more saloons, billiards halls, bowling alley, skating rink, fair-sized hotels, boarding houses, liveries, blacksmith shops, and all the rest that made a first-rate 1850s town click. At Waldo the first water rights for the state was est., as were the first hydraulic mines in Oregon, and Waldo became hub of Illinois Valley mining district. But, after

the climb the fall. By 1915, with gold considerably thinned, Waldo was down to pop. 100, with only sawmill and PS, and sinking further. In 1919 some fastbuck speculators had the bright idea of reviving a Waldo almost gone by forming land development company, selling lots, and building hotel. But the inn was out before it was completed as the speculators ran short of money. Eight years later, in 1927, Waldo paid the full penalty of its former greatness: it was completely wiped out by the hydraulic giants of the mines. And now, only the marker.

* *1.7 m.,* Takilma Jct. (R, *1 m.,* **Takilma,** named for Indian chief. Another former mining town. In 1915 it had pop. 100 and PS. Now only store and back-to-nature colony.

Return to Takilma Jct. Turn for Holland. *4.7 m.,* "T". (To L, *5 m.,* Cave Junction.) Take R. Road goes along Althouse Creek, in the mid-1800s an active mining district. *3.5 m.,* **Holland.** Store. Rather late-founded town (PO est. 1899) but in midst of mining district. There was **Browntown,** *3 m.* off, with no road to old townsite, at its height in 1858; and **Frenchtown Bar,** with

Oregon Caves   *Courtesy State of Oregon*

nothing left of the old mining camp which had its heyday in 1880s; and Althouse itself, all gone. At Holland, turn R for former mining district. *0.5 m., forks.* Take Althouse Creek Rd., L. Along here was frantic mining activity. Drive down 1 m. or so for "feel of the country." Then return to first jct. and turn L for another 1 or 2 m., thru old mining terrain.

Return to Holland Jct. Straight on Holland Loop Rd. (The locals say a lot of pot is grown around here and that growers are trigger-alert, but that visitors have nothing to fear if they stay on paved roads.) *1.5 m.,* Oregon Caves Hwy. Take it, to L. *0.9 m.,* "T". To R, *12.8 m.,* **Oregon Caves.** (See *Cave Junction,* following.) *4.3 m.,* Bridgeview Jct. Straight. *1.8 m.,* US 199, Cave Junction.

1.1 m. — from Waldo Rd. — Rough and Ready Botanical Wayside.

The country thru which US 199 has been traveling and which it will continue to curve its way inland is rich with flora, so where there is no history there is arboreal splendor. Look about and see Port Orford cedar, knobcone pine, sugar pine, incense cedar, canyon live oak, Pacific madrone, California black oak, tanoak and Jeffrey pine.

3.8 m., **Noah's Ark,** formerly Woodland Wildlife Park. Petting animals and caged animals. *0.9 m.,* turnoff for Illinois River SP.

* *0.7 m.,* SP, PA on the fair Illinois River. Fishing.

0.7 m., Oregon Caves Jct., O 46.

* *6 m.,* Siskiyou Vineyards. *14 m.,* **Oregon Caves Nat. Mon.,** labyrinth of weird and beautiful caverns in 7,000 ft. limestone and marble formation in Siskiyou Range. First white to see "The Marble Halls of Oregon" was Elijah Davidson, who came upon the caves in 1874 while chasing a bear. The Chateau, blending with the forest mosaic and moss-covered ledges, looms six stories above canyon floor. Falls of a mountain stream splash into the dining room, are flumed across it, tumble out the other side, and continue toward the sea. Mile by trail from Chateau is Douglas fir more than 12 ft. in diameter.

0.2 m., downtown **Cave Junction,** largest town between Crescent City, Calif., and Grants Pass on US 199. Born in 1930s because of tourism to Oregon Caves, Cave Junction has grown due to consistent increased visitations to Monument and town's strategic position on hwy.

2.1 m., **Kerby.** Town was probably founded to get county seat — and it did, as Kerbyville.. In July, 1857, after dubious election, Kerbyville was declared seat of Josephine County, and so remained until 1885, when voters chose Grants Pass as "permanent location" for county government.

The county itself is noteworthy in that it is the only one in Oregon honoring a woman, Illinois-born Josephine Rollins. Only a change in plans made that possible. In 1850 the 17-year-old Josephine and her family left Missouri for Calif. but switched directions and arrived in Oregon. The next spring the family again took off for Calif. but caught the gold fever before it got there. Josephine accompanied her father and other miners to the Rogue River, where a friendly Indian led them to a creek to the W, in vicinity of Illinois River. When her father discovered gold on the creek he named it after her. Josephine County historians contend that gold was discovered on Josephine Creek before it was found at Jacksonville in Dec. 1851. Josephine Rollins is termed the first white woman to settle in this part of Oregon but it really wasn't for long. A few months after the placer find the miners were warned that hostile Indians were planning an attack. Placing her hide above gold, Josephine, then 18, took off for Calif. and never saw Oregon again, though she had ample time, living to the good age of 79.

For a spell, the settlement was officially designated as Napoleon, at the insistence of hallucinatory doctor who had bought up a big chunk of the real estate. He must have been drinking his own snake oil if he saw any resemblance between the pomp that surrounded jewelry-rich Empress Josephine and the muddy snag of patched tents and hastily slapped together shacks. After a political wrangle the issue was placed in the hands of the state senate judiciary committee — which hasn't yet tackled the problem. By strict legislative legality, then, the town should be Napoleon, but it reverted quickly to Kerbyville. Anyway, the town is Kerby now, and has been for ages, honoring the first postmaster, who spelled his last name Kerbey. In this part of the woods, things are not always what they seem to be.

In 1915 Kerby was bigger; it had two sawmills, creamery, HS, PS, pop. 215, daily stages to Grants Pass and Crescent City.

0.3 m., **Kerbyville Museum,** occupying house built 1878 with second story added later; balconied structure restored 1959. Log schoolhouse built 1898 at base of Elijah Mtn., holding Oregon Caves. Schoolhouse taken apart, log by log, and reassembled here. Grocery store bldg. across road and just E of museum was put up 1876 as IOOF hall. Masonic Temple nearby dates to 1907. Josephine County Historical Society, which operates museum, does excellent job.

2.1 m., on L, Kerbyville Ghost Town, someone's idea of what a rip-roaring mining town looked like way back when.

0.3 m., turnoff L for Kalmiopsis Wilderness Area.

* *16.8 m.,* **Kalmiopsis Wilderness Area.** (See *US 101, Brookings.*)

1.2 m., on L, or W, turnoff for **Eight Dollar Mountain.** (Actually, the Kalmiopsis Road has a fork swinging around the mtn. but turnoff here has special significance.)

  * Turn onto dirt road in open area. *0.2 m.,* up hill, is large, 2-story red farmhouse. Keep on road around it. Go into bottom of draw and turn R. Follow road uphill. *0.4 m.* from farmhouse, park at third driveway to L. Hike *400 yds.* uphill to cabin. Above and around is Nature Conservancy Preserve of Eight Dollar Mtn. Nature Conservancy says: "Eight Dollar Mountain has the greatest concentration of rare plants in Oregon and is known to botanists throughout the country for its diversity. The site is an outstanding example of serpentine soil plant communities. Some of the high priority plants on the preserve include: *Gentiana Bisataea, Hastingsia bracteosum, Senecio*

hesperius, Epilobium oreganum, Calochortus howellii. There are also spectacular *Darlingtonia californica* bogs and a *Deschampsia caespitosa* wet meadow. The preserve also contains azalea thickets, chaparral and Jeffrey pine forest as well."

Apart from its fascinating plant life, the 4,001-ft. Eight Dollar Mtn. has historical and folklore interest. It was the site of an armed encounter in the Rogue River War in late March, 1856 and was the scene of some serious prospecting for gold. No one knows for sure how the mtn. got its name. One story has it that a nugget worth $8 was found on its slope. More in keeping with the craggy terrain is that a man wore out an $8 pair of shoes circling the mtn.'s 12 m. base.

For some years a computer genius lived on the mtn. and it was he who gave the land to The Nature Conservancy. He isn't there anymore. A neighbor said: "He got tired of all the people in Selma nagging him for money so he moved to Sexton Mountain."

Eight Dollar Mtn. is well known to local folks as being haven for marijuana growers. A Selma man said of the pot farmers: "They've got thin nerves and fast trigger fingers." A deputy sheriff cautioned: "Before you get out of the car, lean heavy on the horn."

1.9 m., turnoff R for Lake Selmac.

  * *2.1 m.,* gateway to **Lake Selmac Rec. Area.** Forks. L, *0.5 m.,* store, PA on Lake Selmac. R, *0.6 m.,* CG. *0.1 m.,* PA, BR.

0.6 m., **Selma,** named for town in Iowa. Store. About same size as it was in 1915, when it had daily stages to Grants Pass and Crescent City. Founded in late 1890s, Selma was never more than small hamlet, but for several decades the chrome ore taken by miners in the sharp hills that hem in the vale was freighted thru Selma on its way to the RR at Grants Pass.

Jct. To R:

  * *4.2 m.,* forks. Take R. *0.3 m.,* forks. Straight. *0.5 m.,* site of former splinter village of **Dryden,** named 1892 for 17th century English poet John Dryden. Only a house remains. Return to first forks. Turn R onto Upper Deer Creek Rd. *1.3 m.,* forks. Take L. *1.8 m.,* **Deer Creek BLM CG.** The traveler is now out of the Illinois Valley and into the Deer Creek Valley.

Jct. To L:

  * *7.1 m.* into **Siskiyou Nat. Forest,** forks. Road to forks climbs high above Illinois River and below mica cliffs, exposed by road construction. L at forks. *2 m.,* **Six Mile FS CG.** Small, primitive. *0.2 m.,* **Store Gulch FS CG.** Small, primitive. (*0.3 m.* trail to Illinois River, with sandy beaches banking stream.) *2 m.,* forks. (L, *0.5 m.,* **McCaleb Ranch,** seen first from suspension bridge across river. *4.7 m.,* past headwaters of Chetco River, Kalmiopsis Wilderness.) Straight at last forks: *7.2 m.,* **Briggs Creek FS CG.** Primitive. Here this road ends and Illinois River Trail commences. *27 m.* hike to Oak Flat; *6 m.*

beyond, Agness, at confluence of Illinois and Rogue rivers. (From Briggs Creek CG — hike of *3 m.* to York Creek Botanical Area.)

2.2 m., on R, **Fort Hay Historical Marker.** Here, at the site of a fortified ranch on a DLC, a bitter battle was fought. On March 23, 1856, about 200 Takilma Indians attacked. They got close enough for hand-to-hand combat but withdrew after a night of fighting and were in retreat when reinforcements for the settlers' garrison arrived from Ft. Vannoy, about 20 m. to the NE, in the morning. The makeshift stockade, on the banks of Clear Creek, was in 1852 originally a tavern and stage station. Ft. Hay was later known as Anderson's Stage Station. PO of Anderson est. here 1889. PO moved to Selma 1897. *Oregon: End of the Trail,* pub. 1940, said then: "The window frames of the old building, which quiver as motor cars roar down the modern highway, shook once with the passing of earlier traffic — mule trains from Crescent City with flour, bacon and beans for the northern diggings, and rumbling stagecoaches with mail and passengers, strong-boxes crammed with Oregon gold, and armed guards riding the boots of the cumbersome vehicles. Weathered clapboards cover the original logs of the building." Apart from the marker, there remains not a clue of the fort or the stage station.

1.9 m., summit, Hayes Hill, 1,640 ft.

Fort Hay Historical Marker   *Phoebe L. Friedman*

0.9 m., approximate site of place called **Love.** Like much love, it did not endure.

3 m., **Wonder.** Store. The tale is told that town got its name when John Robinson opened roadside store here in 1902 and the few settlers about wondered where he'd get enough business to keep it going. But the next year a PO was opened. By 1915 the burg had 25 residents and a school, which was also used for church and Sunday school. The wonder today is how long it will take for subdivisions to arrive and bring forth a shopping center.

3.1 m., Wilderville Jct.

    * This is the easy, carefree, scenic way to Medford and will be covered in O 238, immediately following. *0.7 m.*, **Wilderville.** Store, station. Turn R for Murphy. *0.4 m.*, turnoff R for Wilderville Cemetery (*0.2 m.*), 1885 rustic burial ground that seems far from yeoman chores. *4.2 m.*, Fish Hatchery CP, Josephine County scratchout on Applegate River. PA. *1.9 m.*, turn R onto New Hope Rd. *3.1 m.*, jct., O 238.

1.7 m. — from Wilderville Jct. — Merlin Jct.

    * *12 m.*, **Merlin,** on Rogue River. Pleasant auxiliary of Grants Pass.

7.8 m., Grants Pass, O 99, I-5. (See *The Great Heartland*, O 99, *Grants Pass*.) Jct., O 238. (See O 238, immediately following.)

O 238 — Grants Pass to Medford

O 238 is the road of the Applegate Valley, once the apple of S Oregon's eye. In recent years the valley has lost much of its serenity, folksiness and charm because it is being filled up by new homes, so that parts of the valley have begun to look like suburbia. Still, some gentle nuances of the genial past still remain.

Prior to 1853 supplies for the new mining camp at Jacksonville were either shipped by river boat to Scottsburg and then hauled by pack animals to Jacksonville or were brought over the Siskiyou Mtns. from Yreka, Calif. In 1853 a way was found to unload ships at Crescent City, on the Calif. coast. Soon pack trains were inland bound to Sailors Diggings (or Diggins), in the Illinois River Valley, and pushed on to other booming mining camps. A trail was laid out across the Illinois Valley and over the divide to the Applegate Valley, and up that valley to Jacksonville. By 1858 the trail had been widened into a wagon road, which became the paramount artery of commerce for the mining settlements. Today's route from Crescent City to Jacksonville — US 199 and O 238 — closely follows the old trail and wagon road.

O 238 is reached off US 199 from Wilderville Jct. (*10.3 m.*) and begins in the W at Grants Pass.

6.5 m. — from Grants Pass — meeting with Wilderville Rd. *0.3 m.*, **Murphy,** near Missouri Flat, that on a gossamer day is a smoke-whispered vale. Murphy is small sawmill town, settled 1854; PO est. 1875. Store, cafe, station. (For story of

Missouri Flat Cemetery

two beautiful music-makers in area, see "Soul Music on a Rocky Ridge" in author's *A Touch of Oregon*.)

0.1 m. — from Murphy — N Applegate Rd.

* Turn L or E onto N Applegate Rd. *0.6 m.*, turn L onto Kubli Rd. *0.7 m.*, site of **Davidson** (PO 1900–1907 kept in country store). *0.5 m.*, on R, **Kubli,** sometimes called Kubliville, cut thru by Jackson-Josephine county line. Gerald E. Kubli wrote: "My great-grandfather Jacob [Swiss emigrant] settled there in 1868 and my grandfather Kaspar was the only postmaster, starting in 1891. The office closed when RFD came in," in 1907. PO was located in store; nearby was Missouri Flat School. Oldest survivor of Kubli is house Jacob built 1868. *2.2 m.*, jct, N Applegate Rd. *0.1 m.*, **Missouri Flat Cemetery** (1864), with tintype look. *4.2 m.*, O 238 at Applegate.

From Murphy, on O 238:

5.6 m., Williams Jct.

* *4.3 m.*, **Sparlin Cemetery** — 1861. *1.6 m.*, Williams.

1 m., **Provolt.** Entire business district consists of early 20th century country store; county line in middle of road in front of store.

Williams Jct.

* Turn S. *4.6 m.*, Water Gap Rd. Turn L. *1.6 m.*, **Williams,** grouped about colorful rural store that is (at least daytime) social center of fertile Williams Creek Valley. In 1859 an ambitious miner turned entrepreneur, J.

T. Layton, organized a company to bring water to the placer miners. 9 m. of ditch were built. When gold ran out the succeeding farmers used ditch for irrigation. Land has produced crops far more valuable than gold taken here. Jct. Keep R. *0.5 m.,* jct. Curve L onto Cedar Flat Rd. *0.3 m.,* on R, **Hartley Memorial Cemetery** (1851) on early DLC.

From Provolt, on O 238:

2 m., Ferris Gulch Rd.

 * *1.3 m.,* shrouded remains of **Layton Mine,** owned by John Layton. But area was named for Thomas J. Ferris, who settled along here in 1860 to farm. In 1868, when gold was discovered, farming went out. Mining went on for almost 20 years, with water for the hydraulic operation initially supplied by then-celebrated Baltimore Ditch. (Across ridge, to W, was Whiskey Gulch, which somehow never caught fire as gold producer.) Layton was not only mine owner and ditch builder, he was also mercantilist, selling supplies to Ferris Gulch miners. His store stood across road from house, address now 15950 Highway 238.

2.1 m., **Applegate,** in heart of Applegate Valley. Named for Applegate River, which was named for Lindsay, one of three famed Applegate brothers. Lindsay, on his way to Calif. mines in 1848, didn't tarry here, but in those days a soul didn't have to stay around long to be so honored. The most important platinum-bearing gold placers mined in Oregon were in the Waldo-Takilma district. Gold was discovered on Althouse Creek in 1853 and was mined actively until 1917, and less so until 1930. The second, but less important, platinum bearing placer area was on the Applegate and other streams in this vicinity. *Oregon: End of the Trail* says of the Applegate at the time: "The banks of the stream were honey-combed with miners' excavations. On every gravel bar the sunlight flashed upon pans and picks. Fortunes in gold dust were washed out and a considerable amount of placer mining is still evident." The last statement is no longer true. What the book does not say is that many Chinese worked claims and that eventually white hostility drove them from here. Applegate PO was est. 1858 and for the next 30 years had trouble keeping postmasters, running thru 11. Late in life PO became branch of Jacksonville PO. The view N is met by 3,606-ft. Billy Mtn., named for homesteader William Pernoll. The Applegate Valley has become so suburbanized in recent years that the hamlet, once so rustic, now has a micro shopping center. At river bend is Applegate Bridge Wayside, parking for restful stop. Grass, shade, water and restrooms — and who could ask for anything more on a fine summer day?

There begins at Applegate one of the more fascinating off-the-beaten-path journeys in SW Oregon, weaving thru fabled gold country to a land where the dead dreams have been buried and where there is scarcely a sign of the many settlements that once dotted the area.

Take Thompson Creek Rd., named for 1853 DLC settler who 3 years later just plain disappeared. The popular story is that "The Indians got him." At jct., near mouth of Thompson Creek, stood the great entertainment emporium of the Applegate Valley, Rose's Ballroom, built by Orlando Rose, who was to early show biz in these parts what Flo Ziegfeld was to Broadway. Photos of the dance hall show it to be barnlike frame structure but to the dandies and their ladies, who came in carriages to waltz the night away, Rose's was a heavenly place. Creamery also stood at jct. Its relationship to dance hall is vague.

*1.6 m., on R, old **Thompson Creek School,** now residence. Beyond this point there are few houses. Few cars are met. The woods reach out in octopus grasp to cover the land and poke toward the pockets of meadow. Silence here has weight; at places the quiet seems almost overpowering. 6.7 m., forks. Take L, toward Applegate Lake. 0.2 m., on L, **Steamboat Cemetery** (1896). Across road was hamlet of Steamboat. No boats plied Carberry Creek; settlement received its name from a bit of goldcamp folklore. Mines which were found to be unproductive, or whose prospects were built up thru fraud, or were depleted, were said to have been "steamboated." It was gold that brought prospectors here in early 1860s and after the mines "steamboated" some of the miners stayed on to ranch. By 1899 there were enough children in area to organize a school district and log school house was built. A year earlier PO had been opened in front room of homesteader's cabin and consisted of no more than box of postal bins, typical of outlander POs. Later,

Steamboat Cemetery

a small-capacity sawmill, operating on seasonal basis to meet local needs, was constructed. And for a time Steamboat was a stage stop. Apart from the cemetery, there is no evidence here that Steamboat ever existed.

1.7 m., on L, 19th century Culy House, with authoritative W look. Culy children attended Steamboat School. *4.3 m.,* turnoff to Carberry FS CG. *0.3 m.,* jct., Applegate Rd. Straight. *0.7 m.,* turnoff to Seattle Bar FS CG. *0.4 m.,* Calif. state line, in carpet of ferns. Road runs out near here and if a car crashed against a Calif. tree, and a helicopter couldn't make it in, the sheriff or state police would have to come to the site by way of Yreka, Calif. to Phoenix to Jacksonville to Ruch to the accident scene, about 100 m.

Return to jct., Applegate Rd. Turn R, toward O 238. First view of Applegate Lake. *0.4 m.,* **Watkins FS CG.** *0.5 m.,* purportedly near site of **Copper,** named for copper mining area. Here was second "town" of Copper. First was in Calif., near Blue Ledge Mine, and was initially called Joe Bar City, then Hutton. Copper here consisted of store, school (started 1922) and PO (1924–1932). Site of Copper now at bottom of Applegate Lake. *1.4 m.,* near site of **Watkins,** now under water. PO 1893–1920. In 1915 hamlet had PS It somehow seems fitting that last owner of Copper was member of Watkins family. *0.7 m.,* turnoff to **Hart-Tish FS PA.** BL. *0.7 m.,* turnoff to **Swayne Viewpoint** *(0.1 m.),* overlook of lake and Applegate Dam. (Road across dam leads 6 m. on French Gulch Rd. to 160-acre **Squaw Lake,** on side of hill. *0.3 m.,* **Little Squaw Lake,** also recreational.)

2.4 m., **Mule Hill,** well-known to early packers and teamsters. *0.4 m.,* site of **Wright** (PO 1878–88), where Mule Mtn. Trail takes off. *1 m.,* **Bolder City,** someone's parody; a lane of shacks. *1 m.,* **Jackson FS PA.** *1.3 m.,* **McKee,** also known as McKee Bridge. Best recognized for its 112-ft. CB, built 1917, spanning Applegate River. CB was rest stop and relay point for wagoners and their teams hauling ore from Blue Ledge copper mine to Jacksonville. Bridge lasted as vehicle crossing until 1956. Restoration began 1985. With five windows on S side, McKee CB is quite photogenic. Nearby, **McKee FS CG.** Like all such outland places, store-tavern is social center of community and is usually frequented by cheerful people and outrageous liars. McKee was not too long ago considered an outpost in the wilderness but of late is attracting RV owners and other carry-your-home-with-you folks. With all the clean air, quiet and grand scenery here, it's a wonder they didn't arrive sooner.

1.3 m., approximate site of **Pursel** (PO 1898–1904). *0.6 m.,* **Star Ranger Station.** *2.1 m.,* purported site of **Wellesville,** mid-19th century mining settlement and one of three locations of Wellesville sawmill. *1.5 m.,* site of Boaz Ferry at mouth of Little Applegate River. Homesteader Kinder Boaz, rather than search for gold, made good living off prospectors. Legend has it that Little Applegate River was sometimes called Captain because Chinese here called the ferryman captain. *0.1 m.,* turnoff to **Little Applegate River Rec.**

Area. Straight. *0.5 m.,* at 2384 Upper Applegate Rd., on W side of pike, house that is last remaining structure of **Uniontown.**

In 1861 New Yorker Theodoric "Tod" Cameron, 1852 Oregon arrival, opened a store a small distance downstream from confluence of Applegate and Little Applegate rivers. Soon three brothers and a sister came to join him. Together, the Camerons acquired the prime level river bottom land on both sides of the rivers, purchasing some and homesteading the rest. House was built along E side of the Applegate and a town was born. Being solid Republicans and staunch Unionists, the Camerons called the settlement Uniontown. Tod busied himself with politics, mining and sawmilling while his brothers did the building and farming. By the time a frame one-room schoolhouse was built 1871, Uniontown had store, saloon, blacksmith shop and orchard and the Cameron parents had joined their children. Little wonder the settlement was as well known as Cameron as it was Uniontown. But in 1879 name of Uniontown became official when PO opened in store. Village also became supply depot, with one of the brothers delivering food and

McKee Bridge   *Courtesy State of Oregon*

goods to mining camps in the Upper Applegate, to Log Town, and to lumber mill up Forest Creek. Theo Cameron was only postmaster Uniontown ever had. He held that position until 1891, when he moved to Jacksonville to marry a widow with three children. That was the end of Uniontown PO. Store lasted until 1896, school held classes until 1950. Theo's brothers lived out their lives on their ranches. Their children sold out in the 1930s and left the area. The Cameron properties were subdivided and occupied by rural residences. Such is the thumbnail sketch of a pioneer community. (Straight, *2.3 m., O 238*, at Ruch.)

Return to Little Applegate Rd. Turn L, or E. *0.7 m.*, by madrone tree, site of **Uniontown School.** *2.2 m.*, jct., Sterling Creek Rd. At jct., site of **Buncom.** Following discovery of gold at Jacksonville in 1851–52, prospectors branched out all over the Applegate Valley and some found their way to Sterling Creek. Although the claims were held by whites, they were in the main worked by Chinese, veterans of the Calif. gold fields, who paid royalties to the owners. The camp where the Chinese lived became known as Buncom and, as explained by Marguerite Black, an historian of the Applegate Valley, there are two theories as to origin of name: "One source believes that the name originated with the Chinese. Seems they could not pronounce the odd name of a certain white man in the area, and called him 'Buncom.' 'There goes old Buncom,' they would say. Another source states that the name came from a disgusted miner, who found himself the victim of a dishonest deal. The slang word for this sort of thing was 'buncom.'" The name

"Downtown" Buncom

also had another spelling, as seen in the dispatches of mining district progress by two newspapers of the region. The *Oregon Sentinel* reported on 2/9/1861 that "Jackson Creek, Rich Gulch, Poor Man's Creek, Applegate, Williamsburg, Sterling and Bunkum are all doing well. Average $5 to $12 per day. Bunkum has water from Gallagher's ditch, steady all year." On 12/17/1861, the *Southern Oregon Gazette* declared, "Sterling and Bunkum mines are yielding most handsomely." By 1861 village came of age when J. T. Williams opened a saloon, having been granted license to sell "spiritous liquors in quantities of less than one quart, in the precinct of Sterlingville at Buncom." A store was already there. PO followed in 1896. By 1918 the gold was gone and PO closed. Buncom was not as large as some other mining towns or camps in the Applegate Valley and it was not as colorful as most but it is noteworthy today because, even in its feeble condition, it is more a representation of an early town than any other in the valley. The original bldgs. at Buncom burned down but still standing are several early 20th century structures, including false-fronted PO.

3.1 m., to R, on Little Applegate Rd., site of **Crump,** another mining camp of which nary a trace remains. 0.1 m., straight, road to **Little Applegate Rec. Site** (5 m.) and to Sterling Mtn. Trail Heads: **Bear Gulch,** 2.5 m.; Tunnel Ridge, 3 m.; Little Applegate, 4.5 m.

Return to jct. at site of Buncom. Turn R, following Sterling Creek. 0.8 m., on L, site of **Missouri Hotel,** built in 1860s. 0.1 m., on R, tailings of **Sterling Mine,** prominent for hydraulic mining. 3.2 m., forks. Here, at this vacancy, stood **Sterlingville.** The story of Sterlingville, as told by Marguerite Black, reads like an outline for a tale by Bret Harte. "In the fall of 1854 James Sterling [an 1852 Illinois emigrant] and his partner Aaron Davis went over the divide south of Jacksonville to do some prospecting along a small creek. They found exciting amounts of gold in the creek. They returned home to gather supplies and equipment and returned to stake out their claim. On the way they stopped at a ranch where a group of settlers were having a house raising. Somehow the news of the gold find was let slip out, and there was a stampede to look for the site of the find. When Sterling and Davis returned to their claim, they found the creek completely staked out from one end of the creek to the other. James Sterling returned to his farm [at Phoenix, Oregon], and later went to Cottonwood Creek, Calif., where he took up land and lived the rest of his life." Evidently he was never again bitten by the gold bug.

Sterlingville was a prime example of "boom and bust" mining camps. As soon as miners started pouring in, a store was opened. This was quickly followed by a saloon, bakery, boarding house and warehouse. Two years later Sterlingville had grown to about 800 people (it was eventually to reach 1,200) and boasted several stores, gambling house, dance hall, two boarding houses, livery, blacksmith shop, saloons, barber shop and several streets of residences. School district was organized 1869 and continued until 1937. PO had shorter life, 1879–1883. In 1877 the 23-m.-long Sterling Ditch was completed to bring water for hydraulic mining. By then most of the sluice panners had left, with some of those remaining settling down as farmers. Hydraulic mining continued profitably until 1910, when mining became relatively dormant. (By then Sterlingville was a pale shadow of its former self.) The Great Depression of the '30s brought unemployed men to the hills with tools and goldpans. By 1933 about 100 properties were being worked in the area. Hydraulic mining started up again and this time lasted until 1957. Today there is not a stick of wood to indicate where Sterlingville town stood. Sterling Ditch, long unused, is still intact in some places. Farmland around town was abandoned and Sterling Creek grown over with trees and brush. At Griffin Lane and Sterling Creek Rd., site of Sterlingville, take L fork. *0.1 m.,* turn off R to **Sterlingville Cemetery** (1856). At road is plaque giving history of town. From cemetery knoll the evidence of hydraulic mining is clearly visible. *6.1 m.,* "T", at Cady Rd. Turn L. *0.5 m.,* O 238.

From Applegate, on O 238:

0.9 m., turnoff L, or N, to Applegate School (*0.1 m.*). Older part of 2-story brick bldg. put up first part of 20th century. *0.4 m.,* Humbug Creek Rd. Along this creek, for about 3 m., there was some early placer mining. Creek got its name over a quarrel about a mining deal; one of the participants called it "humbug." Ranches replaced mining and in time the ranches were subdivided and occupied by rural homes. *0.8 m.,* on L, old **Kubli Ranch,** now animal ranch. The "settlement" had house, barns, shops, store and water-powered mill to grind grain for fee. *3.4 m.,* on R, or S, **Bosworth House,** built 1858, neighbored by vintage barns and sheds. Here, until her passing, lived one of Oregon's great women, Marie Bosworth, Centennial Mother of the Year and a gentle but passionate advocate of peace and justice. *0.6 m.,* turnoff to **Cantrall Buckley CP.** (*1.2 m.,* CG, PA on Applegate.)

1.5 m., **Ruch.** School district here was originated 1863, more than three decades before there was PO. First schoolhouse, modest frame structure, lasted until 1914 and was on site occupied by present school. In 1896 Caspar "Cap" Ruch built at intersection of O 238 and Upper Applegate Rd. a house, store and blacksmith shop. The next year he was appointed postmaster and given the honor of naming new PO. Being a man who knew his worth, he called it Ruch, and so it has remained. Ruch and his schoolteacher wife operated store and PO until 1939. Ruch Realty now occupies site of old Ruch Store. Frame house Ruch built on hill still stands. But Community Hall, which was directly back of store and was social center of area for many years, is gone and scarcely remembered even by old-timers. For decades Ruch was no more than a store, but suburban explosion in 1970s and 1980s has made of Ruch a bustling bedroom settlement, complete with shopping center.

Jct., Upper Applegate Rd.

* *1 m.*, Valley View Winery. (For details on remainder of this road see earlier this section, O 238, starting with Thompson Creek Rd.) The beauty of taking the Upper Applegate instead of the Thompson Creek Rd. is that the former has much more impressive views of the Siskiyou Mtns.

From Ruch, on O 238:

1.5 m., on R, **Log Town Cemetery.** First recorded burial 1862, of Rev. James Dunlap. Applegate Garden Club members tend yellow rose bushes they planted along fence in 1959. *0.4 m.*, on L, site of **Log Town,** as frequently spelled Log-town. Community, founded in 1850s, had two things going for it: it was on the Jacksonville-Crescent City pike and it was in center of throbbing mining district. Consequently, it had saloons, hotels, blacksmith shops, stores, livery. But it had no school, because few families dwelled here. It is easy to buy the story that settlement derived its name from the many log houses here but place was named for popular miner Francis (Frank) Logg. Site of Log Town today is occupied by mobile homes. *0.2 m.*, on R, marker commemorating **"Maryum's Logtown Rose** 1832–1908." Marker and yellow rose bush are at approximate site where John and Maryum McKee had their home, built 1860s, for many years. (See "The Log Town Rose" in author's *Tracking Down Oregon.*)

1 m., on L, site of **Herling** (PO 1888–1895). Herling was prominent stage stop which burned down about 1895. Brown house was also famous for its "serve yourself" well, with bucket at hand. Herling had one other claim to fame: it was known as "Gallon House" because proprietor had license to sell by the gallon. *1 m.*, on R, Poorman's Creek Rd. Original name, **Poor Man's Creek,** tells better the luck found at this runnel by a down-to-earth prospector. *2.9 m.*, **Jacksonville,** best-preserved historic city in Oregon. (See *The Great Heartland*, O 99, Medford.) *5.2 m.*, downtown Medford.

The Great Heartland

Lying between the Coast Range and the Cascade Mountains, this area contains far more people, industry and institutions than the remainder of Oregon combined. Think of it as a river system, with the main stream being I-5 and its direct O 99 links.

Portland

It is common belief that the Willamette River evenly divides Portland geographically; the truth is that about 80% of the city lies E of the stream.

Another assumption mistakenly shared is that the city was named by one of the first two men to come to Portland. The first white settler in what is now Portland was Etienne Lucier who, upon leaving Hudson's Bay Co, built a small cabin on the E side of the Willamette. A year later, in 1829, he moved to French Prairie, where he became Oregon's first farmer. (See "A Memory of Champoeg" in author's *Tales Out of Oregon*.)

Trappers and traders blazed trails thru the thickets of what became downtown Portland or guided their small river craft past it without anyone bothering to say, "This looks like the real estate of the future." Then came Capt. John H. Couch, and after him the writing was clearly on the wall, though it took a while to recognize the message. In 1841 the 30-year-old Couch (pronounced Kooch), a Mass. seaman since he was 15, arrived as skipper of the brig *Maryland,* on his way to Oregon City and to investigate possibilities of a salmon business. "To this point," he declared at the future site of Portland, "I can bring any ship that can get into the mouth of the Great Columbia River." Without its port, Portland might now be no larger than Salem.

Couch sailed back to Mass. and returned to Portland with an inventory of goods that started him on a successful mercantile career. By then the W side of Portland had its first permanent resident, William Johnson, sailor of the War of 1812, independent trapper, and first bootlegger in the Oregon Country, manufacturing "blue ruin," so dreadful a decoction as to bring about his arrest by the provisional government.

Johnson did not stay long, a year or two by the best estimates. He probably left about the time William Overton, of Tennessee, arrived and shared a claim with Asa Lovejoy, in 1844. Lovejoy was a man of considerable ambition; he had a town in mind. Overton wanted only to hack away enough trees to farm, no more than that. The issue was resolved when the lanky, laconic Overton sold his share of the claim for $100 in goods and provisions to Oregon City merchant Francis Pettygrove, who shared Lovejoy's business aggressiveness.

Together Lovejoy and Pettygrove set out to clear land in earnest. After completing four streets and 16 blocks, which they then platted, they knew they had the making of a city. But a city needs a name and neither would accede to the other the honor of christening the metropolis that would arise from the woods. So they agree to toss a coin, the 2-out-of-3 winner providing the name.

Asa Lawrence Lovejoy, 37 when he stood at the coin tossing, was a graduate of Amherst College, second lawyer to come to Oregon (the first was John Ball), and the first to practice law in Oregon. He was later to have a distinguished public career, serving in many posts and offices, including postal agent of Oregon, mayor of Oregon City, legislator from Clackamas County, and state attorney general — and he almost made governor of the provisional gvmt. Running against George Abernethy, a mission advocate, the non-sectarian Lovejoy lost by only 16 votes, 536 to 520. Only a petty squabble among the anti-mission people provided Lovejoy's defeat.

Francis W. Pettygrove, 43 at the coin tossing, and a native of Calais, Maine, was already in the mercantile world when he and his wife and child and the Philip Foster family took off from New York for the other side of the continent by ship. Landing at Oregon City, Pettygrove opened a store and achieved prosperity. In 1845, 2 years after coming to Oregon, and on the very site Overton had put up a claim shack the year before (at Front and Washington), Pettygrove erected a log store, the first business bldg. in Portland, as a branch of his Oregon City operation. In 1848 he sold his Portland holdings to Daniel Lownsdale for $5,000 in tanned leather, making a 50-fold profit on his investment. Then he took off for Calif. with a load of goods, sold his wares at heart-warming prices, and returned home. Two years later he was foreman of the jury at the trial of the five Cayuse Indians charged with the Whitman mission massacre. (All five were hung.) Restless, then, Pettygrove moved his family to the shore of the Strait of Juan De Fuca, where he founded Port Townsend.

So the coin was tossed and Pettygrove won. He chose to call the new city Portland. Lovejoy would have called it Boston. But Lovejoy's heart wasn't broken. He was a bit of a Maine man himself, having been admitted to the bar in that state. (Had Overton not sold out, the city might now be Nashville.)

There is a bit of irony in that the man who gave Portland its name left the state while the loser remained and is buried in Portland. Still, neither of the men regarded Portland as a hometown enterprise. They had the feelings of an outside investor in the new community, their Oregon roots being in Oregon City. Both sold out, Lovejoy to Benjamin Stark, who arrived in Portland as a ship's purser and later became an ardent secessionist.

By the time Lovejoy died in 1882, Portland had grown phenomenally, considering the time and place. It had stripped off all its wilderness characteristics, heartily commented upon by Elizabeth Dixon Smith Geer in her diary of early 1848: "Portland has two white houses and one brick and three wood-colored frame houses and a few cabins . . . We traveled four or six miles through the thickest woods I ever saw — all from two to six feet through, with now and then a scattered cedar; and intolerably bad road . . . These woods are infested with wildcats, panthers, bears and wolves."

Only 2 years and 8 months later a resident wrote that "Portland has now become the principal town of Oregon. It now outnumbers Oregon City in houses, inhabitants, and as to business there is more done here now than there."

In 1851 the city was inc. and 38-year-old Hugh D. O'Bryant, a Georgian who grew up among the Cherokees where his father had been a missionary, was elected the city's first mayor. He was a good man, founding the city's first public library, but he was either restless or didn't approve of the way the citizenry appreciated him. After his one-year term expired he moved to Douglas County and was elected to the legislature; then he went on to Walla Walla and was named to Washington's territorial legislature; following that, he took off for Calif. and was lost in the crowd.

At the start of 1852 Portland was already the principal port in Oregon, wrote Rev. Ezra Fisher. "The present population is estimated at 700 souls." The city had more than 50 wholesale and retail businesses and half-a-dozen industrial plants. "This is the place where nearly all the immigrants by water land and from which they will go to their various points of destination."

And so the city grew, constantly growing closer to the rest of the nation and incessantly reaching out. In 1883, a year after Lovejoy's death, Portland was finally linked to the E by rail. Four years later saw the last of the Willamette ferry boats when the Morrison Bridge was built to tie together rural East Portland and urban Portland; and in another 4 years, in 1891, when Portland annexed the separate municipalities of East Portland and Albina, the city's pop. was almost 80,000.

Perhaps the most colorful period in the city's history was in the 1920s and 1930s, a long plateau between the past and the future, when Front and First Streets were lined with massive brick structures that looked like they ought to be backgrounds for horse-drawn drays instead of trucks and automobiles.

World War II changed Portland immeasurably. Thousands came here for shipyard jobs and a deep industrial character stayed on. Out of this industrial basis there developed an electronics and services economy that reflected and gave rise to contemporary business architecture. A new era was born. Down went the piles of bricks, the tombs of the early makers and shakers; up bloomed the airy designs to catapult Portland into the world of the moderns.

The aftermath of World War II brought another profound change: the way Portlanders look at themselves. For long decades Portland folk had considered their community more a town than a city. "Portland people are just us folks," was a common expression. Today, however, Portland is a city, not only in size and direction and problems but in attitude. (This state of mind and lifestyle has been encouraged, stimulated and provoked by seeming hordes of newcomers from New York, Chicago, Philadelphia, San Francisco and Los Angeles.) Told what the city would become, Lovejoy might have nodded; Pettygrove would have frowned; Overton would have rushed to his canoe and paddled on.

Because Portland was so far and so expensive for most European immigrants to reach and because the city did not possess the industrial capacity to draw these immigrants, Portland never developed tenement sections, massive apartment housing, row house tracts to more than minor significance, or slums. And for that Lovejoy, Pettygrove and Overton would all be happy.

The conventional way for a quick look at the established prime sites of the city is to follow the 50-m.-long **Scenic Drive,** starting at the Visitor Center, Front and Salmon. (The office gives out free tour guides, city maps and other literature.)

The Scenic Drive carries motorists to the summits of three hills — Council Crest, Rocky Butte and extinct-volcanic Mt. Tabor — which afford sweeping views of Ore. and Wash. Clearly visible on clear days are Mt. Rainier, volcanic Mt. St. Helens and Mt. Adams, all in Wash., and the great peaks of the Oregon Cascades: Mt. Hood, Mt. Jefferson and the Three Sisters.

Other attractions in the Scenic Drive include Washington Park, with its exquisite Japanese Garden, where five traditional garden forms combine to mirror the mood of an ancient Japan; Portland Rose Test Gardens; an imaginative (and misleading) statue of Sacajawea, the young Indian mother of the Lewis and Clark expedition; Oregon Museum of Science and Industry (the beloved OMSI); Portland Zoo, famed for its prolific elephant breeding; World Forestry Center and Hoyt Arboretum, with its Living Memorial to Vietnam War veterans; and the opulent Pittock Mansion; Reed College; and the U of Portland.

More than 200 places have been designated as landmarks by the city's Historic Landmarks Commission. Some of the more interesting, along with others not included, are listed below, with historic name, date of construction and address.

The city has designated two districts as historic: **Skidmore/Old Town** and **Yamhill.** From the standpoint of looking into the past, **Skidmore** is more interesting. Its original focal point was the **Skidmore Fountain** (1888), SW 1st and Ankeny. During the 1890s a common parting was "See you at the fountain," and see each other there hundreds did on warm nights, with men, women, children, horses and dogs drinking from the elegantly sculptured spouts.

Few people meet at the fountain today, certainly not at night. Far more popular is the renovated **New Market Theater** (1872), 50 SW 2nd, the city's great entertainment palace and platform until the mid-1880s. Among the renowned who trod the stage were Madam Madjeska, Robert Ingersoll, E. H. Sothern, Henry Ward Beecher and John L. Sullivan.

Practically adjoining the New Market Theater are the **New Market Annex** (1889) and the **New Market South Wing** (1871), now a sharp and stylish shopping and dining facility.

It is mere coincidence that the Skidmore District, named for an early Portland druggist who gave the initial sum to build the Skidmore Fountain, should merge with Skid Road, now better known as Old Town. Skid Road, whose spine was

Statue of Sacajawea in Washington Park, Portland   *Courtesy State of Oregon*

Burnside Ave., was for decades the ephemeral domain of transient workers, who lived in cheap hotels and flop houses, ate at cheap cafes, drank at cheap saloons, flocked to the "slave market" (casual labor employment office) looking for work and sought solitary entertainment at cheap movies and cheap burlesque shows.

Here came the unemployed loggers, fruit tramps, pearl divers, gandy dancers, seamen, do-anything-you've-got-mister, lugging their tin, cardboard, beat-up leather luggage, coming with their balloons and bedrolls, the suitcase farmers and the bindlestiffs, hoping for enough work to stretch their winter grubstake until things opened up in the spring. And with them came the disinherited, the winos, the bay rum freaks, the crazies, hanging on to a life that stretched only to the next meal, the next drink, the next flop. All together on Skid Road, the proletarians and the lumpen proletariat, the radicals who appealed for unity and action, the beaten, the cynics and the dead-eyed men with scrambled brains.

After World War II Skid Road oozed downhill. There was a marked deterioration in the kind of men who came there. The area was further pinched together by factories and warehouses. The decline accelerated in the 1960s and 1970s, and with hard times devastating sections of the pop., Skid Road, now referred to by the media simply as Burnside, loaded up with homeless who had but a short while ago been industrious individuals and compact families. By the mid-1980s the charitable facilities of Skid Road, such as the Salvation Army, reached the breaking point. In the midst of this tragedy one haven for the homeless, Baloney Joe, located at the E end of the Burnside Bridge, received regional recognition for the health and social services it tried to provide its charges. The director, Michael Stoops, came into the national limelight when he slept on the grates of Congress thru the winter of 1986–87 in an attempt to bring some relief to the homeless of the nation. Later, overcome by scandal, he quit his post.

Following the industrial pinching of Skid Road came invasion of the area by bright, off-beat restaurants and shops, turning Old Town, as the newcomers called it, into a glittery tourist happening. And so, Babylon crosses paths with hell, much to the annoyance of Babylon, which wants the unwashed out of the area.

The Skidmore/Old Town District is also the home of **Chinatown,** pale stuff compared to San Francisco, and includes the bustling **Saturday Market** (also Sunday), an artisan fair under the Burnside Bridge and spreading S-ward.

Among old and interesting structures in the Skidmore/Old Town Historic District are: **Bickel Bldg.** (1892), 233-235 SW Ash (it housed Portland city council until 1895 and was location of Portland's first telephone exchange); **Blagen Block** (1888), 30-34 NW Couch. Historical architect George McMath called it the "largest remaining example of 19th century commercial palaces." Next to it is **Skidmore Block** (1888).

Dielschneider Bldg. (1859), 71 S Oak, good and rare example of pre-cast mercantile structure. Third story added 1878. **Failing Bldg.** (1886), 235 SW 1st; **Fechheimer & White Bldg.** (1883), 233 SW Front; **Glisan Bldg.** (1889), 112 SW

2nd. Last cast-iron bldg. in city, it blends Classical, Romanesque and Gothic styles.

Haseltine Bldg. (1893), 133 SW 2nd; **Lombard Bldg.** (1889), 224 SW 1st; **Merchants Hotel,** SW corner, NW 2nd and Davis. Used as hotel until 1968.

Packer-Scott Bldg. (1890), 1st and Ankeny, across street from Skidmore Fountain. Built as warehouse, now occupied by offices and retail enterprises. **Sinnott House** (1883), 105 NW 3rd; **Smith's Block** (1872), 111-113 SW Front; **United Carriage Bldg.** (1886), 126 SW 2nd, built as livery stable. Only Oak St. facade remains intact of city's oldest surviving brick structure, **Hallock & McMillan Bldg.** (1857), Front and Oak. Perfect example of how to ruin a bldg. thru clumsy and callous remodeling; all four cast-iron columns were removed in the 1940s.

Old Town's most glittering modern structure is **Northwest Natural Gas Co.,** 220 NW 2nd. It had its beginning on 1/7/1859, when Portland Gas Light Co. was granted perpetual franchise by Oregon's last territorial legislature. City's pop. then was 2,874. First gas was produced by carbonizing coal brought from Vancouver, B.C. and later from Australia and Japan, as ballast in windjammers. Unloaded coal was wheeled in handcarts to company's retorts. First gas lights on Portland streets, in what is now Old Town, flickered on in June, 1860.

Also in Skidmore/Old Town Historic District are: **American Advertising Museum,** in 1895 Erickson Saloon Bldg., on 2nd between Burnside and Couch; **Architectural Preservation Gallery,** 26 NW 2nd; **Jeff Morris Fire Museum,** SW Ankeny and Front, at Central Fire Station; **Oregon Maritime Museum,** 113 SW 1st.

To the close N and W of this historic district are **Union Station** (1890), at NW end of 6th Ave. and **US Custom House** (1901), 220 NW 8th.

The **Yamhill Historic District** has as its focal point **Yamhill Market Place,** SW 1st and Yamhill, 3-story atrium, smart shopping complex. At noon hour on weekdays the market, with its Portland avant garde shops, is the fun place to be. It wears a festive hour at other times, too. Among old and interesting places in this district are: **Franz Bldg.** (1878), 124 SW Yamhill; **Harker Bldg.** (1878), 728 SW 1st; **Harker Bldg.** (1880), 824 SW 1st; **Love Bldg.** (1878), 730 SW 1st; **Mikado Bldg.** (1880), 837 SW 1st; **Northrup-Blossom-Fitch Bldg.** (1858), 737 SW Front; **Pearne Bldg.** (1865), 814 SW 1st; **Poppleton Bldg.** (1867), 818 SW 1st; **Strowbridge Bldg.** (1875), 101 SW Yamhill; **Willamette Block** (1882), 722 SW 2nd; **Van Resselaer Bldg.** (1878), 65 SW Yamhill. Upper two stories were added.

Apart from landmarks in the Skidmore/Old Town and Yamhill Historic Districts, the following are among the worth-looking-up places and things in greater downtown Portland:

Pioneer Courthouse (1875), 520 SW Morrison, oldest permanent federal bldg. in NW. Across 6th St. is **Pioneer Square,** a welcome island in a mercantile-financial world and the center of downtown outdoor cultural activities.

Bishop's House (1879), 219 Stark, was originally part of first Catholic cathedral. It has been HQ for Chinese tong and speakeasy. **Blitz-Weinhard Brewery**

(1907), 1133 W Burnside, has the solid, bulldog look of an old brewmaster. **Burrell's Elm,** 111 SW 10th, planted 1870. **Farrell's Sycamore,** NW corner, SW Park and Main, planted 1880. N 125 ft. on same side of street, and in front of parking lot of Roosevelt Hotel, stands oak planted 1877. Parking lot was site of home of Thomas Lamb Eliot (1841–1936), first pastor of First Unitarian Church and founding father of Portland Art Assn. and Reed College. Eliot built his house at location of oak in 1878 and lived there rest of his life. The grandest memorial to him is Eliot Glacier on Mt. Hood.

First Baptist Church (1894), 909 SW 11th; **First Congregational Church** (1890), 1126 SW Park; **First Presbyterian Church** (1890), 1200 SW Alder; **The Old Church** (1882), 1422 SW 11th. Oldest church bldg. in Portland on original site, it was Presbyterian, then Baptist before becoming non-sectarian. Used today for cultural and civic purposes. Free Sack Lunch (organ) Concerts every Wed., 11 a.m.-3 p.m. Portland's version of the "Little Church Around the Corner" is relatively tiny **St. Michael the Archangel** (1901), 425 SW Mill.

Exchange Bldg. (1903), 514 SW 6th, built as Olds and King Store and Portland's first steel frame bldg.; **Portland City Hall** (1895), 1220 SW 5th; **Portland Police Historical Museum,** 16th floor of Justice Bldg., 111 SW 2nd.

A block W of Broadway, and starting S from Salmon, are the 1852–created **South Park Blocks,** lovely landscaped area merging into the Portland State U campus. Facing the blocks are **Oregon Historical Society** and **Portland Art Museums.** Towering above the grass, bushes and benches are original statues of Abraham Lincoln and Theodore Roosevelt. The statues of Lincoln, George Washington (57th and Sandy), and Joan of Arc (NE 39th and Glisan), were given to the city in 1920s by Dr. Henry Wade Coe, whose wife was a compatriot of Abigail Scott Duniway.

Sculpture abounds in downtown Portland. Among the more impressive works of art are the **Elk Statue** on SW Main between Lownsdale and Chapman Squares, whose ginkgo trees are turned by autumn into a brilliant canopy of yellow; **"The Quest,"** Portland's largest single piece of white sculpted marble, in front of Georgia Pacific Bldg., 900 SW 5th; the cast bronze **"Ring of Time"** at entrance of Standard Plaza, SW 5th and Main; and **"Portlandia,"** looking down from the lower reaches of the Portland Bldg., 1120 SE 5th. A cross between the Statue of Liberty and a Valkyrie who has stomped into Portland to lead the masses to only heaven knows where, "Portlandia" surpassed all other sculpture in degree of controversy when complete. Its statistics are impressive: it stands 36' 10", weighs 6-1/4 tons, is second-largest hammered copper sculpture in US, after Statue of Liberty. It is meant to represent Lady Commerce, the darling of the city's seal. Close by her are symbols of Portland's early strengths: a sheaf of grain, cogwheel and sledgehammer. The cogwheel is most compatible for the lady is depicted with trident in hand as a ship enters port. **"Sculpture Mall,"** along N side of Art Museum, Madison between Park and 10th, where a Moore, a Meedmore and a Hepworth are permanent installations, has the most arty atmosphere in town.

Portlandia   *Courtesy Greater Portland Convention and Visitors Association*

In the SW side beyond the SW portion of greater downtown, the largest grouping of opulent old homes is found in the 125-acre **King's Hill District,** bounded by Burnside, Madison, Washington Park and SW 21st. Prominent even here, among the residences of the old merchant princes, is the former **Theodore Wilcox Residence** (1892), 931 SW King.

Among other noteworthy structures in SW Portland are: **Ascension Episcopal Chapel** (1889), 1823 SW Spring; **Cable House** (1886), 1903 SW Cable; **Gov. Curry Residence** (1865), 1020 SW Cheltenham Ct.; **Col. Dosch Estate** (1887), 5298 SW Dosch Rd.; **Espey Boarding House** (1886), 2601-2605 SW Corbett; **Fulton Store** (1880), 7035 SW Macadam; **Haseltine Residence** (1880), 1616 SW Spring; **Jacob Kamm House** (1871), 1425 SW 20th; **Morris Marks Residence** (1882), 1501 SW Harrison; **Piggot's Castle** (1892), 2591 SW Buckingham Terr.; **Milton Smith Residence** (1892), 0303 SW Curry.

Other points of interest on the SW side include: **Portland Children's Museum,** 3037 SW 2nd; **Oregon School of Arts and Crafts,** 8245 SW Barnes, on 7-1/4 acre campus; **Alpenrose Dairy,** 6149 SW Shattuck, working dairy farm that also holds sheep, goats and horses. Visitors, especially children, welcomed at **Dairyville,** the **"Western Village,"** and **Storybook Lane.**

The NW side of the city, from Burnside N to Lovejoy and from 18th W to 23rd, is Portland's Greenwich Village. It is the most genuinely cosmopolitan and sophisticated part of town and one has to walk thru it to experience its eclectic flavor. For years the city's most elegant avenue was 19th St. and its environs comprised Portland's fashionable section. Today it is largely a one-way artery that is a conduit between the industrial NW and downtown Portland but there are still a few sparks of the past left. (For the past, see *Nineteenth Street* by Richard Marlitt.)

Landmarks of interest on the NW side include: **Ayer Residence** (1904), 811 NW 19th; **Bergman Residence** (1885), 2134 NW Hoyt, with 2-story slanted bay windows; **Loeb Residence** (1893), 726 NW 20th; **McKenzie Residence** (1892), 615 NW 20th; **Pittock Mansion** (1914), 3228 NW Pittock Dr.; **St. Patrick's Church** (1889), inspired by the great cathedral, St. Peter in Rome; **Shea-Ayer House** (1892), 1809 NW Johnson; **Temple Beth Israel** (1927), 1931 NW Flanders; **Swedish Evangelical Mission Covenant Church** (1912), 1624 NW Glisan. Throughout the NW side are row houses, townhouses, streetcar-era apts., hovels — from lower middle class to downright poor.

At NW 25th and Vaughn, in the area where the Lewis and Clark Exposition was held in 1905, stands the 11-ft.-tall stainless steel **"Flogger"** statue created by sculptor Frederic Littman in tribute to the industrial worker.

On the SE side, Portland's oldest residence is believed to be the 2-story clapboard house at 1825 SE 12th, built 1862. It was moved here from site near Willamette River in 1902. In the SE section, too, there is located at the E end of the Sellwood Bridge and one block N, **St. Johns Episcopal Church,** built 1851 and moved to this site from Milwaukie in 1961. No longer a church, it is now used for weddings and less chancy occasions. Just N is replica of **Johnson Cabin,** first white dwelling in early part of Portland. Original site was near SW Macadam and Ross Island Bridge. A few blocks away, on SE 13th, N and S of Tacoma, is **"Antique Row,"** in old Sellwood District.

Among other landmarks in SE Portland are: **Allen Prep School** (1905), 1135 SE Salmon; **Barber Block** (1891), 532 SE Grand; **Brainard House** (1888), 5332 SE Morrison; **Buckner-Henry House** (1891), 2324 SE Ivon; **Eliot Hall** of Reed College (1912), 3202 SE Woodstock; **Fenton Residence** (1892), 626 SE 16th; **Kendall Residence** (1894), 3908 SE Taggart; **St. John the Baptist Ukranian Church,** 8014 SE 16th, only one of its kind in the NW, with interior of five pews on each side. Most services entirely in Ukrainian. **Epworth United Methodist Church,** 1333 SE 28th, started with services in Japanese in 1892, now has services in English with translations in Japanese.

Surely, SE Portland's loveliest landmark is **Leach Gardens,** 6704 SE 122nd, public botanic garden created by two extraordinary people, both gone, Lilla and John Leach. Settling on five wooded acres along Johnson Creek in 1931, Lilla the botanist and John the pharmacist and community activist wrought into exquisite form these gardens as a devotion to each other and for the joy of their friends. Lilla was the scientist, John assisted her out of love. Together they wandered deep into seldom-trod wilderness in the 1920s and 1930s in search of unknown plants. She found two genera and 11 species and gained fame in her field for discovery of *kalmiopsis leachiana,* for which the Kalmiopsis Wilderness in SW Oregon is named.

From Leach Gardens, return to Foster Rd., turn R, or E, to 134th, turn R, and *0.6 m.* on stands **Cedar Crossing CB,** first CB in Multnomah County, and dedicated 1/16/82. The 60-ft.-long span was built at the direction of then Multnomah County Executive Don Clark, a man with a feeling for nostalgia and a sense of the whimsical. It was first CB built in Oregon in 16 years and for a moment halted the steady decline of CBs, of which, all told, more than 450 were built.

In NE Portland the paramount point of interest is the **Sanctuary of Our Sorrowful Mother,** at 85th and Sandy Blvd., founded by the Servite Fathers. Covering 60 acres on two levels, 10-story elevator transports visitors to the upper level where, atop the cliff, unfold the Columbia River and Cascade peaks. Focal point

Pittock Mansion   *Courtesy Portland Chamber of Commerce*

Rear of Leach Botanical Garden Manor House *Courtesy Bob Pope*

of the Sanctuary is the Grotto, with the altar set in a large, cave-like opening hewn from volcanic rock.

NE Portland landmarks include: **Freiwald Residence,** 1810 NE 15th; 32-room **Barnes House,** 3553 NE Klickitat; **Chamberlain House,** 1927 NE Tillamook, all built in 1900s; **West Ankeny Carbarns** (1900), 2706 NE Couch; **Loy Sing Yee Residence** (1894), 202 NE Graham.

In N Portland a clump of green cedars, looking to the eye of history weaving like a stalwart platoon of green-clad trailblazers, backgrounds Commemorative Rock, near West Hall on the U of Portland campus. Here, at **Waud's Bluff,** a detachment of the Lewis and Clark party arrived on 4/3/1806, the farthest known point reached by the explorers on the Willamette River. The bluff overlooks the industrial complex of Swan Island, with freighters at the docks.

West Hall (1891), 5000 N Willamette, is the original bldg. on the U of Portland campus. Nearby, at 4333 N Willamette, is 1894 **Mock Residence,** third house on site of pioneer Mock family.

The old **St. John City Hall** (1907), 7214 Philadelphia, now a police station, was the seat of local gvmt. when St. Johns was independent city. Town was founded by James John, 1843 arrival from California, who settled first at nearby Linnton. In 1852 he operated ferry, later opened general store. St. Johns was inc. 1903, had first public land transportation when Willamette Bridge steam trains reached village in 1890, was inc. into Portland 1915.

St. Johns was connected to "mainland" Portland by **St. Johns Bridge,** opened for traffic 6/13/1931 as another link on US 30. When bridge was dedicated, the New York engineer who designed it said span was largest in the world having twisted strand cable, including Brooklyn Bridge. He added that St. Johns Bridge, at 3,800 ft. in length, was largest span of any type W of Detroit and had maximum clearance of 205 ft. Experts have called it one of the seven most beautiful bridges in the world. **Cathedral Park,** under bridge, received top landscaping award in 1981.

Other landmarks in N Portland deserving of attention include sunken rose gardens of Peninsula Park, 6400 N Albina; **Interstate Firehouse Cultural Center,** 5340 N Interstate; **John Palmer House** (1890), 4312 N Mississippi, restored to its original elegance and open for tours; **Albina Saloon** (1895), 4543 N Albina; **David Cole Residence** (1885), 1441 N McClellan; **Dean House** (1894), 4812 N Princeton; **McKay Bros. Block** (1893), 927 N Russell. **Kelly Point Park,** at near confluence of Willamette and Columbia rivers, comprises large grassy meadow and sandy beach. Drive N on I-5 to Marine Dr. Exit, take Marine Dr., and follow signs to park.

The best way for a newcomer, or even a longtime resident, to see the true Portland is simply to drive thru the city at random. Each neighborhood has its own charm and islands of historic interest appear in the most conventional areas. There are streets where strangers will vow they have entered an architectural setting of the 19th century and streets whose surfacing is a century back in time. No part of the city will disappoint the curious and some areas will delight and even astound.

Portland may be the only city in the coterminous US to contain within its corporate limits a "wilderness area." The 5,000-acre **Forest Park** and **Hoyt Arboretum** hold about 50 m. of hiking trails. Best known is Wildwood Trail, National Scenic Trail, that winds 25 m. thru Portland's West Hills. Good starting points are site of World Forestry Center, 4033 SE Canyon, and W end of Thurman St.

The city and its environs are rich in cemeteries; Multnomah County maintains no fewer than 14. Largest and most historic burial grounds in Portland are **Riverview,** 8421 SW Macadam, and **Lone Fir,** SE 26th and Morrison. Riverview is larger, Lone Fir is older, markers there go back to 1846. Between Riverview and Lone Fir the deceased pop. exceeds that of any Oregon city but Portland.

In **Riverview Cemetery** are the Corbetts, Failings, Dolphs, Couches, Terwilligers, Cornells, Skidmores, Pittocks, Scotts, Ladds and other makers and shakers of their time. There is also here the eminent suffragist, Abigail Scott Duniway, sharing a grave with her daughter, Clara Belle Duniway Stearns, who died 29 years before her mother and who in life was often estranged from the great lady. And side by side sleep Frances Fuller Victor, Oregon's finest historian, and Virgil Earp, of Western folklore fame.

Lone Fir holds the remains of Thomas J. Dryer, first editor of *The Oregonian;* George Law Curry, last territorial governor of Oregon and after whom Curry County was named; Dr. J. C. Hawthorne, founder of Oregon's first mental hospital; Harry Lane, one of six US Senators to vote against US entry into WW I; William Hume, founder of Columbia River salmon industry; poet Samuel L. Simpson; Daniel Wright, whose friends planted a redwood at each of the four corners of his burial plot in 1873; and James and Elizabeth Stephens, original owners of first 10 acres of cemetery and upon whose tombstone is chiseled one of the most memorable requiem inscriptions in state: "Here we lie by consent, after 57 years 2 months and 2 days sojurning through life awaiting nature's immutable laws to return us back to the elements of the universe, of which we were first composed." And here, too, are men and women of every race, color, nationality, religion, occupation and degree of pecuniary worth and morality who died in Portland or were carried here from the nearby hinterlands.

Riverside has in its old section more conspicuous tributes to the dead than any other cemetery in the state but Lone Fir is as bountiful in colorful markers. Markers in area set aside for firemen, for instance, have intricate carvings of hooks, ladders, trumpets and shields, signifying the trappings and glory of early fire companies.

Portland's most unusual burial ground is the **Japanese cemetery** at NE 50th and Fremont, contiguous to Rose City Cemetery. Here is a bit of rural Japan for the Issei and their children. Many inscriptions are in Japanese; an oddity is a swastika on a pre-Nazi era grave.

Portland is also rich in carousels, purportedly having more of them than any other city in the US. **Carousel Courtyard,** carousel and museum, is between NE 8th and NE 9th on Holladay St., diagonally across from Red Lion Inn. Other

Phoebe L. Friedman   *Phoebe L. Friedman*

Grave of Frances Fuller Victor in Riverview Cemetery   **Grave of Virgil Earp in Riverview Cemetery**

Lone Fir Cemetery

prominent carousels are at World Forestry Center (see earlier this section); Oaks Park, off E foot of Ross Island Bridge; Jantzen Beach Shopping Center, off Exit 238 of I-5 and near Columbia River Bridge; and Burger King Restaurant, 7601 SW Barbour Blvd.

The only urban preserve owned by the Oregon Chapter of The Nature Conservancy, **Keller Woodland,** is in Portland. The preserve contains an example of a Douglas fir-grand fir-western hemlock/sword fern forest.

From downtown Portland go S on Broadway and follow signs to Terwilliger Blvd. Continue straight past US Veterans Hospital Rd. for 0.6 m. Immediately after moderately sharp curve is gravel pullout on R. Keller Woodland follows the W (uphill) side of Terwilliger for 0.3 m.

On the way up Terwilliger Blvd. there are, on L, or E, remarkable vistas of downtown Portland and reaching to the Cascades, with Mt. Hood just beyond touching distance on a clear day.

Some geologists believe that a fault line runs thru Portland, from the foot of the West Hills thru the downtown area and toward St. Helens.

In 1982, former state geologist Ralph Mason told an audience: "Portland is unlucky in that it has a big, fat fault running right through it, which has been sleeping. If we were to have an earthquake, it would be 6.9 on the Richter scale, last about 45 seconds, and the U.S. National Bank downtown would be the epicenter. We would have access to none of our bridges; none of the north to south roads would be passable; there would be no water system; and gas lines would rupture. Very few homes would be left because few of them are built on solid rock."

Since the San Francisco quake in the autumn of 1989, a possible similar catastrophe in Portland has become TV and cocktail party conversation.

Short Trips Out of Portland
Sauvie Island

For centuries this island, largest in the Columbia, and, in part, washed by the mouth of the Willamette, was a summer and autumn homeland to the Multnomah Indians, and was known later to some whites as Multnomah Island. Lewis and Clark called it Wap-pa-to and Wap-pa-too and to the early whites it was Wapato. In a letter dated April 3, 1835, Nathaniel Wyeth wrote: "This Wappato Island which I have selected for our establishment is about 15 miles long and about average of three wide. On one side runs the Columbia, on the other the Multnomah. It consists of woodlands and prairie and on it there is considerable deer and those who could spare time to hunt might live well but a mortality has carried off to a man its inhabitants and there is nothing to attest that they ever existed except their decaying houses, their graves and their unburied bones of which there are heaps."

Hudson's Bay Co. revived the island and it later became known as Sauvie, for Laurent Sauve, who came from a village near Montreal and was probably foreman of HBC's dairy farm on W side of island. Leaving HBC he moved to French Prairie to farm and died there in 1858 at age 69.

In 1848 HBC withdrew from Sauvie Island and Anglo Americans moved in; by 1855 no fewer than 16 white families had settled on river-fronting claims.

The first link between the island and the mainland was by canoe. Then came the ferry, the most important happening since HBC left. In the late 1960s, then 74-year-old Albert Linder, who had lived with his wife on the island since 1928, told researcher Wayne Gessford: "Everybody used to meet on the ferry — either coming or going. We'd all gather there and catch up on the news. It also served as a lookout. If any game wardens would come onto the island, the news would be spread fast to alert natives to put their fish away."

With Prohibition came white whiskey, "made in the barn and aged in the woods," the natives boasted. It was common gossip that if you couldn't get a jug in Portland you could sure load up on Sauvie Island.

The Great Depression laid a heavy hand on Sauvie Island and farmers resorted to devious means to last out Hard Times. Albert Linder remembered one such enterprising settler:

"Before they put the dike on the upper end of the island, the cars used to come out of Portland and of course there were no roads to speak of. The ruts would get so deep the cars couldn't get out of them once they started down the trail. In one area where the cars had to go, a farmer used to pull the cars out when they got stuck. He made pretty good; he got five dollars for pulling them through the swamp.

"Another farmer questioned him about making so much money. He said he was, but he was getting awfully tired working both day and night. It was found out he hauled water by night to make the swamp muddy, and would pull cars during the day."

In recent years Sauvie Island has become a Portland suburb, a summer recreational retreat (swimming, boating, fishing and picnicking) and, above all, a game management area, designed for wintering waterfowl.

About 10,000 hunters per year use the waterfowl hunting parts of the game management area. More than 20 publicly owned waterfowl hunting areas and as many publicly owned fishing areas dot the island. In addition, some landowners lease duck ponds to hunters.

Raccoon hunting is permitted on the management area other than during waterfowl season. Crow hunting season is generally short. Neither raccoons nor crows are given advance notice that they will be hunted.

Sauvie Island sloughs are noted for their habitation by the painted turtle, recognizable by yellow lines on its dark head and feet and, when turned over, by dark central pattern on red undershell.

Despite all the onslaughts of *Homo sapiens,* Sauvie Island still retains an air of pastoral beauty, except when smog covers it.

Follow US 30 to Sauvie Island turnoff, *10.7 m.* from SW 5th and Morrison, downtown Portland. Along the way the road passes the approach to St. Johns Bridge, most aesthetic span in Oregon, and Linnton, whose founding predates Portland, but now part of the city.

From turnoff to Sauvie Island:

0.3 m., N end of Sauvie Island Bridge. *0.8 m.,* turn R onto Howell-Park Rd. *0.1 m.,* **Bybee-Howell House,** built in 1850s on DLC of Bybee family. For more than a century house belonged to Howell family, hence its name. Classic revival house, restored and now museum, has nine rooms, seven fireplaces. House sits on

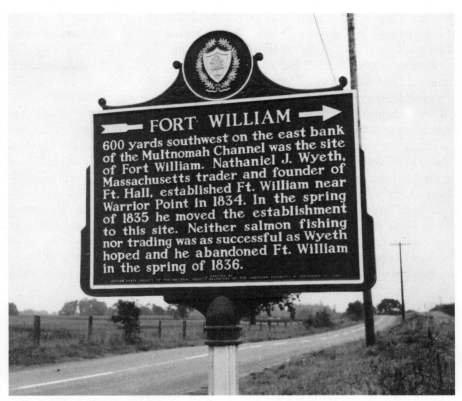

Marker pointing to side of Ft. William

knoll (about 50 ft. above sea level) that is highest point on island. *0.5 m.,* one of largest broadleaf maple trees in world.

Return to Sauvie Island Rd. Turn R. *1 m.,* Reeder Rd. Continue straight. *0.2 m.,* Oregon Fish and Wildlife Dept. office. *1.7 m.,* on L, **Ft. William marker.** In 1834, Nathaniel Wyeth, a Mass. ice merchant who sought his fortune in the Oregon Country, est. a post at Warrior Point, on the NW "neck" of the island. The next year he moved his Ft. William to the Multnomah Channel, about 0.5 m. S of marker. There is no path to the channel and no sign at the channel to indicate the existence of the post.

0.5 m., on L, 13-room house, built between 1890 and 1900. *0.8 m.,* Lucy Reeder Rd. Continue on Sauvie Island Rd., which follows Multnomah Channel, winding wash that departs from the Willamette and empties into the Columbia. Channel possesses some photogenic touches: moorages, log rafts, houseboats, fishing silhouettes and drowsy shades, where clumps of trees snooze above the lazy water. R side of road is great saucer of rich farmland.

2.2 m., Columbia County line. *1.4 m.,* start of **Game Management Area.** *0.2* *m.,* cattle guard. *0.6 m.,* turnoff to Mud Lake and Sturgeon Lake. *0.9 m.,* popular fishing site on Multnomah Channel. *0.4 m.,* turnaround. R for Crane Lake and Gilbert River. *0.8 m.,* **Gilbert River.** Fine fishing.

Return to Lucy Reeder Rd. and turn L onto it. *1.4 m.,* road's end. Return to Sauvie Island Rd. Turn L. *3.1 m.,* turn L onto Reeder Rd. *1.2 m.,* turn L onto Oak Island Rd. *4.1 m.,* end of road at cattle guard. This point is approximately center of Sauvie Island. Take trail across cattle guard. *580 yds.* to forks in grass. Take R. About same distance to Sturgeon Lake. Good view of Mt. St. Helens across lake.

Return to Reeder Rd. Turn L onto it. *2 m.,* stairway to pretty little body of water in wildlife area. Used by swimmers and canoers. *1.1 m.,* Gillihan Rd. Turn onto it. *1.3 m.,* **Reeder Beach.** *0.4 m.,* **Marshall Beach.** *0.8 m.,* entering Columbia County.

2.9 m., stairway to long beach on Columbia River. Beach extends to end of road, *3 m.* From this point, opposite Wash. shore, St. Helens, Adams and Hood are clearly seen. Rainier is visible from some points along beach. The rather narrow road along beach embankment is on a warm day solidly lined with cars.

Return to Reeder Rd. Take it. *6.3 m.,* entrance to bridge linking island to US 30.

East A

From Alder and SW 3rd, downtown Portland, via I-84.

15.3 m., turnoff to Columbia River Scenic Hwy. *1.3 m.,* **Troutdale.** (For Troutdale, see *Short Trips Out of Portland, Columbia River Scenic Hwy.*)

At Troutdale, turn onto Buxton Rd. *0.4 m.,* "T". Turn L. *0.1 m.,* curve R onto Troutdale Rd. *0.9 m.,* Stark St. On SW corner, **Albert Baker Beech Tree** (copper beech), planted circa 1883 by Alfred Baker as corner marker of his farm. Baker came to Oregon from Iowa and for a while was a stagecoach driver E of Cascades. Straight. *1.7 m.,* at triangle, Division St., turn L. *1.5 m.,* turn R onto Oxbow Dr. *1.4 m.,* forks. Turn L. *0.8 m.,* turn L onto Hosner Rd. which is also Oxbow Parkway. *1.7 m.,* entrance gate, **Oxbow Park.** This Multnomah CP, on Sandy River, is quite popular with urbanites who, crowded as the park may be, feel it is still a touch of wilderness. They may have a small point. Oxbow Park has 20 m. of trails and along these reside and visit 220 species of plants, 74 of birds, 30 of mammals, 15 of reptiles. CG, PA. Circular drive around park is 5.2 m.

Between Oxbow and Dodge parks The Nature Conservancy has 532 acres along a 6 m. stretch of the steep-walled gorge, which is in near pristine condition. **Sandy River Gorge Preserve** includes meadows, waterfalls, swales, river frontage, woods. Forest contains stands of old-growth Douglas fir (some as old as 500 years), with Western red cedar and Western hemlock interspersed. Osprey nest is near preserve and bear, river otter, elk and cougar have been sighted in gorge.

Return to Hosner Rd. and Oxbow Parkway. Continue straight on Hosner. *0.5 m.,* turn L onto Lusted Rd. *0.9 m.,* first farm gate on L at foot of hill. This is the only really accessible entrance to **Sandy River Gorge Preserve.** Only persons sincerely interested in studying this unique environment should come here. *0.2 m.,* second gate and start of preserve. No motor, bicycle or horse travel permitted; only pedestrian. *1 m.* hike thru preserve to Sandy River.

Return to Lusted Rd. Turn L. (It should be noted here that this itinerary ought not to be regarded as a point-to-point excursion. All the countryside is lovely, especially in the spring, and there is more of a "nature" atmosphere in these parts than there is around Salem, Albany, Oregon City, Molalla and Woodburn, for example. Those who do not race from one place to another will be the most profited.) *3.5 m.,* bridge across Sandy River. *0.1 m.,* **Dodge Park,** on Sandy River. CG, PA. Another Multnomah County recreationland too heavily impacted inside and outside. But the Sandy flowing thru here is magnificent.

1.8 m., jct., SE Lusted Rd. and SE Ten Eyck Rd.

Straight on SE Lusted Rd.: *0.8 m.,* curve L onto Thomas Rd. *0.6 m.,* **Roslyn Lake Park.** PA. *(0.3 m.,* **Roslyn Lake,** which doesn't seem larger than a good sized mill pond but which bears a large traffic of boaters and fishers.) *0.1 m.,* on L, **Bull Run Grade School,** charming bldg. with airy features. *0.3 m.,* jct., Ten Eyck Rd. and Thomas Rd.

From SE Lusted Rd. and Ten Eyck Rd. jct., take Ten Eyck Rd.: *0.9 m.,* forks, Bull Run Jct. Turn R. *0.6 m.,* turn R onto Thomas Rd. *0.2 m.,* on R, Bull Run Grade School. *0.1 m.,* Roslyn Lake Park.

Return to Bull Run Jct. Turn onto Bull Run Rd. *0.6 m.,* Bull Run River and Bull Run Power Station. **Bull Run** is prime source of Portland's water supply, which Portland water officials claim is among purest in US. Bull Run supposedly received its name from early overlander cattle which escaped from poorly fenced homesteads and ran wild for years. (It was probably the water which gave them their pep.) In 1915 there was hereabout the hamlet of Bull Run, with pop. 100, PS and home of large-scale Crissey "Gladiolus Farm." Village was also terminus of Mt. Hood division of Portland Railway, Light & Power Co. RR.

0.1 m., jct. Straight. *2.4 m.,* site of former settlement of **Aims** (PO 1886–1907.) Old-timers say there was a store here, but not much more. *0.8 m.,* on L, Aims Museum of Relick's," formerly Aims School, then Aims Church. *9 m.,* past sweeping views of the Sandy River, Columbia River Scenic Hwy. (R to Corbett and Multnomah Falls, straight to Troutdale and Portland.)

Return to Bull Run Jct. Turn L. *0.5 m.,* Roslyn Lake Jct. *0.2 m.,* Marmot Jct. — SE Shipley Rd. Turn L. *1.2 m.,* Marmot Rd. Turn R. *1.5 m.,* Ten Eyck Rd. Straight. *0.9 m.,* turnoff to **Sandy River Fish Hatchery** *(0.5 m.).* Large, instructive hatchery in attractive setting. *0.5 m.,* jct., Oral Hull Park. *0.8 m.,* 422nd Ave. *0.8 m.,* **Oral Hull Park,** only park for blind in Oregon. Gardens for the blind, with guide plates in braille, have been, with good reason, much praised. Park was once farm of elderly, childless couple who wanted to leave their land to a good cause but didn't know what. A local justice of the peace, himself blind, convinced them which route to take. Oral Hull Foundation receives no public money; by dili-

Bull Run

gence and quiet persuasion has developed park into well-housed, well-organized retreat for blind and sighted. Return to Ten Eyck Rd. Turn L. *0.6 m.,* US 26. R, *0.3 m.,* Sandy.

From jct., SE Shipley and Marmot Rd. It was at this point that the emigrant wagons on the Barlow Rd., the last leg of the Oregon Trail, turned toward what is now Sandy and continued S on what is now O 211 to the Foster place at Eagle Creek.

4.9 m., site of **Marmot PO.** Erroneously named for marmots, blamed for numerous burrowings at the edges of woods. (Actual diggers were mountain beavers.) PO est. 1886. In 1915 Marmot had pop. 40, PS, sawmill. Site of hamlet so obliterated that most residents along Marmot Rd. have no idea where PO stood.
3.4 m., on R, two dirt roads divided by fence. Walk 40 yds up first road to **Rock Corral,** on R. This large rock, seen only close up, served as centerpiece for makeshift corral on Oregon Trail. A few paces ahead, on L, is Oregon Trail marker.

1.3 m., Barlow Trail Rd.

To R: *0.1 m.,* Sleepy Hollow Rd. Turn L. *0.3 m.,* US 26.

To L, on Barlow Trail Rd. from Marmot Rd.: *1.5 m.,* forks. Take R, or lower

THE KISS OF THE SUN
FOR PARDON
THE SONG O A BIRD
FOR MIRTH
ONE IS NEARER GOD'S
HEART IN A GARDEN
THAN ANYWHERE ELSE ON EARTH

D.F. GURNEY

Oral Hull Park for the Blind

road. *0.2 m.,* E Brightwood Bridge. Turn R. *0.3 m.,* **Brightwood,** at store. First called Salmon (1891), which seems appropriate, since village is practically lapped by Salmon River. But seeing the gleaming forests about town, Brightwood has validity of its own. In 1915 village had creamery and salmon hatchery, which it doesn't have now. *0.3 m.,* from store, turn R onto road at Salmon River bridge. *0.1 m.,* on L, old green house was last civilian residence of WW II hero, Col. Evans Carlson (retired as Brig. Gen.) Scarcely anyone in Brightwood today knows what a towering figure the village could once claim as neighbor. During WW II Carlson's Marine Raiders achieved much success and attention. A political progressive rare in Marine Corps ranks, Carlson had studied guerilla tactics in China, where he was sent by the US to observe tactics of the famous Eighth Route Army. His long-out-of-print book, *Twin Stars of China,* is a remarkable portrayal of war-enveloped north China prior to WW II. (For an account of Carlson's life, see *The Big Yankee* by Michael Blankfort.) Return to Brightwood Rd. Turn R. *0.3 m.,* US 26.

Return to E Brightwood Bridge Rd. Turn R. *4.4 m.,* on R, **"Original Barlow Trail"** marker, plaque on stone. *0.5 m.,* Lolo Pass Rd. Turn R. *1.1 m.,* US 26, at Zigzag. (For return to Portland, see *East B,* immediately following.)

East B

From 82nd and Burnside:

Travel S. *6.3 m.,* Sunnyside Rd. Turn E. *3.5 m.,* 147th. Turn L. *1.1 m.,* Scouter's Mountain gate. Take Scouter's Mtn. Rd. to R. *0.1 m.,* park on gravel turnout at R. Walk *70 yds.* uphill to wooden footgate on L. *450 yds.* hike along birdsong forest path to **Christilla Pioneer Cemetery.**

Originally, this burial ground was called Deardorff Cemetery, after John M. Deardorff, overland pioneer of 1850 who took up DLC in Christilla Valley, now Happy Valley. There are more bodies than grave markers because persons are named on each of several markers. Oldest grave in cemetery said by stone to be 1852. Historical records are vague, stating that a covered wagon emigrant, name unknown, was buried here "before 1857." One of the mysteries of this burial ground is why a headstone was stolen from it.

0.8 m., **Scout Lodge** atop Scouter's Mtn. Lodge overlooks Happy Valley and reserve owned by the Scouts. Nature trails wind thru the approximate 200 acres, open meadows seem virginal, wildlife feels safe here.

Return to Sunnyside Rd. and 147th. Turn L. *1.3 m.,* 172nd. Turn R. *1 m.,* SE Armstrong Circle. Turn R. *0.2 m.,* O 212. Turn L. *0.1 m.,* lane at 17146 SE O 212. (R up lane *0.1 m.,* 16-room **Anderegg Home,** Victorian-style house that becomes more impressive as closer approached. 80-acre farmstead based on three c's: cows, crops, ceramics.)

1.3 m., on R at corner, **Damascus Pioneer Cemetery.** Grave markers go back to 1860s. *0.4 m.,* Foster Rd., Damascus. Turn L. *0.6 m.,* on R, Winston Place, 3-gabled house, part of which was built in 1845 by John S. Fisher, who became first postmaster of Damascus in 1867.

Return to O 212. Turn L, or E. *50 yds.,* on R, in front of **Damascus Community Park,** "Peace Candle," an almost-forgotten — and only surviving relic — of a great ambition in 1959. In that year, Oregon's Centennial, there was a fairly large and generally hapless international exhibit in Portland. Tiny Damascus, then consisting of little more than a country store, provided the only excitement to the rather weary undertakings of the big city by transforming itself into a "Wild West" town, with a few false-fronted structures, staged shootouts, and the like. The great attractions were Sunday buffalo feasts, which brought thousands to the hinterland village. The "Peace Candle" was put up, with an "eternal flame," long extinguished, to symbolize the real meaning of the festivities. Tragedy came

Winston Place, Damascus   *Phoebe L. Friedman*

when the storeowner followed his misguided dream to turn Damascus into an Oregon Knott's Berry Farm. He lost everything in the venture, including his health.

For the genealogical-minded, there is a thread, however slender, between French royalty and Damascus. The town was named by 1854 comer from Iowa, Ed Pedigo, directly descended from the powerful Perigord family of France, and a distant relative of Talleyrand, one-time close associate of Napoleon, Foreign Minister of Louis XVIII, and giant of French diplomacy.

2.1 m., 242nd. (At corner, magnificent view of Mt. Hood.) Turn L onto 242nd, which bobs over undulating meadowland of fine small farms. *2.5 m.,* forks. Straight. *0.8 m.,* 242nd becomes Hogan Rd. Into the 1960s Hogan Rd. was a lovely rural route, as idyllic a stretch of farmland as one could imagine. Now it is only a street of suburbia, with here and there a touch of what it once was. *2.4 m.,* Powell Blvd., US 26, **Gresham.**

What is now Gresham was first settled in 1852 by Dr. John Parker Powell, of Macon County, Missouri, and his wife, Adaline Duvall Powell. Site of original Powell farmstead was at Division and 11th and stump remains of tree he planted, at W end of Olympic Plywood Co. Area was named Powell Valley but PO and town named for Walter Quinton Gresham, Civil War hero and Postmaster at time PO opened in 1884. Not inc. until 1905, Gresham grew slowly, almost lazily. In 1910 it had only about 1,200 people and was regarded as the bucolic prize of Multnomah County. By 1930 town was still small; census showed only 1,348

Painting of first house in Gresham   *Phoebe L. Friedman*

humans. In 1940 pop. had gone to 1,629; by 1950 to 2,434; by 1960 to 3,854, by 1966 to 5,120. Then, almost overnight, Gresham mushroomed. For long, Gresham was site of Multnomah County Fair, and a fine and true fair it was. Then fair was moved to indoor Portland and the land commercially utilized. Shopping centers sprang up like dandelions after rains, and as pretty. In every direction fields were plowed up and orchards uprooted to make way for housing developments. By 1980 pop. had started to move strongly toward 40,000, making it one of largest towns in Oregon, and the Gresham Portlanders loved to visit as a trip to rural sweetness had become just another taffy-stretched suburbia, with no redeemable character of its own.

E on US 26. *1.1 m.,* Orient Jct. Turn onto Orient Rd. *2.9 m.,* **Orient,** cheery little village whose name origin is obscure to historians. (Elderly Japanese say place was first called Oriental, because of large number of Japanese field workers there at turn of century, and later shortened to Orient.) Store. *0.1 m.,* forks. Take L, Bluff Rd. *0.8 m.,* SE Pleasant Home Rd. On R, **Pleasant Home Church,** foundation laid 1884. Cemetery back of church has markers to 1890. Return to US 26. Turn E.

4.7 m., jct., Boring — O 212. (See *Trans-Cascade Roads, US 26.*) *1.8 m.,* Kelso Jct. Turn N onto Kelso Rd. *0.5 m.,* **Kelso.** In 1915 Kelso had two sawmills; none now. Store. Old dance hall, whose country music brought in folks from all parts of the territory, is now warehouse; the dry land boat that served as roadside diner and dished up luscious 20 cent hot dogs disappeared about time suburban flood reached village. Return to US 26. Turn E.

3.4 m., **Sandy.** What a difference a few miles make! Sandy and Gresham were more or less in same pop. category into the 1960s. Then Gresham catapulted ahead while Sandy continued to crawl slowly upward. Closeness to Portland is accountable for Gresham's startling growth and urban alienation. Sandy's ill luck, or blessing, depending upon perspective, is that thus far it is still out of suburbia range. First name of what is now Sandy was Revenue, but Sandy, for nearby Sandy River, won out, since whole area was known as Sandy. Until recently Sandy had been typical market center, with relatively small pop. and large number of institutions. In 1915 Sandy had pop. of only 175 but it had creamery, sawmill and lumberyard, was terminus of three scenic stage lines, had weekly newspaper, four lodges, Grange, Commercial Club and Women's Club. Outwardly, Sandy displays an urbanity reflective of Portland sophistication but below surface there is a lot of the overalls spirit left in town. Jct., O 211.

0.3 m., turnoff to Oral Hull Park, Dodge Park, Bull Run.

Turn N onto Ten Eyck Rd. 0.6 m., forks, Ten Eyck to L. Coalman straight. Take Coalman. 0.8 m., SE 422nd. Turn L. 0.8 m., **Oral Hull Park,** 22-acre beautifully landscaped park, in shadow of Mt. Hood, for use of the blind. Sighted welcome.

Return to forks. Turn R onto Ten Eyck Rd. 0.5 m., **Sandy River Fish Hatchery** (0.5 m.) 0.7 m., bridge over Sandy River. 0.2 m., Marmot Rd. (R, 1.6 m., SE Shipley Rd. Jct. Continue, curving R, on Marmot Rd. For Marmot, Rock Corral

and Marmot area, see *Short Trips Out of Portland, East A*, immediately preceding.)

From Marmot Jct. on Ten Eyck Rd.: *0.2 m.*, on L, **Cliffside Cemetery.** Oldest marker is that of Civil War veteran Herman Anton Poppe, who died 1874. *0.5 m.*, Marmot Jct. — SE Shipley Rd. (Turn R. *1.2 m.*, jct., Marmot Rd.)

0.2 m., Roslyn Lake Jct. (Turn L. *0.3 m.*, Bull Run School. *0.1 m.*, entrance to Roslyn Lake Park PG.)

From Roslyn Lake Jct.: *0.6 m.*, Bull Run. Jct. (Turn onto Bull Run Rd. *0.6 m.*, Bull Run. *0.1 m.*, jct. Straight. *2.4 m.*, site of former town of **Aims.** *9 m.*, Columbia River Scenic Hwy. For this section of trip, see *East A*, immediately preceding.)

From Bull Run Jct.: *0.9 m.*, SE Lusted Rd. Turn R. *1.8 m.*, Dodge Park, on Sandy River. *0.1 m.*, bridge over Sandy River. *3.5 m.*, on R at curve, **Diack Gate,** just beyond Bridlewood Horsemanship Center. (Entrance to Sandy River Gorge Preserve. See *East A*, immediately preceding.) *0.9 m.*, Hosner Rd. Turn R. *0.5 m.*, jct. Straight on SE Oxbow Parkway. *1.7 m.*, entrance gate, Oxbow Park. Return to jct. Turn R onto SE Oxbow Rd., which becomes SE Division. *3.8 m.*, Troutdale Rd. Straight. *2.1 m.*, Burnside St., Gresham. Turn R. *6.1 m.*, 122nd. *2 m.*, 82nd. *4.7 m.*, Burnside and 3rd, downtown Portland.

For completion of this itinerary, East B, backtrack from Oxbow Park to Marmot Jct. Follow *Short Trips Out of Portland, East A*, down Marmot Rd. to Barlow Trail Rd. to Brightwood, to Lolo Pass, and S to Zigzag, at US 26.

At Zigzag, turn W. *1 m.*, Welches Jct. Turn S. *0.8 m.*, **Rippling River Resort,** most grandiose between Coast and Cascades. It is so huge, so much piled upon each other, that the overall picture is that of an upper-middle class Levittown. It is much larger and less pleasing to the eye than its predecessor, Bowman's. A woman who lived near the resort area for more than 80 years lamented, "I liked it best when it was just a cow pasture." *0.2 m.*, on R, turn-of-century house built by William Welch, son of Sam Welch, who settled here in 1882. To rear and W of home is smaller house, which for 55 years was **Welches** PO, with postmaster being either William Welch or his wife Jennie.

In its zenith hour Welches boasted hotel, dance hall, blacksmith shop and store, all owned by William and Jennie Welch. Couple also operated dairy and farm and ran four-horse stage up Barlow Toll Rd. to Government Camp. When she was 80, Jennie Welch recalled, "Summer was the big time. We had 150 people in the hotel and there were hundreds more camping on our grounds. They came clear from Portland by wagon; it took them two days. We had dances on Wednesdays and Saturdays — the dance hall was above the store — and we had sometimes close to 200 people at a dance."

Welches was quite a community then and Jennie Welch thought the name should remain. "I don't know why they call this area Wemme," she questioned, her voice rising. "All the time we had the post office it was called Welches. When I became 70 the government made me retire and, well, it was a political thing. This man down at Wemme was a Democrat precinct committeeman and

Senator Neuberger — you know of him — owed him patronage and that's how our name was stolen. That was a dirty, rotten political trick, stealing our name, that covered this whole district for all those years.

"I don't get my mail at Wemme," she declared resolutely, standing erect. "I drive to Zigzag. That's my post office now."

Jennie Welch lived into her 95th year, running her patrician antique shop until the last, and on Dec. 11, 1985, gracefully leaving the land she had made fairer. But 8 years before she died she had the last laugh. In 1977 poetic justice was done when the PO was removed from Wemme and a new PO built near Welches Jct. It was called, of course, Welches, and Jennie Welch didn't have to drive to Zigzag anymore to do her mail business.

0.5 m., **Wemme,** a scratch on the hwy. Name is not without honor, however. Edward Wemme was prosperous Portland businessman and realtor, owner of first automobile in Portland, and purchaser of every new make and model that appeared, owner of one of first airplanes in Oregon, philanthropist whose funds built Portland White Shield Home for unwed mothers, and good roads enthusiast. In 1912 he bought the Barlow Road for $5,400, improved it, and deeded it to the state. Part of it was inc. into Mt. Hood Loop Hwy. Wemme PO est. 1916, 2 years after Wemme's death.

0.4 m., **Wildwood.** Tavern. *0.4 m.,* turnoff to Wildwood Rec. Area. *0.6 m.,* Brightwood Jct. (Turn N. *1.5 m.,* Brightwood. See *East A,* immediately preceding.) *0.7 m.,* from E Brightwood Loop: *12.2 m.,* Sandy. *11.3 m.,* Gresham. *13 m.,* downtown Portland.

West A

From Burnside and Broadway:

W on Burnside. *2.2 m.,* turn R onto NW Barnes. Follow signs *0.6 m.* to **Pittock Mansion,** one of Portland's great houses, now museum. Completed in 1914 it was built by London-born Henry Louis Pittock, who came to Oregon in 1853 and from then until his death in 1919, with the exception of 2 years (1864–1866) as state printer, was intimately associated with Portland *Oregonian,* starting as printer. In 1860 he was given paper in lieu of back wages and remained its owner and publisher for more than 50 years. Pittock was also a founder of paper making in state. Mansion commands sweeping view of parts of Portland and Cascades.

Return to Burnside. Turn R. *0.8 m.,* Skyline Blvd. Straight on Skyline. *0.5 m.,* on L, **Willamette Stone SP.** Path slopes 220 yds. to spot where, on June 4, 1851, John R. Preston, first surveyor general of Oregon, drove the "starting stake" for all land surveys in the PNW. Stake replaced by stone July 25, 1885. Inscription on stone: "Beginning here, the Willamette Meridian was established running north to Puget Sound and south to the California border, and the base line was established running east to the Idaho border and west to the Pacific Ocean." All the lands of Oregon sectionized from these guidelines. Little is known of surveyor Preston. He was replaced in 1853 and seems to have drifted into obscurity.

1.3 m., NW Cornell Rd. Turn R onto Cornell. *1.6 m.,* **Pittock Bird Sanctuary** of the Audubon Society. Sanctuary includes parking lot E of society HQ at 5151 NW Cornell. Area is year-round home for ruffed grouse, pileated woodpeckers, blacktail deer, pygmy owls.

Return to NW Cornell and Skyline. Straight on Cornell. *2.3 m.,* on L, beyond rustic bridge, delightful little waterfall that cannot be seen from car. Here was site of **Jones Mill,** built 1855. Mill was powered by overshot waterwheel. Logs were drawn by oxen. Lumber was used in Portland homes. Mill dismantled 1892. A local woman, passing by, remarked: "You ought to come here in winter, when it's frozen over. It's sure pretty then."

0.1 m., on L, at 12030 NW Cornell, house built 1876. Original Cedar Mill PO here. John Quincy Adams Young, settler of 1862, built cabin at this site. Later, present house used as store and PO. Young's mill produced cedar siding, shingles, shakes and other bldg. materials that were gobbled up by burgeoning Portland.

0.7 m., center, Cedar Mill, Portland suburb with about as much distinction as average middle-class living room. It may have been more charming in 1915, when pop. was 25.

0.5 m., turn R onto NW 143rd. *0.3 m.,* on L, **Union Cemetery** of Cedar Mill. Markers go back to 1857.

0.6 m., turn L onto NW Union Rd. *0.2 m.,* turn R onto Kaiser Rd. *0.7 m.,* on L, **Bethany Baptist Church,** org. 1881 as First German Baptist Church of Bethany, first church of this specific denomination in Far West. Original chapel (1881) at rear of church kept for sentimental reasons. Not kept was 1928 structure of modified Spanish colonial style with carillon tower. *0.1 m.,* on L, pioneer house, original site of **Bethany.** Swiss-born Ulrich Gerber built house 1876, was PO 1878–1904, with Gerber as postmaster. Place was also overnight stage stop. House passed on thru Gerber family. (See "The Sisters of Bethany," in author's *Tales Out of Oregon.)*

0.1 m., Springville Rd. On NW corner, **Bethany Presbyterian Church** (1904). Turn L, or W, onto Springville Rd. *1.1 m.,* Rock Creek Center of Portland Community College. On campus is **Washington County Museum,** formerly in Hillsboro. *0.4 m.,* 185th Ave.

(L on 185th: *0.4 m.,* Bethany. Store. Turn R onto NW Union. *1.6 m.,* West Union. See later, this section.)

Turn R onto 185th. *1.3 m.,* NW Germantown Rd. *0.1 m.,* on L, **Bethany Bible College,** built 1895 by German speaking immigrants from Germany, Switzerland and Russia as Methodist Episcopal. Until late 1920 services entirely in German. Church became Independent Evangelical in 1960. Back of church is cemetery. In Currier & Ives setting, church has aura of true rural integrity.

Turn R from church. *0.1 m.,* NW 185th. Straight. *0.3 m.,* Cornelius Pass Rd. Turn R onto Old Cornelius Pass Rd. *0.8 m.,* on R, **Rock Creek Tavern,** in 19th century blacksmith shop; one of most colorful taverns in state. Interior has fresh mustiness of light-and-shadow antique shop. Turn L here at Phillips Rd. *0.1 m.,* on R, old **Rock Creek School.** Return to Old Cornelius Pass Rd. Turn L. *0.1 m.,* on L, turn-of-century bldg. that held **Rock Creek PO** and also served as community forum, dance hall, social center.

Return to Cornelius Pass Rd. Turn R. *2 m.,* NW Union Rd. Straight on Cornelius Pass Rd. *1.3 m.,* on R, **Imbrie House.** Six generations of Imbries lived here before house was sold; became restaurant, then roadhouse and brewery. House built 1862–1866; octagonal barn in rear is as old.

Return to NW Union Rd. Here was community of **West Union** (PO 1874–1894). Turn L. *0.8 m.,* on R, **West Union Baptist Church,** oldest Baptist church W of upper Missouri and oldest Protestant bldg. in Oregon still on same place. David T. Lenox, captain of first wagon train to Oregon (1843), donated land for church and cemetery from his original land grant. Congregation org. May 25, 1844 by Elder Lenox in his cabin on site of present church bldg. Founding statement declared that parishioners were those "who have been thrown together in the wilds of West," and thus had gathered to form into union. What must Lenox think now as cars race past the church at above-limit speeds?

First sermon preached in home of Peter Burnett, member of Lenox-captained wagon train. After brief, illustrious career in Oregon, Burnett moved to Calif. after gold was discovered and in 1850 became first governor of state.

West Union Baptist Church

Lumber of the church was hauled by ox team from Milwaukie mills and church dedicated 1853. Well preserved are rafters of cedar poles, joists of fir poles, sills of hand-hewn fir logs.

For third of century the church was a flame in the newfound land, with parishioners traveling from nearby land claims and far outreaches, on foot and horseback and by ox team. But in 1878 congregation was dissolved because of internal politics and that was the end of regular services. Church became active again in 1980s, with morning Sunday services.

Almost since congregation was founded there were plans for school. Finally, on Jan. 16, 1858, the "West Union Institute" was inc. But it was never opened; instead, the Baptists turned to McMinnville for their college.

This area was also home of the **West Union School,** first in Oregon Country est. under school law adopted by territorial legislature in 1850. Bldg. was put up 1851 and lasted until 1900, 9 years after new school was built. There is no trace of the old schools.

Buried in church cemetery are David Lenox; Zephanial D. Bones; Eveline Bones, whose grave was first here (1854); James Imbrie; and two men of Champoeg, George W. Ebbert and Caleb Wilkins. Both were mountain men, farmers, and married to Indian women. Ebbert was first Anglo settler at Champoeg; Wilkins was one of four men to take first wagon from Ft. Hall to Walla Walla. Both arrived in Oregon Country in early 1830s.

0.7 m., Helvetia Rd. Turn L. *0.9 m.,* on L, at US 26, site of **The Five Oaks.** Here the first white settlers on this plain, a small group of mountain men who had settled in 1840, gathered to hold picnics, religious revivals, horse races, and anything else that would bring them together. This first independent American farm community in the Far West was called Rocky Mountain Retreat, then West Union, because of a reunion of the mountain men in a place farther W than the Rockies.

Turn R onto US 26. *2.3 m.,* on R, **Joe Meek Marker.** To L, across road, was where Meek's home stood. (For life of Meek in Oregon, see "The Not So Meek Joe" in author's *Tracking Down Oregon.*)

Return to Union and Helvetia Rds. Straight toward Helvetia:

1.4 m., **Helvetia Tavern,** only business in Helvetia, so named because Swiss families settled here. Tavern attracts customers from several counties because of its sumptuous hamburgers and sober convivial atmosphere.

For practical purposes the tavern marks the breaking point between two options on the West A tour.

Option 1:

1.1 m. — from tavern: There are a number of old, charming houses along this way; among outstanding, on R, 2-story dowager overlooking fields and dales.

0.1 m., on L, **Helvetia Community Church,** org. 1881 as Reformierte Emmanuels Kirche by Swiss and German settlers. Built 1889 in 161-1/2 days at cost of

$832. Spire 65 ft. high. Services held in German until 1942. Became independent community church in 1956. Back and to side of church is cemetery.

0.7 m., Logie Trail Rd. **Logie Trail** was pioneer land route of whites in Oregon. It connected Tualatin Plains to Sauvie Island and was named for James Logie, Hudson's Bay Co. farm overseer on island in 1830s. On NW corner of Helvetia Rd. and Logie Trail is plot of land known to past generations as Cowaniah's Schoolyard. Here was home of Cowaniah, an Indian whom legend records as leading Indians and whites in successful battle against raiding Klickitats. In 1879 first Helvetia School built here. No trace of it now and no longer does Helvetia have a school.

0.2 m., Jackson Quarry Rd. Turn R onto it. *1.2 m.,* on L, quarry. *(0.3 m.,* foottrek — if permission is obtained — to Jackson Falls, pretty picture. Grist mill of John B. Jackson operated in 1850s at foot of falls.)

0.8 m., Mason Hill Rd. This pike was part of Hillsborough-St. Helen's Territorial Rd., hacked out in 1852 to widen old Indian trail. (A "greenery" side trip here is R up Mason Hill Rd., on historic trace to Dixie Mtn., then down Dixie Mtn. Rd. back to flatlands, at Shadybrook. Mileage: 17.7.)

Turn L onto Mason Hill Rd. *0.8 m.,* Jackson Rd. Turn R. *1.1 m.,* on L, **Shadybrook Church,** in pastoral setting except for lumberyard across road. *0.1 m.,* turn R onto Shadybrook Rd. *0.1 m.,* on R, former **Shadybrook School,** horse-age school bldg. now a church.

Return to jct. of Jackson and Shadybrook. Straight on Shadybrook. *1.2 m.,* on L, photogenic old house. *0.2 m.,* on L, 1880s house that seems to be waiting to be put on canvas by sensitive painter.

0.2 m., turn R onto Pumpkin Ridge Rd. All this country is aglow with freshness and the roads weave in and out of vales, into one bowl-shape after another, and with the sun washing the greenery to the bottom, there are Swiss cameos everywhere. "When I first came here, about 1956," said a resident, "the houses were pretty modest. Now there are more fancy homes around here than there are in Portland."

2.9 m., on L, Old Pumpkin Ridge Rd. *0.1 m.,* on R, collapsing pioneer **Pumpkin Ridge School.** *0.5 m.,* on L, **Arcade Cemetery** (1886).

Return to Old Pumpkin Ridge Rd. Turn R. *1.3 m.,* Corey Rd. Turn R. *3.2 m.,* Dairy Creek Rd. Turn R. *2.5 m.,* on L, **Big Canyon Ranch.** Turn L, into ranch and to BLM-managed Big Canyon, a precious bit of "last stand" untouched Douglas fir forest. Trail for hikers and horse riders uphill *1 m.* to skirt of virgin clusters. More wildlife than one would suspect from first observation roam the woods.

Residents hereabouts claim their stamping ground is "secret" of Portland Metropolitan Area. Local of half-a-century claimed, "There's a lot of wilderness around here, only 25 miles from Portland. And hardly anybody knows about us." Asked if he didn't think the publicity would bring in droves of tourists and destroy the calm of his beloved retreat, he replied, "Wouldn't bother me. I'm moving down to Arizona. Too much rain here for my arthritis." Camelot is only in the mind.

0.9 m., turn L onto Meacham Rd. *0.1 m.,* at creek, **Meacham Crossing,** site of pioneer sawmill. Here, in the 1850s, the Military Rd. left the outbound settlements for Astoria.

Return to Dairy Creek Rd. Turn L. *2.3 m.,* site of **Snooseville,** a once-sawmill village that was never on a map. No trace of place now. At Fern Flat Rd. here, turn R. *1 m.,* on R, **BLM Little Bend Rec. Area,** almost liquid green picnic grounds on East Dairy Creek.

Return to Snooseville. Turn R. *4.9 m.,* forks. Take R. *0.7 m.,* on L, pioneer homestead of Jeppesen family. *0.4 m.,* **Bacona** — now only single house. (For story on place, see "Baptism at Bacona" in author's *Tracking Down Oregon.*)

Return to forks. Take R. *7.7 m.,* **Buxton.** US 26 stunted growth of village, bigger in 1915 than at present.

0.9 m., US 26. Turn L for Portland.

Option 2:

From Helvetia Tavern:

1.1 m., on R, on knoll, 2-story pioneer home. *0.1 m.,* on L, Helvetia Church and cemetery. *0.7 m.,* Logie Trail Rd. Straight. *0.2 m.,* turn L onto Jackson Quarry Rd. *1.1 m.,* turn R onto West Union Rd. *0.7 m.,* Jackson Rd. **Jackson House,** on SW corner, built 1880, burned down June, 1986. Turn N, or R, onto Jackson Rd. *0.1 m.,* on L, **Lincoln House,** another Tualatin Valley showcase of the 1880s.

Return to West Union Rd. Turn R. *3.2 m.,* Glencoe Rd. Turn R onto it. *0.2 m.,* Old West Union Rd. Turn R onto it. *60 yds.* on L, **Village Blacksmith Shop.** Charles Walter worked in this shop from 1890 to 1962. He retired at age 90, died 2 years later. Shop is as Walter left it; heritage of horse and buggy days.

For decades there was village here called **Glencoe** (PO 1871–1904). It was on

Phoebe L. Friedman

Village Blacksmith Shop

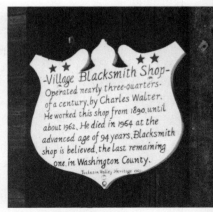

Village Blacksmith Shop

steady course until settlement of North Plains. Then Glencoe stores folded and people began moving to North Plains.

Return to Glencoe Rd. Turn L. *0.2 m.*, North Plains Jct. Turn R. *0.4 m.*, **North Plains,** so-called because settlers considered themselves on N plains of Tualatin Valley. Growing slowly, town advanced from 200 pop. in 1915 to 900 in 1985, average gain of 10 per year. The one block business section is day-to-day large enough for the locals, who go to Cornelius, Hillsboro or Portland for their heavy shopping.

It is given to every town to acquire some sort of legend. In North Plains it was a dog called Hitler, a mutt of dubious ancestry who hung around the tavern. There were many stories written about the pooch, simply because of its name. Almost everyone in the village thought the name funny; when a visitor showed displeasure he was told he lacked a sense of humor.

Return to Glencoe Rd. Turn R. *1.8 m.*, Scotch Church Rd. Turn L. (Old house on L is another pioneer home remodeled into comfortable TV-age dwelling.) *0.5 m.*, **Tualatin Plains Presbyterian Church,** known traditionally as Old Scotch Church and now, sensitive to ethnic concern, addressing itself as Old Scottish (or Scots) Church. One of oldest and certainly most beautiful churches in Oregon. Modest white chapel displays the excellent craftsmanship often found in early Oregon churches. The church, and the cemetery that frames it on three sides, are bordered by grove of firs, oaks and maples. Among those who lie in the old burial ground are early Meek family, including Joe Meek, colorful mountain man, for whom 19th century scribes used the longest, flashiest yarn to spin their patchquilt biographies. But it wasn't all their fault. "Uncle Joe" strung the longest bow in the territory when it came to telling tales. "There's no man like Joe," his Indian wife often said, and from the standpoint of copy-hungry writers, there wasn't. (For more see "The Not So Meek Joe" in author's *Tracking Down Oregon.*)

Return to Glencoe Rd. Continue straight, on Zion Church Rd. (Names change at corners, so that you can be on Road A this side of corner and Road B on the other side. One would hope there is some logic for this scheme. There is enough confusion in Washington County without adding more.)

2 m., Kirkman Rd. Here stood crossroads village of **Schefflin.** Turn R. *0.7 m.*, on R, big old barn full of mellow mirth. *0.4 m.*, on R, **Chalmers House,** reportedly built 1870s. Beyond it is barn as old. *0.3 m.*, turn L. *50 yds.*, turn R. *1.2 m.*, on R, **Harrison Cemetery.** Markers date to 1860s.

Return to Glencoe Rd. Turn R. *1.9 m.*, on L, **Zion Lutheran Church,** strikingly modernistic architecture, quite a change from simple country church that stood at Schefflin, on Zion Church Rd., from 1904 to 1971, and where services continued to be conducted in German until 1941, though English had gradually taken over.

2.2 m., Hillsboro — O 8 — W. Turn R. *3.3 m.*, in **Cornelius,** turn L onto N 10th Ave. *1.8 m.*, on R, old house in faded glory. It is a shame that so many fine old

Tualatin Plains Presbyterian Church   *Phoebe L. Friedman*

houses in Oregon have been turned into rural slum dwellings or have been torn down. *0.3 m.,* on R, white house back of road built 1887.

0.5 m., on R, **St. Peter's Evangelical Lutheran Church,** "mother church" of Lutheran congregations in area and oldest Lutheran Missouri Synod Church in PNW. First church erected 1882 in **Blooming** (PO 1895–1904 in settler's home).

Of Blooming, Lester C. Mooberry wrote in his book, *The Gray Nineties:* "My father always spoke of it as the Lutheran settlement or the Blooming settlement, but later he called it Blooming just as the rest of us did. He seemed to think that calling it Blooming gave it the status of a town but of course it wasn't. It was a settlement with farms and small places, the buildings lining up along both sides of the road that led from Cornelius to Iowa Hill.

"The very center of the community life was the Lutheran Church to which a majority of the people belonged. The church bell rang each Saturday evening at sundown and the sound carried out over the parish.

"A tragedy during the early nineties occurred with the diphtheria epidemic and took the lives of several children in the Blooming settlement. The bell on the German Lutheran Church used to ring and then toll at each death among their membership. The ringing could be heard for many miles, and the people listening remained statue-like as they counted the tolling strokes. They could tell by the number whether it was a child, a middle aged person, or an aged member of the church."

Present church bldg, constructed 1923. Windows, from Italy, insured for $40,000.

Return to O 8. Turn L. *1.4 m.,* at W end of Masonic and Eastern Home, turn R onto Oak St. *1.2 m.,* on L, **Porter Redwood Grove.** The two rows of giant redwoods comprise handsomest private lane in Oregon. They were planted by John Porter, who came here with his parents in 1847. Porter purchased the land in 1854. Around 1870, said Edwin Porter, John's grandson, John planted the seedling trees he raised in his nursery, from sequoia cones he had brought back from Calif.

0.8 m., turn R onto Verboort Rd. *0.1 m.,* turn L. *0.1 m.,* **Visitation Catholic Church,** center of **Verboort.** The 1915 *Oregon Almanac* called Verboort a "Holland Dutch settlement" and described it as "one of the best farmed sections of Oregon." Visitation Catholic Church, flanked by 150 ft. sequoias, was founded 1875; present church bldg. 1959. Verboort comes alive first Sat. each Nov., when annual Sausage Festival is staged, with profits going for upkeep of church school. Food is good and plentiful, which is why lines are long.

0.3 m., on L, driveway to **Black House,** built 1864 and virtually unchanged outside and little changed inside. *0.4 m.,* **Visitation Cemetery.** Stately lane of hedges leads to well-maintained burial ground. Oldest grave is that of Rev. A. W. Verboort (1876). Just beyond cemetery lane is 2-1/2- story white house, one of early jewels of Verboort area.

Return to Verboort Rd. Turn L. *2.7 m.,* on L, **Cornelius Methodist Cemetery.** Markers back to 1860s.

0.7 m., O 8 — E, in **Cornelius,** named for 1845–arriving family. PO 1871. In 1915, when town had only 520 pop. it had seven churches, two lodges, creamery, grain elevator, warehouses, feed mill, sawmill, cider and vinegar works and fruit cannery. It was a staunchly independent town, a key marketplace of Tualatin Valley. Today it is little more than suburb of Hillsboro and Portland.

Monument to Rev. A.W. Verboort, Visitation Cemetery, Verboort

Turn L onto O 8. *2.7 m.,* in **Hillsboro, Pioneer Cemetery.** Large burial ground adjoining W-bound O 8. Oldest grave marker is that of Andrew Jackson Masters, 1856.

6.2 m., turn R onto SW 209th. *0.5 m.,* turn L onto Kinnaman Rd. *0.2 m.,* on R, 20650 SW Kinnaman, **Masters House.** Built 1853 by Andrew Jackson Masters, at cost of $6,000, then princely sum. Masters did not long enjoy comfort and luxury, being shot to death by neighbor in 1856 over land ownership. Dwelling once PO. Years ago local rumor had U.S. Grant having spent night here. *0.1 m.,* on R, **Oakerman Farmhouse,** built 1887. *0.2 m.,* turn L onto 198th Ave. *0.4 m.,* turn R onto O 8. *0.7 m.,* **Aloha.** A rather recent (1912) Portland magnet village, it was suburban then and is no more than moderate shopping center now. For travelers, Aloha is quick hello and goodbye. *2.8 m.*, turn R for Beaverton. Straight, *8 m.*, Portland.

West B

From 6th St. ramp. US 26, Portland:

3.7 m. — along Canyon Rd. — turn onto O 8. This road follows closely a route from the Portland riverfront to the Tualatin Plains opened 1849 as Portland's first "farm-to-market" artery. Opening of the road ensured Portland's eminence in the lower Willamette Valley for without the rich agricultural district of Tualatin Plains it is very doubtful if Portland would have grown as rapidly as it did. So important was this road that in 1851 it was planked by the Portland and Valley Plank Road Co. and 5 years later improved by a state-owned enterprise.

1.6 m., West Slope. *2 m.*, SW Watson Ave., Beaverton. Turn L. *0.1 m.*, SW Farmington Rd. Turn R. *2 m.*, at 16575 SW Farmington, on R, house with water tower. On this suburban road it is an eye-stopper. *1.1 m.*, Aloha Jct. (*1 m.*, Aloha.) *1 m.*, turn L onto Miller Hill Rd. *0.8 m.*, turn L onto Gassner Rd. *0.1 m.*, on R, **Cooper Mtn. Cemetery.** From L side of road, picture postcard views of Tualatin Valley.

Return to SW Farmington. Turn L onto Farmington. *0.5 m.*, Hazeldale. Store. *1.7 m.*, on L, pioneer house in still rustic setting. *0.8 m.*, Tide Flat Rd. (*4 m.*, Kinton, via back road that has moments of succor.) *0.8 m.*, **Farmington.** Store. (PO 1884–1904.) *2 m.*, O 219.

Turn L onto O219. *0.1 m.*, Turn R onto Bald Peak Rd. *0.5 m.*, forks. Take R. *3.5 m.*, Laurelwood Rd.

Turn R onto Laurelwood Rd. *1.6 m.*, **Laurelwood.** When Adventist Academy here closed in 1985, a unique place in Oregon disappeared, even though elegant campus remained. *1.5 m.*, Springhill Rd. On R, collapsing early schoolhouse. Turn R onto Springhill Rd. *0.6 m.*, on R. turnoff to Hill Cemetery. (*0.1 m.*, **Hill Cemetery.** Markers back to 1850s.)

Return to Bald Peak Rd. Turn R. *2 m.*, **Bald Peak SP.** PA. So close a highland retreat is this to the welters of the suburbs below. Under the great parasols of the Douglas firs the grass is mossy soft. Looking E, Mt. Adams, Mt. St. Helens and Mt. Hood seem to drift as clouds above the outreaches of the Tualatin Valley. Facing W, a fruited bowl of shimmering green is tilted toward the notched rims of the Coast Range. Within the bowl a patchwork of shiny meadows jumps the eye from lea to lea.

Return to O 219. Turn L, or N. *1.7 m.*, on R, Burkhalter Rd. Turn R. *0.7 m.*, forks. Take R. *0.2 m.*, on R., Oak Knoll Winery. *0.5 m.*, on L, **Lewis Cemetery** (1847).

Return to O 219. Turn R. *3.8 m.*, **Hillsboro,** at O 8.

Town named for David Hill, 1842 overlander and member of 3-man provisional gvmt. executive committee, whose term of office extended from 7/5/1843 to 5/25/1844. Town went thru names of Columbia, Columbus and Hillsborough before becoming Hillsboro. Seat of Washington County, which has become center of Oregon's hi-tech industry, with Hillsboro near heart of it. **Enschede House,** 801 S 7th, built 1881, one of few reminders of 19th century.

From 1st & Main, go *0.8 m* to 10th & NW Main. Angle onto Cornell. *2.7 m.,* turn L onto Shute Rd. *1.2 m.,* turn L onto Evergreen Ave. *0.5 m.,* turn R onto 263rd. *0.3 m.,* on R, across from Country Gardens, was Methodist Meeting House site, pioneer meeting place in Washington County. According to local legend, several of Joe Meek's children were buried here. Grove in which early settlers gathered for conference and in which early deceased were buried was destroyed in 1985, obliterating all vestiges of Methodist site. **House of Country Gardens,** built 1890, has, as owner put it, "a lot of character."

At jct., O 219, turn W onto O 8. *0.9 m.,* on R, **Pioneer Cemetery** (1856). *2.3 m.,* **Cornelius.** Like many other fruit crop centers in W Oregon, Cornelius is home to growing number of Hispanics and town's community hall is used chiefly as cultural center.

1.6 m., Oak St., **Forest Grove.** Turn R. *1.2 m.,* on L, **Porter Grove,** tall and handsome lane of sequoias. *0.8 m.,* Verboort, famed for annual autumn sausage festival.

Return to O 8 at Oak St. Turn R. *0.9 m.,* campus of **Pacific U,** in Forest Grove. *0.2 m.,* turn R onto College Way. *0.1 m.,* shortest way (into campus) to Old College Hall (1850), probably oldest bldg. in W used continuously for educational purposes. The clapboard structure was raised in 2 weeks in bldg. bee that brought settlers from miles around. Camping on the meadow, the men built while the women took care of the cooking and other domestic chores and the children played. For some years hall was graced by presence of the remarkable Tabitha Brown, who was with first caravan on the cruel Applegate Trail (1846) when she was already elderly and in poor health. (See "The Courage of Grandma Brown" in author's *A Touch of Oregon.*)

Continue N on College Way. *0.1 m.,* University Ave. Turn R. *0.1 m.,* turn L onto Sunset Dr. *0.6 m.,* on R, **Brown-Davidson House,** built 1863 by Alvin Clark Brown, grandson of Tabitha Brown. Apple tree in front of house planted 1848 or 1854 by Orus Brown, Tabitha's son. (Four generations of Brown family lived here.)

In Forest Grove, historic century-plus houses are at 2314 19th Ave., 1604 Birch St., 2126 17th St. — all attractive.

Community called itself Forest Grove in 1851 but from 1850 to 1858 PO was known as Tualatin. In 1915 Forest Grove had pop. only slightly less than Hillsboro; now Hillsboro is more than twice as large. The growing gap reflects look and attitude. Hillsboro looks like a city on or in the make; Forest Grove still has a sort of rustic freshness.

(For more on Forest Grove, see O 47 S, preceding.)

Old College Hall, Pacific University   *Courtesy Pacific University*

From College Way, on O 8:

1.2 m., turn R onto Thatcher-Kansas City Rd. *0.2 m.,* turn L onto Watercrest Rd. *0.6 m.,* **Mountain View Memorial Gardens.** Commanding view of Coast Range and Tualatin Valley. The far-stretching, heart-rising scenery is matched by the glorious symphonies of the wind. Buried here are the founders of Dilley and Buxton towns; the Oregon family of Tabitha Brown; Belle W. Cooke, who crossed plains in 1851 at age 18, was first woman clerk in Oregon legislature, gained regional prominence as poet, was friend and den mother to literary greats of the state; and Rev. Harvey Clark, pioneer independent Congregationalist missionary, early educator, co-founder with Tabitha Brown of first orphanage in the territory, and chaplain of first provisional legislature. Clark gave 200 acres of his land claim toward founding of Tualatin Academy, from which arose Pacific U, and on the rest of his land there grew up the village of Forest Grove. Gravestones back to 1850.

Return to Thatcher-Kansas City Rd. Turn L. *1.2 m.,* on R, **Purdin Cemetery,** family plot, with headstones back to 1858. *1.2 m.,* Hillside Rd. and site of **Thatcher.** First settled about 1847, Thatcher had PO from 1895 to 1902. Not a stick or stone remains to indicate presence of crossroads settlement. Turn L onto Hillside Rd. This pike tiptoes so unobtrusively thru the peaceful undulations that you feel like lowering your voice so as not to disturb the serenity. *3.4 m.,* Clapshaw Hill Rd. On L is Hillside Cemetery (1887). This is Hillside and from the view you can tell why the place was named. There never was a PO here, nor a store; no livery or blacksmith shop — just a viable rural community. Turn R. At R, Hillside Bible Church, org. as Congregational 1884, edifice constructed 1900. *0.1 m.,* **Hillside School.** Built 1877 as one-room, 20 x 20 ft. schoolhouse. Inside is best example of what country schoolhouse was in W Oregon during pre-automobile days. It was turned into a museum by Lawrence Bamford, a farmer who lived all his more than 80 years within 1 m. of school. While school was in operation he was student, teacher, director and clerk. After purchasing the school he restored it into a museum-thru-the-generations, so that each generation is represented, starting with first desks, small iron wood-burning stove, water bucket, slates, lunch pails and maps. Before church was built, school served as area's house of religion and also as its cultural center. After church was built, students played in horse shed at church. On school walls hang photos of teachers, students and classes thru the years. (For story on school and church, see "A Heap of Schoolboy Memories at Hillside" in author's *This Side of Oregon*.)

   0.2 m., forks. (L, follow signs *1.6 m.* to Tualatin Vineyards Winery.) R, *2 m.,* **Kansas City.**

   There was never a town here; not even a PO. Ancient school, long boarded up, is monument to weariness. Community hall, a middle-class solid citizen of its

Hillside School

day, now looks like it's on relief. You may not know you are in Kansas City; vandals rip off the signs almost as fast as they are put up.

Turn L. *0.2 m.*, turn R onto Greenville Roy Rd. *1.5 m.*, on R, pioneer schoolhouse now used as shed and storage area. Bldg. is part of old Greenville. *0.3 m.*, turn L. **Greenville PO** (1871–1907) here on NW corner.

1.1 m., turn R. Portland, *25 m.*

South Suburban
From Union (which later becomes McLoughlin) and Burnside:
4.4 m. Tacoma St. Turn onto Tacoma. *1 m.*, 6th St. Turn R. *1 block*, Spokane St. Turn L. *1 block*, Grand. Turn R. On corner is **Oaks Pioneer Museum,** formerly St. Johns Episcopal Church of Milwaukie. Plaque reads: "Oldest Oregon church in continuous use. Dedicated Dec. 10, 1851." Moved to present site by river barge June 11, 1961. So many weddings have been held here that a bridal dressing room was added. Back of church bldg. are benches to observe Willamette River. Just N of museum is replica of first white residents' dwelling in present W side of Portland — log cabin put up by William Johnson. Original site was near SW Macadam and Ross Island Bridge. Johnson was a British seaman who jumped ship in Boston to join US Navy. Job with North West Co. brought him to Oregon in 1817; in 1835 he returned, joining other former fur trappers on French Prairie. In 1842 he moved to the original cabin with his Indian wife, children and 2 Indian slaves. Here he became a pig farmer and bootlegger, concocting the most heinous brew Oregon lips ever tasted. The stuff was revolting but his customers so eager that the sterner-spirited settlers became worried and threatened to do him in if he didn't close down his still. He did — and quit the place.

Return to 6th and Tacoma. Turn R. Cross Sellwood Bridge. "Fishhook" onto O 43. *1.7 m.*, SW Military Rd.

Turn E onto SW Military Rd. *50 yds.*, forks. Turn R onto SW Military Lane. This street, a page out of an aristocratic countryside village, is architecturally and botanically probably the most elegant enclave in Oregon. *0.2 m.*, **Bishop's Close,** built as residence of affluent Portland entrepreneur, now Episcopalian center. To L are paths leading thru gorgeous floral displays.

Return to O 43. Turn L. *1.3 m.*, turnoff to **Tryon Creek SP**. *1.5 m.*, SP, distinguished for its many nature trails. Also, horse trails, bike trails, FHP.

Return to O 43. Turn R. *0.4 m.*, city center, **Lake Oswego.**

From 1853 until 1959 the town was Oswego, then its residents and those of Lake Grove, at W end of Oswego Lake, merged into city of Lake Oswego. Lake was known to local Indians as Waluga, meaning White Swan. The Yankees, who arrived in the 1840s, named it Sucker Lake. In 1913 it became Lake Oswego.

Although the lake is completely within the city it is not now, as it was several decades ago, visible from the hwy. Only from roads high above it are there adequate glimpses of the water and of the privately-owned residences which encircle the basin. It would therefore seem that only the families and guests of the Lake Oswego Shorefront Committee, which owns the 395-acre lakebed, would have access to recreational use of the water. But a 1975 study — *Pleasure Boating in Oregon* by R. E. Frenkel of OSU — showed that Lake Oswego was the 7th busiest body of water in Oregon and probably the most used by water-skiers.

Oswego was a sparsely occupied settlement until ground was broken in 1865 for construction of the first iron furnace W of the Upper Missouri. Confident that the town would become the "Pittsburgh of the West," some hopefuls built summer cottages on the lakeshore. Permanent homes followed. They remained after the smelter closed down for the last time in 1885, and Oswego continued to grow, though slowly; by 1915 its pop. was 1,000. After WW II the boom started and has not let up.

0.6 m., Ladd St. Turn E. 1 block, Durham St. Of the first two pigs cast by the smelter of the Oregon Iron Co., one is in the Oregon Historical Society, Portland; the other was placed on NW corner of Ladd & Durham. Turn L onto Durham. 2 blocks, Church St. On R is **IOOF Hall** (1909), oldest in town. Return to Ladd and turn L. Follow 0.2 m., keeping R, to smelter in **Rogers Park.** In addition to smelter, which looks like wing, or turret tower, of medieval castle, there are immaculately landscaped gardens, paths to the Willamette; BL; and vistas of dreamy Willamette scene. Across road is Oswego Creek, which empties into river. Upstream on creek is old power plant, and when there is a fisher on the rocks the

Lake Oswego Iron Smelter   *Phoebe L. Friedman*

picture is pure calendar art. (For story of the smelter, see "The Pittsburgh Dream of Lake Oswego" in author's *Tracking Down Oregon*.)

Return to O 43. Turn L. *0.1 m.,* Stafford Jct. Turn W onto McVey Ave., which later becomes Stafford Rd. *1.2 m.,* on R, **Oswego Catholic Cemetery,** est. 1850s, though gravestones do not go that far back. Next to it is **Oswego Pioneer Cemetery.** Stones date back to 1856. *7 m.,* at corner of Wilsonville and Boeckman Rds., **Meridian United Church of Christ,** affectionately known as Frog Pond Church, built 1878. *1.6 m.,* **Wilsonville Memorial Park,** large city park. *0.3 m.,* Wilsonville, which seems spread all over the map. Its incorporation in 1968 symbolized end of the 90-year-old settlement as farm outpost of Portland and its entrance into the jostling family of suburbs.

Return to O 43. Turn R. *0.4 m.,* turnoff E to secular **Marylhurst College of Lifelong Learning,** formerly Catholic institution of higher learning for women. School was outstanding but declining enrollment and higher operating costs forced closure. Shoens Library is architectural gem.

1.3 m., turnoff E to **Mary S. Young SP.** (*0.6 m.,* parking area of SP. PA, bike trail, hiking trails, fishing, FHP.)

1 m., turn W onto West A St. *0.7 m.,* on R, just beyond West Linn HS, entry to **Camassia Natural Area.** Walk *70 yds.* up asphalt, take footpath at wire fence of athletic field. The Nature Conservancy, which owns area, describes it as "Missoula flood relic, scalped of its topsoil, with extraordinary floral and geologic features. Contains vernal and permanent ponds, west side occurrence of quaking aspen and population of pale larkspur. Abundance of rare plant species. Camas are in bloom from early April to mid-May."

Continue on West A to O 212. Across jct. is West Linn Police Station. Take road to E side of it *0.2 m.* to parking lot. Descend stairs that led to walkway of **Willamette Falls Locks.**

A brochure prepared by the US Army Corps of Engineers, which operates the locks, states: "The Willamette River at Oregon City spills about 40 feet over a rocky basaltic horseshoe-shaped reef. The locks were built by the Willamette Falls Canal and Lock Company in the early 1870s to move river traffic around the falls. The state of Oregon raised $200,000 in gold bonds to help pay for the project.

"The locks were opened on New Year's Day 1873. They were operated by a number of owners before the federal government bought them in 1915 from the Portland Railway, Light and Power Company for $375,000.

"The project includes four locks, a canal basin and an extra guard lock used to prevent flooding when river levels are high. The system acts as a fluid staircase between the upper and lower reaches of the Willamette River. Before the locks were built, boats were portaged or towed between the upper and lower river.

"Each lock is 40 feet wide and 210 feet long. Approach guides extend 150 feet downstream from the lower gate and more than 300 feet upstream from the upper gate to direct vessels into the locks.

Willamette Falls Locks

"The locks still function much as they did when they were built, but modern technology has made the job easier. Until the 1940s, the gates were operated manually. Now, the gates are operated by hydraulic pumps controlled by switches in two control stations with the aid of closed-circuit television and radio communication.

"When a gate opens, gravity flow drains 850,000 gallons of water in several minutes into a lock chamber, raising or lowering the water levels necessary for vessels to pass through the locks. Average time for passage is about 45 minutes going upstream and 30 minutes down."

Annual tonnage thru the locks exceeds 1 million, two-thirds of it paper products, logs, and materials used in paper manufacture, and much of that from the paper mill at the locks.

Return to O 212. Turn L. *2.3 m.,* 10th. Turn R. *0.2 m.,* Blankenship Rd. Turn L. *0.4 m.,* forks. Take L. *0.2 m.,* turn R onto Johnson Rd. *0.8 m.,* Tendril Ln. *0.2 m.,* on R, on far side of driveway, blurred signmarker of **Willamette Meteorite.**

It was here, in the autumn of 1902, that Ellis Hughes, a former Welsh miner and then a freelance laborer living with his wife on a small farm, chanced upon

Willamette Locks   *Courtesy Corps of Engineers*

Willamette Meteorite Marker

Replica of Willamette Meteorite

the "big rock" as he was returning from the Willamette School where he had been cutting wood.

Hughes is credited in geological publications with being the "discoverer" of the 15.5 ton meteorite but the Indians had known of it for long. Two Indians then alive told of the Clackamas — by then the tribe was extinct — worshipping the. meteorite as their *tomonowos*, visitor from the moon. One of the Indians remembered that when he was a boy he had been told by Chief Sochimo of the Clackamas that his people washed their faces in the water collected in the crevices of the meteorite and that his young men dipped their arrows into the water before going off to battle with other tribes. The other Indian declared that the stone was the property of the medicine men of the Clackamas tribe.

When a friend told Hughes that the "big rock" was a meteor, he perked up and listened to his wife, who "was afraid somebody would go up and get it the next day." With herculean effort and some ingenuity, Hughes moved the meteorite to his yard, the gruelling chore requiring a full three months. By now Hughes could envision himself a man of affluence. He built a shed over his meteorite and charged 25 cents admission. Hundreds of people came and Hughes was bound for prosperity when Oregon Iron and Steel Co. stepped into the picture. It sued Hughes for possession of the meteorite, claiming that it was found on OI&S land, and that since the meteorite was part of the land, it had been stolen. The jury decided in favor of the company and from then on Ellis Hughes was a bitter man, complaining to one and all of the raw deal he had received in the Oregon courts until his death on 12/3/42.

News stories about the meteorite brought scientists from many parts of the US here. One, Henry A. Ward, gave it the name of Willamette Meteorite, since it was close (2 m.) to the village of Willamette.

Oregon Iron and Steel Co. moved the meteorite to Portland, where it was exhibited at the Lewis and Clark Exposition of 1905. There the "celestial wonder," which Oregonians had hoped to keep in the state, was purchased for $26,000 by Mrs. William E. Dodge II of New York, who presented it to its still owner, American Museum of Natural History. In 1936 meteorite was moved to present location, then newly-completed Hayden Planetarium.

In his 1962 booklet on the Willamette Meteorite, Prof. Erwin F. Lange of then Portland State College, wrote: "To this day the Willamette Meteorite remains the largest and most majestic iron meteorite to be discovered in this country. At the time of its finding, the Willamette was the third largest to be discovered on earth. Today, due to the discovery of other large meteorites, it is the world's sixth largest meteoritic discovery."

In 1938 a small piece, weighing 181.1 grams, was cut from the meteorite and sent to the U of Oregon.

Return to O 212. Turn R. *0.2 m.*, 12th St. Start of business section of formerly independent town of **Willamette.** It runs 2 blocks, to 14th. On SW corner of 14th stands old, attractive **Willamette United Methodist Church.** In front of church is replica (with plaque) of Willamette Meteorite.

Backtrack to 12th St. Turn R. *0.2 m.,* Petes Mtn. Rd. Straight. *0.2 m.,* **Willamette Park,** a roll of greenery. Here Tualatin River enters Willamette.

Return to Petes Mtn. Rd. Turn L. From crest of pike the vistas E are clear and far-reaching. *3.7 m.,* turn L onto Riverwood Rd. *1.2 m.,* **Heeb Park,** above Willamette River. Fine pastoral views of ferry boat crossing river about *0.2 m.* upstream.

Return to Petes Mtn. Rd. Turn L. *0.8 m.,* SW Mountain Rd. Turn L. *0.8 m.,* **Canby ferry landing.** Cross river to E bank.

0.5 m., entrance to **Molalla River SP,** adjoining Willamette River. PA, boating, FHP, trail to confluence of Molalla River.

Return to Canby Rd. Turn R. *1.9 m.,* turn R onto Knightsbridge Rd. *0.1 m.,* on L, **Baker Prairie Cemetery** (1863), one of few burial grounds in PNW that is in heart of residential district.

Return to Holly St. (Canby Rd.) Turn R. *0.4 m.,* **Canby** city center. *0.1 m.,* O 99E. Turn R. *1.6 m.,* across hwy (on E), **Barlow House,** built mid-19th century. The two rows of black walnut trees are the growth of seeds brought 'round the Horn and planted circa 1860 by William Barlow, son of Samuel K. Barlow of Barlow Toll Road fame.

0.1 m., turn R, toward **Barlow,** named for Wm. Barlow. A nothing place now but in 1915 it had PS, two churches, water works, store. *0.3 m.,* on L, **Barlow Pioneer Cemetery** (1856), containing remains of S. K. Barlow and his wife, Susannah Lee.

Return to O 99E. *1.9 m.,* **Aurora.** Turn R at road marked Freeway-Donald. *0.2 m.,* turn R toward Donald. *0.2 m.,* on R., Airport Rd. Turn R. *0.1 m.,* on L, **Keil House** built by William Keil, founder of Aurora Colony. The 3-story home with 2-deck porch across E front was most affluent home of colony.

Return to Donald-Freeway Rd. Turn R. *0.6 m.,* turn L onto Oak Lane. *0.4 m.,* forks. Turn R. *0.1 m.,* **Aurora Community Cemetery** (1862). That the colony was composed in large part of persons of German ancestry is obvious from the names and the German script on the tombstones.

Return to Donald Rd. Turn L. *3.6 m.,* turn L onto Butteville Rd. *0.5 m.,* Donald Rd. *0.2 m.,* city center — if there is such a thing here — **Donald.** "If there was a horse here Donald would be a 1-horse town," a farmer wryly observed. "You can shoot a cannon ball right down the middle of main street and you wouldn't hit a thing or wake a soul."

Return to O 99E by proceeding straight from Donald to Aurora. Turn R. *3 m.,* turn L onto Stauffer Rd. *0.3 m.,* turn L at end of hopyard on L. *0.1 m.,* on R, **Stauffer-Will House,** last original farmhouse of Aurora Colony in place.

Return to O 99E. Turn R. Return to Aurora. Take R on 2nd St. *0.1 m.,* on R, **Ox Barn Museum,** the great relic of Old Aurora Colony. To R of museum is

Stauffer Will Historic Farm

Steinbach Log Cabin, brought in from hinterlands. Beyond museum is **Kraus House,** a more affluent pioneer dwelling, also moved here.

Return to O 99E. Turn R. *3.8 m.,* **Canby,** at Ivy St. Turn R onto Ivy. *0.2 m.,* Township Rd. Turn L. *0.2 m.,* on R, **Canby Evangelical Church,** built 1884, and quite picturesque. *0.9 m.,* on L, **Zion Cemetery.** At R rear is headstone of William Water (Bill) Brown, legendary E Oregon stockman.

Return to O 99E, at Ivy. Turn R. *0.5 m.,* in Clackamas Fair Grounds, **Canby Depot Museum.** RR depot moved here from location about 1 m. S, where it had stood for about a century.

2.4 m., on R, turnoff to New Era. *0.3 m.,* on R, **New Era Spiritualist Camp,** founded 1886. Across road is Anthony Farm (1884), with old-fashioned water tower. Private.

Return to O 99E. *1.1 m.,* on L, paved lot. Park here and look E. Directly ahead and above is rock that looks like head of human. It is generally called **Coalca Rock.**

4.2 m., on L, **Willamette Falls Viewpoint.** Best view of Willamette Falls.

0.4 m., in **Oregon City,** turn R onto Railroad Ave. *0.1 m.,* on R, Municipal Elevator. Ride free from one level to another in Oregon City. At top level, short walk to **McLoughlin House,** Oregon City residence of Dr. John McLoughlin, national historic site. McLoughlin, Chief Factor at Ft. Vancouver, played instrumental role in white settlement of Oregon. Due N of house is **Barclay House,** built 1846 by Dr. Forbes Barclay.

From Municipal Elevator, continue *0.1 m* to 9th St. Turn L. *0.1 m.,* O 99 E. Turn R.

6.4 m., Washington St., in **Milwaukie.** Turn R. *0.4 m.,* at 2746 Washington,

Hager Pond, below 1875-frame house. An urban Walden Pond, bucolic nuance restful to the soul.

Continue on Washington to first corner. Turn L 2 blocks to Harrison. Turn L to 21st. On R, **Milwaukie City Library.** Chief attraction associated with lovely, well-stocked library is duck pond in rear.

0.1 m., O 99E, at Harrison. Turn R. *4.8 m.,* Burnside St., Portland.

(For deeper views and greater detail on places in this tour, see *The Great Heartland, O 99E.*)

Columbia Gorge
(Columbia River Scenic Highway)

Prior to construction of the river level freeway, I-84, the road thru the Gorge, US 30, was on the whole narrow and winding, scary for newcomers and a caution to truckers. Today, as the Columbia River Scenic Highway, much of that road is free of trucks and is basically a tourist excursion, with the most marked attractions being waterfalls. Spongy woods and lushly ferned hills, latticing the sunlight and shading the road, contrast with bulging cliffs and rocky brows to create pastel moods that unreel as a kaleidoscope of fluid imagery. (For an impressionistic glimpse of a young man's meeting with this road on his first journey West, see "In My Beginning" in author's *Tales Out of Oregon.*)

From Alder and SW 3rd, downtown Portland:

14.8 m., Wood Village-Gresham exit. *0.5 m.,* take turnoff to Columbia River Scenic Hwy.

Canby Depot Museum

Coalca Rock

1.3 m., **Troutdale.** John Harlow, a Maine man, stocked trout in a pond on a dale near his home about 1880 — hence the name. At a time when many emigrants were still rafting their wagons down the Columbia, some comers drove their cattle along narrow trails from The Dalles to the nearby Sandy River, and a few settled here. The RR came thru when river commerce was at its peak and the combination made Troutdale a hurdy-gurdy frontier boom town. Anyone too impatient to walk to a corner to find a tavern could locate one in the middle of the block.

Troutdale is not without a few other historic touches. In 1894 a battalion of hungry men, part of Coxey's Army of the desperately unemployed, commandeered a train here to get to Washington, D.C.

In 1913, only year after Oregon women won right to vote, town elected first woman mayor in Oregon. She was Clara Larrson, quarter-Indian daughter of Latourell family of Latourell. Her maternal grandfather had been a British seaman, her maternal grandmother an Indian princess. A year later voters cast their ballots for Prohibition and one of the town saloons closed belonged to Mrs. Larrson's husband. In 1924 Troutdale again elected a woman as mayor. She was deputy sheriff Laura Harlow, daughter-in-law of John Harlow. (See "The Romance Back of Latourell" in author's *Tracking Down Oregon*.)

Old Union Pacific RR station is now town police station and small historical museum containing relics of halcyon RR days.

Downtown Troutdale retains touches of rustic simplicity but few blocks back of it are massive pits of urban development.

0.3 m., on R, or S, **Harlow House,** built 1900, now historical museum. *0.2 m.,* **Troutdale city park,** scenic green on Sandy River. *0.1 m.,* Lewis and Clark SP Jct.

Hager Pond   *Phoebe L. Friedman*

Turn L. *0.3 m.,* **SP on Sandy River.** PA, fishing, boating, FHP. Historical Marker reads: "The two great American explorers, Meriwether Lewis and William Clark, enroute to the Pacific Ocean on Nov. 3, 1805, halted at the mouth of this river which they reported 'throws out emence quantitys of sand and is verry shallow.' Clark attempted to wade across but 'found the bottom quicksand.' They traveled one and a half miles up the riverbank, reaching this general vicinity before returning to the Columbia to make camp on Government Island.

"Homeward bound in the spring of 1806, the expedition camped for six days on 'a handsome prairie' opposite the Sandy 'to make some selestial observations, to examine the Quicksand River and kill some meat.' During this time three men canoed about six miles up the Sandy. While waiting the return of the hunting party, the captains learned from the Indians that they had passed a major tributary of the Columbia for which they had been searching. With seven men and an Indian guide, Clark backtracked to explore the Lower Willamette River. Rejoined by its detachments, the expedition broke camp on April 6 and moved on."

(By 1850 the name of Quicksand River had been shortened to Sandy River)

Bordering the marker are clusters of the state flower, Oregon grape. Park also has a nature trail containing plants named and described by Lewis and Clark while in Oregon.

Thirteen years prior to the arrival of Lewis and Clark, the Sandy River had first been seen by whites. Five months and 19 days after Capt. Robert Gray entered the Columbia River, giving the US its first claim to the vast Oregon Country, Lt. William R. Broughton stood on the banks of the Sandy River.

Gray had had stronger priorities than exploring the Columbia and had sailed on. But word of Gray's finding of the "Great River of the West" spread quickly to other mariners in the north. When Capt. George Vancouver of the British Navy heard of Gray's feat he turned his two vessels, *Discovery* and *Chatham,* south from Juan de Fuca Strait. Off the bar of the Columbia Vancouver opted for the smaller vessel, the *Chatham,* to penetrate the river and do the exploring. Broughton, in command, went up the Columbia about 120 miles and spent 3 weeks in a survey, during which he named a great white mountain to the S after British Admiral Lord Samuel Hood.

On Oct. 30, 1792, Broughton named a stream flowing from glaciers on the S slope of Mt. Hood Barings River, for a prominent British family. That same day he planted the British flag on a nearby island — underwater part of the year — and claimed the Oregon Country for Great Britain. On June 29, 1974, Admiral Sir Charles Madden in Portland to open the Captain Cook Exhibit at the Oregon Historical Society, visited the island named for the *Chatham,* and said of Broughton, "He hoisted the Union flag and grabbed it for King George III. He drank the king's health, romantically by moonlight, in this setting."

(Shading the SP is Broughton's Bluff, a precipice that, wrote Vancouver in his journal, Broughton's crew found to be "high stupendous mountains rising almost perpendicularly from the water's edge.")

Sandy River — Broughton's Barings River — was the landing point for some of the covered wagons on the Oregon Trail floated down the Columbia from points near The Dalles.

Yet Sandy River here is better known for its smelt run than for its history. Smelt season, traditionally between late Feb. and early April, brings out hordes of the eager, who come with nets, buckets, garbage sacks and anything else to dip, scoop and pick, either wading deep into the stream or snatching at the sea- dwelling migrants from the bank. There is, say fish biologists, no known way to predict run size (often entering the Columbia River in the millions), time or arrival, or where the smelt will spawn; some years — 12 in a row, at one stretch — the smelt do not show up at all in the Sandy.

Return to Lewis and Clark SP Jct. Straight — continue E.

2.4 m., Stark St.-Gresham Jct., bridge across Sandy River.

> * First part of road skirts Sandy River Canyon.

2.5 m., **Mt. Hood CC;** *2.5 m.,* Gresham. (From jct., 9 *m.,* Oxbow CP.)

0.4 m., Dabney SP. PA, fishing, FHP. No dogs — except Seeing Eye — or alcoholic beverages. To equate dogs with booze!

1.3 m., **Springdale.** Store, tavern, church, station, school — all the requisites for a rural-suburban entity.

2.4 m., **Corbett.** The two public schools — high and elementary — dominate the town. Its history is basically confined to its being named for 1851 sailing ship arrival Henry Winslow Corbett, who didn't take much time to amass a fortune in Portland. A founding member of the Republican Party in Oregon, the Mass.-born Corbett was staunchly opposed to slavery and secession. He missed the 1860 Chicago convention which nominated Abraham Lincoln only because he arrived late. From 1867 to 1873 he served in the US Senate and would later have served again if not for a dispute between the national GOP and its Oregon membership. The 1896 convention of the Republican Party advocated the gold standard, which riled the Oregon Republicans, who espoused bimetallism. To get even, the Oregon Republicans in the lower house boycotted the session when the legislature met in Jan., 1897 to elect a US Senator. Perturbed, the governor (William Paine Lord) appointed Corbett. But the US Senate refused to seat Corbett, stating that the governor's appointing power existed only where the legislature had not had an opportunity to make a decision. Oregon was then represented by only one senator until Oct., 1898.

A straight line N from Corbett marks the farthest point on the Columbia that Broughton traveled.

0.1 m., Evans Rd.

> * Turn R. 1 m., turnoff to **Mountain View Cemetery** (*0.2 m.*). The long look from this hilltop rolls over farmlands to the suburbs of Gresham and the snows of Mt. Hood. Markers, including that of Jas. Candy, who served in Co. F, 36 Iowa Inft. from 8/14/62 to 8/24/65, go back to 1879.

1.4 m., **Menucha** ("Waters of refreshment" in Hebrew), former estate of Julius

Meier, mercantile prince and governor of Oregon. Now occupied by Presbyterian-owned Menucha Conference Center. River views from estate are breathtaking.

0.3 m., turnoff for Portland Women's Forum SP.

   * *0.1 m.,* **Chanticleer Point.** Watercolor view of Columbia Gorge; clearly visible on clear day are Crown Point, Rooster Rock and Beacon Rock. On a misty day you see less and feel more. Plaque here honors Gertrude Jensen, gentle, lion-hearted guardian of Gorge beauty.

   Inspiring view here calls to mind a verse from a rendition of "Beulah Land" sung by the optimistic pioneers: "Oh Beulah Land, dear Beulah Land,/ As on this mighty ledge I stand./ I look beyond the river's strand/ And thank you, God, for this dear land./ I view the river and shining shore —/ My Oregon for ever more."

0.4 m., turnoff for Larch Mtn.

   * *14.3 m.* — up wind-humming forest corridor — 4,050-ft. elev. parking area of **Larch Mtn.** Corridor traverses 8 m. of second growth Douglas fir and Western hemlock. Near top of mtn., noble fir, silver fir and other high-altitude species appear. Rolling eastward as a sea in the skies, the Cascades break into irregular waves, with Mt. Hood and Mt. Adams towering as tall-masted white ships above the uneven billows. 500 yd. trail, including 125 stairs, to Sherrard Point, cliff aerie with unobstructed views of Mt. St. Helens, Mt. Rainier, Mt. Adams, Mt. Hood, Mt. Jefferson, Columbia River and N strip of Willamette Valley. Trail from PA leads 6.8 m. to Multnomah Falls Lodge.

The scenic, corkscrew Columbia River Scenic Hwy, really begins just E of Larch Mtn. jct.

0.8 m., **Crown Point SP.** This is the place where, on June 6, 1916, at 725 ft. above the river, the Columbia River Highway was dedicated. Crown Point was chosen for the occasion because it commanded — and still commands — the finest views of the Columbia River Gorge. That same year, atop this rocky promontory, construction was begun on Vista House as an observatory and rest stop. Crown Point was once known as Thor's Crown (which seems closer to the poetry of the site) and Vista House cost $100,000 to build. **Vista House** was dedicated May 5, 1918 and in 1974 was entered into the National Register of Historic Places. As part of the 1918 dedication, eight plaster panels gracing the interior of the dome were unveiled. Each is carved with a different motif: chestnut, acorn, pine cone, grape, apple, wheat, Oregon grape, and gingko. (Why gingko, rare in Oregon and of no historic or economic importance, was chosen, remains a mystery.) In center of each motif was inscribed name of a "prominent Oregon pioneer": John McLoughlin, Jesse Applegate, James Nesmith, Joseph Lane, Asahel Bush, Matthew Deady, Jason Lee, and Marcus Whitman. The insensitivity to race by early — and some present — Oregonians is reflected in the eight honored: two were racial bigots and one, Joseph Lane, was vociferously pro-slavery and seces-

Mt. Hood as seen from Larch Mountain *Courtesy Oregon State*

sionist. Vista House is museum and information center. Main floor displays over-size photos of building of road.

2.1 m., Talbot SP turnoff.

* 0.3 m., **Talbot SP,** PA under tall trees in soft green saucers of shade. Straight, old town of **Latourell.** Though no longer cohesive village, it still has three streets running E and W and two running N and S. Practically all the Latourell of yore is gone. (See "The Romance Back of Latourell" in author's *Tracking Down Oregon*.)

0.3 m., **Latourell Falls.** 0.1 m., bottom viewpoint for sheer 249 ft. drop from overhanging basalt cliff. Latourell Creek Trail leads 200 yds. to viewpoint. Beyond: 0.3 m., forks. R: 0.7 m., PA — in ambience of being above it all. L: 0.5 m., Upper Latourell Falls, double spill in appearance because at its middle it is shrouded by thick foliage covering ponderous rock wall. It seems higher, with greater volume, and is more dramatic in tone than Lower Falls; indeed, it is so scenic it looks made for TV beer commercial. Trail to Upper Falls is relatively easy in grade compared to most other Gorge paths.

1.2 m., **Shepperd's Dell SP.** Low waterfall sneaking out of woods treads way

Latourell street scene

into grotto mixing sunlight with shadow. Paths to waterfalls and odd rock formations.

Just E of falls road curves round domed rock known as Bishop's Cap or Mushroom Rock.

0.6 m., on N, magnificent white porticoed house. *0.3 m.,* on S, two-story former lodge. Across road is parking area of Bridal Veil Falls SP. *0.4 m* to wooden platform with face-on view of **Bridal Veil Falls,** one of least seen in area and well worth the hike. Falls surge down in two plops to the creek, which hastily swim for the Columbia.

0.8 m., start of **Angels Rest Trail,** *4.8 m.,* with elev. change of 1850 ft., to jct., Wahkeena Trail. *(1.6 m.,* Wahkeena PA.) At *0.6 m.* from start of trail, side trail of few yds. to precarious overlook of **Coopey Falls,** drop of 135 to 185 ft. *0.1 m.* on, bridge across Coopey Creek. *1.5 m.* on, side trail to Angels Rest Summit.

Jct. Turn L toward I-84.

    * To R of first house is cemetery that for decades was hidden by weeds and legend persisted that it was ancient Indian burial ground. But when weeds were cut, markers revealed deaths of locals in early years of 20th century. A traveler looking for the cemetery was rushed by two pit bulls who jumped high time after time to slide their wet tongues across the newcomer's hands. When he commented on their friendliness to a woman living in a house near the cemetery she replied: "Those dogs can be vicious or gentle, depending on how they're brought up. Around here, all the people are gentle." Another

woman, asked why she lived so far from Swan Island (Portland) where her husband worked, replied: "It's a chore, but we like living in the country." All over W Oregon, people drive long distances to work in cities because they "like to live in the country." *0.2 m.* from jct., **Bridal Veil Community Church** and center of town which had pop. 200 in 1940 but has handful now. Lumber mill village in tiny vale between Scenic Hwy and I-84. Turn L. *0.2 m.,* Bridal Veil PO, doll's house looking across river to cliffs frozen in wrinkles. Due W, along RR tracks, are two pointed rocks, known as **Pillars of Hercules** or Speelyei's Children, the latter the name of the Indian coyote god.

Return to jct. Continue on Scenic Hwy.

0.3 m., **Coopey Falls,** sliver of a village on site, in Indian legend, of battle of giants. On S side, set back off road, impressive cloister of Franciscan Sisters of Eucharist, who politely and firmly tell errant door-comers that they prefer to be private. Best view of Coopey Falls (waterfall) is from road, at E end of convent.

2 m., on R, or S, Mt. Hood National Forest sign. High on slope above it — and slightly to L — is seen **Mist Falls.** On April 9, 1806, Meriwether Lewis noted in his fieldbook: " . . . we passed several beautiful cascades which fell from a great hight over the stupendious rocks which closes the river on both sides nearly, except a small bottom on the South side in which our hunters were encamped. The most remarkable of these casscades falls . . . perpendicularly over a solid rock

Bridal Veil Post Office

into a narrow bottom of the river on the south side. it is a large creek, situated about 5 miles above our encampment of the last evening. several small streams fall from a much greater hight, and in their decent become a perfect mist which collecting on the rocks below again become visible and decend a second time in the same manner before they reach the base of the rocks . . ." The "most remarkable of these casscades" is Multnomah; one of the streams falling from a "much greater hight" and becoming a "perfect mist" is Mist Falls, which drop from a 1,200 ft. cliff top. So thin is the volume of Mist Falls that it freezes over in Nov. Falls is due S of Benson SP pond.

0.3 m., **Wahkeena Falls.** PA looks straight up to falls, which twists down basaltic ribs in 5 flumes. Name may be of Indian origin, meaning "most beautiful." *0.3 m.* to bridge at bottom link of falls. Trail from PA: *0.8 m.,* side trails to **Monument Viewpoint** and 40-ft. drop **Necktie Falls;** *0.3 m.,* 25-ft. drop **Fairy Falls;** *1.7 m.,* jct., Larch Mtn. Trail. (*1.8 m.,* return to Multnomah Falls Lodge.)

0.6 m., **Multnomah Falls,** perhaps the state's single most popular attraction and sheer grace in every inch of its descent, 620 ft. in two stages. (Its source is near the top of Larch Mtn.) Set in a sylvan glen, the long white plume seems a soft scarf of windblown lace against the rugged S wall of the gorge. So ethereal is the falls that every turn of the wind and light gives it new expression, which is why photographers find it exciting. Samuel Lancaster, builder of the old Columbia River Hwy., and a man to know, observed with sobriety: "There are higher waterfalls and falls of greater volume, but there are none more beautiful than Multnomah."

A gvmt. brochure gives geologic history of area: "About 15 million years ago, massive flows of lava began to pour from cracks in the earth in eastern Oregon. The lava eventually covered 25,000 cubic miles of the Pacific Northwest.

"As the lava blocks were uplifted and folded to block its course, the ancestral Columbia River cut down through the basalt to begin creating the great Gorge of the Columbia. It took an ice age to finish the creation.

"Less than 1 million years ago, the Cascade volcanoes began to grow on the horizon. At the same time, great continental ice sheets pushed down from Canada, periodically blocking tributaries to the Columbia River. When these ice dams broke, 500 cubic miles of water rushed through the Columbia Gorge. Huge ice blocks and churning rocks scoured the walls to put the finishing touches on the steep, almost perpendicular cliffs.

"These ice-age floods, combined with continual erosion by the Columbia River, eventually carved a gorge up to 3,000 feet deep and 55 miles long."

The brochure recounts in capsule form one of several supposed Indian tales of the falls: "A legend is told of a terrible sickness that threatened the Multnomah people. An old medicine man revealed that the sickness would pass if a maiden threw herself from a high cliff on the Big River to the rocks below.

"When the Chief's daughter saw the sickness on her lover's face she went to the cliff and plunged to her death.

"Now, when the breeze blows through the water, a silvery stream separates

Wahkeena Falls

Phoebe L. Friedman

Multnomah Falls   *Phoebe L. Friedman*

from the upper falls. The misty stream fashions a form of the maiden, a token of the Great Spirit's acceptance of her sacrifice."

At the **Multnomah Falls Visitor Center,** tourists see and hear of early settlement days along the river, geologic events that shaped the Columbia Gorge, and the area's unique plant communities.

Multnomah Falls Lodge, an impressive stone structure, was built in 1925 at cost of $40,000. Paintings of the forest and waterfalls of the area on the interior of the upper floor were done in Depression days by WPA artists.

In 1915 lumber baron Simon Benson gave the land around Multnomah Falls and the lodge to the city of Portland; in 1943 Portland transferred ownership to the US, with the Forest Service assuming responsibility for both land and lodge.

Trail from lodge to Larch Mtn. PA rises 4,000 ft. in *6.8 m.* (At 1 m. there is trail to viewpoint above falls.) The 6.8 m. trail is not for cardiacs, people in a hurry, or persons not in good physical condition — but it is something special, as evidenced by impressions jotted on the trail: moss-hung vine maple with moody faces, bunchberry dogwood with cheery faces, devil's club bristling with porcupine quill spines, overhangs of basaltic rock stenciled with deer fern, resilient bunches of swordfern, Douglas firs, dogwoods, Western red cedar, hemlock, red alder, snowberries that gleam as though washed by a glacial stream, Oregon grape, the brooch heads of pearly everlasting, mountain rhododendron, water crossings whose bridges are moss-slippery and scowling rocks, mushrooms with caps that look like Japanese lanterns or pans of miniature oil lamps, rotting logs protected by angry tongues of bracket fungi, and lichen to give the feeling of antiquity.

2.1 m., **Oneonta Trail.** Rise of 3,660 ft. in *8.3 m.* to point just below Larch Mtn. PA (At *1.7 m.* from start trail reaches Triple Falls, a triplet cataract scooting about 120 ft. to Oneonta Creek.)

0.2 m., **Oneonta Gorge,** one of true dramatic chasms in state. There is something about Oneonta that may suggest an ancient English castle, its roof long tumbled and its walls coated by centuries of fern and moss growth. Only at midday does sunlight find its way into the brooding hall of rock.

There are, for the geologically-sophisticated, traces on Oneonta's walls, 10 to 15 ft. above bridge, of super-massive basalt flow of Miocene times about 25 million years ago, give or take 5 million years. Fossilized trees, swept up in flow, were entombed on the steep walls and actually grew. But a succeeding tidal wave tore them away, leaving in the walls the holes now seen.

A sign, "Oneonta Gorge Botanical Area," explains more than meets the untutored eye: "From these . . . plants growing here on basalt cliffs just above sea level have come selections and hybrids that are treasured by rock gardeners throughout the temperate world . . . The discerning naturalist, with the aid of field glasses, should be able to locate 50 species of wild flowers, flowering shrubs and trees . . ."

(About *0.5 m.* to Oneonta Falls (65 ft.), but there is no direct trail and only when the creek level is low is it possible to complete the journey — and then only by tricky gymnastics. Oneonta Falls charges down with all stops pulled out, slaps against a sloping shelf, and slides into a pool of frenzy.)

0.3 m., **Horsetail Falls.** Some salty old timer looked at the 176-ft.-high cataract hanging down the butt of the sheer rock wall and came up with the name. On Horsetail Falls trail: *0.2 m.,* forks. Take R. *0.2 m.,* **Ponytail Falls,** swishing more

Oneonta Gorge   *Phoebe L. Friedman*

Horsetail Falls

Phoebe L. Friedman

than 100 ft. down a groove between rock runs to crackle into restless pond below overhanging cave of ox-eyed rocks.

0.4 m., **Ainsworth SP.** PA. *0.6 m.,* Ainsworth SP CG, in fir and hemlock forest at base of 2,000-ft. St. Peter's Dome. Not until 1940 was it first climbed, with one of the six a woman. DS, showers, trails.

0.2 m., jct. Keep R. *0.3 m.,* Frontage Rd. Turn onto it. *0.5 m.,* **Dodson,** once RR station hamlet that time and tracks have passed by.

0.8 m., upper level of Warrendale. (A few nice houses.) *0.5 m.,* jct.

* Turn L, under underpass. Beyond underpass, turn L. *0.2 m.,* and across RR tracks, lower **Warrendale.** In 1915 town had two salmon canneries, large pulp and paper mill, PS, PO. Nothing of that now. Turn R. *0.2 m.,* approximate site of 1870-est. fish cannery that was most prominent on mid-Columbia in its time. Owner Frank Warren received another kind of attention 42 years later, when he went down with the *Titanic.* Some gorgeous homes here now, facing Beacon Rock.

Return to jct. Continue E on Scenic Hwy.

0.4 m., **Yeon SP,** wide spot on a lonely road — but great place to photograph Beacon Rock. Historical Marker reads: "The prominent monolith across the river was named Beacon Rock by Lewis and Clark, November 2, 1805. It marked the beginning of tidewater for early day explorers who used it as a landmark in their journeys. The Indians say that when the chinook winds blow softly up the river one can hear the wailings of unhappy, beautiful Wahatpolitan, the Indian maid who climbed the rock and perished with her child, when given to a chief other than the one she loved."

Actually, on Oct. 31, 1805, Clark jotted down in his fieldbook: "a remarkable high detached rock Stands in a bottom on the Star^d Side near the lower point of this Island on the Star^d Side about 800 feet high and 400 paces around, we call the Beaten [Beacon] rock . . ." Two days later Clark noted: "opposit the lower point of this Island [which Clark called Strawberry] passed three Islands covered with tall timber opposit the Beaten rock." Not until the homeward journey on April 9, 1806, did Clark call it by its present name: "at 2oClock P.M. we set out and passed under the Beacon rock . . ." On the same day Lewis noted that the expedition "departed and . . . continued our rout to the Wah-clel-lah Village which is situated on the North side of the river about a mile below the beacon rock . . ." Lewis also observed, "the hills have now become mountains . . ."

Pierce Island, near Beacon Rock, has been described by The Nature Conservancy as "the best remaining natural island in the Columbia River Gorge," varying in size "from 85 to 200 acres, depending on water level fluctuations caused both by seasonal changes and releases from Bonneville Dam three miles upstream."

This island, which has never been grazed, "is dominated by a black cottonwood/willow woodland community . . . and extensive meadows of tufted hairgrass . . . Both communities are rare in the Northwest, and the presence of the grassland community is especially unusual because it is not found in any other riparian lowland in Washington or Oregon.

"Two rare plants grow on Pierce Island: persistantsepal yellowcress (*Rorippa columbiae*) and riverbank wormwood (*Artemisia lindleyana*)... The island hosts a 68-nest rookery for great blue herons and is a nesting and over-wintering area for the Great Basin subspecies of western Canada goose. Numerous other bird species, bear, beaver, coyote, and deer also visit the island."

Trails from Yeon SP lead to **Elowah Falls.** *100 yds.* from trailhead at parking area — and past water tower — forks. Continue straight. *600 yds.,* forks. Straight, *600 yds.* to Lower Falls. *289 ft.* in summer as misty as a silken scarf waving down the side of a sheer basalt cliff; in winter, when alone, a thick white torrent unleashing its inhibitions and hurling piercing gobs of spray 50 ft. or more. McCord Creek, a mild summer soul, is winter's wrathful giant, roaring challenge to every boulder and tree in its course. As every 4-season hiker knows, the Gorge falls are far more spectacular in late Nov. and Dec. than in July and Aug., bursting with pent-up fury, swiftly changing moods, or, in the case of thinner streams, already beginning their frozen sleep until spring meltdown. R from last forks: *1,200 yds.* to 115-ft. Upper Falls, including lip of cliff, with hikers protected by iron rail. There are no obstacles to gasping vistas of Columbia. For floral lovers, more than 200 species of plants have been identified along paths to falls.

0.1 m., I-84. Take it, E.

2.8 m., turnoff to **Bonneville Dam.**

    * *1.2 m.,* **Bradford Island Regional Visitor Center** imaginatively displays history of Lower Columbia. Tours of dam begin here.

The dam was named after Benjamin Louis Eulalie de Bonneville, an Army officer who, while a captain, obtained military leave to explore the West, which he did from 1832 to 1836. He was in command of Ft. Vancouver, across river from Portland, from 1852 to 1855. During Civil War he was recalled to duty and in 1865 was brevetted a Brigadier General. He was immortalized by Washington Irving in *The Adventures of Captain Bonneville.*

Begun in 1933, the dam was dedicated by Pres. Franklin Delano Roosevelt on 9/28/37 and was first on Lower Columbia. (Oldest dam on the river is Rocky Reach, above Wenatchee, Wash.) Since 1938 there has been further expansion, necessitating relocation of a town on the Wash. side. The dam raised the water level to a point 4 m. above The Dalles, 45 m. E of Bonneville Dam. Many of the river's beauty spots and historic sites, such as the ancient Indian fishing grounds at Celilo Falls, were submerged by this impounding of water.

The need for power has surpassed all other considerations on the Columbia, primarily because of the nature of the river. The enormous flow of water and the rapid fall makes the Columbia the greatest power stream in the

Lower Elowah Falls

Fishways at Bonneville Dam

Courtesy State of Oregon

Americas. One-fifth of the potential horsepower from energy derived from falling water in N America and one-third of this continent's generous portion of potential water power is in the Columbia River. The dam virtually made a lake out of the Columbia in this stretch of the river, as other dams did in their stretches. The lake here extends 48 m. to The Dalles Dam and varies in width from 1/4 m. to 1 m.

The dam was designed so that 718 million gallons of water could spill over it every minute. That is converted into a lot of kilowatts, some of which is sent to Calif. In Central Oregon, towers that hold the cables look like men from Mars descending upon some village or ranch house.

Navigation lock is 500 ft. in length and 76 ft. in width, has lift of from 30 to 70 ft., the filling or emptying time is about 15 minutes, and the largest ship the lock can accommodate is about 8,000 tons.

There has been much controversy about fish ladders at Bonneville and other Columbia River dams. Salmon, steelhead, trout, sturgeon and lamprey make up about 90% of the fish passing Bonneville Lock and Dam. Also, 30 miscellaneous species of fish pass beyond the dam. Five species of salmon are native to the Columbia system: chinook, also known as king, spring and tyee; coho, also known as silver; sockeye, also known as blueback and kokanee; chum; and pink. Largest salmon is the chinook, with length up to almost 5 ft. and weights ranging from 10 to 45 lbs. Smallest salmon is the sockeye, weighing up to 4 lbs. The fish that pass the dam go upstream to spawn; some travel almost 1,000 m. to procreate. All the fish don't go to the same place to spawn — and nobody knows why which fish go where. There is evidently as much to learn about fish as there is about Mars. Migrating fish are attracted to the large flows of water coming from the powerhouse and, on occasion, the spillways. The numerous fishway entrance orifices, or openings, are strategically located adjacent to take advantage of this natural reaction in the collection of fish from the river. Once in the collection system, the fish move via transportation channels to the fish ladders. Each fish ladder consists of an inclined flume, in which are installed a series of weirs. These weirs create successive pools, each of which is 1 ft. higher than the previous one downstream. The fish ladders permit the adult fish migrating upstream to reach the reservoir water above the dam.

Most tourists expect to see a lot of fish jump up the fish ladders. But few fish do. It was discovered that jumping injured the fish, so dam engineers regulated the water flowing down the ladder to induce fish to swim rather than to jump from one pool to another. In each partition between the pools there is a submerged 2 ft. sq. thru which a large proportion of the fish swim without even rising to the surface. Once the fish have moved thru the pools to the top of the dam they pass thru the counting station where they are identified and their passage recorded. From there they pass thru the fishway exits into the reservoir to continue their migration to the spawning grounds.

The white sturgeon is the largest freshwater fish in the Columbia. It reaches lengths of 20 ft. and weighs in excess of 1,200 lbs. It is a long, narrow-bodied fish with an elongated snout. The head and back are covered with rows of bony plates. The sturgeon has changed very little since its ancient origin. It is probably the same color, dark grey, that it was thousands of years ago, and is the old fish of the Columbia. It is generally at least 15 years before it spawns; some reach an age of 80. Few sturgeons are counted passing the dam. But there are sturgeon in the higher reaches of the Columbia and in the Snake River.

Some years ago a maniacal nut came in the dark of night to slash sturgeons in the dam pond, killing most of them. The survivors were better guarded thereafter.

Branford Island is a good fishing spot on the Columbia.

Bonneville Dam and the Columbia River were celebrated in the songs of Woody Guthrie who, according to legend, spent 30 days in the area and composed 30 songs, some with numerous verses. Hired by the Bonneville Power Administration, at little more than appleknocker wages, Woody may have averaged a cent a word for his lyrics. His most famous song of this region is "Roll On, Columbia," with the chorus a ritual of triumph: "Roll On, Columbia, roll on;/ Roll on, Columbia, roll on;/ Your power will turn the darkness to dawn,/ So roll on, Columbia, roll on."

Return to I-84. Turn E.

1.4 m., turnoff to **Cascade Fish Hatchery and Eagle Creek Park.** FS CG, PA

* One of Oregon's most popular trailheads is here. Sometimes it seems there are more people on the trail than ants on their way to work. *1.5 m.,* eye-level view of **Metlako Falls,** a seemingly journeyman drop in these parts. (Actually, more than a 100 ft. descent.) *0.3 m.,* Lower Punchbowl Trail. (You can tell when you get here because jct. is holding area for backpacks.) *0.3 m.,* viewpoint of **Punchbowl.** (Punchbowl, formerly called Devil's Punch Bowl,

Punch Bowl   *Phoebe L. Friedman*

is shimmering kettle fed by powerful columns of fresh water pouring between pillars of basalt. This is one of the few places in state where it is possible to swim below the falls and in summer a lot of young people thrash around in the water or laze on rocks above the falls. Although this falls is low, less than 15 ft., it is, with good reason, one of the most photographed in state.) *1.2 m.*, **High Bridge** (80 ft.) over Eagle Creek. *0.4 m.*, **Skooknichuk Falls,** that in the wind gives appearance of long hair flying in all directions. *2.3 m.*, **Tunnel Falls;** trail passes under it, thru 25-ft. tunnel. *3.3 m.*, **Inspiration Point,** the view not as grand as the name. *4 m.*, 3,732-ft.-high **Wahtum Lake.** CG. Jct., **Pacific Crest Trail.** Distance from trailhead to Wahtum Lake is *13.3 m.* and there are numerous camps and campsites along way. In that distance elevation climbs 3,600 ft. but in the main, trail should not be difficult for average hiker.

Another interesting, but more difficult trail, **Ruckel Creek,** also begins at Eagle Creek, this one E of the main comfort station in the PA. It starts as the **Gorge Trail** but in *0.5 m.* begins on its own. (Take L, up steep ascent of powerline clearing.) *1.8 m.* — from Gorge Trail jct. — stirring view of Columbia River. *3.1 m.*, Ruckel Creek. *0.9 m.*, jct., Pacific Crest Trail. The trail will seem to some up, up — going — and down, down — returning — but there are compensations in hanging meadows completely taken over by wildflowers, a plateau that seems a reprieve for the daring, and the cool and pure water of Ruckel Creek.

Return to I-84 at E end of Eagle Creek. Keep E.

1.4 m., turnoff to Cascade Locks and Bridge of the Gods.

   * *0.4 m.*, turnoff to **Bridge of the Gods.** Here, according to Indian mythology, a natural arch spanned the river. There are several tales: the most popular tells of the terrible judgment rendered by Tyhee Sahale, the Supreme Being, after he learned that his two sons had fought for the love of the fair Loo-wit, whose task it was to guard the sacred flame on the bridge. In a moment of turbulent wrath, Tyhee Sahale commanded that the bridge be demolished — and so it shattered and tumbled into the river, destroying Loo-wit and the two who rivaled for her affection. Out of the massive debris arose the Cascades, and the two sons and Loo-wit were resurrected as Mt. Hood, Mt. Adams and Mt. St. Helens. (For more on the legend, see *The Bridge of the Gods,* a romantic novel by Frederic Homer Balch.) (*0.2 m.* up approach to bridge is Trail Park, jumping off point for Pacific Crest Trail.)

0.2 m., **Cascade Locks,** a town and area rich in exploration, trapper, emigrant, mining and steamboat history. The first white commentaries were on problems with the Indians, who started off by kidnapping Meriwether Lewis's Newfoundland, Scannon, and would have killed him for stew meat had not three heavily armed members of the Corps of Discovery forced release of the dog. Lewis wrote in his fieldbook on April 11, 1806: "these are the greates[t] thieves and scoundrels we have met . . . I am convinced that no other consideration but our number at this moment protects us . . ." Washington Irving, narrating from the accounts of Robert Stuart, who came this way in 1812, called the turbulent waters "the piratical pass of the river." But after the entry of Hudson's Bay Co. into the region, noted Sir George Simpson in 1824, the "Firm and conciliatory measures" pursued by HBC persuaded the Indians to be "peacable and quiet."

So vicious were the rapids here — probably created by avalanches falling from the upper part of Table Mtn. (which broke up the free flow of the Columbia) — that even seasoned Indian canoers and French-Canadian voyageurs often had to portage in this stretch.

Prior to construction of the Barlow Road in 1846, the only way for wagons to reach the Willamette Valley was to disassemble them, load them onto crude flatboats, and float them down the Columbia. But at the Cascades the boats had to be guided to the bank and pulled around the treacherous water by shore lines while the wagons and goods were portaged. Little wonder the Barlow Road, with all its agonies and hazards, was preferred by many to the river passage. (It was also a lot cheaper.)

During the mining booms in Idaho and E Oregon in the 1860s, steamboats became the prime transports of commerce. There were the rapids — but men were inventive. Mule-drawn cars, carrying people and goods, jerked from steamers below the rapids to steamers above it on a water-level wooden-railed portage tramway. The venture being profitable, the promoters replaced the wooden rails with steel ones and imported the *Oregon Pony,* a steel locomotive that was the wonder of its age in the NW. In 1896 the federal gvmt. completed construction of a series of locks here — and this part of the river was tamed. In 1939 the locks were submerged by the backwaters of Bonneville Dam but the town did not physically suffer, though its pop. in early 1980s was less than it was in 1938.

Cascade Locks is sprightly town, with all its tourist accommodations on the single business street. There are no hints of the past on this avenue. (Cascade Locks Cemetery, est. 1875, where many a steamboat man sleeps, is on Lakeside Dr.)

0.3 m., in Cascade Locks, Portage Rd. Turn N onto it. *0.2 m.,* **Cascade Locks Museum,** formerly the 1905–built home of a locks worker. Museum, filled with covered wagon days artifacts, also has true replica of fishing wheel, the kind common on the Columbia for many years. A large wheel was 30 ft. in diameter and caught as many as 3,000 salmon in a single day. More than 40 wheels operated on the Columbia in 1900; in 1927 all fishing wheels in Oregon were outlawed.

In front of the museum stands the *Oregon Pony,* first locomotive built on Pacific Coast (in San Francisco) and first used W of upper Missouri. It was brought to this area in spring of 1862 and operated on 4.5 m. stretch of portage between Turner Creek and Upper Cascades. For long it was on display at Portland's Union Station.

On top of the old locks walls, fishers toss their lines into the channels, place their poles under heavy rocks, to hold them fast, and loaf, stretching out for a

The Oregon Pony at Cascade Locks   *Phoebe L. Friedman*

snooze or lounging in lawn chairs. The river flowing thru the locks sounds like a dog lapping water, which is more soothing for the anglers than the thunderous Cascades were for the Indians, Lewis and Clark, the voyageurs, emigrants and early steamboaters.

At E end of park where stands museum: fee CG, Visitor Center, and dock of sternwheeler *Columbia Gorge,* which plies the Columbia on excursion runs.

* *1.2 m.,* turn R for **Oxbow Salmon Hatchery.** *0.7 m.,* hatchery. Nice people will show you around and tell you everything you didn't know you wanted to know about salmon. *0.9 m.,* Pacific Crest Trail.

Return to I-84 from W end of Cascade Locks. Turn W, toward Portland.

2.7 m., turnoff to Bonneville Dam. *9.1 m.,* Multnomah Falls turnoff. *0.9 m.,* view, on L, of Mist Falls — S of Benson SP. *5 m.,* Taj Mahal view of Vista House, Crown Point. *0.3 m.,* turnoff to **Rooster Rock SP.** *0.4 m.,* on R, Rooster Rock, imaginatively named. *1.2 m.,* viewpoint of Columbia River. *4.9 m.,* turnoff to **Lewis and Clark SP.** *0.5 m.,* Troutdale exit. *16 m.,* downtown Portland.

Mt. Hood Loop

For both out-of-staters and Oregonians, one of the most popular inland tours is the Mt. Hood Loop, which almost circles the mountain. The tour begins in Portland, turns S off I-84 at Hood River onto O 35, and returns to Portland via US 26. The trip is further enhanced by taking the Columbia River Scenic Hwy. to where it enters I-84.

(For the Portland-Hood River section, see *Short Trips Out of Portland, Columbia Gorge,* preceding, and, following, *Trans-Cascade Roads, I-84.*)

The central section of the Mt. Hood Loop starts at O 35, *0.4 m.* from the City Center exit to Hood River, or from Hood River city center, *0.4 m.,* to O 35.

From I-84:

0.4 m., turnoff to **Hood River** city center. Straight. *0.3 m.,* Panorama Point Jct. (This, say the locals, is the "scenic route.")

* *1.6 m.,* **Panorama Point,** probably the finest view anywhere of Mt. Hood and the apple valley. The orcharded Hood River Valley is all year honey and cider to the soul of the eye but at apple blossom time it is downright intoxicating. The gorgeous aesthetic mix of budding life and the suffocation of the senses spurs to mind some lines from Sappho: "Here roses leave shadow on the ground/ and cold springs babble through apple branches/ where shuddering leaves pour down profound sleep."

Perhaps this would be the place to pause for some words on **Mt. Hood.** Geologically it is a stratovolcano that was once from 500 to 1,000 ft. higher than it is now; glaciation has reduced it in size and height. The last major eruption is believed to have been about 2 millennia ago but, according to researchers C. L.

Rosenfeld and H. G. Schlicker, "the continued fumarolic action and the possible relationship of seismic activity to magma movement within the crust would suggest that Mount Hood could erupt at any time." About the year 1800 ash was erupted near the N face of Hood, as evidenced by ring count of trees growing from an ash layer at Tilly Jane FS CG. The most recent activity was Dec. 12, 1974, when crustal seismic shock, with its epicenter near Government Camp, was recorded at a magnitude of 4.1. Scientists could not decide whether the shock was of volcanic or tectonic origin.

Mt. Hood is regarded by some people as an area of geothermal potential. Geothermal leases were taken out on about 2 million acres of land in the Cascade Range and volcanic terrain of central and eastern Oregon. Areas included Breitenbush Hot Springs, Belknap Hot Springs, McCredie Hot Springs, Newberry Crater, Summer Lake, Glass Buttes, Klamath Falls, Lakeview-Warner Valley, La Grande, Burns, Cow Lakes, Vale, Alvord Valley.

The first description of Mt. Hood by a white was given by the man who gave the mountain its present name, Lt. William Broughton, on Oct. 29, 1792. Broughton, a British naval officer, boated up the Columbia at the command of Capt. George Vancouver, who extensively explored the maritime PNW. Broughton's description appeared in Vancouver's *Voyage of Discovery,* whose contents were well known to Lewis and Clark. Broughton reported the following to Vancouver: "A very distant high snowy mountain now appeared rising beautifully conspicuous in the midst of an extensive tract of low, or moderately elevated land, lying S. 67 E., and seemed to announce a termination of the river."

The following day Broughton enhanced his description, as given in Vancouver's book: "The same remarkable mountain that had been seen from Belle Vue point [near the mouth of the Willamette — rf] again presented itself, bearing at this station S. 67 E., and though the party were now nearer to it by 7 leagues, yet its lofty summit was scarcely more distinct across the intervening land which was moderately elevated. Mr. Broughton honored it with Lord Hood's name; its appearance was magnificent; and it was clothed with snow from its summit, as low down as the high land, by which it was intercepted, rendered it visible." Lord Hood was Samuel Hood, distinguished in the annals of the British Navy.

Mt. Hood was first climbed by whites in 1854; among the climbers was Joel Palmer, then Supt. of Indian Affairs for Oregon Territory. Elijah Coalman, who first climbed Hood in 1897 and led climbing parties until 1928, is said to have reached the peak at least 600 times and that number was surpassed by Mark Weygandt, another legendary guide. In 1924, Wells Bennett, the good friend of Weygandt and the man who married Weygandt's widow 6 years after Weygandt's death, rode a motorcycle to the 8,500 ft. high E ridge of the mtn. (See "A Motorcycle on Mount Hood" in author's *A Touch of Oregon.*)

Coalman, as was Weygandt, was indefatigable. Once, after breakfast at Government Camp, he climbed to the summit, went over it, and reached Cloud Cap Inn as lunch was being served. After a hearty meal Coalman arose, went back up to and over the summit, and came down to Government Camp again in time for his 5 o'clock supper.

Elijah Coalman was at his peak when, in 1919, the first aerial photo of Hood was taken. Mark Weygandt was still going strong, in 1936, when the mountain saw its largest climbing party, 401 hopefuls. Both Coalman and Weygandt were dead when six youths from the State School of the Blind in Vancouver, Wash., reached the summit, but perhaps they were driven on by the spirits of both men, each of whom was as famous for humanistic traits as for mountain climbing. In 1986 tragedy gripped the mountain when a group of church high school students from Portland went beyond their capacity and paid for misjudgment in a heavy toll of lives.

From Timberline Lodge to the summit climbers must cover 3.65 miles. The going might be more appreciative if climbers read beforehand the most comprehensive and entertaining book on Oregon's highest peak (11,235 ft.), *Mount Hood: A Complete History* by Jack Grauer.

As can certainly be expected, there is an immense body of folklore and mythology about Mt. Hood. An example, as good, bad or as indifferent as any, appears in a National Forest Service brochure on Mt. Hood Wilderness:

"The original story of the Bridge of the Gods and the mountain, Wy'east, has been altered so many times that many stories exist now. The one most frequently told is from the Puyallup Indians.

"Many years ago, the world was very young and all the people were happy. They had all that they wanted, given to them by the Great Spirit, whose home was in the sun.

"Soon, things were not happy, as two brothers began to quarrel over the land. Each wanted it. So the Great Spirit, to stop the quarrel, took the brothers away one night. When they awoke the next morning, they were in a new land, which was rich and beautiful.

"The Great Spirit told each brother to shoot an arrow in the opposite direction, and where the arrow landed would be their country. The big river (Columbia) would separate the land.

"One brother shot to the south, into the valley of the Willamette River, and became chief of the Multnomahs. The other brother shot north and became chief of the Klickitats.

"After this, the Great Spirit built a bridge across the big river so that the brothers and their people might visit across. The bridge would be a sign of peace, and as long as the brothers remained at peace the bridge would remain.

"The people were very happy and visited back and forth across the bridge. But after a time, the people became wicked and began to quarrel. This made the Great Spirit unhappy, and to stop the quarreling, he kept the sun from shining. The people had no fire, and became cold when the rains came. Soon the people were sorry for quarreling and begged the Great Spirit to return the fire to them.

The Great Spirit relented, and went to an old woman. She had not quarreled when the others had, and still had some fire.

"The Great Spirit promised her anything she wished if she would go out on the bridge and share her fire. The old woman wanted to be young and beautiful again. The Great Spirit told her to always keep her fire on the bridge to remind the people of the kindness of the Great Spirit, and she would be young and beautiful.

"The old woman (Loo-wit) took her fire out to the bridge. The Great Spirit made the sun to shine again, and when morning came, the people were surprised to find a beautiful young maiden sitting beside a fire on the Bridge of the Gods.

"Many people came to see the fire, and the young maiden. Among these were two young men. They visited Loo-wit often, and her heart was stirred by them. One was the handsome chief of the south (Wy/east) and the other was the handsome chief of the north (Klickitat).

"Wy/east and Klickitat became jealous of one another, as Loo-wit couldn't decide which one she liked best. They began to fight with one another, with all of the people joining in. There was much fighting and many were killed. The Great Spirit became angered at the people. He tore down the Bridge of the Gods, which was a sign of peace between the two tribes. He changed the two chiefs into mountains. Even after they were mountains, they continued to fight over Loo-wit. They threw hot rocks at one another, and blew fire.

"Loo-wit was changed into a mountain that still reflects her youth and beauty. She is now called Mt. St. Helens. Klickitat is known as Mt. Adams. And Wy'east was renamed by the white man for Admiral Samuel Hood."

(It is obvious that the above was penned before Mt. St. Helens erupted. But in that there is a nuance of great tragic drama: that the gentle one should turn out to be the violent one.)

(For imaginative poem on mountain and story of mountain man who wrote the ode, see "Mighty Peak of Tremendious Hight" in author's *Tracking Down Oregon.* For folklore of Mt. Hood, see "Old Man of the Mountain" in author's *This Side of Oregon.*)

From N turnoff to Panorama Point:

1.7 m., on E, S turnoff to Panorama Point.

      * *0.6 m.,* East Side Rd. Turn L. *0.6 m.,* take L. *0.1 m.,* Panorama Point.

1.7 m., on E, 2-story white house with "barn-like" features that give it solid character. *0.3 m.,* on E, Pine Grove, tiny, compact service strip. *0.2 m.,* on W, Detham Ridge.

      * 0.1 m., on L, site of first sawmill in Hood River Valley, on Neal Creek. Built 1861; ran until 1887, when it burned down. New mill lasted almost as long before it was shut down.

1.8 m., on E, Sunday Rd.

      * Turn E. *0.2 m.,* 3065 Sunday Rd. On R was home of William Ashley Sunday, known to all America as Billy Sunday, the foremost evangelist of his

day. Born in Ames, Iowa in 1862, Sunday was a well-known major league baseball player from 1883–1891, performing for Pittsburgh and Philadelphia but best known for his tenure with the Chicago White Sox. Upon retiring, he took employment with the Chicago YMCA and then became assistant to prominent evangelist J. Wilbur Chapman. Dissatisfied with his subordinate and seemingly circumscribed role, Sunday launched on an independent career and was ordained by the Chicago Presbytery in 1903. Within a year he was widely known for his sermons, which an historian charitably described as "a crude version of the ultraconservative evangelical theology . . . Earnest and sincere, he preached the divine wrath rather than divine law." It was Sunday who started the practice of "hitting the sawdust trail," a concept derived from his insistence that the floors of the places in which he exhorted sinners to acknowledge their transgressions or be forever condemned to perdition, be covered with sawdust. A windmill, wound-up, colorful preacher, Sunday "saved" hundreds of souls a night; how many reverted to form the next day is uncertain. In 1909 he purchased a farm here, called it the Billy Sunday Ranch, went big into grain and cattle, and built a home and swimming pool. The home, which locals describe as a two-bedroom cabin, was torn down about 1983 to make way for a new residence. By then the swimming pool had long been covered up. Billy Sunday died in 1935 and all that remains on the grounds of his Hood River County home is a garden cart that had been wheeled about by "Ma" Sunday. A "3-hole" outhouse was moved to a farm N of Odell. There are numerous bits of folklore about Billy Sunday and his relatives who lived at or near his home. Some of the stories concern Sunday's brother, supposedly a prodigious producer of corn liquor, and the remains of a still were found on the Sunday property.

0.3 m., Odell Jct.

   * 0.8 m., **Odell.** Settled in 1860s, Odell didn't have PO until 1910 and for year PO was called Newtown. Basically a fruit community, Odell has grown slowly and is today the kind of a 1-business street village Hollywood loves to portray as example of heartland America. *0.6 m.,* N, on R, 2525 Odell Hwy., farmhouse now home to 3-seater outhouse of Billy Sunday. Outhouse has become a sort of shrine for Sunday worshippers. Farm occupant recalled a minister from Lewiston, Idaho, who came here "just to sit on one of the three-holers so he could be closer to Billy Sunday." *2 m.,* Odell Jct. L, traveling SW, *6.7 m.,* Dee Jct. *2.5 m.,* jct. L, Lolo Pass. (To US 26 and Zigzag, *20.9 m.,*) R, *5.7 m.* to forks. Take R fork. *1.5 m.,* **Lost Lake.** Mt. Hood, looking NW and deep into the lake, is always inspiring, especially on a sunlit day. A 3 m. trail of spongy-carpeted fern, cut thru stands of Douglas fir, encircles lake. FS CG, PA, store. Swimming, boating, fishing.

   There is an Indian legend about almost every place in Oregon so, of course, there is one on Lost Lake, as related in *Oregon: End of the Trail:*

   "The shores of Lost Lake . . . were long favorite summer and autumn camp grounds of the Indians. It is told that in days when the oldest grand-fathers were mere papooses, a tribe gathered here for a potlatch. One evening, after the squaws had returned from the berry patches with well-filled baskets, the men had brought in tender venison, and a feast of roast meat had been prepared, a snow-white doe pursued by wolves suddenly broke from a thicket, plunged into the lake, swam to the middle, dived beneath the surface and disappeared. A medicine man pronounced the event an omen of very bad luck. The Indians broke camp and never returned to the lake.

"In 1912 a young Indian couple who had been educated in an eastern college and did not share the beliefs of their elders came here to camp. During a storm a bolt of lightning struck the tree under which they were standing and killed the bride. Today no Indian can be persuaded to visit Lost Lake."

Contemporary Indians are either not aware of the legend or lack this superstition; they come to the lake with the same unworried air as do others. *2 m.,* viewpoint. Anywhere along the road is a grand vista, but this one is particularly fruitful to the eye. *3.6 m.,* Woodworth Rd.

    * Turn W. *1 m.,* Mt. Hood Winery.
0.4 m., Parkdale Jct.

    * *1.8 m.,* Cooper Spur-Parkdale Jct. Turn R. *0.1 m.,* Allen Rd. Turn R. *0.6 m.,* on R, turnoff for **Upper Valley Cemetery.** *0.3 m.,* cemetery — one of fairest burial grounds in Oregon, flanked by apple orchards and under the arc of Mt. Hood. A significant number of graves are of ex-servicemen, the markers giving rank, branch of service and name of war. This would suggest that being in the service was the high point of their lives. It would be nice to see somewhere grave markers etched with symbols of peace. Return to Parkdale Rd. and turn R. *0.4 m.,* **Parkdale PO,** approximate town center. Parkdale is neighborly, spread-out marketplace to which, for good reason, have come retirees, artisans and artists. One has the feeling that if there isn't a community bingo game here there ought to be. Still, Parkdale, like Odell, has as its main business the packing, storage and shipping of apples, and this is evident in the large sheds and freezers seen in both towns. *0.1 m.,* take Baseline Rd. *0.7 m.,* Old Parkdale Rd. jct. Continue straight, now on Lava Bed Rd., to most recent outpourings of Mt. Hood lava. *0.5 m.,* end of road. Return *0.5 m.* to Old Parkdale Rd. Turn L onto it. *0.2 m.,* Red Hill Rd. Turn L. *0.8 m.,* Middle Fork, Hood River. *0.7 m.,* paved road to L. Continue straight. *0.8 m.,* 2nd turnoff to L, at gravel FS road. Here are splendid views of Mt. Hood and Hood River Valley.

    Return to Parkdale-Cooper Spur Jct. Take R. *2 m.,* London Rd. Jess Hutson House on SE corner is veritable rock museum. *6.1 m.,* **Cooper Spur.** Restaurant. Take uphill R for **Cloud Cap.** *1 m.,* turnoff L for Cooper Spur Ski Area (*0.2 m.*) *3.7 m.,* **Inspiration Point.** Grand view of Mt. Hood and large waterfall. *5.1 m.,* turnoff L for Tilly Jane FS CG (*0.4 m.*). *0.6 m.,* trail-head for Timberline Trail. *0.2 m.,* end of road; parking below Cloud Cap Inn,

6,000 ft. elev. Short trail leads to aerie confrontation with **Eliot Glacier,** 2nd largest in Oregon. (For more on Cloud Cap, see *Trans-Cascade Roads, I-84, Hood River.*) *2.4 m.,* jct., O 35.

From Parkdale Jct.:

0.1 m., **Mt. Hood,** open village with homey touch or two and the great mtn. of its name drawing a bead on a calendar art barn that reminds one of words from Whitman: "The big doors of the country barn stand open and ready,/ the dried grass of the harvest-time loads the slow-drawn wagon." (For story of late, famous resident who lived in house just N of barn, see "A Motorcycle on Mount Hood" in author's *A Touch of Oregon.*)

0.8 m., turnoff to Toll Bridge CP.

    * *0.4 m.,* park. CG, PA on E Fork of Hood River.

1.7 m., Parkdale Jct. 4.1 m., Rouston CP.

    * *0.2 m.,* rough CG on E Fork of Hood River.

2.2 m., Cooper Spur Rd. Jct.

    * *3.4 m.,* turnoff to Cloud Cap.

0.1 m., on E, trailhead for East Fork, Elk Meadow and Zig Zag trails. Trail parking. *1.5 m.,* trailhead, East Fork Trail. *0.2 m.,* Sherwood FS CG, PA. *1.4 m.,* Dufur Jct.

    * 26.7 m., **Dufur,** with not a hamlet between. The road sails thru highland greenery into the plains of Central Oregon, paralleling Fifteen Mile Creek part of the way.

2.6 m., **Robinhood FS CG,** on E Fork of Hood River.

Across road from Robinhood FS CG is head of Gumjuac Trail. From here a small network of trails leads into and to the edge of Badger Creek Roadless Area. One trail, approx, 2.5 m., winds thru lupine and penstemon meadows and ridges matted by white sandwort, yellow eriogonum, violet and gold sedums and pastel phlox and past bonzai pines clinging for life on overpowering basalt cliffs to 6,525 ft. Lookout Mtn., 3rd highest in Mt. Hood Nat. Forest. The mtn. is aptly named: every great peak, from Rainier to Broken Top, is sharply etched, as though by a steel quill.

Another trail in this area, approx. 10.5 m. from Badger Lake to Bonney Crossing CG, accompanying Badger Creek, traverses so intermingled a watershed of wet W and dry E that plants and reptiles of both zones occupy same communities, symbiosis in a wild Eden.

3.2 m., turnoff to Hood River Meadows.

    * *0.3 m.,* trailhead R to Elk Meadows and Umbrella Falls. Trailhead L to Sahalie Falls. *0.1 m.,* forks. Take L. *0.7 m.,* on R, **Sahalie Falls.** *0.5 m.,* Mt. Hood Meadows Jct., at O 35.

1.1 m., Mt. Hood Meadows Jct.

    * *50 yds.,* jct. R, *0.5 m.,* Sahalie Falls. E Fork of Hood River, tumbles down 90 ft. with cry of abandon. L from jct., *1.9 m.,* Jct., Hood Meadows, ski complex with head-on view of Mt. Hood. From parking lot, 600-ft. trail descends to basin of **Umbrella Falls,** white-water torrent rampaging down 60 ft. from rocky notch in densely forested hillside.

0.1 m., **Bennett Pass,** at 4,657 ft. highest point on Mt. Hood Loop. *2.1 m.,* **White River,** boulder- jammed glacial cut. *2.1 m.,* **Barlow Pass,** elev. 4,155 ft. *2 m.,* US 26. This marks the end of O 35. Turn onto US 26, W bound.

1 m., Trillium Lake Jct. (**Trillium Lake,** *2 m.*) *0.1 m.,* Snow Bunny, ski facility. *1.1 m.,* **Still Creek FS CG.** A trivia legend has it that people were attracted to Still Creek because its warm waters were advertised as a sort of natural hot spring. All went well until it was discovered that the waters were artificially heated.

0.3 m., turnoff for Timberline Lodge.

* *5.5 m.,* **Timberline Lodge,** most prominent of Oregon's mtn. resorts and center of state's most popular ski slopes. Sno-cats and chair lifts carry passengers high up mtn.

The lodge itself is many things, including a resounding refutation to charges that the Depression-era Works Progress Administration (WPA) consisted of loafers who spent their time "leaning on the shovel." Ground was broken June 11, 1936 and hundreds of unemployed workers, skilled and unskilled, were hired, housed in a tent city at Summit Meadows, 7 miles down the mtn., and trucked to work. On Sept. 28, 1937, 15 months and 17 days after groundbreaking, the completed lodge was dedicated by President Roosevelt. From the start, the lodge was not only a comfortable inn but a museum of arts and crafts. Under direction of Portland designer Margery Hoffman Smith, lodge was furnished with handcrafts in wood, stone, wrought iron and other materials, many of which were found in the area. A total of 119 hand-hooked rugs were made by WPA workers, who also created and produced the sturdy furniture, stained glass and linoleum murals. By 1975 it appeared that the lodge, unique in the nation for its regional artistry and flavor, was badly deteriorating. Only 10 of the hand-hooked rugs remained; the number and condition of applique and woven fabrics was pitiful. This was the year Friends of Timberline was organized and thru the group's unselfish efforts a significant portion of old Timberline Lodge has been restored. So strong is the tradition and reputation of the lodge that it is well-patronized all year. In lobby is Rachel Griffin Historical Exhibition Center, named for former curator of Portland Art Museum and one of Portland's great people.

0.2 m., turnoff to **Government Camp,** alpine village which joins US 26 at W end. Place received name because of what it was: a camp of soldiers in 1849 who had come overland to be stationed in the new political entity of Oregon Territory. When it came time to leave they were forced to abandon their wagons, so they left a warning sign: "Government Property — Do Not Touch."

Now US 26 barrels down **Laurel Hill,** paralleling the last lap and most difficult part of the Barlow Road, opened for commerce in 1846. For some emigrants, Laurel Hill was the most hazardous stretch of the entire way W, and their frightening difficulty here can be realized if it is understood that as steep as US 26 is here, the wagon trace was much, much steeper. William Barlow, son of road builder Samuel Barlow, told how it was: "We went down Laurel Hill like shot off a shovel." In the 2 most precipitous miles there were only 3 levels where oxen could be rested. E. W. Conyers, who traveled the Barlow Road 7 years after it was completed, found it little better than William Barlow had: "The road on this hill is something terrible. It is worn down in the soil from five to seven feet, leaving steep banks on both sides, and so narrow that it is almost impossible to walk alongside of the cattle for any distance without leaning against the oxen. The emigrants cut down a small tree about ten inches in diameter and about forty feet long, and the more limbs it had on the better. This tree they fastened to the rear axle with chains or ropes, top and foremost, making an excellent brake." Actually, the hill should have been called Rhododendron, because of the profusion of that plant here, but the emigrants saw it as the laurel they knew back home.

1.2 m., **Mirror Mtn.,** ski facility. *0.9 m.,* trailhead for Mirror Lake. *0.9 m.,* **Laurel Hill Historical Marker.** *3.7 m.,* **Camp Creek FS CG.** *2.1 m.,* Tollgate. Between two maples is replica of W tollgate of **Barlow Toll Rd.** Zigzag River, aptly named by the emigrants, who crossed it often, makes a Z here. *0.1 m.,* **Tollgate FS CG.** *0.5 m.,* **Rhododendron.** Looking at all the rhododendron shrubs around here, the name becomes obvious. Started as summer colony, it is now all-year town, with good tourist facilities.

0.9 m., **Zigzag,** named for river that is tributary of the Sandy. Ranger station here is one of most-used in state. Jct., Lolo Pass. (See *Short Trips Out of Portland, Lolo Pass,* immediately following.)

1 m., Welches Jct.

* *0.8 m.,* **Welches,** resort in green coves of foothills. (See *Short Trips Out of Portland, East B,* preceding.)

0.6 m., Wemme. *0.5 m.,* Wildwood. *0.4 m.,* Wildwood Rec. Site. *0.6 m.,* E. Brightwood Jct. *1.8 m.,* Brightwood Jct. *0.7 m.,* Marmot Jct. *1.1 m.,* E. Sleepy Hollow Rd. *2.6 m.,* Cherryville Dr. *2 m.,* SE Cherryville Dr. *3.6 m.,* Dover Jct. *2 m.,* turnoff to Oral Hull Park, Dodge Park, Bull Run. *0.3 m.,* Sandy, Jct., O 211. *1.6 m.,* Kelso Jct. *1.8 m.,* Boring- Oregon City Jct. *4.7 m.,* Orient Jct. *1.7 m.,* Gresham — Powell and Main. *13 m.,* downtown Portland.

(For details on US 26 from Government Camp to Portland, see *Trans-Cascade Roads, US 26.*)

Clackamas River

From Burnside and 82nd:

8.1 m., turn R onto O 224 ramp — E for Estacada.

3.5 m., jct., O 212. Continue on O 224. *0.8 m.,* on hillside L. rambling yellow house that seems to sing out, "Put me on the cover of a calendar." *0.4 m.,* **Carver,** formerly called Stone, and site of a once-famous quarry. Leave O 224 to angle R. Cross Clackamas River bridge. (Legend has it that in "olden days" the river here was so thick with salmon the farmers herded their pigs down there to gorge on the fish. Then, legend continues, pigs would have to be fed something to get fish smell out of them. There are less salmon now than there are fish stories.) In 1872 ferry was est. at this crossing but bridge has been here about as long as anyone can remember.

Across bridge, forks. (Road W, toward Oregon City, is away from the thrust of this trip but it is a lovely drive and worth pursuing. Road is pearled with sweet meadows, gentlepeople farms with courtly houses, and fine views of dreamy Clackamas River. Every view here seems a painting. 5. m., on L, Henry Endre's Winery, pioneer in its field. 0.5 m., jct., O 213.)

Return to Clackamas River bridge. Continue straight. 0.2 m. from bridge, turn R onto Hattan Rd. 0.1 m., on R, at corner, plaque on boulder tells legend of Baker Log Cabin.

Take path to R. On L is relocated **Old German Methodist Church,** built 1895 and originally located at Carver. From its opening until its closing in 1924, services were conducted in German. After 1924 the 1-room country church had much use as sheep barn. Moved to present location in 1967, with original pulpit, but organ and pews had been lost and new ones installed in resurrected church bldg. Easter service in 1972 was first time bldg. employed for religious purposes since closing. Tintype of a simple past; seeing it at night one can almost hear an old, warm refrain: "In the sky the bright stars glittered,/ On the bank the pale moon shone,/ And from Aunt Dinah's quilting party/ We were seeing Nellie home."

0.1 m., down lane, **Baker Log Cabin,** perhaps oldest standing log cabin in Oregon. Built 1856 by Horace and Jane Baker, who settled here in 1846. Restored by CCC 1939. Pioneer dwelling has high stone chimney, overhanging roof supported by timbers, second-story covered porch on one side.

Return 0.1 m. to Carver-Springwater Rd. Turn R. 1.3 m., turn L for Barton Park. 0.7 m., on L, 1899 house with water tower. 3.1 m., turn R. 0.1 m., **Barton CP,** immense spread of trees and greenery. CG, PA, BL on Clackamas River.

Return to Barton Park jct. Turn L. 0.4 m., turnoff R for Ingleside Farm and Pleasant View Pioneer Cemetery. 0.1 m., **Ingleside Farm.** Monte Rumgay est. fame here for using horses instead of mechanized equipment. (See "That Wonderful Ingleside Farm" in author's Tracking Down Oregon.) Weather-painted barn is museum of 19th and early 20th century farm artifacts. 0.1 m., **Pleasant View Pioneer Cemetery,** on knoll. Immaculately maintained; sweeping vistas.

Return to road. Turn R. 2.5 m., on L, **Logan Community Church.** 1.3 m., Harding Rd. On L, sprawling frame house with cone-shaped cupola, spool-trimmed porch and splotches of gingerbread. Rare is the first-time traveler who does not at least slow down at sight of this ghostly place, supposedly built circa 1890. (0.1 m. up Harding Rd. to Harding Grange, bingo center of the Upper

Baker Log Cabin

House on Harding Road, Logan, on the way to Springwater

Logan District. Here stood community of **Logan** (PO 1884–1903), named for Major-General John A. Logan, Civil War hero and GOP candidate for vice president in 1884. Oregon youngsters probably heard little of Logan in school but in Illinois every schoolchild in first third of 20th century was taught song with these words: "By thy rivers gently flowing, Illinois, Illinois,/ Came the nation's great immortals, Illinois, Illinois,/ Grant and Logan and thy fame,/ Abraham Lincoln's wondrous name . . ." Or words to that effect. Probably a lot of Illinois kids sang the song without knowing or caring who Logan was.)

2.7 m., on L, **Clackamas Viewpoint.** Stunning panorama of Clackamas River bend, willowy woods, slices of meadow, Cascade foothills and Mt. Hood.

0.4 m., turn R. *0.4 m.,* forks. Take R. *0.9 m.,* on L, old **Viola School,** attended by children of the earthbreakers. *0.2 m.,* **Viola Church,** in "center" of what was **Viola.** PO est. as Clear Creek 1867; 1876 changed to Viola, for early white settler Violet Harding. Place never had more than school, church, store, last-named no more. Return *1.1 m.* to forks. Turn R onto Jubb Rd. *0.2 m.,* on R, **Viola Cemetery.**

"The people here are happy," remarked a woman living near the burial ground. "It's such a beautiful place," she explained, as she pointed to Mt. Hood, appearing to look straight down on the cemetery.

Inscriptions on two of the gravestones reflect the warmth of the prairie folk. That of Lorenzo D. Tracy (1826–1866):

"An amiable farmer here lies at rest/ As ever God with his image blest./ The friend of man, the friend of truth,/ The friend of age, the guide of youth."

And that of Elizabeth E. Kirchem (1825–1866):

"O, let us think of all she said,/ And all the kind advice she gave,/ And let us do it now she's dead,/ And sleeping in her lonely grave."

Return of Springwater Rd. Turn R. *0.7 m.,* turnoff to **McIver Park,** which reaches down to Clackamas River. In 1970, during Viet Nam War, when American Legion convention was scheduled for Portland, authorities feared confrontation between "long-haired" anti-war protesters and legionnaires. Gov. Tom McCall, seeking to abort rumored anti-Legion parade activities, set aside McIver Park for rock festival. Thousands of young people came to the park, to, among other things, listen to music, smoke pot, bathe nude in the river, and dance on the grass. To add to the lovefest, McCall arranged for rose petals to be dropped from a plane. What McCall did not know was that, apart from perhaps some provocateurs, none of the anti-war activists planned to disrupt the Legion convention and that the young people who came to "Vortex I" were not involved in the anti-war movement. McIver SP has CG, PA, DS, fishing, boating, horse trails, showers. Also, fish hatchery.

4.2 m., **Springwater.** Store, Presbyterian Church, Grange hall. Church est. 1889; present church (1904) has modest spire and belfry. Part of Grange hall once part of Springwater School. Bell between church and hall belonged to school. Springwater PO 1874–1914. In 1915 there was spool mill here.

Viola Church

(Straight, *1.8 m.,* **Metzler CP.** CG, PA.)

At Springwater, turn L at corner, S Wallens Rd. *0.4 m.,* on R, 1890s house; impressive. Folklore hints of mysterious past.

0.1 m., O 211. *2.4 m.,* jct, O 224, Upper Clackamas Rd., at edge of Estacada.

(From Carver there is another way to Estacada: Follow O 224 from Carver. *5.5 m.,* Barton. Turn R. *0.3 m.,* Barton CP. Return to Barton. Turn onto O 224. *3.4*

Old house near Springwater

m., jct., O 211. *3.9 m.*, on R, turnoff to River Mill Dam. *1.4 m.*, Estacada city center.

(For Estacada, home of 3-day Timber Festival in July, see *Short Trips Out of Portland, O 211*, following.)

0.3 m., jct., O 211. Continue straight up on O 224, which follows Clackamas River. *1.5 m.* from jct., O 211 — on R, footbridge across Clackamas River to Faraday Lake, 26-acre forebay of Faraday Hydroelectric Project. Bank fishing only, year round.

3.2 m., **North Fork Hydroelectric Project.** PGE says its N Fork Fish Ladder — *1.7 m.* long — is world's largest.

2.7 m., turnoff R to Promontory Park. 50 ft., forks. L: *0.1 m.*, on R, parking area for **Small Fry Lake,** stocked by PGE for children under 14. No charge. *0.1 m.*, PA *0.2 m.*, CG. R: *0.2 m.*, store, BL.

Here the Clackamas is seaweed green, with sunbeams leaping up from the water like fish surfacing to bite. The stream flows thru the mossy, shrubby, fern-stained walls with the silky rhythm of a big cat rippling its muscles.

1.7 m., the river quickly turns churlish here, breaking into whitecaps and lurching across rocks.

Really, there is no point indicating all the places where the Clackamas is exciting, dazzling and rich in shades of green, varied in texture, and topographically exhilarating. There are so many places; one need only look to be rewarded.

1.3 m., to R, Memaloose Rd.

    * Turn onto Memaloose Rd. *11.5 m.* down curvy logging road that climbs and dips thru hills, forks. Turn R. *0.9 m.*, on L, trail to **Memaloose Lake.** Trail marker is more often missing (stolen) than present, but pole generally remains. *1.5 m.* uphill thru forest primeval, Memaloose Lake. FS calls trail "moderate to difficult." For cardiacs, keep nitro close at hand. Memaloose is interesting lake, looking as if an eagle had clawed out a cavity, waited for the rain to fill it, and then flung some fish into the water. Fishers here are scarce.

0.4 m. — from Memaloose Rd. — Lazy Bend FS CG. *3.3 m.*, Bid Eddy PA. *1.2 m.*, **Carter Bridge FS CG,** PA. *0.4 m.*, on L, **Lockaby FS CG;** on R, **Armstrong FS CG.** *0.2 m.*, **Fish Creek FS CG.** (On summer weekends all CGs in this area seem filled.)

0.1 m., forks.

    * R on Fish Creek Dr. *0.1 m.*, Clackamas River trailhead. *7.8 m.* along S side of river to **Indian Henry CG.** Trail slithers thru old growth timber and has fine views of river waterfalls.

    From trailhead point on road: *5.4 m.*, jct., with R fork meandering *6.3 m.* along Wash Creek and L fork twisting *5.9 m.* at side of Fish Creek to Brackett Mtn., and then following tortured route — *15.4 m.* — back to main road. But by then you'll have stopped counting the miles. This is a zesty recreationland and supposedly benevolent to fishers — if you can believe the lot — but it is easy to get confused in.

From turnoff to Fish Creek Dr. and O 224:

2.5 m., **Roaring River FS CG.** *0.8 m.*, **Sunstrip FS CG.** *2.5 m.*, turnoff L to **Three Lynx.**

    * *0.5 m.*, **Oak Grove Hydroelectric Project,** on Three Lynx Creek — an early settler saw three bobcats on bank of creek, hence the name. Parking for fishers. *0.1 m.*, electric utility community that resembles prosperous Swiss village. Schoolhouse is center of social activities for the 65 or so folks who reside here.

1.3 m., **Indian Henry FS CG.** *3.4 m.*, **Alder Flat FS CG.** *0.2 m.*, **Ripplebrook Ranger Station,** only community on road between Estacada and Detroit. No facilities (other than rest rooms) for travelers. Only information, given by friendly personnel.

Just beyond RS, turn L.

    * *3.3 m.*, forks. Take R. *2.9 m.*, **Lake Harriet,** fjord-like figure of Oak Grove Fork of Clackamas River. CG. Road goes on, if navigable, *9 m* to **Timothy Lake** and from there *10.7 m* to US 26 at Skyline Jct.

0.7 m., jct. Take R. **Ripplebrook FS CG** on corner. *2.9 m.*, **Riverside FS CG.** *0.7 m.* forks. Take R — for Bagby Hot Springs. *0.3 m.*, **Two Rivers PA.** *0.5 m.*, **Raab FS CG.** *0.2 m.*, **Collowash River,** looping and twirling and giggling and humming; the self-occupied loner making its own action. *2.7 m.*, jct., **Bagby Hot Springs.** Turn R for hot springs. *1.7 m.*, **Kingfisher FS CG.** *4 m.*, **Pegleg Falls FS**

CG. Falls low (about 40 ft.) but broad, and chanting like backcountry choir. *0.5 m., Bagby Trailhead. (1.5 m.* on gentle trail to hot tub Bagby Hot Springs, volunteer venture which attracts young nature lovers. The way of the trail is reason enough for going to the hot springs. Along a melodic creek that at places is breathtaking to behold, giant firs stand at ease, looking like burly loggers surveying their work for the day. Entire FS trail is 12.5 m., provides access to Bull of the Woods, and winds up at Elk Lake.)

The remotest area in this region is Bull of the Woods — from Ripplebrook R S 19 m. by road and 3 m. via trail. The 10,200-acre sea of forest, at the far headwaters of the Clackamas, contains craggy mtns.; 12 high, small, fish-stocked (chiefly brook trout) lakes, not all of which are accessible by trail; and some old mines. Beware of partially-concealed shafts. This is not an area for the weak or for those lonely away from crowds; the largest number of camp units at any lake is four, at Pansy; five lakes have no camping facilities; and all facilities are primitive. FS tries to keep area as it was when Molalla farmer Bob Bagby shot a bull elk, thus the name, "Bull of the Woods." FS says: "Come prepared to face the extremes of weather encountered in high mountain country. Snow blocks many of the high elevation trails until late June." And it advises: "Bring your own shelter."

Return to jct., FS Rd. 46, near Ripplebrook FS CG. (FS Rd. 46 is the extension of O 224; same road, different designation.)

Turn R, onto FS Rd. 46. *0.1 m.,* **Riverford FS CG.** *2.9 m.,* **Austin Hot Springs.** The natural hot water springs on a utility's 10-acre park was for decades the domain of people. In mid-1980s the word went out, "A resort will be built there," and the groaning began. Money had won out.

8.5 m., jct. *(27.2 m.,* US 26.) Keep straight on FS 46.

7 m., Olallie Lake Jct.

* Take FS Rd. 4690, leaving main hwy., FS 46. *2.7 m.,* 1-way wooden bridge over cheeky creek. *4.5 m.,* jct. — way to US 26. Stay with pike to Olallie Lake. *4.3 m.,* Big Spring, a gushing in the woods. *0.2 m.,* to R, **First Lake Trail.** The lake isn't that great but the modest hike thru the woods is delightful. **Lower Lake FS CG.** *0.7 m.,* turnoff to Olallie Lake Summer Resort. *(0.1 m.,* **Olallie Lake,** reflecting in the sun the white blazing face of Mt. Jefferson. Nowhere is the peak of this mtn. seen with sharper clarity. The largest of the more than 200 lakes and ponds in the vicinity of 7,210 ft. Olallie Butte, the 1 1/4 m. long, 188-acre Olallie Lake, at 4,936 elev., is off-limits to motor powered boats and is well stocked with rainbow and eastern brook. FS CG here.)

0.9 m., **Camp Ten FS CG.** *0.4 m.,* **Peninsula FS CG.** *0.3 m.,* **Monon Lake,** a delicate leaf glistening on the floor of the omnipresent forest. *1.4 m.,* **Horseshoe Lake,** the Walden Pond of the area. *2.1 m.,* Jefferson Wilderness Area parking. Jumpoff point at shore of Breitenbush Lake for one of Oregon's most popular mtn. scenic areas.

(Condition of the road for next 6.5 m. has traditionally been horrific.)

*6.9 m., jct., FS Rd. 46. Turn L onto it.

On FS 46 from Olallie Lake Jct.:

6.7 m., turnoff to **Breitenbush Lake and CG.**

* 6.8 m. lake and CG. Lake, small (65 acres) and shallow (most of it less than 10 ft. deep), is popular with anglers for fine late summer fly fishing. Return to FS Rd. 46. Turn L.

0.4 m., turnoff L for Breitenbush Community.

* 0.5 m., forks. Take L. 0.8 m., **Breitenbush Community,** at what is formally known on maps as Breitenbush Hot Springs. Colorful rustic collection of backwoodsy structures and hot springs bath. Community insists upon advance notice of coming; it rejects notion that it is a casual tourist attraction. Return to FS Rd. 46. Turn L.

50 yds. from Breitenbush Community Rd., **Cleator Bend FS CG.** 4.4 m., **Humbug River FS CG.** 0.3 m., turnoff R to Elk Lake (6.6 m., in rugged country.) 0.7 m., **Breitenbush River.** In many a state, particularly on Great Plains and in SW, this stream would be regarded as major. In Oregon, it is only locally known. 4 m., O 22, Detroit.

Turn W for I-5 and Portland. (For route from Detroit to I-5, see *Trans-Cascade Roads, O 22.*)

Lolo Pass — Lost Lake

Between the real start of this Lolo Pass road and Lost Lake there is nary a house to be seen. But the feeling of being away from it all is not totally present. A huge giant chain of transmission line towers dominates part of the road. In large measure they mar the view of Mt. Hood, but where there are clearings and the forest does not shroud the mtn. there are perspectives of Hood seen nowhere else. And all are impressive.

In autumn the hillsides are aflame with color; some people cut down branches of vine maple to take home for floral display.

Lolo Pass, for some reason or other, was named by a FS official for Lolo Pass in the Bitterroot Range of Idaho-Montana. It was about the most difficult stretch of the Lewis and Clark Expedition, who didn't come anywhere near the Lolo Pass in Oregon.

The Lolo Pass road has its start in the S at Zigzag, on US 26. (From Portland to Zigzag, see *Trans-Cascade Roads, US 26.*)

1 m., on L, Brightwood Jct. The covered wagons bumped down this part of the Barlow Road, the worst behind them. Another two days and they would be in the Willamette Valley.

3.1 m., turnoff to Ramona Falls. (Take it.) 0.6 m., forks. Take R, at bridge. Cross bridge. 0.3 m., on L, **McNeil FS CG.** 0.2 m., forks. (To R, 1.9 m., Horseshoe Ridge Trailhead.) Take L. 1.2 m., Ramona Falls — Lost Creek Jct. 0.3 m., forks. Take R. 0.1 m., **Lost Creek Nature Trail.** A 15-minute walk reveals remnants of a buried forest, variety of plant species and a beaver pond community. Return to nearest forks, *0.1 m.* Turn R. *0.4 m.,* forks. R for **Burnt Lake,** *1.3 m.*

Return to Ramona Falls — Lost Creek Jct. Take road toward **Ramona Falls.** *0.3 m.,* forks. L, *0.2 m.* to Lower Trailhead. R, *1.6 m.* to Upper Trailhead.

From Lower Trailhead it is 4.5 m. round-trip to Ramona Falls. From Upper Trailhead it is 3 m. round-trip to falls, but the road is heinous. (FS states: Road not maintained for passenger vehicles.") FS, which calls Ramona Falls "the most popular day hike in the Mt. Hood Wilderness," describes the trail as "almost flat" and a "good choice for hikers seeking a trail with minimum of obstacles and exertion." Yes and no, depending on heart and lung condition. For the average hiker, the trip from the Upper Trailhead to the falls should take about an hour, the return about 45 minutes — which says something about the grade. Ramona Falls, a 50 ft. swan dive of the Sandy River, and as romantic as its name, is dazzling, electric, lyrical, and ought to remind moviegoers of the 1930s and 1940s of the backdrop to flashy musical comedy dance numbers.

Return to Lolo Pass Rd. Turn R. *6.3 m.,* **Pacific Crest Trail.** From here you can take off on trail up to Canada or down deep into Calif.

25 yds., jct. Turn R, toward Lost Lake. *1.3 m.,* forks. To R, **McGee Creek Trail.** Summer sees McGee Creek sweet as cold soda pop but in early spring it can be a rage. Take L. *4.3 m.,* forks. Straight. *5 m.,* forks. Straight. *2.3 m.,* narrow wooden bridge across W fork of Hood River. *1.1 m.,* Lost Lake — Hood River jct.

Turn L for Lost Lake. *5.6 m.,* jct., Wahtum Lake. *0.1 m.,* jct. If you take L fork

Lost Lake

you'll drive for miles on narrow road thru deep, bristling forest. Interesting, if you have the time. R fork, *0.5 m.*, start of **Lost Lake.** For best view, drive to upper end of lake (*0.6 m.*), where road runs out. On clear day, Mt. Hood reflected in water with near-perfect clarity. Trail around lake (3 m.) is brisk hour hike for those in the pink, but nature lovers will take longer.

As with so many places, there are varying accounts of when whites first saw the lake; dates range from 1850 to 1880. Some accounts say original name was Blue Lake, which seems reasonable and mundane enough from a look at the water, and that the name was changed to Lost Lake because whites who "found" it gave flawed information as to its location.

Indians of the area had a more poetic name for the lake: *E-e-Kwal-a-mat-yan-ishkt*, Heart of the Mountains. That was a long time ago, before the paleface CG, store, boat launches and the rest. At any rate, there are no less than 13 lakes in Oregon named Lost and this 231-acre beauty at elev. of 3,143 ft. is the fairest. (For Indian legend, see *Mt. Hood Loop*, preceding.)

Return to Wahtum Lake Jct. Take Wahtum Lake Rd., narrow but smooth and easy pike to drive if you don't speed. At 30 m. per hour it's a piece of cake. No habitations and only signs of past or present logging activity. *7.6 m.*, jct. (R, 18 m., Hood River.) L, uphill, *5 m.*, forks. Take L. *1 m.*, **Wahtum Lake CG** — quite primitive. *0.2 m.* trail to 62-acre, 3,732 ft. elev. **Wahtum Lake,** which *Atlas of Oregon Lakes* calls "an excellent example of a cirque lake, its basin carved out by glacial erosion." Fishers at the lake say only the true believers come here. *0.5 m.*, turnoff to Scout Lake. *0.5 m.*, **Scout Lake,** another small mtn. lake that attracts the adventurous. *1.9 m.*, from turnout to Scout Lake, **Indian Springs FS CG,** far out in the primitive. For the hardy and the happy.

Return to Wahtum Lake — Lost Lake Jct. Turn L for Hood River. *5.6 m.*, Hood River-Lolo Pass jct. Turn L for Hood River. *2.6 m.*, bridge across Hood River. *1.1 m.*, another bridge across Hood River. *2.5 m.*, jct. Turn L, toward Hood River. *1.8 m.*, jct. Angle R. *0.1 m.*, **Dee,** at lumber mill by RR tracks. In 1915 Dee had pop. 250, with own water works and electric lighting systems, as well as stores and shops. Today it is more of rural area than anything else. Mill and town both started 1906; only mill carries on.

0.1 m., Parkdale Jct. Turn R. (Odell and Hood River to L.) *5.4 m.*, **Parkdale,** at store this side of RR tracks. Return *50 yds.* to Baseline Rd. Take it. *0.8 m.*, continue straight on Lava Bed Dr. Up close are lava mounds, huge deposits of most recent volcanic outpouring of Mt. Hood. Follow pavement 0.5 m. to end.

Return *0.5 m.*, to Old Parkdale Rd. and turn L onto it. *0.2 m.*, turn L onto Red Hill Rd. *0.8 m.*, Middle Fork, Hood River. *0.7 m.*, paved road to L. Continue straight. *0.8 m.*, second turnoff to L, gravel FS road. Here are splendid views of Mt. Hood and Hood River Valley.

Return to Parkdale store (this side of RR tracks).

Parkdale, in midst of orchard country — in spring a fairyland; in autumn a fruited cornucopia — is fitting name. Founded 1910, Parkdale is rather recent

Parkdale Lava Beds

community. The hub of a fruit belt, it sees a lot of seasonal workers, mostly Hispanic these days. Easterners who take a quick glance at the town think it "rustic" and "isolated" and look upon its residents as "hicks," not realizing that Parkdale is full of big city emigres.

From Parkdale store continue *0.5 m.,* to jct. and turn R onto Cooper Spur Rd. *8.1 m.,* Cloud Cap Jct. Turn R, uphill. *1 m.,* turnoff to Cooper Spur Ski Area. *3.7 m.,* **Inspiration Point.** *5.1 m.,* turnoff to Tilly Jane FS CG. *0.6 m.,* **Timberline Trail.** *0.2 m.,* parking below **Cloud Cap Inn,** 6,000 ft. elev. Short trail leads to aerie confrontation with Eliot Glacier, second largest in Oregon. (For more on Cloud Cap, see *Trans-Cascade Roads, I-84, Hood River.*)

Return to Cooper Spur-Parkdale Jct. Straight. *1.8 m.,* O 35 at hamlet of Mt. Hood. Turn L. *6 m.,* Odell Jct. Turn L. *0.8 m.,* **Odell,** another 1-street fruit town.

Return to O 35. Turn L. *0.3 m.,* Sunday Rd. (See *Mt. Hood Loop,* immediately preceding.) 2 m., sliver hamlet of **Pine Grove.** *2 m.,* turnoff for Panorama Point. *1.6 m.,* **Panorama Point,** grand view of Mt. Hood and Hood River Valley. (Rest rooms.) Return to O 35. Turn R. *2 m.,* turnoff to Hood River city center. *0.4 m.,* turn L onto I-84. Follow freeway back to Portland. (See *Trans-Cascade Roads, I-84.*)

Henline Falls — Opal Lake

This is a star-studded truly off-the-beaten-path tour that requires some stamina, strong hands at the wheel, and a keeping of the cool. Few people have been to some of these places and perhaps not more than a score to all of them. Photo opportunities are plentiful and the trip can be broken by (and enhanced with) a dip in a vibrant stream.

Take I-5 to O 22, 2 m. S of Market St. Exit, Salem.

Proceed E on O 22 to Mehama Jct. (For places along O 22, see *Trans-Cascade Roads, Oregon 22.*)

At Mehama Jct. backtrack *50 yds.* (W) to Fern Ridge Rd. and turn N onto it. *1.3 m.*, turn sharp R onto dirt and gravel road. (Cattle guard should be crossed within *0.1 m.*) *1.3 m.*, park at side of road. Look down to R. The cross-forked cataract splashing off a fallen tree is 120 ft. **Stassel Falls.** Across road take path, at R side of Stassel Creek (and not often easy to see from road), *0.3 m.*, gentle trail to **Shellburg Falls,** plunging 100 ft. (or more) from mammoth overhanging rock. One of the more impressive falls in Oregon and good for rolls of film. Path continues around falls and uphill; "good" trail runs out in *0.5 m.* at rustic wooden

Mt. Hood as seen from Panorama Point   *Courtesy State of Oregon*

Shellburg Falls   *Phoebe L. Friedman*

bridge over stream beyond top of falls. Absolutely do not put a foot on trail leading to top of falls! Much too dangerous.

Continue *0.8 m.* beyond Stassel Falls to **Mary Lou Ebert Primitive CG,** on L. The person who described this place as primitive was quite sincere. Bring water — and almost everything else.

Return of O 22. Turn E.

0.7 m., turnoff to **Little North Santiam Rec. Area,** known locally as Elkhorn Rd. This is an exhilarating drive, full of surprises for the adventurous. For the others, the river is recreation enough. It is so lovely that some people come here just to look at it. And look. But the greatest joy is in following it and seeing it from perspectives of water level and from high, high above. There is not a tepid yard to the Little N Santiam, nor is there a nuance of consistent mood. All one can say, heart in thrall, is that morning breaks at every curve.

2 m., **North Fork CP.** PA on mesmerizing stream. Fishers come in droves. *5.4 m.,* on L, **Canyon Creek (BLM) Rec. Site.** CG, PA, fishing. *0.4 m.,* **Bear Creek CP.** *0.8 m.,* on L, **Elkhorn Valley (BLM) Rec. Site.** CG, PA, fishing.

1.4 m., Mile marker 33. Turn L onto gravel road at first lane, 35 yds. *0.4 m.,* on R, and shrouded by brush, beehive-shaped rock known to locals as **King Tut's Tomb,** though it did not always have that name. An anecdotal history of the rock was given by Ray Stout, who first saw it in 1894:

"It became generally known by the people in the community when someone

King Tut's Tomb   *Phoebe L. Friedman*

suggested that it looked like an ancient temple and soon a number of men began working there, blasting and digging in an effort to find a way into the interior. All of this happened in 1894, there were hard times all over the United States.

"About the same time, Jacob S. Coxey was leading a band of about 20,000 unemployed from the middle states to Washington, D.C., and they were receiving much publicity.

"Work at the rock continued for some time and it was publicly reported that they were only a short distance from the interior, and if it did prove to be a temple it should have an owner and Jacob S. Coxey was honored. So it became known then as 'Coxey's Temple.'

"King Tut lived about 1344 B.C. His tomb was not discovered until 1923. Too late for us Old Timers."

A narrow, rocky, uncertain path has frieze-and-panel like formations that seem strangely akin to ancient Egyptian architecture or, to some people, a miniature Temple of the Sun in Mexico. Two cavities in rock could be taken for burial chambers.

Return to Elkhorn Rd. Turn L. *1.4 m.*, entrance to Elkhorn Valley Golf Club, one of fairest courses in state. *0.9 m.*, Elkhorn Woods, just a fanciful cabin. *1.9 m.*, on R, **Salmon Falls CP.** Trail leads to twin waterfalls that make up for lack of

Salmon Falls   *Phoebe L. Friedman*

height with volume and beauty. *0.2 m.,* first opening on R, trail of 300 yds. leads to rock ledge down which Little N Santiam plunges.

0.3 m., said by some old timers to be site of **Elkhorn,** which in 1915 had pop. 150 and was active mining town.

0.4 m., on R, Elkhorn Dr. Directly off Elkhorn Rd. there are few houses. Most of the dwellings are out of sight and the only clue to their existence is found in clusters of mailboxes along road. Many of the dwellings are closed off by steel fences; a resident said, "We're more protective here than we were in the city." Elkhorn Dr. leads in initial stage to colony of affluent river homes. Beyond colony the road turns tough, rocky, ofttimes narrow, climbing, climbing until it seems the road is a thousand, 2,000, 3,000 ft. higher yet above the river. The world

Henline Falls   *Phoebe L. Friedman*

seems to be built of mountains piled upon mountains, with leering faces of mountains so dim you think they could be wiped off the picture if only you had a cloth big enough.

Finally, 6.2 m. from Elkhorn Rd. — it seems much longer — forks. Take L, downhill. 1 m., **Elkhorn Lake.** If anyone else is there, the inclination is to ask, "How did you ever find this unposted place?" Except for the sense of discovery, the lake, small and shrouded by tall timber, can be missed without feeling guilty about it.

Return to Elkhorn Rd. Turn R. 0.2 m., forks. Take R. 0.4 m., entering **Willamette Natl. Forest.** 0.7 m., 1-lane wooden bridge over Henline Creek. 0.6 m., forks. Take L.

0.2 m., first opening on L, FS "road." Turn onto it. 0.6 m., up road to Ogle Mtn. Trail, on L. Follow forest path 0.3 m., to **Henline Falls.** Henline Creek splashes down a cliff into a dancing pool. Sunlight turns the falls into a magic shower hidden in a faerie glen. Alone, singing in the wilderness, dancing with uninhibited verve, the falls combine flair and grace. Falling only about 80 ft., it seems higher, probably because of its buoyant nature. Best photos are taken from below, on rocks and logs in pool. From 50 yds. away there is the illusion — or the reality— of a 3-pronged falls. At path's end, and next to falls, is old mine tunnel, dark and dank, that is best left unexplored. At one time the mines in this area — especially the Bonanza, Silver Star and Black Eagle — were quite active.

Return to Elkhorn Rd. (If you turn L, road goes on in fair condition for 5 m., but there is nothing out of the ordinary to see except pockets in hills to L. These are old mining tunnels and should be avoided, being in varying states of decay and liable to collapse.)

Return to first forks. Turn L, toward Opal Lake. Now begins climax of this tour — one of loneliest and most intriguing drives in W Oregon.

0.8 m., on R, trail downhill to **3 Pools,** on Little N Santiam. Stream here is piercingly translucent, flecked with every color of the rainbow, and gorgeously frothed — and cold. In summer the few who come here sunbathe on rocks, later submerged by autumn rains. From above, river looks like something out of an Italian travel poster, with the stream rushing thru clefts and past cliffs and pillars and battered columns. Send photos of this scene throughout the land and tourists will rush here en masse.

0.5 m., on L, old **Forestry Guard Station.** This is the only house along the road, and most times no one is there.

0.6 m., **Shady Grove FS CG.** Delightful grove on river. Not uncommon for deer to prance by. This is as far up the road as most people go, and it is Paradise for those seeking clean air, crisp water, and uncrowded ambience.

2 m., on R, **Sullivan Falls.** The cool water skips and scoots and curlicues down a vertical gulf between mossy boulders. Fall appears at least 150 ft. (though it has lesser drop); from road you can't see to top — and there's no trail up.

Three Pools
Phoebe L. Friedman

From here the road starts to climb, and if you're afraid of spiraling uphill or of looking down at sheer drops from road's edge, return to Shady Grove and enjoy.

1.1 m., bridge across Cedar Creek. *0.5 m.,* forks. Take L. *0.7 m.,* forks. Take R. Now, for inexperienced rough mountain country drivers, the road becomes scary. The stream seems a mile below, at times the road constricts into a tight knot, at too many other places a slip off the road would be fatal. (there are no shoulders or guard rails and on one side no banks), and the condition of the pike is even more exasperating and ominous than the road to Elkhorn Lake. Beyond the deep canyons, mountains loom ponderously. If one were to write a book, *Where to Hide the Bodies in Western Oregon,* this pike would certainly be included.

4.4 m., wide spot in road — parking for **Opal Lake.** To L, discernible to naked eye, lake is a blue shimmer in a green basin. A trail, if it is not overgrown or wiped out by rain or snow, leads thru woods and bogs to rarely-used lake. It is about 30-minute hike to lake — and the way uphill is not recommended for cardiacs and asthmatics.

From L side of lake it is about a 40-minute tussle to **Upper Opal Creek Falls** thru Douglas firs (some of the giant trees at least 400 years old), hemlock, cedar, Noble fir, anemone, rhododendron, fireweed, wild canterbury bells, huckleberry bushes, Devils club and salmonberry. Upper Opal Falls has descent of about 25 ft. but appears more. It is about 60 ft. drop from bottom of upper falls to ledge of Middle Falls, which has a drop of about 165 ft. From bottom of Middle Falls to ledge of Lower Falls there is a riffle about 65 ft. long, and the descent of Lower Falls is about 170 ft. The only way to get from Upper Falls to Middle and Lower

Falls is by intricate maneuvering and a stout rope, and persons unfamiliar with the woods are urged not to try this trek; if you haven't got time, strength, competent companions and forest savvy, don't go beyond Opal Lake. That has its fill of solitude. At Opal Falls you can stay all summer and may not see another soul. Opal Creek arises from a spring in the hills, flows thru Opal Lake, and erupts in the 3-level falls which, incidentally, are not on official state or FS maps. About 5 m. from falls, Opal Creek unites with Battleaxe Creek to form Little N Santiam. (For heroic story on this area, see "A Name for Opal Creek Falls" in author's *Tracking Down Oregon*.)

A question may be raised about the pike beyond the parking area for Opal Lake. It is a bummer, a car-killer. Anything less than a 4-wheel-drive is doomed.

For the masochistic, a very rugged trail leads to **Phantom Bridge** and a *3 m.* "trail" to **Dog Tooth Rock** (*0.3 m.*, rock, odd-shaped glint in darkling sea of green. *6.5 m.* from trailhead to Dog Tooth Rock), O 22, *0.3 m.* W of Detroit.

Best to turn back at Opal Lake lookover. Return to O 22 and turn W for I-5; proceed to Portland via I-5 or, at N of Salem, O 99E.

Oregon 211

Oregon 211, with its tributaries, forms one of the most historic trips in the Willamette Valley. This is true earthbreaker country and although there is little real evidence of the pioneer days, touches of the spirit remain and fill the air.

Opal Lake   *Phoebe L. Friedman*

Phantom Bridge   *Courtesy US Forest Service*

The trip begins in Sandy, at jct. of US 26. (For road to Sandy see *Trans-Cascade Roads, US 26.*)

0.1 m., on L, delightful **Meining city park.** *2.2 m.,* on R, old **Sandy Ridge**

School, out of Norman Rockwell. Thru the windows, students could look out to Mt. Hood, horses and meadows. *0.7 m.,* turnoff E *(0.2 m.)* to **Sandy Ridge Cemetery;** markers back to 1862. *1.6 m.,* on W, **Forester Cemetery.** Stunning view of Mt. Hood from knoll. Buried here is Rick Sanders, who won Olympic silver medals for wrestling in 1968 and 1972. He was killed in Yugoslavia while hitchhiking. *1 m.,* on R, old **Eagle Creek School,** combined with the new. *0.2 m.* on E, at jct., **Foster Plaque.**

Here was the last great encampment for emigrants coming into the Willamette Valley. From here the wagons spread out in all directions, many going on first to Oregon City.

At jct., near plaque, to L, or E, old O 211, now SE Eagle Creek Rd.

* 0.4 m., at end of shops, on L, turn uphill. *(0.2 m.,* end of road, at private house. Short walk to **Foster Cemetery,** where lie Philip Foster and his wife, Mary Charlotte Pettygrove, the Burtons, other early settlers, and the first two graves, that of Mary Conditt and Nancy Black, both aged 9, who died Sept. 7, 1853, after gorging themselves on the thick, fleshy peaches, hot under the burning sun of that late summer afternoon, in the Foster orchard. They were wrapped in blankets and laid to rest on a hill overlooking the campground. [See "A Corner of History at Eagle Creek" in author's *A Touch of Oregon.*] For permission to take road to cemetery, inquire at shop office.)

Return to old O 211. Turn L. *0.6 m.,* turn L, or N, onto Wildcat Mtn. Rd. *1.7 m.,* "Y". Take R, onto Eagle Fern Rd. *2.2 m.,* Kitzmiller Rd. Turn L. *0.6 m.,* on R, **N Fork Eagle Creek BLM Rec. Site.** A rare CG; so close to settlements and seeming so far off. Return to Eagle Fern Rd. Turn L. *0.1 m.,* **Eagle Fern CP,** a leafy rural gob of goodness on Eagle Creek. *0.7 m.,* jct. On R, bridge over Eagle Creek. There are always some people, especially the young, in the creek on a fair summer weekend. Continue straight. *2.4 m.,* on L, at curve of road, was PO of homesteader burg of **George.** PO started 1880s; long out of business. PO not named for Washington but for US Rep. Melvin C. George of Oregon. He died 1933, about time town did. *0.7 m.,* on

Graves of girls who died at Foster Campground

L, **George Cemetery,** lovingly maintained. Graves go back to 1880s. *0.8 m.,* on R, **George Presbyterian Church,** built 1890s; long abandoned; every year or oftener there is word it will be torn down. Too bad.

Return to jct. of SE Eagle Creek and Wildcat Mtn. roads. Turn L, or E. *2 m.,* on L, store, last of **Currinsville.** Near here PO named Zion was est. 1874. PO name changed to Currinsville and moved here 1884. PO closed 1906. In 1915 town had pop. 150, PS, church, Grange, Equity Assn., Temple and Lodge. *1.8 m.,* forks. (To R, *0.5 m.,* Estacada.)

At forks, continue straight on W 6th Ave., which becomes Coupland. *1.7 m.,* turn L onto Currin Rd. *1.4 m.,* turn R at forks. *2.1 m.,* forks at end of Eagle Creek Bridge. L for Eagle Fern Park *(0.7 m),* R for PO of George *(2.4 m.).*

Return to jct., Coupland and Currin. Turn L onto Coupland. *1 m.,* on L, **Palmateer Farm.** Settled 1853 as DLC. House built 1890. With house came deed signed 1866 by President Andrew Johnson. *0.1 m.,* forks. Turn R. *0.1 m.,* turn R at jct. *1.3 m.* on R, **Garfield Community Church,** last remains of Garfield settlement. PO founded as Leon 1897, closed 1906.

At Eagle Creek jct., near plaque: For better or for worse, this is the center of **Eagle Creek,** stream named 1844. There are several creeks named Eagle in

Winter steelhead fishing below River Mill Dam   *Courtesy Oregon State*

Oregon but no other settlement called Eagle Creek. It is presumed the creeks were named Eagle because eagles were observed at the creeks. Thankfully, the eagles were not always around to inspire the name, otherwise the creeks called Eagle would have to be numbered.

Straight on O 211: *0.1 m.*, on E, site of home Philip Foster built 1845. There now stands home built by Foster's son 1884. In front is largest lilac bush in Oregon, planted before Oregon became a state, and bringing to mind the evocative words of Walt Whitman: "In the dooryard fronting an old farmhouse near the whitewash'd palings,/ Stands the lilac bush tall-growing with heart-shaped leaves of rich green." Across O 211 is house purportedly built 1860 but remodeled. House next to it, on S, built 1880s and also greatly changed.

0.2 m., jct. Take L, O 211. *1 m.*, Wildcat Mtn. Rd. (Take L for Eagle Fern CP. See above.) *2.7 m.*, jct., River Mill Dam.

   * *0.2 m.*, turn L. *0.3 m.*, **River Mill Dam**, on Clackamas River. Built 1911, dam looks like calendar art of early 20th century Americana. PA.

1.5 m., **Estacada**. Why this shady river town, surrounded by greenery, should have been named for the naked, stark plains of NW Texas, the Llano Estacado, only illustrates the misplaced imagination that is so abundant. Close to Portland, town has such bucolic air about it that it is a chore to determine whether it is rural, industrial rural or suburban. (It has elements of each.) To add to complexity, economy is largely based on lumber. When mills are down, unemployment and troubles soar. There have been times when school operation was uncertain because of tendency of hard-hit residents to vote down ballot measures for school financing. Among interesting places in town are **Rock House**, one of oldest bldgs. in community, at SW Lake and Beech, and **Estacada Area Historical Museum**, in city hall.

0.2 m., jct., O 211-O 224. *1 m.*, jct., McIver SP.

   * Turn R. *1.2 m.*, "T". Turn R. *1.2 m.*, **McIver SP.** CG, PA, DS, FHP, showers, boating, fishing, equestrian area. *1.6 m.*, parking for Clackamas River. Turn L. *0.4 m.*, **Clackamas Fish Hatchery** — salmon, steelhead. Evening visitors to hatchery regularly see herons in area. **Milo McIver Memorial Viewpoint**, near front of SP, reveals Mt. Hood in all its glory.

   * From McIver SP jct.: Turn L — for Springwater and Metzler CP. *3 m.*, **Springwater Church**, venerable institution here. Part of Grange hall once was section of old school; bell between Grange and church belonged to school. Springwater PO 1874–1914.

0.5 m., jct. Straight. *1.3 m.*, **Metzler CP.** CG, PA. Park is lovely prairie on crystal clear, carefree creek.

On O 211, from McIver-Springwater jct.:

2.4 m., Springwater Jct.

   * *0.1 m.*, on L, stately house that has such an air of importance and mystery about it that travelers invariably ask, "What is it?" *0.4 m.*, **Springwater Church**, store.

0.5 m., turnoff to Metzler Park.

    * *0.6 m.,* jct. Turn L. *1.5 m.,* **Metzler Park.** *5 m.,* on L, turnoff to cemetery.

    * *0.4 m.,* on R, 1-room country schoolhouse, now **Elwood Community Center.** Across roads are **Elwood Community Church** (1903) and **Elwood Cemetery** (1890). In 1915 this was a thriving little settlement, with pop. 110, two sawmills, PS, United Brethren Church. Now it is just a loose network of rural homes.

4.5 m., **Colton.** Store. Outstanding feature here is Colton (Swedish) Lutheran Church, whose elegant steeple sheds pure beauty over village. *3 m.,* **Cedarvale.** Store. *1.8 m.,* **Meadowbrook..** Store. In 1915 there were two flour mills and PS. PO (1895–1905) had already departed.

Mulino Jct. Turn L for Molalla.

3 m., forks. Take L.

    * *0.3 m.,* jct. Take L. *0.7 m.,* on R, turnoff to Adams Cemetery. (*0.6 m.,* jct. Straight. *0.2 m.,* forks. Straight. *0.4 m.,* **Adams Cemetery,** one of best-kept small town burial grounds in Oregon and, from its repose on knoll, historically one of most scenic. Markers go back to 1852. Here lie the illustrious and the unknown of the Molalla plains, so deeply rooted and yet so unostentatious in Oregon history.)

    Return to S Feyrer Park Rd. and turn R. *0.5 m.,* forks. Straight. *0.6 m.,* on L, **Pacific NW Live Steamers,** a truly free fun spot. From May thru summer, visitors can ride miniature trains on elaborate grid of tracks, picnic on grass (tables provided), enjoy the camaraderie of this friendly hobby place on Shady Dell. Molalla Slough, at rear of park, at first glance appears as roily afterthought. But in late autumn, when the tourists have gone and the shy stream breathes free again, come quietly and look close and you may see a Great Blue Heron swoop down to the water, disgorge a guttural cry, and with a swift unfolding of its enormous wings undercut the wind as it soars toward the waving plume of a tall tree. And in the wake of the heron's flight a beaver snubs upstream toward a jerrybuilt wanigan it will call its winter home.

    Return to S Feyrer Park Rd. Turn L. *0.3 m.,* **Feyrer Memorial CP,** on skipping-along Molalla River. CG, PA. *0.1 m.,* "T". Turn R for Dickey Prairie. *1.7 m.,* **Dickey Prairie Store.** This is approximately the center of what was fertile Dickey Prairie, settled early by hard, obstinate overlanders and probably the earlier site of a Molalla Indian campground and the later scene for *The Earthbreakers,* a novel by Ernest Haycox. Today Dickie Prairie is a suburb of Molalla, which is an extended suburb of Portland. *0.3 m.,* forks. Take R. First lane on R leads *0.2 m.* to site of **Dickey Homestead** (private property). Dickey family plot is *0.5 m.* from house, thru fields. (Private.) There are a number of such family plots around Molalla. Before community cemeteries (and even after their arrival in some cases) it was common for families to bury their dead on their land, often right in the middle of the farming acres. One is reminded of Gray's "Elegy": "Beneath those rugged elms, that yew-tree's shade/ Where heaves the turf in many a mouldering heap/ Each in his narrow cell for ever laid,/ The rude forefathers of the hamlet sleep."

From O 211 and forks that lead to Pacific NW Live Steamers:

0.7 m., main intersection, **Molalla,** named for Molalla Indians. First PO called Molalla est. 1850; PO of Molalla in town of Molalla est. 1875. Town has grown slowly, steadily, its only tourist lure being the Molalla Buckeroo, which in 1940 *Oregon: End of the Trail* called "the largest rodeo in western Oregon." That claim would now be disputed by rival towns. There is a settled "old" ambience about Molalla, as befits a settlement whose hinterland was first staked out by a white 3 years before the first covered wagons arrived in the Willamette Valley. In 1915, Molalla had pop. 350; by 1940 had increased to 655; by 1965 had shot up to 1,650. When pop. soared above 3,000 in mid-1980s, locals boasted that for a small town Molalla was pretty big. **Molalla United Methodist Church,** Main and Sweigle, is typical 19th-century-like house of worship, with attractive bell tower. Bldg. at 112 N Molalla, put up 1875, has been restored to original anatomy. It was used as drugstore, school, furniture store, funeral parlor, barn, speakeasy, meat market, and a lot of other things.

In 1976 Molalla made regional front page news over a stormy "free speech" battle. Briefly: a HS teacher who thought his students should be exposed to a broad spectrum of political ideas and who in the past had invited Republicans, Democrats, Libertarians and John Birchers to speak, found himself under bitter attack for scheduling a 78-year-old Beaverton Communist to address his students. Leading the assault upon the teacher's plan was a private detective who had moved to Molalla 2 years earlier. The private eye, a follower of the Christian Anti-Communist Crusade, formed the ad hoc Molalla Citizens for Better Education and collected 800 signatures urging the school board to bar the Red from speaking in the HS. The board voted to ban, which brought the American Civil Liberties Union, defender of free speech for all persons, into the fray. The matter went to court, the school board's edict was overturned, the Community eventually spoke, and the walls of the HS did not collapse.

On O 211, at main intersection, Molalla:

* Turn L, toward Wilhoit Springs. *0.4 m.,* on R, at 616 S Molalla, **Dibble House,** built in mid-1850s for 1852 comers Horace L. and Julia Ann Dibble of Van Buren County, Iowa. The Dibbles and their children found the house well constructed — the timbers and lumber were all hand prepared — and the two story house commodious, with six rooms, two downstairs fireplaces, parlor, buttery and cellar. Back of the Dibble House was moved the Von der Ahe house, built 1865 and restored by Molalla Area Historical Society. Small structure at rear was the "summer house," used for harvest time canning. *0.7 m.,* forks. Take R. *1 m.,* on L, **Molalla Memorial Cemetery** (1882). *0.6 m.,* turnoff to **Glad Tidings** (*3 m.,* site of where stood hamlet of Glad Tidings. PO 1860–1887. Name's origin remains mystery.) *3.8 m.,* forks. Straight. *1.3*

Dibble House, Molalla

m., site of **Wilhoit Springs.** In 1866 John Wilhoit found land which contained mineral springs. That gave him an idea — to start up a health and recreation resort. In 1882 Wilhoit PO est. About turn of century Wilhoit Springs was becoming one of the great spas of Willamette Valley. Folks from the cities came by train and steamer as far as they could, then rented buggies. Many families loaded children and camping gear into their wagons and traveled for several days or longer to get here. In its prime the spa had resort hotel, rows of cabins, huge campground, restaurant, store, dance hall, bandstand and more. But the mineral springs partially dried up and other attractions arose elsewhere. Nothing now but grass and a sad mineral water trickle at the far end.

Return to last forks, *1.3 m.* Turn L. *1 m.*, jct. Take R. *1.1 m.*, forks. Take L. *0.5 m.*, jct. Turn R. *2.5 m.*, jct. Turn L. *0.2 m.*, turn L onto Crooked Finger Rd. *0.1 m.*, on L, **Scotts Mills CP.** Dazzling waterfall of Butte Creek brightens park and seems to reflect colorful garb of Old Russian visitors from Woodburn-Gervais area. Return to Crooked Finger Rd. Turn L. *4.7 m.* forks. Take L. *0.2 m.*, **Queen of the Holy Rosary Church,** built 1896 on site of Molalla campground. Outside church is great rosary made of floats. Return to forks. Turn L onto Crooked Finger Rd. *1.2 m.*, old country school, boarded up. *0.6 m.*, on R, picturesque farm with windmill. *5.4 m.*, take road to L. *1.9 m.*, on L, obscure level spot, for parking. Walk back 50 yds. to low culvert. Take trail to R. *0.3 m.*, **Lower Butte Creek Falls.** *0.5 m.*, **Middle Butte Creek Falls.** *0.5 m.*, **Upper Butte Creek Falls.** These are among the most spectacular falls in the Willamette Valley, the upper and middle being magnificent in their leap, thunder and beauty. Be cautious on trail.

Scotts Mills County Park

Return to jct. of Crooked Finger Rd. Turn L. *0.1 m.,* **Scotts Mills.** Settled 1850s, named 1866, PO 1887. In 1915 town had pop. 375; fewer today. Christian Church of past is now **Scotts Mills Museum.** Across street, city hall is one of smallest in state. Looks like doll's house. Next to it is frame bldg. from

Our Queen of the Holy Rosary Catholic Church

Upper Butte Creek Falls

long-gone era. On same street, Grandview, 2 blocks uphill to **Friends Church** (1894). On way up, on L, is house that might have been painted by Van Gogh if he had come to Scotts Mills.

Return 2 blocks to road at bottom of Grandview. Turn L. *2.6 m.,* jct. Turn L for Silverton. *1.3 m.,* on L, **Miller Cemetery** (1852), an acropolis of the dead. (Best rubbing here is marker of Samuel Markham, father of poet Edwin Markham.) Chapel, with original pews, is older than most of the buried; it passed century mark years ago.

0.5 m., jct., Abiqua Creek Rd. Turn L. *5.3 m.,* forks. Keep R, on Abiqua Rd. *3.5 m.,* forks. Take L. *1. m.,* jct. Turn L. *0.1 m.,* turn R, up narrow dirt lane. 75 yds., **St. Nicholas Church,** warm pastoral chapel far out in the sticks. Legend has it church was built for benefit of sheepherders. This seems a bit wooly but it makes a nice tale. (Church on private property. Inquire at house below.) Return *1.1 m.* to forks. Take L. *3.8 m.* over narrow, very rocky dirt (and in season muddy) trace thru sparsely inhabited country to where trace broadens. Parking area for hike to Abiqua Creek; trail starts here. *0.5 m.,* sharp, slithery decline to creek. (No place for cardiacs, timid or uncoordinated.) Turn L at creek. *200 yds.* up creek to open-faced view of **Abiqua Falls,** a wide, thundering, 80-ft. cascade. Abiqua Creek leaps over the rim of a solid rock bowl that is cliff from top to bottom. Spectacular is mild for this sight.

0.3 m. from parking area, faint trail to overlook of falls. *50 yds.,* take another trail, to R, *50 yds.,* overlook. You are now on cliff's edge; be cautious. View from here is of Abiqua Creek coming down from L and joined by smaller fall from R before combined water roars down the ledge.

Return to Silverton Rd. Turn L. *3.1 m.,* downtown **Silverton.** (For Silverton, see *Short Trips Out of Portland, O 213,* immediately following.)

On O 211, at main intersection of Molalla, Main and Molalla: Straight toward Woodburn.

1.5 m., jct., O 213. *3.7 m.,* jct., Yoder-Canby.

* L for Yoder. *0.9 m.,* **Yoder.** Store, est. 1915. Yoder family settled here about 1888 and place first called Yoderville. When electric Willamette Valley Southern RR was put thru here, elder Yoder decided to open a store. RR folded after about decade and a half, store stayed on. Yoder never had PO. Lumber mill, started 1891, and still in Yoder hands, has outlived three conflagrations. Yoder also had egg plant once; closed to become part of regional co-op.

* R for Canby. *0.4 m.,* on L, **Smyrna Church** (1891) and **Smyrna Yoder Cemetery.** For several decades church was center of rural life in this area and is still prominent as community hall. *0.5 m.,* Sconce Rd. (Turn L. *1.6 m.,* on R., **Rock Creek Church and Cemetery.** Church, built 1857, is small, weathered, genial-looking, and quickly brings to mind the "church in the dell" hymn. Cemetery, dedicated 1852, was lovingly landscaped and contains some intriguing inscriptions; for example, that on stone of C. G. Wenger, who died 1881: "Shortly before his death a white dove sat on the window sill of his father's sleeping room in Pennsylvania." Continue on Sconce. *0.4 m.,* Barlow Rd. Turn L. *1.1 m.,* O 211.)

* (From Sconce Rd. toward Canby: *4.5 m.,* on L, **Gribble Homestead.** House, not the first residence here, built 1890s. Home sits on Gribble Prairie, named for 1846 overlander John G. Gribble, Carolina born and Missouri farmer who came to Oregon at age 47, next year acquired DLC. *0.7 m.,* Lone Elder. *2.3 m.* O 99E at Canby.)

On O 211 at Yoder-Canby Jct., straight for Woodburn: *2.4 m.,* Barlow Rd.

* Turn L for Monitor. *3.2 m.,* forks. On R, **Nidaros Community Church,** stereotype of white-painted frame rural churches which profusely dot lower Willamette Valley. Take R at forks. *0.4 m.,* on R, example of the comfortable prairie home so common century ago. *0.2 m.,* on L, attractive **Seventh Day Adventist Church,** built in style of 19th century churches. *0.1 m.,* forks. Straight. *0.1 m.,* **Monitor,** one of the small hinterland villages enveloped by fertile land, small farms, and a plenitude of homes. More non-farmers reside between these valley hamlets than do those who work the soil. An old timer, pointing to a row of houses, said: "When I came back from World War II there was still none of this here. It's all changed." Monitor had hopes when

Abiqua Creek Falls

Rock Creek Church and Cemetery

the electric RR bound for Salem came its way. But it never rose above flour mill and pop. 50. Mill is gone and pop. hasn't jumped. Store.

At O 211 and Barlow Rd. Straight for Woodburn. *1.4 m.*, Meridian Rd.

   * Turn L. *0.6 m.*, **Elliott Prairie Congregational Church** (1893), sweet pastoral scene reminiscent of New England churches. The New England influence in rural church architecture spread to the "middle states" of Ohio, Indiana, Illinois and Iowa and carried W to Oregon.

At O 211 and Meridian Rd. — straight. *3.8 m.*, O 99E, at Woodburn. (Follow O 99E N to Portland. See *The Great Heartland, O 99E.*)

Oregon 213

This is another historic road, and enhanced by its many variations of mood. Along its main route and byways it reflects the nuances of the Willamette Valley.

From 82nd and Sandy:

At 82nd and Sandy: On E, formidable former bldg. of **Shriners Hospital for Crippled Children.** E of that, off Sandy, **The Grotto.** (See *The Great Heartland, Portland.*)

2.1 m., Burnside St. (E for Gresham, US 26.) *1.2 m.*, Division St. (E, *12.6 m.*, Gresham.) *0.5 m., Powell Blvd. (E, 12.2 m.*, Gresham.)

0.5 m., Holgate St., **Multnomah Cemetery** (1888). *0.5 m.*, Foster Blvd.

    * *4.2 m.*, on L, **Lakeside Gardens,** restaurant in idyllic setting. *0.6 m.*, **Pleasant Valley.** Store. *4.4 m.*, Damascus Jct., O 212. (L, *4.6 m.*, Boring. R, *2.4 m.*, O 224, Carver-Estacada Jct.)

1 m., Flavel St.

    * E: (Flavel becomes Mt. Scott): *1.2 m.*, **Lincoln Memorial Park,** cemetery that has all the appearance of a swank country estate. One wonders how much cemetery land any country can afford. *0.9 m.*, **Willamette National Cemetery,** the great burial ground of war veterans. *1.4 m.*, **Happy Valley.** Center of village is fire station.

0.8 m., Johnson Creek Blvd.

    * This artery has gained some dubious distinction because the creek is a frequent spillover. Comes a heavy rain, everyone knows the creek will be over its banks and the people on the creek will have renewed headaches.

0.7 m., King Rd.

    * W: *3 m.*, Milwaukie, thru the rear door. More refreshing than the O 99E entrance.

0.9 m., Sunnyside Rd.

    * *2.6 m.*, **Sunnyside.** Store, Grange hall. PO here from 1888 to 1903. *0.2 m.*, on R, big old red barn that looks like it ought to be heaped with pumpkins. *0.6 m.*, 147th St. (L, *1.1 m.*, Scouter's Mountain gate. See *Trips Out of Portland, East B.*) *3.4 m.*, Damascus.

0.7 m., jct. O 224.

    * *0.2 m.*, jct. at overpass. Turn W. *3.1 m.*, Monroe St., Milwaukie. Turn R. *0.3 m.*, city center Milwaukie.

    * From jct. at overpass, turn E. *1.1 m.*, **Clackamas.** PO est. 1873. In 1915 Clackamas had pop. 75 and was known for farming and logging. It is now hip area between freeways. To miss Clackamas is no call for heartbreak.

At jct., O 224 and 82nd, O 213 and O 205 combine.

0.8 m., jct., O 212-O 224.

    * *0.2 m.*, jct. at overpass. *0.7 m.*, Clackamas. *1.5 m.*, Gladstone Exit.

    * *1.1 m.*, **Gladstone.** Not the town you see on O 99E but a hamhock hamlet of an earlier day.

0.8 m., Park Place Exit.

    * Road off exit becomes O 213 again. *1.2 m.*, in Oregon City, turn E onto Abernethy Rd. *0.5 m.*, turn R. *5.1 m.*, **Redland.** Store. PO 1892–1903. Turn L. *3.1 m.*, **Fischers Mill.** Store. This area seems far removed from Oregon City, with its relative lightness of traffic and its abundance of quiet.

From O 213 and Abernethy Rd., continue on O 213.

0.5 m., Washington St. Turn L. *0.6 m.*, 7th St. Angle L. *0.7 m.*, Hilda St.

    * Turn L. *0.3 m.*, **Mountain View Cemetery.** Buried here are Peter

Skene Ogden, Forbes Barclay, William Barlow and Sidney W. Moss. (For more, see *The Great Heartland, O 99E, Oregon City.*)

0.5 m., Warner Milne Rd.

* Turn R. *0.7 m.,* Linn Ave. Turn L. *0.5 m.,* on R, gravel lane *(0.1m.)* to 1851 **Ainsworth House.** Return to Warner Milne Rd. Straight, 1 block, Warner Parrott Rd. Continue straight *0.5 m.* Turn R onto Holmes Lane. *0.1 m.,* on R, 1847 **Rose Farm,** 2 1/2 story dwelling. (Across Holmes Ln., 1898 house.) Return to Warner Parrott Rd. Turn R. *0.3 m.,* Canemah Ave. On L, first lane leads *0.1 m.* to restored 1850 **McCarver House.** First prefab house in Oregon. Return to Warner Parrott Rd. Turn L. *0.6 m.,* South End Rd. Turn R. *0.8 m.,* turn sharp L onto 5th Ave., which becomes Miller. *0.3 m.,* turn onto 4th. *0.2 m.,* L onto Blanchard. *0.2 m.,* gateway to **Canemah Cemetery.** *0.5 m.* trail to cemetery, one of oldest in state. Return to Miller and 4th. Straight on 4th. *0.1 m.,* turn L onto 3rd. *0.1 m.,* R onto Hedges. 1 block, McLoughlin Blvd. Turn R. *0.8 m.,* Main and 5th, downtown Oregon City.

From Warner Milne Rd. and O 213, continue on O 213:

0.1 m., Beavercreek Rd.

* Turn L. *1.3 m.,* **Clackamas CC.** *3.2 m.,* **Beavercreek.** Oregon is replete with creeks named for the beaver, attesting to what was here in the first half of 19th century. Today, more than one Beaver Creek hasn't seen a beaver in many decades. In 1915 settlement had pop. 200, Improvement Club, Grange Society, 8 churches, and the official state almanac reported: "Good country roads lead into this section, making it desirable for automobiles to take pleasure trips from Portland." Beavercreek went into a decline after that but has come back, as center of suburban area. At Beavercreek Store, straight. *0.1 m.,* on L, **Bryn Seion Welsh Congregational Church** (1884). On last June Sunday, church holds *Gymanfa Ganu Blyndol,* Annual Song Fest, with music in Welsh and English. Singing starts after lunch at nearby Grange hall. (For more on church and songfest, see *The Great Heartland, O 99E, Oregon City.*)

Return to Beavercreek Rd. Turn R. *0.8 m.,* bend R. *1.5 m.,* on R, **United Church of Christ,** better known as Ten O'Clock Church. Latter name came about, according to old time officials, because first parishioners were German-born and accustomed to going to church at 10 a.m. in the old country. Therefore, early church here had face of clock painted on church, with hands pointing to 10 o'clock, a reminder for farm families who could see clock from appreciable distance that services started at that time. *0.1 m.,* **Ten O'Clock Cemetery,** est. 1859. *1.4 m.,* Upper Highland Rd. All traces of Highland as a village long ago vanished. *2.1 m.,* on L, **Clarkes Store,** opened 1928. Clarkes PO 1889–1904. *2.3 m.,* on R, **Clackamas Pioneer Cemetery** (1870). *3.6 m.,* O 211, at Meadowbrook. Short years ago the pike between the cemetery and Meadowbrook contained tingling glimpses of a valley seemingly hung in space below — but no more.

From Beavercreek Rd. on O 213, continue on O 213:

1 m., on L, **Clackamas CC.** *2.4 m.,* New Era Jct.

   * Turn R. *1.3 m.,* turn L. *4.3 m.,* New Era. *0.3 m.,* O 99E.

1 m., Kirk Rd.

   * Turn L. *0.9 m.,* on R, **Carus Cemetery** (1851). Here is gravestone of Mary Vowell Adams, who died 1852, soon after crossing plains. At first she was buried in city cemetery in Portland, where Skidmore Fountain now stands. When the city began to spread out, the bodies were moved to other places. Mrs. Adams' remains were taken to homestead est. 2/11/1853 by her husband, Charles, and his second wife, whom he married two months after Mary's death. (For an absorbing account of Mary Vowell Adams, see *Reluctant Pioneer* by Beatrice L. Bliss.) Also buried here are three Buckner girls — Alabama, America, and Missouri.

0.4 m., Carus Rd. **Carus** PO 1887–1907. In 1915 hamlet had two sawmills, daily stage to Oregon City and twice-daily stage to Canby. Today: school, church.

   * Turn L. onto Carus Rd. *1.9 m.,* turn L onto Karmath Rd. *0.5 m.,* **Beaver Creek Cemetery.** Gravestones back to 1887.

3.9 m., **Mulino.** First known as Howards Mill, Mulino PO est. 1882. In 1915 it had flour mill, green house, shingle mill, sawmill, Grange. Baptist church by side of road has that look-feel of old-time religion. Abandoned flour mill is anchor to past. Store, cafe.

Canby Jct.

   * 7.4 m., **Canby.** The county seems so peaceful it ought to be set aside as a rural preserve. The road winds slowly, silently as a cat on a lazy prowl, thru pungent farmlands, eventide softening the land and rubbing the barns and houses and stacks of hay and clumps of cottonwood with a sort of Currier and Ives nostalgia. Summer mornings splash their cargos of sunlight upon the meadows and in the radiance the wrinkles of time seem erased. A woman from Mulino said: "I've never taken this road but that I didn't feel good taking it."

1.4 m., Union Mills Jct.

   * *1 m.,* on R, and back off road, **Trullinger House.** A lot of Trullingers settled in this area, dating back from 1852, when 1847 emigrant Gabriel J. Trullinger took up DLC on Mill Creek. He built sawmill, added wood carding machinery, constructed planing mill, calling his creek industries Union Mills. One of the Trullingers, a Portland dentist, married Louise Bryant, who subsequently left him for John Reed; another, Corinne Trullinger Chamberlin, distinguished herself as a medical doctor, and won the love of thousands of Gresham-area people for her skill and caring. She made house calls to the end and, in the tradition of pioneer doctors, often traveled alone, over dark and unknown roads, sometimes in the dead of winter, to respond to emergencies. Still another prominent member of the clan was John Corse Trullinger, warehouse owner, farmer who pioneered in sowing timothy, flour miller, sawmiller, timberman, and organizer of the Oregon Republican

MISSOURI A. BUCKNER
BORN IN
Torney One) Missouri.
NOV 21 1849.
DIED
DEC 17 1867.

ALABAMA BUCKNER
BORN IN
Clackamas Cou. O.
October 26 1860.
DIED
NOV. 16. 1867.

AMERICA A. BUCKNER
BORN IN
Bates County Missouri.
January 21 1852.
DIED
AUG 19. 1868.

Three sisters in Carus Cemetery

Party, cattleman, town developer, builder and operator of Astoria's first electric lighting plant, and bona fide inventor. Present Trullinger house is not the original but it has tolerable age, which it wears gracefully. Next to house is feed mill, greatly remodeled, which Gabe Trullinger built as flour mill in 1868 or 1877; present Trullingers aren't sure. Mill overlooks Mill Creek, which even in low profile has bubbly cheerfulness. *0.2 m.,* on R, lodge hall, which was schoolhouse, in its elderliness a weary frame with an expression as vacant as the bell tower.

0.1 m., **Union Mills Store.**

From Union Mills Jct., continue on O 213:

0.2 m., on L, site of former Wagon Wheel CP, on the cold Molalla River. People still go there to swim, picnic.

0.5 m., **Liberal.** First PO, est. 1850 by Harrison Wright, 1848 comer, was called Molalla. Liberal PO est. 1893. Village was never more than small earthbreaking settlement. But in 1915, with pop. of only 50, it had Grange, Mother's League, Development League.

Macksburg-Canby Jct.

* To W: *4.4 m.,* site of **Macksburg.** In 1915 burg had pop. 200, two Lutheran churches. One of the churches survives — and there is no town. *4.3 m.,* Canby.

0.7 m., Molalla Jct.

* *2.9 m.,* Molalla. (See *Oregon 211.*)

0.8 m., Needy-Hubbard Jct.

* R on S Barnards Rd.: *5.2 m.,* Needy Rd. First known as Hardscrabble, despite fertility of soil, **Needy** received its name from impoverished state of first white settlers. PO est 1855 but gave up ghost long ago. There is today no sign of where Needy stood when, around turn of century, it had small but brisk commercial district. 6 m., Hubbard.

1.6 m., Jct., O 211 — Molalla — Woodburn.

* E: *1.5 m.,* Molalla. W: *11.3 m.,* Woodburn.

1.3 m., on L, rambling old frame prairie house that ought to be preserved.

5.5 m., **Marquam,** not named for the same Marquam after whom Portland's Marquam Hill and Marquam Bridge are named. For years hop growing was the principal industry here — but no more. Store.

Scotts Mills-Canby Jct.

* S: *2.3 m.,* Cemetery Rd. (*0.3 m.,* Scotts Mills Cemetery, old burial ground.) *0.4 m.,* Scotts Mills. (See O 211.) N: *13.8 m.,* Canby. There is not a settlement between Marquam and Canby and the interlude is lovely.

0.1 m., **Marquam United Methodist Church,** in 1890 simple and dignified wooden structure.

1.9 m., Mt. Angel — Scotts Mills Jct.

* *4.6 m.,* Mt. Angel. *2.6 m.,* Scotts Mills.

1.4 m., **Miller Cemetery.** Many a pioneer of the Silverton country lies here;

gravestones go back to the 1850s. (And many a funeral service was held in the chapel, constructed 1882, with pews built with square nails.) But most impressive marker of all is that of Samuel Markham, and whoever put it up sought fame for Samuel thru his son. For inscription identifies Samuel as "Father of the Poet Edwin Markham" and contains one of Edwin's phrases: "Of all things Beautiful and Good/ The Kingliest is Brotherhood." On a third side of the marker is etched in stone Millet's painting of a bowed, broken French peasant, which inspired Markham to write his monumental poem, "The Man With the Hoe." But the name of Samuel Markham can stand by itself. More fitting than being named father of the poet is a carving, on one side of the marker, showing an ox team crossing the plain. That's what Samuel Markham did, in 1847. He came to the Silverton area just a few years after the first white settler arrived. He plowed, he tilled, he gathered his crops, and when his time came he was laid to rest near

Grave of Samuel Markham, Miller Cemetery

where he had first planted roots in the new land in Oregon. He needed no celebrated son to bring him honor. That he had earned alone.

0.4 m., Abiqua Creek Jct. (For directions to spectacular Abiqua Falls, see *O
211.*)

3.3 m., Silverton — Jct. O 224.

At first glance **Silverton** appears as one more prosaic, tedious town in the
5,000–6,000 pop. class. Its business district still has strong touches of the 1930s,
though it is modernizing — and not always for the best. But even a brief sojourn
thru the town reveals bits of excitement. The library is excellent and a genuine
learning center for the people. **Silverton Museum,** in 1908 Ames-Warnock
House, has exhibits going to back to 1840s. Next to it, at 424 S Water, is old RR
depot, now office of chamber of commerce. Police station was office of Fischer
Flour & Cereal Mills of long ago. At 104 S Water is bldg. that once housed Reo
Cafe, operated by the owners of Bobbie, Scotch collie whose phenomenal feat
made it the most famous dog of its time. In the summer of 1923, when Bobbie was
2 years old, he was taken by Frank and Elizabeth Brazier, owners of the Reo
Cafe, to Indiana, where the Braziers planned to visit their families. In Wolcott,
Indiana, Bobbie disappeared. After a frantic but fruitless search the Braziers gave
up and continued their journey. Nine weeks after their departure from Silverton
the Braziers returned home, convinced they would never see Bobbie again.
Then, on a sunny midwinter afternoon early in 1924, 6 months to the day the
collie last saw the Braziers back in Wolcott, he reappeared in Silverton. He was
thin, exhausted, his paws worn to the nub, and he was in pain — but he had come
home. (For story on Bobbie's incredible journey, see "The Saga of Silverton Bobbie" in author's *Tracking Down Oregon.*)

At 421 and 435 N Water are elegant Victorian houses of 19th century. Gingerbread house at 105 Grant is one of handsomest old homes around. At 314
Jersey stands former Calvary Lutheran Church and Parsonage, now **White Steeple Gallery and Tea Room.** Church was originally conceived in 1887; construction started in 1890 and in 1891 was occupied by First Church of Christ. In 1906 it
was purchased by Lutherans and renamed Norwegian Lutheran Church. In
1926–27 it was remodeled to its present configuration. Sold in 1975; in 1984 White
Steeple Gallery opened for business. Whatever its history, church bldg. is one of
Silverton's fairest sights.

Site of **The Commercial Bank,** 315 E Main, was location of Cottage Hotel,
Victorian-style rooming house, whose most famous occupant was Clark Gable.
William Clark Gable had come from Portland to be with local girl and aspiring
actress Frances (Franz) Doerfler, whom he had met in a theater stock company in
Portland. Here in Silverton he worked for several weeks as a lumber stacker for
Silver Falls Timber Co., located near Hobart Rd. and 2nd St., earning 40 cents an
hour, and known to his co-workers as Billy Gable, "who was always clowning
around." He started Dec. 5, 1922 and worked until mid-January, 1923. After work
on Friday he would walk the 8 miles to the 1870s Doerfler house, still standing, at

13772 Doerfler Rd., and stay there until Sunday evening. For months, in Portland and Silverton, Gable pressed Frances Doerfler to marry him but she bade him wait until they had financial security. Then, after Gable became a pupil of Portland drama teacher Josephine Dillon, whom he later married, he broke with

White Steeple Gallery, formerly Calvary Lutheran Church, Silverton

Courtesy Louis Androes

Frances. (She passed away in a Portland nursing home in 1980.) A feature writer for the Silverton *Appeal-Tribune* wrote of Clark and Doerfler in an article titled, "The Great Romance of Silverton."

Buried in town cemetery, on road to Salem, is Homer Davenport, Oregon's greatest cartoonist. Born on a farm S of Silverton, he fell in love early with the town and even after he became a world traveler, Silverton remained deep in his heart. He once wrote: "The strangest part of Silverton is that it never releases me a day from its hold. A day never passes that I don't hurry over its streets, see its remaining pioneers and in my vision replace those that have gone . . . I have thought of it while seated in the ruins of the Coloseum at Rome, thought of it in London and Paris and Constantinople, thought of it while resting in the deathlike silence and shadow of the Sphinx, and told it near the Euphrates River in Arabia, while among the wild tribes of Anazeh."

There have been many interesting educational experiments in Oregon since the first school opened on French Prairie in 1835. One of the least known and most idealistic took place in Silverton, with est. in 1896 of Liberal University by activists of the Oregon State Secular Union. At a time when all schools of higher education outside the state system were under church control, Liberal University adopted as its credo: "The only religions to have an influence on educational institutions are the religion of right living and the religion of science and humanity" and the articles of incorporation declared: "All education shall be kept forever from and uninfluenced by any kind or form of theology, sectarianism, supernaturalism, Christian or other, and that no religions or religious creeds, catechisms, dogmas, public prayers, masses, sacraments, incantations or religious exercises shall be allowed upon its property or premises under its control." Despite negative reaction to it from some of the townspeople, Liberal U got off to such a strong start that in 1899 it moved into then modern bldgs. on its 44-acre campus. But disputes as to what paths the school should take rent the faculty and supporters and in 1903, when it had become clearly apparent that the breaches could not be closed, Liberal U folded.

From stoplight at jct., O 214, in downtown Silverton, follow W Main St. S on county road.

    * *1.5 m.,* on L, **Evergreen Wayside CP.** *0.9 m.,* on R, picturesque Evergreen School. *2.7 m.,* Sunnyside Rd.

    ** Turn R onto Sunnyside Rd. *0.2 m.,* on L, lane of **Geer House.** Between road and 1847 Geer House stands Riding Whip Tree. Extended Geer family is one of most prominent in annals of Oregon. Homer Davenport, grandson of the Geers of this house, spent his happiest hours here, as he noted in pencil on a wooden slab on W side of house. Inscription begins: "I want to say that from this old porch I see my favorite view of all that the earth affords." The Riding Whip Tree grew from the branch of a cottonwood Homer's mother, Flora, plucked as she rode her horse home one night after a dance in 1853. The next day she thrust the branch into the earth. On 7/12/1936 the tree was

Riding Whip Tree   *Phoebe L. Friedman*

dedicated by a marker. (For story of Davenports, read "A Requiem for Homer" in author's *Tracking Down Oregon*.)
    ** Now the traveler is in the Waldo Hills, so piercingly beautiful with its
rolling topography and luminous swales and clearness of landscape as to

prompt even old Oregonians to gasp, "Yes, this is magical country." In May the green-drenched slopes and dips, so choreographically entrancing in their contours, have to be seen to be believed.

Earliest white settlement in the Waldo Hills was made 1843 by Daniel Waldo. Years later he wrote: "Oregon was just like all other new countries. For a long time we had to pack our own blankets and no place to sleep. There was only a little town at Oregon City. I always kept people without charging them a cent. I accommodated quite a number of people in my house out here on the road. We had not very many beds; they would sleep on the floor anyhow. I would give them supper and breakfast. It was pretty hard on the women but they were healthy . . . There was no sickness. More of the people got drowned in ten years than died . . . We had parties here in the early times and once in a while a dance. They [the settlers] would go 15 or 20 miles and think nothing of it. They would ride at a pretty good jog, men and women both. There were about as many women as men, young and old and married and all kinds . . . There was plenty to eat then; plenty of pork, beef and wheat. We had a fiddle of course."

Samuel L. Simpson (1854–1909), author of the volume of poems, *Gold Gated West,* spent several years of his youth in the Waldo Hills. T. T. Geer, Oregon's first native born governor (1899–1903), was born in these hills 1851. He went to school in Salem but when he was 14 he came back to the farm and made his living on it for 20 years. His book, *Fifty Years in Oregon* (1912) is a classic of pioneer life in the Willamette Valley.

Geer had a novel theory concerning human migration. He believed that instinct, originating in biblical times, pushed people westward instead of eastward. "Human history," he wrote, "does not record a single great movement of people to the eastward in any country." To prove the point, he explained, "The first emigration mentioned in either profane or sacred history is an account of how Cain, after slaying his brother Abel, moved to the Land of Nod, *East* of Eden. This so thoroughly disgusted people that from that day everybody else has been going West."

Frank Bowers, the cartoonist; Margaret Mayo, the playwright; and Margarita Fischer, screen actress, were also from this neighborhood.

** W on Sunnyside Rd. from Geer House lane: *2.7 m.,* on R, first of lovely old houses that continue on for about 1 m. on both sides of road. *1.8 m.,* **Pratum,** Latin for meadows. Area founded by Mennonites; has remained Mennonite stronghold. PO est. early 1887 as Switzerland. Ten years later name changed to Enger; year later to Pratum. Mennonite Church. 8 m., Salem.

* From jct., Sunnyview Rd. — toward Sublimity:

* *0.4 m.,* Victor Point Jct.

** Turn E. Out of the clean fields there springs a wildfire of yellow, a blaze of rape, looking as though it had catapulted out of a Van Gogh painting. The seed of rape (the name taken from the Italian *rapum,* meaning turnip) is shipped overseas, where its oil is used for cooking and industrial uses. At one time rape was fairly popular in Oregon; then became almost extinct; now is making comeback. *3.1 m.,* jct. Turn R. *0.4 m.,* **Victor Point School.** Across road was store, center of Victor Point, which began as Lewisburg for 1851 overlander Daniel Lewis. In 1915 place also had WOW lodge and Union Sunday School. Only school survives, and this one modern.

  * *2.6 m.,* Waldo Hills Dr.

  ** W, *5.2 m.,* Macleay.

  * *1.3 m.,* on E, **Silver Falls Vineyard** *1.2 m.,* jct., O 214 — Silver Falls SP.

  ** Turn E. *9.9 m.,* **Silver Falls SP.**

  * *2.6 m.,* **Sublimity.** Settled early (PO est 1852), town was named by its United Brethren founders, who subsequently moved on to Philomath, "for the sublime scenery in the hills around the town." Scenery is still sublime in the spring — as is all the area between here and Silverton — but it becomes choked and ugly at seed-burning time, after the harvest.

  * The 10th session of the Oregon Territorial legislature on 1/9/1858 chartered Sublimity College, a school of the secondary level sponsored by the United Brethren in Christ. Largely locally supported, school charged tuition of $5 and 50 cents more for each grade above the primary for each 12-week term. For those male students who could board themselves, a "bachelor's hall" was provided. The other students, particularly female, boarded in homes of townspeople. One of the first teachers, perhaps the first, was Milton Wright, father of Orville and Wilbur, both of whom were born after Milton Wright left Oregon. Fierce antagonisms engendered by the Civil War tore apart the college, the church, the town and the farmers of the area and in the early 1870s the school closed its doors for good. (It probably would not have lived much longer, anyway, as almost all such secondary schools were rendered obsolete by growing public education.) Little of old Sublimity remains, except for **St. Boniface Church** (1889), whose front entrance is reached thru archway of greenery. Cross atop steeple is highest man-made point in area. Cemetery to side. Sublimity College is believed to have been across street from St. Boniface Church. Slow to develop,Sublimity grew at average rate of only 14 persons per year from 1915 to 1990.

  * *1 m.,* O 22.

From downtown Silverton, at 1st and Main:

  * Take O 214 toward Mt. Angel. *1.2 m.,* Hobart Rd. Turn L. *0.1 m.,* James St. *0.2 m.,* **St. Paul's Catholic Cemetery.** *0.4 m.,* turn R for Gallon House CB. *0.5 m.,* **Gallon House CB,** last of Marion County CGs, built 1917 at 84' length, over Abiqua Creek. Before Prohibition, bridge was dividing line between "dry" Silverton and "wet" Mt. Angel. At that time Silverton had a powerful temperance organization, The Good Templars, and under its stern persuasion the town enacted under state local option a tough anti-liquor ordi-

St. Boniface Catholic Church, Sublimity

Gallon House Bridge

nance. Mt. Angel, for whatever reason, left the matter of imbibing up to each citizen. Since the drinkers in Silverton didn't want to travel all the way to Mt. Angel to get their booze and since the Mt. Angel suppliers didn't relish hauling their products into snoopy Silverton, it became a matter of tacit agreement that the Silverton drinkers and the Mt. Angel suppliers would meet at the Mt. Angel side of the CB to exchange cash for gallon jugs of "white lightning." (A sort of shed or shack was built there to handle the commerce.) The arrangement worked well until Prohibition became the national law in 1919. Thereafter, bootleggers sprang up like spring daisies in the green meadows in every town, hitherto dry or wet. Return to James St. Turn R. *0.8 m.*, Pine St. Turn R. *1 m.*, 1698 Pine, entrance to **Mikkelson Farm,** at one time scene of regional threshing bees and containing largest collection of steam engine threshers in PNW. *0.3 m.*, forks. (R, *4.1 m.*, Mt. Angel.) Straight, *0.4 m.*, **Bethany Pioneer Cemetery;** graves go back to early 1840s.

From jct., O 214, in Silverton, on O 213:

0.2 m., turn W on to McLaine St. (O 213). *0.6 m.*, **Silverton Cemetery.** Here lies Homer Davenport. Inscription on his tomb reads: "Homer Calvin Davenport 1867–1912. Erected by his friends in memory of Oregon's world-renowned Cartoonist."

4.5 m., Pratum-North Howell Jct. *2.6 m.*, 64th Pl.

   * Turn R onto 64th. *0.2 m.*, on L, **Howell Prairie Cemetery.** Markers back to 1842.

3 m., Lancaster Ave., Salem.

   * R, *1.2 m.*, O 99E.

2.3 m., downtown Salem.

(For return to Portland, take I-5 or O 99E.)

Oregon 214

O 214 takes off from O 99E at Woodburn. (For places along and off O 99E from Portland to Woodburn, see *The Great Heartland, O 99E.*)

From O 99E at Woodburn:

3.5 m., Monitor Jct.

   * *2.3 m.*, Monitor. Store

0.8 m., McKee Jct.

   * Turn R. *1.2 m.*, site of **McKee.** Started as RR station near Pudding River. In 1915 it had pop. 50. Only vestige of settlement now is old McKee School, *0.1 m.*, to R, presently a residence.

1 m., on L, **Simmons Cemetery,** above and partially shrouded from road. Grave markers back to 1852. *0.8 m.*, Calvary Cemetery. *0.5 m.*, Marquam Rd. At corner, on L, **Mt. Angel Cemetery,** est. 1860.

0.3 m., city center, **Mt. Angel.** Settled in the late 1840s, place was first named

Railroad Depot Clock Tower, Mt. Angel

Roy, in 1882. That year a narrow gauge RR came thru and station was called Fillmore. Then, in 1883, there arrived here from Gervais the Benedictine Father Adelhelm Odermatt, a theologian from Switzerland. He built a pilgrimage chapel on a 485-ft. hill the local Indians called *Tap-a-lam-a-ho,* but which whites changed to Lone Butte. Before the year was up, Rev. Odermatt was well on his way to having everyone think of the butte and the community as Mt. Angel, an anglicization of the German Engelberg, for the town in Switzerland where the good father had taken his religious training.

The Mt. Angel area was largely settled by Germans, as a visit to one of the local cemeteries will show. In 1915, when town had pop. 750, community had two German newspapers and monthly magazine. It also had Mt. Angel Academy for girls and Mt. Angel College for boys, Catholic institutions. Mt. Angel has grown slowly, gaining only about 2,000 pop. in 75 years prior to 1990. But good roads have made Mt. Angel practically a suburb of Salem. Some years ago the town made news when a movie, with Alan Alda and Will Geer, was shot here. Otherwise, except for visitors coming to Mt. Angel Abbey, town is quiet all year except during its high decibel Oktoborfest, held in the autumn.

Turn L onto E Church.

*0.8 m., turnoff to **Mt. Angel Abbey.** (0.7 m., past Stations of the Cross,

Abbey complex.) From a Catholic perspective it is logical for the Abbey to be located here since Indians came to this butte to commune with the Great Spirit. Some of the most ethereal views of the Willamette Valley are from butte; those who come only to look at bldgs. are missing a rare beauty. Apart from the magnificent church, points for the tourist include grotto of Our Lady of Lourdes, the Abbey museum (no great loss if it's missed), abbey cemetery and its chapel (oldest bldg. on hilltop), library and Russian Center.

The library, designed by architect Alvar Aalto, combines the face of modernism with the ambience of the scholastic middle ages. Its rare book collection, available for visitors to see thru glass, ought not be passed by. Oldest book, bible in two vols. (language is Frankish, German of that period), was printed 470–473.

Russian Center is museum of Russian "Old Believers," who came to French Prairie region in 1960s, after sojourn which started in the 1920s, when they left their motherland for Sinkiang Province and Harbin, in present People's Republic of China. When the communists came to power in 1949, some Starovery, the Old Believers, moved on to Alberta, Canada. A few years later two other groups left China for Hong Kong, then continued to Brazil, Argentine and Australia. A decade later the two Brazilian groups settled in the Willamette Valley, in and around Woodburn.

The Old Orthodox, as many of the Starovery call themselves, brought with them to Oregon the cultural baggage of centuries past; since the mid-1600s, when they broke with the Russian Orthodox Church because they regarded the reforms there as sacrilegious, the Starovery, as with all persistent minorities, clung adhesively to everything that would remind them of the "true" days. The Russian Center, started by Father Ambrose, a former Benedictine monk who converted to the Russian Old Orthodox faith, is a religious reflection of the scarf-wearing women and long-bearded men, easily distinguished by their embroidered garments, who inhabit the Woodburn-Gervais-St. Paul area. But one must remember that time and American pressures are nudging the children of the Starovery away from the old customs.

Abbey has its own PO — St. Benedict, Oregon.

From city center, Mt. Angel, on O 214:

4.6 m., Silverton. (See *O 213*.)

14 m., **N Falls Viewpoint, Silver Falls SP.** SP supposedly has largest concentration of waterfalls in US — 14, 5 of them more than 100 ft. high, the highest 178 ft.; 10 waterfalls within 3 m. radius. With its many firs, hemlocks, cedars and maples, and acres and acres of grass, and fine facilities, this scenic park is a true Oregon treasure. In addition to CG and PA, SP has DS, trails (connecting waterfalls), swimming, fishing, bike trails, camp showers, boating facilities, FHP. *1.3 m.,* Equestrian Area, Silver Falls SP.

Within expanse of park, on Silver Creek, was village of Hullt (PO 1891–1943),

alongside Silver Falls Timber Co. logging RR. Before est of SP, there was summer resort here. Hullt in 1915 had pop. 150, PS, Christian Church, store.

8 m., Sublimity-Stayton Jct. 2.4 m., Aumsville Jct. (Aumsville, 3 m.) 1.6 m.,
Macleay Jct.

    * 1.2 m., turn R. 1.5 m., turn L. 0.5 m., **Macleay.** Started as narrow gauge
station on Oregonian Railway Co., Ltd. Macleay Country Store in same
location since 1916. 8.5 m., Salem.

From Macleay Jct.:

0.6 m., Aumsville Jct. (Aumsville, 2.8 m.) 0.4 m., **Shaw.** Another place started
as RR station. In 1915 Shaw had two grain mills, which is more than it has now,
but its smallness of pop. has little meaning. Countryside is dotted with homes and
Shaw, like Macleay, is Salem suburb. Store.

1.7 m., O 22. Turn W. 9.8 m., Salem.

(Return to Portland via I-5 or O 99E.)

Shunpiking
West Side — O99W

Before I-5, the high-speed N-S freeway was built, the key routes thru the
Willamette Valley were US 99W and US 99E, both flanking the Willamette
River. At Junction City the roads combined, as they still do and US 99 was the
main artery to the Calif. border. After I-5 was built, US 99W and US 99E were
turned over to the state and became O99W and O 99E. You'll see much more of
Oregon by Shunpiking, taking O 99W and O 99E, as well as roads branching off
them, than you'll observe from the freeway.

West Side Shunpiking

6.6 m., from center of Marquam Bridge, Portland, turnoff to O 99W at N end
of Tigard.

1.5 m., jct., O 217 — the short road from here to US 26. Suffocated with commerce, it is best left alone. 0.2 m., Metzger-Durham Jct.

    * To W: 0.9 m., Metzger, a huddled corner in an industrial wind tunnel.
Bavarian Herman Metzger, who laid out the town in first decade of century,
would probably be surprised. 1.2 m., shopping center called **Progress** (PO
1889–1904). Engulfed by the giant mart of Washington Square. (3 m.,
Beaverton).

    * To E: 2.1 m., Tualatin Jct. Turn L. 0.5 m., on R, old **Durham School**
(1920). Open the front door and you step into the gym, assembly hall, lunch
room — multipurpose. 0.4 m., **Durham,** named for 1847 Oregon comer Albert Alonzo Durham of Oswego, New York, who put name of Oswego on
Oregon map. After making good elsewhere in vicinity, he came to Fanno
Creek and operated sawmill and flour mill. Turn R. 1.3 m., **Tualatin,** famous
for its golf course. The 1915 *Oregon Almanac* described the place as
"Tualatin River, beautiful stream for boating, fishing and picnicking. In a

town of beautiful suburban homes." The river doesn't seem as charming now and, as for suburban homes, Tualatin environs are flooded by forests of subdivisions. Tualatin and its neighbors comprise the Westchester County of Oregon.

* Stay on SW Boones Ferry Rd. *0.3 m.,* "T". To L at "T" is brick bldg. put up 1912 and bearing the stamp of solid, mercantile affluence of early 20th century. Across road, and just back of RR tracks, is beautifully restored **Sweek House,** built 1858, more than a decade before Tualatin had PO and more than half-century before town was inc. Lumber for "Willowbrook," as John and Marie Sweek called their mansion, came from McLoughlin Mill in Oregon City; window was brought 'round the Horn. House has same shape as it did when Lincoln became president. To R of Sweek House is Smith House, 1880s residence of more modest dimensions.

* Turn L onto SW Boones Ferry Rd. *0.2 m.,* Sherwood-Wilsonville Jct.
* Turn R, toward Sherwood. *4.1 m.,* on R, house of worship built as **St. Francis Catholic Church** in 1920s has pastoral look of less ostentatious period. *0.2 m.,* "T" Turn R. *1 block,* city center of **Sherwood.** Platted in 1889 by James C. Smock and named Smockville. But that sounded too hayseed for the ambitious upstarts, so 2 years later name changed to its present. Sher-

Sweek House, Tualatin   *Courtesy Jack Broome*

wood looks like a town designed by Norman Rockwell. It could be picked up and set down in New England and be right at home. Full of artisan shops, Sherwood could also be a stage setting for Thornton Wilder's "Our Town." Nice curiosity piece in Sherwood is Oriental Theater, started in late 1940s as the Robin Hood (a happier name). "Oriental" artifacts came from Oriental Theater in Portland at cost of $750. Seats are from old Molalla Theater — and 299 seats are staggered to provide clear views for all. Old movies shown, and every other week there is a silent flicker with organ accompaniment. Oriental has only 5 manual organ in any theater in US and is "only true Wurlitzer pipe organ around here," say owners.

* From Sherwood-Wilsonville Jct. Straight toward Wilsonville:

* 3.3 m., jct. Turn R onto road skirting Holiday Inn. 1.3 m., Boeckman Rd. Turn R. 0.1 m., "T". Turn L. 1.2 m., on R, **Meridian United Church of Christ,** affectionately called Frog Pond Church, because area was called Frog Pond. Congregation org. 1878; bldg. dedicated 1882; steeple added 1895. Bell brought 'round horn 1855; served old Aurora Colony Church until it disbanded. Belfry lighted every night as "an enduring beacon of faith." Lovely church, with almost homelike interior; the small simple pews adjoining a "living room" with fireplace. Walls covered with large photos of earlier days.

* 50 yds. Stafford Rd. Straight on Boeckman Rd. 0.3 m., SW 60th Ave. Turn R. 0.4 m., curve L. 0.3 m., turn R onto farm road at Abacus Farms. 0.5 m., **Kruse House.** White house to L was built 1857 by John Kruse, first man to put a steam-driven vessel on the river above Willamette Falls. Kruse married Iantha Geer, daughter of Joseph Carey Geer and built log cabin where giant tree looking toward river stood until toppled by Columbus Day storm of 1962. A great Douglas fir at one side of Kruse plot suggests it was a "witness tree," bearing testimonials of first surveyors. 1857 house has been remodeled but brick foundations on sides (and in cellar) are originals. Fine view of Willamette, with houseboats and rolling farmlands beyond, from Kruse House.

* Return to Meridian United Church of Christ. Turn L onto Wilsonville Rd., just beyond Stafford Jct. 2.2 m., on L, **Wilsonville Memorial Park,** city park with acres of recreationland. 0.6 m., **Wilsonville.** First known as Boons (not Boones) Ferry in 1876, after misspelled name of Jesse Boone, great grandson of old Dan'l Boone. Jesse knocked together a ferry boat to span the Willamette and then he cut a road thru the big trees clear to Portland town, and for a time Jesse's route was shortest thru the valley and on to Cal-if-or-ni-ay. Name changed 1880 to present, but Boone's Ferry, across Willamette, served until 1954. A brochure issued by local Booster Club states: "Wilsonville is an unmarked, totally unspoiled area of farms, homes and small businesses." Not quite. The traveler has the feeling here of having wandered into a middle class plastic bubble.

*5.3 m., on R, Ladd Hill Rd. At curve of Ladd Hill Rd., narrow, scarcely distinguishable brambly trace to R up stiff slope leads to tiny **Geer Cemetery** — only two graves now. Joseph C. Geer, veteran of War of 1812, staked his claim here, on Ladd Hill, in 1840s. His property extended to the river. Descendants of J. C. Geer have included T. T. Geer, Oregon historian and state's first native-born governor. Cartoonist Homer Davenport was a great-grandson. Geer's first wife, Mary, died 1847, and lies under a flat, faded marker. (Geer, too, reportedly buried here but there is no indication of his grave.) The other observable grave marker on the slope is that of Ruth Weeks, who was laid to rest in 1859.

* The rustic, winding road, following the contours of the Willamette, is blessed by joyous foliage. Between modern, affluent homes (and estates) is sprinkle of old houses. *2.3 m.,* on L, day use area of Willamette Greenway. *4.3 m.,* Springbrook Rd. House on R corner built 1874 on DLC of 1852. Barn built 1850. *25 yds* beyond Springbrook Rd., O 219. Turn R. *1.3 m.,* O 99W — Newberg.

* From jct., Boeckman-Stafford Rd., at Meridian United Church of Christ: Coming from Kruse Farm, turn R onto Stafford Rd. Coming from Wilsonville, angle L. *1.4 m.,* forks. Curve L. *0.8 m.,* turn onto Newland Rd. *0.4 m.,* **Stafford Baptist Church Cemetery.** Turn R. *0.1 m.,* **Robert Bird Cemetery.** The two cemeteries are as different as day and night. Stafford Baptist is neat, crisp, modern; Robert Bird has the rumpled, weatherworn look associated with pioneer burial grounds. Its markers have the toil-wept, earthy, philosophical characteristics that emerge from *Spoon River Anthology.*

* Return to Stafford Rd. Turn R. *1.7 m.,* **Stafford.** Feed store, tavern. There was more of a community in 1915. Stafford today looks like a hwy. hub of exits and roads spinning off in all directions.

* Turn L, toward Tualatin. *2.1 m.,* "T". Turn L. *1.2 m.,* "T". Turn R. *0.8 m.,* Tualatin. *4.3 m.,* O 99W.

From Metzger-Durham Jct., on O 99W:

0.1 m., turnoff E on Main St. (*0.1 m.,* downtown **Tigard.** There are towns in Oregon one-eighth the size of Tigard which have larger downtowns. Like so many other satellite cities, Tigard is stretched like taffy. A lot of Tigard folks don't see downtown twice a year. If people in a shopping center were told that downtown Tigard had mysteriously disappeared, they would probably mutter "Oh?", and go about their business.)

1.7 m., Canterbury Lane. Turn E, uphill. (*0.4 m.,* SW 103rd. On SW corner is 4-room 1880 house of John Tigard, son of town founder Wilson Tigard, Arkansas traveler of 1852. A century later there were still folks around who remembered the town as Tigardville. In 1915 it had only 300 pop. and its Grange was one of oldest in W. Grange, on E side of O 99W, looks in deep sleep, though it isn't always, and the small village of 1915 might well be 50,000 by end of century.)

0.2 m., Bull Mtn. Rd.

   * Turn R. *3.1 m.*, turn R onto Beef Bend Rd. *0.8 m.*, turn L onto O 210. *0.6 m.*, Vandermost Rd. (L, *0.8 m.*, turn L for Ponzi Winery, *0.2 m.*,) *0.2 m.*, Tile Flat Rd. House on NE corner probably built in 1860s, has original form, tone and gingerbread. Across Tile Flat Rd. is what may be oldest standing schoolhouse bldg. in Washington County, and long used as barn, mainly for sheep. Kinton Grange comes out of Grandma Moses painting. (See "Kinton Has Some Little Lambs" in author's *Tracking Down Oregon.*)

   In **Kinton** vicinity are some marvelous touches: barns that are calendar art, gingerbread houses, contoured fields pregnant with crops, apple orchards sheltered between hay fields, private dirt lanes that climb and wind and wink out of sight around a bend, fences with New Englandish motifs — and oh, so close to Portland. *1.7 m.*, on L, **Flint Farm:** two houses (each built circa 1885, the one on L for the servants) and watertower. One of fairest farm scenes in valley. B. T. Flint, of whom little has been written, was a most interesting man. A midwesterner raised, he had worked on a sheep ranch where Los Angeles is now spread. He purchased land at Scholls in 1865. Five times he crossed the Isthmus of Panama. A sheepman much of his life, he had seen sheep in Calif. suffer for lack of grass. Near the end of his life he extracted a promise from his family that the grass on his grave was never to be spaded. He is buried at Mountainside Cemetery.

   * *0.6 m.*, jct., locally called **Groner's Corner.** Two and one-half story white house on corner across jct. has look of an old, old lady whose face is as wrinkled as the ripples in the sea or as the furrows of an aged wagon road, yet remains sublimely beautiful. House was put up 1880 by John Groner and, at insistence of his wife, Ellen, constructed in shape of cross. Across road is handsome Georgian mansion built 1936 by Ferd Groner, who in 1905 brought first horseless carriage to community of Scholls. From the front windows of the brick mansion the occupants have almost a straightaway look at Bald Peak.

   * Turn L for Scholls. *0.6 m.*, Tualatin River. *0.5 m.*, **Scholls Store,** center of **Scholls,** named for Peter Scholls, who came to Oregon in 1847 but first settled near Oregon City. A grand-nephew of Daniel Boone, Scholls was pioneer in several ways. In 1849 he and James Rowell, one of first two settlers at what is now Scholls, built first sawmill in area, on N side of Baker Creek; it was run by water power. The next venture of Scholls was building raft of cedar logs, which he first operated as hand-powered ferry across Tualatin River. Thus came into being Scholls Ferry, and it placed the tiny settlement on the main route between Portland and Yamhill and Polk counties. Peter Scholls then built a toll bridge to replace ferry. According to *Scholls Ferry Tales,* published by the Groner Women's Club of Scholls in 1976, "It took the people of the Scholls vicinity three days to go to Portland with a load over the Scholls Ferry Road. They traveled in groups of three and five and always

Kinton School

carried a crosscut saw, an ax, and a shovel." In 1871 Scholls Ferry PO was est. In 1895, name shortened to Scholls. At one time Scholls was center of profitable walnut industry and Ferd Groner, who built the Georgian mansion at Groner's Corner, was renowned as "Walnut King of Oregon." But a series of disasters, culminating in the Columbus Day Story of 1962, killed the local walnut industry. Community Church is a long tradition but gone are the old brick and tile factory and the hop growers, and the dirt wagon roads to Hillsboro and Portland are now paved state hwys.

The feeling the people here have for their community was tenderly expressed in three verses of a poem by Ina Rowell Sutherland:

"When it is springtime in Tualatin Valley/ And Nature is at its best,/ I thrill, as I gaze on the landscape — / Most beautiful in the West.

"Chehalem Mountain in horse-shoe shape,/ Surrounds the village called Scholls,/ Where the grass is like the emerald, green,/ And the river Tualatin rolls.

"With friends, old and new, and hearts so true,/ Their friendship will never fail;/ Let me live in the little village of Scholls,/ At the end of the Oregon trail."

* *0.5 m.*, Baker Creek. *0.2 m.*, jct., O 219. Store on R was built as lodge hall around 1905.

* At jct., straight to Newberg, R for Hillsboro, on O 219. (For O 219, see *Cross-Coast Range Roads, US 26, O 219N.*)

From Bull Mtn. Rd. on O 99W:

0.5 m., on W, **King City,** inc. 1966, described succinctly by McArthur as "a planned adult community."

1.4 m., Tualatin — O 212 Jct.

* Turn E. *2.4 m.,* Tualatin. (For Tualatin, see earlier this section.) Turn L at Wilsonville-Scholls Ferry Jct. *1.5 m.,* turn L onto Borland Rd. Now the pike frees itself from the clutches of snazzy suburbia and rolls sweet and velvet thru farm country that is such a relief from the condo syndrome. *2 m.,* Stafford Rd. Jct. Straight on Borland Rd. *3.3 m.,* old settlement of **Willamette,** now part of West Linn. *2.8 m.,* turnoff for Willamette Locks and jct., Oregon City-Lake Oswego. Turn R. *0.2 m.,* Oregon City. (For West Linn, Willamette and environs, see *The Great Heartland, Short Trips Out of Portland, South Suburban* and *East Side Shunpiking, O 99E, Oregon City*.)

From Tualatin-O 212 Jct. on O 99W:

0.7 m., Cipole Jct.

* *0.5 m.,* on L, **Cipole School,** opened 1926 and now office bldg. School was center of onion-growing community of Cipole (Si-pole). Onion growing started in 1870s. "Cipole," or "Cippola," is, more or less, Italian for onion. *1.9 m.,* Six Corners — Sherwood — Scholls Jct.

* E for Sherwood. *1 m.,* Sherwood. (See earlier this section.)

* W for Scholls. *0.6 m.,* on L, **St. Paul's Lutheran Church.** Adjacent cemetery has markers back to 1880s. *1.2 m.,* forks. Curve R. *5.3 m.,* each m. zestful, Scholls. (For Scholls, see earlier this section.) *1.5 m.,* Middleton Jct.

* To E, turn sharp R after crossing N-bound lane of O 99W. *0.4 m.,* on R, **Middleton Pioneer Cemetery** (1874), all that remains to note village of Middleton, which in 1915 had four sawmills, two churches, pop. 75, and was on P.E. & E. Electric RR. *3.4 m.,* Parrett Mtn. Rd. jct.

* To E. **Parrett Mtn.,** a 1,243-ft. outthrust of the Chehalem Mtns., overlooks Newberg and its environs, especially from heights near top of mtn. Road follows form of bell-shaped curve. Realtors and developers are having a field day here and soon houses may be nudging each other for the "amazing" views, which really aren't that amazing anymore. *0.8 m.,* from O 99W turnoff to bottom of other side of hill.

0.7 m., turnoff for Rex Hill Winery (*0.1 m.*); turnoff E for Veritas Vineyard (*0.2 m.*).

1.4 m., Springbrook Jct.

* To R, *0.8 m.,* **Springbrook.** PO est 1893; village named for farm of local settler, prominent pioneer horticulturist Cyrus Hoskins. Springbrook in 1915 had big warehouse, owned by Fruitgrowers' Union, PS, Friends Church, pop. 200. For years town was known for its cannery, now plant for manufacture of pet foods. 1932 school was later sportswear factory; 1888 church is on last legs. But something new has come to Springbrook — the inevitable rows of middle class apt. houses, extension of suburbia.

* To L, *1.1 m.,* on L, 1874 **McKeon House.** Behind it, 1850 barn turned into winery.

0.7 m., Everest Rd.

* Turn L. *0.4 m.,* **GAR, Friends, Pioneer cemeteries,** all in a row. Markers go back to mid-19th century. Buried in Friends Cemetery are Miles Lowell Edwards, "co-inventor of heart valves" and Levi Pennington, for more than three decades beloved president of George Fox College.

0.1 m., jct., O 219S — for St. Paul and French Prairie. (For O 219S, see immediately following O 99W.)

0.1 m., River Rd., **Newberg.**

Turn L. *0.1 m.,* **Minthorn House,** only resident in Oregon to have been lived in by man who became US president. (Place is sometimes called Herbert Hoover House.) Built 1881 by Jesse Edwards, patriarch of most revered pioneer family in Newberg, house was purchased 3 years later by another Quaker, Dr. Henry John Minthorn, uncle and foster father of Hoover. In 1882, Dr. Minthorn and family came to Oregon where he had accepted position as supt. of what is now Chemawa Indian School, then Indian Manual Training School at Forest Grove. Two years later, having become enthused at future of newly founded Friends Pacific Academy, he resigned his post with the Bureau of Indian Affairs to become head of the Academy.

Minthorn House, Newberg   *Courtesy State of Oregon*

Not long after moving into the house on River Rd. the only son of Henry John and Laura Ellen Miles Minthorn passed away. The lad's demise left three daughters but the Minthorn parents ached for a boy. The solution was to bring 10-year-old Herbert Hoover, orphaned several years earlier and living with relatives in Iowa, to Newberg. Young Herbert agreed to the proposal and arrived in 1884. He lived with the Minthorn family in Newberg until 1889, when Dr. Minthorn and his wife moved on to Salem. (Only once after he left Newberg was Herbert Hoover known to have returned to the house where he had lived for 5 years.) Furnishings in the Minthorn House were there when the Minthorns occupied the premises or are period pieces that belonged to other old houses around Newberg. It is presumed that the well and outhouse in back yard are originals. (Neither has been used for many years.)

Newberg's most prominent institution is **George Fox College,** at the edge of the business district. It grew out of Friends Pacific Academy, which was raised to college level in 1891. (Herbert Hoover was a member of the first graduating class of FPA. In 1895 he was in the first graduating class of Stanford U.) In 1893 the Academy became Pacific College. Six years later it received recognition as a standard 4-year college. In 1949 school renamed George Fox College. (In 1984 a member of the wandering curious strolled about the campus of the college, asking at random about George Fox. Of 20 students interviewed, only one knew — and then incompletely — anything about the penal reformer after whom the college is named.)

Apart from the sunny atmosphere of the campus, the college has two attractions for the outsider. One is a tapestry in Wood-Mar Bldg. It depicts William Penn in his traditional role as brother of the Indian; below is the inscription: "The only treaty never ratified by an oath and never broken." The other is the John Brougher Museum. Raised in Silverton, Dr. Brougher (1901–1983) was a meticulous collector of mercantile artifacts, agricultural implements, medical paraphernalia and Quaker possessions, and all are neatly displayed.

At 3rd and College, near Minthorn House, stands **Friends Church** (1892), impressive structure with brick belfry tower.

Velvet Carriage, eatery at 607 E 1st, reflects old-fashioned motif of Newberg, with 1890 to 1910 decor, including mural of 1910 Newberg. Also on display are 1912 Model T Ford with "grandmother's seat" and 1853 piano, used to soften heartstrings of diners.

House at 200 N River is paradigm of solid, conservative homes put up at turn of century.

It is symbolic of changing times that Newberg now boasts that "over 20 wineries are located within a 25-mile radius of the city, placing Newberg at the hub of Oregon's wine-producing industry." One need not have hair white with age to remember when Newberg was the "driest" city in Oregon, boasted of its sobriety and absence of alcoholic beverages, and once created a tempest in a teapot when the painting of a mermaid appeared on a local restaurant. The cry rang out that the mermaid either be harnessed with a bra or the restaurant be closed.

0.1 m., from River Rd., downtown Newberg, on E (1-way lane) of O 99W; George Fox College reached from W lane of hwy.

0.1 m., jct., O 219N. (For O 219N, see *Cross-Coast Range Roads, US 26, O 19N.*)

0.3 m., jct., O 240.

    * *0.1 m.*, corner of N Main and W Sheridan, **Champoeg Valley Mills,** oldest business operating in original location without interruption in Newberg. Mill constructed 1898. One hundred barrel mill was biggest flour shipper from West Coast to port of Houston, company says.

At 403 N Main (N Main and W Sherman) mfg. plant long occupied by **Oregon Nut Growers.** If ever an Oregon structure looked like an English gaol, this is it.

1 block (corner of N Main and W Franklin), 2-story simple white frame bldg. that looks like meeting hall for poor people. Home of **Dunkard Brethren Church.** One can almost hear Aaron Copeland hymn floating from inside the walls.

At 611 N Main, **Gospel Chapel,** built of "wavy-faced" cement blocks in 1908 as St. Paul's Catholic Church.

2.1 m., Sunnycrest Jct. (*1.1 m.*, **Sunnycrest Grange** is last remnant of rural community that never aspired to bigness. Impressive vistas of fecund fields and soft Chehalem Hills on return to O 240.)

1.4 m., on N, **Ewing Young Historical Marker.** (See *Cross-Coast Range Roads, O 47S, Yamhill, O 240.*)

1.7 m., Gaston Jct. (N, 9.6 m., Gaston.) *0.7 m.*, jct. (6.2 m., Lafayette; 5.7 m., Carlton.) *3.3 m.*, on S, photogenic 19th century home. *0.5 m.*, Dewey Jct. (To N, 5 m., Dewey.) *1.7 m.*, on S, 1879 **Carpenter Gothic Victorian House.** *0.1 m.*, jct., O 47S, at Yamhill.

From Newberg, O 99W at 240:

2.3 m., **Dundee,** at 5th St. Scottish William Reid came to Oregon in 1874 and named town he founded after his native city. Although Dundee started as RR settlement, the early comers were more interested in planting fruit and nut trees. Eventually Dundee gave itself the title, "The Prune Capital of Oregon" and later became known as "the nut town," mostly for its filberts.

There is a Great Depression legend about Dundee that only old timers passing thru the town recall. Behind a big tree at the side of the road a town cop (perhaps the entire police force) hid, frequently to race his motorcycle behind a non-resident car, halt the often astounded motorist, and pass out a traffic citation. The revenue coming from the tickets, went the believable legend, kept Dundee afloat during the hard times. Dundee was not the only Oregon town to engage in such devious practices but for a while it was the most notorious and some people went far out of their way rather than drive thru Dundee.

At 5th St., turn W. *0.3 m.*, forks. Take R. *0.3 m.*, turn L. *0.3 m.*, **Dundee**

Pioneer Cemetery. Markers go back to 1860s. Best overview of town and valley is from far end of cemetery. As in many other communities, maintaining the cemetery has been a long-standing problem. Grumbled an old timer whose great-grandparents, grandparents and parents sleep on the hill: "Do you think the young people give a damn about keeping up the graves of their ancestors? They're more interested in their cars and their swimming pools!"

0.3 m. — from 5th St. — 9th St.

   * Turn W. Ahead is a park and a winery. Both fade in comparison to the scenery, the up and down surging hills, with a green and brown and yellow and purple world rising and falling. Going W. the upthrust of the vineyard and orchard-covered slopes is dazzling photographic splendor. Returning E, the road looks down and away to a sun-splotched and misty cut of the valley, the scene resembling an aerial photo. *2.3 m.*, turnoff to **Crabtree Park** and Knudsen Erath Winery. *50 yds*, to L, entrance to park, PA enveloped by tranquility. *0.5 m.*, on R fork, winery.

0.1 m., O 99W and 11th, **Dundee United Methodist Church** has shape and mien of typical Willamette Valley small town churches of early 20th century. *2.6 m.*, turnoff R for Sokol Blosser Winery (*0.8 m.*)

1.1 m., jct., Dayton-Lincoln-O 18.

   * *1.4 m.*, jct., Dayton — O 221. *0.4 m.*, Dayton, at Blockhouse, city park. See *O 221, Dayton,* this section.)

   * From Dayton-O 18 Jct.: *1.3 m.*, Amity Jct. (*9 m.*, Amity.) *1.4 m.*, Amity Jct. (*9 m.*, Amity.) *0.7 m.*, Evergreen Helicopters, whose (at least past) relationship with the CIA has drawn some public protest. *0.2 m.*, on L, **Eagle Hall,** that has every appearance of being early 20th century schoolhouse. *1.5 m.*, turnoff to McMinnville. (*1.1 m.*, McMinnville city center.) *1.8 m.*, jct., O 99W. This O 18 Bypass, which skirts McMinnville, is preferred by many motorists driving from the Portland area to the coast.

From jct., Dayton-Lincoln — O 18 on O 99W.

1.6 m., turnoff to **Yamhill Locks Park.**

   * *1.1 m.*, CP. A marker tells the history of the locks and dams on the Yamhill River here but the most definitive account was written by Ben Maxwell and appeared in the *Oregon Sunday Journal of July 9, 1939:*

   "During the 1870s agitation was afoot in the legislature for improving the upper region of the Yamhill River. Many, indeed, were the ribald jests exchanged between proponents and opponents of the project. Finally, however, the federal government took a hand and constructed a locks comparable to those at Oregon City between the towns of Dayton and Lafayette. The locks were opened by Captain William C. Langfitt, United States engineer, on September 21, 1900, and vindicated those survivors of the Yamhill Transportation and Manufacturing Company who had first undertaken river improvement back in 1872.

   "But, strange to relate, when the locks became operative the need for river

Yamhill Locks

transportation on the upper Yamhill seemed to vanish. About this time a narrow gauge railroad serving the community became standardized and other roads extended feeder lines into the region formerly, but irregularly served by seasonal steamer service. So, for more than a quarter of a century, the locks on the river seemed to exist for no particular purpose.

"In recent years, however, there has been a renaissance in Yamhill river traffic. True, steamboats no longer toot in passing and no new docks have been constructed to replace those fallen into decay or vanished. Rather, powerful towboats with gas and diesel motors churn the turbid Yamhill waters as they strain at log rafts destined for Willamette sawmills and points for off-shore equipment."

Total cost of the locks and the dam was $72,164.83 — far less than what a survey for such a project would cost today.

Tonnage thru the locks here declined from 119,006 in 1944 to 32,966 in fiscal 1953. Almost all tonnage consisted of logs and was rafted by a single company. The Corps of Engineers cut its operating budget from $10,000 to $5,000, removed the lockmaster, and opened the locks only on 24 hours notice to the lockmaster at Willamette Falls. *The Oregonian* editorially commented, "Eventually, the old dam and locks are going to collapse unless an estimated $95,000 is spent for repairs to the structure — and the navigation need does not justify the expense."

A few years later Yamhill County took title from the General Services Administration to the land area surrounding the dam and locks (now the park) and for one dollar took title to the dam and locks. The dam was breached by the Oregon Fish and Game Commission to facilitate passage of anadramous (ascending from the sea) fish in the Yamhill and its tributaries.

There remain only the concrete walls of the 175-ft.-long locks, which provided a lift of 16 ft. to take boats over the falls. There is no evidence of the timber-crib, rock-filled dam.

(As an historical footnote to the above: the land for construction of the locks was given free to the US by Gertrude J. Denny, prominent on two accounts. She was the last survivor of the Whitman massacre of 1847 [she passed away in 1933] and she was the widow of Judge O. N. Denny, credited with bringing the Chinese pheasant to Oregon.)

The shady, grassy park, a perfect picnic area (with casual fishing above and below the falls), is a true delight of the Willamette Valley and one wonders why it is not more fully used.

0.3 m. — from turnoff to Yamhill Locks on O 99W — Jackson St., Lafayette.

Lafayette is one of Oregon's oldest cities. It was founded in 1846 and named for Lafayette, Indiana; has had PO since 1851; until 1889 was seat of Yamhill County. For whatever reason, the town never prospered. In 1915 its pop. was 600; 7 decades later the number had only doubled — gain of less than 10 people per year. Unattractive as it is, Lafayette is crammed with history, though few of the locals know it — or care.

Old schoolhouse at Jackson St. occupies site of pioneer school at which Abigail Scott Duniway may have taught.

* Turn W onto Jackson St. *0.2 m.*, turn R onto 7th St. Exit. *0.3 m.*, turn onto Duniway Rd. *0.4 m.*, on R, **Pioneer Cemetery** (1850). *1.1 m.*, turn R uphill onto country lane. *0.3 m.*, back of mobile homes, house on knoll, built about 1858 by Abigail and Ben Duniway and occupied by them. Circular porch was added later. There was once an apple orchard here. A few aged cherry trees straggle feebly on fringes of knoll. (For more on Abigail Scott Duniway, Oregon's foremost suffragist, see "Battle Hymn of Abigail" in author's *Tracking Down Oregon.*)

1 block, Monroe. House on SE side — **Kelty Estate** — is one of the most distinctive 19th century homes in Willamette Valley. Adjacent walnut grove gives house genteel, rustic atmosphere.

1 block, Madison.

* Turn E. (For places along this way, see itinerary at end of Lafayette.)

1 block, Market St. (Turn W 3 blocks to 6th St. — **Yamhill County Museum.** Bldg. erected circa 1892 as "mission station"; later was known as Evangelical United Brethren Church; in 1937 name changed to Poling Memorial Church. Yamhill County Historical Society took possession of church bldg. in 1970. Furniture includes pulpit chair from Methodist Church of Yamhill and massive walnut Joel Palmer bed from Dayton.)

1 block, Jefferson. (Turn W. *1 block*, 4th Ave. House on SE corner built 1885 and restored. Had been Lafayette telephone office for many years.)

1 block, Adams. (E *1 block*, **Memorial Park.** At SW corner, Adams and 2nd, was site known as the Commons. First court sessions in Yamhill County held

1846 under oak tree called Council Oak. First Federal Court session held here 1848. Bit of folklore has it that elderly woman, about to be hanged from the oak, put a curse on the town. "It will burn three times," she prophesied in dark anger. Twice Lafayette has burned to the ground and the superstitious are awaiting the third conflagration.)

1 block, Bridge St.

    * Turn W. *2.3 m.,* on L, nature preserve. *0.7 m.,* turn R for **Our Lady of Guadalupe Cistercian** (Trappist) **Abbey,** monastery of monks devoted to life of contemplation in cloistered atmosphere. Abbey came to Oregon in 1955. Until Vatican II the monks lived in silence; wore solemn mien; laughter was seldom heard; women were segregated at services. Today monks speak freely, banter and laugh, and women are no longer second class citizens at services.

From O 99W and Madison, turn E for Hopewell, Dayton and Salem:

    * *0.5 m.,* on R, **Amos Cook House,** built 1850. *0.9 m.,* on R, **Francis Fletcher House,** built either 1850 or 1863; accounts differ. Foundation of Fletcher House is hewed log; no stone or concrete. Both Cook and Fletcher were members of the eccentric "Peoria Party," and both arrived in Oregon 1840. Cook was brother-in-law of Abigail Scott Duniway, who often visited here. (For full account of pathetic, ludicrous and mind-boggling "Peoria Party," which was inspired by Jason Lee and propagandized by richness-in-Oregon tales of Indian youth Lee took E with him, see "Long Road to the

Amos Cook House

Cook House" in author's *Tracking Down Oregon*.) *0.1 m.*, turnoff to Dayton. Continue straight. *0.6 m.*, jct., O 18-O 233. Straight on O 233. *0.6 m.*, O 233-Amity Jct.

** (Turn R for Amity. *0.5 m.*, forks. R for McMinnville. Continue straight. *0.2 m.*, forks. Straight. *1.6 m.*, forks. Take R. *5.1 m.*, O 99W. Turn S. *1 m.*, Amity.)

* At O 233-Amity Jct., coming from Lafayette, straight for Hopewell. The road unrolls thru meadowland as fruitful as it is flat, with the Eola Hills on the W running right down to the prairie — a retaining wall against the fields on the other side. In this rich, rich fertile land, exploding with bountiful crops, the pensive traveler remembers that millions of people are in desperate hunger, and wonders why.

* *0.7 m.*, Amity Jct. *0.4 m.*, on E, 1891 house. Morganeidge family plot under maple tree *0.2 m.* back of house. First burial, 1888, was of 19-year-old youth consumed by smallpox. He was instantly interred in the timber, out of sight, and so fearful was the family of the dread disease that they burned their house to the ground. Present house built 3 years later on same site. *0.1 m.*, on R, 2-story house built 1889 and looking older. A museum piece. *0.7 m.*, on R, another early house, and showing its age. *1 m.*, Whiteson Jct. (*5 m.*, Whiteson.) *0.8 m.*, on L, **Monrovia Nursery,** whose plots are gorgeous mosaics of flowers and shrubs. *1.8 m.*, Unionvale Jct. (*3 m.*, Unionvale.) On W, **Fairview School** built 1912, abandoned 1948, now small factory. *0.2 m.*, Amity Jct. Continue straight. *0.8 m.*, Hood View Rd. (W, *2 m.*, Hidden Springs Winery.)

* *0.9 m.*, Church Rd. (*0.2 m.*, to R, **Hopewell Community Church** and **Hopewell Cemetery,** with markers back to 1847. The serenity here is so complete that the transition of the dead from this knoll to the pasture of heaven would meet no obstacle.)

* *0.4 m.*, Hopewell — Wheatland Jct. (E, *1.3 m.*, jct., O 221. Curve R. *0.1 m.*, on E, **Hopewell School,** picture calendar country school built circa 1915; modern school would seem out of place here.)

* *0.1 m.*, **Hopewell.** Store. Founded on great hopes, town never really got off the ground. PO lasted less than 5 years — 6/21/1898 to 1/3/1903. In 1915 Hopewell had pop. of 50, probably more than village proper has today. It also had two stores, blacksmith shop, garage and, at one time, boarding house. One of the stores — the present — was noted for selling moonshine in gallon jugs under the counter. The moonshiner was arrested not for concocting the stuff but for being intoxicated. Hopewell Store has marker stating it was built 1910 but the few senior citizens still around say founding date was more like 1905. In 1985 storekeeper was transplanted Californian. It is remarkable how many Oregon backcountry storekeepers are well-educated Californians. They all say something to this effect: "I'm working at least twice as many

hours for one-tenth the money that I got in California. But this is the good life."

* *3.3 m.*, jct., O 221. (*10.7 m.*, Salem.) (See O *221*, following.)

* From Dayton-Amity Jct., *0.6 m.* S of jct., O 18 — O 233:

* Turn L for Dayton. *1.1 m.*, in **Dayton,** on R, 1890 faded opulent mansion loaded with fan-like gingerbread. 2nd-story covered porch adds elegance. Set back from road, house is tenderly entwined by cedar, oak, plum, walnut, maple and fir trees. *0.4 m.*, (6th and Ferry) on R, **Palmer House,** built 1852 by Gen. Joel Palmer, one of great names in Oregon history. First coming to Oregon in 1845 he laid out town of Dayton on his DLC in 1849. A travel guide he wrote in 1845 and published 2 years later, *Journal of Travels Over the Rocky Mountains,* showed many Oregon-bound emigrants the way to the promised land. He is kindliest remembered as Supt. of Indian Affairs for Oregon Territory. Fair-minded, even-handed, working for conciliation, he believed in making equitable treaties instead of war. After 4 years he was removed from his position because he held back to the best of his abilities the loaded guns of the impatient Yankees and because he had the temerity to regard Indians as human beings. Descendants of Joel Palmer occupied this truly handsome house until 1968.

1 block, house across street from Dayton Grade School built between 1890 and 1900. *1 block,* 5th St. Houses at 426 and 414 5th are examples of old Dayton architecture. (A drive thru and around town is a trip back into late 19th century.) *1 block,* 5th And Church, **Dayton Christian Church,** est 1890. *1 block,* corner of 4th and Church, **Pioneer Evangelical Church,** built 1850s as Dayton Methodist Church, has logs under its clapboards.

1 block, 4th and Main. Turn L onto Main. *1 block,* 3rd and Main, in city park, 2-story blockhouse, built 1856 at Ft. Yamhill (see *Cross-Coast Range Roads, O 22*), and in 1911 moved by 6 wagons from Grand Ronde Indian Reservation. Across street is **First Baptist Church** (1886), wood-frame spire on red brick.

Turn R onto 3rd. Restaurant across street from blockhouse was built as house 1885. *0.1 m.*, 3rd and Ferry. NE edge of city park. Straight onto O 221.

* *0.2 m.*, angle R onto gravel road to **Brookside Cemetery,** opened 1844. Buried here are Joel Palmer and several settlers who voted for American govt. at Champoeg.

* *0.7m.*, Chem-Spray Ln. (*1 m.*, **IOOF Cemetery,** est. 1860.) *0.3 m.*, on R, set back about 100 yds, charming 1885 dwelling — a poem in the eye. An architect described place as "a good old farm house with Victorian influence."

* *5.5 m.*, **Unionvale.** Store, station, cafe. There have been three migrations to this part of Oregon. The first, of course, was that of the Indians, who arrived millennia ago. The second coming was of the Americans, who started setting down roots in the 1840s. The latest wave of settlers are the His-

Ft. Yamhill Blockhouse, Dayton

panics, who work the fields, labor in the warehouses, are starting up small businesses, and occupying run-down, century-old houses built by those who themselves were strangers to the new land. Thus, in the cycling of people is the frontier drama repeated.

　* Grand Island-Amity Jct.

　** L: *0.5 m.,* **Grand Island,** in Willamette River. Island is about 4 m. wide and 7 m. long, domain of small and medium-size farms. A near water level, richly fertile land, with sturdy barns and comfortable homes. Chief crops: beans, berries, sweet corn, hay, cherries. No stores, stations, schools. The only problem — and not a frequent one — is flooding. But when river withdraws it leaves behind precious silt, which contributes to island's productivity. Paved roads web the restful isle; this is the place for the mythical Sunday drive.

　** R at jct: *1.9 m.,* Webfoot Rd. (Turn R. *1.2 m.,* on L, shrouded in a tangle of second growth woods, **Ebenezer Chapel,** a stone husk of a single room 19th century church long abandoned and sometimes used as a barn. All the windows were broken ages ago; not a sliver of glass remains. Branches tangle thru the opening like spiders spinning webs. Best information indicates that Ebenezer Chapel had small but stalwart congregation, most of them German immigrants, and services were conducted in German. [Today there is scarcely anyone in Dayton or Unionvale who has even heard of Ebenezer Chapel.] Back of church, half-hidden in a blurry confusion of close-standing, second-growth fir, scrawny and slopping on each other, lies the cemetery, some of the graves moss-covered and all curtained by the spongy undergrowth and the hair fingers of low branches. Markers back to 1856.)

* Return to Grand Island-Amity Jct. Turn R onto O 221: *3.1 m.,* Hopewell Jct. *(1.5 m.,* Hopewell.) *0.3 m.,* **Maud Williamson SP.** Shaded PA looks like old estate. At entrance is 1860s house with 1890 addition. Exterior restored 1976.

* *0.1 m.,* Wheatland Ferry Jct.

** Turn L. *1.1 m.,* ferry landing. At E side of river a trail R (mostly paved) leads to the river side of **Willamette Mission SP.** Here is approximate site of first mission station in Oregon, est. 1834 by Jason Lee.

** *0.5 m.,* St. Paul-Salem Jct. Turn L for St. Paul. *3.1 m.,* jct. O 219. (See *O 219 from Newberg, O 99W.*)

At St. Paul-Salem Jct., turn R for Salem. *0.8 m.,* on R, **Willamette Mission SP.** *(2.1 m.,* parking area for trail to river. *0.1 m.,* **Willamette River.** Park has PA, bike trail, fishing, swimming.) Return to entrance of SP. Turn R. *2.3 m.,* Hopmere Jct. (*1 m.,* **Hopmere,** started as electric RR station called Chemeketa. Trying to get message across that the place was only a mere hop from Salem, local boosters changed the name. They needn't have bothered to induce people to buy and build homes here. The place was a natural for suburbia — and is.) *3.1 m.,* Keizer — Jct., O 219. (See *O 219, out of Newberg.*) *3.8 m.,* Salem.

* From O 221 — Wheatland Ferry Jct., going S on O 221:

* *2.2 m.,* on E, Day Use Area, **Willamette Greenway.** *3.2 m.,* **Lincoln.** Store. Town was est. by Andrew Jackson Doak, who named it for President Lincoln. Doak ran a ferry across Willamette and town first known as Doak's Ferry. Mail service route was via ferry. PO 1867–1901. At one time Lincoln was important steamboat stop on Willamette, with daily boats bound for Salem and Portland. No trace of docks today.

* Zena Rd.

** Turn R onto Zena Rd. *0.1 m.,* on L, **Brush College Grange.** Brush College is popular name in area between Lincoln and Salem. It all began here about 1860 when the settlers cleared brush and built 1-room schoolhouse which with pioneer hyperbole they called Brush College.

* *1.9 m.,* "Y". Follow L prong. *0.5 m.,* on L, **Spring Valley Presbyterian Church,** atop a rise shared by small, shaded cemetery. Traditional belief is that the bell came year the church was built, 1859. But local booklet, *An History of the Spring Valley Church,* says: "The bell was shipped from England around the Horn in 1884 or 1885. It stood in front of the church for some time until a way to get it up into the steeple could be found. It weighed 800 or 900 pounds. There have been few Sundays in these many years that it has not

Wheatland Ferry

been rung on the Lord's Day, and it was the custom to toll it in case of a death in the valley or any emergency about the neighborhood to alert friends . . . At the turn of the century a group of the neighbors had a night watch . . . and as they rang in the new year the oldest person present and a small child held the rope and rang in the New Century." Pews and floors of church are original. Old pulpit still stands on the old platform. Organ has been in use since about 1900. High ceiling is in keeping with pioneer homes. Eight men (and some of their families) who took up DLCs in Spring Valley are buried in the cemetery.

At foot of church stood village of **Zena,** named for Arvazena Stillman Cooper by her husband, Daniel Jackson Cooper. Her sister's name was Melzena. In 1880s and 1890s Zena had blacksmith shop, general store, grist mill, PO, Grange; church had horse shed and parsonage. All gone.

Return to forks. Cross road. Continue N. *0.7 m.,* first white house on L, built 1853 by 1847 pioneer, John Phillips. Front part is still the original.

** Return to forks. Take L, or W. *1.9 m.,* on N, turnoff (*0.4 m.*) for Bethel Heights Vineyard. *1.1 m.,* on S, **Bethel Cemetery.** Pioneer burial ground (1848) with impressive stones. Here lie Isaac McCoy, founder of McCoy village, and Oscar Kelty, who slew his wife and then was lynched at Dallas (see "The Hanging Tree" in author's *This Side of Oregon.*) *0.6 m.,* on R, **Bethel Church,** last survivor of village in pretty Plum Valley looking up to Eola Hills. Named in 1846, village had enough families around it by 1852 for

Dr. Nathaniel Hudson to start Bethel Academy. At that time there were few public schools in the Oregon outland and academies, some of which taught thru HS grades, sprouted at various places around W Oregon. In 1855 the present bldg. was opened as Bethel Collegiate Institute. For several years it was one of the more profitable institutions in the state. But as "needless" multitudes of academies and colleges sprang up in W Oregon, Bethel's ink turned red and Bethel was merged with Monmouth U, at Monmouth. (See Monmouth, later this section.) By then, too, public schools were opening up in large numbers. *1.2 m.,* O 99W.

    * O 221 from Lincoln.

    0.9 m., Day Use Area, Willamette Greenway. *5.5 m.,* downtown Salem.
From Bridge St., Lafayette, on O 99W:
0.3 m., Mineral Springs Rd.
    * Turn W. *0.6 m.,* on R, entrance to **Lafayette Masonic Cemetery.** Park at gate and walk *0.3 m.,* Gravestones back to 1850s. In season, beware of poison oak. *0.1 m.,* forks. Take R, Mineral Springs Rd. *0.8 m.,* turn to Chateau Benoit Winery *(0.6 m.).*
0.4 m., on R, Mattey Ln.
    * *0.3 m.,* elegant house built 1892 by Joseph Mattey, who lies in Lafayette Masonic Cemetery.
1.7 m., jct., O 47. Two cemeteries at jct.; one to S is older and more interesting.
0.6 m., on R, Farmer's Co-op parking lot. To S, directly in front of Ace Hardware, is area that looks like sunken garden. This is **Malone Cemetery,** about the least-observed burial ground of any in Oregon along a well-traveled state road. Plaque on tombstone facing gate reads: "Location of the first dedicated cemetery between the North and South Yamhill Rivers. It was dedicated as a perpetual cemetery by Madison Malone at the time of his first wife's death in 1850. When a death occurred, the settlers nailed together a board coffin and a simple burial was made. When the first circuit riding preacher came by, a formal funeral service was held. The elements and vandals have destroyed early markers so records are incomplete. The names of 15 people interred here are known. It is believed there are about 25 graves in the plot." The few headstones, cracked and broken, are from the 1860s.
1.4 m., in **McMinnville,** 19th St.
    * Turn R. *1 block,* turn R onto Baker St. *0.2 m.,* turn L onto Baker Creek Rd. *1.2 m.,* on R, house that looks like old-fashioned hat box, with three chimneys, built of square nails, circa 1885. *0.4 m.,* on L, **Shedden House,** built 1852 of lumber brought up from Calif. (In retrospect, this seems like carrying coals to Newcastle.) Two-story white colonial style with handsome veranda. Oldest house in and around McMinnville — and probably most beautiful. *1.2 m.,* forks. Take L. *1.4 m.,* on L, **Ed Grenfell CP.** PA. Cut out of the forest and belonging to it. *1.7 m.,* on L, **E. A. Huber CP.** PA. Rustic

simplicity. Return to Baker St. Turn L. *0.9 m.,* on R, Dyke Studio, NW photos by eminent photographer.

On O 99W from 19th St., McMinnville:

0.9 m., turnoff E on 3rd St. to downtown **McMinnville,** *0.1 m.,* turnoff W on 2nd St. for cemetery.

    * *1.4 m.,* "T". Turn R. *0.4 m.,* turn L. *0.3 m.,* **Masonic Cemetery.** Markers back to 1853.

McMinnville prides itself upon being a quiet, pious city of tradition and respect. The splurges of progress that have erupted along O 99W have thus far not disintegrated the business section.

City was founded by William T. Newby, who came to Oregon with the "Great Migration" of 1843 and named his new home after his old one in Tennessee. Settling here in 1844, he built in 1853 a grist mill on a site which is now city park. Three years later he platted original townsite. (Newby's farmhouse, at 1420 E 5th, has undergone numerous additions but classic revival style has been retained.)

McMinnville's slow and steady growth is reflected in its architecture. Between 1885 and 1910 most of the business bldgs. and fine homes on 3rd St. were built. A large number of the small bungalows were put up between 1905 and 1930.

Most of old McMinnville is seen on a walking tour that embraces the streets between Adams and Johnson and 1st and 7th. Among the most interesting structures in the city are: **Yamhill Hotel** (originally Cook's Hotel), 502 E 3rd, built 1880s; 3-story brick bldg. covered with stucco and painted pale yellow. There is evidence of a former porch and a balcony possibly surrounded two sides. Original hotel had fancy parlor, luxurious bridal chamber, 28 rooms, billiard parlor, dining room.

Frank Fenton House, 434 N Ford, imposing home with Colonial Revival styling; **McMinnville Bank** (1885), 238 E 3rd, brick Italianate commercial structure with elaborate cornice line; **Schilling Bldg.** 238 E 3rd, built early 1880s as saloon, attractive arched windows; **Cozine House,** 105 E 3rd, put up circa 1897, Queen Anne house with "fishscale" shingles and colored glass windows; **Maloney House** (1882), 304 E 1st, rural vernacular house of much interest; **Wiesner House** (1885), 322 E 1st, Italianate style home; **Union Block** 411 E 3rd, built 1890, combines Italianate and Second Empire styling; **Jameson Hardware** (1904), 608 E 3rd, looking almost exactly as it did many decades ago; **Grissen House** (1889), 1004 E 5th, 2-story Queen Anne.

Follow 3rd St. E. Cross overpass onto Dayton-Salem Rd. Turn L. *0.2 m.,* turn R onto Martin Ln. *0.2 m.,* **Altimus House** (circa 1870), and looking, inside and out, as it did more than century ago. Return to Dayton-Salem Rd. Turn R. *1 block* to stoplight. Turn L onto O 18. *0.2 m.,* curve R toward McMinnville. *0.9 m.,* turn R onto Johnson St. (Johnson becomes Lafayette.) *0.2 m.,* turn L onto 10th. *0.2 m.,* Arterberry, Ltd. (cider works) and Eyrie Vineyards (winery).

McMinnville is the seat of Yamhill County, named for Yamhelas Indians and est. July 5, 1843. One of the original four districts of Oregon, it is regarded as the oldest county in the state and originally stretched from the Chehalem Mtns. to Calif. border and from Willamette River to ocean. Present boundaries were est. by 1860.

From 2nd St., McMinnville, on O 99W:

0.6 m., entrance to **Linfield College.** School's origin can be traced back to 1849 when a small group of Baptist pioneers met in Oregon City to form the Oregon Baptist Educational Society, the object being to found "a school of high moral and religious character." But school was est. not in Oregon City but in McMinnville. In 1857 Baptists acquired school started by Sebastian C. Adams in 1855 and the following year McMinnville College was chartered by the territorial legislature. Operations began in 1859. The big boom began in 1881 when 25 acres donated. The next year Pioneer Hall, still used, and probably most historic college structure in Oregon, was built. McMinnville College became Linfield College in 1922 after about $250,000 worth of Spokane property was donated by Frances E. Ross Linfield in honor of her husband, George Fisher Linfield. Noteworthy on the campus in addition to Pioneer Hall is Linfield Observatory, built in 1890s; oldest observatory in PNW, it houses original telescope.

0.6 m., jct., O 18.

* W on O 18. *2.4 m.,* Muddy Valley Rd. Turn R. *0.1 m.,* forks. Straight. *1.7 m.,* forks. Take L. *50 yds.,* on R, entrance to site of **South Yamhill Baptist Church** — third Baptist church org. W of Middle Missouri in 1846.

Church erected here 1850. Only monument marks place. Behind monument is sloped **South Yamhill Cemetery,** better known locally as Muddy Valley Cemetery. Markers back to when Oregon was still Territory. Return to road at entrance to church site. Turn R. *0.4 m.,* on R, turn uphill for 1886-built **McCabe United Methodist Church.** From shaded knoll there is clear and idyllic overlook of the small, golden vale. In the distance, Mt. Hood is delicately etched into another world.

3 m., on L, **Whiteson.** Nothing here now but two streets of houses. But in 1915 town was important shipping point of fruits, walnuts, poultry and vegetables on Portland, Eugene & Eastern RR (electric); had HS and PS, Presbyterian Church, Artisan Lodge, two stores.

5.5 m., jct., O 233 — to Dayton.

0.5 m., Rice Rd.

* Turn E for Amity Winery. *0.3 m.,* turn L onto Jellison Ave. *0.7 m.,* winery. View of saucer-shaped valley from knoll of winery is worth the drive.

0.7 m., **Amity** (6th St.), so named not because of the presence of large numbers of Amish but because of an amicable settlement between two villages over school ownership. Founded 1848 by schoolteacher Ahio S. Watt and named in 1849; PO since 1852. Amity is another of those old Oregon towns which somehow hang on. Yearly festival, held in late July, looks like enlarged garage sale.

And the best bargain is free — friendliness. Amity has the spirit of what towns were supposed to be like in the horse and buggy days.

Turn R on 6th St. *0.1 m.,* on L, **Amity First Baptist Church;** part of it built 1870 and "worked over" in 1920 to, more or less, present shape. *0.1 m.,* **Amity Cemetery** (1854), immaculately tended.

0.1 m., on E, **Amity Church of Christ.** Information board reads: "This congregation was founded in 1846 and is the oldest Christian Church West of the Rockies." Some travelers take this to mean that bldg. was put up 1846; it was erected 1912. Congregation first met at homes of Whiteson members. Three years later, 1849, congregation moved to Amity and met in log cabin. In 1869 congregation worshipped with Baptists, then rented Methodist Church. Finally, in 1870, members built their own church, which in time burned down.

In Amity: turnoff: E to Unionvale and Hopewell, W to Bellevue.

1.9 m., Broadmead Rd.

   * Turn onto Broadmead Rd. *4.6 m.,* Perrydale Jct. *0.1 m.,* **Perrydale.** No commerce, few homes. Community revolves around Perrydale School and Valley Baptist Church. House said by locals to have been erected 1885 must have been beauty in its day. In 1915 Perrydale was really a village: it had flour mill, warehouse, two churches, two stores. Return to Perrydale Jct. Turn L. *0.1 m.,* on R, white rectangular house built 1879 and since occupied by same family. Return to Perrydale Jct. Turn for Broadmead. *0.4 m.,* turn R for Broadmead. *1.1 m.,* just across RR tracks, turn R. *0.1 m.,* site of **Broadmead.** In 1920s there was church and school, both now converted into residences. Even locals dispute where store and PO stood.

3 m., McCoy — Lincoln Jct.

   * To E: Lincoln. (See earlier this section.)

   * To W: *0.5,* **McCoy.** Store bldg. put up 1886; second floor was lodge hall of IOOF. Blue-painted large house, *0.1 m.* beyond store, also built 1886. Town, founded by Isaac McCoy as RR station, was sizeable burg at and before turn of century, when it had pop. 400. Photos of pre-car days show many bldgs., including church, school and homes no longer here. By 1915 McCoy's pop. was down to 130 — probably 100 more than town has today. But in its anecdotage it preserves the feel of a folded page in an Old Oregon album. *1.9 m.,* Perrydale.

3 m., RR tracks. *1.1 m.,* turn R onto farm lane.

   * *0.2 m.,* old farmstead known as **Riggs Place.** House, probably constructed 1880s, was first farmhouse to have gas lights in this part of Oregon. After death of long- time owner Arthur Leppin Sr. in 1979 — he was killed at age 74 in tractor accident — house was abandoned and, vulnerable to time and the elements, faded into a wretched ghost. Outbuildings suffered same fate. On 4/26/1980, an auction was held of things Lippin had collected for half a century. It was a feast for nostalgia buffs: 1926 Model T, farm trucks out of the 1930s, pot-bellied stove, rusty wood cookstove, fertilizer spreader with

The heart of McCoy   *Phoebe L. Friedman*

steel wheels, corn planter of yore, and the like. Before coming here best to
check at Amity.
0.5 m., Smithfield Rd.
       * Take Smithfield Rd. *2.4 m.,* at jct. of Livermore Rd., 1916 warehouse
that was site of **Smithfield,** started as RR station on narrow gauge Oregonian
Railway Co. line, later standardized by SPRR. Since Smith Bros. Ranch
stood here, town named Smithfield. PO est 1893; didn't last long. RR tracks
torn up ages ago.
0.8 m., turnoff E for Glenn Creek Winery (3.7 m.)
0.5 m., turnoff W to **Baskett Slough Wildlife Refuge,** feeding and resting
grounds on the great North-South Flyway for thousands of birds. Baskett Slough
(2,492 acres) is one of three national wildlife refuges in Willamette Valley. They
were est. in 1960s as traditional geese concentration points in the valley following
deep concern over future of dusky Canada geese, whose numbers were being
mowed down by hunters. Nesting only in a small part of the Copper River Delta
of SE Alaska, almost entire dark brown Canada goose pop. winters in Willamette
Valley and along lower Columbia from Sauvie Island to Willapa Bay. Protective
grounds had to be found, and thru sale of "duck" stamps the land for the refuges
was purchased. Baskett Slough Refuge has habitat typical of valley's irrigated
hillsides, oak-covered knolls and grassy field. In addition to several species of
waterfowl, refuge is also home to grebes, herons, hawks, quail, shorebirds, band-

tailed pigeons, mourning doves, woodpeckers and a variety of songbirds. Among mammals seen here are the red fox, black-tailed deer, bobcat, coyote, muskrat, and dusky-footed woodrat. Refuge has horse and foot trails.

1.9 m., jct., O 22.

    * W on O 22: *0.4 m.,* first Dallas jct. *(4.8 m.,* Dallas.) *1.4 m.,* information boards of Baskett Slough Wildlife Refuge. *1.5 m.,* second Dallas jct. (O 223. *3.5 m.,* Dallas.) (For remainder of O 22, see *Cross-Coast Range Roads,* O 22.)
0.4 m., **Rickreall,** at Derry Jct.

Origin of town's name has defied historic accuracy. *Oregon Geographic Names* devotes 40 lines to the controversies — probably a record for that tome. Of at least equal interest is that during Civil War it was called Dixie, because of its secessionist sympathies. PO est 1851 and first postmaster was Col. Nathaniel Ford, 1844 wagonmaster, who kept slaves and who was involved in historic case that laid foundation for Oregon being a free state. (For full story, see "Holmes vs. Ford: A Chapter in Ebony" in author's *This Side of Oregon.*) This early settlement on La Creole Creek never had the muscle to grow. By 1915 it had only 100 pop. and hasn't yet shaken off its lethargy.

    * To E — toward Salem: *0.8 m.,* **Derry,** RR station on SP named by J. W. Nesmith for family home in Derry, N.H. Later efforts to change name to Loganberry failed. Small grain complex here.

    * *0.8 m.,* Morrow Rd. Turn S onto it. *0.3 m.,* turn R. *0.3 m.,* turn L. *0.2 m.,* turn L. Walk *0.1 m.,* to **Pioneer Cemetery,** burial ground in copse. Here lies Nathaniel Ford, his grave marker shattered. It was on this land, the claim of Carey Embree, that John E. Lyle, an Illinois schoolteacher who earlier had started holding classes in the home of Ford, joined with several others to found Jefferson Institute. A description of it is given in *Oregon: End of the Trail:* "The school equipment was modern for the time and place; it consisted of plank benches, puncheon desks, goose quill pens, ink made from oak galls and iron filings, bullets hammered to a point for pencils, and paper from the Hudson's Bay Company store. The textbooks were the Bible, and such books as the settlers had brought with them. The institute was also used for interdenominational service."

    * Return to Derry Rd. Turn E. *1 m.,* Greenwood Rd. Turn N. *0.3 m.,* O 22. Cross hwy. Straight, *2.7 m.,* Farmer Rd. Turn R. *0.3 m.,* Oak Grove Rd. (Straight, *9 m.,* Salem.) Turn L. *0.2 m.,* **Oak Grove Church** (1882), looking as pleasant and wise as an elderly country pastor. Church, school and Grange form trinity of rural community.

0.2 m., turn at N end of Polk County Fair Grounds for Nesmith Park.

    0.2 m., **Nesmith Park.** Path leads to Nesmith Historic Cemetery, PA, Nature Trails. Dominating small burial ground is 16-ft.-tall shaft marking grave of James Willis Nesmith, one of Oregon's early shakers and makers. Grave is on R bank of the Rickreall, in grave chosen by himself for his sepulchre. An early newspaper account rhapsodized: "The sloughing of giant firs, the murmur of the stream join in an eternal requiem." E face of shaft bears under Nesmith's name the inscription: "Born July 23 1820/ Died June 17 1885/ An upright Judge/ A brave soldier/ A wise legislator/ An honest man." W face relates that he was a pioneer of 1843, judge under the 1845 provisional gvmt., US Marshall 1853 to 1855, Colonel of Volunteers 1855, Supt. of Indian Affairs 1857–58, US Senator 1861–67, Rep. in Congress 1873–75. (He was one of the few persons to become a member of the House after serving in the Senate.) What the inscriptions — and most historical accounts — do not say is that on occasion he had a fiery tongue and that some of his opinions were etched in pure acid. He was also an uncompromising supporter of Abraham Lincoln and was the only Democrat in Congress to support the 13th Amendment — the abolition of slavery.

1.1 m., Dallas Jct. 0.9 m., Dallas Jct. (4.8 m., Dallas.) 3.4m., **Monmouth.**

In 1853 Monmouth was settled by contingent of 1852 Illinois comers. As with many other pioneers, they kept the old home fires burning by naming the new village after the town they had left behind. Monmouth was long known as an industrious farm trading center; early in this century "one of the largest and best herds of Jersey cattle in the state" grazed on the rich grass near the town. Downtown still has a rustic look and streets only a few blocks away are occupied by houses which seem ready for a retirement home. Many of them rent to college students. In last few decades the farm town has played second fiddle to **Western Oregon State College,** which the school's catalog calls "the oldest liberal arts college in the Oregon State System of Higher Education."

The early Illini gave 640 acres of land on which to est. the town and a college that would be the educational arm of the Christian Church. And so, in 1856, Monmouth U was born. With few students, times were rough, and in 1865 the school merged with impoverished Bethel College. Later, under church pressure, name was changed to Monmouth Christian College. That didn't make things rosier and in desperation the trustees offered the school lock, stock and barrel for a state university. The legislature wouldn't go for the deal but in 1882 sanctioned the school's bid to become a state-supported institution for the training of teachers. And so Oregon Normal School came into being.

In the 1920s student pop. exploded, reaching enrollment of almost 1,000. Impressed, legislature changed name in 1939 to Oregon College of Education. Old timers remember OCE during the 1930s and early 1940s as bucolic institution, consisting of a few old-fashioned bldgs. and a campus where even a dog fight was exciting news. But the college began to grow at an accelerated rate and broke the barrier of its reputation as a school for teachers. In 1981 it underwent another name change — Western Oregon State College.

The 122-acre campus was some years ago awarded second place among schools of higher education in US for its grounds, which combine charm of 19th century structures with ultra-modern facilities. Outstanding is 1871 Campbell Hall, fronted by giant sequoia planted 1880s. Community Evangelical Church

(1892) at edge of campus has fish-scale shingle steeple, typical of early Willamette Valley church architecture. But without doubt, travelers will find most fascinating the 1985-opened **Paul Jensen Museum,** on campus, artistically-displayed collection of Eskimo artifacts gathered over long decades by Danish-born Paul Jensen, a man as remarkable as the fruits of his labors. Probably finest one-man museum in state and worth driving many miles to see.

(W of Monmouth: 9 m., sands of Spencer Formation have yielded large amounts of shark and ray teeth of late Eocene period.)

W from Monmouth-Independence Jct.:

* 5 m., Airlie Jct. 2.5 m., O 223. Some surprisingly sweeping curves in this short distance — and a lot of good rural scenery.

E from Monmouth-Independence Jct.:

* 2.4 m., **Independence,** named in 1845 for city of same name in Missouri. As neat a 19th century-looking town as there is in Willamette Valley.

* From S Main and S Monmouth, Independence, going S: 0.3 m., Main and I Sts. Turn E toward Salem. 0.5 m., across Willamette River bridge, turn R, toward Buena Vista. 5.4 m., Ankeny Vineyard. 1.2 m., **Ankeny National Wildlife Refuge** (2,796 acres), with fauna characteristic of bottomland farm area of Willamette Valley. Hedgerows, clusters of Oregon ash, some Douglas firs, Sidney Irrigation Ditch and meadowlands draw Myotis and other plainnose bats, raccoons, weasels, minks, skunks, coyotes, beaver, elk and mule deer.

** 1 m., "T". Turn R, toward Sidney (at times spelled Sydney). 1.7 m., **Sidney,** tiny knot of houses. "This is our town all right," boasted a resident, probably tongue-in-cheek. The place, in Ankeny Bottom, started life as station on Oregon Electric RR and at one time had flour mill. It hasn't even memories now. Turn L toward Talbot. 1.3 m., turn R, toward Talbot. 2.3 m., **Talbot,** started as RR station on Oregon Electric RR. Only church, fire station, several homes. But it looks big compared to Sidney. Turn R for Buena Vista. 2.6 m., forks. Take L. 0.2 m., **Buena Vista Ferry,** on Willamette River.

From Monmouth-Independence Jct.:

4.6 m., turnoff W for **Helmick SP.**

* 0.3 m., SP. PA on Luckiamute River, pre-white CG. Several decades ago shark teeth were found in large quantity near the Luckiamute just N of park. Some are still around — but effort to find them is much greater now.

2.8 m., Suver-Buena Vista Jct. **Richards Store** on SE corner has look of old-time country store and has collection of pioneer artifacts. Six micro-rooms or stalls, depicting various forms of rural life — barnyard, schoolroom, kitchen, etc. In addition, large collection of flatirons, dolls, farm artifacts, etc. Lou Richards said: "The young people have no respect for the belongings of their great-grandparents and grandparents. They just throw things out; a lot of our heritage goes to the dump. That's where I get most of my stuff." At intersection is blinking yellow light put in at insistence of Mrs. Richards and her neighbors. "I got tired of picking up dead bodies," she explained.

To W of intersection: *5 m.*, Airlie; *8.8 m.*, Serendipity Cellars Winery.

To E of intersection:

* *0.9 m.*, turn-in-the-road, grain elevator mini-village of **Suver,** founded 1845. It was bigger in 1915, with church, PS, pop. 25. *1.4 m.*, "T". Turn L for **Buena Vista.** Only modern touch here is rural fire dept., with up-to-date equipment and trained force of volunteers. All thru W Oregon the backcountry is studded with efficient, well-supplied fire depts. — a sign of the danger and of the vigilance.

From Suver Jct.:

3.1 m., turnoff E for **E. E. Wilson Game Management Area.** On NE corner, historical marker citing elements and WW II records of Army infantry divisions trained at Camp Adair — 91st (Powder River), 70th (Trailblazers), 96th (Deadeye), 104th (Timberwolf). Many of the troops were not overly fond of the place, which they called Swamp Adair.

* *0.4 m.*, Wilson Game Management Area, best known for pheasant raising. *1.3 m.*, "T". Turn R. *0.9 m.*, Palestine Rd. Turn L. *1.1 m.*, **Palestine Church and Cemetery** (1881).

1.6 m., Tampico Rd.

* Go W. *0.2 m.*, site of **Tampico,** laid out by Green Berry Smith, who appears again in this section on road S of Corvallis. Not a sliver of wood to indicate that here stood a stage station on the Oregon-California Line and was in path of first telegraph line from Portland to the S. *1 m.*, Sulphur Creek Rd. Turn L onto it. A semi-jaded traveler described this rolling, patient pike as "the prettiest road in the state." And at places, looking up and about, the words of Robert Frost come to mind: "The woods are lovely, dark and deep." But here there seem no promises to keep, for the road itself is promise and fulfillment. One might think: "Ah, here is real backcountry where few have trod, and those who reside here are isolated indeed." Not so. People of means have built private road to their homes and along the way live expatriates from the cities, as sophisticated as any of us. *4.1 m.*, on L, **Soap Creek School,** red-painted 1-room schoolhouse now historical bldg. *2 m.*, "T". Take R. *0.2 m.*, turnout at row of rocks. Take path. About *100 yds.* to Sulphur Springs, small creek that isn't much for bathing, (except feet) but in pleasant setting.

From Tampico Rd., on O 99W:

0.3 m., Arnold Ave.

* Turn E. *0.2 m.*, **Adair Village,** community on land once part of Camp Adair. *0.3 m.*, **Adair CP.** PA.

0.5 m., turnoff W for **Peavy Arboretum.**

* *0.8 m.*, Arboretum: Genetics Nursery, School of Forestry, OSU. Since acquiring original 80 acres in 1925 (site of present arboretum), School of For-

Soap Creek School

estry now has close to 11,500 acres — 6,800 acres in McDonald Forest and 4,700 in Dunn Forest. Both forests are wildlife refuges and open to public for hiking and horse riding.

There is a bit of folklore concerning this site of Peavy Arboretum. It goes something like this: Back in the early 1850s a couple of men who had returned from Calif. with gold stuffed the dust into a boot and, afraid they would be robbed, buried the boot near entrance to what became the arboretum. A short while later they were murdered. A few days after that two rough- looking fellows swaggered into the nearest saloon and flashed their wealth. Were they the culprits? Had they found the boot? When the murdered men were discovered a search was set off for the cached gold but there has never been word of it having been recovered.

1.7 m., turnoff W to Peavy Arboretum. *(0.8 m., arboretum.) 1.1 m.,* Lewisburg Ave.

　　* E, *0.1 m.* Turn L. *0.2 m.,* **Mountain View Grange,** last survivor of Lewisburg. In 1915 village had State Game Farm, HS, PS, church, and was lively farm center. Suburbanization has removed all rustic touches.

4.6 m., **Corvallis,** at Benton County Court House.

Settled first in 1845, first town lots were sold in 1849. Town initially named

Marysville, either after Mary Lloyd, first white woman to cross Marys River; Mary Wimple, New York stater who never came to Oregon but was sister of local pioneer; or, most likely, Mary Stewart, better known as Aunt Mary, first white woman to put down roots here.

PO est. Jan 8, 1850 as Avery; name changed to Marysville 9 months later; wound up on Feb. 18, 1854 as Corvallis — "heart of the valley" in Latin — to differentiate it from Marysville, Calif., prominent staging area for the northern Mother Lode mines. (Year before, in 1853, territorial legislature approved same name change.) By then steamers were showing up at ferry landing, with some boats daring as far up the Willamette as Eugene, and a public road to Marysville had opened.

Corvallis commercially bloomed with discovery of gold in the Jackson Creek area, S Oregon, as the main N-S road to the mines came thru the town. When the gold petered out, Corvallis declined as shipping point. But arrival of telegraph line in 1856 bolstered spirits and the next year town was inc. (As an historical footnote, the first jail was built [1859] 4 years before fire dept. was org.)

In January, 1855, the legislature voted to move territorial seat to Corvallis, partly on the assumption that Corvallis was more centrally located and less infested with political venality. It took only the steamer *Canemah* to carry office equipment and baggage upriver to the new site, where all of Corvallis turned out to cheer. Along with the legislators came Asahel Bush and the presses of his *Oregon Statesman*. Everyone was sure Corvallis would be the great political and cultural center of the state. But soon the legislators were complaining that Salem had better accommodations and attractions and in June of same year the capital was brought back to Salem, with the *Oregon Statesman* going along. The Oregon Territorial Capitol stood at what is now 344 SW 2nd St. and plaque on SE corner of bldg. commemorates this bit of history.

In 1864 a battle ensued between Portland, Salem, Eugene and Corvallis for the state capital. Corvallis had the same luck its football teams suffered in the early 1980s and lost by a landslide, Salem emerging victorious.

Before trains and automobiles the Willamette River was very important to Corvallis and it became a great port. In the 1890s you could leave Corvallis at 8 in the morning and by 3:30 p.m. be in Portland. Except for stops at Albany, Buena Vista, Independence, Salem, Lincoln, Wheatland, Fairfield, Ray's Landing, Fulquartz Landing, Champoeg, Butteville and Oregon City, the voyage was uninterrupted.

In early 1853 the legislature appointed a commission to erect a territorial university at Marysville, as Corvallis was then called. But when town was made territorial capital, plan fell thru. But for a notion to move the capital to Corvallis the town might now be the seat of the U of Oregon and Eugene the site of OSU.

A community school started 1859 grew into Corvallis College, which at first was little more than glorified co-educational HS, with faculty of two. In 1865 Corvallis College was taken over by Methodist Episcopal Church, South. (City

Hall is old Methodist Church, S, at Madison and 5th.) Three years later state legislature designated it as recipient of congressional land grant (Morrill Act) of July 2, 1862, to state for maintenance of agricultural colleges. In 1868 Corvallis College became Oregon State Agricultural College. Twenty years later, on 35 acres of land given the state by Benton County citizens the year before, the college, then consisting of a single bldg., moved to its present site on "Campus Hill." Later the school became Oregon State College and, finally, **Oregon State University.**

Prize tourist attraction on OSU campus is Horner Museum, vast repository of Oregon history — natural and human. Museum is located in basement of Gill Coliseum.

Other points of interest on campus: Archaeological Collection, in Waldo Hall, with items from Jason Lee Mission and Fort Hoskins; Archives for History of Science and Technology, in Weniger Hall; Art Department Slide Collection, in Fairbanks Hall; Clothing, Textiles, and Related Arts Collection, in Milam Hall; Ichthyological and Herpetological Collection, in Nash Hall; Kerry Library, containing one of the most comprehensive map collections of the NW; Memorial Union Art Exhibit and Collection Program, in main concourse of Memorial Union; Natural History Collection, in new addition of Cordley Hall; Systematic Entomology Laboratory, in Cordley Hall; University Archives, in Administrative Services Bldg.; Benton Hall, where the college relocated to this site in 1888; Mitchell Playhouse (1898). Education Hall (1902) was Science Hall when 2-time Nobel laureate Linus Pauling studied chemistry and worked as lab assistant. Here Pauling met his wife, Ava, a remarkable person in her own right.

A "moon tree" — Douglas fir seedling, 2 ft. high and 4 years old — was planted in 1975 at the OSU School of Forestry. The seed was collected in Benton County and flown to the surface of the moon by the crew of Apollo 14 Jan 31 to Feb. 9, 1971. The command module "Kitty Hawk" was flown in orbit around the moon by Stuart Roosa, who trained as a smoke jumper at Cave Junction in 1953, while Alan B. Shepard Jr. and Edgar D. Mitchell landed in the Fra Mauro Highlands with seeds Roosa had obtained from Oregon thru the US Forest Service. The seeds were germinated in a FS nursery at Placerville, Calif., then presented to the Oregon Dept. of Forestry. In addition to the School of Forestry, a "moon tree" was planted at the Capitol grounds in Salem, another at the Veterans Hospital in Roseburg, another at Cave Junction, another at the now World Forestry Center in Portland, and the last of the Oregon six was kept at the D. L. Phipps Nursery at Elkton.

Corvallis Chamber of Commerce (350 SW Jefferson) has for free distribution "Historical Guide to Corvallis," which, in essence, is a walking tour and leaves out some important places away from business district and its environs.

From standpoint of historical interest, streets closest to downtown are the more interesting, because houses on them are the oldest, as is the situation in most Oregon towns.

Almost all of the old business bldgs. downtown have been remodeled and, anyway, unless one is an architect, it is difficult to get excited about their appearances, which generally can be described as prosaic.

The most impressive structure downtown is **Benton County Court House** (1888–89), oldest courthouse in Oregon still used for original purpose. Clock tower is best-known landmark in city and clock still uses all the original mechanisms. Architect DeLos D. Neer described his beauty as "High Victorian Italianate architecture with a military influence," which sounds like a poem written by Tennyson, set to music by Verdi, and orchestrated by Sousa. All the brick — more than 800,000 in the exterior — were made in Corvallis. Some of original furniture is still in the courthouse and treated democratically in usage. Some years ago the county commissioners were bent on tearing the courthouse down and replacing it with modern structure. But a vigorous effort to protect the old girl, led by Judge Richard Mengler, blocked the fatuous notion. Instead, the courthouse underwent a renovation — its third. Judge Mengler was honored for his preservationist battle by his name being placed on a bench outside the structure. He has yet to sit on it.

Across Monroe Ave. from courthouse sits town's tallest bldg., **Benton Plaza,** built as Benton Hotel in 1925. At seven stories tall it was "the largest project of its kind ever undertaken in Corvallis" and regarded as "Italian Renaissance at its finest."

Other fascinating structures in Corvallis include: **Dr. H. S. Pernot House** (1896), 242 SW 5th, outstanding example of Queen Anne stick-style architecture; **James O. Wilson House** (1892), 340 SW 5th, picture postcard beauty in its original colors, and its surrounding grounds a true reflection of past; **Dr. George R. Farra House** (1903), 660 SW Madison, now bed-and-breakfast Madison Inn, 3 1/2 story, Princess Anne Style, looking down like a stern but kindly Sidney Greenstreet after a sumptuous meal;

The Church of the Good Samaritan (1889), 700 SW Madison, now **Corvallis Art Center,** eminent example of Vernacular Gothic architecture; **First Congregational Church** (1917), 8th and Madison, Neo-classical bldg. that in 1919 was birthplace of Boy Scouts in Oregon Trail Council; **J. R. Bryson House** (1882) 242 NW 7th, noted for its corbelled top chimneys and boxed-eave roof adorned by intricate brackets with pendents;

Lewis G. Kline House (1884), 308 NW 8th, built for Russian immigrant who brought first sewing machine to Corvallis and built business which stayed in family 90 years; **Biddle House** (1856–57), 406 NW 6th, "a rare example of early Gothic revival architecture" and reflecting the affluent houses of the 1850s; **George Taylor House** (1900), 504 NW 6th, virtually unchanged inside and out;

Woodward-Gellatly House (1871), 442 NW 4th, strikingly handsome and presumptuous Rural Gothic; **Caton House** (1855–1859), 602 NW 4th, only house left in Corvallis built in Classical Revival style, with main entrance of wood frame house at gable end and black walnut tree at SE corner planted about

1859; **Arnold House** (1905), 806 SW 5th, bungalow Variant with Tuscan porch columns and built of "miracle hollow block";

Francis Helms House (1896), 844 SW 5th, Queen Anne style and for most part in original condition; **Hadley-Locke House** (1893) 704 NW 9th, whose locally unique Eastlake style ornamentation and elaborate flare topped chimneys give refreshing architectural interest; **Willamette Valley and Coast RR Depot** (1885), 500 SW 7th, now SP Depot, sole example of Swiss Chalet style architecture in town;

Charles Whiteside House (1922), 344 SW 7th, architecturally probably most original house in Corvallis. Even the untutored will quickly note its strong oriental influence and understand why it is referred to as "Aeroplane" Bungalow architecture.

Outside the central area, the 1856 **Van Buren House** is at 2856 Van Buren; the equally historic **Horning House** at 3701 SW Western Blvd. Author Bernard Malamad, who wrote his excellent novel *A New Life,* partly on the basis of his teaching in the English dept. at OSU, lived at 2860 Harrison.

Corvallis has some very interesting cemeteries:

Catholic Cemetery — take Grant to 36th, where roads intersect to become Witham Hill Dr. Cemetery just beyond intersection. Buried here are Agnes and Julian McFadden, who stipulated in their will that their long-time Chinese servant, Toy Lee, be buried at their feet. Until his death Lee was cared for by a McFadden daughter. One can read various symbolisms in this plot.

Continue on Witham Hill Dr. *1.1 m.* to **IOOF Cemetery** (1857).

Backtrack on Witham Hill Dr., which becomes 36th St. *1.5 m.,* turn R onto Harrison Blvd. *1 m.,* turn L onto 53rd. *0.3 m.,* **Benton County Fairgrounds.** Here stands very old, remodeled Baptist Church. For many decades it stood on bank of Willamette and after being abandoned as house of worship was used as grain warehouse. Continue straight. *1.9 m.,* Plymouth Dr. Turn R. *1. 2 m.,* Mt. Union Dr. Turn R. *0.2 m.,* **Mt. Union Cemetery.**

Marker just inside cemetery reads: "On May 11, 1861, Reuben and Mary Jane Holmes Shipley, former Negro slaves, deeded from their farm purchased from Charles Bales' donation land claim, the original plot for this cemetery."

Buried in Lot 10 are Reuben Shipley, Mary Jane Shipley Drake, Alfred Drake and four Shipley children. Also buried in cemetery are four Newton children, who died within 9 days in Dec., 1876 — perhaps victims of diphtheria epidemic.

From Benton County Court House, going S:

0.5 m., jct. (to W), US 20 — O 34. *0.5 m.,* on E, Crystal Lake Dr. (*0.6 m.,* **Crystal Lake-Masonic Cemetery,** 1842, one of oldest in state.)

1.8 m., jct., **Kiger Island.**

  * Turn E. *0.5 m.,* start of island, at bridge. Booneville Channel, leaving the Willamette, curves around island and rejoins the main stream, which is E boundary of this flat, fruitful food basket. *3.8 m.,* end of public road. *2.5 m.,* on E, Payne Rd.

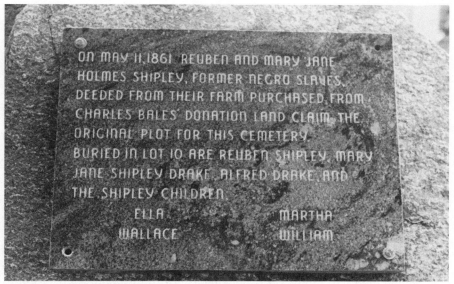

ON MAY 11,1861 REUBEN AND MARY JANE
HOLMES SHIPLEY, FORMER NEGRO SLAVES,
DEEDED FROM THEIR FARM PURCHASED FROM
CHARLES BALES' DONATION LAND CLAIM, THE
ORIGINAL PLOT FOR THIS CEMETERY.
BURIED IN LOT 10 ARE REUBEN SHIPLEY, MARY
JANE SHIPLEY DRAKE, ALFRED DRAKE, AND
THE SHIPLEY CHILDREN.
                    ELLA   MARTHA
          WALLACE   WILLIAM

Mt. Union Cemetery, Corvallis

**Graves of Newton children, Mt. Union
Cemetery, Corvallis**   *Phoebe L. Friedman*

*0.4 m., farmhouse at end of lane. To L, above Booneville Channel, stood **Booneville,** famous river landing of yore. Started in 1853, was still shipping point in mid-1890s. Flooding of Willamette in 1875 altered course of stream; Booneville Channel was until then main channel; after that, main body of river was and is to the E. After 1875 only boats with freight bound for Booneville came up shallow channel. Landing had store, blacksmith shop and warehouse. Except for some old alders and oaks that may have stood here when Landing existed, there is no vestige of pioneer hamlet. Dirt road that curves around stillwater touches home built by Green Berry Smith and still a residence.

2.5 m., Green Berry Rd.

* W: *0.3 m.,* site of **Green Berry** (or Greenberry), RR station named for 1845 pioneer Green Berry Smith, who came to Oregon with Stephen Meek "Lost Emigrant Party" and following year settled in Benton County. There was sawmill and school here. *2.5 m.,* on L, almost inconspicuous stone marker commemorates site of Herbert grist mill (1850) and Inavale, PO 1896–1905. *0.2 m.,* Bellfountain Rd. (To S, *7.4 m.,* Bellfountain.) Turn R, or N, onto Bellfountain Rd. *1.4 m.,* on R, looking as giant mushrooms in dark forest, grave markers of **Oakridge Cemetery.** Here lies settlers of nearby, long-gone Beaver Creek. *4.3 m.,* Plymouth Dr. Straight for Mt. Union Cemetery (see earlier, under *Corvallis*).

1.7 m., on E, **Jensen's Lazy J Ranch,** below Wagner's Butte, known in pioneer times as Winkle's Butte. At foot of Butte stood long-gone and almost completely-forgotten hamlet of **Jennyopolis** (spelled Jenneyopolis in original records.) PO lasted from spring of 1852 to 1857 and was astride main trade route down W side of Willamette Valley. (For story of village see "The Search for Jennyopolis" in author's *Tracking Down Oregon.*) A series of articles by Benton County historian Kenneth Munford in the Corvallis *Gazette-Times,* spring of 1987, detailed the first murder (and its sequence) that came to trial in Benton County. The crime took place near Jennyopolis on May 21, 1852, when Nimrod O'Kelley "did discharge a gun loaded with 40 leaden shot . . . into and upon the breast of Jeremiah Mahoney." O'Kelley was twice sentenced to hang but, in still mysterious circumstances in this most publicized murder affair of territorial years, he cheated the gallows and died of natural causes more than a decade after the shooting.

0.1 m., **William L. Finley Wildlife Refuge** (5,325 acres), named for William Lovell Finley, naturalist, environmentalist, bird photographer and Oregon's first game commissioner and game biologist. Among beauties on Pacific Flyway are the dusky Canada goose; its size and chocolate brown color distinguish it from other types of Canadas found in state. At height of wintering season, Dec.-March, the dusky Canada goose is king (or queen) of the Oregon portion of Pacific Flyway. Over 200 species of wildlife are present throughout year, including black bear (not commonly seen), red fox, gray fox, mountain lion, bobcat, porcupine, elk, mule deer, hares and rabbits. Nearly all species of Willamette Valley

Site of Booneville

Phoebe L. Friedman

Irish Bend Bridge

mammals are represented here because of variety of habitats: Oregon oak and maple woodlands, Oregon ash thickets, second growth Douglas fir, brushy hedgerows, marshes, creeks, meadows and cultivated fields. **Fiechter House,** in refuge, is one of oldest houses still standing in Benton County.

4.7 m., Irish Bend Rd. — Bellfountain Jct.

* To E — toward Irish Bend. *1.6 m.,* "T". Turn L. *0.5 m.,* turn R. *1.7 m.,* **Irish Bend CB,** no longer used. Built 1954 over Willamette Slough at length 60 ft., bypassed 1975. (For more, see "Irish Bend Nightmare" in author's *Tracking Down Oregon.*) Area was named for Irish families who settled on this bend of river.

* To W — toward Bellfountain (Dawson Rd.) *3 m.,* on N, turn uphill for 1859 **Bellfountain Cemetery** *(0.2 m.)* The dead sleep under firs and white birches. *0.4 m.,* **Bellfountain,** wide curve on rural road, with no more than school, church, store, smattering of homes. Yet in the athletic annals of Oregon, Bellfountain is enshrined in gold. In 1937 its HS, now all elementary, won Class B basketball championship of state, permitting it to enter Class A tournament, which it won by defeating Lincoln of Portland. (Tallest Bellfountain player was only 6 ft.) Night of victory was most celebrated in hamlet's history.

* W from Bellfountain on Dawson Rd.: *1 m.,* **Bellfountain CP,** with roofed 85-ft. timber table, giving it "natural-like" ambience. *2 m.,* **Dawson,** site of backcountry mill with flavor of old logging days.

** S from Bellfountain: *2.4 m.,* Alpine.

1.5 m., Alpine Jct.

 * W: *3.6 m.,* **Alpine.** Name is a lot prettier than the town, which looks like time passed it by about 50 years ago. In 1915 Alpine was a lot bigger — and probably a lot nicer to see. Store and tavern divide day and night sociability.

 ** W from Alpine: *0.2 m.,* on N, turnoff for **Alpine Cemetery** (1851) It actually looks neater than the town and, as with some other Oregon cemeteries, does service as lovers lane. *1.5 m.,* turnoff to Alpine Winery (*1.2 m.*) *1.2 m.,* **Glenbrook,** once terminus of branch line of Portland, Eugene and Eastern RR. PO lasted 1898–1905. Now, at best, splinter of bedridden houses. From here the road takes on a personality of its own, a pike for those who seek solitude, who want to poke into a bit of Oregon so close to the heartland and yet so obscure. In sharp turns the road climbs until you feel you are following the flight of an eagle circling in a wheel of air. Much of the silent journey is thru woods dark and secretive — firs and hemlocks and alders and maples; willows and vine maples too. Where the sun catches the rim of the woods the trees explode in a violence of green. *7.1 m.,* **Alsea Falls** BLM CG. *0.3 m.,* Alsea Falls BLM PA. Short trails lead to S Fork of the Alsea and to Alsea Falls, pretty splashes in the stream. *9.6 m.,* downtown Alsea, on O 34. *0.7 m.,* Alpine Jct. (*3.3 m.,* Alpine.)

 0.2 m., on W, Cemetery Rd. (*0.2 m.,* **Monroe Cemetery** — 1863 — in hip-high weeds.)

Courtesy Bellfountain School

0.6 m., at turnoff to **City Hall, Monroe.** Joseph White took DLC here 1846, built small sawmill 1850, started town 1853. First PO, Starrs Point, opened 1852 one m. N in early store. (PO name changed to Monroe 1874.) In its glory days a thriving farm center of Long Tom River Valley, Monroe has been bled by fast road linking Corvallis to Junction City. Between 1915 and 1990 Monroe grew at rate of about one person per year, not quite a pace to challenge Corvallis for supremacy of Benton County. In 1915 Monroe had more to it: sawmill, flour mills, creamery, cannery, brick and tile factory. **Wilhelm House** (1908) at SW corner, 6th and Commercial, biggest, best-looking residence in this part of county.

From Orchard St., at O 99W, turn W onto Orchard. *0.1 m.,* **Monroe United Methodist Church,** built 1910 to replace 1876 church. Belfry, pebble glass windows in front, stained glass windows with religious motifs on E side, and meditative look, like pastor pondering biblical question, combine to give structure full measure of charm. *1.1 m.,* on N, **St. Rose Cemetery.** White markers atop knoll emit image of band of angels holding solemn conference.

0.1 m., S of Orchard St., just beyond forks, tall, graceful steeple of **St. Rose of Lima Church,** which in 1983 celebrated "100 years of God and love of neighbor." From church, S on Territorial Rd.:

   * *4 m.,* turn R onto Ferguson Rd. *2.5 m.,* on R, **Long Tom Grange.** Backtrack to dirt road just E of Grange and on same side. Turn N onto dirt road. *1 m.,* end of road at locked gate. To NE stands **Rattlesnake Butte;** 50 acres of top and upper slopes constitute property of The Nature Conservancy, which says of its site: "Rattlesnake Butte's shallow soils and southern exposure support a rare Willamette Valley grassland type dominated by Lemmon's needlegrass (*Stipa lemmonii*) and the *Rhacomitrium canescens*, and a small remnant of the white oak-red fescue savanna. The rocky south facing slopes are denning sites for a number of reptile species including the Western rattlesnake." Rattlers are particularly numerous in early spring and fall.

At forks, curve L, onto O 99W. *3.6 m.,* **Washburne SP.** PA. *4.1 m.,* O 99 at Junction City.

O 219S — Newberg to Salem

The only state road that passes thru **French Prairie,** the birth basin of white settlement in Oregon, is the S portion of O 219. Before the arrival of the whites the Indians systematically burned the trees and high grass so better to hunt deer, thus the prairie. Superannuated French-Canadian employees of Hudson's Bay Co. gave the prairie its ethnic name. Here was the first school inside the boundaries of what later became the state of Oregon, taught by Solomon Howard and Helen Celiast Smith (see *US 101, Clatsop Plains*); here was held the historic meeting at Champoeg on May 2, 1843; here was built the first Catholic Church in Oregon — and there were many other firsts.

French Prairie has never been a tourist attraction and its really only viable town, St. Paul, is busy but one time a year, at 4th of July Rodeo. Nor is French Prairie oft visited for its history or attractiveness; it remains relatively obscure to the state. Yet it is crammed with history and it still retains nuances of the tingling beauty of some decades ago, before suburbanization, when a lambent mystique hovered over the meadows, no rural house looked real, and in the mystique of stillness there was the hushed expectancy that a voice would sing out from behind a tree and an old voyageur would step forth to offer greetings in French.

From O 99W, at Newberg:

"Replica" of first Catholic Church on
French Prairie

Phoebe L. Friedman

2.4 m., Wilsonville Jct.

 * Turn W. *50 yds.,* Springbrook Rd. On L, red-painted 1872 house. Road then glides with ease thru sweet, fruited, wooded, tilting and turning saucer of green delight and purity. Some of Oregon's finest estates are along this front. *4.3 m.,* Day Use Area, Willamette Greenway. *2.3 m.,* Ladd Hill Rd. On high bank above road at curve is grave of early overland pioneer Mary Geer, died 1847. *5.3 m.,* Wilsonville. (See O 99W, directly preceding.)

1.6 m., **Willamette River.** Just beyond bridge to L is marker indicating site of **Willamette Post.** It stood on closest knoll to E and was first trading post in Willamette Valley. Opened around 1811 by the Astor Co., which est. Ft. Astoria, at mouth of Columbia. Later, British interests took over. The fact that this trading post existed was responsible in some measure for early settlement of French Prairie. After post's days as trading house were ended, it was used by Hudson's Bay Co. as horse relay station for fur brigades until about 1831. In 1861 the Willamette River flooded heavily and carried away every vestige of post.

On R, across O 219S from Willamette Post marker, is ground upon which Etienne Lucier built house and raised first wheat grown in Oregon. The French-Canadian Lucier, who arrived at Astoria 1812 with Wilson Price Hunt overland expedition, trapped for Hudson's Bay Co until 1828, when he left to take up land in what is now the E side of Portland. His next move was to French Prairie, the first permanent white settler here. He was one of the two "swing" votes at the historic Champoeg Meeting of May 2, 1843 and lived until 1853, 4 years after Oregon became a Territory. With him for a while resided the 25-year-younger Francois Xavier Matthieu, the other "swing" vote at Champoeg. (For more on both, see "A Memory of Champoeg" in author's *Tales Out of Oregon.)*

0.7 m., Champoeg Jct.

 * *0.4 m.,* on L, 6259 Champoeg Rd., **Austin House,** built over 4-year period in 1860s by George Eberhard, son of early comer. Black walnut trees, which render parklike setting to house, planted 1870s. In 1985, descendant of Eberhard still occupied house, which retains hand-hewn beans put up 1860s. *1.6 m.,* on R, Jette Court. (*0.1 m.,* restored schoolhouse of pioneer days. Before restoration it had been abandoned for ages and was scarecrow of the thicket.) *0.4 m.,* forks. Take L. *75 yds.,* on L, entrance to **Newell House — DAR Museum.** House was built 1852, only house around to survive 1861 flood. Restored 1955–1959.

Dr. Robert Newell, better known as "Doc" Newell, was one of Oregon's more colorful pioneers. Born in Ohio, he came W as young man and was one of the "Rocky Mountain College" trappers. Tiring of that hungry and precarious life, he proposed to his brother-in-law, Joe Meek, that they leave the cursed occupation and go to the Willamette Valley, where they could farm in peace. In 1841 they brought the first wagon into the valley. Newell was a mercantilist, politician, man of culture, Indian agent, Calif. gold rusher, and peace emissary to the Indians. Together with Andre Longtain he platted town of Champoeg in 1852 and was doing fine as a businessman until flood of 1861 wiped out his profitable property. Discouraged, he moved to Lapwai, Idaho, where he spent the rest of his life, until 1869, farming and working with the Nez Perce Indians. (He had a strong liking for the Nez Perce, his first wife and mother of his first five children being Nez Perce. He was not alone in marrying an Indian woman; many other early trappers and settlers did likewise. The Nez Perce reciprocated his fondness for them, giving him of their own volition the first acreage granted by these Indians to a white. The 5-acre tract is now among the costliest property in Lewiston, Idaho, a fact which would have amused the wry-tongued Newell.)

* On grounds of Newell House — DAR Museum are:

Replica of first brick house W of Upper Missouri, built near Wheatland by George Kirby Gay in 1841. Marker states: "The Gay House was built of native clay, tramped bare footed, molded and burned on the place by Indians. The wood was hand dressed and hand carved." Also on premises: early country school and old Butteville Jail.

* *0.1 m.,* entrance to **Champoeg SP.** CG, PA, fishing, swimming, bike trail, FHP.

Every foot of the park breathes of history, much of it shown and told at the **Visitor Center,** near entrance. One of finest museums in Oregon, it alone is worth visit to SP. Other historic points in park are **DAR Museum** — **Pioneer Mothers Museum Log Cabin** and site marker of Champoeg Meeting, with names of persons who voted American chiseled on stone.

An Indian village, *Cham-poo-ick,* had long been flourishing by the time first white men saw it in 1811. Hudson's Bay Co. had a post here for years, with their first warehouses S of Oregon City, and village was shipping point of Willamette Valley wheat.

These meadows, on S bank of Willamette, are best known in Oregon annals, however, for the event of May 2, 1843. On that day the settlers of Willamette Valley posed the question of provisional gvmt. Contrary to popular history, the occasion was not the impromptu affair the patriots have made it out to be. (If anything, it was a well-organized spontaneous demonstration.) The event was preceded by two "Wolf Meetings," supposedly for devising ways to deal with predators, but the main topics were political independence, that is, placing Oregon under US hegemony. Even earlier than the "Wolf Meetings" was a gathering of settlers presided over by Jason Lee, and the discussion at the funeral of Ewing Young; both took place early in 1841. It seems obvious that for at least 6 years before Champoeg there had been a thrust for wresting Oregon from domination of Hudson's Bay Co.

Why the site of Champoeg? It was a midway point between the leading settlements, it was easily reachable by boat, and it was well known.

The French-Canadians, who worked for Hudson's Bay Co., welcomed the get-together. It was a diversion from their chores and they expected a big feast. When the proceedings turned political many of them walked away in disgust. Had everyone at Champoeg voted that day it is not likely the vote would have gone the American way. But that would not have changed the course of history. The Yankees were pouring in — that year the first wagon train to reach Oregon swelled the American population — and it was only a matter of time, and short time at that, before the British were inundated by the Yankee deluge.

Amidst the debating on that 2nd day of May, 1843, Joe Meek bellowed, in a roaring voice that would have set buffalo stampeding, "Who's for a divide? All in favor of the report and organization follow me!" He then traced a line with his boot toe.

According to popular history the men divided and the count came to 50 on one side and 50 on the other. Then, supposedly, Etienne Lucier and F. X. Matthieu stepped from their neutral ground to the "American side," and the day was won for provisional gvmt. But Matthieu remembered that event otherwise. His grandson, Stephen Matthieu, recalled of the old man more than 12 decades later: "He did not actually say that there had been a nose count, so that they knew he and Lucier were the deciding factors, but he said they decided — Lucier hesitated a moment, and he said, 'Come on, Etienne, let's get over here,' because he certainly didn't want a government organized under the British, since he was a fugitive.

"My grandfather didn't say there were 50 people and 50 people standing and looking at each other, with a line drawn between them, and him and Lucier standing at the side," Stephen Matthieu added. "I never heard him say that. He said they simply moved over to the American side. The count was 52 to 50. He repeated that many times."

The last political meeting at Champoeg took place July 5, 1843. A written constitution was approved and officers elected on May 2 were sworn in. Hudson's Bay Co. withdrew 1852, but settlement continued as river landing, grain market, and mercantile center. Town was platted with roads bearing romantic names, with the main drag being Boulevard Napoleon. Doom struck in Dec., 1861, when Willamette, swollen by heavy rains, all but washed away village. It was never rebuilt.

In 1900 a bit of Oregon became conscious of its Champoeg roots and sought to locate the site of the 5/2/43 meeting. Only one of the survivors was still alive: F. X. Matthieu. He led the governor and the secretary of the Oregon Historical Society to the "precise point" and there the monument was later erected.

How, after more than half a century, did the old man know exactly where the meeting was held? "The only thing he could say as to the exact point," Stephen Matthieu recalled, "was that it was necessary that the meeting be held on high ground. This was way up above the river level." And so are "precise points" determined. But does it really matter?

(For the botanical minded, large specimens of Oregon white oak adorn Champoeg SP.)

*0.4 m., **Zorn House,** also known as Champoeg Farm. Rambling, 14-room residence built between 1867 and 1870 and occupied by at least three generations of Zorns. In 1896 bell tower added to call farmhands to lunch. Windmill tower added same year. Look back about 0.1 m. beyond house for best photo view.

* 0.4 m., on L, picturesque, latticed house supposedly built 1869. Only front exterior has not changed. Rock wall on L near road is remains of 1869 flour mill.

*0.1 m., Butteville-Donald Jct. Curve R. 0.6 m., turnoff to **Champoeg Cemetery.** Markers back to 1853. 0.6 m., jct.

(If L is taken at this jct.: 0.9 m., forks. Take R. 1.1 m., Donald. 3.9 m., on R, turnoff to Aurora Community Cemetery. 0.8 m., Aurora. See O 99E, Aurora.)

* At above jct., straight on County Rd. 415 — Case Rd. 0.2 m., on R, **Tom Case House,** lovely old residence. 0.3 m., on R, and set back 0.1 m. from road, **William Case House,** described by local historical society as "oldest and largest ranch-style house in Oregon." Indianan William Case put 5 years into the bldg., completed 1850, and since renovated. Certainly, the classic of the valley, house is tribute to remarkable skill and patience of builder. 1.3 m., jct., St. Paul Hwy. Turn R, or W. 0.7 m., Champoeg Creek, site of **Mission Mill** built 1839. 1.2 m., French Prairie Rd. 1.9 m., St. Paul.

* From Butteville-Donald Jct., 0.1 m., past old Bailey House: 2.1 m., jct. L for Butteville. 0.4 m., **Butteville,** one of Oregon's earliest towns.

It was named after La Butte, hill to SW a mile away that is only 324 ft. higher than town site. Being on Willamette, Butteville gained early respectability as river landing. Town is probably best-known for F. X. Matthieu of Champoeg fame. He was first postmaster and probably first storekeeper. While his children tended store the old man sat on front porch, always ready to engage customers and passers-by in conversation, especially about past.

Butteville store bldg. goes back in part to 1861. 0.1 m., W of store is mid-19th century mansion built by prosperous grain merchant. Front door faces not road but river because in mid-19th century the key traffic was by steamer. House looks down on Willamette — nostalgic pastoral scene. Near store is old saloon, later garage, later just boarded up. Block from store is stretch of paved sidewalk that testified to importance of Butteville when town was in its prime, before Donald "stole away" its customers. For many years, sidewalk was hidden under weeds. **Butteville Community Church,** built 1930s, on site of previous church, has bell washed down from Champoeg in great flood of 1861. 0.1 m. from store, on L, Linden House, mid-19th century home. Across road is what was **Butteville Institute,** secondary school inc. by legislature in Jan., 1850. Among trustees were such famous pioneers as George L. Curry, J. C. Geer and F. X. Matthieu.

    * 0.6 m., turn L for **Butteville Cemetery.** (0.5 m., cemetery. Those who lie here include F. X. Matthieu, "last survivor of the 52 persons that formed the first civil government west of the Rocky Mountains on May 2, 1843" at Champoeg. He died Feb. 4, 1914, almost 96.)

    * Turn L. 1.2 m., on L, old white house loaded with gingerbread, built 1880s. 0.3 m., on L, 1905 house — lived in by five generations. 0.5 m., Hubbard Jct. (5 m., Hubbard.) On L, glowing lily field. Handsome house back of field built about 1903.

    * 0.5 m., jct. (R, 6 m., Hubbard; L, 20 m., Portland.) Straight. 1.9 m., forks. Take R. 0.4 m., forks. Take L. 0.3 m., on R, **Barlow Pioneer Cemetery.** (See O 99E, Barlow.) 0.4 m., O 99E.

From Champoeg Jct., on O 219S:

4.2 m., **St. Paul,** heart of French Prairie, tranquil town enveloped by lush groves and orchards and fields bursting with wheat, barley, vegetables and flowers.

Coming into St. Paul from O 219 via Champoeg Jct., there is on the L a sign stating that Philippe Decre and Francois Rivet were "Members of the LEWIS and CLARK 1805 Expedition." The pioneers who knew both as French Settlers believed, and so stated in print, that Decre and Rivet had gone to Oregon with Lewis and Clark. (There are people in St. Paul today who believe the same.) The facts are these: Decre and Rivet were boatmen on the expedition and came with Lewis and Clark only as far as Ft. Mandan, N.D. They came to Oregon decades after Lewis and Clark had returned to their starting point. (For more on the legend, see "Two Who Didn't" in author's This Side of Oregon.)

Decre and Rivet are buried here, along with such other prominent French Prairie settlers as Joseph Gervais, Louis La Bonte, Michel la Frambois and Etienne Lucier. Their graves are unmarked but local historians say that when the ground is damp it is possible to locate the graves — though by now no one knows who lies in which grave — by poking a stick into the earth.

Behind rock which holds plaque giving names of the buried here is sculpture crucifixion in memory of Oregon's first Catholic Missionary and Archbishop, Francis N. Blanchet. Statuary was dedicated to "place of the first holy sacrifice of the mass offered up in Oregon, Jan. 6, 1839."

A few yards toward town center is "country-style" red brick bldg. that was St. Paul Creamery for several decades. One block straight, to town center, and a block to R stands **St. Paul Catholic Church,** oldest parish in state and one of most ingratiating church scenes in all Oregon. Seen afar from many points on the prairie, it faces the small town, with the meadows running free behind it.

St. Paul congregation traces its history back to 1836, though efforts to organize a church were made 3 years earlier, when the Canadians, enlisting the services of

St. Paul Catholic Church   *Phoebe L. Friedman*

an unnamed and unknown American, drew up a petition, dated Feb. 23, 1834, to the Bishop of Red River, appealing for a priest.

In the early autumn of 1834 a party of Protestant missionaries, led by Jason Lee from the French province of Quebec, arrived on the E bank of the Willamette and set up shop. If Lee did not at times openly alienate the Catholics of French Prairie he certainly did not shake their faith. Perhaps it was the way he looked at them. In Lee's words, noted by a reporter for the *Peoria Register and Northwestern Gazeteer*, the Protestant missionary, on an 1838 trip E to raise money for his mission, told his Illinois audience that the settlers of French Prairie consisted of "men who had been in the employ of the Hudson's Bay Company, but had taken Indian wives and had settled here to pursue the business of farming. They numbered 15 or 20 families, and had become as uncivilized, nearly, as the savages around them."

On Feb. 23, 1835, the Catholics sent a second petition. It was answered by Bishop Provencher, who directed his message care of John McLoughlin, at Ft. Vancouver. No priests were then available, the cleric stated, but promised that one would be sent as soon as possible. In the meantime, the faithful were to carry on "the best way you can."

Heartened, the Catholics poured their hearts out again in a letter dated March 22, 1836, and proudly declared that "since we Recived youre kinde Letter we have be Gun to Build and to make some preparations to Recive our kind father . . ." Implicitly urging haste, the call noted that "the Countrey is setteling Slowly and our Children are Learning very fast which makes us very eager for Youre assistance." Listed at the bottom of the letter were the "Willammeth Settelers" in the area, together with the number of their children. Eighteen names (with 59 children) are listed; of these, 16 were French-Canadians. The name of Etienne Lucier is spelled as "eken Luceay" and the other non- English speaking settlers suffered similar fate.

The log church built 1836 was, as remembered by Francis Norbert Blanchet when he was Archbishop of Oregon, "70 feet by 30 feet," with 12 ft. by 30 ft. at the back of the altar set aside for two bedrooms, a kitchen and a dining room. It is generally assumed that the log church was built at the site of the present church but the *Sketches* of Archbishop Blanchet suggest that the church was probably constructed several miles to the S of St. Paul and on the E side of the Willamette.

For almost 3 years the settlers waited for a priest. Finally, at 10 o'clock on the morning of Jan. 5, 1839, Fr. Blanchet arrived from a mission on the Cowlitz River. The next day he held mass for the first time in present Oregon. From then until Feb. 3 he performed at 74 baptisms, 25 marriages and one burial, in addition to having the cemetery made and enclosed. Then he left, depressed with living conditions, the unexpected "objections of the Company of Hudson's Bay," the distance the French-Canadians had strayed from the fold, and the Indians, mostly Calapooias, whom he looked upon as heathens.

However, what is the business of religion but to save and to guide? So Fr.

Blanchet must have thought, for he returned in the autumn to become the permanent parish priest and make St. Paul the citadel of Catholic life in Oregon.

"A house of 62 by 25 ft. was raised in March (1841) at St. Paul, to serve as a hall for the people on Sunday and a lodging for the priest," Fr. Blanchet noted in his *Sketches.* But this "peoples' hall" was not popular with all visiting priests; a year after it was put up one of them observed in disgust with St. Paul: "There is yet here only an old chapel which will fall at the first gust of wind on the back of the poor priest, who is lodged in the sacristy."

Things improved in 1843 when, aided by a donation of 4,800 francs from Joseph Laroque, a rich retired HBC fur trader residing in Paris, St. Joseph's College for Boys was founded as a boarding school. In its first term the faculty numbered three, the students 30, all but one of the pupils being enrolled as "sons of farmers," the exception being Andre Hop-hip, son of an Indian chief.

The following year the famed missionary, Rev. P. J. DeSmet, came with four new priests, one lay brother, and six sisters from a Belgian convent, Notre Dame de Namur. The locals were to have a convent finished by the time the Sisters arrived, but it wasn't. Impatient, the nuns grabbed hammers and saws and completed the work. Their eventual prize was Sante Marie de Willamette, with tuition often paid in flour, rice, meat, eggs, potatoes, salt, candles, tea and other commodities.

The years 1844–46 comprised probably the biggest church bldg. boom in St. Paul. On a bluff above Lake Ignatius, now Connor's Lake, the Jesuits constructed a 2-story residence, a second story was added to St. Joseph's College, the N wing of the convent was finished, and a chapel added to the girls' school.

In 1846, too, the log church was replaced by a structure of red brick made in ovens on the grounds. The lofty spire was topped by an iron cross, hammered out by hand by a settler who had been a blacksmith for HBC. Words on the bell state it was presented to the Rev. Father Aloyisius Vercruyise, SJA pastor of St. Paul's Parish, from his relatives in Belgium in 1845, making bell oldest in state. Under its patina, the rich oxidation of age, is inscription, "God, thus your praise go to the end of the earth." Bell was shipped around Horn and unloaded at Mission Landing. The landing, one of crudest on Willamette, was not only key link between Catholic Church on French Prairie and the "outside" but was the point of entry for the many ecclesiastics who came to St. Paul's Parish.

The Calif. Gold Rush siphoned off many French Prairie settlers, forcing the closing of both schools and the Jesuit mission. St. Joseph's College was started again around 1860, again followed by the reopening of the girls' school. But, as the first time, success was not to be had, and the schools closed for good.

Catholic influence on French Prairie has never waned; locals estimate that today 95% of St. Paul is Catholic. The largest families in state must be on French Prairie, it seems, with women in their thirties having five, six, seven or eight children.

St. Paul has grown so slowly since 1915 — about two persons a year — that it seems to stand still. It is now most famous not for its historic interest but for its rodeo, whose prize money is supposedly second only to that offered in Pendleton for an Oregon rodeo. The St. Paul Rodeo was started in the Great Depression year of 1936 by eight men who decided to enliven the town during the summer. They chose a 4th of July Rodeo — a 3- day affair now — and each put in $100 to cover expenses. The first rodeo netted $600 and from then on receipts have mounted.

Asked why St. Paul didn't have a motel, a farmer having a beer at the tavern observed: "It'd do great business for two or three nights and be dead the rest of the year."

The locals boast that no one has been mugged in town in anyone's memory. Many summer residents are Mexican farm workers who send their earnings home to their families in impoverished villages. The Hispanics are almost all industrious, courteous, polite and proud.

Emmett Kirk House, *0.1 m.* E of Main on Mission, is 1889 structure now **St. Paul Mission Museum.** It was supposed to have been torn down to make room for bank but was saved by self-sacrificial efforts of local historian Joe McKay, then postmaster, and moved to present location. In McKay's words, house "evidences the Victorian love for colored glass, filigree wooden trim and patterned shingling." A famous photographer photographed this house to place in a book as most representative of Oregon.

Next to Emmett Kirk House stands **Murphy House,** with back (original) part supposedly built 1832. Thrice moved, Murphy House is also museum; furnishings date back to at least 1836. Window glass said to be among oldest in PNW. Murphy family lived in house from 1856 to 1965. Although Emmett Kirk House is official museum, Murphy House is richer by far in historic memorabilia.

Old City Hall and **Knights of Columbus Hall,** built circa 1900 at 3rd and Oak, 2 blocks E of Main, looks like ancient barn afflicted with arthritis. Silent movies were shown upstairs. An old timer said: "Lots of St. Paul folks met their mates at the dances in this hall."

House on NE corner of 3rd and Blanchet (390 Blanchet) built in 1913 for first banker by Peter McDonald, later postmaster of St. Paul for almost 35 years. (Evidently being postmaster here is not a fly-by-night job. Joe McKay served for about three decades before he retired in mid-1980s.)

For another bit of historic St. Paul, go N on Main from Blanchet. *0.3 m.,* Mission Rd. Take L, or W. *1.1 m.,* on Mission Rd., stop sign. Straight onto private road. *0.2 m.,* down slope, **Mission Landing** — very important in old days; nothing now. Turn L, or S, on Riverside. *0.4 m.,* **Connors House,** built around 1880. Back of house is site of 15-room Jesuit HQ in early days. The famous Fr. DeSmet lived here. Site now occupied by modern ranch-style home. Beyond house is pond known historically as Lake Ignatius, now Connor's Lake. It was favorite fishing hole for the padres. *0.2 m.,* Blanchet Rd. Turn L. *1 m.,* starting point at PO.

Museum of the St. Paul Mission Historical Society

For shortest road to Champoeg SP from St. Paul, take O 219 at Main St. *2 m.,* jct. Turn L or N onto French Prairie Rd. *0.4 m.,* on R, **Cosgrove House,** built 1880s. *0.9 m.,* on L, yellow-painted **Coleman House,** also built 1880s. In 1890 Coleman family operated dance hall and restaurant here. Back addition to house is solar-powered. *2.1 m.,* forks. (On L, opposite corner, **Robert Newell House —** DAR Museum. See earlier, *O 219.*) Turn R. *0.1 m.,* Champoeg SP.

In St. Paul, turn R on Main St., which later becomes River Rd. *0.1 m.,* house at 351 Main built before 1871. *0.9 m.,* Davidson Rd. (Turn L. *0.1 m.,* on R, lawn of modern, Spanish-style **Bustamante House,** gravestone of Augustin Raymond, early settler who died in 1873. His DLC has remained in family, now Bustamante, and farm is oldest in state held by same family.) *0.2 m.,* old house, near fruit stand, is site of former burial marker of Raymond. *4.2 m.,* on R, former **DuRette Farm.** To R and beyond house is granary that was built as Fairfield store in 1856 and moved from original site in 1910.

Fairfield was another Willamette River steamboat landing that grew into a town. D. B. DuRette's father was born in Fairfield in 1860 and D.B. in 1891. "When I was growing up there was still a church, the Cumberland Presbyterian, built in 1872," recalled Mr. DuRette. "And there was still a thriving store and two grain houses. Wheat was shipped by steamboat. There were docks all along the river those days, and the boats burned wood. The Fairfield steamboat landing was washed out years ago.

"At one time," Mr. DuRette continued, "Fairfield had three stores, two warehouses, a saloon, a blacksmith shop, a cooperage, a sawmill, a brickyard, and numerous dwelling houses. The streets were named, and it had been surveyed and laid out in city lots. The year the electric line went in was the beginning of the end of the warehouses. Wheat wasn't shipped by steamboat anymore. When the railroad took over the town declined and the business closed and the town dwindled down to a handful of people, and then it just faded away." (For more, see "Our Landing at Fairfield" in author's *This Side of Oregon*.)

0.1 m., Marthaler Rd. (*4 m.,* St. Louis; *6 m.,* Gervais.)

1.1 m., on L, iron gate. Trail beyond gate leads *0.3 m.,* around hop field to **Fairfield Cemetery.** Four generations of DuRettes lie here. An inscription on a tombstone reflects how most pioneers felt about death: "Parents, sisters, why these tears/ O'er our dull and lifeless clay?/ Could you see our present bliss/ Tears to joy would pass away."

1 m., on R, **Fairfield Grange,** other than the granary the last surviving bldg. of old Fairfield.

0.3 m., jct., O 219S. At corner is eyestopper 2-1/2 story, early 20th century mansion with water tower, home of Nusom Orchards, and engulfed by spacious lawns and orchards.

L to St. Louis and Gervais. Take it.

* 0.7 m., forks. Take L for St. Louis. *1.2 m.,* **St. Louis,** one of those "backstreet" villages unheard of by most Oregonians. As is common with many such places, its past is more interesting than its present. In 1845 a log church was built by the Jesuits and it must still have been sturdy 15 years later, when Sister Alphonse paid a visit, with the eye of establishing school here, for she noted that church was "a wooden building, painted white. The interior is quite nice and the sacristy contains some beautiful vestments. Everything is orderly." In 1847 a resident priest arrived and a parish was organized. Being of French heritage, the priest named the church St. Louis, for the King of France, who was scarcely a saint — but a king adored is a saint on earth. In 1880 or 1890 present church was built. Under it sleeps Marie Dorion, the remarkable Iowa Indian who was first woman to cross plains (with Astor Overland Expedition in 1811) and settle in Oregon. Her body had been removed from Catholic Cemetery here, where she had been laid to rest in 1850. Old St. Louis Cemetery is no more; remains were moved to new cemetery, to R and back of church.

Climer Residence, 1-1/2 blocks NW of church, served as rectory for early priests, is one of oldest bldgs. in state, and is distinguished by log beams, wooden pegs and hand-planed, grooved boards. *0.1 m.,* on R, back of street, old St. Louis School, built 1904 and in use as such until 1968, now residence. It was one of few — if any more — schools which for a time employed nuns as public school teachers.

* 2.7 m., Gervais. *0.4 m.,* O 99E. (See O 99E, Gervais.)

From jct., O 219, at Nusom Orchards.

Turn R for Salem. *1.6 m.*, Wheatland Jct. *(3.6 m.*, **Wheatland Ferry,** probable site of where first farmer in area, James A. O'Neil, resided.)

0.5 m., on R — just past Waconda Fire Dept. station — and across road, one of showplace houses in valley, with round-covered porch and gilded with gingerbread. *4.1 m.*, **Hopmere,** started as RR station and not any more important now. *3.2 m.*, Wheatland Jct. *(6 m.*, Wheatland Ferry.) *1.1 m.*, **Keizer.** Started as appendage to Salem, Keizer has mushroomed into independent community, but its charms seem lost on most travelers. *1.7 m.*, forks. Bear L. *2.1 m.*, Salem — jct., O 219 — O 99E.

East Side Shunpiking
O 99E

From Burnside and Union, Portland S on Union (O 99E), which becomes McLoughlin Blvd.

1.5 m., on L, striking-looking old house which has caught many an eye. *2.8 m.*, Johnson Creek Blvd. *0.4 m.*, Ochoco St.

* Turn R, or W. *0.1 m.*, on L, next to animal clinic, ghostly skeleton of early church.

0.4 m., Milport Rd.

* Turn W. *0.2 m.*, SE 17th. on NW corner, **Milwaukie Pioneer Cemetery.** Oldest grave that of Capt. Frederick Morse, who died Dec. 25, 1850. While celebrating launching of steamboat *Lot Whitcomb,* Morse was struck by fragment of cannon which exploded when fired. Morse and Lot Whitcomb and wife, Irene Chamberlain Whitcomb, were first buried in private Whitcomb cemetery near 28th and Washington, Milwaukie. When land was platted and property sold to make Springside Addition, Morse was moved to this burial ground and the Whitcombs taken to Riverview Cemetery in Portland. Original Morse marker is in Milwaukie Historical Museum.

Also buried here are Seth Lewelling — elsewhere spelled Luelling — and his son, Willie Anton Luelling. Seth's marker has old family name, his son used the new name spelling, the one adopted by Seth's brother, Henderson Luelling, pioneer nurseryman. In 1847 the North Carolina-born Henderson, then operating a small nursery at Salem, Iowa, left for Oregon with his wife, 10 children, and nursery stock of 700 grafted fruit trees, berries and shrubbery planted in open wagon. They arrived in Willamette Valley Nov. 17, 1846 and planted several trees on what is now Waverly Country Club, which borders cemetery to W.

Henderson and his partners — son-in-law William Meek (1848 arrival) and brother Seth (1850 comer) — did very well; in 1851 they had 18,000 fruit trees on the market, operated a traveling nursery, and in 1853 est. several other nurseries throughout Willamette Valley. During the S Oregon gold rush in the early 1850s the partners sold their apples for $1 lb. and their peaches and plums for $1.50 lb. But Henderson was always restless, always reaching. He started a sawmill and flour mill, took a fling at the Calif. Gold Rush, and in 1854 sold his principal interest to Meek and moved to Calif., where he started another nursery and made more money. Still, it wasn't the bigness he dreamt of so off he took himself and his plantation vision to Honduras. There he lost his shirt. Heart-broken, he returned to Calif. and at San Jose began clearing land for one last nursery. He was moving toward his 70th year and starting from scratch again. But before the first plant was set into the earth the lean hand of death stilled his spade.

0.3 m., jct., O 224 — to Estacada. *0.3 m.,* Harrison St., **Milwaukie.**

Turn E. Back of City Hall, on Main between Harrison and Jackson, is stump of ornamental peach tree, first of its kind in PNW. It was sent to Seth Luelling from China in 1869 by Anson Burlingame, first American minister in China. When tree was 75 years old it was uprooted because Luelling home was being torn down, and replanted at present location.

Plaque in front of City Hall honors Henderson Luelling and his son Alfred. On Feb. 5, 1848, Henderson settled on his DLC 1 m. NW of this point and from there began his nursery industry. Another plaque here honors Lot Whitcomb and Joseph Kellogg, 1847 industrialists, and Hector Campbell, first schoolteacher (1849).

Main St., Milwaukie, looks more like small downtown preserved than its site would seem to warrant. The town's past, centered on the Willamette, was more colorful.

Lot Whitcomb, a Vermont man who hacked out farms in Michigan and Illinois before crossing the plains with Henderson Luelling, didn't take long to make waves in Oregon. Before he had been here a year he built a sawmill and grist mill and founded Milwaukie. The next year he went into the boat freight-hauling business and made a pile. With that money he started a newspaper, *Western Star,* in Nov., 1850, and a month later launched first steamer built on the Willamette. It was named for him and it was during the festive celebrations of the launching that Capt. Frederick Morse came to a noisy end.

The *Lot Whitcomb* made the run from Milwaukie to Astoria without stopping at Portland and was one of the first excursion boats, plying between Oregon City and what is now Cascade Locks. Fare was $25 a couple. In 1853 the steamer was sold to a Calif. company for $50,000, exactly $42,000 more than it cost to build her.

Another noteworthy vessel constructed at Milwaukie was the *Jennie Clark,* launched in 1854 as the first sternwheeler on the Willamette. Before then side-wheelers and propellers were the only steam craft on the river. During summer of 1862 the *Jennie Clark* made the first seaside excursion from Portland and until autumn had a weekly schedule, carrying vacationers to the beach for $15 round trip.

Visitors to Milwaukie sometimes ask for walking tour brochure but there isn't any; not that much of interest to see. Still, town has a few encouraging footnotes. **Ledding Library,** Harrison and 21st, looks down upon lovely duck pond in rear. From library, E on Harrison to 37th. Turn R. *0.2 m.,* Adams and RR Sts. Hook L. Right there, at 3737 SE Adams, is **Milwaukie Historical Museum,** in 1865 farmhouse moved to this location. Outside, sheltered from elements, is 1872 horse-drawn Portland streetcar. Behind 1875-built frame house at 2746 Washington is pond that was lifelong task and joy of milkman Paul Hager. Hager inherited from his father the pond, an ancient mill bldg., an old water wheel, a 19th century pumphouse, a mellowed barn and the terraced land flanking the pond. On this acre and a half the Hagers developed for themselves and their friends and Walden-loving visitors a lovely rustic cameo. Here the fish were not caught, the fowl not killed. One day in 1984 the gentle, life-loving, worn-out Paul Hager, suffering from an incurable illness, limped to the barn to feed his milk goat. It was his last gesture on earth. Those who mourned him rejoiced in the way he died, close to one of his pondside friends.

From Harrison and McLoughlin, S on O 99E:

1 block, Jackson St. **Seth Luelling home** stood on SE corner. *0.1 m.,* Jefferson St. *20 yds.* S of SW corner, plaque honors the legendary Father DeSmet, early Jesuit missionary. *1 m.,* **Oak Lodge,** named for roadhouse that stood when the road from Portland to Oregon City wasn't long commercial strip. *2.5 m.,* Roethe Rd.

* *0.1 m.,* on R, **Moore's Flour Mill.** Century-old stone grinding machines from abandoned flour mills in Indiana, Tenn., and E Oregon mill bread flour in 1880 setting. Visitors welcome.

0.2 m., **Jennings Lodge,** platted as townsite 1905. PO named Jennings (for 1847 Oregon comer Berryman Jennings) est. 1910; changed to Jennings Lodge 1911. Part of hwy. strip now.

1.4 m., Arlington St., **Gladstone,** the residential town named for British prime minister William Ewart Gladstone in 1889. Turn E onto Arlington. *0.1 m.,* turn R onto Barton, which quickly turns into W Clackamas and parallels river. *0.2 m.,* on L (E of house at 250 W Clackamas), **Pow-Wow Tree,** huge maple that tradition states was site of Indian councils. Also, tree marked entrance to first State Fair (1861). *0.4 m.,* **Cross Park,** on Clackamas River. Follow W Clackamas *0.2 m.,* around to First St. and turn R. *0.1 m.,* turn R on 82nd Ave. Diagonally across from 82nd, parking lot of High Rocks Park. This is one of Gladstone's greatest joys and its largest problem and most painful embarrassment. The park, on the Clackamas, is indeed scenic but in summer it is marked by heavy drinking, errant behavior and mortalities. "Each year," said a city official, "we find a few bodies floating in the river. People get tanked up, are hot, and jump into the cold river to cool off. Their bodies can't take the shock. So they drown." Return to 82nd Ave. Turn R. *0.3 m.,* turn L onto Oatfield Rd. On R, former grounds of Willamette Valley Chatauqua Assn., founded 1894 as third largest Chatauqua in US. For next 30 years up to 10,000 people — a lot then — participated in annual 2-week program. Among speakers here were William Jennings Bryan and Susan Anthony.

1.2 m., from Arlington St., on O 99E, 10th St., **Oregon City.** *0.2 m., on L, Visitor Center.*

Built on three distinct terraces, or benches, on the sheer bluff along the E bank of the Willamette, Oregon City was initially called Willamette Falls, the settlement being at the break of the Willamette, where the wide, strong-flowing river drops 42 ft. from a basaltic ledge. The falls posed both advantage and disadvantage for the pioneers, making a commercial community here inevitable. The falls provided mill power and, at the same time, created a rupture in the continuity of river transportation, necessitating a portage and later, with the advent of river freighters, a transfer point for goods.

Oregon City has more historic firsts than any other town in the state: first inc. city W of the middle Missouri; first Protestant church, Masonic Lodge and newspaper in the American West; first use of water power in the state; first settlement in Oregon to hear a brass band; first mint in the state; Oregon's first capital. Oregon City also claims to have these firsts in the American Far West: public school, library, Catholic Archdiocese, and court of record, and boasts of being site of origin of first long distance commercial power transmission in US.

There is another first, which local historians have neglected: the first divorce was granted here, to an Oregon City woman, the decree being given in the Provisional court Nov. 2, 1846. After a brief trial a jury found "the allegations as set forth in the petitions substantiated" and to Mary Ann Smith were restored "all the rights and immunities of a state of celibacy."

From the start the river played a crucial role in the development of the settlement. Dan O'Neil of the Mounted Regiment brought to Oregon and stationed at Ft. Vancouver in 1849, left a graphic word picture of early river transportation:

"Navigation in the days of '49, on the Columbia and Willamette, was not only tedious but a sometimes difficult and dangerous undertaking. Steamboats were not in fashion, and as roads were not yet opened for heavy wagon traffic, the only way of getting goods through was by open boats and man power. For this purpose bateaux, belonging to Hudson's Bay Company, were brought into service . . . With a crew of six Indians to each boat, and a load of 5 tons, we would leave Vancouver in the afternoon, making the first landing and camp somewhere near where St. John now stands. On the second night we would reach Milwaukie, and on the next afternoon make our arrival at Oregon City. Getting over the rapids below Oregon City was a tedious but exciting part of our journey, the Indians wading through the current, patient and good natured and willing, as long as they received their dollar a day and plenty of beer . . ."

Oregon City vied with other towns along the lower Willamette for shipbuilding contracts. One of the boats constructed here was the *General Lane,* built in 1849 by John McCullen for the San Francisco run. She went directly to Sacramento with a cargo of lumber from Oregon City. She also had a load of eggs on board which the captain sold to a passenger for 35 cents a dozen. The passenger then sold them in Sacramento for $1 each.

For millennia the Indians of the area had come to the falls of the "Wallamet" for salmon. The whites who shoved them aside continued the tradition. Before the Willamette was thinned of salmon there were tales of the fish being so thick that a big man could cross the river by walking on the back of them. An old timer recalled: "My grandfather told about stopping at the river on the way home from work and catching a salmon for supper." Salmon was for a time so central to the prosperity of Oregon City that Dr. Robert Newell, the "Doc" Newell of the mountain men, noted the fact at a 4th of July barbecue dinner in Salem in 1851 to celebrate passage of the DLC: "Champoeg for beauty,/ Salem for pride;/ If it hadn't been for salmon,/ Oregon City would have died."

There is precious little in downtown Oregon City that is tangible evidence of the historic past. And the charming business district of a few decades ago has all but vanished. In its stead is a street of businesses trying to survive against the onslaught of large shopping centers.

There was a time when folks in Portland and Oregon City could commute by streetcar. Now, as for many years, folks are able to drive around downtown and never pass thru a yard of the business section.

The promoters of Oregon City try to work up a mystique of history about the place. But their efforts have been for nought. Most of the present residents know scarcely anything about the town's history and couldn't care less. They are living for today, with their daily problems, and are not a whit concerned with the false-fronted yesterdays.

Clackamas County Court House, 8th and Main, has on its lawn a plaque memorializing Oregon Trail, Barlow Trail and Oregon City and another paying homage to William Simon U'Ren, "Blacksmith-Lawyer-Political Reformer-Author of Oregon's Constitutional Provision for the Initiative, Referendum and Recall giving the people control of law making and lawmakers and known in his lifetime as Father of Oregon's enlightened system of government."

The plaque does not say that U'Ren, a skilled politician who was called "pussy cat" by some of his contemporaries, because he walked quietly and spoke softly, was also a devoted Single Taxer, a Populist before he became a Republican (the Democrats were too conservative for him), a spiritualist, and a strong believer that you are what you eat and when, echoing a famous dietitian of the day: "Never eat when you are sad or mad, only when you are glad."

Inside the courthouse, photocopies of original 1850 San Francisco plat are sold for modest fee. On SW corner, 8th and Main, **Caufield Bldg.** Oregon's oldest commercial bldg., has housed store of one kind or another since put up in 1848. **Masonic Temple** between 7th and 8th on Main, is HQ for oldest Masonic Lodge W of upper Missouri, with charter brought across plains in 1846. (Present bldg. dates only to 1907.) SE corner, 7th and Main, was site of early Protestant church in Oregon Country. **Methodist Church** dedicated 1844; in winter 1847 provisional legislature met here. On SE corner, 6th and Main, stood first capital of Oregon Territory (1849–1852). After capital was moved to Salem the plain 2-story frame bldg. was used as meeting place of the Masonic Lodge and Sons of Temperance and was county court.

City's most famous downtown structure is **Municipal Elevator,** 7th and Railroad, which carries passengers without fee from lower to upper levels.

Within a decade after Oregon City was platted, houses were arising on the upper level. Access to upper level was reached from a gradual trace S of city but as population grew there arose a need for a more direct foot route between the levels. At first old Indian trails were used. By 1867 a network of stairs were built up the bluff, to be developed and improved over the following four decades. But the climb was still arduous and could not be made by all. Finally, after defeating a bond measure in July, 1912 to build "A Public Elevator at the Bluff," voters reversed themselves 5 months later and authorized $12,000 in bonds. After 3 years of private and political wangling the wooden, water-powered elevator was opened for public use early in Dec., 1915, with 3 minutes required to reach the upper level from the lower. In 1924, electricity replaced water power and the ride was reduced to 30 seconds. As the elevator gained public acceptance the old wooden stairways were removed; most old timers cannot now point out where they stood. In 1954 construction was started on a new elevator. It was dedicated May 5, 1955, one of only four municipal elevators in the world. Elevator makes the foot route between downtown Oregon City and the McLoughlin House an easy stroll.

Clackamas County Historical Society, 2nd and Tumwater, on E of McLoughlin Blvd., just beyond Willamette Falls Viewpoint, is one of newest, largest, best organized county museums in state.

For tour of upper level:

At McLoughlin Blvd and 10th, turn E. *1 block,* Main St., principal downtown thoroughfare. *0.2 m.,* uphill, 7th and Center. On corner is **McLoughlin House,** National Historic Shrine.

In his prime Dr. John McLoughlin was the moving force of the Oregon Country. He and Jason Lee, the pioneer missionary and pro-American plotter, vied for the supremacy of Oregon. The Roman Catholic McLoughlin outflanked the Methodist at almost every turn but, in the end, it was the goal of Lee that won out, though McLoughlin is memorialized as the "Father of Oregon."

Like Lee, McLoughlin was born in Quebec, but their first meeting was 3,000 m. to the W. Educated as a doctor, the Irish-Scottish McLoughlin began practice in Montreal but soon lost his zest for medicine and joined the fur trading North West Co. as a partner.

He was 37 and in charge of the Norwesters station at Ft. William on Lake Superior when NW merged with Hudson's Bay Co. Three years later, in 1824, he was sent W as chief factor of HBC for the Columbia District, with HQ at Astoria.

The following year he moved the HQ 100 m. upstream on the Columbia to a site he named Ft. Vancouver. From 1825 to 1846 he ruled the HBC conglomerate there with firm hand and wise heart as he sought to carry out the mandates as outlined by his superiors. These were: to monopolize the fur trade in the region, control the Indians (thru peaceful means), and prevent the agricultural settlement of the Oregon Country by the restless, persistent and ambitious Yankees.

McLoughlin managed the first until the pelts thinned. And he was successful with the Indians, perhaps because both his spouses were Indian or part Indian. There is little known of his first wife (if he was married to her), a Chippewa woman by whom he had a son. His second wife, the Indian-Swiss Marguerite Wadin McKay, whom he married when he was 28 and she was 37, was the widow of fur trader Alexander McKay. She and McLoughlin had four children.

But on the last of his given duties McLoughlin failed; indeed, he helped create his failure, once he had realized his historic error. "For all coming time," he told Rev. J. L. Parrish, an associate of Jason Lee, two years before the first wagoners arrived, "we and our children will have uninterrupted possession of this country as it can never be reached by families but by water around Cape Horn."

Parrish, the wiser in this instance, replied, "Before we die we will see the Yankees coming across mountains with their teams and families." McLoughlin shook his head emphatically. "As well might they undertake to go to the moon."

Then, according to Rev. I. D. Driver, in his Annual Address to the 1887 Reunion of the Oregon Pioneer Association, "When the first emigrants arrived and

McLoughlin House   *Phoebe L. Friedman*

the news reached the doctor, he laughed and treated it as a joke. When evidence of the fact accumulated that it was true and that a train had encamped on this side of the Cascades, the doctor went and made a personal inspection and after conversing with the emigrants, looking at the dilapidated wagons, torn covers, jaded animals, and sunburnt women and children, he returned, and on meeting Parrish (being a devout Catholic and adhering to all the forms and ceremonies), he crossed himself, using his familiar expression, and said — "God forgive me, Parrish, but the Yankees are here, and the first thing you know they will yoke up their oxen, drive down to the mouth of the Columbia River and come out at Japan."

Instead of seeking to keep the Yankees out of the Oregon Country, which he realized he could not do in any case, he fed them, medicated them, supplied them with tools and seed and gave them the best advice he had.

McLoughlin was not entirely altruistic. In the beginning was the plan to turn the Yankees into customers of HBC. The more Yankees, the richer the HBC. But the newcomers were sharp mercantilists, too, and McLoughlin realized he had lost the game of commerce. So he joined the competition. When a secret agent of the US gvmt. game to Oregon and was instrumental in organizing a company to bring livestock from Calif. to Oregon, McLoughlin was a key principal in the venture.

In turn, a significant number of the pioneers reneged on whatever debts they had incurred, sought to have McLoughlin's land at Oregon City taken from him, made life for him as hard as they could. In dealing with McLoughlin, there is no doubt that anti-catholicism played a strong role in the criticism leveled against him by the settlers.

The decisive figure in the attack on McLoughlin was Samuel Royal Thurston, an 1847 comer who 2 years later was elected Territorial delegate to Congress. There Thurston, supported by the Methodist Mission, inserted a rider in the Donation Land Law of 1850 which, in effect, defrauded McLoughlin of much of his land. After McLoughlin's death some of his land was returned to his heirs.

A tall, striking character, McLoughlin was known to the Indians as the "White-Headed Eagle" and often "Great" was inserted before the appellation. He was innovative, courtly, tough-minded, open to new ideas, and far-seeing. In 1829 he chose a site at the 42-ft.-high Wallamet Falls to build a mill. Here he located a 2-sq.-m. land claim upon which a hamlet was born, starting with retired HBC trappers and voyageurs. In 1842 he had the city platted and gave it its name.

During these years he still managed the far-spread Columbia District of HBC. But his relations with the British-owned, London-based firm grew increasingly difficult as historic perspectives clashed. In 1845 McLoughlin resigned and moved to Oregon City where he became a storekeeper and started work on a 2-story colonial farmhouse. In 1850 he donated to the city the park at 7th and Center. The next year, when resentment against him had ebbed, he was granted US citizenship and was elected mayor of Oregon City, receiving 44 of the 66 votes cast by the Caucasian adult male property holders who went to the polls.

He served only one term. Five decades and 2 years after his passing the McLoughlin House was moved to the park. By then it had been occupied for some time by members of his family and then utilized as hotel and rooming house.

Back of the house, now museum, is a 200-year-old cannon whose only relevance to McLoughlin is a parallel in time. The 18 pounder was made in London in 1789 and supposedly brought to Ft. George (Astoria) by the North West Co. in about 1818 and carted to Ft. Vancouver in 1825. There it remained until 1847, when it was placed on a barge bound for Oregon City. But it rolled off the barge and was not seen again until 1937, when the old channel of the Willamette River near the mouth of the Clackamas River was dredged. Some sharp eye spotted the cannon in 19 ft. of water and gravel. So it was rescued and placed in McLoughlin Park.

Back of the house, too, are the graves of Marguerite and John McLoughlin. She died in 1860 at age 85; he died in 1857, 6 weeks before his 73rd birthday. The McLoughlins were originally buried at the first site of St. John's Roman Catholic Church, at 10th and Water. (For all practical purpose, Water St., W of McLoughlin Blvd., is no more.)

As it often does, recognition and appreciation come posthumously. On Feb. 5, 1889, an oil painting of McLoughlin was presented to the Oregon House of Representatives. The acceptance speech was given by Gov. Sylvester Pennoyer. On Oct. 6, 1905, "McLoughlin Day" was celebrated at the Lewis and Clark Exposition in Portland. In 1907 an elementary school in Oregon City was named for McLoughlin. The dedication address was given by Frederick V. Holman, a biographer of McLoughlin, and ended with: "To this Noble Man, to this Great White Chief, to this Grand Old Doctor, to this savior of the Oregon Pioneer, to this great Humanitarian, the Father of Oregon, to honor and praise for all time." That year the Oregon legislature officially designated McLoughlin as "Father of Oregon."

In 1921 McLoughlin was nominated one of two candidates for the National Hall of Fame and on Feb. 4, 1952, the statue of McLoughlin was dedicated in Statuary Hall in the Capitol of Washington, D.C. Two years later a statue of Jason Lee was unveiled in the same hall. Thus, of the two representatives of Oregon in the National Hall of Fame, one lived in the Oregon Country only 10 years and the other was a citizen for only 6 years. But here, across the continent from where they met and dueled, are the sons of Quebec, closer to their birthplace than to their hour of glory.

Near McLoughlin House (and Municipal Elevator) is **McLoughlin Promenade,** affording fine views of industrial Oregon City, Willamette River and West Linn. McLoughlin deeded this land to city in 1847 and more than a century later stones from the old Commerce Bank of Oregon City were used to build Promenade Wall. At 406 McLoughlin Promenade, 1877 **Miller House;** 306 McLoughlin Promenade, 1880 **Toelman House.**

Next to McLoughlin House (directly N, at 719 Center), is 1850 **Barclay House,** also moved here from original site on lower Main St. House was built by Dr. Forbes Barclay, surgeon at Ft. Vancouver and intimate of McLoughlin. Probably no person served Oregon City as completely as did Barclay. As a doctor, he answered all calls, never deterred by weather or inability to pay. Many a night he rode his patient horse thru the darkling woods or traveled by boat, guided only by lantern, to the scene of sickness. Among the posts he held, Barclay was Clackamas County coroner for 20 years, city school supt. for 13 years, city councilman for 9 years, and mayor of Oregon City for 7 years. When he died in 1873 the entire community mourned.

Across street, at 720 Center, is 1912 **Capt. Phillips House.**

This is the McLoughlin Historic District; area is loaded with 19th and early 20th century structures.

First Methodist Church, 811 Center, is oldest Protestant Church in Oregon Country. Original church, org. 1840, built on NE corner, 3rd and Main. Fine overlook of Oregon City from back of church.

At 8th St., turn R. *1 block,* Washington St. Turn L.

809 Washington, 1889 **Judge Cross House.** 9th and Washington, **St. Paul's Episcopal Church,** org. 1851. 916 Washington, 1896 **Huntley House,** probably most photogenic current residence in District. 1214 Washington, 1894 **Babcock House.**

   (* 101 16th, 1875 **Atkinson House,** built by George Henry and Nancy Atkinson. George est. First Congregational Church; also Oregon City Female Seminary — 1849. 1616 Jackson, 1895 **Vonderahe House.**)

17th and Washington (415 17th), **Hackett House.** *0.1 m.,* beyond 17th and Washington, on R, in Kelly Field, **End of the Trail Marker.** Plaque reads: "Here at Abernethy Green in the fall of 1845, members of the Barlow-Palmer-Rector Wagon Train entered Oregon City as best they could." Barlow and companions started across the Cascades in early October, left their wagons in the mtns., did not reach Oregon City until Xmas day.

At 216 14th St., 1870 **Clark House.**

On or near 12th St.: 712 12th, 1885 **Howell House;** 1216 Jackson, 1892 **Whitlock House.**

On or near 9th St.: 9th and John Adams, **First Baptist Church;** 902 Jefferson, 1893 **Dye House,** home of author Eva Emery Dye; 914 Madison, 1888 **D. C. Latourett House;** 902 Taylor, 1895 **Taylor House.**

From 7th and Center, take Center toward lower numbers:

514 Center, 1886 **Miller House;** 5th and Center, 1896 **McDonough House;** 715 5th, 1895 **Judge Ryan House** — garage in rear is only surviving carriage house in Oregon City; 518 3rd, 1900 **Farr House;** 411 3rd, 1879 **Ross House;** 224 Center, 1869 **Milne House;** 524 High, 1913 **Jones House;** 503 High, 1880 **Charles Latourette House;** 512 6th, 1885 **Jaggar Rental House;** 504 6th, 1911 **Petzold House.**

From McLoughlin House, 7th and Center, take 7th:
1 block, Washington St.

     * NW corner, Washington and 6th, 1907 **Stevens House;** 710 6th, 1925 **Atkinson Memorial Church,** est. 1844 as first Congregational Church in W, architecture patterned after medieval English church; **Oregon Trail Interpretive Center,** 5th and Washington, in basement of Oregon City Senior Citizen Center, has, among other artifacts, original plat of San Francisco; **St. John the Apostle Catholic Church,** 417 Washington, dates from arrival of Father (later Bishop) Modeste Demers in 1843 and was once seat of the Archdiocese; when it was enlarged it covered the McLoughlin graves; tombstones were embedded in foundation. 302 Washington, 1902 **Dr. Stuart House.**

1 block, John Adams St. On corner in front of Oregon City Public Library, plaque honors Edwin Markham as "Poet Laureate of Oregon." Marker placed here 4/23/1952, exactly 100 years after birth of Markham.

     * SW corner, 6th and John Adams, **Ermatinger House,** said to be oldest standing residence in Oregon City; 802 5th, 1893 **McDonald House;** 402 John Adams, 1890 **Trembath House;** 720 4th, 1896 **Carrico House;** 818 4th, 1893 **Koerner House;** 819 4th, 1900 **Erickson House.**

1 block, Jefferson St.

     * 720 Jefferson, 1928 **Zion Lutheran Church;** 610 Jefferson, 1912 **Andressen House;** 902 6th, 1870 **Bacon House;** 415 Jefferson, 1874 **McCown House;** 410 Jefferson, 1913 **Joehnke House;** 308 Jefferson, 1876 **Howell House;** 221 Jefferson, 1890 **Huth House;** 204 Jefferson, 1898 **Busch House.**

1 block, Madison St.

     * 411 Madison, 1872 **Judge Caufield House;** 302 Madison, 1889 **Willoughby House;** 301 Madison, 1892 **Seiler House.**

1 block, Monroe St.

     * 714 Monroe, 1895 **Glass House;** 724 Monroe, 1905 **Erickson House;** 1016 6th, 1870 **McCarver House.**

914 7th, 1892 **Church House.** (Mrs. Mindwell Church was first female deputy sheriff of Clackamas County.) 1108 7th, 1885 **Jones House.** 1204 7th, 1889 **Pease House.**

0.2 m., curve R onto Molalla Rd. *0.7 m.,* turn L onto Hilda St.

0.2 m., **Mountain View Cemetery,** one of Oregon's largest and most impressive burial grounds, looking face-on to Mt. Hood. Here lies Peter Skene Ogden, contemporary of John McLoughlin and his successor as chief factor at Ft. Vancouver. Like McLoughlin, Ogden was twice spoused to Indian women. Unlike McLoughlin, Ogden spent much of his time with HBC in the field and was without doubt the company's greatest explorer. (Ogden, Utah was named for him.)

Also buried here are Wm. Barlow, Dr. Forbes Barclay and Sidney Walter Moss, the last-named an 1842 arrival who surveyed Oregon City with a pocket compass and a piece of rope. (For more on the very colorful Moss, see "Oregon City's Moss" in author's *This Side of Oregon*.)

From turnoff to cemetery:

0.2 m., on R, Warner St. (*0.1 m.,* St. Johns Cemetery. Markers back to late 1890s.)

0.4 m., turn L onto Beavercreek Rd. *4.5 m.,* **Beavercreek,** tiny village that has grown into expanding suburb of Oregon City. Straight at curve. *0.1 m.,* on L, **Bryn Seion Welsh Congregational Church,** built 1884. For first few decades, services were in Welsh, then Welsh and English, then all English. On last Sun. each June church holds *Gymanfa Ganu Blynddol,* Annual Song Fest, with words in Welsh and English. Singing starts after lunch at nearby Grange. To this reunion come former parishioners from all parts of W.

One of the favorite songs is Bryn Myrddin. In English the first verse is:

> Great was Christ the Lord eternal
> Great to wear the flesh of man
> Great on Calvary to languish,

**Grave of man who drowned in "Wallamette falls" —
Mountain View Cemetery, Oregon City**   *Phoebe L. Friedman*

S.W. Moss grave, Mountain View Cemetery, Oregon City

Great to conquer death's wide span;
Truly great His estate
King of Heaven and earth innate.

In Welsh the words are:

Mawr oedd Crist yn nhragwyddoldeb
Mawr yn gwisgo natur dyn
Mawr yn marw ar Calfaria
Mawr yn maeddu angau'd hun;
Hynod fawr yw yn awr
Brenin nef a daear lawr.

Bryn Seion Welsh Congregational Church, Beavercreek   *Phoebe L. Friedman*

Return to Molalla Rd. Turn R, toward Oregon City. At first stoplight, *0.1 m.,* turn L onto Warner Milne Rd. *0.7 m.,* turn L onto Leland Ave. *0.5 m.,* turnoff R onto gravel lane to 1851 **Ainsworth House,** built by John Commingers Ainsworth, steamboat captain, transportation tycoon, banker. 33rd degree Mason and first elected Master on Pacific Coast. White Mt. Vernonish, 4-pillared, balconied house was showplace in its day.

Back to Warner Milne Rd. Cross it. On other side, Leland is Linn. Straight on Linn. *1 block,* Warner Parrott Rd. Continue on Linn. *0.5 m.,* turn onto Holmes Ln. *0.1 m.,* on R. 536 Holmes Ln, white 2-1/2 story **Rose Farm,** gorgeous 1847 restored mansion now museum. ("Rose Farm" name came from multitude of roses grown here.)

It was from the balcony opening off the second floor ballroom that Joseph Lane, Oregon's first territorial governor, gave his inaugural speech on 3/3/1849. Listening to Lane were such luminaries as Dr. John McLoughlin and former provisional governor George Abernethy. The ballroom was the scene of all-night dancing to music of clarinetist and two fiddlers. For victuals the dancers could fall back on beef, bear and elk. 567 Holmes Ln, 1898 residence.

Return to Warner Parrott Rd. and Linn Ave. Turn R onto Warner Parrott Rd. *0.3 m.,* Canemah Rd. Just beyond — 20 yds., on L — dirt lane *0.1 m.* to restored **McCarver House** (1850), sometimes called Locust Farm, because of former adjacent locust grove.

House was put up by Morton Matthew McCarver, native of Kentucky who started W in early manhood. By 1834 he reputedly founded Burlington, Iowa, and was then commissary-general of Iowa, from whence title "General" originated. (Explanation as popular and less accurate was that he was frequently called "General" while in Calif. because he had been a militia officer in Oregon.) He came to Oregon in 1843 with the Great Migration and together with Peter Burnett, later first US governor of Calif., founded Linnton, now part of Portland. McCarver was elected first speaker of the house of the provisional legislature, a distinction some attributed to his immense energy and booming voice. In 1848 he took off for the Calif gold streams, joining the feverish Oregon throng. While in Calif. he was one of 48 delegates who met in Monterey in autumn 1849 to work out a constitution for the new state. McCarver spearheaded an anti-Negro immigration clause and upon its defeat was heart-broken. A sympathetic journalist wrote: "It had been his darling object, his hobby, and Napoleon could not have mourned Waterloo more than did the General the annihilation of his free Negro preventatives." Before the convention adjourned the still boiling McCarver threw a temper tantrum over a minor issue and departed. He left Calif. after supposedly playing a hand in founding Sacramento, on his newly purchased passenger packet, *The Ocean Bird,* which carried an "Aladdin House," cut to measure in Boston. On his Locust Farm McCarver set up his prefab house, first of its kind in Oregon. Less than two decades later he moved to Wash. state and was instrumental in founding Tacoma. Before his death in 1875 he observed blacks around Puget Sound. Anti-Negro to the last, McCarver passed away a frustrated racist.

From Canemah Ave.:

0.6 m., turn R onto South End Rd. 0.8 m., turn sharp L onto 5th Ave., which becomes Miller St. 0.3 m., turn onto 4th. 0.2 m., L onto Blanchard. 0.2 m., gateway to **Canemah Cemetery** (0.5 m.). Chain across start of trace necessitates walking, pleasant hike thru lovely woods. Markers date from 1850s.

Backtrack to Miller and 4th. Continue straight on 4th. 0.1 m., turn L onto 3rd. 0.1 m., R onto Hedges St. 1 block, McLoughlin Blvd. Turn R. 1 m., Main and 8th, downtown Oregon City.

S from Clackamas County Court House, Main and 8th:

0.1 m., **Dr. John McLoughlin Memorial Bridge** — to West Linn. Bridge opened 8/31/1933. Performing christening ceremony was Eva Emery Dye, prominent Oregon City author and historian.

* Turn R, or E. 0.2 m., on L, **West Linn Police Station.** (Behind and to E of it is parking lot. Descend stairs that lead to walkway to **Willamette Falls Locks,** in operation since 1873.)

0.2 m., beyond police station and on O 212 (L at Lake Oswego Jct.), turnoff R onto West A. (0.2 m., on L, on near side of West Linn HS, **Camassia Natural Area,** maintained by The Nature Conservancy.)

Return to O 212. Turn R. 2.3 m., 19th St. Turn R. 0.2 m., turn L onto Blankenship Rd. 0.4 m., forks. Take L. 0.2 m., Johnson Rd. Turn R. 0.8 m.,

Tendril Ln. *0.2 m.,* on R, on far side of driveway, blurred sign marker of **Willamette Meteorite,** "largest and most majestic meteorite to be discovered in this country."

Return to O 212. Turn R. *0.2 m.,* 12th St., start of 2-block-long business section of formerly independent burg of Willamette, now part of West Linn, which has its genesis in 1840 arrival of Robert Moore, member of buffoonish Peoria Party. (See "Long Road to the Cook House" in author's *Tracking Down Oregon.)*

Moore, father of 10, was 59, a rather late age for emigrants, when he reached Oregon, but he was full of get-up-and-go. First off, he purchased a 1,000-acre tract, called the "Green Flat," from Chief Wanaxha of the Wallamut Indians. Then he built a cabin halfway up slope of hill looking down upon Willamette Falls and called it Robins Nest. In 1843, year after Oregon City was laid out and named by Dr. John McLoughlin, Moore laid out his village — he had prior experience in Illinois — and sold industrial and commercial sites along the rocky W bank of the Willamette.

Moore did take time off in 1843 to canoe upstream to Champoeg for the seminal meeting of May 2, where he was one of the famed 52 to vote for local gvmt. (which meant American dominance of Oregon) and for the meeting of July 5, where a system of provisional gvmt. was formulated, with Moore chairman of the legislative committee.

Somehow the plat of Moore's 50-acre townsite was never recorded but it made no difference; 2 years later its name was changed to Linn City, in honor of Lewis Fields Linn, who as US Senator from Missouri championed expansionism. Soon, under the drive of Moore, the village had lumber mill, chair factory, wagon shop, general store, tavern and blacksmith shop.

Discovery of gold in Calif. lured so many men away from Linn City that scarcely an able-bodied man was left. But Moore refused to be faced down by the ghost. He was known as abrasive, opinionated, domineering and stubborn, and it was the stubbornness he put to use. Purchasing a newspaper, he turned it into a booster sheet for Linn City. Gradually the town grew, exploding with energy during and immediately after the building of a canal around the falls in the early 1850s. But in competition for trade and industry Oregon City won out and Linn City was relegated to being little more than a transfer point for river traffic. A disillusioned Robin Moore retreated to his cabin and on Sept. 2, 1857, at the age of 76, he died. A day later he was followed to the crossing of the unknown river by Dr. John McLoughlin, founder of arch-rival Oregon City.

In April, 1861, fire destroyed the industries of Linn City but the town refused to surrender. A freight handling system was built and Linn City began the crawl to recovery. But came Dec., 1861 and the Willamette River, rising 67 ft. from its base, collapsed the breakwater built about a decade before, and smashing everything in its path. When the waters had receded,

Linn City was no more. In its place came West Linn, now a burgeoning suburb of Portland, with its commercial strength along O 43, the road to Lake Oswego.

0.2 m., 14th St. On SW corner, picturesque church. In front is replica of 15-1/2 ton Willamette Meteorite, found in 1902 by farmer Ellis Hughes.

(For details on Willamette Locks and Willamette Meteorite, see *The Great Heartland, Short Trips Out of Portland, South Suburban.*)

Backtrack to 12th St. Turn R. *0.2 m.,* Petes Mtn. Rd. Straight. *0.2 m.,* **Willamette Park,** where Tualatin River ends its course in the bosom of the Willamette.

Return uphill *0.2 m.,* to Petes Mtn. Rd., named for Peter Weiss, who got himself a chunk of slope land in 1868. Petes Mtn. isn't much of a rise, having max. elev. of only 850 ft., but from brow of hill there are, on clear day, sky-scrubbed views of the Cascades and the Tualatin Valley. Turn onto Petes Mtn. Rd. *3.7 m.,* turn L onto Riverwood Dr. *1.2 m.,* Heeb Park, above Willamette. Ferryboat crossing river upstream is nostalgic cameo.

Return to Petes Mtn. Rd. Turn L. *0.8 m.,* SW Mountain Rd. Turn L. *0.8 m.,* Canby Ferry Landing. Cross river to E bank. *0.5 m.,* entrance to Molalla River SP, adjoining Willamette River. *0.1 m.,* SP. PA.

Return to Canby Rd. Turn R. *2.2 m.,* downtown Canby.
In Oregon City, at Main St. and West Linn bridge:

Canby Ferry at mid-crossing

0.1 m., Main and 5th. Straight ahead lies industrial plant of **Smurfit Newsprint Corp.** Some years ago plaques bearing historical notations were fastened to the walls, and bldgs. which linked the historic past to the present still stood. But plaques have been removed (some at office bldg. now) and some bldgs. gone.

The present industrial grounds were once the cradle of Oregon City. Here was erected the first American hotel beyond the reaches of the Upper Missouri, the Old Main Street House, a 14 x 17 ft. cabin operated by Sidney Walter Moss, as flamboyant a character as early Oregon knew. Moss was not much for giving financial credit and when he built another hotel, a 2-story bldg. on the SW corner of 3rd and Main, also on these grounds, he advertised in verse (he was quite a literary fellow and wrote the first novel penned in the Oregon Country): "To all, high or low/ Please down with your dust,/ For he's no friend of ours/ That would ask us to trust."

On these grounds, too, stood the first pulp and paper mill in Oregon, constructed 1866 and using rags and straw to produce less than one ton of paper daily; the first Protestant church (Methodist) W of the middle Missouri; first Masonic Lodge this side of the Rockies; pioneer woolen mill; Opera House, erected 1865; and mint, built by Oregon Exchange co., private enterprise which operated from Feb. to Sept. 1849 and produced $58,500 worth of $5 and $10 gold pieces known as "beaver money" because each was stamped with the likeness of a beaver. The pieces were made from dies and a press constructed from old wagon tires.

Prior to beaver money there was an anarchy of currency. When James W. Nesmith arrived in Oregon in 1843, he recalled later, "Three Mexican dollars was all the money I ever saw."

Emigrants arrived with little US money, which had to compete with Hudson's Bay Co. dollars. Some of the newcomers disdained HBC; others found the consistency of HBC money superior to the uncertainties in dealing with merchants who charged as much as the traffic would bear. When Americans dealt with Americans it was often greed dealing with necessity.

Barter was tried but it worked not well. Various merchants issued their own script and before long there were, among other currencies, "Vancouver Money," "Ermantine Money," "Couch Money," and "Flint Money." The last-named, devised by George Abernethy, Oregon's only provisional governor, was for a time the most popular script.

George Abernethy was a storekeeper for the Methodist Mission in Oregon City when he conceived his system of monetary exchange. What he did was to cut flint rocks to the measurement of dominoes and glue each rock with heavy paper. Upon slip of glued paper he noted in longhand the date, the name "Abernethy," and the value or denomination of each flint rock. This rock money would be accepted by Abernethy in exchange for goods carried in the Mission store. A man with a "pocketful of rocks" was judged to be a man of means.

There was a general feeling that after some of the Oregon settlers returned from the Calif. hills with gold dust in 1848 the crude currency situation would be refined. But from the first there were sharp disputes as to the accuracy of weighing out the dust in the stores. The returnees felt cheated, complaining they had toiled too hard in the chill Sierra streams to be fleeced so handily.

To end the confusion and abrasion the provisional legislature authorized minting of $5 and $10 gold coins and the est. of the Oregon Exchange Co. About then Oregon became a Territory and the coins were declared illegal, since private mintage was in conflict with federal statutes. But the Oregon Exchange Co. was permitted to mint for 7 months and the coins remained in general circulation until 1854, when coins from the US mint in San Francisco arrived. Over the next decade or so the US bought up all the beaver money, with the exception of coins retained individually. These are now highly prized collectibles. As for the Abernethy flint rocks, out of the hundreds or perhaps thousands that were once on hand, only a precious few remain.

Here, too, was located the *Oregon Spectator,* first newspaper in the American Far West, a fortnightly started by the Oregon Printing Assn., a loose-knit group of politically-minded Willamette Valley settlers who wanted a vehicle propagandizing their views and for broadcasting the corporate acts of the local gvmt. The printing plant was obtained in New York by George Abernethy on a visit east in 1845 and boated 'round the Horn. On the sleety day of Feb. 5, 1846 the first edition was pulled from the Washington hand press. Although published less than a decade the *Oregon Spectator* not only reported the hard news of the day but, even more so, reflected in its columns the cultural life of the people. An example is a song that appeared in the issue of Oct. 15, 1846. Titled "To the Emigration of 1845" and written by a "Maj. Sullivan," it was sung to the tune of "The Girl I Left Behind Me."

Too slick and generalized to be real folk music, the song nevertheless was popular with the paper's readers. These are the words:

"As slow our wagons rolled off the track,/ Their teams the rough earth cleaving,/ And drivers all still looking back/ To that dear land they're leaving-/ So loth to part from all we love,/ From all the links that bind us,/ To turn our hearts wher'er we rove,/ To those we left behind us.

"When round the bowl of vanished years,/ We talk of joyous seeming,/ And smiles that might as well be tears,/ So faint and sad their beaming,/ While mem'ry brings us back again,/ Each early tie that twin'd us,/ O sweet the cup that circles then,/ To those we've left behind us.

"And when in other climes we meet,/ Some isle or vale enchanting,/ Where all looks wild, flowery and sweet,/ And nought but love is wanting,/ We think how great had been our bliss,/ If heaven had but assigned us/ To live and die mid scenes like this,/ With some we've left behind us.

"Yet we have made a home once more,/ In the Willamette valley,/ And yet all the boys, both rich and poor,/ May go and court Miss Sally,/ As to myself, I count me blest,/ If you will all excuse me,/ To ease the pain that's in my breast,/ I'll go and court Miss Susy."

On or at the periphery of these grounds, too, stood the stockade John McLoughlin put up to guard his Hudson's Bay Co. stores; the 80 x 50 2-story frame house McLoughlin built in 1846 and which was moved in 1909 to its present location; and the small yellow cottage where famed poet Edwin Markham was born in 1852.

Long years after he departed Oregon City, Markham remembered McLoughlin as "six-feet-six, handsome and impressive." Before Markham was taken by his mother to San Francisco in 1857, McLoughlin died. The 5-year-old lad "was taken into the cathedral in Oregon City when the good man was lying in state," Markham wrote in the foreword to a biography of McLoughlin; "(and) some strong man lifted me onto his shoulder that I might look down upon the face of the great dead."

Edwin Markham never returned to Oregon to live. When he was 69 he visited the state briefly and received much press attention. On his 71st birthday he was named "Poet Laureate of Oregon" by Gov. Walter M. Pierce. It was both a touch of sentiment and a gesture of public relations and the wise Markham, long a resident of Staten Island, N.Y., took the title in stride. He must have reflected,

Salmon fishing below Willamette Falls   *Courtesy State of Oregon*

DR. JOHN McLOUGHLIN
"FATHER OF OREGON"

Bust of John McLoughlin near Willamette Falls   *Courtesy Oregon State*

with a touch of whimsy, that it was his mother, Elizabeth, who was truly the Oregon poet, though her verses were journalistic and topical. She ran a little store and wrote for the local paper, describing whatever events caught her fancy. When she heard a bit of news, about anything from an oversize vegetable to a steamboat grounding, she thrust a sheet of paper on her counter, picked up her pencil, scribbled her rhyming comments, and rushed the copy to the editor.

(For more on this area, see "A Corner of History at Oregon City" in author's *Tracking Down Oregon*.)

From Main and 5th, Oregon City, S on O 99E:

0.5 m., on R, **Willamette Falls,** the closest sight Oregon has to Niagara Falls. (Walk *400 ft.* S along sidewalk adjoining O 99E to bust of Dr. John McLoughlin, his eyes turned upon river.)

From Willamette Falls turnout:

50 yds., turn L onto S 2nd. (Sharp L here, *50 yds.,* Clackamas County Historical Museum.)

* *0.1 m.,* turn R onto S End Rd. *0.4 m.,* slant R onto 5th. *0.3 m.,* turn L onto 4th. *0.2 m.,* turn L onto Blanchard. *0.2 m.,* gate of **Canemah Cemetery.** *800 yd.* auto trace to cemetery, est. 1864 but markers go back to 1850s. Fine view of Willamette from cemetery cliff.

From S 2nd on O 99E:

0.4 m., Hedges St., named for Absalom Font Hedges, Ohio emigrant of 1844 who in 1855, at age 27, laid out town of Falls City, at start and finish of portage around Willamette Falls. Town grew but name was dropped in favor of Indian name of area, *Kanim,* anglicized to **Canemah,** meaning "canoe place." In early 1850s a level portage road was blasted out of rocky bluffs between Oregon City and Canemah and in early 1860s a wooden-strap rail track was built between the two towns. More than 100 tons of freight on cars pulled by mules were hauled each day and so efficient was the operation that it became known as richest RR mile in NW. In mid-1860s iron tracks were laid and Canemah prospered until completion of Willamette Locks, in 1873, led to decreased freight rates. In 1882 Canemah made claim to having first public amusement park in US with Oregon City folks brought here by inter-urban line. Gradually, however, local industry centered in Oregon City and Canemah settled into status of residential district. In 1928 village was annexed to Oregon City. A full half-century later it was listed as National Register Historic District.

In its time Canemah was the great shipbuilding town on the Willamette; during 1850s about a dozen steamboats were built in local shipyards. Here the riverboat captains, the elite of the Willamette, constructed their fashionable Classic Revival style homes, of which only a few remain.

One of the boats built here was the 145-ft-long sternwheeler *Gazelle,* completed in March, 1854. What happened to it was told in the 1961 publication of the Clackamas County Historical Society:

"On April 8, 1854, the Gazelle was ready for the first regular trip up-river to Corvallis. At 6 a.m. in the morning, passengers were loaded at Linn City and the Gazelle then came across the river and tied up alongside of the steamship Willamet at the Canemah docks.

"While the loading of freight was going on and smoke poured from the stacks of the Gazelle, the engineer was reported to have hurriedly left the ship and headed over the hills. He was scarcely out of sight when the boiler of the Gazelle exploded, scattering people, cargo, and debris in all directions. Of the 60 people aboard, 24 were killed and 30 injured. The stores, shops and mills in Canemah closed up for the day as the local residents helped with rescue operations. Of the Gazelle, only the hull was left; the rest was junk.

"A coroner's jury investigated the tragic accident. After testifying, Captain Robert Hereford of the Gazelle was found innocent. The engineer, Moses Tonie, was not to be found as he had reportedly left the territory. The coroner's jury found him guilty of 'gross and culpable negligence.' A mystery still surrounds the activity of the engineer. Unanswered are such questions as: Was this an unavoidable accident? Had the engineer purposely tied down the safety valve on the boiler to form too much steam? Was he hired by a competing company to blow up the ship?

"The hull of the Gazelle was raised, rebuilt and successfully lined over the Willamette Falls. The boat was renamed the *Senorita* and was used on the run to Astoria."

On NE corner of O 99E and Hedges, at 316 McLoughlin, **Stevens House,** 2-story dwelling with two front doors and a chimney at both ends, making it a "double house." On SE corner, 402 McLoughlin, **Capt. Miller House,** moved from its original waterfront location.

  * 1911 **Rakel House,** 210 Hedges, was first residence in Canemah wired for electricity. 402 3rd Ave., 1874 **Louis Paquet House,** 2-story gable-roofed structure. Like almost every house in the Historic District it has undergone modification. 310 3rd, 1864 **Carothers House,** only remaining saltbox-style dwelling in Canemah. 216 3rd, 1918 **Smith House,** square bldg. with multi-paned windows. 408 4th, 1890 **Switzer/Dahel House.** 502 4th, 1867 **Capt. Caseday House,** shiplap-sided dwelling with a delicate porch. 702 4th, 1885 **Davis House;** 707 4th, 1876 **Draper House,** with tall, narrow window openings of Oregon Gothic Revival Style.

0.1 m., NE corner, O 99E and Miller, 1867 Revival Style **Fellows House.** Probably most striking residence in District. Old-fashioned calendar art interior open to public as restaurant and art gallery. Back of it, at 215 Miller, 1859 Classic Revival Style **Marshall House.**

0.1 m., SE corner, O 99E and Jerome (604 McLoughlin), 1868 Capt. **Wilson House.** Back of it, at 214 Jerome, 1915 Bungalow Style **Freeman House.** At 215 Jerome, 1858 Classic Revival Style **Jerome House.**

At 616 McLoughlin, 1870 Vernacular Style **Kent/Canon House.** 708 McLoughlin, 1860 Classic Revival Style **Capt. John Cochran House.** Cochran was captain of *The Clinton,* in 1856 first steamboat to reach Eugene.

816 McLoughlin, 1875 Gothic Revival Style **Isaac Beals House,** greatly modified about 1920. 902 McLoughlin, 1864 Gothic Revival Style **Coburn House,** property of boat carpenter John Coburn and his wife, schoolteacher-journalist Catherine Scott, associate of her sister Abigail Scott Duniway in suffragist movement.

0.5 m., site of **Stringtown,** long vanished. So named because houses were built on narrow strip between RR, close to river, and steep bluff behind.

3 m., on R, parking area for view of **Coalca Rock** (straight ahead from lot) at former RR whistle stop of Coalca. There are, of course, the usual Indian legends about this geological oddity, also called Balanced Rock. The most prominent tells of two Indian chiefs in love with a princess. They met on the cliff to fight to the death for her. The loser was Coalca and he was turned into stone, to forever stare at the river.

One of the loveliest natural sights in area is rough-legged hawk, characterized by long, broad wings and roundish body build.

1.2 m., on L, St. Patrick's Cemetery. Turn L onto New Era Rd.

    * *0.1 m.,* on R, barn reeking with charm. *0.1 m.,* on L, **Herman Anthony Farm** — water tower, barn, prune dryer, house — built 1880. (View from outside.) *0.1 m.,* on R, **New Era Spiritual Camp,** first organization of its kind in US. Founded 1873 by 1844 Oregon arrival Joseph Parrott as The Spiritual Society of the Pacific Northwest. CG laid out 1886, hotel built 1890, still in use. Despite mysticism attached to it, spiritualist camp is friendly place. Visitors welcomed to look around, at Sunday services, and at potluck (or minimal charge) lunch which follows service. *0.1 m.,* on L, at bend of road, house built 1889 was **Grange,** WCTU, and a "Way" or "Wait" House, where farmers who brought their grain to the flour mill nearby stayed until they were unloaded. Gravel road in front of house (Linden Rd., now country road, named for linden trees), was lined with potato cellars and led to steamboat landing and to RR depot. Near end of road was town of **New Era,** platted 1876 and containing school, store/PO and several houses. For 3 months, early in 1870, Parrott Creek, later site of New Era, was most important transportation point in Oregon.

    In the early twilight of Christmas Day, 1869, Ben Holladay's Oregon Central RR pulled into the makeshift terminal at Parrott Creek, farthest advance S the RR had made from Portland. Until RR was extended in the spring of 1870 Parrott Creek was the exchange point between Willamette River boats and RR. The RR continued to stop at New Era and the 1915 *Oregon Almanac* listed New Era as having "daily steamboats in the Willamette River." Today, of course, neither boats nor trains. (For detailed account, see "Great Day at New Era" in author's *Tracking Down Oregon.*) From turnoff to New Era:

1.1 m., turnoff W to Molalla River SP.

    * *1.6 m.,* turn R, toward Canby Ferry. *1.4 m.,* on L, **Molalla River SP,** prairie leading to confluence of Willamette and Molalla Rivers. PA, boating, trails, FHP. *0.5 m.,* **Canby Ferry,** N of three ferries on Willamette.

0.4 m., on L, SE 1st Ave.

    * *0.8 m.,* turn R onto SE Mulino Rd. *6.7 m.,* thru pungent farmland, **Mulino,** minor rural marketplace at jct., O 213.

0.9 m., turnoff to **Clackamas County Fair Grounds.** At entrance stands **Canby Depot Museum** (built 1871 and moved here from central part of town).

Grounds on DLC of 1856 settler Aaron E. Wait, who arrived in Oregon 1847 and was chief justice of first Oregon supreme court under statehood. Canby has been home of county fair since 1908; fair held mid-Aug.

   0.5 m., Ivy St., **Canby.**

      * L, *0.2 m.,* turn L onto Township. *0.2 m.,* on R, 1894 house, possible former parsonage. Directly ahead, New England-looking **Canby Evangelical Church,** built 1894. *0.9 m.,* on L, **Zion Memorial Park,** largest cemetery in area. Buried here is William Walter (Bill) Brown, the colorful stockman of E Oregon. At one time he ran more than 10,000 horses and more than 20,000 sheep. Legends about him could fill a book. The depression following WW I did him in and he sold off his holdings to pay for his stay at the Old People's Home in Salem, where he died Jan. 11, 1941. Despite his place in Oregon history and folklore, Brown is virtually unknown in Canby; a survey of 57 people, including city officials, revealed that not one had heard of him. (For more on Brown, see "Sodbusters and Bill Brown" in author's *A Touch of Oregon.*) Also buried in cemetery is Champing Pendleton, 1846 arrival and first homesteader on Baker Prairie, extending N from Canby to Willamette River.

   At O 99E and Ivy, turn R onto Ivy. *0.1 m.,* turn L onto 3rd Ave. *0.1 m.,* turn R onto Holly. *2.2 m.,* on L, **Molalla River SP.**

   0.5 m., heart of Canby, second oldest city in Clackamas County, outranked only by Oregon City. Named for Gen. Edward Richard Sprigg Canby (1817–1873), veteran of US Army service in Mexican, Civil and Indian wars. He came to Oregon 1870 to command Army's Dept. of the Columbia and was familiar figure at Portland social affairs. Coincidentally, Canby was being platted that year and the citizens sought to hitch their new town to a distinguished name. Gen. Canby was killed April 11, 1873 by Modoc Indians in the Lava Beds hostilities, a victim of frustration and opportunity. (See "Two Apart: Captain Jack and Winema" in author's *Tracking Down Oregon.*)

   Canby was platted by early white settler Philander Lee, whose Lee's Baker Prairie apple orchards stood at present downtown. (Baker Prairie was named for Silas Baker, who moved on from level plateau land claim near where the Molalla joins the Willamette before leaving any kind of record.) Philander Lee felt a touch of claustrophobia in the narrow main street of Oregon City and he resolved that his town would do better. He mapped his 24-block townsite streets wide enough for the turning of an ox team. To determine the necessary width he sent his son out with a team, then measured the turn at 80 ft. So 80 ft became the width of Canby's streets in Lee's plat and if you come to Canby with an ox team you can be assured there is room for a turn.

   Baker Prairie Cemetery on Knightsbridge Rd., *0.5 m.* from downtown Canby, has markers back to 1863. Buried here are William and Louise Mack, 1852 settlers whose name is borne by Macksburg, and Joseph Parrott, founder of New Era. (The Macks lived in 1879 house at 139 SE 2nd Ave.)

Oldest residence in town is now **Chestnut Apts.** 525 SW 4th Ave. William Knight, who built house in 1875 for his bride, Martha Elizabeth Birtchet, was most important man in Canby's history. If there could be a Mr. Everything, he was it. Loveliest of old homes is house at 486 NW 2nd, built by Wm. Knight, 1890.

Christo Chapel, 3rd and Elm, was built 1883, say some local historians, but city records show construction date at 1911. According to legend, church was "papered with tin."

In March, 1933 Canby gained national publicity as city of 900 burned its bonds and celebrated its freedom from debt, while other Oregon towns were defaulting. It was the era when NW 1st Ave. was the Pacific Highway, called "the road of the thousand wonders." When Canby celebrated its centennial it chose as its slogan, "Home of the Good Earth." A resident of 20 years described Canby more realistically: "A nice place to come home to after the excitement elsewhere."

From Ivy St., S on O 99E:

0.3 m., Elm St. *0.6 m.,* Molalla River. *0.8 m.,* on L, **Barlow House,** which may have been built as early as 1854, now private museum. House is fronted by two rows of black walnut trees, brought 'round the Horn circa 1860. Trees owe their residence in Oregon (black walnuts are not native to the state) to Martha Allen, a twice-wed Virginia belle who married William Barlow in 1852 and who importuned her husband to create an environment that would remind her of plantation life back home. When planted, the black walnut trees comprised a 400-ft.-long avenue framing the carriage drive. The cutting hand of humans, particularly in the construction of roads, has had its toll on the house yard and the trees; only about a third of each are left. When the SP was put thru the Barlow land (1,500 acres), one tree, with spread of over 240 ft. and 3-1/2 ft. in diameter, was deemed too precious to be cut down, so it was uprooted, placed on two flatcars, and hauled to the Holladay Addition in Portland, where it was replanted.

0.1 m., S Barlow Rd.

* Turn R onto S Barlow Rd. *0.3 m.,* on L, **Barlow Pioneer Cemetery,** part of Barlow DLC. Here sleep Samuel Kimbrough and Susannah Lee Barlow, overlanders of 1845 and parents of Wm. Barlow. An iron-willed, somewhat pious and rather unconventional Kentuckian, Sam'l Barlow was a full 50 years of age when he took off for Oregon. Arriving at The Dalles, where the Oregon Trail ran out, he was determined that there be a better way to reach the Willamette River than go down the Columbia. Casting his eyes toward the Cascades he resolutely declared, "God never made a mountain that he didn't make a way to get over it." And so, with his family and a handful of other adults (and some children), Barlow set off on an old Indian trail. The weather was so bad and the snow so deep and the ineptness of the party so pronounced that the wagons had to be parked in the mtns. until spring. Ten weeks after Barlow and fellow plodders took off from The Dalles in early Oct., Oregon City was reached. The next year Barlow, together with earlier

comer Philip Foster, obtained a charter and formed a company for the building of what became known as the Barlow Road (or Barlow Toll Road). Many thousands — not all happily, for some regarded Barlow's road (or trail) as the most difficult part of the overland route — entered the Willamette Valley on the trace Barlow pioneered.

At S Barlow Rd. and O 99E, turn L.

* *1.3 m.,* on R, small cemetery, mostly inhabited by Danes. *0.5 m.,* on L, **Kocher House,** elegant 2-story residence unchanged since built 1898. *2.4 m.,* on L, turnoff to St. Josef's Weinkeller, winery. *1.2 m.,* Whiskey Hill Rd. On Ne corner stood old 91 School.

* Turn R onto Whiskey Hill Rd. *0.6 m.,* on L, 1902 house. House diagonally across road probably constructed same year. *0.3 m.,* on L, **Zion Mennonite Church** and cemetery (1890.) Inscription on marker of almost 6 year old Scott Alan Berkey reads:

"A broken doll was sent to me from Heaven up above,/ A broken doll to have and hold, a broken doll to love/ God does send us varied things, he even sent his son:/ Recall the passage in his prayer: thy Will, Lord, will be done,/ God could have sent a perfect doll, but our broken one was blessed./ It's strange how that which seemed so sad should be a joy and fun;/ I thank God for this priceless gift, my broken doll my son."

This is sweet country, settled in large measure by Mennonites, not all of whom adhere to same customs. Almost all are friendly and cheerful.

* *0.1 m.,* on L, big red barn that begs to be painted. *0.3 m.,* Meridian Rd. Grocery store on corner was site of original Whiskey Hill School. First home — small cabin — of Abigail and Ben Duniway was in this area.

* Turn L onto Meridian Rd. *0.8 m.,* turn L onto Miller Rd. *0.8 m.,* on L, turn-of-century home that looks even older. On R, tile factory built 1880s, perhaps oldest tile factory in state. *0.7 m.,* turn L onto Barlow Rd.

* *0.5 m.,* turn R onto Barnard Rd. *1 m.,* Needy intersection. Looking straight ahead and to R was town of **Needy,** with general store (and dance hall upstairs), blacksmith shop, school, PO and residences. All bldgs. burned or torn down. Turn L onto Needy Rd. *0.2 m.,* on L, **Gahler House,** 2-story, L-shaped residence built 1903 by 1888 homesteaders.

* Return to Barnard Rd. Turn L. *2 m.,* turn L onto Dryland Rd. *2.9 m.,* Macksburg Rd., site of **Macksburg,** which in 1915 had 200 pop., two Lutheran churches, PS and Grange, in addition to stores. Turn R onto Macksburg Rd. *0.2 m.,* on R, **Macksburg Lutheran Church.** Prettiest scene around is barn complex across from church. The land hereabouts is flat, so remindful of home to midwesterners. And with a little imagination one can see how beautiful it once was. But now the land is being subdivided, with the pattern of "a house and a horse" replacing farms.

* Return to Dryland Rd. Turn R. *0.1 m.,* curve L onto Macksburg Rd. *0.8 m.,* turn onto county road. *0.4 m.,* on L, white house, built 1896 on site of

Gribble DLC. Locals call architectural style of house "country hoosier." *0.6 m.*, **Lone Elder.** Store. *1.6 m.*, road becomes Ivy St. as Canby is entered. *0.6 m.*, turn R onto Township Rd. *0.2 m.*, 1894 house and 1894 **Canby Evangelical Church.** *0.4 m.*, on R, lane leading to 1880s house that was dairy farm. *0.5 m.*, on L, **Zion Memorial Park,** main burial ground of Canby. Return to Ivy. Turn R. *0.2 m.*, O 99E.

From S Barlow Rd., on O 99E:

1.7 m., **Pudding River.** Like so many other deliciously-named places, there are several stories about Pudding River, which forms a boundary of French Prairie. Most commonly-accepted explanation is that a group of French-Canadian fur trappers, camped in a depressing downfall of snow and cold rains, and short on food, had the luck to spot and shoot an elk, from which their Indian womenfolk made a blood pudding, a favorite French dish. In remembrance, the hunters called the nearby stream *Riviere Boudin,* or Pudding River. Accounts that the hunters and time were Joseph Gervais and Etienne Lucier in the winter of 1821–22 are likely incorrect, since the younger Alexander Henry wrote in his journal on Jan. 23, 1814: "At 11 a.m. we passed a small stream on the left called by our people 'Pudding River.' "

When you have crossed the Pudding River, at the N end of Aurora, you have entered the historic Champoeg District, created by the first organic act of the provisional government. In all this vast area, comprising large parts of what are now the states of Oregon and Idaho and lesser parts of Montana and Wyoming, lived no more than some 200 white Americans. The act of Dec. 22, 1845 changed "District" to "County." Three days before the end of 1847 Champoeg was somewhat reduced by the creation of Linn County, but still ran to the summit of the Rocky Mtns. On Sept. 3, 1849, the first territorial legislature changed the name to Marion County, in honor of the "Swamp Fox" of the Revolutionary War. A popular book among the Willamette Valley settlers then was the *Life of General Francis Marion.* The saga of this nation's first successful white guerilla leader understandably appealed to the frontiersmen, and the few copies of the book were passed around until they had fallen apart.

0.2 m., **Aurora,** site of Oregon's longest-lasting and most successful historic commune. The colony was the last march westward of a dedicated group of old country Germans and "Pennsylvania Dutch," who sought to combine the teachings of Karl Marx with those of Christianity. Initial site of the group was Bethel, Missouri, where commune prospered for decade. Several factors were involved in decision to leave Bethel, including the disturbing observation by the elders of the eroding influence materialism was having upon the young.

Scouts were dispatched W and after much investigation concluded that Willipa Bay, in SW Washington Territory, was ideal location. But upon reaching that area in 1855, the group's leader, Prussian-born, 43-year-old Dr. Wilhelm Keil, and his lieutenants, rejected the new site, finding it too wet, not conducive to good health, and an intolerable distance from markets. Continuing on, now S, after a pause of a year in Portland, where Dr. Keil worked as a pharmacist, the caravan came to the Pudding River in the summer of 1856 and settled on land purchased by an advance party. In 1857 a town was formed and named Aurora Mills, after Keil's daughter; the "Mills" was dropped in 1894.

Despite all noble intentions, and despite its successes that greatly enlarged its land holdings, the colony was doomed from the start, as all American communes have been. The older generation, fixed in an agrarian society, could in the main hold true to the founding principles but the younger generation sought more material wealth, greater expansion, and a larger individuality. Flush in the rise of onrushing capitalism, no commune could succeed. That the Aurora Colony hung together until the death of Dr. Keil in 1877 is a tribute to his strength of leadership.

As is so common with much of romanticized Oregon, misinformation about Aurora is rife. In 1986, 95-year-old Hugo Keil, oldest descendant of Keil family, testily remarked: "All these people come to Aurora and after they live here a few years they think they know it all. They don't know nothin'; it's all baloney they're spreadin'."

And then there is the omission of knowledge which could have been quickly obtained. Example: the otherwise useful *Dictionary of Oregon History,* published 1956, declared in the bio of Dr. Keil, "His wife's name remains unknown." Yet the name of his wife is on her tombstone, next to that of her husband. (Her maiden name was Louise Ritter; she was called Louisa.)

Foremost among the reminders of the colony are the **Ox Barn Museum,** 2nd and Liberty; **Steinbach Log Cabin,** behind the museum; **Krause Colony House,** next to the museum; and past Krause Colony House, last two houses on the block, both put up 1873. In addition, **Fry House** (1863), at 21611 Main and next to it, toward O 99E, the **Colony Store,** for outsiders, built 1872, now antique shop complex. Another colony residence is **Snyder House** (circa 1872), at 3rd and Liberty. In these colony houses dwelt the "hook-and-eye Dutch," so called because buttons were considered frivolous and prohibited in their dress.

It might have amused the elders who built these homes to know that in the 1970s Aurora would suddenly pop up as one of the leading antique shop towns in Oregon; on a per capita pop. basis, Aurora had far more antique shops than Portland, Salem or Eugene. The articles the elders fumbled with, sometimes in frustration, carried — and carry — high prices. But excessive competition and the economic crunch narrow the number of vendors. An Aurora old-timer, who had owned an antique shop for years, said, "I saw what was coming and I told my wife, 'Mama, we've got to get out of the business before we lose our shirt.' People need their money for rent and food."

Unlike most Willamette Valley towns, Aurora has had little growth, averaging a net gain of about three persons per year since 1915. And it had more activity early in the century, when it could boast that it was the center of a prosperous hop-growing area and had HS, Commercial Club, weekly paper and five lodges.

Still, it has police dept. (one officer, a few reserves, two cars for pop. of about 500.) Asked how Aurora could afford a police dept., a city official said grimly, "We can't afford not to."

Take Main St W from O 99E:

* Main St. becomes Ehler Rd. *0.3 m.,* turn R onto Airport Rd. *0.1 m.,* on L, 3-story home with 2-deck porch across E front, built 1860 by Dr. Keil for his son Frederick. (Dr. Keil lived across street in much more modest residence.) Return to Ehler Rd. Turn R. *0.2 m.,* turn R onto Cole Ln. *0.2 m.,* end of lane. Take trail ahead to back of house at end of lane. Turn R. Walk *90 yds.* to ill-kept, almost completely obscured **Keil Family Cemetery.** Here sleep Dr. Wilhelm Keil, his wife, his daughter Aurora, and several others of the family.

* Return to Ehler Rd. Turn R. *0.3 m.,* on L, turnoff to **Aurora Community Cemetery** (*0.5 m.*). Buried here are most of the early colonists, including Keils, Krauses, Ehlers and Stauffers. Return to Ehler Rd. Turn L. *0.1 m.,* Hubbard Cutoff (blinking light). *10 yds.,* turn R onto Boones Ferry Rd. *0.9 m.,* mail box 22430, on L, *0.1 m.,* house built 1879 by four Keil brothers, nephews of Dr. Keil.

* Return to Ehler Rd. Turn R, toward Donald. *1.7 m.,* jct. — straight toward Donald. *1.7 m.,* jct. (To L, *0.5 m.,* Donald Rd. Turn L. *0.2 m.,* Donald City Hall.) To R, turn onto Butteville Rd. *0.9 m.,* turn R onto Fargo Rd. *1.3 m.,* RR tracks, where Fargo Station stood on Oregon Electric RY. *0.2 m.,* "T". Turn L. *0.3 m.,* to R, across field, 2-story frame house built 1886 that looks like the kind of calendar art frame house looking down from many walls. *0.1 m.,* on R, single story residence with bell tower and cross; strange sight to visitors.

* Return to Butteville Rd. Turn R. *0.9 m.,* Champoeg Rd. Turn L. *1.9 m.,* Aurora-Donald Jct. Straight. *1 m.,* **Champoeg SP.**

* Return to Butteville Rd. Turn L. *0.4 m.,* **Butteville,** historic town that just about isn't any more. Cemetery was last stop of F. X. Matthieu, one of first white settlers on French Prairie and last survivor of 1843 Champoeg meeting.

* Return to Ehler Rd. Cross it. Straight. *0.6 m.,* Donald. Turn L onto Main St. *0.2 m.,* "downtown" **Donald,** village with the weary air of 100 years back in time. Still, its antics, which seem like the tales of raw Western history, give it a place in Oregon folklore. Sometimes the whole town has appeared to be involved in political warfare. One wouldn't think that elected office in such a tiny town would arouse so much passion — but at Donald it has. *5 m.,* Aurora, at O 99E.

From Main St., on O 99E, Aurora:

3 m., turn L or E, onto Stauffer Rd.

* *0.3 m.,* on L, **Stauffer-Will Historic Farm,** most authentic 19th century farm complex in W Oregon. Centerpiece is **Will Log Farmhouse,** probably built in mid or late 1860s as part of Aurora Colony. Home for about 20 years,

Grave of Dr. Wilhelm Keil

Grave of Louise Keil

Grave of Aurora Keil

Stauffer-Will House

then used as slaughterhouse. Courtyard-type complex, with farm bldgs. grouped in square. It ought to be turned into SP and operated as working farm in style of life of 1860s.

1.3 m., **Hubbard,** at D St. (On SW corner, **St. Agnes Catholic Church,** delicate cameo of yesteryear.)

Brooding above O 99E is Hubbard's water tower, most distinctive on any road, and for decades and decades the prime distinguishing landmark of town. Long before there was roadside business, travelers could tell they were approaching Hubbard by sight of water tower.

Turn R onto D St. *0.2 m.,* 3rd St., old business part of Hubbard. Laid out along RR tracks, it was core of town until O 99E took away almost all mercantilism and community went into decline. But in 1970s Hubbard began a comeback and today old business part is rejuvenated, with restaurants and light industry. In addition, many new homes have been built and many more refurbished — but, with thanks, the old water tower still stands.

Hubbard Community Church, H and 2nd, built 1892, 45 years after Kentuckian Charles Hubbard settled here. Houses of interest in Hubbard include 2899 A (1886), 3635 5th (1900), 2670 E, 3069 3rd, 2270 J, 2430 J.

From D St., Hubbard, on O 99E:

2.1 m., on L, McLaren School, incarceration facility for youthful offenders. *0.4 m.,* jct.

E, O 211:

　　* *3.7 m.,* turn R or S onto Meridian Rd. *0.6 m.,* **Elliott Prairie Congrega-tional Church** (1893), touch of New England on the prairie.

　　* Return to O 211. Turn R. *1.3 m.,* turn L onto Barlow Rd. *1.1 m.,* turn R onto Sconce Rd. *0.4 m.,* on L, **Rock Creek Church** (1858) and cemetery. Church pews said to be original. About only time some old-timers see each other is at funeral services. There is in this open, flowered burial ground no nuance of melancholy; it is as though the dead are still alive, celebrating the bright afternoons of their lives and intertwined in a camaraderie they did not know before departure.

　　* *1.8 m.,* "T". Turn R. *0.1 m.,* on R, **Smyrna Church** (1891) and cemetery. In the past, church was center of rural community activities, and so it re-mains.

* *0.4 m.,* turn L onto O 211. *5.2 m.,* Molalla.

From O 211 Jct., on O 99E:

To W is jct., O 214.

　　* This route seems to ride on a cushion of air past fields that are as shim-mering green in Nov. as they are in April. The road swings thru French Prairie, always exciting to the eye and so firmly entrenched in Oregon histo-ry. *2.3 m.,* I-5. *4 m.,* curve onto O 219. *4.9 m.,* **St. Paul,** cradle of Catholic history in Oregon. Turn R, continuing on O 219. *7.6 m.,* Newberg, on O 99W. (For details on French Prairie, see O *219S.*)

Much of this area was in the domain of wetlands before the Yankees arrived. An OSU researcher estimated that in pre-European times there were at least 125,000 acres of wetlands in the Willamette Valley. About 1980 there were, he concluded, less than 2,000 acres of undisturbed wetlands, together with native plants and animals, remaining. It goes without saying that as the wetlands have decreased so have the native wildlife and plants that inhabited these acreages.

From jct., O 211 — O 214:

0.7 m., **Woodburn,** at Lincoln.

Turn W. *0.9 m.,* Front St., main business street. *0.4 m.,* **Settlemier House** (1889), at Settlemier and Garfield, now museum of French Prairie Historical Soci-ety. The Queen Anne mansion was built by Jesse Settlemier, who platted Wood-burn and was its first mayor. He was also first horticulturist in area. Having said this dry stuff, a few exclamation marks of comment are in order. The Settlemier House conveys such power of dimension, scope of opulence and extravagance of detail that most people see it only thru a gestalt lens and are impacted by the holistic experience.

Woodburn is one of the tri-lingual communities in this part of Willamette Valley. It is not uncommon to ask for directions here and be told in Russian or Spanish that he or she does not understand English. But allow for another genera-tion and the children of the Hispanics and Old Russians will be as americanized as their Anglo neighbors.

Settlemier House, Woodburn

2.8 m., jct., O 214 — to E.

    * 4.5 m., Monitor Jct. (1.9 m., **Monitor,** flour mill hamlet that hasn't budged in decades.) 2.2 m., **Mt. Angel,** site of Mt. Angel Abbey. 4.5 m., **Silverton** city center.

1.1 m., on W, Belle Paasi Rd. Here, or very near here, stood hamlet of Belle Paasi, creation of 1851 settler Rev. Neil Johnson, who built a **Cumberland Presbyterian Church** and school here. In 1860 a PO est.; name changed to **Gervais** in 1871.

    * Turn R, or W. 0.1 m., **Belle Paasi Cemetery.** Markers back to 1852. One of the most impressive sights in any Willamette Valley cemetery is here — life-size statue of infantryman atop 15-ft. monument sculpted with portraits of US military heroes. Monument, built 1911, honors soldiers of Indian, Civil and Spanish-American wars. By now it could include more hostilities — WW I, WW II, Korean, Viet Nam, Granada and Panama. And coming up, perhaps, who knows?

100 yds. on L, **Belle Paasi Pioneer Site** (1850) marker.

This part of Willamette Valley was a concentration point of DLCs. On Sept. 27, 1850, Congress passed the Oregon Donation Land Act, which granted settlers who would arrive in the territory prior to Dec. 1, 1851, a full section of land (640 acres) if married and 320 acres if single, on condition of occupying and improving the land for 4 years. (A settler was defined as a white male — or half-white, half-Indian — over the age of 18, who was a citizen or who declared his intention of

Monument to Soldiers, Belle Passi Cemetery, Woodburn

Courtesy Marcia Workentine

becoming one. Excluded, at insistence of Samuel Royal Thurston, Oregon delegate in Congress, were males of more than half-Indian stock, Negroes, native
Hawaiians and Asians.) As for single women, they were left out in the cold.

Men who came to Oregon between Dec. 1, 1851 and Dec. 1, 1855, and who
occupied and improved land, were awarded 320 acres if married, 160 acres if
single. They now had to be white — no half-Indian anymore — and at least 21
years of age.

Federal law superseded territorial land law, which meant that single men who
held a section of land under the provisional gvmt. law of 1844 suddenly found
their holdings reduced by half. Consternation and greed combined to send single
men a-howling for matrimony. A woman seen anywhere was besieged by a single
question: Are you married? A commentator noted that schools were emptied of
their girls, some of whom had not yet reached puberty, and land-hungry claim-
ants took to knocking at every farm door behind which dwelt a girl who could in a
few minutes double the hustler's wealth. A wit of the time recorded in verse the
situation of some who had profited from the provisional gvmt. and now faced the
threat of losing half their beloved acreage:

"A crusty old bachelor, lonely and gray
Remarks with a sigh as time passes away,
I hate all women, yet it is quite plain
I must marry real soon or lose half my claim."

(For more on the DLC and the pursuit of single females see "The Bartered
Brides" in author's *This Side of Oregon*.)

0.7 m., Howell Prairie Rd.

 * Turn E. *0.2 m.*, turn L onto Monitor-McKee Rd. *0.6 m.*, turn R onto
Bethelhem Rd. Here is about as close to an Old Russian settlement as
Oregon knows. The people seem to have come out of a tapestry of early
Tsarist peasant days — deeply religious, suspicious of strangers, superstitious, neat, hard-working, rejecting modern "frills," their lives woven
around icons. Few of the adults here speak English beyond a few telegraphic
words. Driving up the street one feels like whistling "The Volga Boatman."
0.1 m., on L, brightly-colored, onion-turreted church enclosed by cyclone
fence and with its gate locked, except for services. This is **Holy Ascencion
Church,** described by its priest as "Old Believer" church. Services are conducted in "Church Slavonic," defined as a "sister language of Russian." Interior is brilliant with icons that convey imagery of flags and shields of medieval
army. Conforming to tradition, parishioners stand during services; there are
no pews. Nearby is Holy Protection of Mother of God which Holy Ascencion priest terms a "prayer house," not a church, "since it has not been officially blessed and has no priest."

All the people in the Bethelhem area are descendants of worshippers who
left Russia following a schism in the Russian Orthodox Church in the
mid-17th century (probably around 1666). Many of the emigrants first settled

in central Europe (most in present Czechoslovakia and Rumania), then moved on to Turkey. In 1963 there was a general exodus from Turkey to New Jersey and 4 years later the Old Russians came to Oregon.

    * From turnoff to Bethelhem Rd.: *0.1 m.,* L corner, Miller Rd., large 1895 house that is old-fashioned mansion of the prairie.

    Beyond, in the web of roads that lead off the pike to Monitor and McKee, the scene is typical rural Willamette Valley: solid houses that conceal their wounds and joys; here and there a blind and toothless barn; and at almost every green thread of the web the munching beef cattle.

1.4 m., on L, **Brown House,** completed 1858. Only a Brown has occupied house since it was built.

0.3 m., Gervais Jct.

    * Turn E. *0.3 m.,* on R, **Masonic Cemetery** contains Old Russian section, with some of the markers lettered in Cyrillic. On other side of road, **Sacred Heart Cemetery.** Gervais Jct. — to W:

    * *0.4 m.,* city center, **Gervais.** Town named for Joseph Gervais, who arrived 1811 with William Price Hunt Party, trapped extensively as hired hand for the various fur companies, was one of the "Men of Champoeg," and lived on French Prairie (but not at Gervais) until his death in 1861 at age 84. He was known to other settlers as a practical, nature-knowledgeable, wise, patient,

Holy Ascencion Church   *Courtesy Marcia Workentine*

unhurried, gentle man who got along very well with Indians (his two wives were Indian). His home was used as first school in what became state of Oregon and he was one of first justices of the peace. Although Gervais had only half the present pop. in 1915 (400 then), it was a more cohesive, integrated community, with Grange, six lodges, more stores and a 100-acre loganberry ranch 0.2 m. from town. As with many other small towns in metropolitan areas, residential growth has far exceeded mercantile development, turning these towns into suburban bedrooms. Influx of Old Russians (easily identified by their dress) and Hispanics has provided Gervais a diversity of languages and lifestyles that has placed it on the frontier of cultural disparity.

   * *0.2 m.,* 7th St., **Sacred Heart Church.** In 1871, transportation magnate Ben Holladay donated a block of land for the bldg. of a Catholic church. Four years later the Parish of Gervais was founded and the following year a bell obtained; it weighed 1,014 lbs., was christened "Patrick" and was then largest in Oregon. The 80 ft. by 40 ft. church, built for less than $6,000, was dedicated June 13, 1875, 3 years after town of Gervais was founded, and to coincide with the name of the town, was dedicated to Sts. Gervasius and Protasius. In 1882, the Very Rev. Prior Adelhelm Odermatt, O.S.B. brought with him from Switzerland to Oregon a group of Fathers, Brothers and candidates and it was in Gervais that they not only found their first home but laid the foundations of what was to grow into Mount Angel Abbey. That year, too, a school was started by the Benedictine Sisters. A decade later the Contemplative Sisters of the Precious Blood were brought here but in 6 months were moved to Mt. Tabor in Portland. All was going well until August, 1894 when, during a 40-hour Devotion, fire completely destroyed the church. But the congregation bounded back. With the $3,000 insurance money from the fire loss, a new church was built early in 1895. It lasted until 1922, when it, too, went up in flames. Third church — the present — dedicated June 18, 1923.

   * *2.5 m.,* **St. Louis,** another of the Catholic-founded communities that dot French Prairie. The first church, built of logs, was put up in 1844, and a town followed. St. Louis was a viable community before the birth of Woodburn, Gervais, Brooks or Aurora and before Salem became Salem. Along the streets facing the church a row of commercial bldgs. housed surveyors, physicians, coopers, blacksmiths, shoemakers, bookkeepers, millwrights and gunsmiths. An 1867 Pacific Coast Business Directory listed the village physician, the town wagon maker, a bookkeeper, a parish priest, a blacksmith, a cooper, the postmaster, the owners of a general merchandise store and harness shop and the keeper of the village hotel. The Marion County Atlas of 1878 showed St. Louis to be a platted town of 20 blocks.

   The coming of the RR, which was laid thru Gervais, doomed St. Louis; when merchants saw their trade going elsewhere they followed. Depleted of commerce, St. Louis faded into a hollow crossroad. PO, est. 1860, folded for good in 1901.

Most Oregonians believe St. Louis was named for the metropolis of Missouri. It was named for king of France; the early settlers were French-Canadians.

Few travelers pause at St. Louis and then only because of the Catholic church (St. Louis). It is the third Catholic church and was built 1885 on site of the 1844 log house of worship.

St. Louis has one other distinction. It is the resting place of Marie Dorion, the celebrated "Madame Dorion" or "Madonna of the Trail," who lies under the timbers of the church, in a place of honor directly beneath the cross on the bell tower.

Marie Dorion, an Iowa Indian, accompanied her hunter-interpreter husband, Pierre, on the long, hungry and agonizing trek W to Ft. Astoria, by the Wilson Price Hunt Party. On Dec. 30, 1811, a day nagged by snow and cold rain, and about 4 m. from North Powder, in Union County, the 25-year-old Marie Dorion gave birth. A few hours later Pierre, Marie and their newborn infant caught up with the others. For some odd reason it is widely held that the babe, mothered by an Indian and fathered by a part-Indian, was "the first white child born in the Oregon Country."

The published legendary courage of Marie Dorion may have been overstated but it is certain that she was resourceful, proud, intelligent, and loyal to the needs of her people, though all her husbands were all or part French-Canadian. After the demise of Pierre Dorion she married a hunter named Venier and after he passed away she wed Jean Baptiste Toupin. She, Toupin and her three families of children moved to French Prairie from the Walla Walla country about 1840 and acquired land near St. Louis. For the next decade she played a strong role in French Prairie affairs and when she died Sept. 5, 1850, at age 64, she was buried beneath the St. Louis log church, the only person so honored.

For more than 80 years her death and burial remained a mystery. In 1932 her great-grandson, J. Willard Gay, of Portland, told researchers that oral history passed down by members of his family indicated that Marie Dorion was buried beneath the altar of the church under the name of Louise L'Egoise. For a definitive answer to the question of when and under what name she was laid to rest, two local historians, McKinly Mitchell and Father Kraus, began a detailed perusal of church records, which dated back to the early days of French Prairie. On page 24 of an old ledger they found an entry referring to the burial Sept. 6, 1850 of Marie Iowa, wife of John Toupin. Back of church is St. Louis Cemetery, where popular lore has it that Marie Dorion was first buried.

    * 1.1 m., "T". Turn R. 3.1 m., jct., O 214, which curves into O 219. 4.9 m., downtown St. Paul.
From Gervais Jct., on O 99E:
2.9 m., Parkersville-Waconda Rd.

* Turn L, or E. *0.7 m.,* on L, **Pioneer School,** built 1938, which makes it one of oldest standing schools in county, though 1938 doesn't seem that far back to old timers. *0.1 m.,* turn R onto 72nd Ave. *0.3 m.,* on R, old country church (whose congregation has sometimes spoken in tongues) and **Pioneer Memorial Cemetery** (1855).

* Return to Parkersville Rd. Turn R. *2.5 m.,* jct., site of **Parker House.** Here stood 2-story mansion built 1850 by William and Cynthia Ann Davis Parker and so majestic on the rude prairie that early settlers called it "The Palace." Parker House was also center of Parkersville, budding village that had its day in the sun. The 4th of July, 1853, was celebrated in Parkersville with parade, feast, and patriotic speeches. Then on May 6, 1854, Marion County convention of Democratic Party assembled on bank of Pudding River, with 10 precincts represented. Historic names at convention included Ralph C. Geer, maternal grandfather of Homer Davenport and soon to be elected to the territorial legislature; John D. Boon, who was to become the last territorial and the first state treasurer; and Richard Miller and George K. Shiel.

Miller, seeking office as county commissioner, had led an attack upon a Molalla village in 1848, killing unarmed women and children. For two decades the story of the slaying was concealed. When truth was finally dragged thru the mire of secrecy, "The Battle of Abiqua Creek" did not seem as glorious as the heroes had painted it to be.

George K. Shiel, a newcomer Irishman, was itching to win public office though he had been in Oregon only a few months, and spent his time at the convention bending every ear that would yield to him. Seven years later he was admitted to Congress, after his credentials had been bitterly contested, and lasted one term. He could not have been elected again. A defender of slavery, he spent much of his energy defending secession and defaming Abraham Lincoln. An attorney, he was barred from the practice of law when he refused to take the oath of allegiance. For the last 30 years of his life he lived as a recluse, subsisting on the handouts of charitable acquaintances. In 1893, when he was 68, he tumbled off the porch of the Willamette Hotel in Salem and broke his neck. By then it was someone with a great trivia memory who could recall the name of George Shiel.

Parkersville's last hurrah was the Marion County Democratic party convention. After that the town slipped rapidly downhill. Wm. Parker, the driving force of the village, died early in 1859, at age 47, and was taken to Silverton for burial. Late in 1861 the PO, est. 1852, closed. Cynthia Ann Parker married twice more before she passed away in 1905 and was laid to rest at Pioneer Memorial Cemetery.

(For full story of Parkersville, see "Parkersville in the Mind" in author's *This Side of Oregon.*)

* Turn R at jct. *0.3 m.,* on L, site of Parker's mills, on Pudding River. *1.7*

Grave of Cynthia Ann Parker   *Phoebe L. Friedman*

m., Mt. Angel Jct. (Mt. Angel, *4 m.*) Straight. *0.4 m.*, forks. Take L, toward Salem. *1.1 m.*, Silverton Jct. Turn L. toward Silverton. *4.4 m.*, Mt. Angel Jct. Straight — toward Silverton. *2.1 m.*, Mt. Angel-Silverton Jct. Turn R, toward Silverton. *0.1 m.*, on L, on bank of Abiqua Creek, **Ames River Ranch,** microcosm of Disneyland. *3.6 m.*, downtown Silverton.

From Parkersville — Waconda Jct., on O 99E:

* Turn W — toward Waconda. *2.1 m.*, at RR tracks, site of **Waconda,** station on Oregon Electric RY. In 1915, place had PO, store, pop. 177. What remain are shell of RR station and 1903 "American Four Square Style" house that was Waconda PO. *0.3 m.*, River Rd. (To L — Salem, *10 m.* To R — St. Paul, *11 m.*) *1.8 m.*, Hopmere, intersection started as RR station. Turn R. *1.1 m.*, "T". (L — Salem, *8 m.*) Turn R. *2.4 m.*, turnoff L to Willamette Mission SP. Willamette River at far end of park is site of Mission Bottom, where Jason Lee and his colleagues est. first mission in Oregon. *0.7 m.*, turn L onto Matheny Rd. *0.4 m.*, turnoff R for Willamette Mission SP BR parking. *0.2 m.*, Wheatland Ferry.

From Waconda Rd., at O 99E:

2.2 m., **Brooks.** Named for 1850 Illinois overlander, Brooks began active life as station on SPRR, never grew beyond cluster of hwy. enterprises.

* Turn R onto Freeway Rd. *0.7 m.*, I-5 overpass. *0.5 m.*, turnoff R to **Antique Powerland Museum.** Open all year but big time is farm fair last week of July, first week of Aug., when there are long daily exhibitions of steam engine threshing, log sawing and operation of gas tractors, all enlivened by old time music.

1 m., on R, Quinaby Rd.

* *1.1 m.*, **Schreiner's Gardens,** nationally known nursery specializing in iris production. *0.6 m.*, River Rd. Turn L. *3.1 m.*, **Keizer,** at Chemawa Rd. Area now city of Keizer was just thinly-populated residential suburbia in 1950s. Now it's the Beaverton of Salem, an appendage that has taken on the problems of a city. Turn R onto Chemawa Rd. *0.7 m.*, turn R onto Windsor Island Rd. *1.3 m.*, turn L onto Naples St. *0.7 m.*, Spong's Landing Park. *0.3 m.*, Willamette River. In 1853 Alexander Spong settled here on a DLC and his farm became known as **Spong's Landing,** because riverboats stopped here, to take on and unload freight from and to the Marion County farmsteads and hamlets in the vicinity and to load wood cut on the Spong place. In mid-1870s the Spongs built a more efficient landing and started operation of ferry. Because of its key location and attractiveness, farm drew many visitors, prompting Spongs to capitalize on the interest by setting aside part of their farm as picnic area. Sign at entrance read: "Admission 25 cents per car, bikers and hikers 5 cents." No admission today.

From Quinaby Rd. at O 99E:

1.1 m., on R, or W, classic white-painted farmhouse with second story porch and water tower in rear. Initial structure was one-room cabin with woodshed and fireplace. Additions made until 1930. Water tower erected 1890.

1.1 m., Chemawa Rd.

* Turn R, or W. *0.3 m.*, on L, **Chemawa Indian School,** founded 1880; students from seven continental Western states and Alaska; grades 9-12. All

old bldgs. that gave school "reservation" look are gone; facility now resembles college campus. 2.7 m., River Rd., "downtown" Keizer.

0.3 m., **45th Parallel,** halfway point between Equator and North Pole.

4.1 m., downtown **Salem.** In 1840 Methodist missionaries led by Jason Lee abandoned their station on the Willamette bottomland because of a "great sickness," and moved about 10 m. S to a rich prairie ripe for cultivation. Here the missionaries platted a town, which they called Chemeketa, the Calapooya word for "place of rest."

As a last hope for survival, the missionaries, discouraged by their lack of success, established Oregon Institute, opened as a "literary and Religious Institution of learning," and sold lots, purchased with wheat, to finance the new school. Oregon Institute carried on precariously until 1853, when its successor, Willamette U, was chartered.

Because the original settlement was on Mill Creek, the community was as often called the Mill, and after Oregon Institute was opened, was more often called the Institute.

After the mission was dissolved in 1844, a new name was chosen. It was Salem, Biblical word for peace and harmonious with the English translation of Chemeketa. In the coming decades there was as much controversy and turmoil as peace, but the name Salem remained. Many a name indicating tranquility or fraternal love has been the scene of a bloodier battleground. In 1849 PO was est. but only a few years after it opened resolutions were introduced in the territorial legislature to change name, with about half-a-dozen favorites pushed forward as candidates. The matter was finally resolved early in 1854 and Salem remained.

In 1851 territorial legislature voted to move the capital from Oregon City to Salem, an act the missionaries had long advocated and supported by *Oregon Statesman* editor Asahel Bush. Opposing change was *Oregonian* editor Thomas J. Dryer as well as the governor, two members of the territorial supreme court, and a minority of the legislature, who argued that the act was unconstitutional. Since Dryer was a Whig and the governor, John P. Gaines, an apointee of Pres. Zachary Taylor, was regarded as sympathetic to the cause, the fiery Asahel Bush, more burning than Moses in his fiery denunciation of those who scorned his commands, wrote with a torch that Dryer, Gaines and their followers were "a squad of federal nullifiers" and "lickspittles and toadies of official whiggery."

One might wonder what influenced the legislature to shift to Salem. Oregon City was a relatively large town then while, according to J. W. Nesmith, "there were perhaps half a dozen families living in Salem."

Once the legislators observed Salem at close range they began to look about for another location. In 1855 they voted to move to Corvallis and the entire territorial gvmt. boarded the steamer *Canemah* for the new home. But after one session the lawmakers returned to Salem, finding they cared less for Corvallis than for Salem. (Corvallis, in turn, wasn't enthused about most legislators.) More important, Congress had appropriated money for the state capitol to be in Salem and the

Comptroller of the US Treasury was not about to release money for the building of a capitol anywhere other than Salem. Though an arsonist (rumors said it was a fellow from either Oregon City or Corvallis) burned down the capitol in the same year the legislature returned to Salem, the city continued on as state capital, seeing its way thru floods and fires. On April 25, 1935, the capitol, a classic Greek statehouse that had served Oregon for more than five decades, was destroyed by fire (no arsonists this time) but another, larger edifice was on Dec. 4, 1936 under construction. It was completed in 1939 at a cost of $2.5 million.

Truly impressive is the modern **state capitol,** with its marble, sculpture and murals. The walls of the rotunda, rising 106 ft. from the floor to the ceiling, are in rose travertine marble from Montana. So are the halls. The floor of the rotunda and the stairs are of Napoleon gray marble from Missouri. The baseboards and ramps of the great stairways are in Vermont radial black marble. The sculpture and the murals are depictions of Oregon history. Some, to be sure, are ultra-heroic and fanciful, such as Leo Friedlander's work of Capts. Lewis and Clark being guided to the Pacific by Sacagawea. But all are strikingly handsome.

About the best overall view of Salem and its environs is had from the capitol tower, reached by stairs from 4th floor.

**A mural in the Oregon State Capitol Rotunda shows
Dr. John McLoughlin welcoming Narcissa Whitman and
Eliza Spalding to Ft. Vancouver in 1836**   *Courtesy State of Oregon*

A block from the capitol stands the **State Library,** a treasure trove for researchers. The archives are laden with documents of Oregon history. Planted on the capitol grounds is one of Oregon's "moon trees," Douglas firs which traveled in seed form to the moon and back with astronaut Stuart Roosa in 1971. Beyond the capitol is campus of **Willamette U,** oldest W college. **Mark O. Hatfield Library,** named for US Senator, champion of peace, has section containing mementos of his political life, including a passel of honorary degrees from PR-minded schools, perhaps repeating the old adage, They honor who would be recognized. (Hatfield entered politics while on the WU faculty.) Waller Hall on WU campus, built 1867, is in National Register, as are many other Salem structures.

Eastern gray squirrels seen scampering about capitol grounds and WU campus are, compared to the W gray squirrel, relatively foreign to Oregon. They were brought here in early 1920s thru the fancy of then Gov. Ben W. Olcott. On a visit to capitol of Penn. at Harrisburg, Olcott was so fascinated by the gray squirrels he saw in the park that he arranged to have 48 shipped to Oregon's capitol grounds. Only 20 squirrels survived the trip but their families have done quite well, not only on the capitol grounds but throughout Salem.

Salem's great museum is **Marion Museum of History,** better known by its old name of Mission Mill Park, located on grounds of Thomas Kay Woolen Mills, first part of which was put up 1889. Museum grounds — on Mill between 12th and 14th — contain **Jason Lee House** (1841), moved here from original site 2 m. away; parsonage of **Willamette Methodist Mission** (1841); **John D. Boon**

Jason Lee House   *Phoebe L. Friedman*

House (1847); **Pleasant Grove Pres. Church;** and a complex of retail shops (some in Thomas Kay Woolen Mills).

In this section of Salem are also located: **Honeywood Winery,** 501 14th, founded 1933, oldest establishment in Oregon's wine industry, specializing in fruit wines.

Webster House, 901 13th, restored Victorian dwelling.

Deepwood, Mission and 12th (1894), one of most impressive houses in Oregon; looks like ante bellum mansion designed by a New England architect given carte blanche in ideas and expenditures. A lot of people would consider themselves lucky to live in the carriage house. Estate includes cultivated, formal, informal and wildflower gardens. Originally called Port House, for first owner Dr. Luke A. Port, it was christened New Year's Eve, 1935, as Deepwood, and so registered as legal farm name with secretary of state. Name came from Albert Bigelow Paine's children's book, *The Hollow Tree and Deep Wood Book,* and was bestowed upon estate by Alice Bretherton Brown, who, after death of her husband, house's third owner, married Keith Powell, whose first wife (deceased) was daughter of second owner. Deepwood now museum.

Bush Pasture Park, 600 Mission St. SE (near Deepwood), contains 89 acres of natural park grounds, is site of **Bush House,** one of finest Victorian houses in W, built 1877–78 for pioneer Salem banker and publisher Asahel Bush, and now preserved as museum and, near it, **Bush Barn Art Center,** remodeled from farm barn built 1880. Bush House has marble fireplaces, original wallpaper, original and period furnishings.

Salem has two historic cemeteries. The first is **Lee Memorial,** D and 21st St. NE. It holds graves of Jason Lee and members of his immediate family, including his two wives. Life was hard for women: Lee's first wife, Anna Maria Pittman, first white bride in Oregon Country, died less than a year after marriage and only a day after death of their 2-day-old baby, first white child born in Oregon. Lee's second wife, Lucy Thompson, died 3 weeks after birth of only child and less than 3 years after marriage. Lee, son of a Vermont Revolutionary War soldier, came to this land in 1834 as first Protestant missionary and left 10 years later under order from his superiors, who had become disenchanted about him from reports of his shift from religion to politics and his weak administrative performance. After 10 days of intensive questioning by the Board of Managers of the Methodist Missionary Society he was exonerated from charges circulated by some of his former co-workers in Oregon. Since a replacement had already been selected Lee could not return, but was permitted to retain his title, "Missionary to Oregon." He died March 12, 1845, of tuberculosis and strictures of the intestines and was buried in the small cemetery of his native Stanstead, Quebec. At his passing he was but 42; it had taken him only a decade in Oregon to become the most controversial figure in the annals of the state. His admirers agreed with a line in the obituary penned by his nephew, Daniel Lee, who had come to Oregon with Jason in 1834: "His sun has gone down at noon." His critics felt he should have left Oregon at mid-

Grave of Jason Lee   *Phoebe L. Friedman*

morning. Jason Lee's body was returned to Oregon in 1906 and given permanent burial at this cemetery.

The likeness of Anna Maria Pittman Lee is etched in stone above her grave. We see a plain-looking, large-boned face, eyes fixed patiently to her goal, a plodder more than a zealot. She had come by harsh travel to a far-off land to serve her Lord and if that meant marrying Jason Lee, or anyone else, so be it. Thru him she would fulfill her role as missionary to the unwashed.

The poignant inscription on the flat stone reads: "Beneath this sod the first ever broken in Oregon for the reception of white mother and child lie the remains of Anna Maria Pittman, first wife of Rev. Jason Lee and her infant son. She sailed from New York in July, 1836. Landed in Oregon June, 1837. Was married July 16, 1837 and died June 26, 1838. Aged 35 years."

Jason Lee, also etched in stone, is shown as tall, strongly built, long of face, full of beard, energy churning in his impatient frame, a strider, a would-be maker and shaker, a trampler for his single-mindedness. He had the build sculptors love for heroic statues and, indeed, a statue of him, representing Oregon, is in the halls of Congress.

(For more on Jason Lee, see "Long Road to the Cook House" in author's *Tracking Down Oregon*.)

Lee's second wife, Lucy Thompson, lies under a much smaller and simpler marker, and without more identification than her name and date of her life span (1809–1842).

Others in the circular, enclosed Lee plot within the cemetery include Alanson Beers, blacksmith and lay missionary who arrived by boat in the spring of 1837 as the first reinforcement to the Willamette Mission of the Methodist Church; Josiah L. Parrish, a "Man of Champoeg," who came in 1840 aboard the sailing ship *Lausanne*, bringing to Oregon the first white clover seed, and who was later first Oregon producer of pure-bred sheep; Harvey K. Hines, author and clergyman, who organized the First Methodist Church at The Dalles in 1856; and Nehemiah Doane, Methodist preacher who came to Oregon in 1849 as principal of Oregon Institute.

It seems a bit illogical that buried outside the Lee "ring" is Gustavus Hines, brother of Harvey. Another arrival on the 1840 journey of the *Lausanne*, he was a close associate of Lee, and after the death of Lucy Thompson, Hines and his wife Lydia, who had lost their only child, a daughter, raised Lucy, the Lee's daughter.

Near the "ring" lies Margaret Hadley Irvine, whose inscription reads like a short and proud poem in a *Spoon River Anthology:* "Wife of Jess Irvine, Mother Irvine-Clagget Clan, Born Baltimore, MD 1794, Crossed the Plains in Covered Wagon, Died Salem, Oregon Oct. 13, 1852."

The second historic Salem cemetery is **Pioneer** (aka IOOF) at SE Commercial and Hoyt. Probably more veterans of the 1843 Champoeg "Divide" meeting lie here than in any other cemetery. Although some historians state that this burial ground was not est. until 1854, first burial here was of Mary A. Leslie in Feb., 1841.

Pioneer Cemetery is replete with remains of the illustrious. Among them are: Tabitha Brown, the courageous Grandma Brown of the Applegate Trail and a strong link in the chain that led to the founding of Pacific U; Virgil Pringle, Tabitha Brown's son-in-law and another member of the near-disastrous Applegate Trail caravan; Capt. Charles Bennett, whose tombstone states that he was discoverer of gold in Calif. (He was with James W. Marshall at Coloma when Sutter's Mill was being constructed.)

Rev. David Leslie, who came to Oregon in 1837; was one of two magistrates for the Oregon Country S of Columbia River, in 1839; in 1841 was chairman of committee to draft code of laws for the Oregon Country; was a trustee of Oregon Institute; in 1844 opened first frame church in Oregon City; and in 1849 was chaplain of first territorial legislature.

Asahel Bush, editor and publisher of *Oregon Statesman,* prominent banker, and one of the "power elite" of Oregon until start of Civil War; Dr. William Holden Willson, 1837 arrival and one of the "Men of Champoeg"; John Daniel Boon, 1845 arrival and Methodist minister who became last territorial and first state treasurer; Joseph Holman, one of the absurdist Peoria Party who finally made it to Oregon in 1840 and thereafter was an engine at full steam. He cut the first timber on the site of Salem, was at Champoeg that fateful day of May 2, 1843, helped found Oregon Institute and taught there, was an original trustee of Willamette U, pioneer flax-seed grower and breeder of purebred sheep, successful Salem businessman.

Reuben Patrick Boise, 1850 comer who held judicial posts (including chief justice of state supreme court) for almost 25 years, was five times master of Oregon Grange, founded Ellendale Woolen Mill, co-prepared first code of Oregon laws.

John Pollard Gaines, governor of Oregon who had previously served in War of 1812, was a major in Kentucky cavalry, fought in Mexican War, and was member of Congress from Kentucky. He wanted to be remembered as an ardent patriot and a kind and indulgent husband and father and "in every relation and station of life as an honest man."

Inscription on tombstone of Hon. Saml R. Thurston, born in Maine, reads: "Here rests Oregon's first Delegate / a man of genius and learning / a Lawyer and Statesman / His Christian values equaled his wide philanthropy / his public acts are his best eulogies." Encomium omits reference to Thurston persuading Congress to limit free land in Oregon first to male, adult whites and half-Indians and then to male whites (over 21 only). He was first laid to rest at Acapulco, Mexico in 1851 while en route home. Two years later, by order of territorial legislature, his body was brought to Salem.

Still standing, and now coffee house, is first **Oregon State Treasury,** at 888 NE Liberty. Across street from rear of 1860-built treasury bldg., which was also Boon Store, is "Salem Began Here" marker. In 1840 the Oregon Methodist Mission under Jason Lee dammed Mill Creek below the bridge and erected a lumber mill. Two years later a flour mill was added. In 1856 Mill Creek was also site of first power-operated woolen mill on Pacific Coast. In spring of 1841 the missionaries built the first house in Salem which, with additions, stood at 960 Broadway. (It is now grounds of Marion Historic Museum.) Occupied by four families, including that of Jason Lee, it later housed Salem's second store, first PO and treasury of Territory of Oregon.

Chinook salmon spawn within Salem in Sept. Mill Creek site is on State St. at intersection with O 22. Pringle Creek is located further W on Mission St., then N on Liberty, and E on Mill to parking area. Path along creek provides fine close-up viewing.

Marion Square Park, 3 acres of forest park near downtown Salem, was platted as a dedicated park even before Salem's articles of inc. became official in 1860. Park, between Marion, Front, Union and Commercial, is noted for more than its Douglas firs, which go back to about 1850; Marion Square trees are listed in American Forestry Assn. book, *Famous and Historic Trees.*

Waldo Park, at corner Union and Summer, contains only one tree, a redwood, planted by William Waldo in 1872. In 1936 the American War Mothers were instrumental in having the redwood and the ground around it dedicated as city park.

Civic Center, 535 Liberty, SE, has fountains, sculpture, art, fancy landscaping, bike and foot paths along Mill and Pringle creeks.

First United Methodist Church, 600 State, originated 1841 with 13 members. Today's sanctuary, built 1878, boasts 185 ft. spire, highest edifice in Salem.

Downtown Salem combines the usual glittery modern with the rarer passing old. The closer to the river, on W side of town, the older the bldgs. Most attractive and historic of downtown structures are Ladd & Bush Branch of **US National Bank of Oregon, Reed's Opera House Bldg.,** and **"Castle Tower."**

The Ladd & Bush Branch, at Commercial and State, was built 1869 and nearly identical to Ladd & Tilton Bank built in Portland a year earlier. The Portland bank was demolished in 1954 and ironwork saved from bldg. was used by architects in restoration and expansion of the Salem bldg., making it largest cast-iron fronted structure on Pacific Coast. Bank has two floors of cast iron columns, arched windows and decorations. Architects say Ladd & Bush Bank was styled after 16th century Venetian library, *Libreria Vecchia.*

Bldg. at SW corner Court and Liberty was constructed in 1870 as Reed's Opera House. Salem then was a village struggling to emerge from muddy streets and wooden sidewalks. Town had less than 1,200 persons (but it did have 13 bars, three drug stores and 15 groceries, in addition to a few hotels, liveries and blacksmith shops). So raw was the town that nobody thought it odd for an Indian encampment, of bark and brush wigwams, to be located on river bank. Into this swirling, noisy milieu came the 3-story Reed's Opera House, which for 30 years was the great cultural center of the mid-Willamette Valley, though its patrons froze in winter and sweated in summer. In cold weather, two wood burning stoves were put to use but they provided little heat. Proper dress was overcoat and blanket. Today, shops occupy ground floor of the old emporium of the arts.

"Castle Tower," on 3-story NB Bldg. at 129 Commercial, built 1892, is eye-gripper, the alpish, elfish touch being so incongruous here.

Other old structures downtown include: 233 Commercial NE (1867); 240 Commercial NE (1889); Bush-Brey Block, SW corner Commercial and Court (1889); Strong Bldg., 179 Commercial (1890s); 147 Commercial NE (1889); 129

Commercial NE (1896); 110 Commercial NE (1870); 327 State (1874); 356 State (1880s); 351-373 State (1890); 362-372 State (1880); 229-237 State (1870); 105 Liberty NE (1891). These bldgs. have been remodeled to large extent and to have any notion of what they looked like when built, observe upper portions.

Also of interest downtown are: **Elsinore Theatre** (1926), built in Tudor Gothic style, 170 High, and old **Odd Fellows Bldg.** (1900), which replaced Reed Opera House as cultural Mecca of Salem.

Historic and impressive structures elsewhere in Salem include **Smith House** (1859), 606 High; **Collins-Downing House** (1886), 241 Church NE; **Durbin House** (1870s), 448 Walter NE; **Gilbert House** (1887), 116 Marion NE; **John Minto House** (1869, 1922, 1926), 821, 835 and 841 Saginaw S; **Wilson House** (1861), 434 Water NE; **Elijah Colbath House** (1877), 334 Wyatt Ct. NE; **Burggraf-Burt-Webster House** (1895), 901 13th SE; **Curtis Cross House** (1924), 1635 Fairmount S; **Benjamin Harding House** (1884), 1043 High SE; **Daniel Jarman House** (1929), 567 High SE, the residential palace of Salem; **David McCully House** (1865), 1365 John S; **Jones Sherman House** (1913), 835 D NE; **Smith-Omhart House** (1870), 2655 E Nob Hill St. SE; **William Lincoln Wade House** (1870), 1305 John S; **Robert Witzel House** (1875), 6576 Joseph SE; **Samuel Adolph House** (1878), 2493 State.

Oregon State School for the Deaf, 999 Locust, has museum containing old furniture, records and memorabilia of school.

Oregon State Hospital, 24th NE and Center, was est. 1883. First structure, Bldg. "J," 4-story pile with clock tower, stands opposite Administration Bldg. First patients came from Portland hospital of Dr. J. C. Hawthorne but within a decade patients began arriving from all parts of state. Those coming by stagecoach were laden with incoming mail; those arriving by RR were shipped in baggage car. In 1890 inmate pop. consisted of, among others, 69 housewives and 63 farmers, compared to two saloon keepers, two preachers, a lone cowboy, a single harlot, and one spaced-out woodchopper. Certainly there were a lot more farmers and housewives than other folks, and this tells a lot about the lives of both. Inside main office in Administration Bldg. is prop from movie made here. Inscription reads: "This is the hydrotherapy control module used in the movie, 'One Flew Over the Cuckoo's Nest' which was filmed at Oregon State Hospital in early 1974." Will Sampson, who played the Indian, actually threw this 70-lb. mockup out the window. Visitors are invited to try lifting it.

A quaint bit of history took place E of Salem in Sept. 1860. When the first state legislature met on the 10th day of that month, six pro-slavery, pro-secession legislators fled from the capitol in the dead of night to prevent a quorum and the election of anti-slavery, anti-secession Edward D. Baker to the US Senate. (Congressional representatives were then elected by legislatures.) Five of the six hid out in the barn built few years before by farmer Nick Schrum. Barn, built on trap rock foundation, had wooden-pegged oak timbers and stood strong and sturdy for more than 100 years. Evidently the fleeing lawmakers felt the barn would provide them protection from their colleagues. A statement by Stephen Douglas Democrats, who voted to send Baker, a Republican, to the US Senate, charged the six absconders with "concealing themselves like hunted malefactors in farm and outhouses, subsisting on cold victuals stealthily conveyed to them from tables of charitable partisans." Eventually the six were tracked down and returned to Salem, where business was resumed.

The barn is no more. The Columbus Day Storm of 1962 destroyed it and the wood was carted off. Near where the barn stood is lovely 2-story home, said to have been constructed about time barn was built. Take State St. to 62nd Ave. SE. Turn R. *1.1 m.,* Macleay Rd. Turn L. *0.2 m.,* Sonia St. Turn L. House is at end of gravel road. Caution: occupants of house do not want to be disturbed.

One of the really charming mid-19th century homes in Willamette Valley (or anywhere in the state) is **Straub Home,** so-called because of its long occupancy by Robert Straub, a governor of Oregon, and his wife, Pat. There is history enough in the old bones of the house for at least one book. Here came political power brokers, Indian chiefs, merchant princes, the rogues and the righteous. There is so much character in the rambling, rocking-chair house (with its inspiring overview of the valley and the Cascades) that one wonders why it is not besieged by photographers. But remember that the occupants cherish their privacy. Take Marion St. Bridge and turn R at W end, Wallace Rd. *0.6 m.,* Orchard Hts. Rd. *1.5 m.,* on R (2087 Orchard Hts. Rd.), Straub House.

Another historical dwelling in Salem area is the **Brunk House.** (On O 22, from Marion and Commercial, in Salem, *6 m.,* on R.) Harrison Brunk was the typical migrating Yankee, who moved in slow stages until he reached the frontier, then leaped across it to the other side of the continent. Born in Kentucky, he went on to Illinois (where he married Emily Waller), then to Missouri, and then, in 1849, with five children, made the big jump to Oregon. Settling in Polk County he took up DLC at what is now Baskett Wildlife Refuge. Brunk was typical, too, in that he settled near someone he knew, a distant cousin. And his life runs the pattern of pioneer land tenure; he sold his DLC in 1858. In 1860 he contracted with a neighbor to have the present house built, for the sum of $844 in gold. The residence was completed the following year and most welcome, for by then the Brunk family numbered 13. In Sept., 1891, a Brunk son, Thomas W., and his wife, Clara, purchased the home place from Harrison who, now alone, his wife dead and his children long grown and gone, padded thru the big house in bent, spectral vacancy. Four years later he and Emily were reunited in earth. It was Thomas Earl Brunk, grandson of Harrison and Emily, and born here in 1893, who left the house in trust to Polk County. The Friends of Brunk House try to maintain it in the period 1859–1920, roughly between statehood and the triumph of the automobile, which completed the close of the pioneer era.

From Court and Commercial, Salem:

6.1 m., Commercial Ave. (O 99E) empties into egress wing of I-5.

1 m., Sunnyside-Turner Exit.

* Take exit. *0.2 m.,* "T". Turn R. *0.9 m.,* Sunnyside. Scarcely anything left of village but Sunnyside School, built 1925. (Earlier school put up 1889.) Bright yellow structure is now Montessori Children's House. Looking W from school, the sunlight seems to drip down the side of a billowy grass swell.

* Return to "T". Continue straight (E). *1.1 m.,* turn R onto Enchanted Way. *0.7 m.,* **Enchanted Forest,** bit of Disneyland off freeway. Return *0.7 m.,* to head of Enchanted Way. Turn R onto Delany Rd. *2 m.,* at stop sign, turn R onto 3rd St. *0.3 m.,* turn L onto Chicago St. This is "city center" of **Turner,** born of the RR, but now dependent on truck traffic for its existence. *1 block,* turn R onto 2nd St. *1 block,* turn L onto Denver. In this area are the oldest houses; at 1st and Boise lived Henry L. Turner, after whom town was named. *1 block,* at 1st and Denver, on R. **Christian Cathedral,** built 1890, in its time a bastion of bourgeois puritanism. Adjacent parsonage of same vintage. *0.2 m.,* on R, **Turner Memorial Tabernacle** (1891) on Turner Memorial Grounds, "Historic Meeting Place, Oregon Christian Churches, Since 1885." *0.2 m.,* turn L onto Witzel Rd. *0.4 m.,* on L, **Twin Oaks Cemetery** (1851). Here are graves of Henry L. Turner and of Dean Cromwell, most famous track and field coach in American history, for decades coach at USC and coach of US Olympic team. Cromwell, who was raised in this area, often yearned to return here for good, and in death he did.

From Sunnyside-Turner Exit, I-5:
3.6 m., Jefferson Exit.

Turner Tabernacle

Grave of Dean Cromwell, Twin Oaks Cemetery

* Take Jefferson Exit. *0.2 m.,* "T". Turn L, or E. *0.1 m.,* Turner Jct. (Turner, *6.9 m.*) *5.2 m.,* Marion Rd.

Turn L onto Marion Rd. *0.1 m.,* on R, N 3rd St., **St. Thomas Catholic Church,** appearing as though it had been moved from SW. Separate services for Hispanics — in Spanish. *0.1 m.,* straight onto Cemetery Hill Rd. *0.3 m.,* uphill, **Jefferson Cemetery** (1850). Buried here is veteran of War of 1812. One of best-maintained small town cemeteries in state.

Return to Marion Rd. at Cemetery Hill Rd. Turn onto Marion Rd. *2.6 m.,* Scio Jct. (Green Bridge Rd.) (Scio, *8.8 m.*) *0.3 m.,* on R, large white house that combines pioneer flavor with modern convenience. *1.8 m.,* **Marion Store,** "downtown" Marion. In past: general store and Grange on corner of Marion Rd. and A St. Across street, in front of RR tracks, was **Marion Hotel,** built 1870s and to R of it, RR depot. There is a legend in Marion that the family who gave land for the SP to run its tracks thru town stipulated that each passenger train stop in Marion for 5 minutes. The agreement ended upon death of last member of family.

Stayton Jct. (Stayton, *8.1 m.*) Turn R onto Stayton Rd. *0.2 m.,* on L, **Marion Friends Church** (1889).

Return to Marion and Stayton Rds. Turn L, toward Jefferson. *1 block,* turn R onto A St. Cross RR tracks to Duck Flat Rd. Turn L. *1 block,* turn R onto Marion Hill Rd. *0.4 m.,* on R, **Marion Friends Cemetery** (1893).

Return to Marion Hill Rd. and Duck Flat Rd. Turn L onto Duck Flat Rd. *1.4 m.,* turn L onto Pearson Rd. *1 m.,* turn R onto Parrish Gap Rd. *0.9 m.,* on L, above slope, **Hunsaker Cemetery** (1850). *1.9 m.,* on far side of flowering home, turn L onto Cemetery Rd. *0.3 m.,* **Cloverdale Cemetery.** Here lie: Isaac Morris, who served in Co. D 8 Iowa Inf. in Civil War; three children of J. M. and C. C. Morris who died between Aug. 31 and Oct. 21, 1855; two not-yet-named children of M. J. and N. E. Duncan, whose headstones read simply, "Infant" and "Infant Duncan," who died 1878; and four Delaney children, aged 4 to 18, who perished within 15 days in Oct., 1877.

Also buried in this cemetery: Daniel Delany Sr., who crossed plains in 1843, bringing with him the last of his Tennessee slaves, a young black woman named Rachel Belden, first black woman in Marion County. Early in 1865 Delany was murdered by two men, George P. Beale and George Baker, who had heard he kept a substantial wad of money under his bed. Beale and Baker were tracked down, arrested, and on May 17, 1875 hung in Salem. Seeking to recover the stolen money, the Delany family sued the attorneys for Baker and Beale, accusing the lawyers of taking the money from their clients and keeping it themselves. Although the attorneys were acquitted, Beale sided with the Delany family. "I stole the money from Delany and the lawyers stole it from me," he said.

Grave of a veteran of War of 1812 in Jefferson Cemetery

Return to Parrish Gap Rd. Turn L. *0.6 m.,* on R, **Cloverdale School;** the older part, still used, built 1910.

In 1910 Cloverdale teachers were paid $35 to $40 a month and boarded with families in area; children walked to school, wore shoes only in winter, sat two to a desk, carried lunches in pails, drank water from same dipper, drew their water in pails from spring near school, played on grass and dirt, started class by chorusing "Good Morning, Teacher," had to stand in the corner when they misbehaved, and on Fridays played special games and memorized poetry.

Head of household occupations thru the years reflects the changing character of the school district. At beginning, farming was dominant. As late as 1942, about half of the occupations listed was "farmer." In that year, in a distinctive break with the past, four of the fathers moved to work in the shipyards. That's where the money was. Two of the fathers were loggers.

In 1961 only two of the heads of household were farmers; seven were associated with wood products industry; five were in construction; two were bottlers, none had what could be called a white collar job. And, for the first time, women were listed as parent or guardian. One labored at log ripping. Another, who worked at home and had six children, listed her occupation as "zoo keeper."

In 1986 Cloverdale joined mainstream America in observing the fact of single parent and two-income families; occupations of parents were divided into Father and Mothers. Not a single farmer appears on the ledger. Occupations for fathers include administrator, minister, builder, sales contractor, air traffic controller, insurance, realtor; for women, office manager, child therapist, secretary, Adult Parole and Protection Services. Cloverdale was now occupational suburbia.

0.5 m., on L, elegant, ample 2-story mansion that dominates vale. Handsome portrait. *2 m.,* on L, at Chicago and 4th, in Turner, gawky 2-story bldg. of type common for lodges at turn of century. This was built by Masonic Order, last used as church. *0.2 m.,* "downtown" Turner.

* Return to Stayton St. in Marion. Straight for Turner. *0.2 m.,* on R, white house built 1853–54. Under Oregon ash in front yard is buried most famous Jersey cow in Oregon history, Vive La France. At one time it held three world championships for milk and butter fat production. Marker put up over grave is now at Poultry Bldg. in State Fair Grounds, Salem. Local legend has it that Vive La France died in calfbirth and that calf, which also died, is buried 50 yds. back of farm's barn. Other sources say famed Jersey died of disease. *50 yds.* farther, behind farm fence, is 1853 barn of first Holstein ranch in Oregon. Again, this is local lore.

* Return to head of Marion Rd. (2nd St.) in Jefferson. Turn L. *0.1 m.,* on L, **Jefferson Elementary School,** occupying original site of Jefferson Institute, private school teaching some HS classes; opened 1857, moved 1899 to Main

Vive La France marker, State Fair Grounds, Salem

and Union and false front added. Bldg. later became cafe; still later burned. Across street, **Jefferson Evangelical Church.** Parsonage has demeanor of sweet, old-fashioned lady. *0.5 m.,* Scio Jct. Turn R onto Main St. and heart of Jefferson.

Self-styled "Frog Jumping Capitol of Oregon," Jefferson was once head of navigation on the Santiam, though boats had a difficult time except in high water. David Douglas, the great botanist, found, among other plants in this area that fascinated him, native tobacco. *1 block,* Ferry St. (L, *1 block* to Santiam River and site of first ferry.) *0.1 m.,* on L, fairest of the nostalgia in Jefferson, **Jacob Conser House** (1854), first frame bldg. in town, now town library, city hall, senior center. Conser, typical of the versatile pioneers, crossed plains in 1848, est. ferry 1851, became postmaster of downstream Syracuse City and then Santiam City, donated land for Jefferson Institute, platted the town, was member of territorial legislature. With all that, he fathered 10 children by first of two wives. Jacob Conser Memorial Bridge across Santiam honors the man. **Methodist Church** (1871), Church and 2nd, is one of oldest in Santiam Valley. Houses that go back to turn of century and beyond are present in Jefferson but none stands out.

From O 99E and Main (at food market), turn R onto O 99E. *0.1 m.,* **San-**

Parsonage, Jefferson Evangelical Church

tiam River. *1 m.*, turn L, or S, onto Scravel Hill Rd. Cross RR tracks. *2.3 m.*, on R, **Silas Haight House** (1846), locally known as "Little White House" because it was supposedly inspired by original in Washington, D.C.

Return to O 99E. Turn W. *0.8 m.*, jct. Keep L. *0.3 m.*, forks. Take L. *1.3 m.*, **Millersburg Store,** "core" of Millersburg. Across Conser Rd. is strikingly modern city hall. Turn R onto Conser Rd. *0.7 m.*, turn R onto Woods Rd. *0.8 m.*, on R, Box 558, Isom House, early frame dwelling shaded by large maple trees. *0.4 m.*, on L, **Miller Cemetery** (1850).

From Jefferson Exit on I-5:

1 m., Ankeny Hill Exit.

   * Take Ankeny Hill Exit. *0.2 m.*, "T". Turn R, or W, on Ankeny Hill Rd. *0.1 m.*, curve R. *0.1 m.*, on L, **Anderson House,** started 1853, completed 1855. Early settlers told of fierce animals roaming Ankeny Hill.

   ** At curve near Anderson House, S for Buena Vista. *0.9 m.*, jct. Straight for Buena Vista. *0.3 m.*, **Ankeny Wildlife Refuge.** *1.4 m.*, Talbot Jct. (To L: *1.1 m.*, **Talbot.** Community church, fire station and faint dribble of houses comprise burg now, started as RR station on Oregon Electric RY.) Straight: *1.3 m.*, site of **Sidney,** once another station put up by Oregon Electric. "This is Sidney," says an amused resident, and sweeps his hand over near nothing. Turn L for Buena Vista. *2.2 m.*, Buena Vista Ferry, on Willamette.

From Ankeny Hill Exit on I-5:

2.5 m., Rest Area. *0.4 m.*, Santiam River. *0.9 m.*, Dever-Conner Exit.

* Take Dever-Conner Exit. *0.2 m.,* "T". Turn L. *0.4 m.,* on L, and *220 yds.* thru field, **Milton Hale** (aka Syracuse) **Cemetery** (1856), with most headstones toppled. Hale arrived in 1845 to stake a claim; returned with family in 1846 and est. ferry, which he operated for years. It was on key route of travel S on E side of Willamette. Hale founded Syracuse, first town in Linn County, on his claim, and probably short distance E of cemetery. But soon, on N bank of Santiam, a rival town, **Santiam City,** arose on Samuel S. Miller's claim. PO at Syracuse est. 1850; name changed to Santiam City 1852. Great flood of 1861 wiped out both villages and PO moved, with name change, to Jefferson. Flood, and changes that followed, so altered course of Santiam that the old sites do not have same relationship to river that they did before. There hasn't been a burial at Hale Cemetery since early 1900s; place is really dead.

* Return to Dever-Conner Jct., taken off I-5. Continue straight, W. *1 m.,* curve W onto Dever-Conner Rd. *0.3 m.,* on L, **Bill Case Farm,** Box 33010. (Obtain permission of residents.) *0.5 m.,* thru mint field, **Allphin Cemetery** (1848), scarred headstones of three members of Allphin family secreted in thick blackberry bushes.

Continue W. *0.7 m.,* site of **Dever,** station on Oregon Electric RY. There was also store here as nucleus of farming community. Nothing now but tracks. *0.2 m.,* **Dever-Conner Community Church.** Strangers invited to join pot luck after Sunday services. *0.5 m.,* Groshong Rd. Straight on Dever-Conner Rd. *0.1 m.,* on R, old **Dever School,** rural tintype. *1.4 m.,* turn R onto Black Dog Rd. *1.1 m.,* end of road. Trail beyond gate (obtain permission from home occupants here) leads to approximate site of Black Dog Landing, Willamette River steamer wharf. (Keep in mind that the river changed its course since then, leaving the present slough.)

Return to Groshong Rd. Turn R onto it. *1.4 m.,* Millersburg Rd. Turn L. *1.3 m.,* **Miller Cemetery** (1850). Turn R onto Woods Rd. *1.2 m.,* turn L onto Conser Rd. *0.8 m.,* **Millersburg Store.** Turn R. *1.2 m.,* turn R onto Old Salem Rd. *1.7 m.,* three cemeteries: to W, on N, **Waverly Memorial;** to W, on S, **St. Johns** (aka Jewish or Hebrew), 1877; many early Jewish settlers from Germany buried here; some stones have Hebrew inscriptions. To E of road: **Houston** (aka East Albany), 1851.

From Dever-Conner Exit on I-5:
1.2 m., Scio Exit.

* Take Scio Exit. *0.2 m.,* "T". Turn L. *2.7 m.,* Jefferson. Scio Jct. (Scio, 8.8 *m.*)

From Scio Exit on I-5:
2.8 m., Millersburg Exit:

* Take Millersburg Exit. *0.2 m.,* turn R. *0.3 m.,* turn L. *1.2 m.,* Millersburg Store. Turn L onto Conser Rd. *0.8 m.,* turn R onto Woods Rd. *0.9 m.,* on R, the once elite Isom House. *0.3 m.,* on L, Miller Cemetery (1850).

From Millersburg Exit on I-5:

1.2 m., O 99E Exit. 0.3 m., Knox Butte Exit.

    * *0.2 m.,* turn E. *2.2 m.,* turn L onto Scravel Hill Rd. *0.6 m.,* on R, **Knox Butte Cemetery** (1853). View W from here, across green prairie, would be ethereal if not for those omnipresent, churlish clouds billowing from industrial plants. Some people say the clouds have the odor of rotten eggs boiled in castor oil but to the folks who work here, "It smells like money."

    Return to Knox Butte Rd. Turn L, or E. *2.3 m.,* turn R onto Harbor Rd. *0.6 m.,* turn L for **Santiam Central Cemetery** *(0.2 m.),* 1852.

From Knox Butte Exit on I-5:

0.2 m., Albany Ave. Turn R *1 block* for three cemeteries: **Houston** (aka East Albany), 1851; **Waverly Memorial;** and **St. Johns** (aka Jewish or Hebrew), 1877. How St. Johns can be reconciled to Hebrew is a mystery unless one grants residence of the ecumenical spirit in hearts of the pallbearers.

0.1 m., **Waverly Lake,** the nautical experience of Albany.

Dever School

Hebrew inscription on stone in St. Johns Cemetery, Albany

0.8 m., jct., US 20 — E, and Albany city center.

From Exit O 99E on I-5:

Take Exit O 99E. *0.4 m.*, Albany Ave. Turn R. *0.1 m.*, three cemeteries. (See immediately above.) *0.1 m.*, Waverly Lake. *0.9 m.*, E Albany Jct. — Santiam Rd. (Turn R, or W. *0.5 m.*, at Santiam Rd. and Main, **Faith Bible Church** [1892], with grandfather-faced belfry.) *0.9 m.*, turnoff to city center. *0.6 m.*, city center, **Albany.**

No city in the Willamette Valley has so leathery and elegant a feel of history as Albany. The town has about 100 structures built before 1900, and driving or walking thru the old areas — Monteith, Hackleman and Downtown historic districts — creates the sense of strolling thru the halls of an art gallery and looking at the etchings of distinctive solid middle class American architecture, with all its touches of mercantile pomp and conspicuous consumption (or display).

Walter and Thomas Monteith were not the first white settlers in the Albany area but they remain the most memorable, precisely because a house they built still stands. In 1848 the Monteiths arrived at what was soon to be the site of Albany and purchased for $400 and a Cayuse pony the Smead claim. The following year the Monteiths built the first frame structure in Albany and it remains the only surviving original 2-story house with full length, 2-story porch in Linn County. When completed, in 1850, it was considered the most opulent residence in Oregon. First remodeled in 1918, it bears no striking similarity to the original design.

During its long years the **Monteith House** served as single family dwelling, church, apt. house and rooming house, and out of sheer necessity became in Albany's youth the civic, cultural and social center of the town. Historians know it best as having been the site of the organizational meeting of the state Republican Party in 1857, where for the first time the issue of slavery was brought up in earnest at a political gathering. Fifteen years later it was HQ for the 5th Regiment of Oregon Volunteers. Presently it is a museum at the original site, 518 2nd Ave. SW, 1 block from Albany's main business street.

The Monteiths laid out town lots on their land and a new community was founded, named for the New York state capital the Monteiths had left behind. In 1850 Abram Hackleman laid out 70 acres on the land E of the Monteith claim and to this day there is W Albany and E Albany.

In 1853 the folks of E Albany talked the territorial legislature into changing the name of the town to Takenah, a Calapooia word supposedly meaning "deep pool," where the Calapooia River enters the Willamette. The W Albany settlers, scoffing at the Indian name, acidly quipped that Takenah really meant "hole in the ground," or a translation closer to human physiology. After 2 years of suffering jibes the legislature decreed that Albany it should be, then and forever.

The first steamer arrived in the early 1850s and Albany became one of the most famous Willamette River landings of the steamboat days, but nothing remains to indicate that putative glorious era. In 1860 the California Stage Co. chose Albany as a major point on its Portland to Sacramento run; fare from Albany to Portland was $10. (Steamboat fare between the two cities was cheaper, only $1 in 1870.) The RR reached Albany in 1870; in 1888 the world's longest wooden RR drawbridge was built for the Albany-Corvallis run, and by 1910 no fewer than 28 passenger trains departed daily from Albany, routed in five directions.

In 1867 Sam Simpson, a young Albany attorney, was moved by the vistas of the wide river here to write, "Beautiful Willamette," an ode taught in every Willamette Valley school in the 1880s and 1890s.

Simpson was Albany's prodigal son, dying an alcoholic, and is little recognized by the town. Far better known and far more honored is Delazon Smith, who in 1859 founded Albany's first newspaper, which continues on as the Albany *Democrat-Herald*. Smith and Joseph Lane were the first US senators from Oregon and, like Lane, Smith was pro-slavery to the core. His contempt for black people was boundless; he said of the Negro: "His heels stick out too far; his forehead retreats too much; his smell is too strong." But Albany historians don't talk about that.

Other Albanyans of prominence would include the fiery J. Quinn Thornton, a provisional supreme court judge, and George Earl Chamberlain, who finished his term as Oregon's first attorney general before moving on to Portland, where he was elected governor and then US senator. The bldg. where Sam Simpson studied law with Thornton was already a musty old sneeze in the 1930s and is long gone. The house built for Chamberlain in 1884, when he was district attorney for the 3rd judicial district, still stands, a grand 2-1/2-story example of the Stick style, at 208 SE 7th.

Despite its traditional conservatism, it was in Albany that the Free State Republican Party met on Aug. 20, 1856, and adopted a platform fired up by the burning declaration: "Resolved that we fling our banner to the breeze, inscribed, free speech, free labor, a free press, and Fremont." Yet, though the Republicans convened here again 6 months later to place the issue of slavery square before the people for the first time, Albany was probably the strongest Southern stronghold in the valley during the first 2 years of the Civil War.

In addition to its architectural nostalgia, Albany is distinguished by its Timber Carnival, centered on July 4, which draws competitors from as far off as Australia, and by its stinking fumes. You can drive up and down the Willamette Valley blindfolded and every time you come thru Albany, particularly the N outskirt of town, you will know where you are. In this area is also an inversion corridor which holds the heaviest fog in the valley.

Albany's attractions include: **Bryant Park,** W end of 3rd Ave. and across bridge at 3rd and Vine. On L, at E end of bridge, power plant over Calapooia River built 1912. Plant is part of, or here stood, **Magnolia Mills and Warehouse,** built 1852. David Douglas, the great botanist, camped in what is now Bryant Park in 1826.

At W end of 7th Ave. are **Riverside Cemetery** (1847) and **Masonic Cemetery** (1853).

Albany Fire Dept. Museum, 120 34th St. E, has bell made in San Francisco in 1877 for Albany Engine Company No. 1. For years the bell summoned volunteer firemen by ringing out the number of the district in which a fire had been reported. In 1939 the city sold the bell to the county for placement atop the new courthouse. In May, 1982, the bell was taken down.

Albany Regional Museum, in basement of downtown city library, 302 Ferry St. SW, is good place for research start.

At foot of Calapooia St., Willamette River was first bridged. At or near here, Sam Simpson composed his well-known poem, "Ad Willametum," better known as "Beautiful Willamette." (See "High Tide for Sam Simpson" in author's *Tracking Down Oregon.*)

Other places of note: **Creative Art Guild Gallery** in old Oregon Electric RY station, SE corner, 5th and Lyon; first HS in Albany, now **First Baptist Church,** Jackson and 3rd; **US Bureau of Mines,** Queen Ave., on site of old Albany College. Albany's oldest standing church is at 238 3rd Ave. SE. Built 1875 as **St. Paul's Methodist Episcopal Church South,** and moved in 1878, it has served several denominations and looks like gaunt and feeble resident of nursing home.

In the summing up, what is most charming about Albany comprises its structures, starting with the Monteith House, described by architectural historian George McMath as being "Rural Vernacular/Pre-Classic Revival." Other architectural styles found in the historic districts include Classic Revival, Gothic Revival, Italiante, Queen Anne, Eastlake Style, Stick Style, French Second Empire Baroque, Colorful Revival Period, Bungalow, Transitional Box and American Renaissance. McMath said: "Virtually every style and type of house that was built in the Northwest during the 19th century is represented in Albany."

Guides to the historic structures of Albany are available from Albany Chamber of Commerce, 435 1st Ave. All houses except the Monteith are private and are open to visitors only once a year, on last Saturday in July. A Christmas tour, conducted by Historic Albany Tours, is held Sunday evening before Christmas Eve and is designed to permit visitors to see interiors of several historic homes.

Among distinctive structures in Monteith District are: **Stick Style house** (1885), 724 Broadalbin, painted in authentic historic colors; **Francis Redfield House** (1860s), 808 Calapooia, featuring hand-hewn beams, six-over-six double-hung windows, and weatherboard siding; pioneer-era houses at 538 and 528 2nd (adjacent to Monteith House and built circa 1865); **Whitespires Church** (1891), 510 5th, probably most observed structure in Albany; **Armstrong-Jones House** (1868), 516 Elm, best example of Gothic Revival style in Albany; **Marshall House** (1898), 540 6th, Queen Anne Style at its best; **Samuel Train House** (1886),

540 SW 6th Avenue, Albany

704 Ellsworth SW, with octagonal corner tower and variety of shapes of windows.

Exemplary structures in Hackleman District include: **Wolverton House** (1889), 810 Lyon SE; **Ralston House** (1889), 632 Baker, most elaborately decorated structure in Albany; **Chamberlain House** (1884), 208 7th SE, tallest home in Albany; **Hand House** (1886), 319 7th SE, with dormer windows and Mansard roof; **Hochstedler House** (1889), 237 6th SE, most expensive ($6,000) of the Cottage Souvenir pattern book houses authored by G. F. Barber of New York; **Allen House** (1880), 208 6th SE, first house in Albany to have electric lights; **Gothic Revival house** (1865) 240 4th SE, one of Albany's earliest existing residences; **Goltra House** (1893), 331 Montgomery SE, best example of Italiante Style in Albany; French Second Empire Style apt. house (1885), 606 2nd SE, has original porch and columns; **Queen Anne house** (1878), 404 Jefferson, with porch and W wing added 1897; **Parker House** (1875), 638 5th SE, Gothic Revival with steeply pitched roof and lancet windows; **Bean House** (1878), 505 5th SE, one of handsomest Stick Style houses in city; **Althouse Home** (1868), 118 5th, only Classic Revival structure in Hackleman District.

Most of the interesting structures in the Downtown Historic District are on 1st Ave., which looks like updated stage setting of "The Music Man." Bldgs. of note on 1st: 442, 208–210, 222, 301–305, 333, 343, 406, 401, 415–421, 434. Other historic bldgs. at 211 2nd, 214 2nd, 136 Lyon, 213 Water.

From jct., US 20-W and downtown Albany:

0.7 m., Queen Ave.

   * Turn W. *0.6 m.,* on L, **US Bureau of Mines.** Campus was site of Albany College, which had long and distinguished stay here. In 1858 Albany Academy was inc.; 8 years later it became Albany Collegiate Institute. Year later, 1867, Albany College est. under auspices of Presbyterian Church. In 1925 campus was moved to site here, where it remained until 1937. Old 99E ran past the campus and many a hitchhiker of yore took his (and on rare occasion her) wait here, heading for somewhere or nowhere while watching students move about the campus. In 1934 a jr. college had been est. in Portland and a few years later the entire college moved to the big city. In 1942 the estate of Lloyd Frank, on the hills of SW Portland, was purchased and name of college changed to Lewis and Clark. Administration Bldg. is site where William J. Kroll and associates developed process for making ductile zirconium, pioneering new age of modern extractive metallurgy. Specimen of first extruded zirconium on display inside.

2.5 m., on W, **Linn-Benton College.** *1.2 m.,* on W, former **McFarland School,** built in early 1930s, say old-timers. Typical of rural schools that grew addition by addition. *0.9 m.,* jct., O 34. E for Lebanon, W for Corvallis. (For both, see *Cross-Coast Range Roads, O 34.)*

1 m., Oakville-Verdure Jct.

   * *2.8 m.,* **Verdure,** site of RR station built early in century on Oregon

United Presbyterian Church, Albany

Electric RY. *0.5 m.,* Western Star Grange, *0.5 m.,* forks. Take L. *0.6 m.,* forks. *0.4 m.,* on R, turnoff to Oakville Cemetery, pioneer burial ground *(0.2 m.)0.6 m.,* Church Dr. Ahead is **Oakville-Willamette United Presbyterian Church,** one of oldest and fairest in Willamette Valley. Turn R onto Church Dr. *1.3 m.,* Peoria Rd.

0.3 m., turnoff E to old "downtown" **Tangent.** *0.1 m.,* traditional Tangent "business district": fire dept., PO. Yellow house back of fire station built with square nails — but age is unknown. Town had more to it in 1915, and it didn't have much then. *1 block* to E, Birdfoot Rd. and Blackberry Ln. *1 block,* on R, century-plus-old structure built as church, used in recent years as shabby habitat. Like other small towns in valley, Tangent is "fenced in" by wheat and rye grass. SE of Tangent the first domestic rye grass in US was planted by Wm. Felzer and John Roberts.

From Tangent to Harrisburg the road runs straight and lonesome thru flat, silent land, and the RR tracks do not curve for 20 m. There is a mystique here that sometimes seems unworldly, as though all motion was suspended and that you have found yourself on the plains of another planet. And then there is the feeling that this is an Oregon of the past frozen in time. And yet, and yet — it can thunder rain here when a gentle sprinkle is falling on Albany. And the wind can suddenly, angrily rise, like a lion awakened before its slumber is complete, and paw up a tunnel of dust so thick you cannot see 6 ft. ahead of you, with headlights on.

A concise cameo of the geology and paleontology S of Tangent is given in *Oregon: End of the Trail:* " . . . the prairie-like expanses are dotted at intervals by dome-like buttes. Formed by volcanic upthrusts, it is believed that at one time they formed islands in the waters that formerly filled this valley. Their upper strata abound with marine fossils, including the tusks and teeth of mammoths and mastodons. In the surrounding foothills petrified rock is frequently exposed by the weathering of crumbling volcanic tufa."

These buttes add to the ghostly abstraction of the plain and invest the land with the esoteric of the unconquered.

0.1 m., on W, colonial-style house of kind fairly common at turn of century. Across road, house may be as old but is poorer in concept and structure. *0.3 m.,* on W, 1898 house that looks like prototype of scores that dotted the plain about 1900. Probably less than 5% of fine houses of that period still remain in this area; yet the illusion survives that there are many.

0.5 m., on L, **Jenks Hatchery,** oldest (1910) and largest poultry hatchery in state. Fertilized eggs are shipped here from Arkansas. About 1 million eggs under incubation at all times; 200,000 chicks hatched weekly; 4,000 chicks vaccinated (by automatic units) per hour. Chicks delivered to contract fryer farms from Eugene to Seattle, where they are raised to 4-1/2 lb. fryers in less than 7 weeks, then marketed and sold as fresh Oregon and Washington grown fryers.

1.7 m., **Calapooia River.** The name of this stream has been spelled enough ways to please — or displease — everyone. *3 m.,* on E, Plainview Rd., at outskirt of Shedd.

**Albany Research Center, US Bureau of Mines,
formerly Administration Building, Albany College**   *Courtesy Bureau of Mines*

* Take Plainview Rd. E *1.5 m.,* on L, **Thompson's Mill.** A few folks from Mass. settled here in 1858 and started village of Boston Mills. That year flour mill built; for almost 120 years mill operated by Thompson family. Boston Mill was supply center for early farmers and travelers. PO est. 1869. When RR built thru Shedd 1871, Boston Mills was done; only mill remained. It is oldest industrial plant in Oregon and at one time the prettiest, with water-wheel, millpond-gliding ducks, and a picture postcard of serenity. House adjacent to mill was 19th century built.

* *0.1 m.,* on L, or N, Norman Rockwell barn (1881), part of Hallelujah Acres. *0.4 m.,* on R, **Savage Butte** (aka Bunker Hill) **Cemetery.** Squeezed between huge slabs of rock, and far from public eye, are faded and broken gravestones of early homesteading Savage family. *0.3 m.,* I-5 overpass. *0.1 m.,* the booms that shake you here are not sonic but gunfire at the shooting club range. Turn L. *2 m.,* Tangent Jct. (Tangent, *6.8 m.*) *0.8 m.,* jct., Seven Mile Lane. (S to Brownsville.) Straight: *0.8 m.,* **Plainview Mennonite Church,** in the core of Mennonite country. *0.2 m.,* on L, site of **Plainview** RR station. Tracks taken up and no sign now that RR came thru here. Plainview once had two stores, PO, PS, United Brethren Church, blacksmith shop. Now there are only seed cleaning and fertilizer plants in addition to Mennonite

Thompson Mill

Church. *1.2 m.,* "T". Turn R. *0.1 m.,* Lebanon Jct. L to Lebanon, straight to Brownsville. When a farmer was asked, "How come one road goes south to Brownsville and another east to Brownsville?" he replied, "Around here you can get to any place in a lot of different ways." (L to Lebanon: *2 m.,* on L, old **Rock Hill School.** *3 m.,* turnoff to Sodaville *[1.6 m.] 1.2 m.,* **Crowfoot.** Grange, church. *0.5 m.,* US 20. L, *1.6 m.,* city center, Lebanon. Straight from Lebanon Jct.: *6.2 m.,* Brownsville, thru the back door.)

From Plainview Rd. and O 99E:

On NW corner of Fayetville Rd., across O 99E from Plainview Rd., **Shedd Methodist Church,** est. 1853. Structure built 1873 and has been in continuous use as Methodist Church.

     * Take Fayetville Rd. W. *0.1 m.,* on L, **Porter House,** two stories with full attic, built 1874, Shedd's largest and most grandiose residence. *1 m.,* on R, late Victorian, boxlike house built circa 1880, moved here from Shedd 1897. *1.7 m.,* **Fayetville,** site of former RR station. These stations were important to farmers as loading depots. *2.4 m.,* "T". Turn L. *0.6 m.,* Peoria.

1 block S of Plainview-Fayetville Rds., on O 99E, on E, former Presbyterian Church, most impressive structure in Shedd. Some years ago, with its iron-grilled balcony, it looked like a haggard, confused, run-down dreamer still wearing her jewelry. For a while this was an antique shop; entire bldg. is precious antique. On W side of hwy. are two houses, 30056 and 30444, that smack heartily of past.

1 block, at 30030 O 99E, grumpy centenarian of a dwelling. At corner, on W side, **Shedd Masonic Lodge,** started 1882; present bldg. put up 1929; presumptuous white porticoed structure strangely out of place here.

1 block, on W, **WOW Hall,** with its rectangular simplicity looking like it belongs on the prairie.

You are now in the heart of Shedd, which started as Shedd in 1871, was changed to Shedds and then changed back to Shedd. The naming business is about all the indecision the town has suffered.

E of Shedd are two prominent buttes of area: Wards, 858 ft., and Saddle, 646 ft.

"South of Shedd," it is written in *Oregon: End of the Trail* (pub. 1940), "the swales are blue in springtime with the hyacinth-look blooms of the camas, Indian food-root. The carrot-like white-flowered Indian *Yampah,* the *carum* of the botanists, also abound; the slender plants spring from crisp, nutlike bulbs that were also relished as food by the natives."

No more, say the old-timers; the swales are now in rye grass. But in spring the camas and the *Yampah* still spring to life "along the road between the fences."

Between Shedd and Halsey winds can whip up suddenly, and scooping up thousands of particles from the fields, make dark the brightest day.

0.8 m., turnoff W for **Shedd** (aka Pugh) **Cemetery.**

     * *1.1 m.,* cemetery (1853), in a sublimely peaceful setting, as though death is a hymn to comfort the evertoiling.

100 yds., turnoff W for **Pugh House** (*0.1 m.*), an Oregon Gothic, tenderly

Former Presbyterian Church, Shedd

landscaped. *0.4 m.,* on W, another **Pugh House,** built 1870s as mark of affluence and now model of nostalgia. *0.4 m.,* on E, back of road, home built early 1880s and still hale and hearty. *2.5 m.,* on W, paved road.

  * *0.4 m.,* "T". Turn R. *0.1 m.,* **Smith Farm House** (1864), multi-gabled, one of loveliest old homes in Oregon. Barn built 1870s; used to train horses for police and fire depts. of nearby towns. Black walnut tree is about 100 ft. high and magnificent in spread. Altogether, farm is Willamette Valley gem.

1 m., jct., O 228, Halsey.

O 228

  This is a true mid-Willamette Valley road; flat between haunting buttes; the heartland of seed fields, where the land is raging green in spring and black as coal after the summer burning and where the pillars of smoke in August look like a circle of oil refineries on fire or, worse yet, a nuclear cloud moving inexorably on its path of doom; a house here and a house there, suddenly come upon, that were built in the 19th century; once virile settlements that are now but hazy fragments of memory in the blinking minds of octogenarians; young families who have taken over from elder farmers and with gritted teeth are working against strong odds to beat the game; no answer when you knock on doors because the women are working to help support the farms; the continuum of history lost in the quick forgetfulness of television; a cordiality that says, Move on, time's-a-wastin'; the numbing quiet of alienation; the confused sense that yesterday is only the burial ground—but where are most of them? O228 is a road not for the traveler or the historian but for the poet and the artist.

From O 99:

2.4 m., I-5. 3.3 m., on S, **The Living Rock Studios,** incredible museum built by Howard and Faye Taylor. One part of the outside resembles a castle and the interior of bldg. is equally compelling. Taylors estimate that "the total weight of the building material used may surpass 800 tons" and that 8 tons of reinforcing steel were used in main bldg. Their dream of Living Rock Studios, the Taylors wrote, "has become a reality in a tree of life formed of petrified wood, pioneer relics, mineral specimens, wood carvings of the native woods of Oregon, paintings of the history of Oregon, but most importantly the scriptures in illuminated stone that depicts biblical events."

0.6 m., **Brownsville.** *(0.5 m.,* to N. downtown Brownsville.)

The S end of city park along Calapooia River, was Kirk's Ferry, Brownsville's original name, and on the supply trail from Willamette Valley to Calif. gold fields. Town settled in 1846; PO est. 1850 as Calapooya. First postmaster was Rev. Henry Harmon Spalding, who with his wife, Eliza, came across plains in 1836 with Marcus and Narcissa Whitman.

Consider Henry Harmon Spalding, a man who wandered in the shadows. His start was son of a wedless mother who was as deserted by affluence as she was by a man. Henry was raised in poverty and low esteem. But when he was 19 he saw the light, converted to Christianity, and set his eyes upon the foreign missionary field. He had a crush upon the attractive, mercurial Narcissa Whitman but when she opted for the dashing Marcus Whitman, Henry swallowed his pride, married Eliza Hart, as plain and pious as himself, and the four set off toward the far sea, Narcissa and Eliza being the first white women to cross the Rockies.

The Whitmans est. a mission station near present Walla Walla, Wash.; the Spaldings went on to settle among the Nez Perce near present Lewiston, Idaho, and one of Spalding's first converts at his mission was Chief Old Joseph, father of the celebrated Chief Young Joseph.

When the Cayuse Indians rose up against the Whitmans, on Nov. 27, 1847, one of those who escaped the massacre was Eliza, oldest daughter of the Spaldings. She was attending the Whitman mission school and her knowledge of Indian linguistics, limited as that knowledge was, made her useful as a translator between the Cayuse and their 53 captives.

After the uprising the Spaldings received orders to close down their mission at Lapwai. At odds with their new situation, they moved to Oregon City and debated their future. They did not have too many months to wait. Hugh L. Brown and Capt. James Blakely, uncle and nephew Brownsville pioneers of 1846, invited Spalding to open a subscription school and provided Spalding with a firm foundation by giving him part of their claim.

Spalding hoped to found a town on part of his land (now N Brownsville). He named the place Amelia, after his youngest daughter, who later married the son of Hugh Brown. In 1849 Spalding started the first school in Linn County. Later the little log schoolhouse was the site of the first session of Linn County, Oregon Territory, Probate Court. And Spalding was named first school commissioner of Linn County, which at that time took in all the land W of the Rockies, N of the now Calif.-Nevada boundaries, E of the Willamette River and S of the Marion County line.

Eliza Hart Spalding died early in 1851. She had been a good wife: hard-working, patient, supporting her spouse's dogged determination for success and respect. She was probably a better mate for him than the strong-willed, individualistic Narcissa would have been.

By then Spalding was also an Indian agent as well as a farmer. But something was missing for him in Oregon and in 1859 he returned to the Nez Perce country in Idaho. In the late 1860s he returned to Brownsville to be with his daughters, but left in 1870, returning again to Lapwai, once more to preach. He died on Aug. 3, 1874, still trying to win the Indians to the white man's God.

Spalding never blazed his way into the sunlight; he was a plodder compared to the flair-soaked Marcus Whitman. But the West and the Nez Perce had turned Henry Harmon Spalding from a dour, narrow, humorless missionary into a wise, flexible, tolerant man whose affection for the Nez Perce was boundless. If only they were more open to the teachings of Christ . . .

In 1859 the PO name was changed to Brownsville, and so it has remained, honoring the father-in-law of a Spalding girl. Town grew up on the output of woolen milling and in recent years has been seeking to revive image of prosperous "mauve decade" of the 1890s. Stores and other bldgs. in business district are false-fronted, in period style. Balconies of Masonic Hall were put up in early 1960s to give older structure an older look.

Most visited place in town is **Moyer House** (1881), built in Italian villa style popular at the time. **First Baptist Church,** Main and Walnut, org. 1853; present edifice put up 1906. Store at Stanard and Main occupies Brownsville's first brick bldg. (1903); upper floor was for long home of local WOW, later Masonic order. **Brownsville General Store** (1880) in oldest existing commercial bldg. in town. **IOOF Bldg.** put up 1908 of local brick. **Linn County Museum** with pioneer rooms and shops recreated in former depot, is gathering place of storytellers.

Moyer House, Brownsville

Phoebe L. Friedman

First brick building in Brownsville

Tellers cage in Brownsville Citizens Bank dates to 1870s; came from Bank of Independence. Store at S end of bank block has fireproof walk-in vault, left over from days when Bank of Brownsville, town's second brick bldg., occupied premises. City park (**Pioneer Park**) includes site of first ferry and is home of state's oldest annual celebration, Pioneer Picnic, started 1887, held in June. Food is good, reminiscing even better.

Other places of interest in Brownsville: 105 Stanard, office of one of first doctors; 628 Main (1880s), upper story built 1890s, doctor's residence and office, served as town's only hospital for years, with nurses residing upstairs; 711 Main (1890), simplified Italiante style; 804 Main (1900), Queen Anne home built by merchant O. P. Coshaw, whose entrepreneuring included construction of 500-seat Opera House in town; 822 Main (1890s), one of the "fancy" houses of its time; 215 Depot (1891), long a hotel for stage and train workers; 721 Oak (1890), "Oregon style" home of local editor; 707 Oak (1890s); 627 Oak (1890s); 618 Oak (1890s); 229 Spaulding (1860s); 232 Kirk; 1119 Kirk; houses in 300 block on both sides of Kirk (1880–1910), especially 320 Kirk (1889), where "Indian Lize," last of the Calapooia Indians, spent the close of her centenarian life in small 2-story addition behind this house. There were hundreds of her tribespeople when whites arrived to settle; within few decades only she was left, and with her passing the entire tribe ceased to exist. **City Hall** was once Methodist Church. **Howe Bldg.** (1908) bears on E wall scars of 1919 fire that burned much of business district. **Brownsville United Presbyterian Church** est. 1857.

At Kirk St., first corner S of Moyer House, turn L, or E. *0.9 m.,* forks. Straight. *0.5 m.,* **Pioneer Cemetery.** First to be buried here was Eliza Hart Spalding, in 1851. More than 60 years later her remains were disinterred for reburial at side of her husband, Henry Harmon Spalding, at Lapwai, Idaho, to which they had come in the flower of their lives. Still buried at Brownsville are the Spalding girls, Eliza Spalding Warren and Amelia Spalding Brown, as well as several grandchildren, and the early families of the town, the Kirks, Blakelys, Browns and Cooleys.

0.1 m., going S from Kirk and Main, on R, **Brownsville Christian Church** (1892), on knoll looking down at Calapooia. In the spring of 1846 Alexander Kirk started a ferry, no more than small flatboat just big enough to hold team and wagon. Kirk stretched rope across river and loaded ferry was pulled by hand. Clearly visible from bridge, looking W, is tall broken-topped tree that still bears rope burns of ferry. Take path 75 yds. along top bank and below are remains of old bridge, site of Kirk's ferry. Just in back is broken-top tree.

Largest bloc of houses in Brownsville is S of O 228. These 19th century homes include: **Cooley House,** Blakely and Robe, said to be oldest house in city; SE corner, Blakely and Templeton; SW corner, Cooley and Robe (1878); SE corner, Robe and Templeton.

From jct., Main and O 228:

    * *1 block* W to Washburn St. Turn S. *2 blocks,* on NE corner, Washburn

Linn County Museum, Brownsville

and Blakely, **Blakely Monument,** where 1846 overlanders Hugh Brown and James Blakely started first store, in 1850. PO in store, and town named for Brown. Capt. Blakely, born in 1812, passed away in 1913 at age 101. What changes he had seen!

  * The road now becomes the Gap Rd. of yore, part of Territorial Rd., which led from Oregon City to Pleasant Hill, following Indian trails along E foothills of Willamette Valley. *2.3 m.,* on E, **Union Point** plaque, set in foundation stone from old church. Here is the true nothingness of what in its prime was a contender for county seat, now held by Albany. On slope beyond marker once stood a town between 200 and 300 people, with store, blacksmith shop, gun shop, church and subscription school — first school in Linn County, opened 1848. Here was the home for several years of one of Oregon's most remarkable and least-known achievers, Rev. Wilson Blain. In 1850, a year after preaching his first sermon here, Blain and his parishioners, who had followed him to Oregon from Indiana, org. Associate Reform Presbyterian Church. In 1852 it united with Willamette Congregation of Oakville to become United Presbyterian Church of Oregon, first of this denomination. In 1854 Blain founded Union Point Academy, granted charter same year by territorial legislature. But academy was weak from start and in 1859 its resources were transferred to Albany Academy, which became Albany College, which is now Lewis and Clark College in Portland. After Blain's death in 1861 Union Point went swiftly downhill, with both S Brownsville and N Brownsville (united in 1895) forging ahead. So you look at the plaque and raise your eyes to the slope and find it hard to realize that here were planted the seeds of two important Oregon institutions.

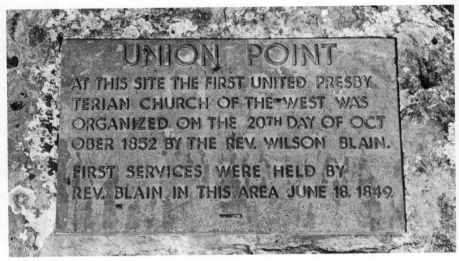

Site of Union Point

* *0.1 m.*, on W, turn onto Ranch Rd. *1.6 m.*, Stubbs Rd. Straight. *0.1 m.*, turn L onto farm road. (*0.4 m.* past farm gate, **Blain Cemetery** — 1855. Wilson Blain buried here.)

* Return to Gap Rd. Turn S. Now, as the pike rolls thru fields of wheat and rye grass and hay wheels, the eye looking W is met by hills soaring into green swells on the bosom of the prairie: Twin Buttes, and Indian Head Buttes, and Bond Butte. Old-timers of yore told tales of area occupied by grizzlies. Book published in 1940 said they were "now almost extinct." They sure are now.

* *3.8 m.*, turn W onto Belts Dr. *1.3 m.*, Belts Dr. curves to L. Straight. *0.1 m.*, past house on corner, farm gate. Thru farm gate, *300 yds.* to **Luther White Cemetery** (1847), small burial plot on seed field knoll, and kept watch by two maples.

* Return to Gap Rd. Turn S. *1.6 m.*, forks. (R, *8.8 m.*, Harrisburg.) Take L — Gap Rd. *2.7 m.*, Gap Rd. becomes Placeboro Rd. *3.3 m.*, Coburg Rd. Continue straight on Placeboro Rd. *0.8 m.*, on L, 32344 on mailbox, house that is last vestige of old settlement of **Priceboro**. *0.2 m.*, on L, stood RR station, 12 ft. by 16 ft. "depot," where passengers waited for train. When RR was abandoned, contractors took up tracks and where tracks had been, road was patched over.

* Return to Coburg Rd. Turn S. *2.3 m.*, on E, **West Point Cemetery.** Buried here is Hulings Miller, father of famed poet Joaquin Miller. Plaque says West Point Cemetery dedicated 1885 but grave markers go back much further.

* *3.6 m.*, on L, or E, Wilkens Rd. Plaque on NE corner contains brief history of area. It states that Eastside Old Territorial Road 1848–1865 and the old stage road ran along base of hills. Osage orange trees were planted along roadside in 1854. Due E was home of 1848 pioneer, whose house was also Willamette Forks PO. Take Wilkens Rd. *1.4 m.,* turn R. *0.3 m.,* end of road. On R, farmhouse was site of Sunny Ridge, where Miller House stood. In 1882 another house was put on top of old foundation. Cincinnatus Heiner (Joaquin) Miller lived here on family farmstead from 1854 to 1856, between ages 13 and 15. The shining mtns. to the E, he wrote, were "topped with wonderful fir trees that gloried in the morning sun, the swift, sweet river, glistening under the great big cedars, and balm trees in the boundless dooryard."

    * Return to Coburg Rd. Turn L, or S. *1.8 m.,* turn R. *0.4 m.,* Coburg. *0.1 m.,* turn L for freeway. *0.7 m.,* I-5.

From Brownsville Jct. at O 228:

1 m., on R, **Atavista Farm,** built 1875 for John and Amelia Spalding Brown. Termed "one of the restorations of the Italiante form of the villa house in Oregon," Atavista Farm is beautified by 2-story bay windows, asymmetrical mass, and several small porches. The firs and the black walnut are believed to have been planted by the Browns.

5 m., on S, **McKercher CP.** PA, fishing in Calapooia River. *0.7 m.,* **Crawfordsville CB,** over Calapooia. Built 1923; has length 105 ft. Hasn't been used by car since 1963. *0.1 m.,* **Crawfordsville.** Store. Named for Philemon V.

Crawfordsville Bridge

Crawford, native of Indiana. Coincidentally, there is a Crawfordsville, Ind. In 1915 town, with pop. 300, was much larger than it is now. It then had two sawmills, flouring mill, HS, PS, three churches.

The fields are flat and reach their ends only at the low hills, which rise up to contain the spreading plain. The trees rush to the road like agitated ostriches and suddenly halt, peering wide-eyed at the passing cars.

0.4 m., Marcola Jct.

    * This is the road thru the Mohawk Valley, which begins where Linn County turns into Lane County. There was a time, up to the 1950s, when the Mohawk Valley was really rustic, and had a secretive air about it. It is now becoming pure suburbia.

    * *12.5 m.,* turnoff R to **Shotgun Creek Rec. Park.** *(1.6 m.,* on R, rec. site, BLM day use area.)

    0.9 m., on L, or E, Paschelke Rd. **Ernest CB** over Mohawk River. Built 1938 at length of 75 ft. This span replaced original CB put up 1903. CB was filmed in movie "Shenandoah." (Cross bridge. Turn R. *1.4 m.,* Wendling Rd. Turn L. *1.9 m.,* **Wendling CB,** built 1938 with length of 60 ft., across Mill Creek. *0.4 m.,* site of Wendling, former lumber town; PO est 1899. In mid-1930s one of biggest sawmills in all NW was here; the hills were thick with timber; camp houses of loggers lined the road. Nothing now.)

Ernest Bridge

Wendling Bridge   *Phoebe L. Friedman*

* From jct., Marcola Rd. and Paschelke Rd.: *2.2 m.,* Wendling Rd. (Up Wendling Rd., *3.5 m.,* Wendling CB.)

* *0.3 m.,* **Marcola,** settled in second half of 19th century and first called Isabel. Supermarket, station, but it is no longer the independent market town of Mohawk Valley; too close to Eugene and Springfield. House on NW corner of Marcola Rd. and Whitmore St. built 1872, oldest house in Mohawk Valley, was home of Mary Cole, after whom Marcola was named, in 1885.

0.6 m., on R, or W, turnoff to Marcola Cemetery (*0.1 m.*) *3.1 m.,* Mohawk Jct. Turn R onto Hill Rd. *0.1 m.,* **Mohawk.** Store. With area settled in 1860s, Mohawk grew into thriving little town and in 1915 had 200 folks living in and around burg, possessed a privately owned electric light system, had PS and Grange (still has Grange), and was shipping point for hops and clover. *1.2 m.,* on R, turnoff to **Valley View Cemetery** (*0.1 m.*). Now the road curves gently thru rural residential slopes, the kind of suburbia where there always seems to be a lawn or garage sale taking place. *2.9 m.,* jct. (Straight: *6 m.,* Springfield.) R: *6.1 m.,* bridge over McKenzie. L to Armitage SP; R to Coburg, and back to Brownsville, for nice round trip.

* From Marcola and Hill, S-bound.

* *5.8 m.,* jct. Straight. *1.9 m.,* jct. Straight. *1.6 m.,* Springfield.

From Marcola Jct. on O 228:

0.1 m., on R, or S. turnoff for **Crawfordsville Union Cemetery.** (*0.6 m.,* 1852–est. cemetery, on knoll.)

3.4 m., **Holley.** Store. **Holley Christian Church** has "Come as you are welcome sign" and evidently means it. Area is noted for petrified wood and semi-precious stones, with "Holley blue" highly regarded. To side of church is Old

Holley Rd. *1.5 m.*, down road, on R, small farm open for commercial digging of petrified wood, jasper, etc.

3.8 m., turnoff R to **Ames Cemetery** (100 yds. on L), est. 1863. *0.6 m.*, jct., US 20, at **East Linn Museum,** treasure house of pioneer mementos. *0.2 m.*, downtown **Sweet Home.**

Return to Halsey on O 99.

Flat on the prairie, **Halsey** has the piercing tang of a page out of a midwestern novel by Edna Ferber. You know that on a cold December day the farmers coming into town slap their hands together and the steam of their breath seeks warmth against sturdy mackinaws. The farmers don't, of course; they brisk out of their cars and pickups and hurry into the store, cafe or bank. But the lay of the land, with its indrawn air, compels a reach out for the fiction of the past rather than the facts of the present.

Halsey started life in 1871, when RR came thru, and has since led a slow-poke life, barely doubling 1910 pop. of 375 in 1990. And maybe that is good, because town is a rich and thick album of the way things were.

0.2 m., — from jct., O 228 — on SW corner, D ST. and O 99E, which is 2nd St. in Halsey, stands **Grace Bible Fellowship,** formerly Halsey Christian Church, and as such oldest in town, and the kind pictured on wall plates. Gaunt, simple-faced prairie house on 1st St., just S of O 228, has the straight, stark lines of a parochial pioneer dwelling and seems more in tune with this land than is many a fancier house.

0.1 m., F St. (*1 block,* 3rd St., **United Methodist Church,** veteran of the plains.) *2 blocks,* H St., "heart" of Halsey. On H St. turn R. Houses on SE and SW corners of H and 3rd built late 1870s. Houses on SW and NW corners of 4th and H built early 1880s. All four built by same man.

1 block, I St. Houses on SE and SW corner of 3rd and I are handsome residences old-timers like to remember. At W end of I St. is kind of big, bucolic house Grandma Moses liked to paint. And she would have loved the barn behind it.

1 block, J St. Turn W onto J St. *1 block,* house on SW corner is beauty of Halsey in its prime. Turn S onto 3rd St. *0.1 m.,* on R, 1365 3rd, 1880s house. *0.1 m.,* O St.

* Turn W onto O St. *0.4 m.,* Powerline (also seen as Power Line) Rd. Turn S. *1 m.,* turn R onto farm lane. Walk *300 yds.* along fence to **Halsey** (aka Smith and Rust) **Cemetery,** est. 1855. Cows trampling thru cemetery-pasture have toppled headstones.

Return to Powerline Rd. Turn R, or S. *0.2 m.,* turn W onto Lake Creek Rd. *3.2 m.,* Peoria Rd. On SE corner, Grange. N and E of intersection, **Lake Creek Mennonite School,** grades 1 thru 10. Children dress in traditional Mennonite attire.

* Return to Powerline Rd. Turn R, or S. *1.9 m.,* on L, entrance gate to **Cogswell-Foster Preserve,** 90 acre tract on Little Muddy Creek that has

Barn at west end of I Street, Halsey

never been plowed or logged. (Until mid-19th century it was maintained by periodic burning.) Sterling example of natural white oak and ash forest that existed before white settlers entered Willamette Valley. There is not even a trail thru this multi-bird species nesting area given The Nature Conservancy by the late Mrs. Lee Foster, whose grandfather came here in 1872. *0.4 m.* farther up road, 1898 **Foster House.**

From O 99E and O St:

3.2 m., Cartney Rd.

    * Turn R, or W. *0.4 m.,* Powerline Rd. *2 m.,* **Cartney,** site of RR station built to serve grass seed warehouse on Oregon Electric RY. *0.4 m.,* Peoria Rd. 1898 house on NE corner is pure calendar art. Straight across Peoria Rd.: *1.5 m.,* forks. Straight. *0.6 m.,* **McCartney CP,** on Willamette. Park named for 19th century settler J. M. McCartney, after whom Cartney Station was called. There is no record to indicate why the Mc was dropped at the tracks.

    * From O 99E — E, across RR tracks. *2.2 m.,* "T". Turn R. *1.5 m.,* site of **Rowland.** In 1915, when Rowland was on E Side line of the SP, it had PS, HS, three saloons, livery stable, hotel, blacksmith shop, stores, cluster of residences. A native of the area recalled that "Years ago people come from Portland on the railroad to Harrisburg, rent a rig, and drive to Rowland and rent rooms in the hotel. Then they'd just step outside the hotel and start duck shooting. The peculiar conditions brought a lot of ducks here and Rowland had a great reputation for duck shooting." There is not a printed or scrawled word along the road to indicate that a settlement once existed here. In 1986 the tracks were taken up but Rowland as a town had died long before. Only a few weary houses and shacks stand where the ducks landed — and the ducks haven't been around for ages.

From O 99E and Cartney Rd.:

0.6 m., on W, **Alford Cemetery** (1853). On DLC of Thomas Alford. There was a settlement here, born of the RR, called Muddy, for Muddy Creek, which seems to slink thru Linn County like a stray cat clinging to shadows. Muddy Station PO est. 1874, lasted 1 year. For 2 years area was served by Liverpool PO, also long gone. Muddy changed to Alford in 1900. But death was in the wings.

Turn E onto Powerline Rd., at N edge of cemetery.

* *0.3 m.,* on R, **Masonic Cemetery** (1851). *0.2 m.,* on L, **Workman Cemetery** (1885). *1.3 m.,* Diamond Hill Rd. Turn L. *0.5 m.,* Harris Dr. Turn L. *1.2 m.,* on R, ghostly house emblazoned with graffiti, the branded outcast on the plain. *1.2 m.,* site of Rowland.

Turn R onto Rowland Rd. *1 m.,* turn L onto Diamond Hill Rd. *0.9 m.,* I-5 overpass. *2.7 m.,* forks. Straight. Diamond Hill Rd. becomes Gap Rd. *1.7 m.,* Belts Rd. Turn L. *1.3 m.,* forks. Straight on Tub Run Rd. *0.1 m.,* large yellow house. Beyond it, along fence line, *200 yds.,* small **Wiggle Cemetery** (1853) typical farm burial grounds.

Return up Belts Rd. to Gap Rd. Turn L onto Gap Rd. *3.8 m.,* turn L onto Ranch Dr. *1.5 m.,* Stubbs Rd. Straight. *0.1 m.,* turn L into farm drive. *0.4 m.,* past farm gate, **Blain Cemetery** (1855). Buried here among other noteworthy Oregonians are Wilson Blain, prominent pioneer clergyman, and George A. Waggoner, well-read author of his times.

* Return to Gap Rd. Turn L. *0.2 m.,* on R, tablet marking site of **Union**

"Ghost" House on the Prairie   *Courtesy Marcia Workentine*

Point, where on Feb. 10, 1852, and under leadership of Wilson Blain, two branches of Presbyterian Church in Oregon united. Being on the Old Territorial Rd., Union Point was favored by travelers, and for a while the village prospered. But good times were short-lived; PO only from 1854 to 1858; "big town" of Brownsville captured the trade. *2.4 m.,* O 228-Brownsville.

From Alford Cemetery, on O 99E:

3.1 m., Peoria Rd. *0.2 m.,* in **Harrisburg,** Territorial Rd.

 * Turn E onto Territorial Rd. *0.3 m.,* turn L onto 7th St. *0.2 m.,* turn R onto Diamond Hill Rd. **Diamond Hill** was last stand of Grizzly bears in Linn County, 1856, old records say. PO 1858–1869. As late as 1950s, wagon tracks of old Territorial Rd. of 1840s and 1850s still identifiable. *4.7 m.,* Rowland Rd. *1 m.,* Harris Dr., site of **Rowland.**

0.1 m., Smith St., center of **Harrisburg.** Town first known to 1852 settlers as Prairie Precinct or Prairie City; then Thurston (1853); in 1855 it acquired present name except for "h" ending, which the years discarded. First steamboat, *James Clinton,* reached Harrisburg in 1856 and thereafter until RR finally put end to river transport, town was important Willamette port.

Turn W onto Smith. *0.2 m.,* at end of street, **Harrisburg Landing;** PA and restrooms. Across street, at 1st and Smith, is bldg. that held pioneer May and Sender General Store.

Other landmarks of past: **IOOF Hall** (1889), SW corner of 2nd and Smith. On NW corner, first bank bldg. (still has bank vault), then first telephone exchange. Bldg. at 172 Smith built 1885 and, said local wit, "held together by termites clasping hands." At 730 2nd is large, elegant, 2-story 19th century mansion with 4 gables, porch and basement levels adorned with fancy millwork — oldest, most attractive house in Harrisburg and attractively landscaped. **Christian Church,** 6th and Smith, is early forum of religion here.

From 3rd and Smith:

0.3 m., on L, La Salle St.

 * Turn E onto La Salle St. *0.3 m.,* 6th St. Turn R. *0.3 m.,* on R, **Davis House,** built 1850s, as was adjacent barn. *10.3 m.,* Stallings Rd. On L, house built 1880s, moved here in 1950s; house on R embellished by 1901 pump house. *0.3 m.,* on L, 1851 **Macy House,** oldest in **Coburg,** a charming mixture of past and present, urban and rural, dynamic and laid back. It seems hard to believe — but it is true — that Coburg's pop. in 1990 was smaller than its pop. in 1915 (800). Without even trying to imagine 1915 traffic, Coburg's today has to be a lot heavier.

 Century-plus architecture at 163 S Willamette and house adjacent to it on S; 209 (Coburg Inn) N Willamette; 422 N Willamette; IOOF Hall, N Willamette and Mill; 173 W Dixon; 355 E Dixon.

* From E Pearl and S Willamette, turn L for freeway.

0.6 m., I-5.

 * From E Pearl and S Willamette: straight. *0.9 m.,* on R, 1895 house. *0.3*

m., on L, turnoff to **Coburg Cemetery** *(0.2 m.).* In small, darkling grove at rear of cemetery, hoary grave markers date back to 1856; headstones here of three Bryant children, ages 19 months to 8 years, who died within two-month period in 1877. *0.5 m.,* on L, house which local historians say was built by early ferryman in 1848. *0.4 m.,* **McKenzie River.** *0.2 m.,* **Armitage SP,** on McKenzie. PA, fishing, BR, FHP. At or near here was tiny hamlet of Armitage, named for 1848 arrival who est. first ferry across McKenzie. When McKenzie PO was est. early 1854, at site of Armitage, postmaster was ferryman George H. Armitage. (From turnoff to Armitage SP — Springfield, *5.3 m.;* Eugene, *5.5 m.)*

From La Salle St. and O 99E, **Harrisburg:**

0.1 m., **Willamette River.** First "mass transportation," in 1848, was by crude ferry. Not until 1925 was bridge built.

0.7 m., on R, McMullen Lane. This is approximate site of **Hogem,** named for large hog-feeding pen owned by man who also had flour mill here; built 1865, closed down in early 1870s.

0.9 m., **Lancaster.** Nothing now but store — but in its prime Lancaster was fightingest town on river because of bullying, obstructionist tactics to make landing head of navigation on river. In 1852 a burly fellow named Woody opened roadhouse and soon locale was known as Woody's Landing, or Woodyville, with most prominent bldg. being Woody's crude, candle-lighted saloon. It thrived on rivermen who wanted to look down on something stronger than water and on road travelers who were inclined to wipe off — or wash down — the dust. Woody had a lot of kinfolk, with the manners of the Dead End Kids and the scruples of the 40 Thieves, and cargo unloaded here at twilight was mysteriously missing at dawn. Anyone even hinting that the "Woody Bunch" might be responsible was inviting mass attack. In 1858 PO of Freedom opened. About then Woody sold out to another gang of toughs and crooks, Mulkey & Co., and a warehouse was built and settlement grew. A few years later — probably 1864 — the town took its place on the "big road" from Corvallis to Oakland by way of Eugene, when the California & Oregon Stage Co. moved its station here from Milliorn, *1.5 m.,* to W. By then, however, town had been severely damaged by 1861 flood and separated from stream when Willamette changed course. In 1866, PO name changed to Lancaster. Coming of RR to Junction City performed last rites on Lancaster as a viable community and in 1872 PO moved to Junction City.

1.9 m., jct., O 99E and O 99W, becoming O 99.

O 99

0.6 m., main intersection, **Junction City,** 6th and Ivy.

Junction City received its name not from merger of roads but, in 1871, anticipation of unfulfilled jct. of two RR lines. In 1915 Junction City was complete market and distribution center for large agricultural area and there were gobs of open space between the town and Eugene. Today, distance between Eugene and Junction City is one long hwy. commercial and industrial strip and it is likely that in the foreseeable future it will be difficult to tell where one city ends and the other begins. Big annual event here is four-day Scandinavian Festival, held early Aug., one of great folk festivals of W US.

Attractions for the curious in Junction City include **Junction City Historical Society Museum,** 655 Holly, between 6th and 7th, on Holly, in town's oldest house, built by Dr. Norman Leslie Lee, first physician here, about 1870. Close by is **Junction City Boarding House,** 290 W 7th (7th and Holly), built 1871 as **Cumberland Presbyterian Church. Bushnell House** (1875), 248 Holly, is another survivor in good health. **Finland Station,** on NE corner, 5th and Holly, has old steam engine. Album page train depot at SW corner, 5th and Holly.

At 6th St., E to Deal St. Turn N. *0.5 m.,* R onto Dana Ln. **Soren Jensen House** (1890), 29323 Dana Ln., looks like derelict or dowager, depending on upkeep efforts of tenants. House at 29361 Dana Ln. has settled for dowager status.

At 1st St., first traffic light S of main intersection, 6th and Ivy, turn W.

* *0.1 m.,* turn L onto Prairie Rd. In same block, on R, **Gideon Millett House,** largest and most lavish of Junction City's old houses. Return to 1st St. Turn W. *0.5 m.,* on N, small **Junction City Cemetery** (1859). 1st St. becomes High Pass Rd. *3.4 m.,* stop sign at Veneta Rd. Turn N. *0.5 m.,* on E, **Rest Lawn Memorial Park** aka Junction City IOOF Cemetery (1874). Return to High Pass Rd. Turn W. *0.4 m.,* on L, **Danish Lutheran Cemetery** (1901).

Junction City Boarding House

518   IN SEARCH OF WESTERN OREGON

Letters and diaries of the pioneers in this area frequently speak of rain; in this the area was typical of all W Oregon. Rain made it difficult to work in the fields, rain poured into cabins and houses not rainproofed, dampness was hard on arthritis and other infirmities, rain piled up the gloom, rain churned the land into rivers of mud, making travel laborious, exasperating and painfully slow, rain kept people at home, where they developed cabin fever.

The settlers vented their displeasure with the excess rain in many ways; one was by lamentably singing a song titled "Webfoot Land" and put to the tune of "Beulah Land," which, in turn, copied the music of "O Tannenbaum." The song became a favorite throughout the Willamette Valley and remained so until gravel and paved roads replaced the horrible old pikes. And it went like this:

"I've reached this land of mud and rain/ And all its riches hard to gain,/ And since I've reached this very spot,/ Sometimes I wished that I had not.

"Oh, Webfoot Land, wet Webfoot Land,/ As in my house I sadly stand/ And gaze throughout the dripping pane,/ I wonder when twill cease to rain./ And since I've reached this very spot,/ Sometimes I wished that I had not."

(In arid E Oregon the lyrics were, in true folk lore style, changed to reflect the specific conditions. Thusly:

("Oh Bunch Grass Land, Oh Bunch Grass Land/ As on the highest point I stand,/ I look away across the plain/ And wonder if twill never rain/ And view the dried and shriveled wheat/ And wonder what we'll have to eat.")

From Ivy and 6th, Junction City:

0.3 m., turnoff L for Santa Clara.

    * This is the "river drive" along River Rd., so peaceful and rustic in the 1950s and so super-suburban now. *6.6 m.,* on L, 1898 house, rural beauty. Red barn behind it looks at least as old but it was built in 1930s. *1.6 m.,* on L, **Awbrey Rec. Area,** pleasant rest stop. *1.8 m.,* **Santa Clara,** "river" suburb of Eugene. *3 m.,* Eugene.

1.5 m., on R, jct., O 36 — to Coast. (See *Cross-Coast Range Roads, O 36.*)

On L, Prairie Rd.

    * Take L, Prairie Rd. *2.5 m.,* Meadowview Rd. At or near here was site of **Grand Prairie** (PO 1854–1860). In truth, no one in area knows location of Grand Prairie and rare is even the old-timer who has heard of it. *2.7 m.,* Irvington Rd. Turn L. *0.1 m.,* on R, **Irving Christian Church,** built 1853, moved here from site of Irving. Return to jct. Cross road. *0.1 m.,* site of **Irving.** In 1915 it had pop. 100, stores, HS, PS, three churches, Grange. Now there is nothing to indicate existence of town.

6.6 m., turnoff L to Santa Clara (2 m.).

Turnoff R to Alvadore (5.8 m.) and Fern Ridge (6.1 m.).

4.4 m., jct., O 126, to Coast. (See *Cross-Coast Range Roads, O 126.*)

1.5 m., Willamette St., downtown **Eugene.**

Eugene is really three cities, or three populations, that both neutrally and symbiotically exist in the same general terrain, providing a provocative and baffling stage setting and scenario. It is an international city, the only international city in Oregon, where one feels that this part of Eugene could be moved to various parts of the world and be at home there. Secondly, it is an American city, where so many people from so many regions of the nation have settled and intermingled here that one can stand on a downtown street corner and watch the faces of America go by. Thirdly, it is an Oregon city, which has gathered to itself the proletariat and the former farm folk from every corner of the state. Quintessentially, what is distinctive about Eugene is its intrinsic lack of definable identity. This might be said about some other cities as well, but in Eugene, once one enters the realm of reality, the fact is glaring.

Had New York State-born Eugene F. Skinner not yet come to the end of his wanderings here, there surely would have been a town and then a city — geography dictates as much — but, obviously, the place would have a different name. From Illinois, where he had lived for several years, the 36-year-old Skinner and his wife of 6 years, Mary Cook Skinner, wagoned to Calif. in 1845. Had he stayed around he might have become rich but he did not like what he saw and, too, he was still restless. So N he traveled until he came to Polk County. That area wasn't good enough for him, either, so he hit the trail again, nudging his way S and a little E. He did set down roots, then, at the foot of a 681-ft.-high hill now known for long as Skinner Butte and overlooking the Willamette River. (After WW II the site was next door to a U of O student housing project. Skinner would have liked that, being a great believer in education.) So there, in 1846, the Skinners built their cabin and in it came into the world their daughter, Leonora, first white child born in Lane County. Like most pioneers, Skinner was a jack-of-all-trades, picking up a dollar, or what went in lieu of such, wherever and however he could. He farmed, but that didn't provide his growing family with much more than food. He started a ferry service and that brought in some cash. In 1850 he opened a PO, named Skinner's, and that added a few cents to the family larder. Then, in 1852, seeing destiny in front of his eyes, he and another fellow laid out a town, so PO name was changed to Eugene City. Looking ahead, Skinner donated some of his land for county bldgs.; he was county clerk for a while. And he practiced law, all of which provided for financial solvency. The future of Eugene City was assured on March 3, 1857, when the *James Clinton,* first steamboat to ascend the Willamette River to Eugene, arrived safely to huzzas of the settlers. Now linked to the Willamette Valley towns and cities by the most efficient transportation of its time, Eugene City was on the way to bigness. On May 22, 1889, Eugene City became Eugene. By then Eugene F. Skinner was a quarter of a century dead; Mary Cook Skinner followed him to the grave 17 years later.

Growing steadily, Eugene in 1915 had pop. 12,083 and university enrollment of 2,000. It also had a Bible School, Catholic Academy, School for Girls, business college, two daily papers, was terminus of electric line from Portland, was pivot point of several RRs, and boasted street railway system with interurban line to Springfield.

The nationwide shift in pop. following WW II brought profound changes in a large number of Oregon communities with none more affected than Eugene. The real explosion began in the 1950s, and on the heel of it came an architectural redesigning of downtown and the creation and flowering of dazzling middle class residential areas on the outer spokes of Eugene. Concurrent with the rapid growth of the city was prominence of U of O track team, coached by Bill Bowerman, a crusty individualist with a genius for inspiring his athletes. Bowerman's runners and Bowerman himself developed running into more than a sport and a cult; running became a pronounced lifestyle and Eugene crowned itself "Jogging Capital of the World." (So limited is fame in Oregon, however, that when Bowerman, a staunch conservative, sought election to the state legislature, he was turned down by the voters. They would cheer his champions but they did not want him to represent them as a lawmaker.)

The U of O's most celebrated track star was Steve Prefontaine, up there with the best of world class distance runners. Still a young man, he was killed in a single car accident but the legends live on, and memorializing the pride of Eugene and hometown Coos Bay is the Prefontaine (Jogging) Trail.

Eugene (together with most of Lane County) has a national reputation for its progressivism in energy control and distribution, environmental preservation and management, and feminine issues. Politically, it has given the state (and in at least one case the nation) some of the finest legislators of the century, including Wayne Morse, Charles O. Porter, Edward Fadely, Richard Eymann and Margie Hendrickson.

The best place to start seeing the historic sites and fascinations of Eugene is downtown. Noteworthy are **Hult Center for the Performing Arts** (6th and Willamette), finest facility of its kind in the state; **SPRR Depot** (1908), at N end of Willamette; **McMurphey House,** better known as Castle on the Hill (circa 1888), 303 Willamette, and the most striking old house in town; **Oregon Electric RY Passenger Station** (1914), 27 E 5th, now restaurant; **Palace Hotel** (1903), now Lane Bldg., 488 Willamette; **Smeede Hotel Bldg.** (1885), oldest surviving brick bldg. in Lane County, 767 Willamette; brick facades at 859 Willamette were put up between 1872 and 1888; **McDonald Theater Bldg.** (1925), 19th and Willamette, is typical of movie houses of that period; **Quackenbush Bldg.** (1903), 160 E Broadway; **Telephone Pioneer Museum** 112 E 10th; **Christian House** (1855), 170 E 12th, oldest residence in Eugene; 433 E Broadway (1868), now restaurant; house (1868) that was home of the widow Skinner, 260 W 6th; **Miller House** (1870), 246 E 3rd; **Koppe House** (1890), 205 E 3rd; **Watts House** (early 1900s), 335 Pearl; **Campbell House** (1890s), 252 Pearl; **Ankeny House** (1890s), 212 Pearl.

Downtown Eugene is noted for its two colorful shopping marts: **Fifth St. Public Market,** High and 5th, a 3-story collection of boutiques and restaurants in historic preservation area, and **Saturday Market,** 8th and Oak, an artisan cornucopia.

Close to downtown is **East Skinner Butte Historic District.** It includes **McAlister House** (1904), last of the large Victorian-period residences to be constructed in the East Butte area, at 286 High; **Henderson House,** oldest example of Greek Revival architecture in Eugene, and SW portion of it built 1857 as part of Heatherly and Bailey Tavern, and moved in 1909 from original location on NW corner of 8th and Pearl, where it had been a private school before turned residence, and now at 260 High; **Cogswell-Miller House** (1884), 246 E 3rd; **Mims House** (1867), 330 High.

High St. leads into **Skinner Butte Park,** running E and W along S bank of Willamette. Park, delightful day use area, contains replica of 1846 cabin built by Eugene and Mary Cook Skinner. Beyond park is **Owens Rose Garden.**

Other Eugene structures of interest include: **Condon Residence** (1878), remodeled house of what was for years home of Dr. Thomas Condon, world-famous geologist, at 1258 Jackson; **Peters-Liston-Wintermeier Home** (1860s), locally renowned for its "Rural Gothic" style, originally located at SE corner, 10th and Pearl, before being moved to present 1611 Lincoln; **Chambers House** (1876), built for $2.,300, 1006 Taylor; **Smith Home** (1902), 2065 Lincoln; **Masterson House** (1857), all wood construction, 2050 Madison; **John Scott McMurry Home** (1880–1886), 21st and Kincaid, moved 3 blocks from original location near 24th; **U of O Faculty Club** (1886), built as Collier Home on SW corner, 13th and University; **Abrams Cider & Vinegar Mill** (1883), 602 E 8th; **Maude Kerns Art Center** (1895), in oldest church structure in Eugene, 1910 E 15th; **Patterson House** (1903), 751 E 11th.

The **U of Oregon,** moderate stroll from downtown, is famous for its Museum of Art, Museum of Natural History, Summer Festival of Music, Bio-Social Research Center, trees (400 varieties), and campus sculpture. Pioneer bldgs. are Deady Hall, which became first U of O facility when it was erected in 1876 (it was guaranteed to last a millennium so it still has almost 9 centuries to go), and Villard Hall (1885). Adjoining UO is Northwest Christian College, which was Eugene Divinity School when volcanic stone administration bldg. was constructed 1907.

Almost enclosed by UO is **Pioneer Cemetery,** 18th and Potter, which has sections devoted to veterans of Civil War.

Lane County Historical Museum, in county fairgrounds, 740 W 13th, has excellent displays. Back of it is pioneer **Lane County Clerk's Office,** built 1853 in classic revival style of Oregon territorial period. Has been moved four times; was scene of first jury trial in area conducted by noted Judge Matthew Paul Deady.

Willamette Science & Technology Center (WISTEC) and **Lane ESD Planetarium,** 2300 Centennial Blvd., near Autzen Stadium. Planetarium is largest facility of its kind between San Francisco and Vancouver, B.C.

Hendrick Park, Summit Dr. and Skyline Dr., is famed for its beauty and profusion of rhododendrons. **Greer Gardens,** 1280 Goodpasture Island Rd., has one of nation's largest collections of rhododendrons. **Alton Baker Park, Lane CP,** Day

Pioneer County Clerk's Office   *Courtesy Lane County Historical Museum*

Island Rd. and Garden Way, on N bank of Willamette, has excellent day use facilities.

Oldest house in Lane County (1851) is **William Stevens House.** At exit of Ferry St. Bridge, stay on Coburg Rd. *1 m.,* turn R onto Harlow Rd. *2.1 m.,* turn L onto Game Farm Rd., in Springfield. *0.3 m.,* on L, **Immanuel Baptist Church.** Part of it was 2-story Stevens House, unique for its double flight of stairs and innovated kind of turned baluster.

Take Willamette St. S. At 24th, turn L. At University, turn R. At corner of University and 25th stood first school in Eugene area, erected 1850s. Teacher Sharon Ann Moore rode her horse from Goshen to school and back every school day, come rain or come shine. Up slope, **Masonic Cemetery** (1859). Contains graves of Eugene Skinner; John Whiteaker, first governor of Oregon statehood; and S. F. Kerns, noted overland pioneer of 1852.

Return to 24th and Willamette. Turn L. *0.5 m.,* turn R onto Crest Dr. At 595 Crest Dr., **Morse Ranch Park,** 6-bedroom house built 1936 by Wayne and Mildred (Midge) Morse. Until his death, this was home of Sen. Wayne Morse, one of the truly great senators in the history of this nation. He exemplified many of the characteristics that distinguish Oregon to the nation: independence of thought, courage, resolution, integrity and devotion to peace and justice.

Grave of Eugene Skinner, Masonic Cemetery, Eugene   *Phoebe L. Friedman*

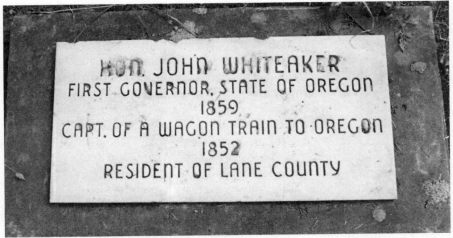

Grave of John Whiteaker, Masonic Cemetery, Eugene　　　　*Phoebe L. Friedman*

Return to Willamette. Turn R. *3 m.,* thru gorgeous suburbia and along over-looks of shimmering vales, parking area (on L) of 2,065-ft. **Spencer Butte,** area's highest viewpoint. Hiking trails lead from parking lot to top of butte.

For **Willow Creek Preserve,** owned by The Nature Conservancy, go W on 18th to Bertlesen Rd. Cross rd. *0.2 m.,* at point of high voltage lines, park on L side of rd. Willow Creek Preserve is to L. The Nature Conservancy calls the preserve an "excellent example of a native, unplowed grassland, containing *Deschampsia cespitosa* community, which is a relic of pre-settlement prairie-oak savannah mo-saic once extending nearly the entire length of the Willamette Valley and now existing only on about nine other sites. The preserve is unique in that it serves as habitat for the highest proportion of all known individual plants of the critically endangered species *Aster curtus,* and one of three known viable populations of *Lomatium bradshawii.*" A lady living nearby said, "I don't know what the fuss is all about. It's just a weed. It's been around here as long as I can remember."

* For a breezy side trip out of Eugene, backtrack from Willow Creek Preserve (toward Willamette St.) and turn R on Chambers. *1.6 m.,* turn R onto Lorane Hwy. *4.1 m.,* turn L for Lorane. The road has the contours of a rope twirling in a stiff breeze. *8.5 m.,* forks. Take L. *5.7 m.,* **Lorane,** two stores. On hillock, *0.1 m.,* stand pioneer lodge hall and, next to it, Lorane Christian Church, est. 1889. There is little to Lorane but it is hub of roads to Coast, Drain, Cottage Grove, Veneta and Noti. There was more to town in 1915, when it had two churches, two lodges, HS and PS.

From 7th and Willamette, Eugene, on O 99.

1.9 m., jct., O 126. *0.7 m.,* enter I-5. *3.4 m.,* turnoff to O 99. *0.1 m.,* turnoff E to O 58. *0.2 m.,* **Goshen,** a crossroads dot on the highway. Settled in 1870s as Land of

Promise, its dream fell short from the start. Old Goshen Church, built 1898, now residence.

5.5 m., **Cresswell,** named by transportation tycoon Ben Holladay for then postmaster general John A. Creswell in 1873. Creswell grew as independent town and in 1915 had pop. 550 (good sized then) with HS and PS, four churches, at least four lodges, Grange, weekly paper, bank, Boys and Girls Industrial Club and band, Commercial Club, place on main line of SPRR. Today, with almost four times 1915 pop., Cresswell is still a stable market town but has drifted into the shadows of Eugene suburbia.

5 m., Davisson Rd., site of **Walker** (PO 1891–1925).

> * Turn R on Davisson Rd. *0.2 m.,* on knoll, **Walker Union Church,** sole survivor of town. Classic simple white house of worship, with fish scale steeple and all, born with Walker. Cemetery back of church.

0.1 m., on W, old **Walker Schoolhouse,** now shed and shop. *1.3 m.,* **Saginaw.** Store. Settled in late 1890s, Saginaw long a mill town but never became more than site of mill. In early 1980s Saginaw had brief moment of regional glory when several promoters staged a quasi-rock "Woodstock West" on farm just E of Saginaw.

> * Turn E on Saginaw East Rd. *0.8 m.,* "T". Turn L onto Sears-Delight Valley Rd. *0.6 m.,* on L, century-plus house. *0.1 m.,* forks. Straight, on Meyer Rd. *0.9 m.,* on R, was scene of festival, on farm of Verel "Slim" Murrell. "Woodstock West" was not the smash success its promoters had predicted. About 60,000 tickets were printed but only 6,000 people showed. So ephemeral in this revolving door society is fame (or notoriety) that few people in Saginaw area have heard of the festival and fewer know where it was held.

2.8 m., **Cottage Grove,** once divided into two towns by the Coast Fork of the Willamette. During last quarter of 19th century a battle raged between the W siders, who had PO called Cottage Grove, and E siders, who had RR station and who inc. town of their own, first under name of East Cottage Grove and then, wanting independent status, under name of Lemati, Chinook jargon for mountain. If it hadn't been so grim it would have been comic opera — as it appears now. Imagine the marshal of Lemati jailing the marshal of Cottage Grove because the latter had the temerity to wear his badge while meeting the mail train.

Cottage Grove, generally regarded as the S or upper anchor of the Willamette Valley, developed as lumber town. In 1915 25 mills were tributary to the city, which had pop. 2,700, about one-third of 1990 pop. It was also the distributing and shipping center for immense lumber and mining area, including the Bohemia District.

Probably the most extraordinary and puzzling writer in Oregon history was resident of Cottage Grove. She was Opal Whitely, whose family moved to Walden, *3 m.* from town, at jct. of Mosby Creek and Row River, shortly before Opal's 5th birthday in Dec., 1902. Opal attended 8th grade and HS in Cottage Grove.

526   IN SEARCH OF WESTERN OREGON

Apart from her stay in Cottage Grove, Opal grew up in a logging camp and early became conversant with nature. At the U of Oregon she saturated herself in geology, biology, physical geography and botany. One of her professors wrote: "She may become one of the greatest minds Oregon ever produced." At the same time, deeply religious, she was taking courses at a divinity school.

In 1919, at the age of 21, Opal Whitely breezed into the office of the *Atlantic Monthly* in Boston with a copy of a book she had written and had paid to be published. Editor Ellery Sedgwick took a look at *The Fairyland Around US* and decided immediately that it was amateurish. But he became interested in Opal and soon learned from her that she had a diary, written when she was 6 or 7, and that it had been torn to shreds and was heaped up in boxes in Los Angeles. The boxes were sent for, Sedgwick read the scraps, was intrigued, and told Opal to assemble them into a story. Starting in March, 1920, the *Atlantic Monthly* began serializing *The Story of Opal: The Journal of an Understanding Heart*. It immediately made Opal and Cottage Grove famous while confounding distinguished editors and eminent psychologists.

Opal, who would have been a great subject for today's psychics and tabloid writers, comes thru as a child wonder, a female Peter Pan, a titanic literary elf. The background she gave of herself was enough to boggle the mind; she claimed she was a changeling of royal parentage and that Ed Whitely, the astounded logger, was not her real father. Her imagery was as startling: she lived free in the woods among her friends — Peter Paul Rubens, an affectionate shepherd dog; "my most dear wood rat" named Thomas Chatterton Jupiter Zeus; Brave Horatius, the pet pig who followed the girl everywhere; a gossipy cow called Lars Porsena of Clusium; and Michael Angelo Sanzio Raphael, a charming, sympathetic fir tree.

After a round of bizarre adventures, during which Opal lived in the luxurious palace of the Maharajah of Udaipur, Prince Rajputana, in India, as Her Royal Highness Francoise Marie Bourbon-Orleans, for about 5 years, the eccentric and colorful Opal dropped out of the limelight. But her memory lingers on; to this day there is contention as to whether she was genius or fraud.

Most interesting part of town is S on River Rd., reached from Main St., key business street. Greenway along Coast Fork of Willamette is fun place, with kids and adults "shooting the rapids" in rubber rafts, on tires, and whatever else is deemed riverworthy. Vintage houses (1890s) at 553, 625 and 653 S River. On other side of street are, *0.2 m.*, from Main, **Dr. Snapp House** (1866), with "witch's hat" front and used as museum during Bohemia Days celebration in mid-July; *0.1 m.*, on L, swaying footbridge across Coast Fork of Willamette; *0.3 m.*, on L, CB which locals claim to be only RR CB in US

Cottage Grove Historical Museum, in 1897 former Catholic Church at H and Birch, supposedly only octagonal-shaped public bldg. in NW. Yellow house at Ash and I has venerable look of affluent Cottage Grove in late 19th century. Restored **Cottage Grove Hotel,** 8th and Main, built early 1900s, is now complex of specialty shops. **First Presbyterian Church,** 216 S 3rd, founded 1851 but present structure reflects modernistic architecture. Complex comprised of 1-story chapel, taller square sanctuary with plain cross on wall above communion table, and simple parish house, all located around courtyard with polished rocks set into Japanese-style gardens. Church bell stands on supporting redwood frame carved with religious symbols.

For **Shields Cemetery,** go to 16th and E Main, turn R, go under freeway, take R fork. *(0.4 m. from 16th and E Main.)* Gravestones back to 1871.

One of the most adventurous off-the-beaten-path trips in Oregon starts at Cottage Grove. It touches three CBs and winds thru the more historic parts of the 225-sq.-m. Bohemia Mining District. This heavily timbered region of gorges, streams, wooded scarps and jagged peaks is home to turbulent mtn. streams and to wildlife which have been pushed back into the dark recesses of the diminishing forest primeval by the relentless incursion of man.

On a spring day in 1863, a so-so luck proprietor and miner named "Bohemia" Johnson, supposedly hiding in the Calapooya Mtns. after killing an Indian, accidentally discovered gold. There followed the usual stampede; within 2 years, 100 claims were staked. No great finds were made but old-timers insist that there is more of the major metals remaining than were taken out —silver, lead, zinc and copper. And there is the common lore of "lost" mines — in this area the Lost Frenchman, Lost Dutchman, Lost Lode of Trestle Creek, Lost Mine of Fiddlers Green.

* From Main and Pacific (O 99) go E. *1.7 m.,* turn L. *0.2 m.,* Row River Rd. Turn R. *1.7 m.,* on R, **Currin CB** (1925), over Row (rhymes with cow) River.

* For another way, turn E toward freeway, *0.8 m.,* N of Main St. *0.6 m.,* turn R. *0.2 m.,* **Village Green,** renowned as splendid hostelry. Next to it is station for Oregon Pacific and Eastern RR, which makes 1914 vintage steam engine 35 m. trip on summer weekends to foot of Calapooya Mtns.; Diesel on weekdays. Among shops near Village Green is "The Round House," 1551 E Main, featured in Ripley's "Believe It Or Not." *1.5 m.,* USFS station; good for information. *0.3 m.,* on R. turnoff to **Sears Cemetery** (1853). *0.9 m.,* on R, Currin CB, at Layng Rd. Turn R onto Layng Rd. *0.9 m.,* on L, private lane for *(0.1 m.)* **Mosby House,** built 1862 on 1853 DLC. Continue *0.4 m.* to Mosby Creek CB (1920).

* From Layng Rd.: *1 m.,* Mosby Creek Rd. Turn R for **Mosby Creek CB.**

* *1.1 m.,* forks. Take R. *0.5 m.,* **Dorena Res.** turnoff, to L. *2.5 m.,* **Baker CP,** on Dorena Res., lake created in 1947 by Corps of Engineers for recreation and flood control. This excellently designed park has various use areas so set apart as to make life comfortable for all. *3.8 m.,* on R, **Dorena CB** (1949), over Row River.

2.1 m., **Dorena.** When lumbering is down this hamlet looks dead. With its row shacks, it seldom looks prosperous. *1.6 m.,* **Culp Creek School.** *0.4 m.,* jct. Here is where the traveler intent upon making the Bohemia Mining

District tour must come to a choice: either straight toward Disston or R on Sharps Creek Rd. The latter route is now recommended.

3.1 m., **Sharps Creek Rec. Area,** wayside retreat in clump of alder, cedar, Oregon hazel and vine maple, with abundant undergrowth of huckleberries. *3.2 m.,* **Staples Bridge.** *3.7 m.,* turn L onto Sharps Creek Rd. Creek was named for dour hermit named Sharp who homesteaded near Staples Creek. *1.7 m.,* **Fairview Creek,** small CG and great place for picnic.

Here stood **Mineral,** the place where miners and freighters stayed overnight, generally at the 2-story hotel, before starting the gruelling ascent up 6-m. Hardscrabble Grade to Bohemia Saddle, where they would descend to the Musick Mine. Only four horses were needed to pull freight wagons from Cottage Grove to Mineral (which was reached second day out of Cottage Grove), but 6-or 8-horse spans were required to get up Hardscrabble. The grade was one of the most difficult stretches of mtn. road in all the mining W and the miners and freighters reached Bohemia Saddle exhausted. Today the hardest part for cars is descending, because of possible brake failure. (For account of Hardscrabble Grade and the Bohemia Mining District, see "No More Elephants in the Bohemia" in author's *Tracking Down Oregon.*)

3.2 m., **Glenwood.** Miners living and working near Shane Saddle left mail here to be picked up as well as lists of items needed. Nothing of Glenwood now. *1.3 m.,* site of Vesuvius Mine; just a marker now, unless you go probing

Bridge over Row River

about, which you shouldn't. *1.2 m.*, **Bohemia Saddle.** Here the miners would cry "We've made it!" Here, too, is division between drainage of Willamette River and Umpqua River.

Turn L toward Fairview Lookout. *1.2 m.*, Fairview Lookout Tower, 5,933 elev. Climb stairs to top of tower for far-away views: Coast Range, Three Sisters, even Crater Lake.

Return to Bohemia Saddle. Turn R. *0.1 m.*, **Bohemia CP,** small PG with restrooms.

Return to Bohemia Saddle. Turn R on lower road. *0.6 m.*, forks. Turn sharp R on this side road. *0.6 m.*, sad remains of **Bohemia City** and the once-mighty Musick Mine. Last survivors: **Bohemia General Store — PO** and the **Lundberg Stage House.**

Return to forks. Keep R. The road becomes almost startlingly level — and for good reason. Here was narrow gauge electric RR which hauled Musick ore to Champion stamp mill. *0.3 m.*, from last forks, Champion Creek Rd. Turn L. *1 m.*, Champion Mine, one of the great producers of the region. As late as 1960 the mining camp was going strong. Not a bldg. stands, but there is ample evidence all about of mining.

2.5 m., Golden Curry Mine, which started out as the Gould and Curry and became corrupted in oral commerce. Nothing now but a hole in the ground. *0.3 m.*, site of Arkansas Mine. *0.3 m.*, site of Trixie Mine. *1.1 m.*,

Mosby Creek Bridge

Marker at bottom of Hardscrabble Grade

Lundberg Stage House, Bohemia City

Remains of Musick Mine

Bohemia Smith Falls, sprightly little cascade with a legend. Miner Bohemia Smith took off with a jug from Lundpark for the Champion Mine, where he worked. Tripping his way thru the dark, he stepped off the edge of a cliff and tumbled onto a net of boughs on a probably astonished tree. Rescuers found him clinging to his jug and singing uproariously. And so, at this spot, Bohemia Smith Falls.

2.2 m., **Noonday Trail.** Before Hardscrabble Grade and the Champion Creek Trail were gouged out, freight was brought up to the ridge by this route. 0.2 m., **Champion Creek Bridge.** Here was the site of power dam, removed to make passage for migrating fish, and, on opposite bank of Brice Creek, across the road, a flume.

Take Brice Creek Rd. just after crossing the bridge, 0.3 m., Trestle Creek, one of the several "lost mines" of the Bohemia. 1 m., **Lundpark,** named for Alex Lundberg and Alex Parker, who operated a way station for men going up to the mtn. There was here a hotel, barn, warehouse and 2-story log store. Nothing of the old remains; now CP. 1.4 m., **Cedar Creek CG.** 4.5 m., **Disston,** a child of the Bohemia and orphaned by its collapse. Store; E terminus of old Oregon Pacific & Eastern RY. 0.7 m., jct. Keep L. 2.5 m., **Stewart Rec. Area.** 0.6 m., turn R. 0.7 m., **Wildwood Falls Park,** scene of pure joy. Return to Row River Rd. Turn R. 0.3 m., Sharps Creek Rd. Jct., where the tour of the Bohemia began.

4.1 m., on L, **Dorena CB.** Forks. Take R, to swing around opposite side of

Dorena Res. *11 m.,* past Harms CP and Dorena Dam, Village Green. *1.6 m.,* downtown Cottage Grove.

Another motor excursion out of Cottage Grove leads past Cottage Grove Res. and to the site of former London.

* In Cottage Grove, turn E onto 6th St. *3.2 m.,* turnoff to **Taylor-Lane Cemetery.** *0.2 m.,* turn R. *0.1 m.,* on L, cemetery. Here lies S. B. Shortridge, born 1796, only 4 years after Robert Gray sailed into the Columbia River. He died in this peaceful valley 1877. Return to London Rd. Turn R. *1.8 m.,* jct., Cottage Grove Res. Turn L. *1 m.,* **Cottage Grove Dam.** *0.4 m.,* **Southridge Park.** *1.1 m.,* **Pine Meadows CG,** on Cottage Grove Res. *0.7 m.,* **Primitive CG.** *0.1 m.,* **Wilson Creek Park,** on Cottage Grove Res. *1.2 m.,* jct., London Rd. Turn L.

* (On London Rd., from Cottage Grove Res. jct.: *4 m.,* S jct., Cottage Grove Res.)

* From S jct, Cottage Grove Res.: *2 m.,* London Grade School. *0.1 m.,* on L, Church at London; est. 1857, built 1898. *0.1 m.,* on R, **London Grange.**

Wildwood Falls, Row River   *Courtesy State of Oregon*

London PO 1902–1919. In 1915 it had pop. 70, store, and was gateway to nearby Calapooya Mineral Springs.

2 m., **Amos.** PO 1898–1902. PO moved 2 m. and named changed to London. Another fine side trip out of Cottage Grove is to Lorane:

* W on Main St. from O 99: *1 m.,* turnoff R to Cemetery Rd. *0.2 m.,* **Fir Grove Cemetery.** Burials back to 1861. Inscription on marker of Blanche Churchill, who died 8/12/1890 at age 14 years, 2 months, 16 days, reads: "We have folded her hands across her breast./ We have kissed her marble brow,/ And in our aching hearts we know/ We have no Blanche now." *11.6 m.,* **Lorane.** The W half of this road is curvier than an exaggerated image of Lillian Russell. Or, as a local wit put it, "This is the way to vertigo."

From Main and O 99, Cottage Grove:

0.3 m., on W, **Lea House** (1891), on SW corner of O 99 and 6th.

Turnoff E to Cottage Grove Res. and London. (See preceding.)

3.3 m., turnoff to Cottage Grove Res. (*4 m.*) and London (*11.2 m.*)

* *0.7 m.,* on R, **Latham School.** In vicinity was Latham PO (1878–1888).

2.3 m., enter I-5. *5.2 m.,* take turnoff to Curtin and Pass Creek Park.

0.2 m., stop sign.

* Turn L. *0.2 m.,* E side of **Curtin.** Store, PO. Return to stop sign. Turn R for **Pass Creek CP** (*0.1 m.*), CG, PA.

Return to turnoff for Pass Creek Park. Turn R. *0.1 m.,* W side of Curtin, which had its start in lumber and in 1915 had four sawmills. Today it is little more than a freeway stop and a modest shopping and service area for folks in the nooks and crannies of the low hills.

0.2 m., "T".

* Turn R for cemetery. *1 m.,* turn R. *0.2 m.,* gate of **Comstock Cemetery** (*0.2 m.*). Markers back to 1876. Return to "T". Straight. (Coming from I-5, turn L.)

0.7 m., Lorane Jct.

* Turn W on what is essentially a logging road. *8 m.,* on L, **Lorane IOOF Cemetery,** last home of the lodge members. *1 m.,* Lorane.

From Lorane Jct., on old 99: *3.4 m.,* on E, eye-catching house near what was **Leona.** Leona PO est. 1901; long closed. In 1915 Leona had pop. 300, with store, PO, PS. It may still be on the official Oregon hwy. map but practically everything about it has been completely erased. Interviews with 24 residents in area disclosed that 20 had never heard of Leona and the other four had no real notion of where the hamlet had been.

2.2 m., **Drain,** at jct., O 38. Visitors often ask, "How could a town endure such a name?" To many people Drain sounds depressing or self-vilifying and the prosaic character of the town has provoked some cynics to remark that the settlement has "gone down the drain." But truth has its own version. Town was named for pioneer Charles Drain, who in 1850 purchased DLC from Jesse Applegate.

House on SW corner of 1st and A has cupola, gingerbread and spooling of later

19th century homes. House was once a chapel. Next house S on A St. (305) has the Rural Gothic style of turn-of-century residences in these parts. Just beyond this house is **Pass Creek-Krewson CB** over Pass Creek, rebuilt 1925 at length of 61 ft. Original bridge crossed here in 1870s. Marker states bridge was on route of Overland Stage line to Scottsburg from Roseburg and Jacksonville. Since there was little at Scottsburg in 1870s, one wonders.

From downtown, take B St. E. *0.1 m.,* turn R onto Main St. *0.2 m.,* Alta Vista. Ahead, "**Drain Castle,**" oldest and most distinguished-looking structure in these parts, now school district office.

E on Alta Vista. *0.4 m.,* curve R onto Cemetery Rd. *0.5 m.,* **Drain Cemetery.** Buried here are members of Drain family; most striking tombstone is that of John C. Drain (1843–1891), who at age 31 was speaker of the state house of representatives for 1874 session.

Return to B St. Turn E. *0.1 m.,* grade school, at or near site of one of Oregon's first normal schools. (Drain old-timers do not know exact location.)

At jct., O 38, take O 38 W.

6.7 m., on L, or N, and *0.1 m.* off hwy. and on private property, **Roaring Camp CB** over Elk Creek; built 1929 at length of 88 ft. Legend behind name is that many years ago there was a roadhouse near here called Roaring Camp.

"Drain Castle"

Roaring Camp Bridge

On O 99 from Jct., O 38.

3 m., on W, **Jesse Applegate Marker.** Home of one of Oregon's foremost sons stood *0.5 m.* W of here. It was used as first court of provisional gvmt. The seldom-seen grave of Jesse Applegate, in Applegate Family Cemetery, is on knoll of Yoncalla Hill, nearest rise W of road above site where Applegate house stood. According to Jesse's daughter, Roselle Applegate Putnam, hill was named after Indian chief. Another version is that Yoncalla is compound of two words and means game birds on a hill. The hill was so thick with wildlife that within 2 years after arriving here, Jesse Applegate killed two bears and more than 40 deer on it.

What coming of the whites did to the Indians in the Yoncalla Valley was graphically detailed by Roselle Putnam in a letter dated Jan. 25, 1852:

"The hill is called after a chief who with a numerous tribe once inhabited these valleys — among the few remaining survivers of this tribe that occasionally came to beg a crust of bread or an old garment that is getting worse for the wear — there are some old ones who remember the chief, say that he was a great physician and skilled in witchcraft — which is a belief still prevalent among them — his men hunted bear and deer on this hill and caught salmon in the streams around it and the women dug roots in the valleys and gathered nuts and berries on the hills — they were a numerous and happy nation — but now the busy multitudes are low and still — the dense forest whose echoes were then only wakened by the war

Grave of Jesse Applegate   *Phoebe L. Friedman*

song and the wolf's howl are now half demolished by their enterprising successors — the game is frightened away by the sound of the axe and the crack of the whip — the acorns, nuts and roots are yearly harvested by their hogs so that if these ancient owners were still living they would be deprived of their means of sustenance."

The acrocephalic Jesse Applegate came with the first wagon train in 1843 and gained some literary acknowledgement for his *A Day with the Cow Column*. A highly opinionated, inveterate letter writer to newspapers and politicians, Applegate was recognized as "The Sage of Yoncalla." His home was open house to travelers, especially those who agreed with him. He can be remembered in many ways: a pioneer across the plains, a surveyor, co-opener of the Applegate Trail into S Oregon; member of the provisional gvmt.; strong mover for territorial gvmt. and statehood, foe of slavery, champion of Abraham Lincoln, farmer, scholar. In later years he suffered "misfortune and poverty," a decided waning of his popularity, and a loss of sanity. He died in 1888, 7 years after the passing of his wife, Cynthia Ann, who had borne him 13 children. A few months after she was taken from him he said of the woman to whom he had been married for almost half a century: "She was a safe counsellor, for her untaught instincts were truer and safer rules of conduct than my better informed judgment. Had I often followed her advice, her pilgrimage on earth might have been longer and happier; at least, her strong desire to make all happy around her would not have been cramped by extreme penury." (For more on Jesse Applegate, see "Pioneers! O Pioneers!" in author's *Tracking Down Oregon*.)

2 m., on E, **Halo Trail.**

 * *0.5 m.*, turn L onto Applegate Rd. *0.5 m.*, on L, house built 1852–56 by Charles Applegate, one of the three illustrious Applegate brothers.

0.3 m., **Yoncalla,** at City Hall. PO est March 14, 1851; 7 months later Jesse Applegate became postmaster. Since 1915 town has grown at a rate of 5.71 persons each year. At that rate it will reach 1,000 pop. in 2020. However, precisely because of its small townishness, Yoncalla has gained regional exposure thru a single person, Dr. Lydia Emery, a compassionate, gentle and wise medical provider who for decades charged patients only a dollar a visit.

At City Hall, turn W onto Applegate Ave. *0.2 m.*, turn L onto Douglas St. *0.3 m.*, following paved road, **Yoncalla Cemetery.** Here the Applegate name is plentiful among the gone. Charles Applegate lies here, put to rest in 1879 at age 73. Documentation on tombstone of Milton Applegate bears pathos. Between 1880 and 1889 he and his wife, Sara, lost three children, none of whom lived more than a year. Then, as though his heart had been broken in finality, Milton died in 1889. Sarah lived on until 1932. Below the hillock burial ground there is secreted a gentle vale, bordered by maples and oaks rising to a higher meadow which, in turn, is fenced in by a loftier slope. In Oct., when color is churning in the leaves, the scene is dazzling magic.

2.7 m., — from S side of City Hall — Rice Hill Exit.

 * *0.2 m.*, **Rice Hill,** complete tourist facilities. Just N, on old road, are some vintage barns.

5 m., Rest Area. *3.1 m.*, take Oakland Exit to 99.

0.5 m., on L, grass divider strip, marker dedicated to memory of Rev. J. A. Cornwall and family. "They built the first immigrant cabin in Douglas County near this site hence the name Cabin Creek. The family wintered here in 1846–1847. Were saved from extreme want by Israel Stoley a nephew who was a good hunter. The Indians were friendly. The Cornwalls traveled part way westward with the illfated Donner Party."

50 yds., turn L toward Old Oakland.

 * *0.5 m.*, on R, 1856 house, oldest original residence in Oakland area. Knoll to SE of house and across Calapooia River was where stood Old Oakland. Town named for groves of Oregon white, or Garry, oak, clumped with broad-leaved mistletoe, that were profuse in the valley. (PO located in oak grove; trees later blasted out to clear land for prune orchard; had PO come in later it might have been called Pruneland.) Started in 1852, town was key stop for California Stage Coach Line and hub of horse-carried mail routes leading

A barn near Yoncalla   *Phoebe L. Friedman*

to Jacksonville, Scottsburg, Eugene and Corvallis (then called Marysville). In 1872 RR came and town moved to new site, to be near rails. Old Oakland eventually became a vague memory — if that much. *0.1 m.,* make sharp L turn onto old wagon road. *0.3 m.,* **Masonic Cemetery.** Under the scrub oaks sleep the founders of white valley settlement. Markers back to 1860.

1.1 m., **Oakland** city center. Little-publicized, Oakland attracts visitors because of its naturalness. It is the most unaffected historic town in the state, looking like a 19th century daguerreotype. This community of less than 1,000 pop. has more than 50 structures built in 19th century and going back to 1855: **James Dearling House,** originally a saloon in Old Oakland, now at 2nd and Maple. **Stearns Hardware** has been at same location since 1877. Photogenic Victorian house at 218 SE 5th. **City library** in 1890 bldg. that was drugstore. **Z. L. Dimmick House,** 1880 Queen Anne style, is calendar art. Oregon and California Warehouse built 1870. Structures moved from old Oakland include: **Pichette House** (1860), **James Mullings House** (1868), **Walt Kincaid House** (1860), **Rosie James House** (1870), **Deardorff Hotel** (1860), **Deardorff House** (1858). Most of these structures are along N end of O 99 in Oakland. (Walking maps are available at several businesses, including Tolly's.)

Oakland has a town museum, but it seems a redundancy; the whole town is a museum. Yet, Oakland has some surprising modern touches. It has a theater group that performs at the community center. Oakland Studio of Dance Art, in 1899 furniture store, has excellent reputation for its ballet teaching. A school of ballet in Oakland! The Carriage Works builds horse-drawn vehicles for sale to three continents; it, too, is in bldg. with patina of nostalgia. Tolly's may be the most delightful restaurant-antique shop-art gallery in state.

From Locust St., on O 99:

0.1 m., turn W onto road marked as leading to I-5.

   * *2 m.,* turnoff L for I-5. Continue straight. *1.7 m.,* forks. Turn R. *0.1 m.,* **Rochester CB.** Built 1933 at length of 80 ft. over Calapooya River, remodeled 1969. With its gently curved top, this roofed span is a charming side attraction.

2.5 m., **Sutherlin,** at State and Central.

Sutherlin Bank Bldg. has been at intersection since 1910, a year before the 455 pop. inc. into a city. The 2-story bldg. constructed of sandstone hauled to site from quarry at Deady, few m. S of Sutherlin. Since the RR tracks wound up 2 blocks short of the bldg. site, horses pulled the stone blocks the rest of the way on temporary rails by railcar. Bank cost $10,000 to build; was originally topped with stone cornice removed in 1949 because of erosion and damaged done by nesting swallows.

Turn L, or E, on Nonpareil Rd.

   * *0.2 m.,* on R, **City Park;** holds steam locomotive and ancient caboose, which served lumber camps. *0.3 m.,* Waite Ave. Turn R. *1.6 m.,* turn R for Cooper Creek Res. *0.6 m.,* **Cooper Creek Res.; Douglas CP;** PA, BL. Return to Nonpareil Rd. Turn R. *2.6 m.,* turn R onto Plat I Rd. *0.4 m.,* on L, turn onto Valley View Dr. *0.6 m.,* **Valley View Cemetery.** There lie here, looking down on a valley that still has the hard-knuckled expression of the recently tamed frontier, the Sutherlin clan, founders of the town. Coming

Main Street in Oakland   *Courtesy Terry Tollefson*

Courtesy The Carriage Works

Buggies built by The Carriage Works, Oakland

Rochester Bridge

Courtesy Terry Tollefson

from N Carolina, they must have picked the townsite because it reminded them of a closeness to their native hills. Return to Plat I Rd. Turn L. *0.4 m.,* Plat I Dam. Return to Nonpareil Rd. Turn R. *2 m.,* Plat B Rd. Turn L onto it. *0.2 m.,* **Fair Oaks Cemetery.** Markers back to 1860s. Return to Nonpareil Rd. *3 m.,* **Nonpareil,** name of no-longer-existent silver mine. PO 1882–1884. Nonpariel Store — and that's all there is. Owner says: "I don't know why it's spelled that way. That's the way it was when I bought it."

From State and Central, in Sutherlin:

Turn R, or W. *0.1 m.,* O 99 turns S. Straight.

   * *1.2 m.,* O 138. *0.4 m.,* Fort McKay Rd. Take it. *0.9 m.,* Church Rd. (Turn R onto Church Rd. for best view of Ford's Pond.) *1.8 m.,* turn off Fort McKay Rd. onto Scott Henry Rd. *0.1 m.,* **Calapooya Country Church** (1906), white patrician beauty, now crafts shop. From Fort McKay Rd, on O 138: *1 m.,* at Church Rd., start of **Ford's Pond,** largest stocked log pond in Douglas County.

A round-about way to get from Sutherlin to Roseburg is thru a shining vale tucked away in an inaudible cloud of sleep.

   * Take Elkton Rd., O 138. At Ford's Pond, turn L for Umpqua and Cole's Valley. *6.3 m.,* **Umpqua.** (For rest of way to Roseburg, see *Cross-Coast Range Rds.,* O 38.)

Sutherlin S from O 99 Jct.:

4.9 m., on E, Wilbur Cemetery Rd.

   * *100 yds.* to R, lane to **Wilbur Cemetery** *(0.1 m.).* Markers back to 1850. Inscription of tombstone of Mary Ellison reads: "Dear is the spot where Christians sleep,/ And sweet the strain that angels pour./ Oh why should we in anguish weep,/ They are not lost but gone before."

0.2 m., at SW corner of O 99 and Oak Hill Rd., in **Wilbur,** former **Wilbur Tavern,** oldest standing structure in Douglas County. First floor built 1851–52. In 1870s, second floor added. When completed, 2-story bldg. preserved Classical Revival lines of original 1-story bldg. Lumber from second floor of Wilbur Academy used in second story of former Wilbur Tavern.

0.1 m., on W, at 8642, late 19th century house. *0.4 m.,* jct., N Umpqua Hwy.

   * *0.1 m.,* on R, **Wilbur United Methodist Church,** est. 1853. In front of church is monument: "In Remembrance of the Umpqua Academy 1857–1888 founded by Rev. James H. Wilbur, D.D."

0.3 m., on L, first site of **Umpqua Academy,** later called Wilbur Academy. (There were two other sites; both off O 99.) Despite dates on church monument, the evidence is not that simple. Umpqua Academy is said to have been opened as early as 1853 and closed as late as 1900. What is certain is that its founder, commonly known as Father Wilbur, came to Oregon from New York by way of Cape Horn in 1847, at age 36. An ordained Methodist minister and an appointed missionary to Oregon, he had several accomplishments before he took up pastoring at Wilbur in 1853. He had organized the Taylor St. MR church in Portland in 1850 and the Portland Academy and Female Seminary in 1851. Umpqua Academy was probably opened in 1854 and was only school of its kind then between Salem and Sacramento. Contrary to popular local opinion, Father Wilbur did not remain for many years with his academy. In 1860 he was named Supt. of Education on the Yakima Indian Reservation and until 1881 worked on the reservation, for a time as Indian Agent at Ft. Simcoe. He passed away in 1887 and he, his wife, and their daughter are buried in Lee Mission Cemetery, Salem.

Oregon: End of the Trail gives a graphic thumbnail sketch of the academy at this site: "The first building was a rough log structure with a few rough pine desks. Like other Oregon pioneer places of learning, the 'Rules' of the academy prohibited: 'Profane, obscene or vulgar language or unchaste yarns or narratives, or immoral gestures or hints; any degree of tippling anywhere; any sort of night reveling.' The pupils from the academy came from southern Oregon, from about Jacksonville, Leland, Canyonville, Cow Creek, Lookingglass and from the northerly parts of the county, from Yoncalla, Elk Creek, Green Valley and the classic precincts of Duck Egg, Tin Pot and Shoestring."

From the site of the first academy, the N Umpqua Hwy. breaks into a free-spirited, open, little-traveled, first class road swooping thru wooded hills and past stock meadows, with rarely a house on or near the pike all the way to O 138. At points the N Umpqua River, often far below, bursts into view, affording inspiring vistas. Why this road is not popular — many people living in O 99 towns near the road have never taken it — would be a mystery if not for the knowledge that there is little in Glide to attract people around Sutherlin, Wilbur and Winchester on daily basis. In autumn this N Umpqua road is afire with remarkable color.

10.5 m., on R, **Jackson Wayside,** on N Umpqua River. *4.5 m.,* site of Carsena A. Huntley claim. (Huntley Creek, named for him, runs thru what was the middle of his property.) Carsena Huntley was an uncouth, insensitive grabber who in 1849, to obtain more acreage, took as bride the 14-year-old Mary Priscilla Avery, and proceeded to treat her as dirt. In 1858, when she was 23, Mary divorced Huntley, in what was regarded on the frontier as a scandalous affair, and went on to a life of her own. She was the first female medical student at Willamette U. Denied a diploma because of her sex, she enrolled at Women's Medical College in New York and, logically, was not denied a diploma there. She married C. M. Sawtelle, who did receive a medical degree from Willamette and the two doctors practiced medicine together in San Francisco. Mary Sawtelle published a medical journal for 8 years, was an early feminist, and lobbied successfully for the right of married women to hold property in their own names.

1 m., Frear Bridge, over N Umpqua. *0.4 m.,* O 138. (E, *1.5 m.,* Glide.) From jct., N Umpqua Rd., on O 99:

Winchester Dam *Phoebe L. Friedman*

2.1 m., parking area at N end of 884-ft.-long N **Umpqua Bridge.** Stairway leads to Winchester Fish Counting Station. Good viewing for fish in season: May thru Aug.: chinook and summer steelhead; Sept. thru Nov.: coho, fall chinook, summer steelhead; Dec. thru May: winter steelhead, squaw fish, suckers, lamprey. Exciting watching a salmon and steelhead climb fish ladder on way to spawning areas in N Umpqua. Neat dam.

0.2 m., on R, entrance to **John P. Amacher CP,** on N Umpqua. CG, PA, trailer hookups, FHP.

0.2 m., **Winchester.** Town, if it can be called that, was seat of Douglas County until 1854, when Roseburg took over. Thereupon many businesses were moved to Roseburg — and Winchester hasn't been the same since.

3.5 m., in Roseburg, jct., Garden Valley Blvd.

    * Turn R, or W. *0.4 m.,* on L, turn onto Hick St. *0.2 m.,* **Memorial Gardens.** Buried here are Gen. Joseph Lane, after whom Lane County was named, and Aaron Rose, founder of Roseburg. Lane, an imperial character, lies above ground, in a sepulcher that from a distance looks like a summer cottage. Rose, the affable merchant, more modestly lies below ground, his grave marked by a simple tombstone.

Return to O 99. Turn R, or S. Just below Garden Valley Blvd., on L, or E, at 1387 Stephens, **Hunt's Chain Saw Museum,** related to the development and use of chain saws in the lumber industry. One of a kind — at least in Oregon.

1.2 m., jct., O 138. *0.6 m.,* downtown **Roseburg.**

First known as Deer Creek, PO est. 1852, changed to Roseburgh 1857, and finally to present spelling in 1894. Irreverent citizens call city "Poseyville" because of the community's small town spirit, which can reach a frenzy of astounding proportions when it comes to high school athletics. ("It's the only game in town," said a policeman.) Town named for Aaron Rose, who came here in 1851. As successful as he was colorful, Rose was town's first saloonkeeper, operating tavern in his home. Douglas County Court House is on site of Rose's land claim.

Roseburg is full of folklore. When town was only a village, cows were almost as common as people and they wandered at will, their neck bells clanging sleep away. A local bit of witticism declared that the noise increased consumption of alcoholic beverages but other citizens stole out into the night and removed the bells from the cows. In 1889 the city fathers (no city mothers then) decreed that the use of bells on all domestic animals was unlawful.

Several years earlier the city council was concerned with the proliferation of laundries. It seems that some women were using the laundry business as a blind for other ventures. So, of course, an ordinance was passed, and it read: "Any woman who had been lawfully married and had a legitimate child or children to support may operate a hand laundry upon the recommendation of the committee on health, and police."

Like many Oregon cities, Roseburg has been wracked by disaster. But no Oregon city in recent times was as rocked as was Roseburg in the early hours of Aug. 7, 1959. A fire in a lumberyard detonated a truck loaded with explosives and before calm settled, 14 persons had lost their lives, 57 more had been injured, and property damages exceeded $12 million — a goodly sum for Roseburg. A plaque at the entrance to the parts dept. of Riverside Motors, Pine and Oak, marks the site of the explosion.

Most prominent landmark in Roseburg area is **Mt. Nebo,** formerly famed for its goats, which ranged entire length of rim. Visitors are told that best place to view goats is from downtown Roseburg, along E bank of S Umpqua River: Look W toward Mt. Nebo. But goats are presently very scarce; too many sauntered down hill to venture into paths of cars.

Lane House, now museum operated by Douglas County Historical Society, at 544 SE Douglas. Gen. Joseph Lane did not live in this house but he resided nearby and sometimes took his meals here with his daughters. The house Lane lived in was sited where Douglas County Farm Bureau Cooperative stands.

Willis House, 744 SE Rose, built 1874; became city library 1924; used as city hall between 1959 and 1973. **Methodist Episcopal Church,** old-time beauty at 809 SE Main, houses The Main St. Gallery. **Hamilton House** (1895), SE Lane and Kane. A block N on Kane (at Cass), is turn-of-century house of affluence. **Umpqua Valley Arts Center,** in classic bldg., at 1624 W Harvard Blvd. **Nathaniel Curry Estate,** 1458 Quail Lane, massive Queen Anne style home built for San Francisco businessman, completed 1894.

From architectural and historical perspective, most interesting part of Roseburg is **Mill-Pine District,** 33-sq.-acre area of land once owned by Aaron Rose and symbolic of RR's heyday in city. The roughly 7-block by 3-block district, anchored by SE Mill and Pine, looks more like working class section of an Eastern city than an Oregon town. Many of the bldgs. here are turn-of-century darlings that look like they have been on the relief rolls for past few decades. Out of this area have emerged some prominent citizens, among them John A. Buchanan, author of "Oregon, My Oregon," the state song.

Parrot House, also known as the "Castle," two main stories and cupola, and built circa 1870, is at edge of Mill-Pine District. It is *0.1 m.,* on L, where O 99S and O 99N merge — *0.7 m.* from city center on Pine.

Douglas County Museum, S of city and off I-5, is architecturally most striking historical depository in state.

A side trip for the curious out of Roseburg begins at Washington St., downtown.

> * Take Washington St. W off Stephens St. *0.6 m.,* Washington becomes Harvard. *1.8 m.,* turn L onto Lookingglass St. *6.1 m.,* "T". Turn L. *0.1 m.,* on R, white house, built circa 1885, oldest house in Lookingglass area. *0.1 m.,* **Lookingglass Store,** the business section of Lookingglass. There was more in 1915, and even more before then. Place was on Coos Bay Wagon Road and in 1970 old-timer Andy Jacoby remembered the stagecoach days, when as a boy he sold water for five cents a dipper to coach passengers. He also remembered when drunks in the livery stable and saloon across road from each

Parrott House, Roseburg   *Phoebe L. Friedman*

Douglas County Museum, Roseburg   *Courtesy State of Oregon*

Round barn at Lookingglass

other exchanged shots. "Bullets would fly across the road but they were too drunk to hit each other. The kids had to take a different way to school, though, or they'd get hit by the bullets." Turn R onto Coos Bay Wagon Rd. *0.3 m.,* on R, white house of simple utilitarian beauty, probably as graceful today as when built around turn of century. *0.7 m.,* round barn, only one in these parts. Built around 1860, barn was mortised with wooden pegs and square nails, had dirt floor; legend says it has never been painted.

From Pine and Washington, Roseburg:

6.5 m., crossing of S Umpqua River.

    * At S end of bridge turn L, or E, onto Winston Rd. *0.1 m.,* turn L onto Pepsi Rd. (so-named because of Pepsi Cola plant.) *0.1 m.,* on L, white, 2-story **"Winston House,"** assertedly built in late 19th century by town founder. Area is where settlement of Winston began.

0.6 m., turnoff W for **Wildlife Safari.**

    * *0.2 m.,* turn R onto Safari Rd. *1.8 m.,* **Safari Village.** The 600-acre preserve contains more than 600 animals and more than 100 species of birds, including tigers, lions, elephants, cheetahs, yaks, ostriches, camels, hippopotami, rhinoceroses, cape buffaloes, cranes, peafowls and flamingos. These animals and birds are seen by driving thru the preserve. Some years ago manager Al Hooten called his wild animal park a specialized zoo, ideal for keeping, displaying, breeding and studying larger mammals. Similar wild animal parks exist in the S and E US, England, Europe and S Africa. Wildlife Safari isn't the Serengeti Plain but it is the closest thing to it in W US.

0.5 m., jct., O 42.

Ostrich and rhinos stop traffic at Wildlife Safari

Courtesy Wildlife Safari

* Turn W for **Winston.** *0.2 m.,* **Winston City Hall.** Apart from it being associated in location with Wildlife Safari, Winston's only distinction is that it is a pleasant bedroom of Roseburg. *0.7 m.,* **Lookingglass Creek.** *0.8 m.,* on S, **Brockway.** PO est 1881 as Civil Bend, sarcastic reference to uncivil conduct of the inhabitants and to a sassy turn in S Umpqua River. Store built 1890 *0.2 m.* N on Brockway Rd. and facing S. Moved on skids in 1921 to present location and now facing N. Store, which has been in same family since 1890, is one of homiest in state, loaded with antiques and character. Old PO (long vacant) remains in corner of store. In 1915 Brockway had pop. 300 and PS. Only store survives.

** Turn N onto Brockway Rd. *0.2 m.,* turnoff L. *50 yds.* on R, white house built 1869. Across rd. is another white house, more photogenic in its fancy gingerbread but not as old. *0.2 m.,* up road, on R, large house fronted by three large trees — cedar, fir and maple — built between 1850 and 1864, dates depend on old-timer queried, but surely oldest structure in area.

From jct., O 42, on O 99:

0.6 m., S **Umpqua River.** Along S Umpqua are found here and there the rare and lovely Oregon myrtle. With its glossy evergreen bright foliage, its symmetrical closely branched crown, and its aroma of bay, the myrtle is not hard to recognize. Unfortunately, many, much too many, have been cut down.

1.1 m., **Dillard,** named for 1852 Missouri DLC settler John Dillard, who lived on his farm 40 years, until death. Dillard is another of those lumber burgs that would drift away if the mill closed. *1.3 m.,* on W, **Roseburg Lumber Co.,** at one time the largest lumber plant — 8 acres — under one roof in nation. *5.6 m.,* O 99 dissolves into I-5. *0.5 m.,* Rest Area.

3.2 m., turnoff to Myrtle Creek and O 99. Road to Myrtle Creek from I-5 crosses 547-ft.-long **Myrtle Creek Bridge.** This concrete deck, arched bridge was built in 1922 on old 99 and is still rendering yeoman service.

0.7 m. — from I-5 turnoff — **Myrtle Creek,** which calls itself "Gateway to the 100 Valleys of the Umpqua." Myrtle trees on Myrtle Creek, which flows into S Umpqua, attest to town's name.

Myrtle Creek claims a lot of history, beginning thousands of years ago, when giant mammals roamed these parts. One of them left behind a fossil tusk 10 inches in diameter at the butt and 6 ft. long; it was not until 1927 that someone came along to find it.

On a note of more recent history, the first long cattle drive in US came thru here in 1837 on the way from SF Bay Area to Willamette Settlement, near Newberg. Almost a decade later a trail-breaking party led by Jesse Applegate and Levi Scott passed thru, opening a wagon road into S Oregon. (A 400-ft.-long section of the South Road starts just N of Main St. near Dole Rd. But there is nothing to suggest the historic trail.)

Came 1851 and the site of Myrtle Creek had its first white settler, James B. Weaver. Itchy-footed, as were many pioneers, Weaver sold out the first year to

Covered Bridge over South Fork of Myrtle Creek   *Phoebe L. Friedman*

one J. Bailey for a yoke of oxen. The next year Bailey, no more stable than Weaver, sold all the section to Lazarus Wright, who stayed with the 640 acres until 1865, opening a bank and store while farming. Then Wright sold half his land to John Hall, who had the area surveyed, platted and subdivided. And Myrtle Creek was on its way to becoming a town, although it was not inc. until 1903.

Though its pop. is less than 3,500, Myrtle Creek has a general hospital, a 24-hour police force of eight officers, the only fire dept. training facility in Douglas County, an old-style hotel that was familiar before motels became standard, and an all-night cafe, whose breakfast business starts at 2 a.m. "Because that's when the log truckers start hitting the road."

Historical structures in town include **Aksarben Gas Station and Cabins** (1923), first gas station and "motel" in these parts, at Main and 4th; **Charles**

White House (1890s), at Oak and 3rd; **Stanfield House** (1880s), at 3rd and Pleasant; **Phil Rice House** (1890s), Italiante cottage on Heard near Morrison; **Fred Buell House** (1890s), on Heard and Morrison; **First Christian Church** (1890), Rural Gothic at 2nd and Hall; **Stephenson House** (1890s), 2nd and Pleasant; **Myrtle Theater** (1917), first movie house in area, Main near 2nd; **Ferd Gabbert House** (1880s), 1st and Hall; **Methodist Episcopal Church** (1892–93), Gothic Revival, and **ME Parsonage** (1895), 2nd and Division; **John Hall House** (1870s), Oak, near PO.

At S end of Main, turn E onto Riverside Dr. *0.2 m.*, on R, 6-gabled wooden 2-1/2-story house with shake roof built by occupant of house. Interesting. *0.5 m.*, turn R onto Neal Lane. *0.4 m.*, **Neal Lane CB,** built 1929 at length 42 ft.; only CB in state having kingpost truss design, and with window on either side.

Return to O 99 — Riverside Dr. Turn S.

3.2 m., **Tri-City,** supposedly for Myrtle Creek, Canyonville and this long strip of roadside business and dwellings between. It should have been called String-town. Ask 10 people the location of the town center and the usual reply is "Wherever you are."

1 m., Riddle Jct.

   * Turn R for Riddle. *0.4 m.*, I-5. *2.6 m.*, **Riddle.** Named for 1851 settler, Riddle is generally known as Oregon's "nickel town." Only a short drive from the freeway, the settlement nevertheless appears self-contained. It is certainly nobody's bedroom. **Riddle Masonic Lodge,** originally hotel known as Riddle House, built 1866 by J. B. Riddle and his wife, Mary Catching, first white child born in Cow Creek Valley, has the solidity of sound business.

   * At 6th and Main, take 6th. *0.5 m.*, turn L onto county road. *0.3 m.*, turnoff to **Riddle Cemetery** (*0.2 m.*) Markers back to early 1850s. *0.1 m.*, on L, office of **Roseburg Forest Products,** largest plant under one roof — 18 acres — in state. *2 m.*, forks. Take R. *0.8 m.*, **Hannah Nickel Smelter,** only nickel smelter in US. Smelter built at base of Nickel Mtn., only outcropping of nickel in US. Mtn. now so reduced, company is "scratching to get more," in words of local historian.

   * Cow Creek Rd. goes on to Glendale, creating "horseshoe bend" between the two towns. It is 38 m. between Riddle and Glendale and there is little to be seen but the pike twisting between trees.

   * Return to downtown Riddle. Continue toward Canyonville. *5.5 m.*, Canyonville.

From I-5 turnoff to Myrtle Creek:

3.5 m., turnoff to Riddle (*3 m.*)

4.2 m., turnoff to Canyonville. *0.3 m.*, O 99. Turn S. *1.1 m.*, **Canyonville.**

Climb to the top of the grassy slope above the tennis courts in city park and you see the true meaning of Canyonville — cupped in the lovely and far-stretching Umpqua Hills. City park has pedestrian CB, across Canyon Creek.

Canyonville is sited at N end of Canyon Creek Canyon (or Coldstream Canyon or Canyon Creek Gorge) and known to early pioneers as Umpqua Canyon. Settled in 1851, Canyonville (in its first few years also called Kenyonville) developed as supply post on California-Oregon State route and experienced flurry of excitement and growth when rich ledges of gold-bearing quartz were discovered on tributaries of S Umpqua. Earlier, Canyonville had felt the boots of the fur brigades of Hudson's Bay Co., who were in area as early as 1832. And then, in 1846, had become the betrayed, bedeviled South Road caravan, seeking a S road into the lower valleys of W Oregon. Canyon Creek Canyon was undoubtedly the most horrendous part of the "Applegate Trail" in all its length. From the pass at the head of Canyon Creek, to the S, the canyon plunges 1,300 ft. to Canyonville and into this treacherous gorge the innocents stumbled, cursing Jesse Applegate to the last ember of their fury. He had sold them on a "short cut" to Oregon and they had left their main road Oregon Trail comrades to follow Applegate and his associates. Long before they had reason to regret their decision; now they wondered what madness had led them into this hell.

Tabitha Brown, who is regarded as one of the founders of Pacific University, was 66 when she followed Applegate into the wilderness. She could endure the Nevada wasteland and the thorny ranges to follow: " . . . sixty miles of desert without grass or water, mountains to climb, cattle giving out, wagons breaking, emigrants sick and dying, hostile Indians to guard against night and day," but in Umpqua Canyon she almost reached the end of her rope.

She remembered to her grave the grim spectacle in the gorge, whose length would be debated by the pioneers — 12 m. or 15 m. "I rode through in three days at the risk of my life, on horseback, having lost my wagon and all that I had but the horse I was on. Our families were the first that started through the canyon, so that we got through the mud and rocks much better than those that followed. Out of hundreds of wagons, only one came through without breaking. The canyon was strewn with dead cattle, broken wagons, bed, clothing, and everything but provisions, of which latter we were nearly destitute. Some people were in the canyon two or three weeks before they could get through. Some died without warning, from fatigue and starvation. Others ate the flesh of cattle that were lying dead by the wayside."

(For more on the ordeal, see "The Courage of Grandma Brown" in author's *A Touch of Oregon*.)

Beyond Canyonville the pioneers entered the S Umpqua River Valley and the Beulah Land of Oregon became real to them.

Another famous name associated with Canyonville is Joseph Hooker, later a prominent Civil War general. He made his HQ here while improving the wagon road up the canyon in 1858.

Canyonville Cemetery, 0.6 m. N of town, contains graves of some eminent pioneers, including Horace B. Myrtle, who died early in 1863. It would have seemed more logical to have had him buried at nearby Myrtle Creek. 0.2 m., N of cemetery, Evergreen Motel. Just N of office is old log cabin, on tract owned by Cow Creek Indians.

Late in 1982 the then 645-member Cow Creek Band of the Umpqua Indian Tribe, HQ'd here, was granted tribal recognition by US, reversing action taken in 1954 when the Cow Creeks, along with 111 other bands in nation, had tribal recognition terminated. Cow Creeks, who ratified treaty with the gvmt. in 1855, thus became the 5th tribe in nation to either gain recognition or have its recognition restored after 1954 termination.

Canyonville United Methodist Church, 2nd and Pine, dedicated 1876, 8 years after construction started. House at 305 and 325 Pine built in 1870s or 1880s, old-timers say. Pioneer house, typical of early dwellings here, across street from bus depot.

Largest institution or business in town is **Canyonville Bible Academy,** "an independent self-supporting Christian coed boarding high school of Full Gospel persuasion," founded 1924; its eight bldgs. occupy 10-acre campus near heart of town. Although sports are limited due to small enrollment, CBS holds 11 state track records and its cross-country team is generally tops in state in its division. With all the hills around Canyonville to run on, cross-country should be a natural here.

At Canyonville city center, jct. O 227.

O 227

0.2 m., in city park and across Canyon Creek, pedestrian CB, built by Canyonville Lions 1976. *1 m.,* on N, **Canyonville Park.** *4.1 m.,* on S, old farmhouse with gingerbread porch. *1.9 m.,* S Umpqua River. *0.2 m.,* on N, **Days Creek Community Church,** once ME Church, built around 1900, stands on knoll overlooking valley. *0.2 m.,* **Days Creek,** tiny hamlet settled 1851 by Patrick and George Day. In 1915 burg had pop. 150, a lot more than it has now. But location is sure pretty.

3.6 m., on N, across from mail box #17, lane leading *0.4 m.,* to **Bland Mtn. Cemetery** thru genuine farm spread. Burial ground in horse pasture. Markers back to 1874, though cemetery est. 1867.

2.6 m., on N, across from mail box #29, uphill lane *0.3 m.,* to **Van Norman Cemetery.** (At first fork of dirt road, park car and walk *50 yds.* uphill to cemetery, on L.) Burial ground unusual because almost every grave has cross; because graves, hidden in high grass, suggest a forgotten site; and lastly, and perhaps most importantly, vistas from cemetery, in all directions, are, to say the least, spectacular: narrow valleys slotted between green hills, churns of mtns., a world afloat in contours. Somehow the image is of Wales.

2.5 m., Carl C. Hill Wayside — Douglas CP; PA on S Umpqua.

1.2 m., on S. **Milo Academy CB** — Oregon's only steel CB capped with wooden superstructure — spans S Umpqua as entrance to Milo Adventist Academy.

CB span replaced venerable 100-ft. bridge that existed at site since 1920. When old bridge was replaced with new steel structure in 1962, area residents felt they had lost part of their heritage, so span was modified and a new white cover emerged. **Milo Adventist Academy** is only Seventh Day Adventist boarding academy in state, was founded 1955, its campus of 410 acres equals many a small college for size and attractiveness. Aim of academy summed up in sentence taken from catalog: "Deans, teachers, work supervisors — all the people connected with Milo — see it as their privilege and duty to do all they can to make Christ real for students."

Academy is about all there is to Milo, which doesn't have PO or store suggesting a hamlet. Begun as Elk Creek in 1884, name of PO was soon changed to Perdue and remained that way until 1920, when postmaster was given the boot because he moonlighted as census taker. Three years later Milo PO started. In 1915 Milo had PS, pop. 23, and its own identity.

5.5 m., **Tiller.** Store. Turn-of-century hamlet, Tiller never made if off the ground. In 1915 it had pop. 25 and PS. *0.3 m.*, S Umpqua River. This stream is sister to O 227 and helps to green its fair fields and abundant forests.

Red Mountain Lookout, Tiller Ranger Station   *Courtesy Umpqua National Forest*

0.1 m., on N, **Tiller FS Range Station.** Just to E of RS, on knoll, is **Red Mtn. Lookout,** moved here in fall of 1985 and dedicated 6/14/1986. Cupola style lookout was put up on Red. Mtn. in upper Cow Creek Valley in 1928, replacing lookout tree which had been functioning since 1921. Lookout, measuring 12 ft. by 12 ft. sq. and surmounted by 8-ft.-sq. cupola, was sited at elev. 4,797 ft. and was utilized to detect fires in surrounding mtns. and valleys of upper Cow Creek and Applegate drainages. Red Mtn. Lookout's most famous firewatcher was a local rancher, Henry Looney, whose spread was 4 m. from the big hill. Looney served 19 years and acquired reputation as crack firewatcher and as a powerful hunter of wolves and ringtailed cats. His food and supplies were packed in by his wife, Gertrude Looney, who some years was paid as much as $5 per month for her labors. One of the items that intrigues visitors is the glass legged lookout stool, to be stood on during lightning storms.

After Tiller, O 227 turns twisty, weaving thru thick timber. *5.2 m.,* **Drew.** Nothing but a few houses. Drew has always seemed isolated. In 1915, when it had PS, which it doesn't now, it was 32 m. to nearest RR point, at Riddle. *7.8 m.,* **Threehorn FS CG.** *13.4 m.,* jct., O 62. (Short distance past jct., on O 62, Trail.) Return to O 99.

O 99 — Continued

0.1 m., from Canyonville city center, turnoff to I-5.

10.3 m., turnoff to Azalea.

*0.2 m., "T". Turn E on Cow Creek Rd. *4.2 m.,* on R, **Longfibre CP.** *2.7 m.,* **Galesville Dam,** one of first dams in US built (at cost of $35 million) of roller-compacted concrete. Behind dam is reservoir, known to few outsiders. Near dam, according to local historian, there stood PO of **Starvout** — but that is as uncertain as sites of other jumping-around POs. (Beyond dam a county road of varying condition passes thru what was the PO of **Anchor** — scarcely anyone in the area has heard of it — and turns S, driving an erratic course thru sparsely-occupied terrain to jct. *10 m.* NE of Wimer and *10 m.* N of O 234 at Sams Valley. *2.1 m.* below jct., on way to Wimer, was micro-dorp of **Bybee Springs.** Memory of it has also been near obliterated. Few folks living in Wimer or Azalea have ever taken this county road full route and those who have are generally not anxious to repeat the performance. And beware of logging trucks!

*0.2 m., W from "T," **Azalea,** named for profusion of this warm-hearted flower in area, which is also favored by fir, alder, oak and yellow pine. For what little it has, Azalea is a right lively place, folks constantly coming and going.

1.8 m., turnoff to Quines Creek.

*0.5 m., **Quines Creek.** Restaurant. Galesville PO est. here or near here

Tuller Marker

Text on marker:

PIONEERS' GRAVES

In this vicinity are buried:

Jeremiah G. Tuller, born in Ohio in 1822 and died in 1895, came to Oregon in [...] and served in the Cayuse Indian War or [...] 1848.

His wife, [...], born in Il'inois in 1826 and died in 1907, ca [...] regon in 18[...] via the Barlow Road.

Their dau [...] Clementine Bell, M D, born in 1852 and die [...] 901, graduated from the University of Oregon Medic[...] School in 1899.

The family home, located on the south side of the road, was destroyed by fire in 1931.

1854; closed 1916. In 1915, burg had HS, PS, blacksmith shop, store, boarding house. All gone.

3.9 m., turnoff to Rest Area. *1.3 m.,* turnoff to Glendale.

 * *3.2 m.,* **Glendale,** originally called Julia, is an "album" of the 1930s, its one-sided business street facing the RR tracks, as so many towns did when the RR was king. Glendale has no shopping centers, no malls, no edge-of-town or suburban commerce. It is a modern portrait of nostalgia. In 1915 Glendale was bigger than it is today. Decline may have started in 1928, when much of business district was consumed by fire.

Fastest growing commerce in Glendale, as everywhere in Oregon, is rental of video recorders and movies. Other observations on recent trends in Oregon: most marked mercantile shift: extension of hours by food stores, with 24-hour marts now current even in small towns; biggest change in merchandising: the full-circle combining of small food stores and gas stations; fastest growing institution in state: senior citizen center; strongest current in Oregon employment: minimum wage area jobs.

Glendale Cemetery, *0.1 m.* up 1st St. from Montgomery, holds graves of pioneers of 1849 and 1852.

At Shell Station, take Reuben Rd., which becomes Cow Creek Rd. *4.7 m.,* site of **Reuben,** former RR siding mappoint. *2.7 m.,* on L, **Tuller Marker.** Buried near here are Jeremiah G. Tuller, 1844 arrival from Ohio and veteran of Cayuse Indian War of 1848; his wife, Miriam, an Illinois native who first married at the age of 18 and at 19 came to Oregon with her husband, Arthur Hale Thompson, who was killed by Indians near Mormon Island on the American River of Calif.'s Gold Rush Country in spring of 1849 at a place subsequently known as Murderers Bar, and who in 1850 wed Jeremiah Tuller; and a Tuller daughter, Clementine Bell, MD, who at the age of 47 received a medical degree from U of O Medical School, and who is the "mystery" of the family, there being no evidence to determine if she divorced Arthur Bell, whom she wed in 1880, or whether Bell died. Two years after she started practicing medicine she passed away.

The Tuller Marker has been targeted by vandals since it was put up 7/14/1977. Lyman Deich, archaeologist for the Medford office of Bureau of Land Management, recounted earlier history of marker:

"The original was a wooden post. Approximately three weeks later, vandals cut the post with a chain saw and threw the marker over the embankment.

"The sign was reinstalled in August, 1978. Again, it stood for about three weeks before it was attacked. This time it was apparently battered down with a pickup or 4-wheel-drive vehicle and considerable damage was done to the sign.

"Whether or not the sign will be reinstalled is uncertain. Some area residents feel that to not replace the marker would indicate acquiescence to the lawless elements of the community. On the other hand, if we do reinstall it we may be merely playing a game with the vandals in which we devise ever more secure (and expensive) ways to install the sign and they devise ever more ingenious and violent ways to destroy it."

A new marker was placed near the grave site and it was soon riddled with bullets.

From PO, **Glendale,** backtrack toward I-5. *0.6 m.,* turn L onto Glendale Hwy. *0.5 m.,* Glendale HS. *1.4 m.,* site of **New Odessa Colony,** commune founded in 1882 by group of young Russian Jewish exiles from city of Odessa who hailed themselves as followers of Karl Marx. (Marx would have winced at the naivete of the colonists, who had absolutely no understanding of scientific socialism.) The group took the name of "Am Olem," meaning "The Eternal People."

A variety of factors influenced the decision to settle at Glendale, which somehow seemed logical, since a Jew, Solomon Abraham, a right-of-way agent for the RR, had platted Glendale. Abraham was also a pioneer merchant in Douglas County. Probably the most decisive element in choosing Glendale was the advice given by RR mogul Henry Villard, a close friend of Michael Heilprin, a New York author and scholar who befriended the emigres upon their arrival in America.

The New Odessa Colony lasted only from 1882 to 1887. Given the times and the weak political maturity of the colonists, failure was inevitable. But all remembered their commune days with warmth and pride and all partook in liberal and humanitarian causes the rest of their lives. All — or almost all — became professionals: lawyers, dentists, doctors, engineers, chemists and educators and all retained their passion for culture. Joseph Havitt, a dentist, was responsible for bringing to the US the noted Russian dancer, Nazimova. The last of the colonists, Peter Fireman, a brilliant chemist and inventor and the most successful of all the Glendale group, passed away in the 1950s at the age of 94.

From Glendale turnoff to I-5:

4.1 m., turnoff to Wolf Creek.

0.7 m., **Wolf Creek.** Place first gained fame because of its pioneer **Six Bit House,** crude hotel that charged only 75 cents per night, compared to the $1 assessed by other local innkeepers. As with most other rural hotels of its period, the Six Bit couldn't afford night clerks. Instead, candles were left at the registration desk or on the mantle of the living room fireplace. As each guest arrived he (no shes came alone) picked up a candle and hied himself to the second floor. Here he pounded on each door until he found one where there was no response. Then he entered and made himself to home for the night.

Town has for decades been best-known for its **Wolf Creek Tavern,** whose date of construction has not been definitively established. Legend has it that inn was put up 1857 by transportation tycoon Ben Holladay as stage stop. A bit of folklore suggests that Chinese miners constructed it in 1860s to hide their gold operations. Researchers of the Oregon State Parks believe inn was built about 1873 by Henry Smith, local businessman. In 1915 and again in 1922, additions were made.

Rumors persist that bldg. stands on foundation of old placer gold diggings, a tale as romantic as the nature of its construction. It was built of ripsawed lumber, all hand-planed. The large timbers were fastened with wooden pegs, with old-fashioned square-topped nails to hold the planks in place. Beams and panels were hand-hewn and carved by artisans.

Legend reports that during the time of the 16-drag stagecoach trip between San Francisco and Portland, the stage stopped overnight at Wolf Creek Tavern. That may or may not have been; it certainly could not have been before 1873 and by then the route was pretty well set.

As Wolf Creek Tavern entrenched itself into the romanticism of Oregon, the names of more illustrious persons were added to the guests of the past. The list includes President Hayes, who passed thru Wolf Creek at about 10 a.m. and kept going; Jack London, who is supposed to have resided here while completing his novel, *Valley of the Moon* (more competent researchers believe London and his wife, Charmain, stayed here while she typed the mss. of his *The End of the Story*); Sinclair Lewis, who allegedly was here for a spell, in search of local color for his writing; Mary Pickford and Clark Gable; and, of course, U. S. Grant, supposedly a guest while a 2nd Lt. in US Army. Grant, who seems to have slept almost everywhere in W Oregon, to hear the local folksayers, could not have been here; he exited the PNW long before Wolf Creek Tavern was built.

In 1975 the state of Oregon acquired Wolf Creek Tavern, by then shoddy from unchecked deterioration of age. Restoration began in 1977 and in 1979 the tavern, under lease, was again opened. Restoration reflects various time periods of inn's existence, giving it air of continuity. First floor central stairway, ladies' parlor and men's sitting room were given authentic 19th century ambience and, in general, bldg. emerged as living, changing mirror of tavern as it evolved from 1870s wayside to ultra-smart place it is today.

Local folks say they have never heard of Ft. Bailey, but the meticulous Oregon historian, Frances Fuller Victor, in her *Early Indian Wars of Oregon,* places this camp by the Oregon Mounted Volunteers in the campaign against the Rogue River Indians in 1855–56 as being at or close to today's settlement of Wolf Creek.

Looking down upon the community is 3,000-ft.-high **London Peak,** named for Jack London, who supposedly had fondness for butte, two decades after his death. 2 m. trail to top begins at Wolf Creek CP.

From Wolf Creek Store:

    * 0.3 m., turnoff E on Coyote Creek Rd. 3.2 m., on R, **Golden School,** built circa 1885, now privately owned. Interior is schoolroom of that period in Oregon though many desks came from Kansas. 0.1 m., on R, 1884 house. 0.7 m., **Golden,** mining town of yore. PO 1896–1920. In 1915 it had stamp and quartz mills, PS, church. Church, picture of gaunt, elderly lady, non-denominational now, was Christian in 1915. Standing also, but shabby compared to dignity of church, and now residence, is former general store.

There is a longer, more rugged trip out of Wolf Creek, into another section of the mining country:

    * Take Wolf Creek Rd. W for Grave Creek, Almeda and Galice. 10.1 m., on R, faltering log structure that looks like early day trading post. 4.9 m., confluence of Grave Creek and Rogue River, at fine, seemingly out-of-place concrete bridge. Jct. here, with R fork heading NW to branch into lanes that dead end in the Rogue wilderness, lead to coastal Gold Beach, or eventually reach Coos Bay. 3.8 m., heading E from Grave Creek bridge, unmarked viewpoint. Across Rogue the paltry remains of old Almeda Mine rest in sun and rain. That gouge in ledge on reddish hillside sweeping back from Rogue was mine's entrance. 0.2 m., **Almeda Bar Rec. Area,** CP on river. 3.3 m., Galice. (For Galice and rest of this trip, see *Cross-Coast Range Roads, Rogue River Road.*) 0.4 m., Galice Creek bridge historical marker. 4.5 m., **Indian Mary Park.** 1.3 m., **Hellgate Viewpoint.** 5.8 m., Merlin. 3.5 m., I-5. S, 4.5 m., downtown Grants Pass. 0.4 m., I-5 N. (16 m., Wolf Creek.)

S on O 99 from Coyote Creek Rd., Wolf Creek:

0.2 m., I-5. 4.3 m., turnoff to Sunny Valley.

    * 0.3 m., jct., **Sunny Valley,** formerly called Grave and Grave Creek.

Store, modest tourist facilities. For many years **Radio Park Store,** folksy establishment heated by pot-bellied stove, was even better known than Wolf Creek Tavern to residents of this area. According to oldtimers, store was called Radio Park because during the 1930s, when bldg. was dance hall,

Church at Golden

the only radio in the valley was here. Settlers would come from miles around to listen to their favorite programs. But Radio Park Store was succeeded as food market by newer, up-to-date mart. *Sic transit gloria* or, as the old hoboes would say, "That's all she wrote."

* At Sunny Valley Jct., turn E, toward Leland. *4 m.,* just beyond concrete bridge, **Leland.** Only couple of houses now. A fifth generation native of Leland said that, in its prime, when RR was being built and mining was flourishing and farming was strong, Leland had pop. of 3,000, with several hotels, including a 2-story one, a hotel perched on slope of steep hill, so that the roomers slid down to the road; section house for RR workers; RR depot, a swag of saloons and stores; and more.

The figure of 3,000 seems a bit much, even given the temporary inpouring of RR workers. One thing is certain: what ballooned quickly came quickly to earth. By 1915 Leland's pop. was down to 50. As with so many early POs, Leland was in more than one place. Originally it was near Sunny Valley and was called Twogood's, then Ft. Leland and Grave Creek House.

From Jct. at Sunny Valley:

* E, *0.3 m.,* **Grave Creek CB,** built 1920 at length of 105 ft. Bridge, which can be seen from I-5, is one of handsomest in Oregon, its six Gothic-style windows on either side give it a look of class. Stream was named for grave of 14-year-old girl named either Josephine Crowley or Martha Crowley Leland, member of first wagon train to enter Oregon from S, in 1846. She was buried

Grave Creek Bridge   *Phoebe L. Friedman*

in spot covered by present roadway. Legend has it that five Indians killed in 1853 were buried in the same grave, which is why the stream has sometimes been called Graves Creek. The site is loaded with history. NW of bridge was fought Battle of Hungry Hill — also known as Battle of Bloody Springs — where on Oct. 30, 1855, red and white men clashed. Supposedly, six Oregon volunteers and three regulars were slain. County historians say that five soldiers lie in graves near here — but the graves are unmarked and no one knows their locations. Near here, too, was site of **Ft. Leland,** post used during Rogue River Indian uprising of 1855–56. And just beyond bridge and 100 yds to NE stood **Harkness and Twogood Stage House,** built 1857. Among its guests were Pres. Hayes and Gen. Sherman —maybe. Probably Ft. Leland stood nearby the place for, like many other "forts," it was first a stockade designed to protect settlers who fled here for safety. It may have been extension of Grave Creek House, built earlier by Harkness and Twogood and reinforced with heavy timbers after the Battle of Hungry Hill.

There is always folklore in the wake of dramatic events. Mrs. Mary E. Cobb, Jefferson librarian, recalled in 1984 something of the CB and area:

"We lived there when the bridge was built. The workmen camped along the creek and bought eggs, milk and butter, and vegetables from my mother. We walked to school up the road a short way, where the old road turned left down to Leland. The road we took turned right to Placer. On a ways further was an old cemetery. While we lived there a man named Brown bought the farm. He piled all the tombstones against the fence and plowed and planted the small field which was the cemetery. All the neighbors were quite upset but nothing was done about it. The story we were told was Josephine Leland (the pioneer girl) died and was buried. The Indians took her body and hung her by her hair up in this tree. When the road was widened (more cars) the oak tree was left — seemingly planted in the center of the road. A few years later it was paved and the tree had to go."

*Just beyond CB turn R onto Placer Rd. *3.5 m.,* **Placer.** If it weren't for the roadside marker you wouldn't know you were at the site of what, at turn of century, had been a small but lively placer and quartz mining town. Only a few scattered houses and shacks.

(For more on area, see "Sunny Valley Scene" in author's *Tracking Down Oregon.*)

From turnoff to Sunny Valley on I-5:

5.2 m., turnoff to Hugo.

* *1 m.,* turn onto Three Pines Rd. *0.8 m.,* forks. Take R. *1.4 m.,* forks. Take R. *0.1 m.,* **Hugo.** Store. Settled rather late, PO not est. until 1896; no longer there. At one time Hugo had hotel, two stores, RR depot, PS. In 1915 it had pop. 100; fewer now.

You look at places like Hugo that were towns and you realize the concept is only an illusion of nostalgia. Hugo isn't a town anymore and hasn't been for years. Like other Hugos throughout W Oregon, this one is an "area" or "district" now. Hugo today is a rural store that doesn't look different from a neighborhood store in a city, and that's what it is, a neighborhood rural store.

5 m., **Louse Creek.** In the 1860s there was prominent stagecoach stop here. There is a bit of lore about booty taken in a stage holdup and cached along the creek, with clue supposedly being blaze in oak tree. *0.2 m.,* possible site of Winona, on Jumpoff Joe Creek. PO 1897–1905. In 1915 it had sawmill.

Turnoff to Merlin.

* *0.2 m.,* turn R. *0.2 m.,* turn L. *3.1 m.,* **Merlin,** on Rogue River and last outpost of suburbia before heading W toward coast on sparsely traveled high road. Merlin today is expanding bedroom of Grants Pass.

From I-5 and Merlin turnoff:

2 m., turnoff to Grants Pass. *2.5 m.,* **Grants Pass.**

When, during Civil War, news reached the muckers laboring to improve the California Stage Route "pass" N of town that Vicksburg had fallen, the unionists celebrated by christening the road summit Grants Pass. So goes the legend. PO est. 1865. From 1910 to 1940 Grants Pass actually lost pop. but since close of WW II has been growing steadily and is in danger of losing its image as a "just folks town," especially with the burgeoning of the unincorporated areas, which have made a minor metropolis of Grants Pass.

City profits dollar-wise from its position as E gateway to Oregon Caves Nat'l. Monument and the Redwood Forest. Boat trips of varied duration, and led by experienced white river guides, are popular on the Rogue and bring many people to Grants Pass. In this town lived the greatest of Oregon's river runners, Glenn Wooldridge, more closely associated with the Rogue than anyone else. (See "Old Man of the River" in author's *This Side of Oregon.*)

Grants Pass has the dubious distinction of being the capital of the largest mari-juana-growing area in state. But, on brighter side, Grants Pass boasts oldest amateur theater in Oregon, the Barnstormers, founded 1952.

Riverside Park, on Rogue, is without a doubt one of the most beautiful parks in state. **Grants Pass Art Museum,** prominent for its traveling exhibits, is in park. **Josephine County Historical Society,** one of state's best, in 1890 Schmidt house, corner, 5th and J. **Wilson House,** on R side of NE Jackson and 6th, impressive turn-of-century baronial manor. **New Methodist Church** (1890), oldest church structure in town, 6th and B. Victorian-style **McLean House** (1898), built by first Presbyterian minister, was used as hospital 1913–1921; **St. Luke's Episcopal Church,** 224 NW D, dates back to 1895; **First National Bank of Oregon** Bldg., 208 NW 6th, built 1890. **Kienlen-Harbeck Bldg.** (1900), 147 SW G, originally saloon and rooming house, was meat market for 40 years. **Rogue River Brewing Co.** (1884), 509 SW G, closed when city voted itself dry in 1917. Thereafter, bldg. was used as saddle harness shop, granary, grocery store and art gallery. First story of **Newell House,** 591 SW G, built 1885. **Ahlf House** (1902), built in Queen Anne style at 762 NW 6th, is largest historic residence in Grants Pass, containing 5,000

Croxton Park Grave Memorial Landmark, Grants Pass

sq. ft. Most interesting part of town is G St. 4th to 7th, on S side, because of its many late 19th and early 20th century bldgs. On N side of street was RR depot.

Croxton Pioneer Cemetery, on Memorial Way, near Lincoln School, has markers back to 1856, including B. H. Baird, "killed by a grizzly bear" in 1864 and McDonough Harkness, killed by Indian April 21, 1856, at age "39 years, 1 mo. and 5 days." Harkness, a special express manager employed by US Army, was scalped and mutilated in the most gruesome way, an expression of complete revenge by the Rogue River Indians for Harkness' part in the 1853 murders of six Indians on Grave Creek.

Croxton Memorial Park is most unusual burial ground in Oregon. Park was once cemetery and the graves are still here, but now covered by grass. Markers were taken up and placed in concrete border enclosing rose garden, as a grave marker monument. Near monument is plaque on a rough cut stone with poem, "Oregon Trail Breakers," written by Percy T. Booth:

"If in my haste I chance to pass/ Smug with speed in chrome and steel/ I'll mark the place where last you sleep/ Tucked in with flower blankets sweet/ Soft touched by breath of early spring/ As altar cloth, unfurled in peace/ Across the pain of yester years/ Your debt is full paid, your work complete/ This land you loved and held so dear/ Now holds you safe, in warm embrace/ And in the place He fixed for you/ He hung an arch of promise there/ And shared His robe of royal blue/ A piece of sky, torn loose and tossed/ With loving gentleness across/ Your throne, a godly gift to you/ O Pioneer, have patience please/ With those of us who in our ease/ Forget your fingers brushed the dust/ Of unreached stars, then passed to us/ A heritage of precious hope/ That we might face our tasks today/ Because you walked ahead of us/ And broke the trail and led the way."

For one of the most unusual animal places in Oregon, turn W onto G St. from

6th and G. *1.3 m.*, turn L onto Lincoln. *0.5 m.*, curve R onto Lower River Rd. *6.9 m.*, on L, **Whitehorse CP,** on Rogue River. CG, PA, trailer facilities. *4.3 m.*, on L, **Wildlife Images Rehabilitation and Education Center,** holder of coveted and rarely given special award from Izaak Walton League of America for wildlife conservation efforts.

The non-profit Wildlife Images, operated by long-time, ardently dedicated conservationists, Dave and Judy Siddon, and a staff of volunteers, has as its prime mission the rehabilitation of wild animals and birds who have been shot or otherwise injured and unable to survive in their natural habitat. When the patients are restored to health and are judged capable of existing on their own, they are transported to areas conducive for their best chance of life and released. Animals and birds incapable of making it outside this rehabilitation home are kept as "show" exhibits, primarily for schoolchildren, to better acquaint them with nature.

From city center, Grants Pass, on O 99:

0.8 m., jct., US 199; jct., O 238. (See *Cross-Coast Range Roads, US 199.*)

O 99 winds along Rogue River, which has lost some of its charm in recent years because of relatively dense build-up but still retains enough enchantment to make the ride pleasurable. But not for drivers; too much traffic.

5.4 m., on L, **Weaksu Inn.** Guests have included Clark Gable, John Wayne, David Nivens, Ann Sothern, Gabby Hayes and Herbert Hoover. When Gable was alone he occupied Room #4 upstairs and when he was with Carole Lombard he rented Cabin #6. He was in room #4 when he was given the news that Carole Lombard had been killed. He stayed in the room without leaving for a week, then moved to Cabin #6 and remained secluded for two more weeks. His meals were brought to him by Rainbow Gibson, owner of the inn and a good friend of Gable.

Walk *100 yds.* past inn and downslope to **Savage Rapid Dam,** on Rogue, dedicated 11/6/1921. Prime site to view migrating salmon during May and June. Observation platform above fish ladder.

3.5 m., jct., city of Rogue River. At jct., Fleming Rest Area. PA.

* *0.4 m.*, city of **Rogue River,** aptly named, being on stream. Prior to 1876 the place was irreverently called Tailhold by gusty miners, freighters and homesteaders. In that year it became the respectable Woodville and remained so until 1912, when some PR-minded citizens cashed in on name of river. Some decades ago the town was best known for being across the river from a "farm" holding 8,000 rattlesnakes, the rattlers raised to provide meat for epicurean dining and venom for medicinal purposes. In recent years town has been prominent for its tongue-in-cheek National Rooster Crow, held in June. Rapid communications and transportation have made Rogue River a virtual suburb of Grants Pass and it has no striking characteristics as a town, but its idyllic location in the Rogue River Valley gives it a charming ambience. Town is gateway to Valley of the Rogue SP, on river. CG, PA, dumping station, fishing, BR, FHP.

* In city of Rogue River, take Pine St. It becomes E Evans Creek Rd. *7.3*

m., turn R. *0.8 m.*, **Wimer and Wimer CB.** Founded in 1880s, Wimer some-how never developed into a viable marketplace. In 1915 it had only store and PS and doesn't have much more now. But hills and woods are adequately peopled. Old-timers insist CB was first built in 1892 but documentation at-tests to 1927; present bridge dates from 1962, is 85 ft. in length, and from a certain perspective appears as a barn floating on water.

    * Retrace route *2 m.* to Minthorne Rd. Turn R onto it. *0.2 m.*, cross Evans Creek. *0.7 m.*, turn L onto W Evans Creek Rd. *6.2 m.*, **Palmerton Park,** local arboretum. *0.3 m.*, "T". Turn L onto Foothill Blvd. *0.3 m.*, Pine St. Ahead, bend onto Main St. *0.5 m.*, on L, Wards Creek Rd. (Turn L onto it. *0.1 m.*, **Woodville Cemetery,** adjacent to adult village. Markers back to 1880.) Return to Main St., which is now N River Rd. Turn L. *2.9 m.*, turnoff to **Valley of the Rogue SP** (*0.3 m.*). *2.7 m.*, **John B. White House,** 1859. General store of hamlet of Rock Point (PO 1859–1912) sited at present corral of White House. Other businesses of mid-19th century dorp included shops and houses. Next to White House is **Rock Point Stage Station,** built 1863. Until 1883, when RR came thru, tavern was colorful wayside and every stage deposited a cast of characters seemingly fresh from a Bret Harte tale. Stage station at jct., O 234. (R, *50 yds.*, **Rock Point Bridge,** named for beehive rock formations below.)

From jct., O 99 and city of Rogue River:

2 m., on R, or S — just before Birdseye Creek — white-painted **Birdseye House,** redone log structure put up 1856, with many of logs taken from original stockade of short-lived Ft. Birdseye (1855), which stood less than 0.1 m. back of house. Oldest home in S Oregon still in use. Please do not trespass on grounds.

1.6 m., **Foots Creek,** cheery roadside mercantile gathering place, the kind of coming together rural neighborhood shopping that reminds old-timers of their

City Hall, Wimer

Wimer Bridge   *Phoebe L. Friedman*

Rock Point Stage Station   *Phoebe L. Friedman*

youth. Foots Creek PO est. 4/5/1878; lasted until 7/7/1879. In 1885, PO of Bolt started here; closed late 1896. After span of some years, community again became known as Foots Creek, completing the circle of nomenclature.

3.2 m., start of O 234; O 99 and O 234 run as one to Gold Hill.

0.3 m., **Rock Point Bridge.** *0.1 m.,* jct., N River Rd. (L on River Rd.: Rock Point Stage Station (1863), John B. White House (1858), both close to jct. See earlier.)

0.2 m., from Rock Point Bridge, turnoff L to **Rock Point Cemetery** *(0.1 m.)* Markers back to early 1870s.

0.3 m., Sardine Creek Rd.

   * 4.3 m., on R, commercial **Oregon Vortex,** also advertised as "House of Mystery." Originally gold mining assay office, house puzzles optically illusioned tourists though it has been scientifically debunked.

1.6 m., **Gold Hill.** Sign at entrance to town reads: "A Quiet City. All Loud and Unnecessary Noises are Prohibited." That says something about the town.

Named for the gold mining in hills above town, first quartz mill in Jackson County was built here or near here. Remains of old gold mines can be detected with binoculars on Nugget Butte, due N of town. Vine-covered brick house at 719 2nd Ave., built 1880, and is most photogenic home in town. Bldg. at 320 2nd Ave. built 1885. First two houses off 4th St. on 1st Ave. put up around 1890. House

Birdseye House

Gold Hill entrance sign

at 535 4th Ave. was saddlery when original town stood on N side of RR tracks. **IOOF Bldg.** put up 1891; front remodeled. **Grange,** 275 4th Ave., dates back to 1890. Tavern at 4th Ave. and 4th St. was **Gold Hill Hotel,** built 1884, originally had 32 rooms, restaurant and bar. Bar built with single mirror 5 ft. high and 12 ft. long placed in bldg. 1903. **Metzel House,** 125 3rd St., really looking its age, was probably a very decent appearing residence when new in 1882.

Gold Hill is surely one of the most interesting looking town in W Oregon, having so frank a tintype face of the past. There is nothing pretty about the town; it has rugged, coarse-grained features, but it will bring sparkle to eyes of Oregon history buffs.

Jct., downtown Gold Hill, O 234. Here O 234 separates from O 99.

0.6 m., public boat landing on Rogue. *2.2 m.,* **Gold Nugget Rec. Site,** on Rogue. *1.2 m.,* on R, Gold Rey Ranch. Not too long ago, as time passes, this was a buffalo spread.

3.7 m., Old Sams Valley Rd. *(1.4 m.* up road, on R, old **Sams Valley School** and **Sams Valley Grange,** last remains of hamlet of **Sams Valley,** named for Chief Sam of Rogue River Indians. PO — 4th class — closed 1953 as "economy move.")

0.6 m., Table Rock Rd. From here can clearly be seen the flat-topped butte where dwelt the Rogue River Indians. On Sept. 10, 1853, at foot of butte, Table Rock Treaty was signed by Gen. Joseph Lane and the Rogue chiefs. Around the butte raged battles between Native Americans and paleface newcomers, who had driven away the game the Indians had hunted for meat for centuries, and who were starting to plow up the fields whose plants was traditional nourishment for the first people.

* Turn R onto Table Rock Rd. *2 m.,* on R, Wheeler Rd., parking for *1 m.*

steep trail to **Lower Table Rock Preserve,** property of The Nature Conservancy. *0.5 m.,* on L, **Table Rock Monument,** near where Table Rock Treaty was signed. *1 m.,* site of town of **Table Rock.** *2 m.,* **Tou Valle SP,** on Rogue. *0.9 m.,* Antelope Rd. Turn L. *1.8 m.,* O 62, at White City. (For Table Rock Rd. details, *see Trans-Cascade Roads, O 62.*)

2.7 m., Antioch Rd.

    * Turn L. *1 m.,* on R, **Antioch Cemetery** (1867). *1.3 m.,* Beagle Rd. Old hand-dug well on NW corner is all that remains of hamlet of **Beagle.** In 1915 it had pop. 50, PO, PS, Baptist Church. In early years, G. W. Stacey was the town's blacksmith, E. H. Thornbrue the barber, and the Wilhite brothers ran the general store. When Camp White — now site of White City — was activated during WW II, Beagle area was bought up by US for heavy artillery range, doing away with PO, rest of hamlet, and all farms and homes in area. After WW II, land sold back by US and now plenty of homes around. But Beagle stayed down the well.

4.9 m., jct., O 62.

Resume O 99 at O 234 jct., in Gold Hill:

Former Grange Hall, Gold Hill   *Phoebe L. Friedman*

0.3 m., jct., I-5.

* Turn R and cross over freeway. *0.6 m.,* service station. Walk back *0.1 m.,* toward freeway. At far end of guard rail on R, turn R. *100 yds.,* beneath maple and screened from freeway by pines, **Dardanelles plaque.**

* Plaque marks site of pioneer village of Dardanelles, founded by the colorful William Green T'Vault, who came to Oregon with Stephen Meek's Cutoff Party in 1845 and went on to become a driving force in Oregon politics before his career was halted by his unbridled devotion to slavery. He had been Oregon's first postmaster general and first editor of Oregon's first newspaper, *The Oregon Spectator,* before he moved to S part of state. (While at Jacksonville he was twice prosecuting attorney for First Judicial District.)

On Oct. 19, 1852, T'Vault opened Dardanelles PO in his cabin on his DLC here. Some other settlers joined him in est. a voting precinct and on April 4, 1853, first election was held. The next year a grocery store was opened but not for another 7 years and after the discovery of gold did anyone apply for permit to sell "spiritous liquors." With gold, Dardanelles mushroomed. Its crowning glory was the Adams House, later known as the Dardanelles House, one of fanciest of S Oregon inns. By then T'Vault had been a territorial legislator from Jackson County and recognized as an advocate of the Confederacy. Together with Joseph Lane he was implicated in somewhat nebulous plans to create a "Pacific Republic," meant to dismember the W flank of the Union. T'Vault died of smallpox in 1869 and today is remembered only by keen students of Oregon history. As for Dardanelles, it returned to its earlier obscurity when the mines became exhausted. When The Dardanelles House burned in 1876, it was the signal for last rites. Other bldgs. were removed from the site, leaving only a few houses. PO closed 1864, reopened 1877 by some Johnny-come-latelys, the next year shut down for good. Today most people in Gold Hill know of Dardanelles only because service station bears that name.

* Turn R in front of station onto Frontage Rd. *1.6 m.,* Hodson Rd. Turn L. *0.2 m.,* turn R onto trace. *0.1 m.,* **Hay Cemetery,** aka Hay & Gall Cemetery, est. 1856, but surviving markers back only to 1880s.

From O 99 at jct. to I-5 and Dardanelles:

O 99 becomes Blackwell Rd. *0.4 m.,* on L, late 19th century house called **"Munster House"** by some locals because of its odd design.

4.3 m., at **Tolo Tavern,** site of Tolo. Among first white occupants here were soldiers of Ft. Lane, built 1853 by Capt. Andrew J. Smith. Fort was military HQ in region until 1857, when soldiers moved out. In 1864 Willow Springs PO est. in ranch house, and mines, quarries and mills started to open. Fort was relinquished by Dept. of Interior in 1871 and then purchased by private owners, who anticipated that Willow Springs would become one of the big cities of S Oregon. In 1886 name of Willow Springs changed to Tolo. (It seems an important resident wanted to honor former county of Yolo in Calif. but postal authorities in Wash.,

Table Rock   *Courtesy State of Oregon*

D.C. mistook the Y as a T. Two years later town was platted by Paine Page Prim, Tennessee-educated lawyer who had served on state supreme court, 1859–1880, 6 years as chief justice. A year after platting Tolo he died and was buried in Portland.)

Around turn of century two brothers from New York, Col. Frank H. Ray, a financier, and Dr. Charles R. Ray, medical practitioner, began operation of rock quarry that gave Tolo unofficial title of "Construction City" of S Oregon. Rays also constructed Gold Ray Dam, area's first hydroelectric plant, built on Rogue River (1902–1904), that brought electricity to the town. Still, despite the quarry, a sawmill, brick plant, RR depot, and several on-and-off gold mines, Tolo could not grow into the city its promoters expected. In 1915 town pop. was only 150 and burg was headed downhill. PO, which closed in 1897 and had reopened again 1898, and was in Max Jacoby's "Groceries, Confectionaries, Etc." store for years, shut down for good on Dec. 4, 1918. That same year RR depot closed. In 1925 a HS student researching Tolo described the depot as having "gone to ruin like the rest of Tolo." About that time a combination hotel/boarding house burned down and another 12-room hotel had few occupants and sometimes none at all.

The legal death of Tolo came on April 1, 1986, when the Jackson County commission returned to public ownership a plat that contained 474 bldg. lots and several public streets. In essence, Tolo was officially effaced from the map and the way was clear for persons to buy up large tracts of land within the townsite without having to worry about title.

　　* L on Tolo Rd. *0.2 m.,* on L, grove in which gypsies camped in 1920s and 1930s when they came thru Tolo. *0.6 m.,* **Ft. Lane Monument,** under oak trees and near snag of lowland ponderosa pine, here called bull pine.

1.6 m., jct., I-5 and O 99. Straight on O 99.

1.4 m., Scenic Ave., Central Point.

　　* *0.8 m.,* **Crater Rock Museum,** fascinating collection, artistically displayed, of arrowheads, petrified wood, semi-precious stones, ancient rocks, and much more.

0.4 m., turnoff for downtown Central Point.

　　* *0.2 m.,* downtown **Central Point,** closet of Medford. Actually, Central Point was settled before Medford but Medford emerged as focus of commerce and transportation. The time is swift approaching, if not already here, when the lines between Medford and Central Point will be so blurred as to defy individuality.

　　1908-built school at Ash and SW 4th, now for 5th and 6th grades of Central Point, is genuine illustration for "This Was Oregon." School is 2-story brick pile topped by 2-story wooden tower.

2.8 m., jct., O 62. (See *Trans-Cascade Roads, O 62.*)

1.4 m., downtown **Medford;** jct., O 238.

Medford is another of those Oregon cities that owe their birth and at least early prominence to the RR. Before the line was built thru S Oregon, in 1883, there was virtually nothing at what is now the state's fourth largest city. The new town not only took away the business from storied Jacksonville but, in 1926, the county seat as well. Jacksonville sneered at the upstart, called it Chaparral City. Medford ignored the insult all the way to the bank. Though it has industry, Medford is perhaps best known as the processing center for a prosperous orchard area.

　　Points of interest in Medford: **Medford RR Park,** Table Rock Rd. at Berrydale Ave., miniature train rides; **Mini Park,** corner of E Main and Central, downtown, where downtown workers gather for lunch; **Bear Creek Nature Trail,** which starts at Barnett Rd. just E of I-5; **Medford Elks Bldg.** (1915), designed by noted architect Frank Chamberlain Clark in neo-classical revival style; **Frank Clark Jackson House,** 1917 E Main; **Rogue Village Art Assn. Gallery,** 40 S Bartlett; **Edgar Haver House,** now Perl Funeral Home, 426 W 6th St., built around 1906 in Colonial Revival style with unusual windows, facades and columns. Most beautiful residential district is along E Main and its immediate tributaries E of Lindley Ave.

　　From Central and Main, W for Jacksonville on O 238:

0.3 m., Oakdale Ave.

* Turn S on Oakdale. House at 615 (1885) is oldest of old houses in this part of Oakdale Ave.

0.2 m., on S side of Main, **Dr. Pickel House** (1895). Dr. Edwin D. Pickel was a Mr. Big of his time and an innovative fellow; he had first telephone in Medford and his number was, of course, 1.

1.4 m., Oak Grove Ave.

* Turn S. *0.3 m.,* turn onto Madrone Ln. *0.7 m.,* on R, down dirt lane, 1876-built, restored **Whetstone House,** at 3438 Madrone Ln. Walls are three bricks thick and rise from dug foundation to two full stories, with 12-ft. ceilings. Red brick rectangle's solid facade broken with 35 round-top windows.

1.7 m., on L, 1887 **Bybee House.** On R, Hanley Rd.

* *0.9 m.,* on Hanley Rd. The **Willows Farm Museum,** operated by S Oregon Hist. Society. Major attraction is 1875 (or 1872) **Hanley House,** large and handsome white frame mansion filled with period furnishings. Prior to construction of Hanley House here there were other structures and of these only crude stone-piled spring house remains, under farm's singular willow.

1.5 m., city center, **Jacksonville.**

Whetstone House, Medford

Site of the first great gold rush in the Oregon Country, following placer gold discoveries in 1851–52, Jacksonville had PO in 1854. Gold mining and the mercantilism, transportation and finance which grew up around it, attracted the most diverse pop. of any mining area in Oregon. Among the miners were large numbers of Chinese who, according to the testimony of old-timers, dug a tunnel that still runs under Jacksonville. The Chinese, working the longest hours and under the most difficult conditions at the most reluctant dirt, were subjected to such prejudice and harassment that finally, early in this century, they departed for San Francisco. (See "Jacksonville Voice of the Past" in author's *A Touch of Oregon*.)

Long after Jacksonville had formally given up on gold, gold became a means of survival for some families. During the Depression of the '30s, desperate farmers turned chunks of their good meadowland over to gold dredgers, receiving a 10% cut of all gold mined. The people of Jacksonville who didn't have acreage to lease to the dredgers dug shafts in their backyards and pulled out the buckets with a hand windlass. The dredging activity was halted in 1941, when the federal gvmt. set about building military camps and decided it had more need of men and equipment than of gold.

A living museum of the second half of the 19th century, intelligent restoration has made Jacksonville perhaps the most fascinating tourist town in Oregon. Artisans occupy bldgs. once holding people of earthier trades. Most of the interesting places are on the main stem, California St. Just stroll about town; there seems to be a plaque on every other bldg.

Among historic sights: **Jacksonville Museum,** occupying the courthouse built in 1884, and a must for visitors; The **Old Jail,** since 1979 a museum for children, and a marvelous one at that; **Methodist Church** (1854), oldest church in S Oregon consistently used as house of worship; **St. Joseph's Catholic Church** (1858) and **Rectory** (1861); **Dowell House** (1859); **Table Rock Saloon** (1859); **U.S. Hotel** (1880), the downstairs of which is now a bank. Pres. Hayes stayed at the hotel once and when presented his bill the next morning by the owner, a very volatile lady, Hayes is said to have replied, "Madam, I stayed here only one night. I did not purchase the hotel."

Other historic structures: **IOOF Bldg.** (1855), whose upstairs was used by Jewish pioneers as a synagogue and later, according to legend, by the Chinese as a gaming hall; **Brunner Bldg.** (1855), now town library; **Wade Morgan & Co.** (1861); **McCully House** (1860); **Beekman Bank** (1862), now a museum; **Beekman House** (1880), another museum; **Plymale House** (1865); **J. W. McCully Bldg.** (1855); **Redman's Hall** (1884); **Orth Bldg.** (1872); **Kahler's Law Office** (1875); **Herman Helms House** (1878); **Love House** (1854); **Orth House** (1850); **Ben Drew Warehouse** (1856); **Harness House** (1858); **Ryan E. Morgan Gen. Store** (1863); **Minerva Armstrong House** (1856); **First Presbyterian Church** (1881); **Glen Drum Hotel & Gen. Mdse.** (1858); **Miller Gunsmith Shop** (1858); **Martin & Zigler Blacksmith Shop** (1859); **Belle Union Saloon** (1856); **Sachs Brothers Dry Goods** (1861); **Anderson & Glen Gen. Mdse.** (1856).

Jacksonville Museum   *Courtesy State of Oregon*

Fitting in neatly with pioneer structures on California St. is **F. A. Stewart Bldg.,** put up in late 1970 by Universal Studios for filming of "The Great Northfield Minnesota Raid."

At California St., turn R onto SW Oregon.

0.2 m., on L, turnoff to **Jacksonville Cemetery** *(0.3 m.).* One of the great burial grounds of Oregon, cemetery divided into three sections: Catholic, Jewish, Protestant. Graves include those of W. G. T'Vault, the spectacular and disputatious history maker; C. C. Beekman, the legendary banker; and Peter Britt, early pho-

Beekman Bank, Jacksonville *Courtesy State of Oregon*

tographer, artist and horticulturist, honored with exhibits at Jacksonville Museum.

0.2 m., from turnoff to cemetery, on L, **Nunan House** (1890), Jacksonville's oddest structure. The 3-story, 18-room dwelling was constructed of local brick, sandstone, sugar pine, hardwood, cement, and iron grill ornamentation. It has 9 gables, stained glass windows and porch gazebo. It looks as though a committee of architects, each with own style and taste, was simultaneously set to work on constructing this bizarre creation. The story in these parts is that the owners sent off to Sears Roebuck for house plans. If so, different people must have read different catalogs.

Concerts of the annual Peter Britt Music Festival, staged in summer, are held in the air-conditioned ballroom of U.S. Hotel and on greensward of Peter Britt Estate.

Among the several distinctions of Jacksonville is that in 1856 it had a women's liberation movement of sorts, with the women carrying "pepperboxes," small pistols to protect themselves against the toughs who roamed the streets. One night, after the women had had it up to the gills, they held a meeting at which they castigated the men of the town for not providing enough defensive measures. While they were hotly airing their protests and demands, some of the men got a feminine undergarment and ran it up the flagpole. When the women emerged from the meeting, they were incensed and fired off their "pepperboxes" in rage. Fortunately, no one was injured and the garment came down. The next morning, however, two effigies were found high in a tree. The meaning was obvious, since the one representing a man was much higher than that of the woman. No one could be found who would take the effigies down but they finally fell apart thru aging.

For a short way to Ashland from Jacksonville: Take E California. *7.2 m., O 99.* Turn S.

From Central and California, Medford, on O 99:

2 m., on E, **Harry & David,** "the world's leading shipper of fine food and fruit gifts (tour thru plant) and **Jackson & Perkins Co.,** "World's largest rose grower."

3.5 m., **Phoenix,** originally known as Gasburg, or Gastown; there is no conclusive evidence for either name. Most popular legend is that name was sarcastic

Old sign at Jacksonville Cemetery   *Courtesy Ray Neufer*

tribute to stage station waitress who talked incessantly. Less accepted but more sympathetic tale is that in its very early years there were several young men but only one young woman around. She was more articulate and sharper of wit and better informed than any of her male hangers-on, thus the crude exaltation. The origin of Phoenix, too, is of dubious certainty. One point of view is that the village arose out of its ashes after a disastrous fire; the other is that the town was named after a company sign in the window of the local insurance agent, who was also the postmaster.

Settled in or about 1850, community felt itself endangered during Rogue River War and built stockade, where 15-man contingent was soon under siege. After hostilities ceased, stockade was abandoned. In 1862, Camp Baker (known of today as Fort Baker) was constructed to house First Oregon Volunteer Cavalry. Facility was terminated after Civil War; not a stick of it remains.

Phoenix is porch of Medford but has some inducements for the historical-minded. On NW corner of 2nd and Main, **Grange Hall** has shape and mien of such early 20th century halls. **Phoenix Cemetery,** 5th and Rose, est. 1857; surviving markers back to 1860s. **Samuel Colver House,** Oak and Main, built of logs sheathed with sawed lumber in 1855 by first settlers, has been stagecoach stop, inn, distillery, store, residence, antique shop.

2.5 m., from Samuel Colver House, **Talent,** initially called Wagner Creek Forks for first settler Jacob Wagner, who arrived 1852, acquired DLC, and the next year completed his house. (Name changed to Talent, for A. O. Talent, who platted town in early 1880s.) In mid-1850s, Ft. Wagner was built, at what is now 226 Talent Ave. In his diary, early overlander Wellborn Beeson wrote: "The

Nunan House, Jacksonville

Wagner 'fort' was Wagner's house with a hurriedly built heavy wall of logs as a barricade to protect the house and the people within." The only structure of Talent's pre-RR era (1880–1900) still existent is Baptist Church at 303 E Main. Other historic places, most in or near business center (0.3 m. W of O 99), include **A. P. Talen House** 108 S. Front; **Talent School/Community Hall,** 204 E. Main; **Talent Hotel,** 101 W Main; **Oddfellows Hall/Confectionary/Talent Cafe,** 201 Talent; **Knighten House,** 54 Talent; **Boarding House,** 104 I St.; Rural Gothic houses at 300 W and 110 E Wagner; Queen Anne house and Simple Queen Anne house, 316/400 Wagner Creek Rd.; **Walters Store,** W corner of I and Wagner; **Methodist Church and Parsonage** 204 and 206 S 1st.

  0.4 m., from turnoff to city center, Rapp Rd.

  * Turn W onto Rapp Rd. *1 m.,* Rapp Rd., which turns into Wagner Creek Rd. Straight. (On NW corner, **Water Irrigation History Marker:** "Near here in March 1852 Jacob Wagner diverted water for the irrigation of 69.4 acres and thereby established the first known water right in Oregon") *0.3 m.,* on L, old farmhouse, with water tower and windmill. *0.6 m.,* turn R onto Anderson Creek Rd. *0.1 m.,* on L, **Stearns Cemetery,** est. 1857; markers back to 1860s. Buried here is John Beeson, one of the great Indian reformers of the 19th century, who was driven from his home by vigilante-minded Indian haters. His simple gravestone bears humble inscription: "Pioneer and Man of Peace."

From O 99 and Rapp Rd.:

2.2 m., on W, **Jackson Hot Springs,** resort whose swimming pool is filled with 82–84 degree (F) mineral water from hot springs.

  0.8 m., on E, turnoff to Jackson House.

  * *0.4 m.,* on R, **Jackson House,** built 1854 as Eagle Mill Warehouse; of late a restaurant.

1.4 m., downtown **Ashland,** centerpiece of what is probably Oregon's most charming city. It is large enough to be more than tourist attraction and small enough to retain its grace. First settled about a decade before statehood, town was named for either Ashland, Ohio, or Ashland, Virginia; local historians disagree. PO first called Ashland Mills, because of grist mill.

A strong thread of artistry and culture runs through Ashland's history. First postmaster, Abel D. Hellman, was vociferous reader and so were some of the other pioneers. Marble works were est. 1865 and Ashland's marble craftsmen were widely recognized. Ashland was scene of annual Chautauqua series. And so it seems logical that the famed Oregon Shakespearean Festival should have been founded here. After the Chautauqua bldg. had been condemned and its dome removed, Angus Bowman, initiator of the Shakespearean Festival and for a long time director of the Shakespearean Theater, observed that the old bldg. bore a rather striking resemblance to the Globe Theater of Shakespeare's day. And so, with a "16th century" stage built, emerged the Elizabethan theater.

Contemporary Ashland has progressed quantitatively and qualitatively into

Scene from "Love's Labours Lost"　　　　　*Courtesy Oregon Shakespearean Festival*

Oregon's foremost theater city, at least on a per ratio pop. basis. The Oregon Shakespeare Festival presents plays at three theaters; in addition, several other production companies are active; one offers its works at a former church turned into a cabaret-theater. Today's Shakespearean Festival "season" is moving toward year-round performance and, with the other drama groups, show time has become anytime in Ashland. Along with its drama, Ashland has produced two excellent contemporary regional historical writers: Kay Atwood and Marjorie O'Harra.

The city, looking up to the green ramparts of the Siskiyou Mtns., is preciously located and fortunately endowed with all the requisites for natural beauty. In addition, human creativity and shrewd taste have combined to make **Lithia Park,** once famed solely for its fountains of lithia water, a decorous and utilitarian green of pleasure. Swans are traditional symbol of Lithia Park but there are also, on Ashland Creek, which runs thru park, resident woodducks and mallards.

Pioneers of lower Rogue River Valley lie in these cemeteries here: **Hargadine** (1850), at top of Sheridan St.; **Ashland** (1871), E Main and Martin; and **Mountain View** (1904), *0.5 m.,* on O 66 from O 99.

Apart from its celebration of the bard, Ashland is best-known for **Southern Oregon State College,** which almost everyone in area calls SOC (pronounced

Sock). SOC can trace its lineage back to 1869, when a quarterly conference of ME Church, held at Ashland, voted to est. Ashland Academy. But before the bldg. was completed, funds failed and the enterprise was suspended. After that came a series of ups and downs, mostly downs, until, in 1926, was ushered in Act 1 of the modern era with the opening of Southern Oregon Normal School.

On campus are **Museum of Vertebrate Natural History** and **Chappell-Swedenburg House Museum,** once the largest and most opulent residence in area.

Ashland is loaded with 19th and early 20th century homes, some of which have been turned into bed and breakfast places, and other quasi-pioneer structures. Suggested places to see for the curious, historic-minded include: Victorian houses at 115, 125, 131, 137 and 159 N Main; **Winchester Inn,** 2nd and Hargadine; **Minger House,** 80 Hargadine; **Old Pink Church,** 1st and Hargadine, now caba-ret-theater; **Baldwin Beach House** (1884), 348 Hargadine; houses at 138 and 142 Siskiyou; **E. V. Carter House,** 505 Siskiyou; **Carter Fortmiller House,** 514 Sis-kiyou; **Taverner House,** 912 Siskiyou; **James Ragland House** (1888), 91 Gresham; house at 1521 E Main (1856), 269 B St. (1889); **Mikalis Home** 455 B St.; **Petrozzi Home,** 86 Granite; **McCall House** (1883), 153 Oak; Iris Inn, 59 Man-zanita; **Morical House,** 668 N Main; old bank bldg. at 76 E Main; **Trinity Epis-copal Church** (1895); **Mark Antony Hotel;** historic old RR district.

1.4 m., — from Ashland city center — jct., O 66.

3.1 m., O 99 goes into I-5.

6.6 m., turnoff for **Mt. Ashland.**

* 0.1 m., on R, narrow uphill dirt road, slit in hillside. Park car and walk *0.1 m.* up dirt road to RR tracks. Turn L. Walk *0.1 m.* to RR tunnel. What happened here is told graphically and economically in *Oregon: End of the Trail:*

"On October 11, 1923, the three D'Autremont brothers, Hugh, 19 years of age, and Roy and Ray, 23-year-old twins, swung onto the tender of the south-bound Shasta Limited No. 13 just outside the small station of Siskiyou and ordered the engineer to stop the train, which he did at the southern end of Tunnel Number 13. Under the leadership of Hugh, the amateurs of crime shot and killed the engineer, the fireman, and a brakeman. When the mail clerk opened the mail-car door in answer to the order to come out, they shot at him but he managed to close the door in time. Unable to enter the car the bandits dynamited it, but the gases and flames from the explosion further thwarted them, and they fled into the rough Siskiyou wilderness without a penny for their efforts. In their haste, they left some supplies and other arti-cles behind them. The most important to detectives was a pair of overalls, in a pocket of which was the receipt for a registered letter signed by Hugh.

"Immediately the railroad's telegraph wires sizzled with the news. The U.S. Post Office Department threw out the largest net it had ever cast for fugitives. The Southern Pacific and the American Railway joined the state of

Oregon and the Federal government in offering dead-or-alive rewards that totaled $5,300 for each culprit. Bulletins and posters bearing pictures of the brothers appeared conspicuously in every railway station and post office in the country. Canada and Mexico also posted 'wanted' notices. The search spread to all parts of the world and descriptions of the men were issued in seven languages.

"Many fake clues were followed before a soldier early in 1927, landing in San Francisco after serving in the Philippines, noticed the resemblance between the picture of Hugh D'Autremont on a post office circular and a soldier in the 31st Infantry in the Islands. The authorities were notified and Hugh was captured on February 12 and was brought to Oregon, where he was indicted for murder.

"The trial opened on May 3 at Jacksonville, becoming the town's most important event since the gold stampedes of the 1850s. A mistrial resulted when one of the jurors died, and a second trial began on June 6 and ended on June 21, when Hugh was sentenced to life imprisonment.

"Meanwhile, the search for the twins continued and on June 8 they were arrested in Steubenville, Ohio, where they had been living and working as the Winston brothers. Ray had married and had one child. They had heard of Hugh's capture and after first denying their identity, waived extradition and were returned to Oregon, where they confessed to the crime. Hugh then admitted his guilt. The twins were also given life sentences."

At the point where the dirt road from the hwy. reaches the RR tracks stood station hamlet of **Siskiyou,** PO 1895–1932. In 1915, PS. On Dec. 17, 1887, at 5:04 p.m., a golden spike driven here completed the Siskiyou line of the SP.

The impressive name of Siskiyou deserves more noble word origin than is the case, but the vision of the heroic seldom appears in the inspiration of place names. Siskiyou is an Indian word, Cree to be exact, meaning a particular kind of horse, spotted or bobtailed or both, and perhaps a pack horse as well. In 1828, while Archibald McLeod was leading a Hudson's Bay Co. fur brigade across the mtn., his pack train was caught in a fierce snow storm. When the fury abated McLeod found that most of his pack animals, including his favorite, a bob-tailed horse, had been lost. His French-Canadian packers, in a tribute to McLeod, called the place where the storm struck Pass of the Siskiyou. In time the name was shortened to Siskiyou and extended to cover the mtn. range (which geologically is part of the Klamath Mtns.) as well as the plateau to the S (Siskiyou County, Calif.)

* From parking spot, turn R at "T". *0.7 m.,* Mt. Ashland-Colestin Jct., at 4,310-ft. Siskiyou Summit. Turn R. *1.3 m.,* turn L down Colestin Rd., a tight, twisty, bumpety backwoods pike plunging into a thorny wilderness. Let caution reign. For first 3 m. the land seems deserted. Then the road snakes into a narrow valley occupied in part by some rather affluent-looking homes. *3.4*

m., former **Hotel Colestin,** last remainder of old Colestin. Bldg. is "rural baronial," three story, with porch around second story. There is bear-like hugeness and hugness to the structure, which suggests a warm welcome and relaxed stay. People came here for the therapy of the mineral springs and a plant here bottled "Colestin Natural Mineral Water," advertised as "Recommended for kidney, stomach and rheumatic troubles, biliousness, etc." The motto of the bottler was, "A sparkling table water unequaled for medicinal properties." The village was also famous as a camping ground. (Private property.) *l m.,* site of **Deter,** whose story is told by Geraldine Deter, an in-law of the founding family:

Tunnel 13, Siskiyou

"Deter post office was established 20th March, 1920, in the home of David Milton Deter and Grace Bray Deter, his wife, who was the postmaster till the office was closed 31st December, 1931. In order to get to Deter by motor vehicle it was necessary to drive on highway 99 over Siskiyou Pass to Hilt, California, proceed north on the valley floor up Cottonwood Creek for about 5 miles. Colestin, a former soda springs resort, was another mile north. Colestin lost their post office when most of the people moved away. Deter was established consequently. There was a flag stop, siding and section house and crew at Gregory but because there were several offices by that name postal authorities agreed to the name of Deter. As usual it was an in-house office and store. The postmaster received her pay by stamp cancellations. Mr. Deter was paid to carry the mail bags to Gregory, a distance of about 100 yds.

"The main source of transportation was the Southern Pacific railroad, which had three passenger trains, numbers 12, 14, 16 north and 11, 13, 15 south each day. Numbers 11 and 12 were through trains but the other four could be flagged down. There were three or four freight engines each way every day. They required helper engines to push freight up the mountains from Hornbrook. After the Natron cut-off through the eastern part of the state, the trains were greatly decreased, the people moved away. The Deter school was reduced to two pupils in 1930. In 1928 and 1929 I had 12 pupils. The school district transported the few remaining children to Hilt, Calif.

"The Greek brothers, George, Theodore and Gust Avgeris, operated quite a large sawmill just west of Deter. The post office was again moved to Colestin where the Avgeris families now lived (1932), another in-house office-store. When it was discontinued the mail came from Hilt. When the Deters sold their ranch they moved to Medford and the P.O. was discontinued.

"Logging was the principal industry which made Deter a busy little place in fair weather. The Deter School District #97 was a very rich one, a very large area with land owned by Southern Pacific, U.S. Forest Service and Fruitgrowers Supply Co., who maintained several logging camps and miles of railroad for carrying logs to their sawmill in Hilt, Calif.

"The valuation of Dist. #97 in 1929 was assessed at $415,384.89, with a school tax of 1 mill. School census was 20 with average daily attendance of 11.1. D. M. Deter was chairman of the board; Grace Deter, his wife, clerk. Geraldine Redmond, who later became a Deter, was the teacher in 1928 and 1929. Because of the bad roads in the winter school opened in March and closed in November. At that time, 1929, there were two other "summer" schools in Jackson County, Climax and Pinehurst. In later years the county graded the roads and a northbound road from Colestin to Siskiyou Summit was made. This eliminated the Hilt detour and the children now meet the bus on the Ski Bowl road and are transported to the Ashland School."

Thus the small saga of a mtn. community of which no trace remains.

* From Colestin Rd. W: Mark Lawrence, resident and student of Jackson County history, wrote: "Two tenths of a mile beyond the Colestin Rd. turn-off the 1863 telegraph line passes overhead. A marker which I helped set on the right hand side of the road marks it and the old toll road. About a quarter

Mt. Ashland Ski Lodge   *Courtesy State of Oregon*

of a mile south was the site **Riddleburg** (Hell Town). The last stagecoach passed through here in the fall of 1887 with the completion of the railroad. All written reports indicate that Riddleburg was a very tough place. However, if there were any saints running stagecoach lines or constructing railroads, I never happened to read about them." *7.5 m.,* **Mt. Ashland Ski Lodge,** at 7,523-ft. Mt. Ashland. With or without skiing, whatever season, the views of wild mountains and forests and skies that seem larger than ever are a gallery of Turner paintings, Beethoven's Ninth, a sea of wind, a triumph of roses. Return to old 99. This is the way it was before the freeway — sharp rises and falls, deceptive curves, 2-lane. *4.9 m.,* I-5. *0.8 m.,* Calif. line.

Via I-5 from Siskiyou Summit: *4.3 m.,* Calif. line.

Trans-Cascade Roads

I-84
Portland to Biggs Jct.

I-84 is the great river road of the Pacific Northwest, running with the Columbia to the open plains of Eastern Oregon. In the west the land is moist and timbered, with cliffs and mountains narrowing the range of the sky. Beyond The Dalles, the land flattens and the sky is enormously enlarged. To be sure, hills and buttes and cliffs live there, but they seem ancient, remote, and looking as though they were stenciled into the landscape.

Along this river came a procession of history: Indians of a dozen tribes, Lewis and Clark, the Astorians, trappers and traders of furs, caravaners bound for their Beulah Land, the iron horse that bent time.

There are no mountains to cross from Portland to the eastern counties. Beyond the rush of traffic west of The Dalles there is only the spread-out land and its vibrating silence and loneliness. The river is the road's constant, yet the river of the wheatlands is not the river of the woods. Sun gives way to shadow, the journeyman changes into the artist. Traveling east, the oil painting is removed, leaving an empty picture frame. The Columbia changes faces as though it were a slide presentation. And that, too, is what the road is, a slide show. One has the feeling that at any moment the lights will be turned on and the illusion will disappear.

From Portland: Alder and SW 3rd. (Cross Morrison Bridge.)

11 m., turnoff to Blue Lake Park, Fairview, Gresham.

3.8 m., Wood Village — Gresham turnoff.

  * *3.1 m.,* Gresham.

0.5 m., turnoff to Columbia River Scenic Hwy. (See *Columbia River Gorge,* preceding).

.5 m., Troutdale exit. *1.1 m.,* turnoff to Lewis and Clark SP. (See *Columbia River Gorge,* preceding.)

2.6 m., Chatham Island, in Columbia. *1.5 m.,* Corbett exit. (See *Columbia River Gorge,* preceding.)

Now the traveler is fully into the Columbia River Gorge, surely one of the scenic beauties of this nation. So remarkable are the vistas, going E or W, that one who has passed thru the gorge a thousand times is no less moved on the thousand and first passage. The gorge is never twice the same: light and wind and point of perspective and river pastels see to that.

Probably the most vivid imagery of the Columbia Gorge was penned in 1843 by John C. Fremont as he led a small party to probe southern Oregon and northern Calif.:

"Mount Hood is glowing in the sunlight this morning, and the air is pleasant, with a temperature of 38 degrees. We continued down the river, passing through a pretty green valley, bounded by high precipitous rocks . . .

"The canoe sailed smoothly down the river; at night we encamped upon the shore, and a plentiful supply of comfortable provisions supplied the first of our wants.

"We enjoyed the contrast which it presented to our late toilsome marchings; our night watchings, and our frequent privation of food. We were a motley group, but all happy, three unknown Indians; Jacob, a colored man; Mr. Preuss, a German; Bernie, creole French; and myself.

" . . . The wind rose to a gale after several hours; but the moon was very bright, and the wind was fair, and the canoe glanced rapidly down the stream, the waves breaking into a foam alongside; and our night voyage, as the wind bore us rapidly along between the dark mountains, was wild and interesting. About midnight we put to the shore on a rocky beach, behind which was a dark-looking pine forest. We built up large fires among the rocks, which were in large masses round about; and, arranging our blankets in the most sheltered places we could find, passed a delightful night.

" . . . We glided on without interruption between very rocky and high steep mountains, which sweep along the river valley at a little distance, covered with forests of pine, and showing occasionally lofty escarpments of red rock. Nearer the shore is bordered by steep escarped hills and huge vertical rocks, from which the waters of the mountains reach the river in a variety of beautiful falls, sometimes several hundred feet in height. Occasionally along the river occurred pretty bottoms, covered with the greenest verdure of the spring."

In recent years, there has been a struggle as to the future of the Gorge, with conservationists and private ownership tugging for the very soul of this monumental glory.

2.3 m., on N, Rooster Rock, obviously named. 0.4 m., turnoff to **Rooster Rock SP.**

> * 0.6 m., SP. PA, swimming, fishing, boating, FHP. The park gained increased attention when part of the beach become a mecca for nudists. In the beginning some of the garbed and curious brought field glasses, then the scene became old hat. Lewis and Clark camped here on their return journey and made another note of Beacon Rock (the first made when headed W.) Fur trader Alexander Ross, who passed by some years later, called the monolith Inshoach Castle. But this sentimental gesture to his native Scotland did not survive, and Beacon Rock it remained.

2.6 m., on S, two sharp-tipped rocks between which pass RR tracks. Rocks are commonly known as **Pillars of Hercules** but to the early settlers they were equally known as Speelyei's Children, in honor of the mythical Indian coyote god.

0.4 m., turnoff to Bridal Veil and Bridal Veil SP. (See Columbia River Gorge, preceding.)

2.7 m., turnoff to **Benson SP.**

* *0.4 m.,* SP, a surge of open-wooded greenery facing pond and looking up to cliffs. Clearly seen is **Mist Falls,** winging off a 1,200 foot-high escarpment. PA, swimming, fishing, boating, FHP.

0.5 m., turnoff to **Multnomah Falls.** (See *Columbia River Gorge.*)

4.1 m., turnoff to Ainsworth SP.

* R on Scenic Hwy. *0.4 m.,* turn L. *0.2 m.,* **Ainsworth SP CG.** *0.4 m.,* Ainsworth SP PA. Return to jct. Straight. *0.3 m.,* turn R onto Frontage Rd. *0.5 m.,* Dodson, orphan hamlet looking for a ghost. (See *Columbia River Gorge.*)

2.3 m., turnoff to **Yeon SP.**

* SP. Trails to two impressive waterfalls. (See *Columbia River Gorge.*)

2.8 m., turnoff to **Bonneville Dam,** which celebrated its 50th anniversary in the summer of 1987. The dam was authorized in 1933, at the height of the Great Depression, as a federal works project. With 13 million unemployed in the US, the $20 million given for construction of Bonneville Lock and Dam was a lifesaver for the region. Pres. FDR dedicated Bonneville Dam Sept. 28, 1937. Then, the same day, he was driven to Timberline Lodge and dedicated that facility. At the time Bonneville Dam was dedicated, a segment of the media sneered at it as the "Dam of Doubt" and "Roosevelt's White Elephant."

* *1.2 m.,* **Bradford Island Regional Center,** where orientation tours of dam complex start. (See *Columbia River Gorge.*)

1.5 m., turnoff to **Cascade Fish Hatchery and Eagle Creek Park.** FS CG, PA, one of best-known Oregon trailheads. (See *Columbia River Gorge.*)

2 m., — from W exit or *1.4 m.,* from E exit — turnoff to Cascade Locks and Bridge of the Gods.

* *0.4 m.,* turnoff to Bridge of the Gods. *0.2 m.,* Cascade Locks. (For both, see *Columbia River Gorge.*)

1.4 m., Wyeth turnoff.

* *0.3 m.,* jct. Turn L. *0.1 m.,* site of what was **Wyeth,** never more than a "tie pickling plant," or a plant applying creosote to ties. Thus was honored Nathaniel J. Wyeth, the Massachusetts ice merchant who came W in 1832 and 1834 to make a fortune and returned home both times empty-handed. Among those in his 1834 party were naturalists Thomas Nuttall and J. K. Townsend, both important names in pioneer Oregon science, and John Ball, first school teacher in the Oregon Country and an early — though brief — settler on French Prairie. Unlike most other entrepreneurs of his time, Wyeth was a man of vision, who thought big and intended to stay in Oregon rather than return home as soon as he had made a fortune. But he could not win for losing; everything he bent his hand to turned sour. (For more an Nathaniel Wyeth, see *Trips Out of Portland, Sauvie Island,* this book, and "A Wayward Marker on Sauvie Island" in author's *A Touch of Oregon.*) In 1915, place name of Wyeth reached zenith, with PS and pop. of 80. When creosote plant moved out, people followed.

 * Return to jct. Turn R. *0.1 m.,* **Wyeth FS CG.** Wyeth Trail begins in park. *6.2 m.* hike to jct., Mt. Defiance Trail.
4 m., turnoff to **Starvation Creek SP.**

Starvation Creek Falls   *Courtesy State of Oregon*

*0.2 m., parking for SP. PA, FHP. 0.2 m., **Starvation Creek Falls,** a pretty picture any time of the year. Starvation Creek pushes thru cleft in a Cascade wall and ricochets and spumes and plumes in windblown waves about 80 ft. to a shelf, then leaps about another 80 ft. to a jumble of rocks, then rolls as a creek again thru the park. A marker in park reads:

"The plaque below was originally displayed on the Columbia River Scenic Hwy. at Shell Rock Mt., a little more than two miles to the West.

" 'Construction of the Columbia River Highway began here in 1912/ Funds were contributed by Simon Benson/ Labor was performed by Honor Men detailed by Governor Oswald West.' "

It seems rather obvious that the "Honor Men" were convicts who weren't stirring up any trouble at the state pen. At least that is the message most readers of the plaque receive.

From the parking lot a trail paralleling I-84 at trail's start leads 400 yds. to **Cabin Creek Falls,** another 800 yds. to **Hole-in-the Wall Falls,** and 4.5 m. on to summit of 4,960 ft. **Mt. Defiance.**

Starvation Creek received its name from a then widely publicized episode. Across freeway, at RR tracks, a train in 1884 was marooned for two weeks in 30 ft. snowdrifts. Passengers burned all the coal, then the car seats, finally whatever combustible materials they could find to keep from freezing. Folklore has it that some people were boiling their leather shoes for victuals. A rescue party prevented starvation.

From where the train was stalled there is a magnificent view of the Columbia Gorge.

0.9 m., turnoff to **Viento SP.**

* 0.4 m., SP. CG, PA, showers on Viento Creek. Viento is Spanish for "wind" and the wind here can throw cars around like paper plates when its temper is up. However, according to McArthur's *Oregon Geographic Names,* RR station here received its name by taking the first two letters of three men prominent in RR building: Villard, Endicott, and Tolman. In 1915 a hamlet had arisen about the RR station: it had store, PS, was minor market for farm, livestock and fruit growing, had daily boats to Portland, and boasted pop. 41.

6 m., turnoff to West Hood River.

* 0.9 m., jct. Turn L onto Westcliff Dr. 0.1 m., turn L again, continuing on Westcliff Dr. 0.2 m., **Columbia Gorge Hotel,** historic inn whose site as a rest for travelers (now tourists) dates back years before Robert Rand, Hood River businessman, built his Waw-Gwin-Gwin Hotel, in 1903. Rand remembered:

"This used to be a great meeting place for the Indians in the early days ... It was taken up by John Dye and his squaw. I bought it from a man named Amen and paid twenty-eight hundred dollars for forty-three acres. People thought I was an easy mark to pay that amount for forty-three acres of rocks and oak trees that stretched along the bluffs which overlooked the Columbia. They didn't know that sunsets and waterfalls, rugged old oaks and huge heaps of weather-worn rocks had any commercial value, but for every nickel I put into this place, I will take a dollar out."

During the years of passenger vessel travel on the Columbia, steamers approaching the hotel would announce the number of room guests on board by tooting the whistle — two for two room guests, six for six room guests. Given the word, or the whistle, maids would make up the appropriate number of rooms.

In 1920, Rand sold his Waw-Gwin-Gwin Hotel and the 23 acres surrounding it to lumber baron Simon Benson for $35,000. Rand's place was torn down and on the site was constructed the Columbia Gorge Hotel, a three-story stucco bldg. with Spanish-style red tile roofs, towers and long sun porches, perched on the edge of a basaltic cliff.

Benson had originally agreed to put up $300,000 for the hotel but before he shelled out the last dollar for construction and furnishings, he had spent between four and five hundred thousand. Do not weep: Benson got his money back and, in addition, the project added to his stature as a champion of tourism and a devoted friend of the state. With Cecil Rhodes, Benson could have said, "Philanthropy is all very well but philanthropy plus ten percent interest is much better."

Fluctuating with the economic winds, the hotel has had several changes of ownership and from 1952 to 1978 was retirement home operated by Neighbors of Woodcraft. Legend has it that among the celebrities hosted here were prominent Hollywood personalities, including Rudolph Valentino, who supposedly used the inn as a hideaway. Capitalizing on this bit of trivia, the hotel has a Valentino Lounge.

The original hotel received its name, Waw-Gwin-Gwin, Indian for running water, from a small waterfall, which somersaults 207 ft. to lagoon rubbing shoulders with the Columbia.

* From hotel, return to first turn from hotel, turn R, across freeway, take first road to R, Country Club Rd. 1.5 m., turn R onto Post Canyon Rd. 0.4 m., turn R onto Westwood Dr. 0.4 m., **Hood River Vineyards.**

* Return to Country Club Rd. Follow 1.9 m. to Oak Grove Park. At edge is **Oak Grove School** (1912–1969), four-room, two-story school now residence. Occupants are besieged by visitors, many of them former students, some who walk into the house without knocking.

On I-84, from West Hood River turnoff:

1.6 m., Hood River City Center exit.

* 0.4 m., **Hood River** city center.

* The stream Hood River was first known as Dog River because some starving travelers ate dog meat on its banks. Undoubtedly a good many explorers, voyagers, trappers and mariners passed this way before 1854, when

Nathaniel Coe and family arrived from New York, together with the brothers Nathan and James Benson and William Jenkins and his wife, but little was written about the area, Mt. Hood excepted. Where is now the city center is where the Coe farm was developed; the home was the community center for many years. Town's first industry was making oak kegs for whiskey trade in gold mining country of Idaho and E Oregon. There was probably more drama in the early days, when transportation was by river steamer and the only overland route was a rough trail to The Dalles.

Probably prize tourist attraction in town is **Hood River Museum,** in 1978 bldg. near waterfront — lovingly organized documentation of life in county from Indians to apple growers. Inscribed in Japanese on steel outside museum are lines from poem, "Morning", by Shizue Inatuski:

Stele outside Hood River Museum

In the light of the morning sun
On the Columbia River
A wheat-laden tugboat is sailing.
Look! A Japanese ship is anchored.

"Morning" reflects a 180-degree turn in Hood River County attitude toward Japanese Americans, whose property was greedily pounced upon when they were shipped off to desert camps during World War II and who, even servicemen, were vilely treated at War's end.

In recent years, Hood River has advertised itself as sailboarding and windsurfing "Capital of the World." The activities have revitalized Hood River's economy and brought a swath of flair to the otherwise staid community. All the necessary ingredients, including steady winds at high speed and plenty of water, are here for windsurfing.

In 1987, 81 years after the line opened, the 22-mile-long Parkdale branch of the Union Pacific was purchased by the city of Hood River. In the spring of 1988, passenger travel resumed after a long absence, with the focus on tourism.

* From 4th and Oak, Hood River: W to 13th and Oak. Turn L. *0.4 m.,* turn L. *0.1 m.,* turn R. *1.5 m.,* three cemeteries adjacent to each other: **Mountain View, Catholic, Hood River,** all founded circa 1875. *1.2 m.,* turn L. *2 m.,* Odell Jct. Straight, *0.6 m.,* on L, 2525 Odell Hwy., farmhouse prizing three-seater outhouse that once belonged to famed "sawdust trail" evangelist Billy Sunday. (See *Trips Out of Portland, Mt. Hood Loop,* preceding.) *2 m.,* **Odell,** cheery little apple town brimming with entre-nous social activities. R at jct., *0.4 m.,* **Tucker CP,** PA on Hood River. *6.3 m.,* Dee Jct. Started as company sawmill town, **Dee** had pop. 250 in 1915, together with privately owned water works and electric lighting system and was on Hood River RR. By 1940 pop. down to 100. Gradually, Dee declined to rural neighborhood. R at Dee Jct.: *5.5 m.,* on L, **White Bridge Park.** CG in woods. *2.5 m.,* jct. L, Lolo Pass. (To US 26 and Zigzag, *20.9 m.*) R, to forks, *5.7 m.,* Take R fork, to Lost Lake. *1.5 m.,* **Lost Lake,** one of prettiest lakes in state and on a clear day a perfect mirror of Mt. Hood. FS CG, store. (See *Short Trips Out of Portland, Lolo Pass.*)

* L at Dee Jct.: turn for Parkdale. *6.6 m.,* Baseline Rd. Turn R. *1.2 m.,* **Lava Beds,** among most recent flow of Mt. Hood. Jumbled mass of volcanic rock is 0.5 m. to 0.8 m. in width. Average height of flow above E side farms is 100 to 200 ft.; elevations vary from 1800 ft. on N end to 2900 ft. at eruption overlook at S. End. Return to Parkdale Rd. *0.1 m.,* **Parkdale,** aptly named. An open village settled in first decade of this century, Parkdale has all the charm of a country marketplace in a most enchanting setting. Few areas in all Oregon can equal the beauty of the undulating Hood River Valley, with its quick streams, sun-spiked woods, sponged green meadows and, above all, orchard after orchard plunging and rising until lost in the maw of Cascade

shadows. And Parkdale has a bit of history: Early on it became N terminus of Mt. Hood RR and was RR point for tourists going to Cloud Cap. In recent years, the most conspicuous change in Parkdale has been the seasonal influx of Hispanic workers, who in the gentle warmth of spring arrive to turn Parkdale into a bilingual village.

* *0.5 m.*, to S, Cooper Spur Jct. Take R, Cooper Spur Rd. *2 m.*, London Rd. House on SE corner, owned by Jess Hutson, is rock museum, gathered by man who vows he traveled 900,000 miles, thru every vein of the W, to assemble his collection,. Visitors welcome. *6.1 m.*, turn for Cloud Cap. (On L is alpine-image restaurant. This area has exploded in recent years, with high-priced homes arising as the woods are slashed away.)

* On Cloud Cap Rd.: *1 m.*, turnoff to Cooper Spur Ski Area. (*0.8 m.*, ski area.) *3.7 m.*, **Inspiration Point.** (Turnout for parking.) Exceptional views, including one of Wallalute Falls, from 5,000 ft. elev. *5.1 m.*, jct. To L, *0.4 m.*, **Tilly Jane FS CG,** high in the high trees. According to ring-counts on trees damaged by volcanic ash, Mt. Hood last erupted about 1800. Return to Cloud Cap Rd. *0.6 m.*, Timberline Trail. *0.2 m.*, parking below **Cloud Cap Inn.** At 6,000 ft. elev. here you feel much higher, so pure is the air and so far-reaching the vistas.

The rustic log cabin, anchored to the mtn. by cables so as to withstand winter winds, was built 1889 as a six-room hotel. The trip from Hood River was often made in one day. An 1890 schedule had the journey this way: From Portland to Hood River via the Union Pacific or the steamer *Bailey Gatzert*. The next morning, stagecoach for 10 m. to Little Luckamas, arriving in time for lunch. Stage with four fresh horses to Elk Beds. There, six fresh horses hitched to coach and these pulled passengers to Cloud Cap Inn. Later, passengers took train at Hood River all the way to Parkdale and completed journey by stage. It must have been a trying undertaking for the horses and no doubt some of the passengers had apprehensions. In 1941 the inn was closed and would have been torn down if not for intervention of Crag Rats, mtn.-climbing group. Former inn is today basically rescue operations HQ and when Hood climbers are missing the alpine structure is a very busy place. Short hike from inn to end of rock-strewn path leads to aerie confrontation with Eliot Glacier.

* From Cloud Cap Rd. jct.: *2.4 m.*, jct., O 35. (See *Short Trips Out of Portland, Mt. Hood Loop*.)

From City Center Exit, Hood River, on I-84:

0.5 m., jct., O 35 (see *Mt. Hood Loop*) and White Salmon Bridge, across Columbia. *2.5 m.*, W-bound access only, **Koberg Beach SP.** PA, fishing, FHP. *2.8 m.*, Mosier Exit.

* *0.4 m.*, **Mosier,** yawning village of about 400 whose city center is the gas station. Settled in 1850s as stage station, town grew into marketplace of prosperous fruit-growing area that achieved recognition for its delicious apple

cider. By 1915 it had grown to pop. 750, with HS, PS, four churches, five lodges, Development League, Farmers' Union, weekly paper and privately owned electric lighting plant. But hard times struck, people moved away, and in 1940 pop. had dropped to 192. From service station, turn R. One-half block on L, marker denoting remnant of wagon trail built in 1872 from The Dalles to Sandy. Turn L at corner. One block, **First Christian Church** (1910), Mosier's most important historic landmark.

* *0.3 m.,* just beyond bridge, dirt trail on R uphill 200 yds. to split rail **Pioneer Cemetery.** Six markers, the oldest 1865. *1.7 m.,* on L, **Mayer Mansion,** three-story white house with graceful columns, reminiscent of antebellum mansions of mid-South. House built 1914 by Portland businessman Mark Mayer as country home on farm of 250 acres; has four bedrooms on 2d floor, three on 3rd.

The **"Scenic Loop,** which is what this road is called, winds up to and along a plateau that affords moving views of the Columbia and its basaltic cliffs and rock canyons as cannot be seen from the freeway. This was once US 30 — the main road in these parts — and squirming around it at 30 m. per hour you can understand why a water-level route was desperately needed. There is yet a pioneer character to the tawny plateau, which breaks into ridges and drops into deep defiles.

* *4.3 m.,* turn R for **Rowena Crest.** The viewpoint is a semi-circle that seems suspended in mid-air. Seen here is the graceful geometry of the road at three levels; the imperial march of the Columbia; and, on the Wash. side, groaning cliffs, the wind-bleached town of Lyle, and the Klickitat River pushing into the Columbia. It's quite breezy on the Crest, so hang on to your whatever.

* *0.3 m.,* turn R on Rowena Crest Rd. *0.1 m.,* on L, **Tom McCall Preserve,** overlooking Rowena Plateau and the Columbia. The preserve, a part of The Nature Conservancy network, was dedicated early in April, 1982, a few days after McCall's mother, Dorothy Lawson McCall, passed away, at the age of 93. Ten months later McCall himself was dead, another statistic of cancer. The preserve contains 167.19 acres, extends from the freeway to the plateau, and contains, in the words of The Nature Conservancy, "biscuit scablands as well as Missoula Flood remnants, a tremendous spring wildflower display and permanent and seasonal ponds. Columbia lomatium (*Lomatium columbianum*) and Hood River milk vetch (*Astragalus hoodianus*) are found on the site, both of which are Columbia River endemics."

On Rowena Dell Plateau, New York artist Michelle Stuart and her artist helpers produced a form of art little known in Oregon, sculpture in terms of piles of rounded stones, interfaced in imaginative configuration. *Oregonian* reporter Beth Fagan described it best: "The 100-foot-wide circle, with pyramidal sunrise and sunset, cairns atop mounds on its perimeter, opposite their stone siting circles, is called 'Stone Alignments — Solstice Cairns.' "

2.1 m., turnoff L for **Mayer SP.** *(0.6 m.,* SP, on Columbia. PA, fishing, swimming, boating.) The turnoff marks end of "Scenic Loop" but for more off-beat terrain continue on old road. *1 m.,* **Rowena,** a fuzz of houses, striking up the whimsy of a gypsy camp. The loose enclave is about midway in Rowena Gap, geologic formation created by the Columbia cutting 4 m. thru the anticlinal ridge of these hills.

It is rather universally conceded that The Dalles was the end of the Old Oregon Trail, meaning as far as wagons could go W without detouring, as on the Barlow Trail. In reality, the wagons could go as far as Rowena Bluffs. From here on W, voyage was by river craft, often rafts. Even with experienced mariners and study oarsmen, the journey rarely took less than four days and, with the river becalmed or exceptionally furious, could take more than two weeks.

A sentry of Cloud Gap

* From Rowena, 8.8 m., downtown The Dalles.
From Mosier Jct., on I-84:
4.3 m., Rest Area.

On W-bound side is **Memaloose SP** (CG, DS, showers, FHP), noted for its bit of romantic history centered on a small island in the Columbia. For hundreds of years this rocky intrusion in the river was an Indian burial ground and was known to the Warm Springs tribe as "Island of the Dead." At one time, the isle was covered with burial houses but these were destroyed by the high water of 1894. When it became known that Bonneville Dam would raise the river and cause it to overflow much of the island's three acres, the last bones of the deceased Indians were disinterred from the sandy grave pits and removed to the Wash. mainland. On the shrunken half-acre isle there is now only a white granite shaft. Under it sleeps a white man, Victor Trevitt, and therein hangs a tale.

The New Hampshire-born Trevitt, after learning the printer's trade in Ohio and serving in the Mexican War of 1847, came to Oregon with the American Rifle Regiment. He first lived in the Willamette Valley, most notably at Oregon City, where he reentered the printing trade. In 1854, at age 27, he moved to The Dalles, where he became a land promoter, tavernkeeper, gambler and politician. He was a member of the first state legislature and served in the state senate from 1866 to 1874. His first wife, from whom he was later separated, was part Indian; his second, the widow of a judge. Between the two are encompassed Trevitt's philosophy and his stress upon stature. (Not for the sake of humility did he delight in being called "Major.")

In The Dalles, Trevitt deepened his sympathies and his love for the Indians and at a time when anti-Indian fever ran high, Trevitt was sometimes their lone white partisan in town. His views and semi-bohemian life brought on the adjectives of "colorful" and "eccentric" and he was more at home in cosmopolitan San Francisco, where he died on Jan. 23, 1883, at age 56, four months after his second marriage. His body was brought back to The Dalles and then carried to Memaloose Island.

The request to be buried there, put down in writing, shows the direction to which his heart pointed: "I have but one desire after I die, to be laid away on Memaloose Island with the Indians. They are more honest than the whites, and live up to the light they have. In the resurrection, I will take my chances with the Indians."

(According to historian Edwin D. Culp [*Oregon The Way It Was*] the Indians, rather than feel flattered, resented the intrusion of a white man and "never again buried their own dead on the island; in fact, many removed their relatives, believing the area had been contaminated by allowing a white man to be buried here.")

(There is a story in The Dalles told by the descendants of persons who knew Victor Trevitt. He died in the winter and all that season his body was kept at The Dalles because the Columbia was frozen. Came spring, his male friends chartered a sternwheeler and, with a brass band playing and beer rapidly being depleted from kegs, Trevitt's body was taken to Memaloose Island for a rousing burial.)

Champions of Victor Trevitt proclaim him to be a man completely free of racial prejudice, a noble characteristic for a Westerner of his time. Not quite. Trevitt was openly bigoted toward blacks and carried his hostility into the state legislature. For example: in 1868, as senator from Wasco County, he introduced a resolution rescinding legislative approval two years earlier of the 14th Amendment.

2.5 m., turnoff to Rowena and Mayer SP. *7.6 m.,* turnoff to city center, **The Dalles.** (*0.8 m.,* city center.)

Without shadow of a doubt, The Dalles is the most interesting city between Portland and the Idaho line on I-84 and one of the most historic-laden in the state. Almost every literate person who came thru, even before there was a white settlement, wrote of the site. Here, where the rapids and narrows formed an interstice between navigable portions of the Columbia, travelers were awed and terror-stricken. William Clark wrote that "a tremendious black rock Presented itself high and Steep appearing to choke up the river . . . at this place the water of this great river is compressed into a channel between two rocks not exceeding forty five yards wide and continues of a 1/4 of a mile when it again widens." With the agreement of the party's most experienced waterman, the one-eyed fiddler, Peter Cruzatte, Clark gambled on getting his canoes thru the cauldron: "accordingly I deturmined to pass through this place notwithstanding the horrid appearance of this agitated gut swelling, boiling + whorling in every direction, which from the top of the rock did not appear as bad as when I was in it; however, we passed safe to the astonishment of all the Inds . . ."

The Indians, who gathered here from as far W as the Oregon Coast and as far E as the Bitterroot Mtns. (and perhaps the plains beyond) called this place *Winquatt* and *Wascopam.* To Lewis and Clark the site was "the great [Indian] mart of all this country." Clark was more specific: "Ten different tribes who reside on Taptate [Yakima] and Catteract [Klickitat] River visit those people for the purpose of purchasing their fish, and the Indians on the Columbia and Lewis's [Snake] River quite to the Chopunnish [Nez Perce] Nation visit them for the purpose of tradging horses buffalow robes for beeds, and such articles as they have not. The Skillutes precure most of their cloth knivs, axes, + beeds from the Indians from the North of them who trade with white people who come into the inlets to the North at no great distance from the Tapteet."

Here, too, was probably the first toll passage in the Oregon Country, Indians with muscle forcing on other Indians a fee for the privilege of continuing their journeys. Those Indians who did not trade profited richly in fishing, and then there were those who lived by glib tongues and swift hands. Nathaniel Wyeth observed that the Wascopam were genial but "habitual thieves." Other white travelers had stronger words. What the Indians thought of chauvinistic whites was not recorded, but one can imagine.

The Dalles received its name from French speaking *voyageurs* of Hudson's Bay Co. who saw in the basaltic walls of the narrows a reflection of the flagstones *(les dalles)* in their villages far away. Some years ago, the local Chamber of Commerce issued a brochure purporting to give a true derivation of The Dalles and to this end quoted a talk given by Dr. William C. McKay to the Ladies Aid Society in 1869:

"The early French *voyageurs* knew the falls of the Columbia at the Indian fishery six miles above this place as *Le Dalle,* signifying a trough — literally a trough of the Columbia. It has always been regarded by them as the most dangerous point in navigating the river, and it was customary at the proper stage of the Columbia to run their boats down the rapids, which always required great courage, dexterity and experience. But often, with all these accomplishments, many a poor *voyageur* found a watery grave in the whirlpools, and none can tell of his resting place. Within my own recollection many have perished in its turbulent waters. It is a noted point and much dreaded by them; consequently, they gave it the name of *'Le Grand Dalle de la Columbia'* — The Great Trough of the Columbia." (The brochure added: "It is now covered by the pool behind The Dalles Dam.")

There is only one problem with the above: neither Dr. McKay nor the Chamber of Commerce took the time to consult a French dictionary — there is no word in the French language resembling *dalles* as trough.

Some of the more daring *voyageurs* shot their canoes thru the rapids but the cautious used their own labor power or Indian help to portage. Nathaniel Wyeth hired about 50 Indians to carry his party's boats about a mile around the falls, paying each "a quid of tobacco."

Jason Lee passed this way in 1834 and four years later his nephew, Daniel Lee, together with another Methodist ordained minister, H. K. W. Perkins, est. the 2d mission in the Mid-Columbia country. (The first was founded on the lower Walla Walla River by Dr. Marcus Whitman in 1836.) Not to be outdone, the Catholic padres followed in 1841 and the battle for souls was on. So intense was the rivalry that little time was available to Christianize the Indians, which probably did the Indians no harm.

Much of the drama of early Oregon was centered in and around The Dalles. Here soldiers gathered to organize war against the Indians and here, as an official point, the emigrants pulled up their wagon trains on the last mile of the Old Oregon Trail. John Minto, writing in Oct., 1844, observed: "We got to The Dalles and went into camp near the mission. We found it was Sunday, and we had camped right against the log building in which service was held in preaching to the Indians. We felt like trespassers, and had no right to complain of cold treatment, as our disregard of the Sabbath was an added obstacle to the objects of the missionaries."

George A. Waggoner (*Stories of Old Oregon*) arrived eight years after Minto and observed a wild Western scene: "After weary days we reached the place on the eighth day of October. The first of the immigration had crossed the Cascades with their teams, but the snow now lay deep on the summit, and no one could cross it. Several hundred were trying to get boats to go down the Columbia River, and each day some were starting down in Canoes which they bought from the Indians. Some made flatboats, and some were being taken in yawl boats. There were no permanent residents at The Dalles, but some soldiers were building a log fort there. We secured two large Indian canoes, fastened them about six feet apart, laid a floor of boards across them, and with some others we paddled out on the great Columbia with our novel craft. What a bliss it was to move along without the pain of walking on sore feet."

By 1852, when Waggoner arrived, the Barlow Toll Road had been open for six years. It had been laid out by Kentuckian Samuel Kimbrough Barlow, who vowed, "God never made a mountain He didn't make a way to get over it." The road, built in partnership with Philip Foster, who ran a large emigrant stop at Eagle Creek, led S from The Dalles to Tygh Valley, where a trail was cut thru the timber to the W, and emerged at Laurel Hill. (Only 12 years earlier another Samuel Barlow, a Mass. doctor, had proposed a RR from NY to the Columbia.)

On Jan. 11, 1854, Wasco County was est. by the territorial legislature; name derived from Wascopam word "wacq-o," meaning cup or bowl, a description fitting the geography of The Dalles. When created, the county was the largest in the US, embracing all the land lying E of the Cascade Range, between the Columbia River and the Calif. line, to the summit of the Rockies, taking in all of Oregon E of the Cascades, most of Idaho and parts of Wyoming and Montana.

The Dalles has had numerous firsts. At least two are worthy of mention: the first newspaper (*Journal*, 1859) between the Upper Missouri and the Cascades, published by the commandant of Ft. Dalles, and the first coeducational institution of learning (Wascoe Independent Academy, 1882) at HS level E of the Cascades. On a footnote of trivia, it had the first plant W of the Mississippi to bottle Pepsi-Cola.

With the rise of stock ranching and discovery of gold in E Oregon and Idaho, The Dalles bloomed as never before. It became a febrile transportation and supply center, with the streets choked with freight wagons and stage coaches and the docks crowded with steamers. Hotels, taverns, boarding houses, livery stables and blacksmith shops sprouted in very corner of town.

So much gold flowed thru The Dalles that the US govt. built a mint here but not a single piece of money was ever coined. By the time the mint could be put into operation the mines of E Oregon and Idaho had petered out to a point where the mint was not needed, and the gold continued on, as before, to the mint in San Francisco.

When the Oregon Short Line, a branch of the Union Pacific, was completed in 1884, it marked the downturn of river and stage travel. (For more, see "Saddlemakers and Steamboat Days" in author's *A Touch of Oregon*.)

From supplies and transportation The Dalles turned to salmon packing, cherry packing and agriculture (chiefly livestock and grain). Today the city is diversified and is the cultural center of the Mid-Columbia. For a town of approximately 12,000 it is as modern as modern can be but its greatest charm still resides in its storied past.

The best place to start a tour of historic The Dalles is at the original **Wasco County Courthouse,** located adjacent to the Chamber of Commerce near W 2d and Pentland. Before reaching its (hopefully) final destination, the courthouse was shunted about as often as a boxcar and before restoration was as seedy as a Skid Road derelict down to his last gulp of hair tonic.

The courthouse was built in 1868 at 3rd and Court, where stands the present city hall. It housed a sheriff's office and three jail cells on the first floor and a court upstairs, entered only by an outside staircase. It was also used as a public meeting place and church until 1882, when a new, large brick courthouse was built at 3rd and Union. On July 4, 1977, the restored Original Courthouse was dedicated and has since served as museum and interpretive center.

(It is fitting that the courthouse be close to Mill Creek, for near where Mill Creek flows into the Columbia, *0.5 m.,* from the courthouse, is site of **Rock Fort,** where the Lewis and Clark party found rest and repose on Oct. 25, 26 and 27, 1805. Here, at this hollowed-out piece of earth rimmed by huge boulders, the elkskin trailblazers mended their canoes, killed deer for food, and reconnoitered the river below. They also had one other task, as noted by Clark: "The *Flees* which the party got on them at the upper + great falls, are very troublesom and dificult to get rid of, perticularly as the men have not a Change of Clothes to put on, they strip off their Clothes and kill the flees, during which time they remain nakid." The expedition also paused here April 15, 1806 on their return voyage.)

Walk to 2d Pl. and turn R. The Italiante-style house at 420 (1867) and the Victorian house of same period, at 422, are picture postcard dwellings of bourgeois gentility. Other striking houses in area are at 209, 215, 415, 419 and 505 3rd Pl.

At 6th and Trevitt is marker locating site of **The Indian Mission of the Methodist Episcopal Church.** Across street is 1890s **Victorian house,** with cupola and iron fence, big and eye-catching, the fanciest old house in The Dalles. From any perspective — historic, architectural, botanical, scenic — house and grounds are exemplary.

At 316 W 4th and 313 W 4th (1860) are two more venerable reminders of local history. House at 218 W 4th, built 1867, was home to Northwest Cattle King Ben Snipes, who at one time owned 125,000 head and had an 800 m. cattle trail ranging from the Yakima Valley to the Fraser River and beyond in British Columbia.

St. Peter's Landmark, formerly St. Peter's Church (1898), 3rd and Lincoln, has atop its 146-ft.-high spire, tallest in town, 6-ft.-high chanticleer weathervane, in commemoration of the cock that crowed after Peter's denial of his Lord.

Thompson House, 209 W 3rd, built 1889–1897, Victorian structure of Queen

St. Peter's, The Dalles

Phoebe L. Friedman

Anne and Eastlake motifs, served as family dwelling until 1949, then became boarding house, is now business office.

Brick bldg. at 3rd and Union, housing **Smith-Calloway Chapel** on first floor and lodge on 2d floor, was 2d county courthouse. **St. Paul's Chapel,** 5th and Union, carpenter Gothic church built 1875, is distinguished by stained glass windows and exquisite interior. **Victor Trevitt House,** on Union between 5th and 6th, was moved from 215 W 3rd. It dates back more than a century.

Wasco County Library, 7th and Court, on site of first white child born in The Dalles, was built around giant sycamore. Sterling example of modern NW architecture. Works of local artists exhibited in gallery.

City Park, 6th and Union, has etched on boulder the words: "End of the Old Oregon Trail 1843–1906." Why the end date was chosen is a good question.

Classic house at 216 E 5th has leaded windows and leaded door. **The Dalles Art Center,** originally Carnegie Library, opened 1910, Washington and 4th. House at 202 E 4th built as boarding house is symbolic of early 20th century life. Mansion at 106 E 4th was constructed in classical revival style, big and self-important, now filled with offices of professionals. It seems out of place in The Dalles, unless one assumes that in this eclectic town nothing is out of place. **The Dalles City Hall,** 3rd and Court, was built 1908 on site of first county courthouse. House at 514 Court was winner of Beautification Award presented by Mid-Columbia Board of Realtors. Early 20th century home at 515 Court was turned into The French House Restaurant, marking epicurean high for The Dalles.

Pulpit Rock, natural lectern of upthrust conglomerate, at 12th and Court, has marker commemorating est. of Methodist Indian Mission by Daniel Lee and H. K. W. Perkins on March 22, 1838. Legend has it that early Methodist missionaries preached here to emigrants and Indians. In more recent times, Pulpit Rock used for Easter Sunrise Services.

Government Mint, made of native sandstone (see earlier) is now rear section of warehouse at 710 E 2d.

Most noted pioneer site is **Ft. Dalles,** first est. as Camp Drum in 1850, then the only post between Ft. Vancouver and Ft. Laramie. Renamed Ft. Drum in 1853, Ft. Dalles in 1855. Abandoned as fort in 1867. Only surviving bldg. is Surgeon's Quarters, now museum, at 15th and Garrison.

From Ft. Dalles continue *0.1 m.* to Trevitt and turn L onto it. *0.2 m.,* Trevitt becomes Scenic Dr. Continue. *0.8 m.,* **Sorosis Park,** 15-acre green span and PA, with magnificent overlooks of city, river and hills. *0.4 m.,* entrance to **Judson Baptist College** campus. *0.2 m.,* **Pioneer Cemetery;** markers date back to 1860s. Buried here is D. G. Leonard, whose marker states he passed away Jan. 18, 1878 — exactly two weeks after he had been shot in the head at his John Day Fording station. Arrested for the murder was Leonard's wife, Mary; the trial that followed was one of most sensational in county's judicial history. (For more, see "Ghostly Sequel to the John Day Fording" in author's *Tracking Down Oregon.*) Inscription on gravestone of Mary M. Kimsey, dead at one year, five months and 11 days, in early 1879, reads: "Weep not Papa and Mama for me,/ For I am waiting in Heaven for thee." Inscription on grave of Ida Elnora Davis, who died Sept. 4, 1879 at age two years, 11 days, reads: "This lovely bud, so young, so fair,/ Called home by early doom,/ Just came to show how sweet a flower/ In Paradise would bloom." *0.6 m., turn R, 50 yds., angle R and stay R. 0.1 m.,* on L, round barn, only one of its kind in area. Built 1932, 66 ft. diameter, by William Howard McNeal, who authored a number of historical books, following long career as rural mailman. Once home of The Dalles Masqueraders, theater group.

From 2d and Union, downtown, go S on Union to ninth. Turn R. Go to Mt. Hood St. Turn L onto it. At forks, take Mill Creek Rd. *0.7 m.,* turn R onto farm lane. Drive to farmhouse at end of road. Ask for directions to **Treaty Oak,** ancient tree amidst cherry orchard, where Treaty of the Tribes of Middle Oregon was signed. By signing, confederated Indian tribes agreed to cede to US their "right, title and claim to all and every part of the country." In exchange, they were settled on barren plateau of Warm Springs Reservation.

From City Center Exit, The Dalles, on I-84:

Grave of D.G. Leonard, Pioneer Cemetery, The Dalles

2.8 m., jct., US 197 — to S — and The Dalles Bridge, to N. (See *US 197*, following I-84.)

0.5 m., on W-bound side of freeway, Portage Inn. To E and N of motel stand small, weathered **Indian Shaker Church** and several outbuildings. The Shakers originated in Little Skookum Bay, near Olympia, Wash. as a sect that consciously and subconsciously sought to redefine Indian Christianity and to return to the origins of Indian religion. Sociologically and historically it was a rejection of white experience and exploitation, as was the more famed Ghost Dance of the Great Plains, which followed later. (See *The Ghost-Dance Religion* by James Mooney.) The small band at Little Skookum Bay was not the first of the Indian Shakers and not the first to organize its own pharmacology, concentrating on remedies. But for mesomeric healing the sect, as the name implies, engaged in spasmodic shak-

Indian Shaker Church and Lone Pine, The Dalles

ing. In the second half of the 1880s the Shaker influence spread to the Yakimas and to other tribes E of the Cascades. It had no difficulty crossing the Columbia to The Dalles but that was about as far S as it penetrated. A white student of the Shakers in The Dalles concluded that the sect "practiced the strictest morality, sobriety and honesty."

1.3 m., turnoff for **The Dalles Dam** (0.1 m.)

A brochure issued in 1966 by the Corps of Engineers declares that the dam "was the fourth stage of navigation development of the Columbia River in the turbulent reaches below Celilo Falls" and gives this bit of history: "Prior to 1863 the link between boats operating on the upper river above Celilo, and those with their terminal at The Dalles, was an old wagon road portage. Then in the spring of 1863, the Oregon Steam Navigation company completed a 13-mile iron-railed portage along what previously had been known as Thompson's portage, between The Dalles and Celilo on the Oregon shore. The Dalles-Celilo railroad operated regularly and at a profit for a number of years. With the aid of a telegraph line, installed parallel to the track, the train could always be on hand to meet incoming boats and speed their cargo in either direction. Increased traffic, especially on the upper river, soon justified the construction of The Dalles-Celilo Canal, which went into operation in 1915, at a cost of $4,840,000, just a little more than the initial appropriation for construction of The Dalles Dam. Today, the obsolete navigation moves unimpeded over the earlier works of man and nature." A train excursion of the dam is a tourist delight.

Now the land, so vastly different than two score m. westward, has nuances of the Grand Canyon country and Monument Valley. Among the differences between green W Oregon and sandblown E Oregon is the sound, or, in the case of E Oregon, the lack of it. The hills are hushed, quiet in stoic whisper, everlastingly old, with the silence of parched age. And the river speaks only when it trembles.

8.1 m., on S, view of **Long House, Celilo Village.** When Celilo Falls was a fever of fishing, the village throbbed. Fish hung out to dry formed grids within grids, smoke rose from every hut and shanty, children were as numerous as whirls of dust, women chatted and mended and cooked in conspicuous rhythm. Here was a settlement alive and even when visiting Indians returned home, the remaining villagers kept alive the spark of activity. The Long House was the scene of social, community and political life: here were held the ceremonial dances, the powwows, the stick games, all that went with the amalgam of Indian culture. The original Long House burned down decades ago and the present structure is a pale presence compared to the gusto of the first. As for the village, the broken dreams have gone, replaced by those who still occupy the place with a stubborn will to hang on. (See "At Celilo Village The Road Runs Out" in author's A Touch of Oregon.)

0.2 m., jct., O 206.

* L, 0.2 m., **Celilo Park,** greensward on the Columbia, and site of Celilo Falls. For centuries this was the great traditional fishing grounds of the

Yakima, Celilo, Klickitat and Warm Springs Indians, who netted and speared salmon from cliffs. Here the river dropped suddenly, plunging down a cleft, and it was in this trough that the Indians found their catch. Fishing places on the cliffs were passed on from generation to generation and the Indians were guaranteed by the US that their rights were inviolate so long as the river ran and the sun rose in the east. But the trough was flooded by construction of The Dalles Dam and Indian fishing here came to an end. What survives is one of the best-known photos of Oregon: Indians fishing above the turbulent waters.

* R from jct., *0.3 m.,* Celilo Village.

* O 206 — Celilo Jct to Wasco:

2.7 m., **Deschutes River.** This was a key crossing on the Old Oregon Trail. Pioneer accounts tell of Indians ferrying the emigrants across in return for brightly-colored shirts and dresses. W of the river the wagon trains took to what is still an obscure, rough trace. It climbs the bluff and goes along it, looking down on Celilo Village. Faint traces of wagon wheel ruts are still evident. *0.1 m.,* **Historical Marker,** telling of emigrant crossing. *0.2 m.,* **Deschutes River SP.** Camping in copse or out in open meadow, Oregon Trail display, PA, fishing. *1.5 m.,* jct. (Straight, *3 m.,* Biggs.) Take R for Wasco. *6.2 m.,* on S, **Locust Grove Church,** for decades used as sheep, pig and hay barn. It was opened 1895 as United Brethren Church and after 1900 was affiliated with Methodist Church. Its last known use was in 1914 as funeral for Carl Minkler's infant son. A Portland woman, Amanda S. Lind, recalled teaching at Locust Grove School, across road, in 1921–22. *3.8 m.,* jct., US 97. (*8.7 m.,* Biggs Jct., *0.2 m.,* I-84.) *0.8 m.,* **Wasco,** at 400–odd pop., first and largest community in Sherman County. First PO, est. 1870, was called Spanish Hollow; name changed to present 1882. Wasco produced first woman bank president in Oregon — and 3rd in US. She was Marie Barnett Cooper, who was also first female automobile dealer in Oregon. Grandest sight in town is three-story **Crosfield House,** built somewhere between 1896 and 1906; once served as hospital. Crosfield Store, long, long abandoned, has markings of when it was in the flivver business. Across street is old **Barnett Bank;** much, much later, beauty parlor that occupied premises was only one in state to have bank vault. Everything about Wasco suggests setting for wheat country Andy Hardy movie, from sleepy depot to the comfortable houses which never appear to have anyone at home. (For more, see "Portrait of Van Glider" in author's *Tracking Down Oregon.*)

* From Wasco take Airport Rd. *4 m.,* to **Klondike.** Gordon Hilderbrand, oldtimer of area, related a bit of anecdotal history about this place: "Klondike's first business was established in 1897 — two years later sold to Antone B. Potter, who established a post office there in 1899 and he operated it till his death, then his son George Potter ran it till the 1950's. A. B. Potter had a phone line to McDonald. Most of it was on barbed wire. One time a man

Locust Grove Church

bought some gas for his auto and did not pay for it, so A. B. (As Mr. Potter was known) called McDonald on the phone: 'Tell him not to let him cross.' But I guess McDonald figured if he didn't let him cross the ferry he wouldn't get the toll so he let him cross and A. B. was out the gas." All that remains of "downtown" Klondike is skeleton ghost of **Geo. A. Potter General Merchandise Store.**

** Facing Potter store, turn L. *0.3 m.,* old brick school house, remembered as active only by elderly. *4.7 m.,* slant R. *5.1 m.,* on R, Oregon Trail sign. *3 m.,*

Crosfield House, Wasco

The remains of Klondike

Phoebe L. Friedman

Old school near Klondike — empty for decades

Oregon Trail Marker. *0.2 m.,* where Oregon Trail emigrants forded John Day River. (For detailed account of fording, see "Fording On the Oregon Trail" in author's *Tracking Down Oregon*.) Near fording was **McDonald,** tiny river hamlet built around inn. In 1915, it had PO, est. 1904, closed 1922.
From Celilo Jct., on I-84:
7.2 m., Biggs Jct., one of largest truck stops on Oregon section of this freeway. Also, fine accommodations.
Jct., US 97.

US 197 — The Dalles To Shaniko
O 216 — Tygh Valley to Grass Valley

9.8 m., past Eightmile Creek, turnoff E to Boyd.
* *0.8 m.,* **Boyd,** early flour mill village with nothing but a couple of old shacks to show for the past. In 1915 Boyd for pop. 50, PO (opened 1884), PS,

ME Church, Farmers' Union. (For pioneer telling of hamlet, see "A Tolling Bell at Boyd" in author's *Tracking Down Oregon*.)

1.4 m, turnoff W for **Endersby** (*2 m.,*), whose PO (1892–1906) was Endersly. In 1915 it had PS. Nothing now.

0.5 m.,, turnoff to **Star #23 Rebekah Lodge Community Cemetery** (*0.2 m.,*), on hillock. From here the horizons seem flapping in the last curvature of earth, nailed down only at sunset.

1.2 m., turnoff to **Dufur.** In early part of century Dufur boasted that the apple orchard here then, at N of town, was largest in the world. In 1921, 194 cars of apples were sold off this orchard and in 1922 crop was estimated at more than 125,000 boxes. Crew of 125 men was regularly employed and in picking season another 400 men were hired. Almost 100 horses were kept for orchard work. There are several reasons why the orchard failed; the most logical reason was that there wasn't — and isn't — enough moisture for growing apples year after year. What was orchard is now wheatland. *0.5 m.,* downtown Dufur.

First settler in area arrived 1852. In 1863 first house at what is now Dufur was built. PO opened 1878. By then the valley was known as Fifteen-Mile because Dufur was 15 wagon m. from The Dalles. In 1910 Dufur had pop. 700, two hotels, was terminus for the Great Southern RR, had an auto stage which made two trips daily to The Dalles, was up to date with telephone and daily mail. By 1915 town had slipped to 600 pop. but had HS, PS, three churches, Farmers' Union, five lodges, Development League, weekly paper. More than 7,000 acres had been planted with apple, pear and cherry trees in the past three years. The official *Oregon Almanac* raved: "Mt. Hood and the forested slopes and rolling hills on

Old homestead at Boyd

both sides of the valley are in full sight and make the city especially attractive from a scenic point of view. Winters are mild and short and summer nights are always cool." With all that, Dufur's pop. in 1990 was below that of 1915. **Balch Hotel,** constructed 1907, was grand hostelry in its time. The three-story brick bldg. with front porch and 2d-floor balcony supported by square wood columns is now private residence. Town comes alive at Steam Engine Threshing Bee in Aug., to celebrate wheat harvest. (For folklore history of Dufur and Balch Hotel, see "A Dreaming at Dufur" in author's *Tracking Down Oregon.) 1.3 m., US 197.*

In spring the hills from here to Maupin are so moist green you think you can squeeze the color out of them. Later they turn golden, rust, black, and, in winter, white.

6.7 m., Friend Jct.

*5 m., **Friend.** Only abandoned "The Friendly Store" stands as last whisper of this gentle ghost. Hamlet came rather late on the plain, in 1903, and died in middle age. Friend was once the S terminus of the 41-m.-long Great Southern RR, built 1904 and starting from The Dalles. The trip took two hours and 45 minutes and along the way the train had regular or flag stops at Three Springs, Annalore, Dufur, Boyd, Rice, Wrentham, Neabeck, Freebridge, Brookhouse, Fairbanks, Petersburg and Seuferts. (Only Dufur is still a town.) In 1936 the line was sold by the Wasco County Court for junk to cover unpaid taxes. In 1915 town had pop. 100, PS, Farmers' Union, Commercial Club, Methodist Church, was terminus of Great Southern RR, which had

All that was mercantile Friend   *Phoebe L. Friedman*

pushed N beyond Dufur. *0.5 m.* beyond Friend, at first road, turn R. *0.3 m.*, on L, behind barbed wire fence, old bank vault. A grocer planned on building a bank at Friend but got no further than the vault, where he kept his store receipts. On corner of Clark Mill Rd. is abandoned weatherbeaten Friend school house, prairie relic of the three R's. Turn L. *0.1 m.*, **Friend Cemetery.** Buried among the weeds and sage and wildflowers are some of Friend's first, including George J. Friend. (For more on Friend, see "A Friend in Time" in author's *Tracking Down Oregon*.) From Friend to Tygh Valley: *4 m.*, jct. Turn R. *2.2 m.*, jct. Turn R. *1.6 m.*, US 197. Turn R. *5.5 m.*, Tygh Valley - Jct. O 216.

From Friend Jct., on US 197:

3.6 m., **Tygh Ridge Summit** (2,697 ft.) The hwy. corkscrews down in a show of abandon, twirling thru the buffalo-hide stubbled hills. *5.7 m.*, on L, home of colorful All-Indian Rodeo, held in mid-spring. (For graphic account of the rodeo, see "The Chute Boss" in author's *A Touch of Oregon*.) On ridge across road from rodeo grounds the battered wagons of Meek's Lost Emigrant Party of 1845 ground on toward The Dalles. *1.2 m.*, jct., O 216.

To **E on O 216:**

4.1 m., turnoff to **Tygh Valley SP.** PA, fishing. Short walk from parking area to overlook of one of most impressive waterfalls and river scenes in Central Oregon. Double waterfall here: in background the water comes over a spillway in shimmering lace pattern; in foreground a torrent pours joyously down a scrubbed wall of rock. An abandoned power plant E of the falls is a sign of another time. The White River here — which is swallowed up by the Deschutes a short distance E of the power plant — calls up the first lines of Sidney Lainier's *Song of the Chattahoochee:* "Out of the hills of Habersham,/ Down the valleys of Hall,/ I hurry again to reach the plain,/ Run the rapid and leap the fall . . ." *3.5 m.*, **Sherars Falls.** Here Native Americans dipnet for chinook salmon from home-made platforms or from rocks above the Deschutes River. Under permit by federal treaty, members of the Confederated Tribes of the Warm Springs Reservation fish on both sides of the stream, using their traditional methods, from July to Oct. The Deschutes, a frothy, greenish stream, whirls and ripples thru a low, rocky canyon. Cinder-hued ledges extend from the cliff to form a trough, so that the stream has to fight its way thru the tight pen, creating riffles and caldron boils as it battles out of its encagement. The Deschutes, formerly spelled Des Chutes, gained national prominence early in the century when, in the Dec. 1909 issue of *Hampton's Magazine,* John L. Matthews described the Deschutes as "in many ways the most remarkable in America" and that it contained the potential of "a greater energy than is possessed by any other river of this capacity in the world." RR tracks above river seem passive now but this area early in 1900s was site of bitter and bloody RR war between two of the "most earnest grabbers of the Northwest," robber barons James J. Hill and Edward H. Harriman. *0.2 m.*, **Sherars Bridge.** As early as 1827, there was a bridge here, made by the local Indians of slender wood.

White River Falls

Phoebe L. Friedman

Peter Skene Odgen tried to cross it and five of his horses fell thru the span. A bridge built by whites in 1860 was carried away by high waters and had to be rebuilt two years later. Joseph Sherar, a legendary name in central Oregon, bought the bridge in 1871 for $7,040 and spent $75,000 improving roads to it. He charged toll that some thought exorbitant, and ran an inn, store and livery here. There was also a stage station and PO. As late as the 2d decade of this century a toll bridge stood here. *0.2 m.,* Maupin Jct. *0.5 m.,* jct., Deschutes River Access Rd.

     * This access road follows the white-capped waves of the Deschutes as it breast strokes toward the Columbia. Along the stream are cliffs in a variety of formations, hills that bulge like camels or seem to be following the water in an elephant walk, and garishly painted slopes. *10.3 m.,* **Beavertail Rec. Site.** *7.3 m.,* **Macks Canyon Rec. Site** — and end of road. CG, restrooms. Sign reads: "An Indian village once stood here. The depressions you see are ruined pithouses, some dating back 2500 years. Last to live here were the Tenino Indians, a hunting and fishing people." Nearby Cedar Island is blue heron rookery.

     * From jct., Deschutes River Access Rd., on O 216:

Beyond this point the road switchbacks to a high plateau and then catpaws

Indians fishing from platforms near Sherar's Bridge

Courtesy State of Oregon

Deschutes River Canyon   *Phoebe L. Friedman*

thru formidable and grim rock formations until it strikes windy, barren landscapes, which it shudders across until reaching fields of grass so high that the
pioneers could claim that a man on horseback could not be seen if he were in the
middle of a field. *0.3 m.,* from jct., start of a four m. steep ascent up a long sloping
canyon that is breathtakingly deep. The descent has greater awesome power. *4
m.,* the rolling wheatlands that begin E of the canyon have a remoteness upon
them which is made more mysterious by the incessant shadows. *15.6 m.,* Grass
Valley, at US 97.

W from jct., O 126:

* *0.3 m.,* **Tygh Valley,** home of late-summer Wasco County Fair. Once
site of Indian village and later center of famous hop growing area (district
received three medals from international expositions for quality of hops
grown), Tygh Valley probably reached its peak in 1915 when, though it had
only town pop. of 152, it had two flouring mills, HS, PS, two denominations
using same church bldg., three lodges, Grange, several stores and shops.
Today, store.

To this point the traveler on US 197 has been following the Barlow Toll
Rd., designed to be a short cut from The Dalles to Oregon City. US 197
either adheres to that trail or keeps it in sight. At Tygh Valley, the road
turned W and went to present Wamic. Then it continued W and NW to
where Barlow Pass is on O 35, *2 m.* N of US 26. From there the Barlow

Cutoff zoomed down Laurel Hill. Later, the emigrants sought a better way to reach Laurel Hill and cut a trail down to and along the White River.

5.7 m., **Wamic.** Store. Here was the E gate of the Barlow Toll Rd. (For road from Wamic to White River Jct. on US 26, see *Trans-Cascade Rds. US 26,* following.) The pike to Rock Creek CG, at Rock Creek Res., is well paved. From there W, take FS Rd. 48 *25.5 m.* to O 35. To L, Barlow Pass. The present FS Rd. vaguely follows the route of the Barlow Trail. Along that route, and in the most difficult section, there still stand trees with rope marks dug into them that point to places where wagons had to be lowered. Leander H. Baker, pioneer of 1853, described the travail 67 years later in vivid detail, so searing was the experience:

"I remember that James Biles, our captain, donated two of his oxen, valued at $400 — a great deal of money in those days—to be killed so we could use their hides as ropes. When we were crossing the Cascades, we had to lower the wagons down some of the canyons and finally our ropes were wore out. We were at a loss what to do till Biles said, 'Bring me one of my oxen.' They killed it and plaited the hide into ropes, but they were not long enough so Biles gave us another of his oxen and then we had rope sufficient. Through the Cascade mountain forests we did not make more than three miles a day and the notches we cut in the great trees so that the wagon wheels could pass may still be there. We were told there was a road, but we had to clear every inch of the way of underbrush so the wagons could get through, sometimes having to cut down whole trees."

From Wamic Jct. on US 197:

1.6 m., crossing of White River. *2.2 m.,* Oak Springs Jct. (To E: **Oak Springs Fish Hatchery** — rainbow trout, summer steelhead, winter steelhead.)

2.9 m., jct., O 216 — W. (See *Trans-Cascade Rds, US 26 — O 216* following.)

2 m., **Maupin,** named for Howard Maupin, celebrated in central Oregon as the "fearless plainsman" who slew the "notorious" Chief Paulina, after whom Paulina Lake was later named. Legend has it that Paulina and friends stole some of Maupin's stock, Maupin followed in hot pursuit, caught up with the old chief, and let the bullets fly. Maupin town sits on a naked plateau above the Deschutes River and is buffeted by wind and seared by sun. Most travelers find Maupin barren and unpalatable but somebody must like it: since 1915, when it had pop. of 150, town has grown at rate of five persons per year. On April 12, 1976, Maupin was shaken up when earthquake of magnitude 4.8 occurred NE of town. It was first earthquake ever recorded in area and most intensive of any recorded quake in all central Oregon. Seismic waves were detected as far away as Gilmore Creek, Alaska. (For more on town, see "A Reason For Maupin" in author's *A Touch of Oregon.*)

Beyond Maupin, going N, US 197 uncoils in sweeping braids down and down to the Deschutes River and then climbs to the naked, thorny plateau, windy and eerie on a winter night, and so rocky that post holes cannot be dug and barbed wire is held in place by rock-anchored boxes.

0.7 m., from Maupin, Bakeoven Jct. (Original site of Maupin, at mouth of Bakeoven Creek, near where Howard Maupin operated ferry.)

* On Bakeoven Rd.: *0.3 m.*, Deschutes River Access Rd. *8.6 m.*, on W, **Bakeoven Cemetery,** last dry leaf of hamlet which derived name when "a German baker, stranded with his flour and other supplies after the Indians had stolen his horses, set up a rough clay and stone bakeoven and made bread which he sold to miners and prospectors on their way to the Baker district." (*Oregon: End of the Trail.*) In 1915 Bakeoven had pop. 20, PS, tri-weekly stages to Maupin and Shaniko. *17.3 m.*, thru pretty ranch country, **Shaniko,** Oregon's best-known "ghost town."

* On Deschutes River Access Rd.: *3.2 m.*, Handicapped Fishing Ramp, with picnic tables by riverside. *4.2 m.*, view of Sherars Falls. *0.4 m.*, O 216. (See *O 216*, above, this section, for remainder of Deschutes River Access Rd.)

From Bakeoven Jct. on US 197:

16.4 m., Snow Cap Identifier. Name dials pointing to the great peaks of the N Cascades. *4.5 m.*, jct., US 97.

* On US 97 toward Shaniko: *6.6 m.*, on R, or S, cattle guard entrance to oldtime ranch spread, about as natural and pungent a cattle country scene as there is in Oregon. (On this narrow, rocky road, don't leave gates open and be very cautious about cattle.) *0.5 m.*, forks. Take L. *2.4 m.*, along fence line, stile on L. Park and cross stile to **Lawrence Grasslands,** one of Oregon's finest, as well as last, stands of natural grasses, especially bluegrass/wheatgrass, located on geological formation known as biscuit scabland. Looking W and then letting your eyes roam N and S, you have one of the finest views of

Lawrence Grasslands

the Oregon Cascades. In early autumn, a good time to be at the Grasslands is on a warm day as the sun drops behind the range. One moment it is delightfully warm and the next a chill sweeps across the thorny flats.

* From turnoff to Lawrence Grasslands: 6.2 m., Shaniko.

US 26— Portland To Madras
O 216 — US 26 to Maupin

US 26 is a popular Trans-Cascade road simply because it is a direct route out of Portland and has numerous ski facilities. It is not, except for views of Mt. Hood and Mt. Jefferson, an especially scenic pike, and it is not the easiest route to traverse. Mountain-view travelers bound for Bend go on I-5 to Salem and latch on to O 22. But for ecology, the graphic transition between the flora and the land characteristics of the moist W and the arid E, US 26 is most interesting.

From Powell Blvd. and 82d:

4.5 m., 164th Ave. On S, **Meadowland Dairy.** House built 1882, was once PO of Kronenberg (1893–97.) 7.5 m., on S, SE Walters Dr.

* 0.1 m., cemeteries containing graves of early Gresham-area settlers: on L, **Gresham Pioneer** (1851); on R, **White Birch** (1888).

0.2 m., **Gresham,** Powell and Main. (Here or near here was PO called Camp Ground, which lasted just three weeks in 1884. Folded when postal officials realized there was another PO in vicinity, Gresham, opened about same time.) This is about the only part of Gresham that even mildly links the present hodgepodge of suburban sprawl to the pleasant village it was even into the 1960s. This is where the town center was, small and compact, with genteel demeanor. Today Gresham is a maze of shopping strips and residential hives that cancel out the traditional concept of town. In two decades it mushroomed from a modest-size, stable settlement to one of the largest cities in the state and it bodes to become larger yet thru boundary expansion and in-migration. (For more, see *Short Trips Out of Portland, East B.*)

1.3 m., jct., US 26 and Powell Valley.

Another way to reach open US 26:

Take I-84 to Wood Village turnoff (12.8 m., from downtown Portland.) 0.2 m., turn R onto 238th Dr., which becomes Hogan Rd. 2.8 m., turn L onto Burnside St. 0.7 m., US 26 at Powell Valley Jct.

0.4 m., Orient Jct.

* 2.9 m., **Orient.** (See *Short Trips Out of Portland, East B.*)

4.7 m., jct., Boring — O 212.

* 0.2 m., "T". (L, 2 m., Kelso.) Take R. 1.3 m., jct. Turn L. 0.2 m., **Boring.** Residents deny it is so, but some visitors, appraising the grainy suburb that looks like it belongs a long way from Portland, might demand proof. Boring in 1915 might have been livelier, with four lodges and summer stage line to Mt.

Hood resorts. *4.6 m.,* **Damascus,** settled in the 1860s, which makes it a little younger than the other Damascus. In 1915, it was one of the few towns in state to have Dunkard Church. Shopping center has taken charm out of feed store village. (For more, see *Short Trips Out of Portland, East B.*) (From Damascus, *9.8 m.,* Oregon City center.)

1.8 m., Kelso Jct.

* *0.5 m.,* **Kelso.** Store. (See *Short Trips Out of Portland, East B.*)

1.6 m., Sandy — O 211 Jct. (See *Short Trips Out of Portland, O 211.*)

0.3 m., jct., Oral Hull Park, Bull Run, Dodge Park. (For the above and Sandy River Gorge Preserve, Roslyn Lake, Bull Run, Aims and Marmot Rd., see *Short Trips Out of Portland, East B.*)

2 m., jct., Dover District.

* *0.7 m.,* forks. Turn R onto SE Firwood R. *3.4 m.,* on R, old **Dover School,** a beggar hiding its rags. *0.1 m.,* **Dover Community Church,** center of what was Dover, named for Dover, England. No white cliffs here — but lots of nice berry country. PO 1890–1911.

3.6 m., SE Cherryville Dr.

* *1.2 m.,* **Cherryville,** genteel vacancy of the past. There may have been a flurry of wild cherries here once but they went out with the burg. In 1915, pop. was all of 50 and town had PS, church, Commercial Club. Oregon State Immigration Agent, laboring to bring folks here, noted: "Water supply from mountain streams, always cool and pure." Water still good. *0.5 m.,* first lane on L from Nickels mail box, turn for **Cherryville Cemetery** (1888), but appearing older, thru path back of farm.

4.6 m., E Sleepy Hollow Dr.

* This run is distinguished by the many fine houses along it. In many parts of Oregon there is greater residential density on shrouded county roads hidden from main pikes than on parallel hwys. *1.1 m.,* Barlow Trail. Turn L. *0.1 m.,* Marmot Rd. *1.2 m.,* on L, Rock Corral. (See *Short Trips Out of Portland, East A.*)

1.1 m., E Sleepy Hollow Dr.

* The shorter way to Marmot. *0.3 m.,* Barlow Trail. Turn R. *0.1 m.,* Marmot Rd. Turn L. *1.2 m.,* on L, **Rock Corral,** where Oregon Trail caravaners over-nighted their stock. (See *Short Trips Out of Portland, East A.*)

0.7 m., Brightwood Jct.

* *0.2 m.,* **Salmon River,** one of many streams in the state called Salmon. On far side of bridge, turn L. *0.1 m.,* old green house on L was residence, Sept., 1946 to May, 1947, of late Evans Carlson, Marine Corps hero of WW II and founder of famed Gung-Ho Carlson's Raiders. This was his last home. Sent by US govt. to observe Communist Army in Japanese-occupied China, Carlson became warm friend of Communist leaders and adapted their methods to create effective force of Marine guerrillas. Forced by illness to leave Marine Corps (as Brig. Gen.), Carlson became ardent post-WW II progres-

sive. (For more, see *Short Trips Out of Portland, East A.) 0.4 m.,* **Brightwood.** First called Salmon, PO est. 1891. Store, tavern.

0.4 m., Salmon River. *1.4 m.,* E Brightwood Jct. *(0.5 m.,* Brightwood.) *0.4 m.,* **A. J. Dwyer Roadside Preservation Area.** *0.2 m.,* turnoff to Wildwood Rec. Area.

   * *0.3 m.,* CG, PA, trails thru woods and to Salmon River.

0.4 m., Wildwood. *0.5 m.,* **Wemme,** diminished by nearby shopping center. *0.6 m.,* Welches Jct.

   * *0.8 m.,* **Rippling River Resort,** site of old Welches. (For story of Welches, see *Short Trips Out of Portland, East B.)*

1 m., Lolo Pass — **Zigzag.** Village derived its name from Zigzag River, branch of the Sandy, because for several m. the stream, along Barlow Rd., zigged and zagged, forcing emigrants to ford it more than once. Town is supported by tourists, skiers, some retired folks, and people who work in Portland.

   * On Lolo Pass Rd: *4.1 m.,* turnoff for Ramona Falls. (For Ramona Falls, see *Short Trips out of Portland, Lolo Pass — Lost Lake.)*

0.9 m., **Rhododendron.** The name is a natural, as anyone who explores the town environs can see. Developed as summer colony it is emerging into year-round community.

   * At E end of Rhododendron turn S on 20 Mile Rd. Cross bridge over Zigzag River and continue *0.8 m.* along summer houses to Rd. 20 E. Turn L and park at Flag Mtn. Trail sign. The 2 m. trail begins sharply, in switchbacks, but after 0.3 m. settles into gentle rise; elevation gain is only 600 ft. Views along Flag Mtn.'s ridge include Zigzag, Reid and Sandy glaciers on Mt. Hood, Hunchback Mtn., Devil's Peak, Zigzag Valley. Rhododendrons are massed like cheering throngs along trail and lined up with them are vine maple, Oregon grape, bracken fern, salal, alder, and hemlock, while, overhead, hawks, owls and jays, blue and gray, together with aerial armada of other birds, patrol the skies.

0.6 m., **Tollgate FS CG.** *0.1 m.,* on S, **Tollgate on the Barlow Trail.** W collection gate of Barlow Toll Road. (See "Tollgate on the Oregon Trail" in author's *A Touch of Oregon.)*

2.1 m., **Camp Creek FS CG.**

Now the road really begins to climb up Laurel Hill. When the wagons came over the Barlow Trail the slope on Laurel Hill was as steep as 60 degrees and one stretch of the descent, a 300-ft. drop, was so awesome that some comers wondered aloud if they would survive it.

2.6 m., on R, **Zigzag Forest Fire Area marker.** Information on 1952 fire, which consumed 1,750 acres of Mt. Hood Nat'l Forest in less than 40 hours. "It will take decades to restore the value destroyed. SOMEONE'S CARELESSNESS CAUSED THIS FIRE!"

1.1 m., on S, Oregon Trail Historical Marker — Laurel Hill. *0.9 m.,* trailhead for Mirror Lake. Cross bridge on Camp Creek by foot.

Barlow Road Tollgate

Mt. Hood from Laurel Hill

Courtesy State of Oregon

2 m. gradual climb to Mirror Lake and views of Mt. Hood and Zigzag Valley. FS says: "On weekends, this is one of the most popular and crowded day hike destinations around Mt. Hood."

0.8 m., turnoff to Mirror Mtn. W, part of Mirror Mtn. Ski Area.

* *0.2 m.,* Mirror Mtn. Lodge. *0.2 m.,* US 26. *0.4 m.,* turnoff to Government Camp.

* *0.7 m.,* village of **Government Camp,** alpine settlement which joins US 26 at W and E ends. In 1849, a contingent of US troops, leaving their wagons here for the winter, gave the site its name by posting a sign: "Government Property — Do Not Touch." *0.1 m.,* Rest Area. *0.1 m.,* US 26. (Turnoff also leads to Mirror Mtn. E.) At site of Government Camp was PO of Pompeii, est. 1902 and perhaps never used. *Oregon Geographic Names* states that name given by long-time guide O. C. Yocum for "volcanic soil in the vicinity."

0.2 m., turnoff to **Timberline Lodge,** Oregon's most famous ski lodge, the nation's first summer ski resort, and having the longest skiing season in the US and Canada. (For details, see *Short Trips Out of Portland, Mt. Hood Loop.*)

An almost continuous forest extends E from here, on US 26, consisting of Douglas fir, western hemlock, mountain hemlock, Alaska cedar, western red cedar, silver fir, noble fir, grand fir, alpine fir, western white pine and, further E, ponderosa pine, western larch, incense cedar and juniper. There is a fascinating transition in tree composition in the E move from here. The trees gradually become smaller, older species are left behind and newer ones appear, the woods become thinner, and then there are no trees at all. The transition, of course, is due to the changes in precipitation, from moist W to arid E.

0.3 m., **Still Creek FS CG.** Local gossip held for decades that the creek was a hideout for bootleggers but long before that, according to *Oregon Geographic Names,* emigrants at confluence of this stream into Zigzag River noted how calm the creek was compared to the agitated Zigzag, hence the name.

Along this part of the hwy., in late spring and early summer, the necks of squaw grass perched on the banks above the road look like curious geese staring at passersby.

1.1 m., Snow Bunny Lodge, ski facility. *0.1 m.,* turnoff S to Trillium Lake.

* *2 m.,* **Trillium Lake.** FS CG. Located on S slope of Mt. Hood and providing from its shore a dazzling view of the mtn., lake is a favored recreational site, particularly for Portland-area residents. Originally, seven-acre pond, accurately named Mud Lake, was as appealing as a burned-out lawn. In 1960, its life changed when Mud Lake was dammed and the lake increased to 57 acres and made clear. Naturally, name had to be changed. Rainbow trout are planted yearly; stocked, too, are brook trout and cutthroat trout. Because of its shallow water, Trillium Lake is liked by fly-fishing anglers.

0.4 m., jct., O 35. (See *Short Trips Out of Portland, Mt. Hood Loop.*)

4.6 m., turnoff to **Frog Lake.**

Trillium Lake, below Mt. Hood *Courtesy State of Oregon*

Mt. Hood reflected in clear waters of Frog Lake *Courtesy State of Oregon*

* At first sight, no larger than a frog pond, with typical FS CG. View of Mt. Hood from upper end, especially in the morning, is really something. *0.2 m.,* Wapinitia Pass— 3,949 ft. *1.3 m.,* Blue Box Pass, 4,024 ft. *0.9 m.,* turnoff to Clear Lake FS CG.

* *1.2 m.,* **Clear Lake,** one of eleven lakes in Oregon with the name. This clear lake is not in the most scenic setting but a lot of fishers come here. *1.6 m.,* jct., Skyline Blvd. — Timothy Lake — Olallie Lake.

* Skyline Blvd. zips thru massed woods that refuse to part for meadow or house. It is a recreational road, one of many such which lace the Oregon Cascades. *3.9 m.,* jct. (R for **Little Crater Lake CG,** a minor jewel in the forest. Road to it may be blocked with snow until late spring.) *4.1 m.,* **Joe Graham Horse Camp;** bring your steeds and ride thru the woods. *0.1 m.,* jct. (To R: *1.4 m.,* Oak Fork FS CG. *0.2 m.,* Gone Creek FS CG. *1 m.,* **Hoodview FS PA,** on **Timothy Lake.** The 1,282 acre Timothy Lake is really a reservoir, formed when Portland General Electric dammed the Oak Grove Fork of the Clackamas River in 1956 for generation of electric power. Prior to then Timothy Meadows, which the impoundment flooded, had been a favorite area for summer grazing of sheep. Sheepherders spread Timothy grass

Timothy Lake   *Courtesy State of Oregon*

to enrich the natural grasses, hence the name. The rather circular lake rests behind a 110-ft.-high, 740-ft.-long dam.) (To L at jct.: *0.1 m.*, **Clackamas Lake Historic Ranger Station.** *0.3 m.*, turnoff to **Clackamas Lake CG.** *24.7 m.* Olallie Lake. From jct. it is *30.5 m.* to Breitenbush.)

2.1 m., jct., White River — Wamic.

  * Another fine recreational road, with not a house on it until Wamic is approached. *2.8 m.*, turnoff to Clear Creek CG. (*3.8 m.*) *0.1 m.*, jct. (L, *9 m.*, O 35.) Turn R. *4.4 m.*, jct. (To R, *1 m.*, Forest Creek CG.) *2.3 m.*, jct. (L, *10.5 m.*, **Badger Lake.** The 4,472-ft.-high, 40 acre Badger Lake, looking from the air like a footprint in the woods, is good rainbow trout lake and is yearly stocked. Lake veterans say fly fishing is best in autumn. FS CG.) *4 m.*, on R, Old Barlow Rd. Not recommended for pleasure driving in typical passenger car. *2.1 m.*, turnoff to another rough section of Old Barlow Rd. *2.3 m.*, jct. (L, *0.2 m.*, Rock Creek CG, on Rock Creek Res.) *0.6 m.*, jct. (To R, *4.8 m.*, Bonney Creek CG.) *5.4 m.*, **Wamic,** W gate on the Barlow Toll Rd. Wamic is almost a dividing point between the forested W and the dry lands E. As such, it is scenically sited, but the village is rather nondescript. In 1915 it had pop. 150, which is more than it could boast more than 70 years later. *5.7 m.*, **Tygh Valley,** US 197. Once site of Indian settlement, Tygh Valley was, later, CG on Barlow Rd. A gentle sort of micro marketplace, it is rare to come across anyone who, knowing the village, doesn't speak kindly of it.

Entering **Warm Springs Reservation.** If you think that on this road thru the reservation you will see tipis and storybook Indians, think again. The only tipis are at the Kah-nee-ta resort, and they are for tourists.

A bit of history on the Warm Springs Indian Reservation, est. 1855. Thru treaties negotiated by Gen. Joel Palmer, first commissioner of Indian Affairs in Oregon, members of the Tenino, Wasco, Paiute and Klickitat tribes were herded here. Today the reservation is occupied by three peoples — Paiute, Wasco, and Warm Springs — who comprise the Confederated Tribes of the Warm Springs Reservation. The name Warm Springs comes from the warm springs at Kah-nee-ta. The Paiutes say it is a woman's name; the Wascos say it means "hidden valley." To the Warm Springs tribe, the name, appropriately, means "hot water.")

About 1940 the Reservation covered 300,000 acres, mostly barren. About 1,100 Indians lived here on govt. rations since the crops were too poor to support even this relatively small number of people. Today the Reservation covers about 600,000 acres and pop. has increased, though some Indians go off to the cities for employment.

Literally, the Indians have pulled themselves up and out of dire poverty. The Reservation is one of the most viable in the nation. The Tribal Council of the Confederated Tribes has est. a large scholarship fund to provide college and trade school education for its younger members. Indians who would have left the Reservation in the past for low-paying menial jobs in the city now work here in developing the enterprise.

One of Oregon's highest peaks, 10,495 ft. Mt. Jefferson, is on SW corner of Reservation. The SW border is formed by the Metolius, one of Oregon's swiftest and best fishing streams.

0.7 m., jct., O 216.

O 216

This is a delightful road, easy to drive, traffic generally light, and the countryside pleasant. Many of the people who come this way are campers and mushroomers.

2.1 m., turnoff to **Clear Creek CG** *(3.1 m.) 1.1 m.,* turnoff to Camas Prairie and Keeps Mill CG.

    * *0.8 m.,* jct. To L, *1.2 m.,* **Camas Prairie,** a bit of meadow in the woods. Informal camping. Straight, *2.8 m.,* **Keeps Mill CG.**

0.5 m., **Bear Springs FS CG.** *1 m.,* turnoff to McCubbins Gulch FS CG *(1.8 m.)*

7.3 m., **Pine Grove.** Store. For years this stretched-out village was known only for its roadhouse; now it is a sprawl of houses and shanties, each seemingly tossed at random from the sky. N and S the place is probably not more than 100 yds. but W and E it stretches on to the amazement of newcomers. It is 1.1 m. between the store and the trailer camp and that's only part of the string. *(0.6 m.* from store, old Pine Grove school house.)

At Pine Grove the road breaks onto the unclothed plateau. A traveler observed, "It's like stepping from a greenhouse into a sandbox." *1.8 m.* from trailer camp, jct., White River. (N, *3.8 m.* to White River, a stream deep in Oregon-bound lore.)

3.5 m., thru Juniper Flat, present **Wapinitia.** Store: Wapinitia, or the more probably correct Wapinita, is a Warm Springs Indian word referring to location, perhaps — between tree and barren land. There may be some substance to this because the village was once known as the self-explaining Oak Grove. Wapinitia was an early Central Oregon homesteader village. In 1915 it had pop. 50, PS, United Brethren Church. By 1940 village was down to 35 people. And the original Wapinitia has been ghostly since.

From present Wapinitia a road juts N to Simnasho, Kah-nee-ta and Warm Springs, the last on US 26.

    * Not too many years ago this road traversed poor land of wretched poverty. The changes since have been remarkable. Even the land looks better. And the homes along the way are considerably better than the shanties of old.

    1 m., site of **old Wapinitia.** On R at crossroad is long-deserted stagecoach inn. (L, *0.1 m.,* church bldg., now sagebrush ghoul.) *12.2 m.,* **Simnasho.** Originally pronounced as though spelled **simnassa,** the word supposedly means

Old Wapinitia Stage Station

thorn bush, of which there is plenty about. At one time, the people of this small Indian community marched to the church of the United Presbyterian Mission, reaching it by a short boardwalk, and then trooped to the Long House, where they engaged in the rituals of their forebears. The UPM church, the pastor's residence and the board sidewalk have been played out

Old church at Simnasho

and the Long House burned down years ago. But the Simnasho of despair has also disappeared. The village has a school, a large community center, and a growing number of comfortable homes.

The road to Kah-nee-ta first rides a high, naked plateau exposed to long and indelible panoramas of the Central Cascades. The range is seen as a continuum, rising from valley floors and stretching as a barrier far as can be seen. Then the road enters a sea of yellowish, reddish, purplish, salmonish, brown-green rock-cropped hills, the painted waves achurn above the raw-sculptured gorge of the Warm Springs Canyon. Geologically, the colored cliffs point to eons-ago volcanism, spouting geysers, scalding springs, rocky terraces and ancient pools of bubbling mud that turned to stone. Some millennia ago the valley of the Warm Springs was a gorge swamped with steam. Mineralized hot water, racing down cliffs, formed terraces that are today strikingly apparent.

* *11.2 m.*, jct., Fish Hatchery. (Turn R. *1.7 m.*, **Warm Springs Nat'l Fish Hatchery,** 298 m. from Pacific.)

2.1 m., Kah-nee-ta Jct. (*1.2 m.*, **Kah-nee-ta,** gorgeous spa operated by Confederated Tribes of the Warm Springs Reservation. This warm water oasis in a saucer of juniper hills has become one of the top-flight resorts of Oregon. Indians had come to the hot pools of the Warm Springs River for centuries before the first white chronicler, John C. Fremont, with 25 companions, arrived via a common Indian trail in late 1843. Fremont noted that "springs on the left, which were formed into deep handsome basins, would have been delightful baths, if the outer air hand not been so keen." The pools he tested varied in temperature from 89 degrees to 134 degrees. The spring water for the Kah-nee-ta swimming pools is cooled by the Warm Springs River and hovers at about 80 degrees.

Return to Kah-nee-ta Jct. The road climbs out of the canyon to charge across a generally arid plateau. *9.3 m.*, on R, rimrock wall of kind often seen on Oregon desert. Top resembles fortress parapet. *1.1 m.*, Warm Springs, administrative center for the reservation, on US 26.

From Wapinitia store, on O 216:

* Take dirt rd. *50 yds.* E of store. *1.2 m.*, jct. (To L, *8.8 m.*, **Smock Prairie,** on plateau which affords striking views of Cascade peaks. For some people the terrain and what it holds — flat plain and sparse ranchsteads — is boring; for others the ambience is exciting, for here is a back-country Oregon still pungent with the past.) *1.2 m.*, turnoff R to **Kelly Cemetery.** (*0.5 m.*, burial ground of homesteaders.) *8.5 m.*, Tygh Valley.

From Wapinitia store, E on O 216:

7.2 m., US 197. (*2 m.*, Maupin.)

US 26 — Continued

On US 26, from jct., O 216:

4.2 m., **Bear Springs FS CG.** *6.9 m.*, turnoff N to Simnasho Butte. *0.2 m.*, 45th Parallel. *2.1 m.*, Simnasho — Kah-nee-ta Jct.

    * *6.5 m.*, Simnasho. (See earlier this section.)

0.4 m., Warm Springs River. *7.5 m.*, **Mill Creek Canyon,** spectacular lava gorge over Mill Creek. The deep, rugged canyon is so deceptively noncommittal from the road that few people pause to look down. In many another state it would be a tourist standout.

0.1 m., on S, **Historical Marker.** Reads: "From ancient days trails made by the first Indians of the region crossed this plain. Over them passed Peter Skene Odgen in 1825 and 1826 with his trapping parties bound south for the Crooked River and the John Day Rivers, the Harney and the Klamath Basins. Nathaniel J. Wyeth, fur trader, went south in 1834 and returned in 1835. Captain John C. Fremont used the trails in his southland exploration into Nevada and California in 1843 and Lieutenant Henry L. Abbot, leading a Pacific railroad survey party, followed them in September 1855."

3.7 m., turnoff to Blue Lake, one of 11-such-named lakes in Oregon.

    * *5.1 m.*, jct. Straight. *16.2 m.*, Blue Lake. L, *13.8 m.*, Trout Lake.

3.8 m., look to S. On the long plateau the junipers appear as tipis. *2.3 m.*, on N,

Catholic Church, Warm Springs

Warm Springs Catholic Church, a warm landmark above the road for many years. *0.4 m.,* Kah-nee-ta Jct. (Kah-nee-ta, *11.6 m.* See earlier, this section.)

0.2 m., **Warm Springs.** The commercial town is divided into two sections, almost two m. apart, and dissimilar in mood. The W part is most important, it being location of Warm Springs Reservation Administration Center. In recent years Warm Springs has grown affluently and its middle-class residential sections would be looked upon with favor anywhere in Oregon.

* From E end of service station at W end of Warm Springs: Turn R. *0.1 m.,* turn L. *0.3 m.,* at four-way crossroads, turn R. *0.2 m.,* forks. Take R, West Hills Dr., adorned with handsome homes. *0.6 m.,* on L, **Warm Springs Cemetery.** Buried here is Billy Chinook, legendary scout of white trappers and trailblazers. Inscription on his tomb reads: "A faithful and true friend of the white men, William Chinook died at the age of about 65. He was one of the chiefs of The Dalles band of Wascoes, and a signer of the Indian treaty dated June 23, 1855." Best to inquire at Agency HQ before entering cemetery.

1.8 m., **Deschutes River.** Most of the time there seem to be some fishers around. At one time the Oregon Trunk RR (no longer there and the rails long ago torn up) ran down the E side of the Deschutes. To the N, about *1.5 m.,* was Vanora (PO 1911–20). In 1915 it had pop. 20, PS, was shipping station on RR. To the S, about *1.3 m.,* was **Mecca,** shipping station for the Warm Springs Reservation. PO 1911–24. In 1915 the *Oregon Almanac* noted: "Steel bridge over Deschutes River on shortest auto road to Central Oregon from Portland." Although Vanora in its prime had fine water system and Mecca was the point at which the old wagon road crossed the Deschutes, there is nothing but nothing to indicate the once-presence of these hamlets.

2.2 m., jct., Pelton Dam — Lake Simtustus.

* This "side trip" off US 26 could easily take much of the day. It exposes the traveler to some of the finest and rarest scenery in Central Oregon.

* *0.6 m.,* forks. Straight. *1.6 m.,* **Pelton Dam,** 200-ft.-high concrete arch structure built 1958 by Portland General Electric. As creator of what is sometimes called Pelton Reservoir, it is power-generating facility on main tributary of Deschutes River. Lake name Simtustus was chosen by Warm Springs Indians to honor fellow tribesman who scouted for US Army against Paiutes in 1867–68 campaign. *0.6 m.,* **Pelton Park** PGE CG, PA, marina, BR. Fishing license required from Warm Springs Indians; Warm Springs Reservation on W side. Lake resembles eel, being 8 m. long and no wider at any point than 0.3 m.

The road swishes past bouldered creeks that jump into the lake and run under huge rock outcroppings on slope before rising to a plateau of wheatlands, showing another face of the varied land. *6.2 m.,* Belmont Lane. Turn R. *1.5 m.,* SW Mountain Dr. Turn L. *1.7 m.,* turn R for Round Butte Dam Observatory. *0.7 m.,* **Round Butte Dam Observatory.** These are the views from the precipitous lookout: Round Butte Dam; below, to L, beyond juniper, Metolius River; directly below, Lake Billy Chinook, which holds the waters of the Metolius, Deschutes and Crooked Rivers; beyond Billy Chinook gleams Lake Simtustus, amalgamation of the rivers under name of Deschutes.

    * Return to SW Mountain Dr. Turn R. *1 m.,* Butte Dr.; two gorgeous views of Three Sisters at turn. *2.7 m.,* on R, viewpoint. *0.9 m.,* on R, viewpoint. The vistas, from the viewpoints, of the water-carved, wind-eroded, sun-browned canyon are telescopic and powerful. From one, the Deschutes and the Crooked are seen, together with a patch of the Metolius, forming Billy Chinook Lake. In summer, the waters are specked with power boats, each with its own shimmering peacock tail. From another, 7 million years of Central Oregon geology are visible above the confluence of the Deschutes and Crooked Rivers. The formation, with its yellow, brown, gray and black bed, contains volcanic and sedimentary characteristics. And then there is the center-front look at a high tongue of land, now called "The Island" and known to early homesteaders as "The Plains of Abraham." Nothing grows

Metolius River arm of Lake Billy Chinook.
Mt. Jefferson in background   *Courtesy State of Oregon*

on it but sage and juniper. According to the inevitable oldtimers of the area, several homesteaders tried to make a go of it on "The Plains of Abraham" but Providence was not on their side.

0.6 m., jct. (L, *3 m.,* Culver.) Take R. *0.7 m.,* forks. (On L, below and bending back, CG.) *1 m.,* jct., **Cove Palisades SP Marina.** Straight. *0.6 m.,* parking area for PA of **Cove Palisades SP.** Picnic area here, on hillock overlooking Lake Billy Chinook, is one of the most delightful in state. The vistas are panoramic, the grass is soft, the breeze wanders in and out like a restless puppy, clean tranquility occupies the scene.

* Return *0.6 m.,* to marina jct. Take R, lower road, not going directly into marina but just to L of it. *0.9 m.,* to L, high on cliff, waterfall. *1.2 m.,* Lake Billy Chinook Bridge across Crooked River Arm. *1.3 m.,* on L, **Petroglyph Rock,** giant boulder covered with baffling small-ringed craters, sunbursts, insect designs and curlicues. Perhaps several thousand years old, but its age remains as much a mystery as its meaning. Boulder was found about 1 m. N, near former rapids of Crooked River. In the cliff above Petroglyph Rock are several caves, but it is dangerous to climb to and enter them. *0.2 m.,* **Cove Palisades SP.** PA, swimming, BR, FHP. *0.1 m.,* Cove Palisades SP. CG, dumping station, FHP. *0.5 m.,* Cove Palisades SP. PA, swimming, BR, FHP.

Lake Billy Chinook from Cove Palisades State Park.
At right are the Plains of Abraham.   *Courtesy State of Oregon*

Possible site of Geneva

1 m., Lake Billy Chinook Bridge across Deschutes River Arm. Beyond, the narrow road fishhooks up a cliff to a mesa, climbing and edging thru scrawny pines, a sea of sagebrush that the wind rustles into waves, and rocks that are scattered as one would throw out seed from a sack. *2 m.,* **Lake Billy Chinook Village.** Store, in season. And there is an "airport" here, which a villager called Interstate because a daring pilot flew in a light plane from N of the Columbia.

   * *1.5 m.,* jct.

   ** Straight. *0.5 m.,* R at crossroad stood **Grandview School,** all gone except for thick-walled cement outbuilding and rock walls. Turn L. *2 m.,* crossroad. Turn R. *1 m.,* on L, **Grandview Cemetery.** There are graves here from the last two decades, which means that some deceased have been brought here from relatively long distances since, apart from Lake Billy Chinook Village, there isn't a house around for miles. And flowers on the graves indicate people come here from fairly long distances to remember their departed. *1 m.,* crossroads. Turn L. *1.6 m.,* purported site of **Geneva** early 20th century homesteader settlement. Boards of homes only clue of past. *12. 9 m.,* past Squaw Creek Canyon, jct. at pavement. This lonely dirt pike winds thru wasteland writhing in the wind and sun, with a rare blossoming of meadow, an unexpected tableaux of cows, and a ranchstead. Turn R. *2.5 m.,* Camp Polk Rd. *3.1 m.,* jct. Turn R. *1.3 m.,* Sisters.

   * At Grandview School — Geneva Jct.:

   * Turn R. *1 m.,* jct. (To R: *1 m.,* at "T", site of what was **Grandview.** The homesteaders, who came in the big rush of the early 1900s, tried transforming

acres of rocks into dry farming and stock raising, but one by one they gave up, leaving behind the grand view and broken dreams. A few cellars, a few foundations — and the wind.)

* Turn L. 7.8 m., jct. (To L: Lake Billy Chinook Rec. Area, 3 m.; US 20, 24.3 m. — 5.4 m., Sisters. This is another sparse pike, with little pleasing scenery and scant habitation. It seems more frequented than the earlier road to Sisters.)

* Straight from Jct.: 0.1 m., turn R onto auto trail. 0.1 m., makeshift parking space in cut out of sagebrush. Walk W 0.1 m., to cavity, or scalloped indentation in plateau, for **Balanced Rocks of the Metolius.** A most dramatic geologic formation — and so defenseless. Easy prey to vandals, who shoot at the rocks. Please take nothing but the beauty the scene affords and kindly leave the area intact and clean.

* 2.4 m., **Perry South FS CG,** on Lake Billy Chinook. W of it flows the Metolius river.

Beyond CG there are no habitations along road but there are unequivocal looking fences and signs that speak in unmistakable terms that the private property here — and there is a lot of it — is not to be disturbed. The houses

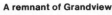

A remnant of Grandview

— several small colonies of them — are down on the river, in an Elysian setting. *9.9 m.,* road ends.

(For US 97, backtrack to Culver Jct. and continue E.)

From Pelton Dam Jct., on US 26:

10 m., US 97. *(0.5 m.,* Madras.)

There is uncertainty as to who named **Madras** and why but it is a fact that the accent is on the first syllable, whereas the Madras of India is accented on the second and last syllable. This difference is the least between the two cities.

Even being the seat of Jefferson County has not swelled the pop. of Madras. But it has sought to keep up with the times. In 1915, though the town numbered only 400, it had five churches, three lodges, was HQ of the county Farmer's Union, and could boast in the *Oregon Almanac* that it possessed commercial garages.

The Great Depression all but turned Madras into a ghost town. Erskine Caldwell, traveling the US as a journalist, described Madras as beaten and deserted and used as a symbol of the town's devastation a broken screen door of an empty store creaking in a sere wind. By 1940 the pop. was down to 291.

General economic recovery and water brought Madras back from the grave.

Balanced Rocks of the Metolius

Irrigation attracted a new era of farmers and in their wake came the support services and the mercantile facilities that would provide Madras with the chemistry of life. But Madras has remained the smallest of the "major" cities of Central Oregon, not even reaching 2,500 into the closing years of the 1980s.

The city itself is attractive when viewed against its natural background. A few blocks from the main street the traveler can be into the outland. Madras itself has nothing to hold the traveler — it is an antiseptic, prosaic town that seems to have been placed there in error — but its environs are impressive. For starters, it is the gateway to Cove Palisades SP and a vast recreational area. Seldom-traveled roads lead W to the former homesteader villages of Grandview and Geneva and to the incredible Balanced Rocks of the Metolius. Dirt roads E scruff through sleepy sage and hills as frozen-eyed as a porcelain cat to Ashwood, Horse Heaven and Mitchell, traversing some of the most photographically exciting "Western" country in the state.

O 22

Salem to US 20

This smooth road, a silky corridor thru meadows and woods, is one of the heaviest-traveled pikes of the Cascades and one of the easiest to drive. The road climbs steadily and without effort from the Williamette Valley to its confluence with US 20 and as it glides past the shoulder line of trees the air seems to rustle. Even if there was nothing of scenic or historic interest along or back of O 22, the route itself would be attractive.

From Market St. exit on I-5, Salem, *2 m.,* to O 22 exit.

From O 22 of I-5:

0.7 m., turnoff to Turner.

   * *0.2 m.,* jct. Turn R for **Turner.** *1.8 m.,* Release Center of State Correction Division. *0.4 m.,* turnoff R to **Western Baptist College.** *0.5 m.,* Administration Bldg, nerve center of friendly, Hoosier-looking, old-fashioned WBC campus. Robert S. Allen Archaeology Museum in library. Return to Turner Rd. *1.7 m.,* turn onto Witzel Rd. *2.4 m.,* on R, **Turner Twin Oaks Cemetery.** Grave markers back to 1857. Buried here is Dean Cromwell, track and field coach at USC from 1908 to 1948 and head coach of US Olympic track and field team in 1948. He died in 1962, age 83. Why Cromwell here? He was brought up in Turner and loved the place. *0.4 m.,* Turner Jct. Turn R. *0.2 m.,* **Turner Memorial Tabernacle** (1891), impressive structure that has spellbinder look to it. This has been "Historic meeting place of Oregon Christian churches since 1885." *0.1 m.,* turn R onto School Ave. *0.1 m.,* turn L onto Chicago St. (To R, at Chicago and 4th, pioneer lodge hall used as church.) *0.1 m.,* turn R onto S First and Boise, **Turner House,** built by George Turner, who was 12 when his family arrived in Marion County from Scio, Ohio in 1852; oldest house in area. Turn L onto Boise. *0.1 m.,* turn L

onto Aumsville Rd. *0.2 m.,* 7840 and 7850 3d, on L, two of Turner's pioneer homes. Backtrack to Boise. Straight from Boise on Aumsville Rd. *3.9 m.,* turn R onto Aumsville Rd. *2.8 m.,* turn L. *0.2 m.,* O 22.

From turnoff to Turner:

3 m., on R, State Correctional Institution. *2.8 m.,* jct., O 214 — Silver Falls SP.

  * *0.2 m.,* "T". To L: *1.7 m.,* **Shaw.** Store. Silver Falls, *14.8 m.*

  * From "T", turn R: *0.1 m.,* jct. Turn L. *2.9 m.,* **Aumsville.** Originally called Hoggum, because of pig proliferation, first PO est. 1862 as Condit, renamed Aumsville six years later to honor late pioneer Amos Davis, whom friends called Aumus. Out of such triviality is the permanence of local history born. Although pop. is more than double that of 1915, town had more community services then. This is the story of many small towns, which have surrogated their services to the cities. Turn toward Stayton. *0.8 m.,* angle L for cemetery. *0.3 m.,* turn L. *0.4 m.,* turn L onto Dead End Rd. *0.4 m.,* **Aumsville Cemetery.** Markers back to 1848. View from cemetery knoll is of pleasant Grant Wood Scene. Return to Stayton Rd. Turn L. *1.7 m.,* "T". Take L. *25 yds.,* O 22.

2.5 m., Aumsville Jct. *(0.8 m.,* Aumsville.)

2.7 m., Sublimity — Stayton Jct.

  * To L: *1.5 m.,* Sublimity. Turn R on Main. *0.2 m.,* patrician **St. Boniface Church** (1889). (For more, see *O 213, Sublimity.*)

  * To R: *1.5 m.,* jct. Turn L. *1.1 m.,* jct. Turn R. *0.6 m.,* **Stayton.** Founded 1872, Stayton has grown slowly, steadily, from 100 pop. in 1875 to 900 in 1915 to 4,500 in 1990. House at E Burnett and N 3rd (1889) seems to have stepped out of Mother Goose. Turn L. *0.8 m.,* **Lone Oak Cemetery** (1876). Backtrack toward downtown. *1 m.,* Florence. Turn L. *0.1 m.,* **Paris Woolen Mills.** Company started 1876, has had string of owners. Present plant built 1905; complex looks like 19th century mill town back East. From E 3rd and Marion, turn L for **Stayton Pioneer Park** *(0.3 m.).* Rebuilt **Jordan Creek CB** (see *US 20-O 226* immediately following) links Pioneer and Wilderness city parks; CB spans Salem Ditch, diversion of N Santiam River. Trail in natural wooded area of Wilderness Park leads 400 yds. to small dam. Return to N 3rd and E Marion. Straight *0.1 m.* to N First and Marion. Turn L, toward Kingston. *1.1 m.* site of **Kingston,** started as station on Corvallis and Eastern RR. In 1915 it had store and Christian Church. Nothing now.

2.5 m., Stayton Jct. *(2.3 m.,* Stayton).

7 m., on L, Fern Ridge Rd. (For Shellburg and Stassel Falls, see *Short Trips Out of Portland, Henline Falls — Opal Lake.*)

35 yds., on R, Mehama — Lyons Jct.

  * The "business heart" of **Mehama** is virtually at the intersection of O 22. Named for Mehama Smith, wife of pioneer ferryman. PO est. 1877. In 1915 Mehama had three churches, two lodges, was summer resort. Now it's just a semi-wide spot on road — but it is still shady nook on N bank of Santiam. *1.2*

Grave of 1842 settler in Aumsville Cemetery

m., **Lyons.** In 1915 it had only 100 pop., just a mite bigger than Mehama. Today pop. is 1,000 and town has smart little business street. Continue on Lyons-Mill City Rd. *0.4 m.*, turn L onto 13th St. *0.7 m.*, **John Neal Memorial Park.** CG, PA. On Sundays, when service stations might be closed, only rest rooms open to public could be here. Return to Lyons — Mill City Rd. Turn L. *0.9 m.*, on R, Fox Valley Rd. Here was site of **Fox Valley,** PO 1874–1907.

Sole survivor of dorp is no-longer-used Fox Valley School, built 1914. *5.4 m.,* **Mill City,** name inspired by sawmill in 1888. Before forests were cut back, Mill City lived off its big sawmills. Early in century, town also boasted large hospital. First Presbyterian Church, downtown, has New England look — white, frame, simple, belfried. Stewart's Grocery, in 1914 bldg. is type of general store common in 1920s and 1930s. Upstairs is lodge hall for four fraternal organizations. Mill City is a charming town that looks like it could have served as the setting for *The Music Man.* Listen close and you can hear "Seventy-Six Trombones" rattle down the street. But chief distinction of burg is that it is in two counties — Marion and Linn. *0.3 m.,* O 22.

From Mehama — Lyons Jct.:

0.8 m., jct., **Little N Santiam Rec. Area.** A most delightful play and explore area. (For details, see *Short Trips Out of Portland, Henline Falls — Opal Lake.*)

3.2 m., **N Santiam SP.**

   * *1 m.,* SP. PA, fishing.

2 m., **Fishermen's Bend BLM Rec. Site.**

   * *0.1 m.,* Rec. Site. CG, PA. Dine on picnic table more than 80 ft. long, whose top is one board, cut from giant Douglas fir.

1.6 m., turnoff for Mill City *(0.3 m.)*

2.8 m., **Gates.** Around 1915 Gates was center of gold, silver, lead and copper mining in these parts. PO has jumped around in place and name. Started on S side of Santiam, in Linn County, in 1882, with name of Henness. Next year it became Rock Creek. Nine years later postmaster moved across river to village there and changed name to Gates, to honor old settler Mary Gates. This infuriated the

House at East Burnett and North Third, Stayton, built in 1895

Courtesy Richard Jungwirth

elders who been around as long as Mrs. Gates and they drew up petition to return to name of Rock Creek. But fellow entrusted with petition had too much to drink one day, and when he sobered up he couldn't remember where he had last seen petition. So PO — and town — remained Gates.

    * Turn S at Horeb St., where PO is located. *0.4 m.,* forks. Take R. *0.7 m.,* turn R onto Kingwood. *0.6 m.,* on R, **Fairview Cemetery.** Burial ground looks down and up to woods, which seems logical, since so many loggers were laid to rest here. Among departed are Wm. Thomas of "Oregon Vols Indian War" and members of the Rambo family, whose thoughts on how their name has been used would be interesting.

1.7 m., **Minto CP,** another thickly wooded refreshing recreational area along river. There was tiny settlement here, named for John Minto, one of those Oregon pioneers with an iron in every fire. PO here 1892–1904. In 1915, PS.

0.2 m., **The Maples Rest Area.** Nature trails meander along river in sylvan setting. *1.1 m.,* **Packsaddle CP,** fine get-away-from-it-all place for people who really don't want to get-away-from-it-all.

1.6 m., **Niagara CP.** A century ago some minor industrialists coughed up what appeared to them a great notion: They would dam the N Santiam here to produce power to run a mill to make paper from straw. In 1974, Sid King, editor of *The Oregon Motorist,* graphically described the place where the masonry dam was constructed: "The river charges down against the basalt dike across its path and over thousands of years it has painstakingly sliced a bulb-shaped channel through nature's dam. The gorge, called the Narrows, is only four feet three inches wide at mean water level but it broadens out to a width of 25 feet to 40 feet below the surface of the river. The river tips up on edge to slip through this narrow gorge and in doing so provides one of the outstanding compact-size canyon-cascades in the northwest."

High water destroyed the dam, leaving standing a section 50 ft. high and 40 ft. wide, with wing walls on both sides.

PO was first spelled Niagora and in its time Niagara was known as having smallest PO in US — 6 ft. by 8 ft. — "not enough room to change your mind," as a postmaster wryly said. But town wasn't lonely: seven logging camps were located within five m. In 1915 Niagara had pop. 45, store, hotel, tavern, PS, and 10,000 horsepower hydro-electric plant under construction.

There is a legend that Niagara Dam was built by Chinese laborers, but this is not true. A letter printed in the Dec. 24, 1959 issue of the Salem *Statesman* and written by two men on the scene reads in part: "I, Chris Knutson, 78, worked on the Niagara Dam project during its construction. I never saw a Chinese man on or near the site.

"I, Lang Stafford (another Gates oldtimer), spent many happy days with my cousins, the McClery boys, on the Niagara Dam location, while our Dads worked on the masonry. After the right-of-way, and roadbed for the railroad through

Gates was finished, Chinese labor was brought in to help place the ties and rails. We would like to have the record straight."

Walk down the stairs from the path for a straight-on view of Niagara Dam. The N Santiam rolls free, rising and crying in turbulent scorn as it sweeps past the hunk of wall. But there is a wash of beauty here: a brief but striking corridor of stone beyond which, on a slope across the river, the eye finds a waterfall.

2.7 m., **Big Cliff Dam.** 1.7 m., turnoff for Detroit Dam Powerhouse.

* 1 m., powerhouse. Road to it passes Big Cliff Lake.

1.3 m., **Detroit Dam.** Overlook of Detroit Lake. People fish from railings. Behind dam the N Santiam is backed up 8.5 m., creating Detroit Reservoir (or Lake); when filled, a winding, dreamy deep blue lake with mystic coves.

4.1 m., turnoff to **Mongold Park.**

* PA, BL on N Santiam, water skiing, swimming.

1.8 m., **Detroit Lake SP.** CG, PA, swimming, fishing, boating, showers. 0.1 m., Detroit Ranger Station. 1.6 m., Breitenbush — Olallie Lake Jct. (See *Short Trips Out of Portland, Clackamas River.*)

0.2 m., **Detroit,** which the lake turned from farming village into tourist stop. To S, in middle of lake, was old Detroit (PO 1891). It had stores, RR station, cluster of homes. Construction of Detroit Dam put town 100 ft. under water.

3 m., Blowout Rd., laced with trails.

* 0.9 m., **Hoover FS CG,** on N Santiam. 2.1 m., **South Shore FS CG. CG,** PA, BR. Road continues on 21 m. before wending its way back to O 22.

1.5 m., **Idanha.** The grand plan to build the Corvallis & Eastern Oregon RR from the coast to Bend ended here, with Idanha becoming E terminus of aborted line. Until tourists arrived, Idanha was a quiet sleep along the road. Now it is so modern it couldn't pay its electric bill some years back. Store looks like Grandma Moses laid it out.

4.1 m., **Whispering Falls FS CG.**

* 0.2 m., FS, CG. The whisper of the falls, on S side of N Santiam, is drowned out by the strong chatter of the stream.

5.9 m., **Riverside FS CG,** in forest on river. Peaceful place to study war no more. 2.1 m., on S, Marion Forks. Restaurant. On N, turnoff to Marion Lake Trailhead.

* 0.1 m., **Independence Rock Trail.** 2.5 m., one-way bridge over Puzzle Creek. 2.1 m., trailhead for Marion Lake (2 m.) in Mt. Jefferson Wilderness. En route is **Marion Falls,** a water gymnast, and 1 m. to N, lacy Lake Ann. The 261-acre 4,130 ft. high **Marion Lake** has for decades been one of the most popular back-country lakes in the state. *Atlas of Oregon Lakes* calls it "the largest lake in Oregon not accessible by automobile" and adds: "Indeed, with the exception of massive Waldo Lake it is the largest natural lake in the Williamette Natural Forest on the west slope of the Central Cascades." Although rainbow trout, brook trout and cutthroat trout are in abun-

dance, few people who hoof it to Marion Lake are fishers. Most come simply for the wilderness experience.

0.1 m., turnoff to **Marion Forks Salmon Hatchery.**

    * *0.1 m.,* Hatchery. About 500,000 spring chinook smolts are released each year.

2.8 m., Straight Creek Rd.

    * This is the "direct" and lonely (!) way to reach US 20 from O 22 in these parts. Few travel this road for the sole purpose of getting from one hwy. to another and rarely anyone at night, for the pike is almost completely deserted then and there is not a house, service station or telephone on the route. This is a recreation road, for the fisher, boater and camper, and though it is paved it is to be treated with respect, for much of the way it twists like a showoff snake wiggling thru a three-dimensional world of forests. *23.3 m.,* bridge across Quartzville Creek.

    0.9 m., another bridge across Quartzville Creek.

    0.8 m., turnoff R to site of **Quartzville** *(2.1 m.,),* first settled in 1864 and site of several minor gold flurries. *50 yds.,* jct., FS road to Detroit Dam — the rough and scenic way, and not for "Sunday drivers." (See *US 20,* following, for more.) *0.4 m.,* **Quartzville Optimist Club Park.** *1.2 m.,* **Yellow Bottom Rec. Site.** *3.7 m.,* jct, Yellowstone Access Rd. — to Crabtree Valley and O 226. (See *US 20,* following, for details.) *2 m.,* **Dogwood Rec. Site.** *7.1 m.,* **Whitcomb Creek Park.** *1.7 m.,* **Thistle Creek Ramp.** *4.6 m.,* **Green Peter Dam.** *3.7 m.,* **Sunnyside Park.** *1.5 m.,* US 20.

Quartzville Marker

Thistle Creek Ramp, Green Peter Reservoir

The transition from Douglas fir to the higher-altitude species on the W side of the Cascade divide, and white fir, Western larch and ponderosa pine down the E slop, is seen on 22, and US 20, from here to Sisters.

11.4 m., start of lava deposits on O 22. Flow is from Nash Crater — estimated to be 3,800 years old.

1.2 m., jct., US 20. (For rest of way to Sisters and Bend, see *US 20,* following.)

US 20 — Albany to Bend

O 226 — US 20 to O 22 (near Lyons)

US 20 is a pioneer road that for long was State 54. From Albany to Bend it has changed dramatically since the 1950s and today it is completely modern. Towns in its 99E vicinity have been netted by the centrality of Albany; Sweet Home and Lebanon experienced rapid growth (which came to an end in the early 1980s); Green Peter Dam was built, with a plethora of recreational facilities as a natural consequence; Cascadia SP was opened, as a follow up to Cascadia Resorts; the high lakes became popular with casual tourists; and the enclave of Black Butte added a touch of Yankee royalty to the scene.

US 20 from I-5, at Albany:

4 m., turnoff N for **Santiam Central Cemetery.**

0.5 m., turn R. *0.2 m.*, cemetery (1853).

1.6 m., jct., O 226. (See O 226 at end of this section.)

3.3 m., on S, Spicer Dr.

   * *1.1 m.*, turn R onto Spicer School Rd. *0.6 m.*, Bolhken Rd., site of **Spicer,** first called Leng and started as RR station in 1880s. PO 1886–1904. School and store long gone. Return to Spicer Rd. Turn R. *1 m.*, Tallman Rd. Turn L. *1.7 m.*, just beyond RR tracks, take gravel road that follows tracks. *0.2 m.*, site of **Tallman,** another RR station burg gone with the choo-choo. (For more on Tallman, see *Cross-Coast Range Rds., O 34.*)

0.5 m., on L, old school house converted to dwelling. (*2 m.*, turnoff L, or N, for **IOOF-Masonic Cemetery 1871).**

   * *0.1 m.*, cemetery. Oldest part is *0.1 m.*, ahead.

0.7 m., turnoff L on Dodge St. for Pioneer Cemetery (1850).

   * *0.1 m.*, Grove St. Turn R. *0.1 m.*, turn R onto Park St. *50 yds.*, **Pioneer Cemetery,** smack in residential area.

0.1 m., jct., O 34 — E terminus of that road.

0.3 m., downtown **Lebanon.** A pioneer homesteader town, Lebanon started life in 1848 as Kees Precinct. It was an important supply point on the Cascade Wagon Road and its first wealth came from outfitting wagon trains. In 1851, Jeremiah Ralston, who surveyed the site, named it after his birthplace in Lebanon, Tenn. Three years later the Methodists opened Santiam Academy, chartered by territorial legislature, in log cabin. A few years later a two-story, four-room school house was completed. In 1864, the year a bell was brought 'round the Horn, peak enrollment of 105 was reached, and everyone concerned agreed that the road ahead was even brighter. But est. of PS in 1870 sent the

Grave of 105-year-old woman in Pioneer Cemetery, Lebanon

House at 3rd and Ash in Lebanon, built in 1852

academy into decline and in 1907 it went out of business, with bldgs. and grounds taken over by Lebanon School District. In 1915 Lebanon had pop. 2,180 but by 1940 had dropped to 1,851. After WW II pop. spurted and by 1980 had reached more than 10,000. In 1890 Lebanon jumped into industrial age with construction of paper mill. For decades it was renowned mill town, boasting "largest plywood mill in the U.S.A." But hard times took its toll and as mills closed in the 1980s, an exodus began and people, recalling the happy days, saw a ghost town, though none was on the horizon. Pioneer homes, in diminishing number, dot residential streets, mostly near business section. **Crandall House,** 488 2d, is loveliest vintage house in town; probably built 1870s or 1880s. House at 3rd and Ash, built 1892, has flamboyant characteristics of late 19th century nouveau bourgeois conspicuousness. Old houses at 310 and 515 Grant and 136 Rose. **City Library,** 2d and Ash, was formerly hospital with 26 bed capacity. Annual June Strawberry Festival, topped by "World's largest strawberry shortcake," crowds the town.

0.8 m., on S, Airport Rd.

* 0.6 m., Stoltz Rd. Turn L. 2 m., at bend, take Blueberry Hill Rd. 0.5 m., turn R. 0.2 m., **Dodge Cemetery** (1877). Seen from cemetery: haunting desert-like wheatlands and low buttes — the Chimney Rock scene of the valley. Return 0.2 m., to road. Turn R. 0.2 m., former **Rock Hill School,** strikingly placed atop a knoll. For years the old school house was used as barn.

1.1 m., on S, Crowfoot Rd.

* 0.5 m., **Crowfoot;** name suggested by crowfoot image of intersection of

Pioneer house at 515 Grant, Lebanon

Rock Hill School

Phoebe L. Friedman

roads. When college at nearby Sodaville was abandoned, women's dormitory was moved to Crowfoot and became Grange. The traditional store, school and church comprise the other community institutions.

1.3 m., on S, Sodaville Jct.

* *1.5 m.,* **Sodaville.** The name came naturally, from the cold soda water springs. It was the raison d'etre of **Sodaville Springs SP,** est. on land donated in 1871. People from all parts of the Willamette Valley would come here for the water; the two bathhouses that held the spring-fed mineral baths were always filled in season. Farmers buggied from miles around to the Spring House, on site of present city hall, to picnic and then fill water containers before starting home. Located at Sodaville from 1892 to 1904 was Mineral Springs College, Presbyterian normal school consisting of classroom bldg., on knoll, and, below it, Ladies Hall. The campus had been gouged out of a forest and beyond the campus the woods ran into the sky. In 1895, enrollment was 125 — probably the high water mark. That year rent was $2 to $4 per month for a cottage and students were advised they "can board themselves at from one dollar to one dollar fifty cents per week." There is no open trace of Mineral Springs College now — hasn't been for decades— but there are people around the state whose parents and grandparents were proud graduates of this valiant little school. Its campus was where the Sodaville School is now sited and foundation stones of the classroom bldg. are buried beneath underbrush on knoll back of PS.

With the soda springs active and the college vibrant, Sodaville was an A-1 town. It had three hotels, three stores, two blacksmith shops, three churches, skating rink, a saloon or two, ice cream parlor and confectionery, PO, drugstore. It also had horse race track. But then the springs began to dry up and the college folded. In 1915, construction of present US 20 between Lebanon and Sweet Home doomed Sodaville, say the oldtimers. But this may be nostalgia after the wish. Just before pike between Lebanon and Sweet Home was built Sodaville's pop. had declined to 150 and town was down to school, church and Grange. Today it still has PS (though more modern) and the church (Evangelical). Only mercantile establishment is small store. The SP, pioneer in state system, is now city park and from time to time the city posts notices that the spring water is contaminated. Small as it is, about 200 people, town has the typical big city alienation of so many Oregon communities. A resident of 35 years, living 1 m. from city hall, confessed to being in ignorance about local affairs. "I don't know what those people in town are up to," she declared with an air of exasperation. Although many historical traces have been removed in recent years, house at 2307 Maple, reputedly built 1872, compels attention — two-storied veranda with gables facing in all directions. House nearby, at W end of Maple, was started in 19th century and built in stages. Original owner had openings cut into walls so that spirits wouldn't be

"Ghost House," Sodaville

trapped. One day he hung himself from a sturdy oak limb outside his home and since then the place has been called "Ghost House."

* At city park, take Waterloo Dr. *2 m.,* turn R onto Buckmaster Rd. *0.2 m.,* turn L onto gravel road. *0.1 m.,* **Klum Cemetery** (1865). Return to Waterloo Rd. Turn R. *0.8 m.,* on N, Waterloo Jct.

2.2 m., on N, Waterloo Jct.

* *0.7 m.,* **Waterloo.** Name comes not from site of the famous battle but for its outcome — defeat of the arrogant. After some thorny litigation a town jester quipped that the village ought to be named Waterloo because one of the court contestants, as pompous as Napoleon, had been badly beaten. In 1990 Waterloo had almost doubled the pop. of 1915 (96), which proves the triumph of virtuous persistence. *0.4 m.,* **Waterloo CP,** with mineral spring (inundated in winter) on N shore near river and low falls — with caves beneath them — of S Santiam. More than a century ago there was flour mill and sawmill on river, using low falls for power. In 1877, the machinery was moved. In 1892 a hosiery mill was built on the site of the earlier mills. This was found to be unprofitable and hosiery mill was converted to woolen mill — which also disappeared.

* Turn R for Berlin. *1.3 m.,* Berlin Rd. Turn R. *0.3 m.,* turn L onto Bellinger Scale Rd. *0.9 m.,* turn R at mail box 32059. *1.1 m.,* **Bellinger Cemetery**

(1854). Here lie a host of Bellingers, pioneers of area. Some years ago, according to locals, man from the neighborhood committed suicide here. In explanation for the choice of site, a nearby farmer explained: "He didn't like to travel far."

    * Return to Berlin Rd. Turn L. *2.7 m.,* **Berlin Union Church,** all that is left of the **Berlin** that was. Town's name was begotten in odd way. Horse races were held near home of Josiah Burrell, merchant-farmer of means. He fed spectators for free and so lavishly that he soon started worrying about going broke, with folks coming as much for the feasts as for the races. So he started to charge for his meals and shortly was in the restaurant business. What had been a quiet home became known as Burrell's Inn. When PO was considered, locals wanted to name it Burrell's Inn, since Burrell's home was to be PO. But PO officials thought otherwise. Eventually a compromise was reached: Berlin. In 1944 some outsiders began move to change name of village to Distomo, Greek town destroyed by Nazis earlier in WW II. Name change was to be accompanied by barrage of national publicity, but when townsfolk heard about the plan they strongly protested and won the day. About all the town ever had, beside the church, was store and school, both gone.

    * *0.1 m.,* forks. Straight. *0.9 m.,* just before mail box 4982, turn L onto narrow dirt road. *0.1 m.,* Powell — **Berlin Cemetery** (1893), last stop for Burrell and friends, their graves sometimes smothered in bracken ferns.

This is Berlin

0.8 m. — on US 20, from Waterloo Jct. — turnoff N to McDowell Creek CP.

* *0.9 m.,* forks. Take L. *2.9 m.,* S Santiam River. *4.8 m.,* **McDowell Creek Falls CP,** plethora of waterfalls in various sizes and configurations. Trail from parking lot leads 400 yds. uphill thru woods to 119 ft., three-stage **Royal Terrace Falls,** a dazzle of beauty. Path continues 1,000 yds. (and across paved road) to **Majestic Falls,** a single, sloppy-showered cataract, reminding one of a big, shaggy dog shaking off the rain. Along path are picnic tables and benches for viewing and just relaxing. *0.5 m.,* from first parking lot, parking for Majestic Falls. Steps lead to observation platform at top of falls and to bottom of falls.

3.7 m., Liberty Rd.

* Turn R, or S. *0.7 m.,* "T". Turn L. *0.1 m.,* Liberty School. Turn R. *0.3 m.,* on R, **Indian Council** (or Pow Wow) **Tree,** giant Douglas fir that measures upward of 25 ft. around. (Also known to locals as "Wolf Tree" because it stands alone and separate from trees of its kind.) Starting at about 6 ft. up the giant becomes a one-tree forest, with ten trunks of at least 18" diameter growing out from the main trunk and three more larger than 12" growing up from the branches, as far away as 25 ft. from the main trunk system. Many horizontal "branches" are at least 2 ft. in diameter, and every limb seems to aspire to be a tree. Legend has it that the Calapooia Indians came here twice a year; once to"pow wow", or hold council, and again for the camas festival. Camas grew abundantly in swales of valley, and after the harvest the Indians would camp under or by the tree and feast, race, trade, and gamble. Tree is also supposed to have been a "pow wow" site for whites and Indians to iron out problems but, considering the fate of the Calapooias, this seems hard to digest. When conquerors and conquered meet, the "pow wow" is simply a matter of the conquerors dictating terms. More legend has it that hill above tree was burial ground for Calapooias. One of the graves was occupied by body of a beloved chief. Each year, at Calapooia "pow wow" time, the Indians left gifts on and around the grave of the chief. But when the whites began to rip off the gifts and denude the grave, the Indians quietly removed the body to a new location and kept the site a secret from the whites. There are still oldtimers in the Liberty district who remember climbing the tree in their youth and finding arrowheads imbedded in the mighty fir. Whether their memory is pure or clouded by legend is uncertain. The Calapooias were a small tribe — no more than 600 when the first wagon train arrived. Soon their numbers began to decrease. Less than 80 years after the first overlanders came this way, the last of the Calapooias died.

* *0.5 m.,* — from tree — forks. Straight. *0.5 m.,* Liberty Rd. Turn R. *0.3 m.,* **Liberty Cemetery** (1860).

From Liberty Rd. turnoff:

4.3 m., jct., O 228. On SE corner is **East Linn Museum,** in bldg. that was first a

Royal Terrace Falls, McDowell County Park

school, then church. Museum, unpretentious reflection of area's past, is warmly arranged.

0.5, **Sweet Home** city center.

Some of the oldtimers still call the town Buckhead, supposedly its first name. PO est. 1874, though area settled by sodbusters almost 30 years before. About 1880 the stores and PO moved from what is now E part of town to Ames Creek, in the W part, where the Buckhead saloon did thriving business, and somehow Buckhead became Sweet Home.

In prehistoric times a mighty forest was spread in this area. All that's left of it now is silicified fossil wood — some of it gorgeously colored with clear marked grain and rings structure. Other lures that bring rockhounds to environs are banded agate, chameleon agate, crystal-lined geodes, and fire-engine red jasper.

Sweet Home's most famous resident, though some deny it, was Klondike Kate, "glitter girl" of the Yukon Gold Rush, who achieved fame and life-long legend as singer and dancer in mercurial Dawson. From 1951 to 1957 she lived in Sweet Home with her husband, W. L. Van Duren, an accountant, and died in her sleep in at their home, 2226 Main, on Feb. 21, 1957. She was 80 but since she

Pow Wow Tree

Foster Dam   *Courtesy Corps of Engineers*

had for decades subtracted four years from her age, her obituary listed her as 76. A woman who had been at ease in several different social spheres, Kate could roll her own cigarettes with loose paper from a Bull Durham pouch and pour tea as fastidiously as any lady. More than a quarter-century after her death a friend in Sweet Home remembered her thusly: "Kate had all kinds of rummage sales. She acted reserved but she liked to be in the public eye. When they had the parades and things she got dolled up and tried to make a big splash and everything. She could tell stories about the gold rush days as long as you wanted to listen, but she never pushed herself on you. She was a nice, sweet lady."

Sweet Home has had the same ups-and-downs as rival Lebanon. In 1915 its pop. was 300 but by 1940 had dropped to 189. After WW II, town grew steadily, to pop. of about 7,000 in 1980. Then came lumber slump. Businesses suffered and real estate plummeted. A merchant gloomily noted: "You can buy a house for half its value but what good is it if you don't have a job?"

2.4 m. — from city center — on S, 47th Ave.

    * *0.3 m.,* turn L onto Airport Rd. *0.3 m.,* on L, **Gilliland Cemetery.** Older part, upper L, back to 1854.

0.4 m., **Foster.** If you glance in the wrong direction you'll miss the village. It wasn't always this small, though. In 1915, it had two sawmills, grist mill, electric light plant, HS, PS, Union Evangelical Church.

0.5 m., on N, Foster Dam — Fish Hatchery Jct.

* *0.6 m.,* **Foster Dam,** rockfill structure with concrete spillway and powerhouse containing two generators. *0.3 m.,* forks. Take L. *0.3 m.,* **South Santiam Fish Hatchery.** Return to forks. Take L, onto N River Rd. *0.5 m.,* on R, **Lewis Cemetery** (1850), overlooking Foster Lake. *0.5 m.,* Gedney Creek Ramp. *1.5 m.,* **Lewis Creek Park,** water sports site.

0.4 m., Foster Lake Viewpoint. *1.8 m.,* Green Peter — Quartzville Jct.

* The scenery that lies ahead is so striking that one would have to be an absolute idiot to come without a camera and a lot of film — preferably color. The multitudinous views of water and mtns., seen in a thousand shapes and imageries, can boggle the mind.

1.5 m., on R, **Sunnyside Park,** Linn CP on Middle Fork of Santiam. CG, PA, BL. *3.7 m.,* **Green Peter Dam.** Behind it, Green Peter Reservoir, which extends N more than 10 m., to Quartzville Creek. Corps of Engineers-created lake is recreational favorite and though there are formal CGs and PAs it is evident that the entire reachable shore is one continuous fishing and/or rest site. In spring, bear grass and rhododendrons hold sway as Lords of the Mountains and Douglas firs, not yet doomed by the faller, seem to stretch toward the clouds. And then there is the columnar basalt, which journalist James Magner aptly described as looking "like it is made up of black loaves of ossified bread."

4.6 m., turnoff to Thistle Creek Ramp (*0.3 m.,*). *1.7 m.,* turnoff to Whitcomb Creek Park. (*1.2 m.,* thru a winding in the woods, BL on Green Peter Lake.) *7.1 m.,* **Dogwood Rec. Site,** located on gravel bar which was locale of placer mining from 1890s thru 1930s.

2 m., on L, jct., Yellowstone Access Rd.

** On Yellowstone Access Rd.: This pike, part of it downright miserable, is in its first stretches pure wilderness and, in the E portion, passes thru stands of firs up to 900 years of age. Conservationists have long sought to preserve Crabtree Valley — and undoubtedly will be honored for their courage and foresight after the old growth is gone.

** *6.9 m.,* forks. Take L, away from paved road, which appears more attractive. *2.3 m.,* spur road on L. Take it. *0.4 m.,* forks. Take L. *0.1 m.,* **Crabtree Lake,** a dip in the mountainous woods. All about are patches of the ancient timber. Return *0.5 m.,* to the "main" road, which loggers know as Snow Peak Rd. Continue W. *3.4 m.,* forks. Take L. *1.5 m.,* forks. Straight. *5.1 m.,* site of former **Snow Peak Camp,** once giant logging operation. Beyond here the road is as gentle as a house cat. *14.2 m.,* Bond Rd. Turn R. *0.5 m.,* turn L onto Griggs Dr. *1.1 m.,* turn R onto Brewster Rd. *1 m.,* O 226.

* From jct., Yellowstone Access Rd., going N:

3.7 m., **Yellow Bottom Rec. Site.** CG. *1.2 m.*, Quartzville Optimist Club Park. *0.4 m.*, jct., FS Rd.

** This FS road is the adventurous way to Detroit Dam and O 22 and is not recommended for the faint hearted. But the trip is something not soon forgotten. Cascade peaks swim in the E sky, hills seem piled upon hills, an oncoming vehicle is a rare happening, and at points the road challenges you to take sides. And more: This road looks down with brilliant clarity upon Detroit Lake and then comes around the S shore of it. It also affords some exotic mtn. views, especially when clouds foam across the sky and the peaks seem to be adrift on some far spacious islands. *16 m.*, Detroit Dam.

50 yds., forks.

** Take L, uphill. *2.1 m.*, site of **Quartzville,** a rather minor mining town in the history of the state but in the mid-19th century and about turn of century there were flurries of gold rush fever. Not much gold and lesser folklore seem to have come out of area. Still, there were some odd touches. Because Quartzville was relatively close to pop. centers of the Willamette Valley, it attracted an uncommon number of tenderfeet and holiday prospectors. Families would come for a week or two, to camp as they would for picking hops or attending a revival meeting, and scrounge for gold. Business-

Short Bridge

Lower Soda Falls

men would come up by carriage for a weekend, muck in the creek, and return home poorer but feeling a bit adventurous. There was more money to be made picking hops and more joy in a revival meeting but there was something glamorous about a gold stream that could not be duplicated elsewhere. It was the big lottery of some lives.

* Return to Green Peter Rd. Continue N. *0.8 m.*, bridge across Quartzville Creek. *0.9 m.*, another bridge across Quartzville Creek. Now the road and scenery change in character. The rod turns twisty and the scenery mundane compared to what was before. *23.3 m.*, O 22 — 2 m. E of Marion Forks.

From Green Peter — Quartzville Jct., on US 20:

6.9 m., on N, High Deck Rd.

   * 0.1 m., **Short CB** (1945), last of the Santiam CBs and survivor of wooden shingle roof species. Formerly known as Whiskey Butte Bridge, which has snappier ring. Length: 105 ft.

1.6 m., **Cascadia SP** entrance.

   * 0.5 m., forks. (L — 0.2 m., Cascadia PO, est. 1898). R — 0.1 m., CG. Across restroom at first CG is trail to **Soda Creek Falls,** once mineral spa. Giant firs rising back from giggly, dimple-faced S Santiam give park its character. View from bridge in summer is always that of young people sunbathing on rocks in stream. After the 10th trip one gets the feeling that these are the same people doing the same thing. Park has CG, PA, fishing, FHP. Back of Camp 14 is trail that leads 1,200 yds. to Lower Soda Falls, a thin, gurgling, sloping, rope-like water that snakes down a cleft squeezed between moss-covered massive rock falls, dropping from 140 to 175 ft. in three shelves. Backtrack about 300 yds. to creek crossing and go about 1,000 yds. to Upper Soda Falls, another eye-filling drop on creek.

4.7 m., turnoff S to S Santiam Wagon Rd. Now basically a logging road, it has little interest for travelers.

2.7 m., **Trout Creek FS CG,** amidst Douglas fir ensemble, with maple and dogwood and hazel brush profuse, on S Santiam. In spring this is a blaze of color, and in summer huckleberries abound.

0.1 m., on N, **Trout Creek Trail.** Up Trout Creek into hills. 0.3 m., on S, **Yukwah FS CG.** Rustic CG in lush 2d growth woods. 2.2 m., on S, **Fernview FS CG,** on S Santiam. Even on hot day this place is cool, screened from sun by big leaf maples, Douglas firs, hemlocks, choke cherry and vine maples. 0.2 m., on N, **Rooster Rock Trail,** rising from 1,317 ft. to 3,567 ft. in about 1.5 m. 1 m., **Upper Soda.** Mountain House was familiar name for more than century.

1.9 m., turnoff S to House Rock FS CG.

   * 0.2 m., turn R for CG. 0.3 m., across straight ahead bridge, CG on Sheep Creek, tributary of S Santiam. At near side of immediate bridge, House Rock Loop Trail. 90 yds., forks. Turn L. Cross Bridge. Turn L. 0.1 m., on R, **House Rock,** large rock shaped like a bowl turned upside down, which leaves a large (and damp) room under the rock. Beyond it, 750 yd. trail to **House Rock (Little Cross) Falls,** keep L at forks about halfway up trail. House Rock (Little Cross) Falls: an uninhabited splash bouncing down a knobby rock face and joyfully joining the choric waters of the stream. (S of House Rock FS CG — 2 m. by FS Rd. — lies Three Creeks Drainage, where some of the oldest trees in Oregon are located.)

7.6 m., on S, view of Jumpoff Joe Rock, giant outcropping that looks like timbered El Capitan of Yosemite.

1.8 m., on S, view of Iron Mtn. A formation up there has the configuration of a chimney — or somebody perched on ledge and ready to leap — or CIA agent surveying the road and pretending to be a rock.

2.9 m., on N, Iron Mtn Trail. From parking area a *1.6 m.* FS trail winds very gently into sloped woods, and alpine flowers bug the summer days.

0.3 m., **Tombstone Pass** — 4,236 ft. *0.4 m.,* **Cone Peak Trail.** Not recommended for folks who stay close to nitro tablets, but for the hearty the views of great.

South Santiam River roaring through a cleft   *Courtesy State of Oregon*

50 yds. **Tombstone Prairie Historical Marker.** In the sleepy swale below road Indian tribes of area met to swap goods and gossip, so first whites called place Indian Prairie. In 1871 a teen-age lad accidentally shot himself, was buried here, and so Tombstone Prairie. After wagon road was built across Cascades, prairie was favorite stopping point for freighters.

3.3 m., **Lost Prairie Historical Marker,** which reads: "Lost Prairie was named by a group of Willamette Valley settlers who camped here in April, 1859, while

House Rock (Little Cross) Falls

searching for a cattle trail over the Cascade Mountains to central Oregon pastures. The expedition was led by Andrew Wiley. To reassure less stout-hearted members, who felt the party was lost, Wiley climbed a tree on a nearby mountain and was the first white man to view the Santiam Pass from the west side of the mountains."

Lost Prairie FS CG, park-like area that can be taken for a beaver homestead. *1.6 m.,* Hackleman Creek Rd.

* *4.8 m.,* turning L at every forks, thru heavily logged country, O 126, at Clear Lake.

2 m., turnoff N of Lava Lake.

Geologists say the rocks here — indeed, along US 20 from Lebanon to about 15 m. E of here — erupted some time ago, between 15 and 30 million years to be exact. Evidence of that eruption comes in the form of mudflow deposits, ash beds and lava flows. Starting with jct. of O 126 and extending E for several m., US 20 cuts over the N portion of Sand Mtn. lava field. More than 20 minor volcanoes form almost a straight line, from about 1 m. N of hwy. to about 7 m. S of it. Trees along here that were killed by an eruption have been dated to be 3000 years old.

0.6 m., jct., O 126.

0.3 m., panoramic view of Three-Fingered Jack. *0.9 m.,* on S, **Sawyers Ice Cave,** shallow lava tube in basalt that erupted about 3500 years ago. Cold inside! About *100 yds.* uphill is much larger ice cave — part of lava tube system traversing this area.

0.4 m., crater flows typical of area. One has the feeling that the ruins of another world lie here. If some civilization were to survive a nuclear war, this is the kind of thing people might see a thousand years after the holocaust.

0.8 m., Little Nash Sno-Park. Cross-country skiing popular here. *0.9 m.,* Jct., O 22.

1.8 m., on N, **Lost Lake FS CG,** by a lake that normally stays frozen until late spring. Geologists say red and black cinder cones were red hot about 2,000 years ago. Lost Lake seems an American reflection of a Karelian lake, with its tundra ambience imagery. Arkhippa Perttunen, whose runes provided much of the core of the Karelian national epic, the *Kalevala,* which inspired Henry Wadsworth Longfellow to write *The Song of Hiawatha,* probably had lakes such as this Lost Lake in mind when he sang: "Then the Frost/ his songs recited,/ And the Rain/ its legends taught me;/ Other songs/ the winds have wafted;/ Or the ocean waves/ have drifted;/ And their songs/ the birds have added,/ And the magic spells/ the tree-tops."

3.4 m., on N, **Historical Marker.** It reads: "The old grade crossed by the Santiam Highway at this point was built as part of the Corvallis & Eastern RR by T. Egenton Hogg in 1888 and was to have connected Newport and Boise. Hogg Rock, the solitary eminence just west, is named for Hogg." The shadowy "Colonel" Hogg, one of the least-defined entrepreneurs in Oregon history, was great for promoting and raising money until all that he promoted went down the drain.

Mt. Washington from Santiam Pass

Courtesy State of Oregon

Three years after he was ousted form the RR venture, he died in Philadelphia, which some Oregonians then did not regard as a compliment.

0.3 m., turnoff S to **Hoodoo Bowl,** one of NW's finest ski areas, and Big Lake.

    * 0.5 m., Ray Benson Sno-Park. 0.4 m., magnificent view of Mt. Washington. 1.3 m., turnoff 0.5 m. to Pacific Crest Trail. Straight. 0.3 m., turnoff to **Big Lake FS CG.** PA, BL. Big Lake has full-scale reflection of Mt. Washington. (Returning to US 20, excellent view of Three-Fingered Jack).

0.3 m., **Pacific Crest Trail.** 0.5 m., **Santiam Pass** — 4,817 ft. On clear day, unless blocked by trees, fine snapshots of 7,841 ft. Three-Fingered Jack and 7,802 ft. Mt. Washington.

3 m., turnoff to **Elliott R. Corbett II Memorial SP.**

    * 0.8 m., jct: turnoff to Circle Lake (3.6 m.,) and to Corbett SP; hiking access only to SP, in primitive area. PA. No CG.

3.3 m., turnoff to Suttle Lake — Marina. 0.3 m., turnoff for Suttle Lake, Blue Lake and Scout Lake.

    * 0.9 m., turn R to Blue Bay CG (0.1 m.), BL. Return to road. Turn R. 0.1 m., turnoff R to South Shore CG — BR (0.2 m.) Return to road. Turn R. 0.2 m., L for Scout Lake. 0.7 m., **Scout Lake FS PA** and Swim Area. No dogs. Return to last jct. Turn L. 1 m., **Link Creek FS CG,** BL on Suttle Lake. 25 yds., turn L. 0.4 m., **Blue Lake.** Return to last intersection. Turn L. 0.2 m., **Suttle Lake FS CG,** on Suttle Lake.

This Blue Lake, one of 11 in state by that name, is only 54 acres in area but, because of its depth, greater at maximum than 300 ft., is well-known as "the Crater Lake of the Central Oregon Cascades." Geologists say the aquamarine crater was blasted out of solid rock by cataclysmic steam explosions. Part of the rocky, forested S and W shores of the lake are occupied by Corbett Memorial SP, wilderness area with only water and toilet installations provided. Link Creek, outlet stream of Blue Lake, has cut thru crater wall to travel 0.4 m., to Suttle Lake. Although Blue Lake reflects the corniculate peak of Mt. Washington, most first-timers here exclaim, "So blue!" Newcomers to Suttle Lake gush, "How lovely!"

Blue and Suttle Lakes occupy the same basin but Suttle is glacial in origin. Much larger than Blue Lake, Suttle (253 acres) is not nearly as deep (only 45 ft. at maximum). One does not have to inquire why Blue was so named, Suttle is a misspelling; tribute was paid to John Settle, closely associated with "building" of Willamette Valley and Cascade Mountain Military Wagon Road, swindle of the 1860s. Unscrupulous promoters have a long history in Oregon.

Both lakes are key elements of this very popular tourist area, which is wound in hiking and horse trails; boasts excellent fishing (trout and salmon); is almost as well known for swimming, water skiing and small boating; and is abundant with resorts and CGs. Winter brings a decline in visitors, but not dramatically.

0.9 m., turnoff to Mt. Jefferson Wilderness Trailheads.

2.7 m., Metolius River — Camp Sherman Jct.

    * *2.7 m.,* jct., Metolius River — Camp Sherman. Turn R for Metolius River. *1.7 m.,* turn L. *0.2 m.,* parking for **Metolius River.** Sign at start of 400 yd. trail reads: "Down this path a full-sized river, the Metolius, flows ice cold from huge springs. The springs appear to originate from beneath Black Butte. However, geologists say this is misleading and believe the springs have their origin in the Cascade Mountains to the West. The unusual fault which created Green Ridge is thought to have brought the springs to the surface, thus releasing the beautiful Metolius River."

    The Metolius begins humbly, a swish of water thru barefoot grass, and for a quarter of a mile brushes against and thru the grass, awakening and stretching its arms. Then, though still a narrow stream, it begins to free itself from the green entanglement and find a clear path ahead. From the base of 6,415 ft. Black Butte the coursing rivers points N for 20., aiming at 10,495 ft. Mt. Jefferson. It zings thru open woods of ponderosa pine and western larch, dotted with incense cedar, Douglas and lowland fir, and Engelman spruce. About halfway thru its 46 m. length, the Metolius bends E, forming the S boundary of the Warm Springs Indian Reservation. Then, in a dramatic climax, it rushes thru a rocky gorge, more than 1,500 ft. deep at points, to pour into Lake Billy Chinook, the creation of Round Butte Dam, where the Metolius is merged with the Deschutes and the Crooked. The Metolius, an Indian word for "white fish" or "light colored spawning salmon," is regarded by true Izaak Waltons as one of the best rainbow trout streams in the W (only fly fishing permitted). But you do not have to be a fisher to rejoice in the beauty of the stream and the land thru which it passes. Painters and photographers insist the Metolius was made for art — and few with clear eye will disagree.

    * Return to Metolius River — Camp Sherman Jct. *1.3 m.,* jct. Turn R. *0.4 m.,* on R, **Chapel in the Pines,** non-denominational church which started life as a boxcar church for a "community on wheels" that went along with a company's logging operations in the Cascades. It was brought here in 1956. *0.2 m.,* **Camp Sherman,** year-round rustic village that is center of Metolius River recreation area activities. Camp Sherman has stores, restaurants, resorts, growing number of residences. Square dancing at Community Hall brings together dudes and wranglers. Bridge here is fine spot for aiming cameras at the Metolius, with its frothy background.

    * Turn for Wizard Falls. *0.4 m.,* **Camp, Sherman FS CG,** in the pines and along the river. *0.6 m.,* **Allingham FS CG.** *0.3 m.,* **Smiling River FS CG.** *0.4 m.,* **Pine Rest FS CG.** *0.3 m.,* **Gorge FS CG.** *0.6 m.,* jct. Turn L. *2.1 m.,* jct. Turn L for **Wizard Falls Trout Hatchery.** *0.2 m.,* across Metolius, hatchery. Wizard Falls is little more than a fast riffle in the river but because it breaks the flow of the stream it has a sense of audacious beauty. If you look

**Metolius River at its source. Mt. Jefferson
in the background.**

Courtesy State of Oregon

close you may see the riffle as a big fish somersaulting downstream, with its white belly flashing in the sun.

*Return to intersection. Turn L. *0.6 m.,* **Allen Springs FS CG.** *1.6 m.,* **Pioneer FS CG.** *0.7 m.,* **Lower Bridge FS CG.** *0.6 m.,* turn L onto FS rd. *0.8 m.,* at spur to L, park car. Trail of 400 yds. to oxbow of stream, **Metolius River Nature Conservancy Preserve.** Nature Conservancy states: "A low elevation, sphagnum bog occurs here. As well, an Engleman spruce bottom-land forest is present, harboring seven conifer species. The largest reported population of *Penstemon peckii,* an endemic to Oregon, occurs here. Peak of flowering is in mid-June."

From turnoff to Metolius River — Camp Sherman, on US 20:

2 m., **Black Butte Ranch,** exclusive sanctuary for the well-heeled.

2.1 m., **Indian Ford FS CG.** Historical Marker reads: "Here was a ford on the Indian trail mentioned by Lieutenant John C. Fremont. Evidently the only whites to have used it consisted of an early day surveying party led by Lt. Henry L. Abbot and Pacific RR survey party in Sept., 1855."

4.8 m., Historical Marker explaining that in this vicinity Indian trails from all parts of the area and as far N as The Dalles converged here.

0.8 m., jct., O 242.

50 yds., on R, O 242, Historical Marker of McKenzie Hwy. *0.1 m.,* on L, **Patterson Ranch,** largest herd of llamas in W.

At jct., US 20 and O 242, Sisters Ranger Station (USFS).

Chapel of the Pines, Camp Sherman

The Nature Conservancy Preserve at Bend of the Metolius

Llamas at Patterson Ranch, Sisters   *Courtesy US Forest Service*

0.3 m., from jct., downtown **Sisters,** which knots together the strands of US 20, O 126 and O 242. Because of its proximity to Three Sisters — originally named by early Methodist missionaries as Mounts Faith, Hope and Charity — Sisters is one of Central Oregon's most attractively-sited cities. But the village has tried to improve on nature — for reasons of commerce — by becoming a "True Western" town thru false-fronting the main street stores and shopping mall. This works fairly well in tourist-heavy summer but the rest of the year, even accounting for winter sportspeople, Sisters has its problems. "Behind the glitter there's trouble," said a middle-aged woman working as a waitress because her husband and son were unemployed. "There's no industry here," she explained. As bustling as the main drag is in the daytime, so markedly does it become deserted after the sun goes down. A merchant said in June: "Between eight and ten p.m., Sisters has increasing cardiac arrest. After ten it's dead."

For one of the more spectacular drives of Central Oregon, start out from Elm St., near old-fashioned Sisters Hotel. Magnificent views of Three Sisters and Broken Top. Road thru pine forest is mysterious and enticing, beckoning one to a world unseen.

* *8 m.,* **Black Pine Spring FS CG.** *1.3 m.,* on L, pine-covered 4,998 ft. Melvin Butte, named for homesteader J. L. Melvin, who accused a neighbor of putting sawdust in his irrigation ditch, got into fight with him at site of butte, killed the man, and was charged with murder. But jury, which knew importance of pure water, cleared Melvin, who then became sort of folk hero. *4.6 m.,* face-on view of Tam McArthur Rim, on Broken Top. *0.7 m.,* **Three Creek Meadows FS CG;** elev. 6,300 ft. *0.3 m.,* forks. L, unimproved road goes to Todd Lake. Straight: *0.8 m.,* **Driftwood FS CG.** Three Creeks

Hotel Sisters in Sisters

Lake, forest-fringed basin, looks up to rim named for Lewis A. "Tam" McArthur, original author of *Oregon Geographic Names*.

An historic side trip leading out of Sisters is to site of old Camp Polk.

* From city center, Sisters, drive *0.3 m*. E on US 20 to Locust Ave. Turn L, or N, on Locust Ave., which becomes Camp Polk Rd. *2.8 m.*, Indian Ford Rd. Straight on Camp Polk Rd. *0.3 m.*, bear R on Camp Polk Rd. *0.4 m.*, on L, cattleguard. Turn L, across cattleguard. *0.2 m.*, barn, oldest standing structure in Deschutes County, that is on site of **Camp Polk,** military outpost built and occupied in winter of 1865–66 under command of Capt. Charles LaFollette of Polk County, Oregon. Neither he nor any of his 40 men of Co. A, first Oregon Volunteer Infantry, ever engaged the Indians in battle or ventured into the High Desert to seek out the dreaded foe, Chief Paulina. In 1870 first white settler came along and in 1875 Camp Polk had a PO. In 1880 PO moved to Sisters and given new name. *0.2 m.*, **Camp Polk Cemetery** (1875).

* For an experience even more soul-satisfying, return from Camp Polk to Indian Ford Rd. Turn R. *1.3 m.*, turn R onto Stevens Canyon Rd. Mail box marked "Staender" is at corner and across road is ranch. *2.1 m.*, tire tracks to R. About *25 yds.* down trace may be chain across dirt track and a small Nature Conservancy sign by chain. If chain is unlocked, drive l m. up trace to parking area at backwoods shanty called Wildhaven House. If chain is locked, park near it and walk the distance to Wildhaven House. Beyond house is **Wildhaven Preserve,** described thusly by The Nature Conservancy:

Three Creeks Lane

Camp Polk Barn

"This preserve contains two predominant communities: western juniper/ bitterbrush/bluebunch wheatgrass, and Ponderosa pine-western juniper/ bitterbrush/ Idaho fescue. The western juniper on the site are extremely old, with some individuals dated at between 800 to 1,000 years of age, making some of them the oldest in the state. The understory condition is extremely rare due to its lack of disturbance. The preserve is located at 3,300 feet elevation on the eastern slopes of the Cascades, in one of the driest regions of the state with annual precipitation of 10 inches."

There are paths to tread and photographs to take and all the while one has the feeling of walking on sacred ground — bits of nature not yet savaged by the hand of Progress.

From N Locust on US 20:

0.1 m., Sisters City Park. PA.

0.2 m., jct., O 126. (See *O 126,* following). *0.1 m.,* **Sisters City Park.** CG. *4.9 m.,* Cloverdale Rd.

 * L on Cloverdale Rd. *2.1 m.,* Jordan Rd. On far R corner, remains of old stage coach station, one of most authentic Old West sights in Central Oregon.

5 m., turnoff to Cline Falls SP. (SP, *11.1 m.,*)

5 m., **Tumalo Emporium.** Turn L. *1 block,* turn L. *5 m.,* **Tumalo Community Church,** built 1917 and oldest standing church in Deschutes County — proof of how relatively new is white settlement in this land. Organ is only one of three of its kind in PNW. Church stands in former town of **Laidlaw,** platted 1904.

0.2 m., Tumalo SP — Cline Falls SP Jct.

 * R, *1.2 m.,* **Tumalo SP.** Hot as the days may be, nights can be windy and chilly. L, *9.8 m.,* Cline Falls.

Old stagecoach station near Sisters

0.2 m., Deschutes River. *1.7 m.,* Tumalo SP Jct.
    * *1.5 m.,* the back way to Tumalo SP. More interesting than the other way.
1.7 m., US 97. (S, *3 m.,* city center, Bend.)

Still the fairest city of the plains, despite a surge of urbanization and the ensuing problems of the unprepared and of the bigness-is-greatness mind set, **Bend** is the gateway to a vast and varied recreational area. Scenic Drive is a good way for people is a hurry to see the city. The route includes Pilot Butte, a 511-ft.-high cinder cone above the plateau. It was this landmark which the emigrants took as their compass point when crossing the desert bound for the Willamette Valley, thus the name.

When the comers reached the Deschutes River here they named the place Farewell Bend, as a fond goodbye to a pleasant place. But before moving on many of the overlanders climbed to the top of Pilot Butte, to look with awe upon the range of snow-capped mtns. extending N and S across their line of march. The vistas today are as equally impressive. Almost the entire range of Oregon's Cascade peaks are visible, blazing white above the hazy, blue-green forests and the ocher plain. Facing E, the earth tilts and changes from a geometry of irrigated farms to burnt-up slope buttes and cones.

Bend was commonly called Farewell Bend until PO of Bend was est. early in 1886. After a tug of war between the names of Deschutes, Pilot Butte and Farewell Bend, Bend survived. But not until the late spring of 1904 was the plat of the town filed for record.

As the key crossroads settlement of Central Oregon, Bend was a natural to grow. By 1915 its pop. was 1,800 and it was the S terminus of a RR, the center of an irrigation district, and the trading and distribution hub of the area. It had five sawmills (being located at the edge of a vast timber belt), two planing mills, flour mill, brick yard, refrigeration plant, electric light and water works systems, HS, PS, public library, four churches, Grange, Commercial Club, Women's Club, a host of fraternal organizations, two banks, weekly paper. By 1940 its pop. had zoomed to almost 9,000 and thereafter began a drive toward 20,000, which it appeared certain to reach when hard times struck. At that, Bend could lay claim to being the largest city E of the Cascades (and down to the Great Heartland.)

As with all cities in a rush, Bend's growth came largely with uncontrolled housing and with shopping centers that left the traditional business section looking orphanish. Thus, some of the city's charm was lost, but its environs remain stupendous.

There are several noteworthy scenic and recreational trips out of Bend; the most memorial — combining the attractions of the Central Cascades — forests, lakes, camps, mtns., trails, rivers, resorts, wild life, lava formations, plants — is the Cascade Lakes Hwy., long known as Century Dr.

Turn W on Franklin Ave. *0.6 m.,* turn R onto Tumalo, *0.5 m.,* turn L onto NW 14th. *8.1 m.,* Viewpoint. *8 m.,* full-faced view of 9,060-ft. Bachelor Butte. *4.4 m.,* Bachelor Butte Jct. (Turnoff to well-known ski area.) *1.6 m.,* Todd Lake Jct. (*1 m.,* **Todd Lake,** elev. 6,150 ft., looking up to 9,152-ft. Broken Top, ruggedest

Tumalo Church

formation in Central Cascades. Lake named for John Y. Todd, Mexican War veteran and early day settler near present Bend. First called Lost Lake, popular early name for many lakes. Covers 29 acres; has max. depth of 60 ft. FS CG.) *0.4 m., lava flow. 1.9 m.,* Sparks Lake Jct. *(0.7 m.,* 779-acre **Sparks Lake;** max. depth 7 ft. FS has two sites here.) *0.6 m.,* Green Lake Trailhead. *(5 m.* trail reaches three **Green Lakes,** mounted in saddle between S Sister and Broken Top.) *0.8 m.,* **Devil's Garden,** mtn. meadow near Satan Creek. FS CG. *0.5 m.,* on R, lava pile. *0.2 m.,* **Devil's Lake,** alpine mirror so close to dead forest of Hells Creek and purgatorial remnants of past volcanic action. Elev. 5,446 ft. Lake covers 30 acres at rather shallow depth of 9 ft. Hwy. here is on old Indian trail. *0.7 m.,* turnoff to Devil's Lake FS CG. *(0.2 m.,* FS CG. Trails take off here for S Sister and Wickiup Plains.) *1.4 m,* Mirror Lakes Trailhead. *1.3 m.,* **Quinn Meadow Horse Camp.** Horses are might popular in these parts — almost as common as sail boats and fishing rods. *1.4 m.,* Sunset View Jct. *(1.4 m.,* **Sunset FS PA.** Splendid view of Elk Lake and the eminences above it from E. Fine swimming.) *0.4 m.,* Elk Lake Resort Jct. *(0.2 m.,* **Elk Lake** and **Elk Lake Resort.** Elk Lake covers 405 acres with max. depth of 62 ft. Lake has no surface outlet. With more than 100 rainbow and Eastern brook trout lakes within 10-m. radius, Elk Lake is regarded as recreational center of Cascade lakes loop. Sail boaters seem to come here in droves. The lofty peak of S Sister, a portrait of grandeur, is mirrored in the waters of Elk Lake; beyond E shore, Bachelor Butte appears as a phoenix arisen from the ashes of its extinct crater. Pack trains for explorations into Three Sisters Wilderness make up at Elk Lake Resort. Point FS CG nearby.) *0.7 m.,* Beach Picnic turnoff. *(0.2 m.,* on Elk Lake, Beach FS CG.) *0.7 m.,* Six Lakes Trailhead. *0.5 m.,* **Horse Lake** — E Elk Lake. *1.3 m.,* turnoff to BR on Hosmer Lake. *(0.1 m.,* 198-acre **Hosmer Lake,** max. depth 12 ft., stocked with Atlantic salmon. *0.2 m.,* forks. L, *0.1 m.,* **Mallard Marsh CG;** R, *0.1 m.,* South CG.) *2.7 m.,* Lava Lakes Jct. *(0.6 m.,* "T". L, *0.4 m.,* **Big Lava Lake;** straight, *0.4 m.,* **Little Lava Lake.** FS CG. Lava Lakes comprise source of Deschutes River.) *1.5 m.,* Lucky Lake Trailhead. *2.2 m.,* Deschutes Bridge Jct. *(0.1 m.,* Deschutes Bridge PA. This is the first near-road glimpse of the river.) Beyond this point the road is accompanied for several m. by the Deschutes, which is here no wider than a small creek as it cuts in and out of glades and woods. *3.7 m.,* Crane Prairie FS CG Jct. *(0.8 m.,* jct.: *3.1 m.,* 156-acre, max. depth 55 ft. **Little Cultus Lake.** *3.8 m.,* Taylor Lake to S, Irish Lake to N, two glittering tarns. FS CG at each lake. Crane Prairie FS CG, *5.8 m.*) *0.7 m.,* Cultus Lake Jct. *(1.8 m.,* forks. L, *0.3 m.,* **Cultus Lake Resort.** Straight, *0.2 m.,* **Cultus Lake FS PA.** *0.8 m.,* CG. The 792-acre [max. depth 211 ft.] lake seems to have been designed for a resort; it is postcard scene of recreation, cooled by breezes sifting thru stands of ponderosa, lodgepole and white pine.) *0.4 m.,* Quinn River FS CG — Crane Prairie Res. Jct. *(0.2 m.,* **Quinn River CG,** stone's throw from Quinn River and Crane Prairie Res. This is as good a place as any to see osprey nests in **Crane Prairie Osprey Management Area.** The fish hawks — often mistaken for bald eagles — are scattered thruout the large area. The tall, reedy, gray, naked snags of trees killed when the reservoir was flooded in the early 1920s make excellent nests for the osprey, a rare species said by environmentalists to be threatened with extinction. Other birds which find shelter in the management area include bald eagles, cormorants, blue herons and kingfishers. You will need a telephoto lens to get a readable picture of an osprey in its nest.) *0.5 m.,* Osprey Point Observation Trail turnoff. *(0.2 m.,* parking area. *0.5 m.,* bog trail of 200 yds. to **Crane Prairie** and dead trees. The bog hiking isn't always easy and the view from bog's end isn't any better than Quinn River site, just passed.) *1.1 m.,* Rock Creek FS CG turnoff. *(0.3 m.,* CG on Crane Prairie Res.) *2.5 m.,* jct. (Straight: *20 m.,* O 58.) Turn L for US 97 and remainder of Century Dr. tour. *2.5 m.,* Crane Prairie Dam Jct. *(1.7 m.,* **Crane Prairie Dam.** Historical Marker here reads: "Seeking a railroad pass through the mountains Lieutenants R. L. Williamson and Phil Sheridan with Dr. J. S. Newberry and an escort, passed here August 29, 1855, camping that night on the old Ranger station site four miles north. The next day they camped at Little Lava Lake. Returning, Williamson and Sheridan passed here en route south Sept. 26, 1855.") *1.3 m.,* — past FS CG — Wickiup — Twin Lakes Jct. (Between here and Wickiup Dam, *6 m.,* are N Twin Lake and its CG, Sheep Bridge CG, S Twin Lake and it CG, and Gull Point FS CG on Wickiup Res.) *5 m.,* jct. Turn R for Pringle Falls and remainder

Elk Lake, with South Sister in background   *Courtesy State of Oregon*

"Osprey trees," Century Drive

of this tour. *5.3 m.*, Wickiup Dam Jct. *(4.1 m.,* **Wickiup Dam.**) *2.5 m.*, Fall River Jct. (L, *3 m.*, **Fall River;** R, CGs.) *0.4 m.*, **Pringle Falls,** rapids in the Deschutes. Rapids are spectacular about *200 yds.* downstream. *0.2 m.*, Pringle Falls CG turnoff. *(0.1 m,* CG on Deschutes.) *7.2 m.*, US 97. *25.3 m.*, Bend.

O 226

This road, contrary to others, has been laid out in the format of a "tour," simply because it seems the efficient thing to do. Otherwise, the format would lead to convolution and confusion. The largest concentration of CBs in the state is located in this area, as is one of Oregon's rarest waterfalls. Obviously, then, O 226 is not a road to be swept over casually.

O 226 takes off from US 20 *5.6 m.* from the I-5 overpass, at Albany.

2.5 m., Crabtree Jct. Turn L onto Cold Springs Rd. *0.4 m.*, Crabtree Dr. Turn L. *0.8 m.*, Gilkey Rd. Turn R. *1.9 m.*, on R, white 2-1/2 story house, built 1870, that smacks of earthbreaker time. *1 m.*, on R, three chimney house that looks asleep in great-grandmother's photo album. *1.2 m.*, jct., Kelly Rd. — Gilkey Rd. Take L, Kelly Rd. *1.2 m.*, to R. off road *100 yds.*, site of **Weddle CB,** 120-ft. span built 1937 across Thomas Creek and demolished in October, 1987 despite strong protest.

Return to Kelly Rd. — Gilkey Rd. jct. Go straight, onto Gilkey Rd. *1.2 m.*, **Gilkey CB,** 120-ft. span built 1939 over Thomas Creek. Until 1970 CB stood next to RR CB. At this point stood RR station which served as shipping point for local products. Youth from vicinity jump from CB into Thomas Creek.

Return to Cold Springs Rd. and Crabtree Dr. Continue E on Crabtree Dr. *25 yds.*, turn L onto Hungry Hill Rd. *1.6 m.*, **Hoffman CB,** over Crabtree Creek, built 1936, with length of 90 ft.

Return to Crabtree Rd. Turn L. *0.1 m,*. **Crabtree,** back-country quiet burg that seems stuck in the ambience of the 1930s. Tavern, with wooden sidewalk in front and on side, has gentle neighborliness of village taverns in W Oregon. This one, though, seems special. **Crabtree Church** organized 1909, 63 years after John Crabtree, Linn County's first recorded land owner, est. farm near here.

0.6 m., O 226, at forks. Take L. *0.9 m.*, Brewster Rd. Turn onto it. *1.8 m.*, Griggs Rd., at Willamette Industries Office.

(Turn L. *1.1 m.*, Bond Rd. Turn R. *0.5 m.*, two roads go L, side by side. Nearest has sign reading "Private Road . . . Persons Using This Road Do So at Their Own Risk." This pike, known as Snow Peak Rd., is near suicidal to drive on weekdays, when logging trucks barrel along it like Patton tanks. The virtue of this road is that it passes thru **Crabtree Valley,** a stand of very old timber which conservationists are vigorously trying to protect. *14.2 m.*, site of former **Snow Peak Camp,** legendary logging operation. *10 m.*, [Crabtree Valley], spur road to R. Take it. *0.4 m.*, forks. Take L. *0.1 m.*, **Crabtree Lake.** Around it are trees hundreds of years old. Return *0.5 m.*, to main road. Continue E. *2.3 m.*, forks. Take R. *6.9 m.*, Green Peter — Quartzville Rd. L for O 22, R for US 20. See *US 20*, this section.)

Hoffman Bridge

From Griggs Rd. and Brewster Rd.: S on Brewster Rd. *1.5 m.,* Lacomb Jct. Turn L onto Baptist Church Rd. *1 m.,* turn L onto Richardson Gap Rd. *2.3 m.,* on L, **Providence Church and Cemetery.**

The interdenominational frame church, looking benignly down upon the valley from a knoll, is kinder in disposition than the log church built 1854. That had an air of vigilant righteousness, as though erected by Jeremiah and maintained by avenging angels. The analogy may not be too far-fetched. The church was built as Baptist by a sturdy band of moralists headed by Elder Joab Powell, pioneer circuit rider and one of the most colorful figures in Oregon's ministerial lore.

Tennessee-born (1799), he had been preaching for six years when he moved to W Missouri in 1830. There, between working on his 640-acre farm, he "did the Lord's business" for more than 20 years, until wagoning to Oregon in 1852, where he took a DLC at the forks of the Santiam. Once established on his stock ranch he returned to preaching; his voice was not stilled until his death early in 1873.

A powerfully built man, with broad shoulders, piercing blue eyes and graying hair, Powell was known thruout the region for his booming voice, fiery tongue and burning evangelism. It was said that when he preached in Scio his sermon

The church of Joab Powell

could be heard in Jefferson, almost 10 m. away. No farm household short of being stone deaf could fail to tell Powell was coming by his off-tune rendition of "The Judgment Day, the Judgment Day is rolling on, Prepare, O prepare!"

Although he could scarcely read (and write), he had a sponge-like memory and needed to hear a biblical passage or a hymn only once to remember it word for word (though not note for note.) He seemed never without a bible; he could not go to the outhouse, his contemporaries said, without taking the good book along.

"Uncle Joab," as his parishioners called him, was anything but prosaic. First off, he was a formidable sight, packing 300 lbs. into an above 6-ft. frame covered by homespun garments. Before he started his preaching, usually in shirt sleeves, he'd jam a chaw of terbacky into his mouth and pull on his galluses. Then he'd open with, "Well, breethring, I will sing you a little song! I am the Alpha and the Omegay," accenting heavily the last syllable. Whenever his sermons didn't properly arouse his listeners he lamented, as though consigning the unenthusiastic to perdition, "There is not much rejoicing in Heaven tonight."

Mattoon's *Baptist Annals of Oregon* said of him: "He traveled all over the Territory, and was well known everywhere, and whenever it was announced that he was to preach, he was sure of a crowded house. He had no education . . . He murdered the English grammar, and used figures of speech that were certainly original. Yet he did a vast amount of good. His sermons were full of earnest appeals, and he would exhort, sing, pray, and entreat, until his audience was sometimes in tears and sometimes in smiles . . . With his ready wit and uncultivated humor, he was always ready for interruptions, disturbances or emergencies . . . It was claimed that with his own hand he baptized nearly or quite 3000 persons."

A bit of poetry about him made its way into *Rural Rhymes of Olden Times* (edited by Martin Rice):

"And who of you that ever heard/ Joab Powell preached the word,/ But had his better feeling stirred,/ by plain and simple talk."

Not all who heard Powell speak did so out of sincerity or even curiosity. There were those who, poking fun at Powell's crudeness of speech, came to snicker and jeer. Once, when a town dandy had gone too far, Powell halted his sermon and rendered this rebuke: "Young man! You feller leaning agin that post! You're the one I mean; you'd better go to praying than be standing there a-laughin' at me, you poor, miserable sinner, you!"

On one occasion Powell was invited to act as chaplain of the state legislature; he responded by issuing the shortest prayer in the history of that body: "Lord, forgive them, for they know not what to do."

Powell's circuit riding life is now part of pioneer history and Oregon folklore but almost completely forgotten is as equally a serious side of him. Though Southern-reared and long an inhabitant of a pro-slavery area, he was an ardent abolitionist and consistently flailed against slavery and unequal treatment of blacks.

The cemetery, back of the church, is laid neatly on the quiet hill, with seldom any sound but the wind to reach the graves. Both Powell and his wife lie here, under simple stones. The epitaph on Ann Beeler Powell's marker may be a commentary on the death of her restless, relentless, fire-and-brimstone spouse: "There remaineth therefore a rest to the people of God."

Return to Baptist Church Dr. Turn L. *3.3 m.*, "T", at Meridian Rd. Turn R. *0.2 m.*, **Lacomb,** a compromise on Tacoma, which PO authorities rejected. In 1915, this dorp had pop. 50, sawmill, HS and PS, and daily stage to Lebanon and Albany. Today it is only store. Tourist interest here: old Baptist Church. (*4.1 m.*, US 20, at Lebanon.)

Return to Brewster Rd. Turn L. *2 m.*, **Brewster.** Store. (*2.9 m.*, US 20, at Lebanon.)

Return to O 226, at Brewster Rd. Turn R. *0.3 m.*, turn R onto Fish Hatchery Rd. *3.1 m.*, Richardson Gap Rd. Turn R. *1.1 m.*, **Providence Church.** In vicinity of church there were in 1890s ocher paint mines in operation.

Return to Richards Gap Rd. and Fish Hatchery Rd. Straight on Richardson Gap Rd. *1.3 m.*, **Bohemian Hall CB,** over Crabtree Creek, built 1947, span of 120 ft. Locals call the span Richardson Gap Bridge. The name Bohemian Hall came from lodge Czech settlers built here.

Return to Fish Hatchery Rd. Turn L. *3.3 m.*, forks. Take L. *0.2 m.*, **Larwood CB,** over Crabtree Creek, built 1939, with length of 105 ft. Near bridge, Roaring River empties into Crabtree Creek, only place in nation a river flows into a creek, say both locals and Ripley "Believe It or Not." (Locals refer to span as Roaring River Bridge.) Across bridge is **Larwood Wayside,** fine for picnicking, swim-

House near Brewster

Bohemian Hall Bridge

Larwood Bridge

ming, fishing and just lazing. *0.1 m.*, "T". Turn R. *0.6 m.*, **Roaring River CP.** More greenery on the splash-happy stream. *0.6 m.*, **Roaring River Fish Hatchery.** Albino cutthroat trout and large rainbow brood trout present all year. "Herman" the sturgeon, a centenarian displayed at the State Fair since 1932, resides at the hatchery.

0.4 m., forks. Take R. *0.5 m.*, at end of pavement, turn sharp L uphill on rocky rd. *0.5 m.*, spur rd. to L. Keep straight. *1.6 m.*, forks. Take L. *0.2 m.*, on R, tiny stream gurgling down bank. Below it is culvert, unseen from car. (Culvert is *50 yds.* before rd. bends to R.) Here, to L, is jumpoff for veritable find. Arduous passage thru woods, following S Fork of Roaring River, leads to **Staircase Falls,** one of least-known, lesser-even-seen waterfalls in state. Approximately 100 ft. from drop to bottom, river literally descends a flight of rock stairs. Spectacular, to state the obvious. But a strong word of caution: only persons in excellent physical condition and properly garbed should attempt hike, which takes, round trip, from 40 to 90 minutes, depending on skill and durability of hiker and on condition of terrain. There are no paths. You have to make your own. You must climb over and under fallen logs, push thru fern-dominated woods, cling to plants and branches that hopefully will not give way and, from the top of the falls, worm your way down to a precipitous descent. If the ground is wet you may be in trouble. (See "A Climb Down Staircase Falls" in author's *This Side of Oregon*.)

Staircase Falls

Return to Fish Hatchery Rd. at O 226 and turn E onto O 226. *3.5 m.,* on N, turnoff to **Franklin Butte Cemetery** (*0.1 m.*) Markers go back to 1860s. Section contains a dead village of Czech-born settlers of Scio area.

Return to O 226. Turn E. *1.4 m.,* O 226 — Scio Jct. Straight. *0.3 m.,* **Scio,** compact little town of 600 named for Ohio home town of flour mill builder in 1860. In 1915 town, even with only 500 pop., must have seemed larger. It had five lodges, weekly paper, Commercial Club, annual Linn County School Children Industrial Fair, annual June Rose Show, and a regular stage met all trains; the Southern Pacific came within 2 m. of Scio and the Corvallis & Eastern, 3 m. At C & E stop was Munkers, with PS. Czech immigrants found Scio area similar to their homeland vales and settled here, establishing Z. C. B. J. lodges. Roughly translated: Western Fraternal Brotherhood. A surviving lodge hall is near O 226 jct. The brief main street is a tintype of some decades back, with its small stores and some false front bldgs. **Scio Museum,** at 1st and Ash, is in old West Scio Depot, built late 1880s and moved and restored after it had spent about 25 years on nearby farm. Much of museum's small storage is taken up with complete set of issues of the Scio newspapers going back to 1890. Museum in Chapin Park, wayside on Thomas Creek. Traditional big days in Scio: Linn County Lamb and Wool Fair (coupled with Northwest Champion Sheep Dog Trials) in May.

(Take Jefferson Rd., downtown. *0.8 m.,* turn R onto Miller Cemetery Rd. *1.4*

Shimanek Bridge

Hannah Bridge

m., **Miller Cemetery.** Markers back to 1853. *0.6 m.,* turn L. *0.2 m.,* site of no-more **Shelburn,** hamlet of yore. In 1915 it had pop. 75, PO, store, blacksmith shop, PS, two churches. *1 m.,* forks. Take L. *0.1 m.,* at forks, take L. *1.3 m.,* West Scio. Store. Turn R. *1.5 m.,* forks. Take L. *3 m.,* Jefferson.)

Return to O 226 — Lyons Jct. Turn L, toward Lyons. *2.2 m.,* Richardson Gap Rd. Turn L. *0.7 m.,* **Shimanek CB,** over Thomas Creek, built 1966, with span of 130 ft. First CB built 1904 at cost of $1,150. Red-painted, old style portal design and louvered windows make Shimanek the best-looking CB in Linn County and one of most photogenic in state.

Return to jct. — Richardson Gap Rd. and O 226. Turn L onto O 226. *4.4 m.* on R, *50 yds.* into Camp Morrison Dr., **Hannah CB,** over Thomas Creek, built 1936, with length of 105 ft. *1.6 m.,* site of former Jordan CB, over Thomas Creek, built 1937, with span of 90 ft. (Rebuilt CB stands in Stayton.) Dam (long inactive) and the intriguing rock formations below it make very pretty sight. Near here was small lumber mfg. complex, store, PO (1874–1905). Turn R. *0.9 m.,* at "T", site of community of **Jordan.** Presently: church, school. Local historians say Jordan Valley was named by Joab Powell out of respect for the Holy Land.

Return to O 226. Turn R. *6.3 m.,* Lyons. (See *0 22,* preceding.) *1.2 m.,* O 22.

O 126 — Eugene to Redmond
O 242 — O 126 to Sisters

Better known as the McKenzie River Hwy., O 126 is the most intimate of Trans-Cascade routes. This may be because of the numerous hamlets along the road; or of its affinity to the McKenzie River, so clear green as to surprise and awe at every view; or of the road itself, which seems more a back-country pike than a major hwy.; or the woods, which belong more to everyday experience than to glossy photography.

At Exit 194A on I-5, S of Eugene, turnoff to O 126.

1.2 m., turnoff to **Springfield** city center.

1.1 m., edge of city center. Continue on S 2d St. *1.1 m.,* end of street. Cross street 50 yds. to gravel jct. Take R. *0.1 m.,* **Briggs House** (1898) and start of **Dorris Ranch,** 250 acres donated by Dorris family and developed by Springfield's Wilamalane Park and Recreation Division as a "living historical farm." Return downtown. **Springfield Museum,** 6th and Main. Best part: "Old Springfield," on 2d floor.

There is scarcely a soul around Springfield now who remembers town in 1930s, when it had quiet, folksy main street which fell asleep at night when sidewalks were rolled up. (See "In My Beginning" in author's *Tales Out of Oregon*.) Today this city, built upon lumber, is a maze of shopping centers and subdivisions and one actually has to look for downtown to find it. Once the burly, rustic, only half-acknowledged cousin of Eugene, it is now almost as sophisticated. In 1957, Springfield inaugurated mid-July Broiler Festival that has become one of major events of Willamette Valley.

From 6th and A, one block from museum, turn E.

2.8 m., Jasper — Marcola Jct.

    * Turn S for Jasper. *0.8 m.,* "T". *2.5 m.,* site of **Natron,** named for mineral found near where RR station was built. 1915 Natron had PS, Grange. Just neighborhood now. *1.9 m.,* Pleasant Hill-Oakridge Jct. (*3 m.,* Pleasant Hill.) *0.1 m.,* **Jasper,** named 1880 for son of pioneer who sank roots here in 1846. Refreshing suburb with store, station, Grange and pretty park (fee). From Jasper SE: *5.8 m.,* Fall Creek; *4.8 m.,* Lowell and Lookout Point Dam; *1.8 m.,* O 58, *1.7 m.,* E of Dexter.

At Jasper-Marcola Jct.:

    * N for Marcola. *1.6 m.,* "T". Turn R. *9.9 m.,* Marcola, in Mohawk Valley. (For Mohawk Valley, see *The Great Heartland, East Side Shunpiking,* O 99E, O 228.)

1.5 m., at 57th St., jct. with passby O 126.

From City Center Jct. on Freeway O 126:

5.2 m., Springfield Jct. *0.5 m., Thurston District.* Thurston named for 1847 infant comer George H. Thurston, son of Oregon's first territorial delegate in

Congress, Samuel Royal Thurston. In 1915, Thurston had PS and Christian Church.

3.1 m., Thurston Rd.

   * *1.9 m.,* Thurston School, in old Thurston District, now part of Spring-field.

1.6 m., **McKenzie River,** first glimpse along this route of what the late Prince Helfrich, a famous river runner, called "the most beautiful clear green river in America."

0.2 m., **Hendricks Bridge SP Wayside.**

   * *0.1 m.,* Wayside, on river. PA, fishing, boating, FHP. A CB here was claimed to be longest span of its kind in the country. It has been gone for seeming ages but Lane still has more CBs than any other county, though greatest concentration is in Linn.

0.1 m., Walterville Jct.

   * *0.7 m.,* "T". Turn R. *0.3 m.,* Millican Community Hall. *0.2 m.,* **Walter-ville** business district: store. Walterville named by early settler George Milli-can for his son Walter. The Millicans later moved to central Oregon, and a crater and PO were named for George Millican.

0.9 m., Walterville. Now the road wends thru lovely, simple pastoral land, dotted by small farms of sheep and cattle.

7.2 m., on S, Public BL. *0.3 m.,* **Leaburg,** earlier (1877) known as Leaburgh and (1907) Deerhorn. In 1915 hamlet had pop. 75 and HS and PS and was a more homogeneous community then. *1.3 m.,* on S, turnoff to Greenwood Dr.

Leaburg Dam

Goodpasture Bridge   *Courtesy State of Oregon*

      * *0.3 m.,* **Greenwood Cemetery,** with markers back to 1887.

1.2 m., BR on McKenzie. *0.7 m.,* McKenzie Fish Hatchery. *1.9 m.,* Leaburg Dam.

      * Cross bridge to **Water Board Municipal Park** (PA) and **Leaburg Fish Hatchery.** Pond shore E of dam is alive in summer with anglers.

1.7 m., **Goodpasture CB,** 165-ft. span across McKenzie. Built 1938 at cost $13,154. Bridge, with Gothic style windows on both sides, is one of most photogenic and photographed CBs in state.

Beyond bridge the McKenzie ripples sweet and dimplish in summer, a far cry from the snow-bloated, mad demon of early spring.

0.9 m., **Vida,** minuscule hamlet with about same in-village pop. as 1915. Store, station, cafe. Another of the "neighborhood" towns strung along the river.

0.5 m., on S, **House of Horses Museum,** exhibiting the folk genius of 1895-born self-taught painter and wood carver Martha Shelley.

1.7 m., on S, Thompson Lane.

      * *0.2 m.,* Prince Helfrich BL. (For story on Prince Helfrich, see "The Lost Hunter" in author's *Tales Out of Oregon.*)

0.6 m., **Ben and Kay Dorris SP.** PA, swimming, boating.

      * *0.3 m.,* BL.

3.1 m., Rennie Public BL. *1.7 m.,* Silver Creek Public BL. *0.5 m.,* **Nimrod.** In the bible, Gen. 10: 8-9, Nimroad, son of Cush, is alluded to be a great hunter. On

Rafting on McKenzie River off Dorris State Park

the banks of the McKenzie one would think a term for a fisher would be more appropriate, unless the name meant a hunter of trout, though deer were common until people became more common. Store.

1.3 m., **McKenzie Village,** breathing deep of the river. Cafe. All places McKenzie honor Donald McKenzie, partner with John Jacob Astor in Pacific Fur Co., which founded Ft. Astoria. In 1812 the 300-plus-lb. McKenzie, known to his colleagues as "Perpetual Motion" and to his Indian wife, Princess Choin, daughter of chief Concomly, as a "good man," explored the Willamette Valley and its major streams.

1.8 m., **Morton Memorial SP.**

 * *0.1 m.,* SP. PA, fishing, no water.

0.3 m., on S, **Finn Rock.** Legend says the formation was so named because it resembles shark's fin. Alas for legend, place named for early settler Ben Finn. *0.1 m.,* Finn Rock Store. *1.7 m.,* on N, Blue River Jct.

 * Turn onto Blue River Dr. *1.2 m.,* turn L onto Blue River Rd. *0.4 m.,* forks. Take L, toward Viewpoint. *1.1 m.,* **Blue River Dam** and **Reservoir Viewpoint.** The 320-ft.-high earth fill dam holds back 975 acres of water area. Return to Blue River Dr., also known here as Cascade Hwy. and Main St. Turn L. *0.2 m.,* village of **Blue River,** the "big town" on the upper McKenzie. Blue River Tavern, which calls itself "A Working Man's Bar" and "Best Watering Hole on the River" may not have loudest Saturday night country western in county, but at worst it comes close. Town's com-

munity park, volunteer project, has picnic tables and barbecue stoves in grove of firs, and innovative playground equipment.

1.2 m., Forest Glen BL. *0.1 m.*, Blue River Jct.

* *0.1 m.*, **Blue River.** Village was born of mines in area and large stamp hills commonplace decades ago. Almost quarter century after mines were opened, Blue River PO est., 1886. *Lucky Boy,* mining camp on Quartz Creek, *2.5 m.*, beyond Blue River Dam, had PO 1901–06. Site is reached by rough road but there is nothing to show where camp stood.

2.7 m., turnoff N to **Blue River Reservoir.**

* *0.9 m.*, Res. *2 m.*, CG, BR.

1.6 m., jct., **Cougar Reservoir.**

* *0.2 m.*, turnoff R to Delta FS CG. *1 m,* CG and Nature Trail. Return to Res. rd. Turn R. *0.2 m.*, forks. Turn R. *0.4 m.*, S Fork, McKenzie River. *2.4 m.*, jct. (To L, *3 m.*, Echo BR.) Take R. *0.2 m.*, Viewpoint, near dam. **Cougar Lake** is highest Corps of Engineers project in Willamette Valley drainage, with elev. of 1,690 ft. Practically all area around lake remains in pristine state. The 6 m.-long-lake, created by 452-ft.-high dam, seems to exist in a world of silence. *1.8 m.*, Wilderness Vista. *2.4 m.*, parking for hot springs. (*0.5 m.*, comfortable trail to hot springs, first known as Terwilliger, after first

Blue River Reservoir   *Courtesy Corps of Engineers*

white man to see them; then as Capra, after Californian who came across them in 1870s; and now as Cougar. If you insist upon floating in the nude, confine yourself to allotted corner of pond, separated from the conventional by log barrier. CG *0.5 m.* from hot springs.) *2 m.*, S Fork, McKenzie River. *0.1 m.*, forks. (L — *1 m.*, Slide FS CG.) (R. *1.4 m.*, French Pete FS CG. *51.1 m.*, O 58. A slow drive thru a small universe of trees, creeks, buttes and flats. Your gas tank ought to be at least half-full and you ought to have a supply of food — just in case.)

1.1 m., turnoff S to McKenzie River Dr.

   * *0.4 m.*, **Rainbow,** a rather late settlement, named for rainbow trout. Village consists of some houses and noted Holiday Farm, 19th century stage coach stop and farmhouse converted into inn. *0.4 m.*, **Belknap CB,** 4th CB at this point: 1st in 1890, 2d in 1911; 3rd in 1939 and washed out during Christmas flood of 1964; present, built 1966, is 120 ft. in length and has louvered Gothic windows on S side for interior illumination. *0.4 m.*, jct. (L — *0.2 m.*, O 126.) Straight — along river, — *1.8 m.*, O 126.

2.8 m., turnoff S to Rainbow.

   * *2.2 m.*, Belknap CB. *0.4 m.*, Rainbow.

0.7 m., McKenzie Bridge FS CG.

Cougar Dam and Reservoir   *Courtesy Corps of Engineers*

Horse Creek Bridge

* 0.2 m., CG, BL.

0.6 m., **McKenzie Bridge.** Store. *0.2 m., on S, Horse Creek Rd.*

* 1.2 m., on L, **Horse Creek CB,** built 1930, 105 ft. span across Horse Creek. Hasn't been used since 1968. One of the more mundane looking CBs in state. *0.1 m., jct, Cougar Res. (10 m.) 0.3 m., Horse Creek FS CG.*

0.2 m., **Jennie B. Harris SP Wayside.** PA, fishing — but no water. *1 m.,* McKenzie River Trail. *1.5 m., Foley Ridge Rd.*

* 2.5 m., forks. Take R. 3.9 m., turn R on spur road for Rainbow Falls. 0.3 m., trailhead for **Rainbow Falls.** 1,700 yds to viewpoint. Roar of falls is powerful but binoculars needed to see them — and only if FS has trimmed foliage screening viewpoint. A spectacular scene — if it can be seen. Getting down to Separation Creek, which runs thru valley below, is hazardous and should not be attempted by amateurs this side of sanity.

0.8 m., on N, **Paradise FS CB.** Large camping area deep into woods — and raft launch on McKenzie. *0.5 m., Raft Launch Unloading Area.*

0.8 m., jct., O 242.

(For O 242, see this section, following O 126.)

1 m., Belknap Springs Rd.

* Turn W. 0.3 m., turn R for **Belknap Woods,** upper area of Belknap Hot Springs. *0.1 m., Belknap Woods. 0.1 m.,* **Belknap Lodge.** Belknap Hot Springs started in late 19th century. McKenzie River ripples and sings past lodge — refreshing and captivating sight.

1.8 m., Frissell-Carpenter Rd.

Sahalie Falls   *Courtesy State of Oregon*

    * McKenzie River bridge — the stream so photogenic here.

    4.3 m., **Olallie FS CG,** tent and trailer retreat providing feeling of seclusion on bank of swift rippling McKenzie.

    2.1 m., Smith River-Trail Bridge Res. Rd. Jct.

        * *0.2 m.,* Trail Bridge Dam. *0.3 m.,* **Trail Bridge FS CG.** *0.4 m.,* forks. (L, *0.1 m.,* Trail Bridge Res. BL.) R: *3.4 m.,* **Smith River Dam.** *0.1 m.,* Smith River Res. BL. *(2 m.,* by boat only, **Lake's End CG.)**

    2.6 m., turnoff E to Robinson Lake, small and sleepy.

2.5 m., turnoff W *(0.3 m.)* to Carmen Diversion Res.

0.1 m., turnoff W to Ice Cap FS CG — Koosah Falls.

* *0.1 m.,* forks. L, *0.4 m.,* Carmen Res., dreamy pond-like water that seems completely isolated. Straight from forks: *0.1 m.,* take L. *0.1 m.,* **Ice Cap FS CG.** R at forks: *0.1 m.,* **Koosah Falls.** Koosah (Chinook for sky) was once called Middle Forks, being the 2d of three falls created when ancient bed of McKenzie was blocked by a number of lava flows from Belknap Crater, more than 10 m. off. It happened no longer than 1,500 years ago. Koosah drops about 100 ft. in strong volume over burnished escarpment.

0.4 m., turnoff to **Sahalie Falls.**

* *0.1 m.,* parking for falls, reached by easy, short walk. (Wheelchair accessible.) Once called Upper Falls, Sahalie thunders out of pine hill clefts to cascade about 140 ft. into ponds backed by glistening, springy moss.

0.6 m., turnoff to Cold Water Cove FS CG.

* *0.6 m.,* **Cold Water Cove FS CG,** on S shore of Clear Lake.

1 m., turnoff to Clear Lake Day Area and Resort.

* *0.4 m.,* FS Day Area. *0.1 m.,* Clear Lake Resort. The transparent lake, in a 2,000-ft. depression formed many years ago by the vast McKenzie lava flow, which piled up a dam across the old Santiam Valley — the flow came from a rather modest size cinder cone volcano approx. *3 m.* E — is fed by giant springs gushing up from the NE shore, the same springs that created the McKenzie River. The lake, about 100 ft. deep, is not only the coldest in the Cascades — almost a constant 41 degrees F — but the clearest. The drowned trees still rooted in bottom of lake have been judged by radiocarbon analysis to be about 3,000 years old. (This is one of 11 lakes in state called Clear.)

1.8 m., **McKenzie River Trail.** The almost 25 m. trail, usable almost all year because of its low elevation, is reached from many points. It has the proud designation of National Scenic Trail.

0.4 m., turnoff W to **Fish Lake FS CG** *(0.1 m.)* Except for the rainy springs, Fish Lake is no wetter than a meadow.

From Fish Lake to US 20, both sides of the road are at the edges of deep fields of lava.

1.5 m., jct., US 20.

29.8 m. — O 126 and US 20 are one — Sisters. (See *US 20,* preceding, for details.)

From Sisters, at Sisters Hotel:

0.5 m., jct. Take O 126, to L.

10.7 m., Tumalo Jct. (Tumalo, *11 m.*) *4 m.,* Deschutes River. *0.1 m.,* **Cline Falls SP,** on Deschutes. PA, fishing, FHP.

1.9 m., on N, **Reindeer Farm.** Offspring of reindeer brought from Alaska several decades ago roam pastures here, except when they are on show at shopping centers and such.

On S, Helmholtz Way — the road to Petersen Rock Garden.
  * *3.4 m.*, "T". Turn R. *0.5 m.*, turn R onto SW McVey. *2.5 m.*, **Petersen Rock Garden.** The outgrowth of hobby of Danish immigrant farmer, all in native rock, is imaginative construction of form real and fancied.
2.3 m., US 97, Redmond.

O 242

This is primarily a summer road and a tourist road. Commercial travel is discouraged — and is self-discouraging. The road has more curves than a forked-tongue politician and is slower than the delivery of a campaign promise. Speeds of 20 m. per hour can seem fast here and many a person has reached the end of this road with the vow never to try it again. Open only five months of the year, it doesn't possess a single tourist facility. The loneliest, most vulnerable and most spectacular road across the Cascades, it is heaven to the true gypsy and hell to the freeway addict. On the W slope the road, always narrow and never out of sight of the next bend, passes thru woods dominated by fir; the E slope is pine forest, quiet and fragrant and cool, with the shoulders of the road covered by pine needles. No one who would claim to be in search of the soul of Oregon should pass this road by.

O 242 is the only state or federal hwy. touching the Three Sister Wilderness. In addition to the Three Sisters (10,085-ft. North Sister, 10,047-ft. Middle Sister, and 10,358-ft. South Sister), the Wilderness contains such other mtns. to climb as 9,175-ft. Broken Top, 7,524-ft. The Husband, 7,051-ft. The Wife, and 7,810-ft. The Little Brother. Only 154 ft. from the crest of S Sister — the favorite climb of the Three Sisters — there is a lovely lake in a crater. Collier Glacier, between N and Middle Sister, is 1-1.5 m. wide and 0.75 m. long, making it not only the largest of the 14 glaciers found in the Three Sisters but the largest in Oregon. Broken Top is the best example in the coterminous PNW of the effects of advanced glaciation. Within the Wilderness are more than 300 lakes, spread around except for two major groups. The Mink Lake group, in the S, near the boundary line of Lane and Deschutes counties, and on the Pacific Crest National Scenic Trail, contains about 15 lakes, the largest being 360-acre Mink Lake. The Horse Lake group, N of the Mink Lake group, and also near the Trail, consists of about seven lakes, 60-acre Horse Lake being the largest. The fairest of all lakes is probably 5-acre Mirror, befriended by Lancelot and Camelot Lakes and shimmering in the shadow of 6,745-ft. The House Rock, beyond which stretch the Wickiup Plain. Close to the Pacific Crest National Scenic Trail in the north center of the Wilderness, Linton Spring bursts out of solid rock at the edge of Linton Meadows and in the twinkle of an eye is a full-grown creek that runs swift downslope and across enormous fields of grass before emptying into Linton Lake, near Alder Springs on O 242. Between Engelman spruce, western hemlock, white fir, and western red

Icy springs flowing from base of South Sister
feed the Green Lakes in the Three Sister Wilderness

Courtesy State of Oregon

Broken Top Crater, in the heart of the Three Sister Wilderness   *Courtesy State of Oregon*

cedar grow lupine, Indian paintbrush, heather, pine dandelion, cats-ears, Jacobs-ladder, swamp laurel, larkspur, bluebells and host of other wildflowers.

1.4 m., **Limberlost FS CG,** in swath of pure forest. *5.5 m.,* grand view of Three Sisters. *2 m.,* turnout for Proxy Falls.

* *0.5 m.,* trail into Three Sisters Wilderness to **Upper Proxy Falls** and the same distance — the trail splits — to **Lower Proxy Falls.** Upper Falls forks

Upper Proxy Falls   *Courtesy State of Oregon*

around island of firs and splashes in twin columns down terraces that are so evenly spread they seem hand-made. Then, united, Upper Falls spills lustily over thickly green-mossed stumps to a pool which has no visible outlet. Geologists say the water drains into porous lava and reappears elsewhere — no one knows where — as a lake, stream or spring. Total drop of Upper Falls is about 125 ft. Lower Falls is even more impressive. Like Upper Falls, it de-

Lower Proxy Falls

scends in two branches, but its drop, about 200 ft., is steeper and the flow fuller. It emerges from a thicket to race down a bulging wall, leaving an "island" of trees in the middle. Once on the canyon floor, it reforms as a stream and heads for the Pacific. Both falls were formed by a lava dam that can be traced to a volcanic flow originating from Collier Cone.

1.5 m., **Lower Alder Springs FS CG,** small, old-style CG in maw of forest. This is the check-in point for the *1.2 m.,* trail to **Linton Lake,** one of the gems of the Cascades. Contributing to the lake is **Linton Falls,** which leaps down a mtn. side in a staggered and brilliant dazzle of cascades and ripples.

0.1 m., **Alder Springs FS CG.** Even smaller than Lower Alder — and more intimate. During wagon road days it was corral for stock being driven across the range.

0.1 m., Western show gate. From end of Nov. thru end of June, gate is generally closed.

Beyond this point the road groans up Deadhorse Grade, so named because a draw horse keeled over dead on this spiraling (and for some, agonizing) ascent. In less than 5 m. the road climbs almost 1,200 ft. Some people get so dizzy from all the winding that it has been suggested a detoxification center be established halfway.

3 m., on R, magnificent views of Three Sisters. *1.9 m.,* turnoff to Frog Camp.

  * *0.3 m.,* **Frog Camp,** trailhead for Obsidian Trail, which leads into Three Sisters Wilderness.

Three Sisters from O 242

0.5 m., **Scott Road Historical Marker.** It reads: "In 1862 Felix Scott led a crew of 50 men who blazed a trail across the Cascade Mountains, following an old Indian trail which skirted lava flows. Scott hoped to use the new route to take supplies to gold fields in Idaho. His trail was difficult for wagon trains, and in 1866 an easier route was found, which is now the approximate location of the present state highway across McKenzie Pass. In Scott's day this area was known as Summit Prairie. Portions of his old trail, found 1,000 feet north at this point, are still maintained by U. S. Forest Service and used by hikers and horsemen."

There is here an excellent view of Three Sisters.

0.2 m., turnoff for Scott Lake.

0.7 m., **Scott Lake,** deep in the woods and eminently popular. FS CG on shore.

2.5 m., **Belknap Crater View.** Cinder cone on L is Big Belknap Crater; lava cone on R is Little Belknap Crater, responsible for the vast dumps of lava in foreground. Some geologists believe that out of Belknap Crater were belched billions of tons of lava, making the Mt. St. Helens eruption minor in comparison.

Scott Lake, watched over by the Three Sisters   *Courtesy State of Oregon*

Belknap Crater

Belknap Lava Flow   *Courtesy US Forest Service*

Gnarled pines struggle to survive in the lava
fields off O 242   *Courtesy State of Oregon*

Two fiery streams covered the land and from them came many of the falls and lakes and land formations along and spread out from the McKenzie River. Almost everyone has an immediate yen to climb onto the lava fields but caution is strongly advised: the rocks are sharp and sometimes slippery and the going is tricky.

1.3 m., Historical Marker honoring pioneer mail carrier John Templeton Craig, whose route extended from McKenzie Bridge to Camp Polk (Sisters.) While carrying the Christmas mail in 1877, the 56-year-old Craig was caught in a sudden snow storm and sought shelter in a rude cabin. A search party found him frozen to death. A path from the marker leads to cement tomb and to rock where cabin stood. They were placed here by the Oregon Rural Letter Carrier Association in 1930.

Beyond the marker the great lava fields begin and continue for several miles. The wonder is not the high-waved sea of volcanic deposits but the trees, frail and spindly, which stubbornly push their way thru the coral black rocks, reaching for the sun as they battle centimeter by centimeter for life. Out of a harsh soil, thru a prison of rock, in a land of little rain, they battle daily for survival and emergence. Thus do these children of nature's ghetto extend their arms to the sky.

2.2 m., — from Historical Marker — 5,324-ft. **McKenzie Pass** and **Dee Wright Observatory.**

For almost everyone the observatory is the climax of O 242. Reached by flights of stone stairs, the lookout bldg. has two levels. The first — interior — is a series of narrow windows spaced about the lava walls, with each window framing a

Craig Tomb

specific mtn. peak, with name and distance from the bldg. carved into the stone. Larger windows provide panoramic views of much of the Oregon Cascades. The upper level is open to 360 degrees view. Rising above McKenzie Pass, the observatory is in the center of the most extensive lava flows in the state. Astronauts destined for the moon came here to practice.

"Nowhere in the continental United States," says the Forest Service, "is there a more impressive view of recent volcanic activity or a greater variety of volcanic forms than at McKenzie Pass. On a clear day one can see the crest of the Oregon volcanic Cascades from Mt. Hood to Three Sisters. Broken, rugged lava flows cover seventy-five square miles, and cinder cones, land islands and glaciers dot the landscape."

Mt. Hood is 78.5 m. from the observatory; Mt. Jefferson is 28.5 m. off. North Sister, Middle Sister and Mt. Washington are all less than 10 m. away. Some of the clearly observable landmarks have fascinating names: Bald Peter, Horsepasture Mtn., Little Brother, The Husband.

The observatory was named for a simple, unflinching honest, always-ready workingman, who from 1910 to 1934 was a Forest packer and then straw-bossed the CCC crew which built the observatory. Before it was completed, however, Dee Wright died. His monument has not been altered since then; quite an oddity in Oregon affairs.

The 0.5 m. Lava River Trail, starting and ending near the observatory, is, at least in places, part of the McKenzie Salt Springs and Deschutes Wagon Road,

Dee Wright Observatory

North Sister from Dee Wright Observatory

constructed between 1866–72. The road was built across the lava fields, despite the torturous terrain, because it was 1,000 ft. lower in elevation than the older Scott Trail (1862), which crossed the summit near N Sister. Upon completion, toll was charged. Last toll collected was in 1894 at Blue River, formerly known as Craig's Bridge. In 1910 the first automobile wheezed over the summit; in 1917 the state took over the hwy. Some folks say it hasn't improved much since then — but neither has the scenery deteriorated.

A marker on the Lava River Trail reads: "You are standing near the western edge of a lava flow from Yapoah Crater. The flow is eight miles long and about a half mile wide . . . Geologists believe this flow is about 2700 years old, one of the most recent in the area."

For those persons who have gotten nervous coming up the road or want to diminish their tensions before starting down — and others — there are rest stations near the observatory.

O 242 uncoils down the E slope of the Cascades and, when the lava runs out, rushes of ponderosa pine fill the space. Although the Yapoah flow is secreted from the hwy. by the pines, it is close by, to the N.

0.6 m., turnoff to Lava Camp Lake, Millican Crater and Pacific Crest Trail. *2.8 m.,* Black Crater Trail. *3 m.,* Western snow gate. *4.4 m.,* **Cold Springs FS CG** *(0.2 m.),* in open pine. *3.6 m.,* **Patterson Ranch,** the great llama spread of Oregon. The curious llamas approach the fence and coolly survey the human starers. Ranch also home to camels, who generally stay in background. *0.3 m.,* Historical Marker detailing history of transportation of McKenzie Hwy., beginning 1862. *0.1 m.,* jct., US 20.

0.2 m., city center, **Sisters.** Town was named for Three Sisters, which FS calls "the most majestic alpine group in the Cascade Range." First whites to observe peaks were probably in party of peripatetic Peter Skene Ogden of Hudson's Bay Co. At least he recorded the observation in Dec., 1825. In the 1840s Methodist missionaries stationed at Salem wandered E far enough to see the peaks and, properly awed, named them Faith, Hope and Charity. Evidently later observers, believing that mtns. did not possess such noble traits as are endowed to humans, changed name to present calling. Sisters started slowly and then went into decline. In 1915 pop. was 150. By 1940, it had dropped to 130 and was so isolated that *Oregon: End of the Trail* said of it: "This is the last point for 35 miles at which any kind of supplies may be procured." Real revival of Sisters, and its subsequent growth, began in the 1970s, when artists, artisans and semi-Bohemians moved in to est. a mtn. Carmel and innovative merchants false-fronted business structures to give downtown that "genuine Western" look. Despite the surge of showmanship, pop. of Sisters in 1990 was about same as 1950, when town was best-known as habitat of the retired.

O 58
Goshen Jct. to US 97

Prior to the construction of I-5, O 58 was the most feasible route from the Willamette Valley to San Francisco. It is still the prime road to Klamath Falls. Although not singled out in travel literature as a recreational pike, O 58 is heavily recreational in summer. A counting of the lakes, camps, trails, and woods that follow will explain why. There are few settlements; the largest, Oakridge, has about 4,000 people and from Oakridge to US 97, a distance of 50 m., there is no town. But truckers who travel the route, and lots of them do, are known for their hwy. help.

From I-5, at Goshen Jct., S of Eugene:

2.8 m., Coast Fork, Willamette River.

1.7 m., **Pleasant Hill.** Coming into this sweet valley between the Coast and Middle Forks of the Willamette in 1846, the 58-year-old Virginia-born Elijah Bristow, veteran of the War of 1812 and the Creek Indian War, looked about and exclaimed, "What a pleasant hill! Here is my home!" It must have been mighty pretty; he had come up from Calif., to which he had emigrated from Illinois a year earlier. Thus he and his family, including his wife of 34 years, the former Susannah Gabbart, became the first settlers of Lane County. Bristow donated five acres of his claim for "church, school and cemetery purposes," and in the winter of 1849–50 the first school in Lane County was opened at Pleasant Hill. PO est. 1850 with Bristow as postmaster. In these parts the rugged woodsman and sharpshooter was a man for all seasons. As late as the 1950s there were still a lot of oldtimers around Pleasant Hill, and at their reunions they delighted to talk about the days when the latchstring was always out, folks knew each other and cared about each other, and there was much more fun at socials than watching TV or going to the movies. Today, Pleasant Hill, having been shorn of its rustic innocence, is just one more up-to-date suburb of Eugene and Springfield.

0.4 m., on S, historical marker honoring Elijah Bristow — fireplace made of bricks Bristow used in 1846. *0.2 m.,* on S, **Pleasant Hill Church,** oldest of First Christian denomination in state. *0.5 m.,* on N, **Pleasant Hill Cemetery,** one of Oregon's oldest burial grounds, with **2d Pleasant Hill school house** on ridge. Buried here are Elijah Bristow, who died at age 73, and his wife, Susannah. Their simple, austere gravestones, side by side, portray a pioneer American Gothic of the dead.

0.6 m., Jasper Jct.

  * *2.2 m.,* jct. (To R, *0.2 m.,* **Jasper CP,** a big roll of green on the rolling Willamette.) Straight: *0.7 m.,* jct. Turn R. *0.1 m.,* **Jasper,** one of those Toonerville Trolley towns that never took off. Settled before mid-turn of 19th century, it survived as RR station on SP's Cascade line. In 1915 it had 150 pop. and two lodges; today, its business district is a suburban store.

2.9 m., turnoff N on Rattlesnake Rd.

* *0.2 m.,* jct. (To L: **Rattlesnake** PO est. 1868; name changed to Trent 1875. **Trent School** nearby is all to suggest existence of hamlet.) (To R: *0.7 m.,* turn L into **Elijah Bristow SP.** *0.8 m.,* parking area for PA. SP also has Willamette fishing, horse trails, FHP.)

1 m., Dexter Jct.

* *1.5 m.,* **Dexter,** settled in 1848 and first called Butte Disappointment. In 1848, when Elijah Bristow and five other Pleasant Hill men were hot in chase of some Indians, they aimed for a butte, to pick up trail. But high waters of the Willamette prevented them from reaching the butte, hence the name. PO est. 1872; name changed to Dexter three years later. In 1915 town was one of few in state to have Athletic Club. At foot of gentle Lost Valley, Dexter seems pleasant place to live. Today it is another rural suburb, with store. Without the store, the sites of so many Oregon towns of past would be difficult to locate.

1.6 m., on N, Dexter Park. BL.

0.3 m., Dexter-Lost Creek Jct.

* *5.5 m.,* keeping on Lost Creek Rd., site of **Zion** (PO 1899–1913.) *2 m.,* site of **June** (PO 1895–1907.) In 1915 it had pop. 50 and sawmill.

1.7 m., on N, Lowell-Fall Creek Dam Jct. At jct. is **Lowell CB,** over Middle Fork of Willamette. Ferry across stream until 1907, when first bridge put up. Present span — 165 ft. — constructed 1945; no longer in use.

* *0.7 m.,* Main and Pioneer, **Lowell.** (To R — 50 yds., Lowell Gen. Store,

Second Pleasant Hill School, now a storage building at the Pleasant Hill Cemetery

Graves of Susanna and Elijah Bristow, Pleasant Hill Cemetery

Lowell Bridge

put up 1907; still has sunbonnet cheery look.) Straight on Pioneer: *1 block*, N Shore Dr. Turn L onto it. *0.7 m.*, **Lowell Park.** BL on Dexter Reservoir. *0.6 m.*, Dexter Dam. *2.7 m.*, BL. Return *2.9 m.* to N Shore and Moss. Turn L. *1.9 m.*, **Unity.** Store. Across road, **Unity CB,** 90-ft. span over Big Fall Creek, built 1936. Turn R at Unity onto Winberry Creek Dr. *0.4 m.*, jct., Big Fall Creek Rd. — Winberry Creek Rd. Here was **Winberry,** which in 1915 had pop. 25, PS and ME Church. *0.1 m.*, turnoff to Fall Creek Dam (*0.2 m.*) *1.1 m.*, turnoff to North Shore BR (*0.2 m.*) Return *1.2 m.* to Winberry Creek Rd. — Big Fall Creek Rd. jct. Turn L, onto Winberry Creek Rd. *0.7 m.*, viewing area of **Fall Creek Dam.** *0.4 m.*, turnoff to Winberry Creek Park (*0.2 m.*) on S side of Fall Creek Lake. PA, BL.

1.5 m., viewpoint of **Lookout Point Res.** *11.2 m.*, turnoff N for Hampton FS CG (*0.1 m.*). BR on Lookout Point Lake.

1.5 m., on N, **Black Canyon FS CG.** Richly wooded, with BR on lower end of Lookout Point Lake. FHP. One of most delightful FS CGs in Cascades.

1.9 m., on S, **Shady Dell FS CG,** haven of songbird tranquility, with many old, tall trees.

2.2 m., on N, Westfir Jct.

   * *0.5 m.*, jct. Turn L. *1.8 m.*, on L, **Office CB,** 180-ft. span across N Fork of Willamette, built 1944 as private entrance to mill. Alas, mill burned down in Dec. 1984, a bitter Christmas present to people of the area. *0.1 m.*, **Westfir,**

Unity Bridge

est. 1923 by Western Lumber Co., whose main product was fir. Store. *1.8 m.*, Oakridge Jct. Straight. *1.1 m.*, "T". *0.5 m.*, Oakridge.
2.1 m., on N, Westfir Jct.

    * At corner, **Ferrin FS CG,** on Middle Fork of Willamette. *1.3 m.*, jct. Straight. *1.8 m.*, Office CB. *0.1 m.*, Westfir. *3.4 m.*, by back road, Oakridge.
2.1 m., **Oakridge,** biggest town on or off O 58 and a true logger's stronghold, though travel-through services keep city alive when lumber is down. Few tourists see old business district, which is above O 58, on old hwy. Museum, little open, near center of town, delineates Oakridge's past, which isn't all that much.

    * Turn N from O 58 onto Crestview. *0.3 m.*, turn R onto 1st St. *1.8 m.*, turnoff R to Rigdon FS RS. *3.4 m.*, turnoff R to **Salmon Creek Falls CG** (*0.2 m.*). Mill stream-like waterfall is icing on cake for this bouncy creek.
0.8 m., turnoff S to **Green Waters Park.**

    * *0.1 m.*, city park on Salmon Creek. PA.
0.9 m., turnoff N to **Willamette Fish Hatchery.**

    * *0.9 m.*, hatchery. About 224,000 rainbow trout and about 5 million spring chinook salmon are raised here annually.
0.1 m., on S, Hills Creek Dam Jct.

    * *0.5 m.*, forks. Straight. *1.3 m.*, **Hills Creek Dam.** *1.2 m.*, view of Diamond Peak. *0.7 m.*, C. T. Beech FS PA, on Hills Creek Res. *0.5 m.*, Hills Creek, at East Shore bridge. Return *3.7 m.*, to forks. Turn L. *0.3 m.*, Middle Fork of Willamette. *1.2 m.*, Hills Creek Res. Viewpoint.
7.4 m., **Blue Pool FS CG** (*0.1 m.*) CG, PA on Salt Creek. Area once noted for McCredie Hot Springs, long-ago dried up.
10.6 m., view of Diamond Peak. *1.2 m.*, turnout for **Salt Creek Falls** trails. Camera Viewpoint — *50 yds.* Top of Falls — *50 yds.* Bottom of Falls — *0.3 m.* At drop of 286 ft., Salt Creek is, in the opinion of some, the most spectacular falls in state, because of sheer descent and heavy volume.

Office Bridge, Westfir

0.2 m., turnoff to Salt Creek Falls FS CG.
      * *0.2 m.,* CG. Trail to Salt Creek Falls.
2.3 m., on N, Waldo Lake Jct.
      * *2 m.,* on L, Mt. Fuji Trail. *1.7 m.,* on L, Mt. Ray Trail. *1.7 m.,* on L, Betty
Lake Trail. (Across rd., Bobby Lake Trail.) *0.9 m.,* on R, Twin Peaks Trail.

Salt Creek Falls   *Courtesy State of Oregon*

0.4 m., Shadow Bay Jct.

* L for Shadow Bay Jct.: *1 m.,* Waldo Lake Trail. *0.7 m.,* on R, **Shadow Bay FS CG,** on Waldo Lake. *0.5 m.,* Shadow Bay BR. Shoreline Trail begins here.

* **Waldo Lake,** with 6,298 acres, is Oregon's 2d largest lake, behind Upper Klamath, and the state's 2d deepest lake, behind Crater; Waldo's max. depth is 420 ft. and its mean depth 128 ft. The cobalt blueness of its water gives Waldo a surface beauty rarely matched in Oregon. Because of its untouched quality, it was listed as one of the Virgin Lakes on a survey map drawn in 1863. Until 1969, the lake could be reached only by trail or 4-wheel drive. Waldo is regarded as the purest lake water in the state and "one of the cleanest and purest lakes in the world," according to an information marker. On a clear day you can see to depths of 100 ft.

* Straight from Shadow Bay Jct.: *4.3 m.,* turnoff to **Charleston Lake** *(0.3 m.) 1.7 m.,* "T".

* L from "T": *0.9 m.,* Waldo Lake Trail. *0.3 m.,* **Islet FS CG.** BL.

* R from "T": *0.3 m.,* on L, **North Waldo FS CG.** Turnoff to R: *7.8 m.,* **Taylor Burn FS CG.** Straight from turnoff to Taylor Burn CG: *0.6 m.,* BL.

On occasion Waldo Lake is the happy hunting ground of very large and very voracious mosquitoes, a trait it shares with a number of other high mtn. lakes (Waldo is at 5,414-ft. elev.) but Waldo seems to breed champions. *1.4 m.,* on S, view of Diamond Peak and Mt. Yoran. *1.1 m.,* on S, Forest Vista.

Waldo Lake

Turnout for view of two prominent peaks: Diamond Peak (8,744 ft.) and Mt. Yoran (7,100 ft.) *0.1 m.*, turnoff N to Gold Lake and Gold Lake CG.

    * *1.2 m.*, on L, Marilyn Lake Trail. *0.8 m.*, **Gold Lake FS CG,** on S tip of 96-acre Gold Lake, described in *Atlas of Oregon Lakes* as "one of the scenic and botanical treasures of the Willamette National Forest." Because of the prime wetland and rare vegetation contiguous to the lake, a 463-acre tract extending upstream from Gold Lake has been set aside as the Gold Lake Bog Research National Area. Only people with strong scientific interest are permitted to visit the bog. On Gold Lake itself, no motors on boats and fly fishing only.

  0.6 m., **Willamette Pass,** 5,128 ft., and Willamette Pass Ski Area. *0.3 m.*, Odell Lake Jct.; W Access.

    * *1.8 m.*, Yoder Lake Trailhead. *0.2 m.*, **Trapper Creek FS CG.** *0.3 m.*, turn L for resort. *0.1 m.*, Shelter Cove Resort, on **Odell Lake.** Oddities at resort grounds include foundation of burned-down Cascade Summit Lodge; Cabin A, supposedly built in 1882; and the kind of gas pump common in the 1920s and 1930s.

    The glacial trough that is Odell Lake, with 3,582 acres in surface area, is one of the largest in the Oregon Cascades, and all around it is an extended family of firs: Douglas, Pacific, silver, subalpine, white and Shasta red. Between the firs grow western and mountain hemlock, ponderosa, lodgepole, white pine and Engelman spruce. Blackberry bushes run riot, with picking free. Fishing for mackinaw and rainbow trout is popular but most fishers are bent on kokanee.

  1.3 m., turnoff S to **Princess Creek FS CG** (*0.1 m.*), on Odell Lake. *2 m.*, on S, viewpoint, Odell Lake — Diamond Peak. *1 m.*, on S, **Sunset Bay CG** (*0.2 m.*) on Odell Lake. *0.6 m.*, jct., Odell Lake — CG — Resort — Marina.

    * *0.5 m.*, **Odell Lake FS CG,** on lake. *0.1 m.*, Odell Lake Lodge — Marina. Crater Butte Trailhead.

  1.9 m., turnoff to Crescent Lake.

    * *2.3 m.*, jct. To R: *0.4 m.*, turn L for **Crescent Lake FS CG.** *0.2 m.*, CG on Crescent Lake. Straight: **Spring Creek CG,** 6 m.; Conorta PT CG, 2 m.; Summit Lake, 4 m.

    * From first jct.: Straight: *0.2 m.*, forks. Turn R. *0.1 m.*, forks. Take L. *0.4 m.*, **Simax Beach,** on Crescent Lake. PA. At jct. to Simax Beach: Straight: *0.3 m.*, **Crescent Lake Lodge.**

    Crescent Lake, 5 m. long, 4 m. wide, and with max. depth of 265 ft. is regarded by vacationers as an aquatic recreationland, but it also has another function. It is of significant importance in watering land in the Bend area.

    Trails from the lake lead into the roadless Diamond Peak Wilderness, a delight for seasoned hikers.

  2.3 m., on N, turnoff to Davis Lake.

    * *9.9 m.*, **Davis Lake,** on E slope of Cascades. The 3,906-acre lake, a

Cabin A, Odell Lake

waterfowl habitat, is engulfed by a ripping meadow behind which waves a forest of ponderosa pine. 10 m. beyond lake is Wickiup Reservoir, created 1949, and a home of the osprey.

10.7 m., on N. turnoff for **Little Deschutes FS CG.** *4.3 m.,* US 97. (S, *7.8 m.,* Chemult.)

O 138 — Roseburg to US 97

Locally known as the Diamond Lake Hwy., O 138 can with more than a mere measure of justice lay claim to being the most recreational road in the state. For one argument in its favor, it passes close to Diamond and Crater lakes. For another, it reaches out to a brilliant ensemble of traveler, camper and fisher delights. For a third presentation, the road is excellent, as well designed as any state road in Oregon.

Having said the above, the traveler who has crossed every Cascade road in the state is faced with this admission: No sooner is an ecstatic tribute penned to one pike than another is taken and proves as beautiful. What can one do but accept without discrimination a folio of joy?

From Stephens and O 138, Roseburg:

3.7 m., on S, Buckhorn Rd.

  * *0.8 m.,* jct. *0.8 m.,* on R, **Pine Grove Church,** early 20th century house of worship. *0.3 m.,* **Dixonville,** named for Dixon family whose spread was biggest in these parts. They raised cattle, which were driven over Cascades and across High Desert to great shipping port of Winnemucca. Hamlet was never very much; in 1915 it has only store, PS and church. Now the store is Dixonville.

In this country sheep seem everywhere and, say ranchers, are often prey to cougars and eagles. They say "It takes two lambs a week to feed two eagles." So, since there are some eagles in the hills, predatory rate is high. Ranchers say: "Every two-week lamb taken by an eagle represents a loss of $50."

* Turn R (or W) at store. *0.9 m.,* on L, 2-1/2 story white house that, say locals, was "classiest around" at turn of century. Barn is older. *0.4 m.,* on R, **Wilbur Brown House,** said to have been "lived in for a spell" by time 20th century arrived.

* Return to Buckhorn Rd. Turn R, or S. *0.6 m.,* on R, **O. C. Brown Park.** Millstones at entrance to park were, according to local lore, brought around the Horn but did not belong to Brown family. *0.1 m.,* O. C. Brown Rd. On L, last remaining original structure (barn) of Dixon Ranch. Turn R onto O. C. Brown Rd. *0.6 m.,* on R, lane into farm. Last house on L was home of the O. C. Browns. Couple served as schoolteachers when they weren't ranching.

* Return to Buckhorn Rd. Turn R. *1.1 m.,* on L, double-bay window early home. *0.3 m.,* on L, two-story white house that was mark of affluence in early 1900s.

0.1 m., on N, Temple Brown Rd.

* *0.4 m.,* on L, **Temple Brown House,** built about 1880, oldest house of the three Brown brothers, prominent Deer Creek citizens. They were all well-educated and all pioneer ranchers. Mrs. Temple Brown stirred a lot of tongue-wagging because she was, for many years, what is contemporarily known as a professional student. She would teach school for two or three months, then go off to college for a while. House greatly remodeled.

0.6 m., Buckhorn Rd.

* *0.8 m.,* **Pine Grove Church.** *0.3 m.,* Dixonville.

7.4 m., turnoff L for Whistler's Bend CP.

* *2.8 m.,* **Whistler's Bend CP.** CG, PA, BR on bank of N Umpqua River, which surrounds park on three sides. Hiking trail, forest, meadows — an uplifting ambience.

4.5 m., on S, Little River Rd., gateway to one of the loveliest off-the-beaten-path trips in this fairyland country.

* *1.9 m.,* on R, old log pond. *1.1 m.,* bridge across Little River, rich-bodied green stream. *2.6 m.,* **Peel Country Store.** (Peel PO 1882–1921.) One of very few places in W named for Confederate soldier. In 1915 Peel has PS, daily stage to Roseburg, pop. 75. *1.2 m.,* **Cavitt Creek CB,** built 1943 with length of 70 ft. Turn R across span onto Cavitt Creek Rd. *2.7 m.,* **Cavitt Creek Falls Rec. Site.** (*0.2 m.,* PA. **Cavitt Creek Falls,** at short path from PA, on small, splashy creek. Swimming hole below 12-ft. falls is popular with those in the know.) *6 m.,* **Shadow Falls Trailhead.** Moderate 0.8 m. trail thru old-growth Douglas fir, braided by subtly hued wildflowers in spring and summer, to triple waterfall which rushes 75 to 95 ft. down photogenic grotto.

* Return to Little River Rd. Turn R. *4.1 m.,* trailhead for **Wolf Creek**

Falls. (*2,400 yds.* to falls on up and down trail. Along way are several unusual rock formations, some looking like they belong on Easter Island. Aficionados of waterfalls will want to check out Wolf Creek: upper falls drops 75 ft.; lower falls, 50 ft. Not high — but powerful.)

* *1.3 m.,* **Wolf Creek CG.** (*1 m.* nature trail begins at bridge spanning Little River. Direction markers are periodically vandalized, so it isn't that difficult to go astray.)

* *0. 1 m.,* old logging camp, now used by Little River Christian Camp. *0. 7 m.,* **Emile** (pronounced E-Mile) **Creek BLM Rec. Site,** another fine outing spot of area. *1.4 m.,* **Cool Water FS CG,** in forest setting along Little River.

** Across from Cool Water FS CG is jct., FS Rd. 2703. Follow 2703 *4.8 m.* to FS Rd. 2703-150. Take that road *2.1 m.* to trailhead for **Grotto Falls** (*0.5 m.,* to 100-ft. falls, which pours into Emile Creek).

** Take FS Rd. 2703 *7.1 m.* to FS Rd. 2703-750. Turn L. *0.2 m.,* **Emile Big Tree Botanical Area,** grove of Douglas fir whose median age is about 400 years. Big Daddy here is 235-ft.-tall, 9 ft., 10 in. diameter fir named for William Howard Taft, no stranger to girth. Continue up FS Rd. *3 m.* Turn R onto FS Rd. 4711-835. *0.5 m.,* **Willow Flats Sump.** Things to enjoy: beaver dams below sump, 2-acre shallow lake stocked with 3 in. rainbow fingerling trout, subalpine meadows, wildflowers galore, berry picking. FS advises comers to boil all sump or stream water.

* Return to Little River Rd. Turn onto it. *0.4 m.,* Red Butte Lookout Rd. (*0.2 m.,* **White Creek FS CG.** At 1,600 ft. elev., cool in summer. Good beach, shallow water provides fine swimming for children. Across rd. from CG, Overhang Trail — *0.3 m.* easy trail which derives name from passing under basalt rock overhang covered with maidenhair ferns. Wildflowers curl up to old-growth-Douglas firs along trail.) 10 m. up road, Red Butte Lookout, great place to see a world of forest below.

* *7 m.,* Willamette Meridian. *2.5 m.,* **Lake in the Woods FS CG.** Caught in the rain, 1907 trail cabin is sturdy shelter. Lake in the Woods has grandiose sound but this man-made lake, four acres in area and with max. depth of only 8 ft., appears as nothing more than small pond. Two stirring waterfalls close by. Near cabin, trail twists 0.5 m. to **Hemlock Falls,** 80-ft. drop into Hemlock Creek. Across rd. from CG, *0.8 m.* trail to 70-ft. **Yakso Falls,** created by a dive of Little River. Yakso Falls is split by protruding rocks so that it takes on the imagery of a fan breached by sunlight.

* *5 m.,* **Hemlock Lake FS CG.** The 28-acre man-made reservoir, 33 ft. at its deepest, is a quiet water, its tranquility made manifest by no motors allowed. Fishers come here for rainbow trout and kokanee. A 1 m. trail loops around Hemlock Lake and the Yellow Jacket Loop Trail is a 5 m. lasso, with a 1 m. side trail out to Flat Rock Mtn., once used as emergency lookout. *0.5 m.,* **Hemlock Meadows FS CG,** on E arm of Hemlock Lake. BR for Hemlock Lake at Hemlock Meadows.

From Little River Jct. on O 138:

0.1 m., on L, or N, **Colliding Rivers.** Here the N Umpqua and Little River meet head on in dramatic encounter. Picnic tables at viewpoint face this meeting of the waters.

1.3 m., **Glide,** stretched out hwy. burg with modest tourist facilities. PO est. 1890. Despite smallness of town, there seem to be homes everywhere back of hwy.

0.1 m., on S, Lone Rock Rd.

   * *1.1 m.,* on L, turnout for pleasant overlook of N Umpqua.

3.3 m., **Idleyld Park.** Store. PO was called Hoaglin until late 1932. Probably only Oregon settlement named for amusement park, which stood here early in century.

0.1 m., **The Narrows CP.** Douglas County has many parks and the site of each was wisely chosen.

0.7 m., on N, Rock Creek Rd.

   * *5.2 m.,* **Millpond Rec. Area.** BLM CG, PA on Rock Creek. *1.8 m.,* **Rock Creek Rec. Site,** also on Rock Creek. Both areas are very popular on summer weekends.

0.2 m., turnoff S to Swiftwater Park.

   * S side of bridge is much-used for fishing. *0.4 m.,* **Swiftwater CP.** PA. Mild trail tiptoes thru woods within sound of N Umpqua. *0.5 m.,* hike is tranquil nature walk. Another trail — downhill and switchback — descends to stream.

East of the turnoff to Swiftwater Park, O 138 travels for about 35 m. thru area of volcanic rocks of the W Cascades spread out between 35 and 20 million years ago. There is no clear clue along this section of the hwy. to indicate the existence of the original volcanic mtns., erosion having molded them into harsh ridge and ravine terrain so conspicuous today.

In an approximate 500-sq.-mile area along the N Umpqua and its tributaries, an endangered species of the white-tailed deer, the Columbian, roam the oak-covered hills and valleys.

In this region, too, is found the ringtail, one of Oregon's least-known furbearing animals. Inhabiting brush canyons and rocky outcrops, they are social loners, denning with whomever or whatever occupies the habitat, even skunks and rattlesnakes. Ringtails were known in the mining camps of yore as "miner's cats" because of their reputation as tenacious mousers. If you catch one in your headlights — it can be mistaken for a raccoon or small fox — do your best to let it live. It deserves life.

0.1 m., on N, turnoff to fish hatchery.

   * *0.2 m.,* **Rock Creek Fish Hatchery.** Raised here are spring and fall chinook, summer and winter steelhead, cohos and rainbows. Hatchery releases about 250,000 lbs. of fish each year.

0.3 m., W boundary of fly angling; for the next 31 m., fly angling only.

Near here, cataracts and riffling white water of the N Umpqua combine for striking river scenery. At points the riffles look so clean they appear to have been washed and so rich in texture they seem to be fresh cream or pure snow.

0.4 m., on S, **Cable Crossing CP.** In next 4.3 m., there are three more CPs, all PAs. Distances from one to another: *0.3 m., 1.2 m., 2.8 m.*

1.3 m., from last CP — Smith Springs — Susan Creek BLM Rec. Site. PA.

  * On N side of road from PA, trailhead for **Susan Creek Falls.** 1,300 yd. trail of mild graduation to falls, spirited 50-ft. plunge framed by fallen fir. Falls

Fishing the North Umpqua   *Courtesy State of Oregon*

Susan Creek Falls

are in a "twilight zone," encased on three sides by moss-lined rock wall which is always moist and never feels sun upon it.

    * Beyond bridge at falls, a tougher trail, of 700 yds., climbs to **Susan Creek Indian Mounds.** The "mounds," enclosed by cyclone fence, is jumble of rocks almost obscured by brush. Here, so goes the legend, Indian boys who had been sent out alone to prove themselves as men, and who had to survive on their own, fasted and performed activities to please the Spirits, such as piling up rocks, until the vision was bestowed upon the youth, which is why the Mounds area is also called Vision Quest Site.

4 m., on N, trailhead for Fall Creek Falls.

    * *1,200 yds.* to **Fall Creek Falls** on easy trail. Almost halfway up is sturdy bench for resting. Below bench, Job's Garden Trail takes off from falls path to wind down thru Douglas fir forest to bottom of basaltic, columnar-rock outcroppings. Fall Creek is a pretty double waterfalls, about 35 to 60 ft. Even if falls weren't there, walk thru old-growth forest is rewarding.

In this country of stellar performers, the river remains the star. The Umpqua is a temperamental stream and from bend to bend its behavior is unpredictable. It will be smooth as glass, a pool without a ripple in it, and suddenly it will clash against rocks, break into white-topped, blue-bellied riffles, swirl, froth and snarl.

And then it will be peaceful again, the face of innocence. The road almost hugs the river for more than 30 m. and there is always the thick, real forest.

2.4 m., **Bogus Creek FS CG.** PA. *3.5 m.*, **Steamboat.** Though on official state map, Steamboat is only an inn — chic resort and candlelight and champagne dinner place — but it is a widely known landmark on O 138. Jack Hemingway, brother of Ernest, and himself a famous fisher, called the N Umpqua upstream from Steamboat "the greatest stretch of summer steelhead water in the United States." Among the prominent who fished here was Zane Grey.

0.5 m., on L, or N, Steamboat Creek Rd.

    * *0.4 m.*, **Canton Creek FS CG.** *0.2 m.*, jct., Canton Creek Rd.

    ** On Canton Creek Rd., L fork: *3.1 m.*, **Scaredman Creek Rec. Site.** *6.2 m.*, Upper Canton Creek Rd. (Ahead on Canton Creek Rd: *21.7 m.* to Bohemia Saddle, *39.7 m.* to Cottage Grove, *39.5 m.* to Oakridge. A lot of uninhabited country is seen but little of it is striking.) Turn onto Upper Canton Creek Rd. *3 m.*, turn R onto FS Rd. 2300–600. *0.4 m.*, on R, Canton Creek Trail. *1.5 m.*, of generally rough, choked, overgrown trail to **Canton Creek Falls,** 100-ft. descent secreted in bristling canyon flanked by protective "bodyguards" of Douglas fir and western red cedar.

Little Falls of Steamboat Creek near confluence with North Umpqua

Courtesy State of Oregon

* Return to jct., Steamboat Creek Rd. Turn L. *0.7 m.,* **Little Falls,** 5-to-10 ft. rupture in the flow of Steamboat Creek. Big attraction here is watching fish jump up the falls to move on. *4.3 m.,* turn R across bridge for Steamboat Falls CG. *0.1 m.,* forks. Take L. *0.5 m.,* turnoff L for **Steamboat Falls CG.** *0.1 m.,* CG. Brief, level trail to viewpoint. Steamboat Creek finds opening in wide rock bed, executes 90-degree turn, slices in sheer tide into small pen, and roars almost 30 ft. down a wall that looks like the exterior of a SW pueblo. Though the drop isn't impressive, the sound and fury and odd geology comprise an arresting happening.

From Steamboat Creek Rd. on O 138:

1.1 m., **Island FS CG,** on N Umpqua. *2 m.,* **Jack Falls,** a trio of descents, 20 to 70 ft. on Jack Creek, which flows into N Umpqua. No trail to falls and they are obscured from road by brush. *1.5 m.,* **Apple Creek FS CG.** *3.1 m.,* **Horseshoe Bend FS Rec. Site** (*1 m.,* on river.)

1.8 m., on N, **Dry Creek Store,** another landmark on O 138. Back of it has grown up a little settlement, one of the micro-communities that have sprouted like weeds along this hwy. in past two decades.

* Follow Bradley Trail back of store for *3 m.* — an arduous climb — to **Dog Creek Indian Cave.** Trail passes above grave of William "Bill"

Steamboat Falls

Bradley, who died in 1909 at age 48 while attempting to subdue a wild horse. He had lived here alone for 28 years. At time of his death, the nearest road was 35 m. off. (For Bradley's story, see "A Grave Marker to Ponder On" in author's *Tracking Down Oregon*.) (For grave, follow fence along R turn *35 yds*. It is surrounded by brush and not easy to see from road-trail.) Inside walls of Dog Creek Cave are covered with pictographs, some suggesting hunting scenes. Vandals, of course, have done their work, profaning humanity and nature. In its higher stages the trail winds thru virgin timber, salal, and fern, and Oregon grape and fir needles carpet the red soil. Rock chimneys and natural arches are within short hiking distances. And, in spring, the purple

Eagle Rock   *Courtesy State of Oregon*

blooms of the rare kalmiopsis are found. When the wind is still and there are no voices on the ridge, the chant of the Umpqua is heard as a call coming from the far end of a tunnel. Early curiosity seekers carted away all easily removable artifacts from cave. FS would like to protect cave but doesn't have the money. Money for overkilling seems more important than the preservation of our heritage.

1.2 m., remains of old bridge across N Umpqua. *1.1 m.,* Eagle Rock FS CG. Towering above it is **Eagle Rock,** one of the most photographed rock formations in state. Top can be envisioned as head of vigilant eagle but from appreciable perspective it looks like Crown Point (and Visa House) on Columbia River Scenic Hwy. *0.7 m.,* turnout for fine views of Eagle Rock and its companions, Old Man and Old Woman Rocks, described by geologists as volcanic plugs.

1 m., **Boulder Flat FS CG.** *2.7 m.,* on N, Soda Springs Res. Rd.

Entrance to a school community

* Take 1st rd.—Copco Rd.—20 yds. from O 138—to L. *0.9 m.*, **Soda Springs Res.** *0.1 m.,* **Soda Springs Dam.** *0.3 m.,* power plant. Most people come up this road to fish res. but some drive here to see fluted cliffs at power plant. These perpendicular pillars of volcanic rock, colored by lichens, have been oft photographed but those who expect the cliffs to look like the color photos of 2 or 3 decades ago will be disappointed; time has taken its toll and the pillars aren't half as interesting now.

1.9 m., turnoff N to Toketee Falls School.

* *0.2 m.,* **Toketee Falls School,** neat country schoolhouse that draws kids from along N Umpqua and its branches. Adjacent to school is "village of **Frostbite Falls.** "Where are the falls?" a visitor asked a local watering his lawn. "You're looking right at it," came the reply as the man pointed to his hose.

0.4 m., on N, small marker giving story of 10,000-year-old lava flows — the intracanyon basalts. *1.6 m.,* Toketee Jct.

* *0.2 m.,* jct. Take L. *50 yds.* Take L. *0.1 m.,* trailhead for **Toketee Falls.** *450 yds.* of easy trail to Toketee Falls. "Toketee" is Indian for graceful and the falls is surely that. The first leap of the water is pretty but otherwise uneventful, about 35 ft. drop. The next leap, over sheer wall of basalt and down into deep "punchbowl" is about 100 ft. and possesses an artistry of nature. 200 yds. from fall, bench on trail overlooking N Umpqua, deep, deep below, in brooding canyon.

* Return to Toketee Rd. Turn L. *0.4 m.,* **Toketee Dam and Res.** The shallow 75-acre Toketee Lake, formed by damming of N Umpqua, is annually stocked with rainbow trout and is also home to some brown trout and eastern brook. *0.9 m.,* turnoff to BL on Toketee Lake. *2 m.,* forks. Take R, FS Rd. 3401. *3.2 m.,* Deer Creek. *0.4 m.,* take turnoff *1.1 m.,* to parking area of **Umpqua Hot Springs.** (Before taking dirt rd. to Hot Springs, check terrain. Low cars may run into a peck of trouble. Better to walk and avoid possible mishap.) From parking area, hike *0.6 m.* to Umpqua Hot Springs. Setting is primitive but pool is blessing for irritable muscles.

1. 9. m., turnoff N to Toketee Ranger Station. *0.3 m.,* on S, turnoff to Watson Falls, highest in S Oregon, with drop of 272 ft.

* *0.2 m.,* on R, **Watson Falls FS PA.** *0.1 m.,* on L, trailhead for Watson Falls. *0.2 m.,* up fairly steep trail, forks. To L, bridge for viewing. To R, *0.2 m.,* Upper Viewpoint. **Watson Falls,** is more of a spray than a heavy gush and the spray seems to take on the form of ospreys diving in pursuit of breakfast. The spray splashes on and bounces off black rocks which appear to have been cringing for centuries. Lower slopes, rocks and fallen trees are moss-covered, taking on an art form of a green and brown mosaic.

4.8 m., turnoff N to **Whitehorse Falls FS CG.**

* *0.1 m.,* CG. It's only a few steps to **Whitehorse Falls,** double-fauceted shoot of about 15 ft. into rilly pond of Clearwater Creek.

1.1 m., on S, Stump Lake, at 3,875 ft. elev. The 11-acre 10-ft.-deep lake is stocked bi-annually with brown trout.

2.5 m., turnoff S to **Clearwater FS CG.**

* *0.3 m.,* CG. *0.1 m.* trail to **Clearwater Falls,** loud, brashy, splashy chaotic tumult of water that looks like a bunch of fire hydrants gone berserk. At top of 30 ft. cascade the subterranean water pours out every which way and "pot holes" show the stream alive. Only a strong network of roots keeps earth from collapsing. Above the falls, alongside penned-in Clearwater, is one of nicest CGs in W Oregon. Reach by rd. Most people who come to the falls zip out their little cameras and take photos of each other posing against the cascades' backdrop. Since the lighting isn't very strong and the shooting is done from a distance of about 15 to 30 ft., it is doubtful if many sharp negatives emerge.

2 m., on S, marker explaining that O 138 is now in a lodgepole pine forest. That is soon made evident by rows of these skinny pines standing at dress formation.

1.2 m., turnoff N to Lemolo Lake Rec. Area.

* *3.1 m.,* jct., **E Lemolo FS CG,** Straight: *1 m.,* turnoff to **Poole Creek FS CG.** *0.3 m.,* turnoff to Thorn Prairie Rd.

** For impressive waterfall, take Thorn Prairie Rd. *0.4 m.,* turn R onto FS Rd. 3401. *1.7 m.,* on R, lane to trailhead for Lemolo Falls. *700 yds.* to parking area (some people walk). From trailhead, *1,000 yds.* to **Lemolo Falls.** In Chinook jargon Lemolo means "wild" or "untamed," and it is not difficult to see why the falls were so named. The drop has been estimated to be from 75 ft. to 168 ft; call it 150 ft. and enjoy. Spearing into the N Umpqua, Lemolo Falls seems to have been designed for creative people impelled to record the spiritual impulses of their visual impressions.

* Return to Lemolo Lake Rd. Turn L. *0.6 m.,* turnoff R to Lemolo Lake Resort. *0.1 m.,* resort on **Lemolo Lake,** 450-acre reservoir, with 8.3 m. of shoreline, a depth in some places of 100 ft., and at 4,142 ft. elev. Lake is well stocked with German brown trout, kokanee, eastern brook and some rainbows. Resort open all year and in winter caters to snowmobilers and cross-country skiers, both of whom enjoy vast tracts of terrain for their sports.

* From jct., E Lemolo FS CG (Loop trip.):

** *2.2 m.,* **E Lemolo FS CG.** *0.3 m.,* **N Umpqua River.** *0.1 m.,* **Inlet FS CG.** *0.1 m.,* jct. Turn L toward Lemolo Lake Resort; rd. runs alongside Lemolo Lake. *1.8 m.,* **Bunker Hill FS CG,** on lake. *0.5 m.,* forks. (To R — N Umpqua Trailhead.) Take L. *0.1 m.,* **Lemolo Lake Dam.** From here, sharply-etched view of Mt. Thielsen. *0.3 m.,* turnoff to Lemolo Lake Resort (*0.1 m.,*) *0.6 m.,* turnoff on Thorn Prairie Rd. for Lemolo Falls (see above, this section.) *0.3 m.,* turnoff to Poole Creek FS CG. *1 m.,* turnoff to E Lemolo FS CG. *3.1 m.,* O 138.

0.8 m., turnoff N to Pacific Crest Trail (*13 m.*) *5.1 m.,* turnoff S to Diamond Lake Rec. Area.

Lemolo Falls

* *0.4 m.*, jct. To R: W Shore. Straight: E Shore. Either way is the first link of a loop around **Diamond Lake.** Most people prefer the E shore route because (1) they may not get farther than the resort; (2) the lake is closer that way; (3) the road on the E side of the lake is better.

* On E shore: *0.6 m.*, turnoff to Diamond Lake Resort (*0.1 m.*) Resort is largest on or off O 138 between the Coast and Crater Lake and has more

utilization than Crater Lake, being open year-round. In addition to its summer activities, resort is center of large winter sports region, particularly skiing, cross-country skiing and snow-mobiling. Along O 138, meaning an area 10 m. N and 10 m. S of hwy., there are hundreds of sq. m. for cross-country skiing and snowmobiling. Sno-Parks are numerous and the road is kept clear. Diamond Lake Ranger District has more than 55 m. of designated Nordic trails in Diamond Lake and Lemolo Lake areas. Trails range in elev. from 4,200 ft. to 8,365 ft. at top of Mt. Bailey. All trails marked at trailhead and along route by blue trail signs. Mt. Bailey is favorite ski area of Diamond lake winter resorters.

Diamond Lake, at elev. of 5,183 ft., covering 3,214 acres in a lovely glacial valley between Mt. Bailey and Mt. Thielsen, and stocked with several kind of trout, is a pure and popular rec. area. In addition to the resort, shoreline of lake holds well-developed CGs and PAs and rather sizeable summer home colony. Lake rec. area seems to belong closer to city than to middle of Cascades but excellent roads to lake eliminate gap between urban and wilderness.

Lake was not named because of its shape — it isn't at all diamond in imprint — but bears the signature of John Diamond, early Coburg settler who was a member of party of pioneer road builders involved in opening a wagon wheel passage between the Willamette Valley and Idaho. An 8,750-ft. mtn. was called Diamond Peak in 1852 because John Diamond climbed to the top. While at the summit he spotted a lake, more than 30 m. to the S as the crow flies, and so the lake was named for him too. But to assert, as historical writers have done, that Diamond was the "discoverer" of Diamond Lake, is to slander the Native Americans who lived around the lake.

* *1.2 m.*, on R, **Diamond Lake CG.** On L, **Diamond Lake Information Center.** *1.4 m.*, RV Park. *0.3 m.*, jct. (Straight: *0.7 m.*, jct. R — O 230. L, *0.2 m.*, O 138.)

* At lst jct. (S Shore) take R. *0.4 m.*, **S Shore FS PA.** Fun spot on lake and magnificent view of **Mt. Thielsen.** *0.3 m.*, **Broken Arrow FS CG.** *0.9 m.*, Silent Creek. *3.2 m.*, Thielsen View FS CG— another great view of Mt. Thielsen. *3.2 m.*, jct. end of loop.

From Diamond Lake Jct., on O 138:

2.9 m., on N, trailhead to Mt. Thielsen:

* *4 m.* trail to top of Mt. Thielsen, rising from 5,400 ft. elev. to 9,182 ft. at peak. The last stretch — approx. 65 yds. — is the most difficult and a climax to the increasingly steeper trail. Only by fingering and toeing around the boulder heap in the last stretch can the peak be reached. From Diamond Lake the volcanic peak of Mt. Thielsen looks too narrow to support a single climber. In actuality, the spire is 10 ft. by 40 ft. and can hold several people. As would be expected, the view from the top is panoramic, extending S to Mt. Shasta in Calif. and N to Mt. Jefferson. Sited astride the "ridge" of the

Cascades, the views W are of Douglas fir and hemlock; the view E of park-like pine forests. The best time to ascend Mt. Thielsen is about from mid-Aug. to mid-Sept., when the mosquitoes have had it for the year and the snowmelt has revealed the trail. But a note of caution: only experienced climbers and only persons in excellent physical condition and accompanied by experienced climbers should attempt to reach the spire of Mt. Thielsen — or even the boulder line below it. Incidentally, Mt. Thielsen, which sepa-rates Douglas and Klamath counties, was named in 1872 for Hans Thielsen, early RR engineer. Earlier, it had been know as Big Cowhorn and still earlier, before the Yankees arrived, the Indians called it *His-chok-wol-as,* which sounds best.

1.4 m., jct., O 230 to Medford. (See O 62—O 230, following.)

3 m., Crater Lake Jct.

* *0.9 m.,* entrance to Crater Lake National Park. *8 m.,* Rim Rock Jct. *6.1 m.,* Crater Lake Overlook.

0.9 m., on N, N Crater Trailhead — part of Pacific Crest Trail. *0.5 m.,* Cas-cade Pass — 5,925 ft. elev. *13.6 m.,* US 97. (N, *9 m.,* Chemult.)

Mt. Thielsen above Diamond Lake   *Courtesy State of Oregon*

O 62 — Medford to US 97 (near Chiloquin)
This is the high road from the Rogue River Valley to Crater Lake National
Park and is used by more people, particularly Californians, to reach the park than
is any other pike. O 62 is swift, much of it is unfettered by recreational deviations,
and is without sharp curves. It is in every sense a delightful road to drive, even
without the magnet of Crater Lake.
From downtown **Medford:**
1.3 m., angle R onto O 62. *3.6 m.,* Central Point Jct.
    * *2.1 m.,* on L, **Central Point Cemetery** (1868). *0.7 m.,* turn R toward
Central Point. *1.2 m.,* downtown Central Point.
2.4 m., jct., O 140. (See O 140, immediately following.) *0.3 m.,* White City,
industrial appendage of Medford, on WW II Camp White.
    * To R, or E, on Antelope Rd., **Agate Desert.** The Nature Conservancy
describes Agates Desert as "a flat, gravelly outwash plain of quaternary al-
luvium. Small depressions in the surface result in vernal ponding in an otherwise dry environment. This is an important natural area with unique geologic features and a highly specialized flora." Unfortunately, Agate Desert is
being built up. Of the acreage The Nature Conservancy would like to preserve, it says: "The site has the best population of *Limnanthes floccossa* ssp,
grandiflora, a rare plant restricted to this region, and also has three special
plant occurrences of state concern, *Microseris acuminata, Pilularia americania*
and *Arenaria californica."*
    * To L, or W, on Antelope Rd.: *1.8 m.,* turn R onto Table Rock Rd. *0.9
m.,* on R, **Tou Valle SP,** on Rogue River. Large day use area, fishing, boating. *2 m.,* on L, **Table Rock Bible Church,** formerly Table Rock School.
Site of town of Table Rock, between mesas of Upper Table Rock and Lower
Table Rock. Table Rock PO est. 1872, form changed to Tablerock; discontinued 1906. In 1915, Table Rock had PS, church, Improvement Club, Farmers' Telephone system of 300 phones, pop. 250. Except for school turned
church there is absolutely no trace of where Table Rock village stood. *1 m.,*
on R, **Table Rock Monument.** Near here, on Sept. 10, 1853, Treaty of Table
Rock was signed by the Yankees, led by Gen. Joseph Lane, and including
Joel Palmer, J.W. Nesmith and Samuel Colver, and the Rogue River Indians, led by Chiefs Sam, John, Jim, Jo, and Limpy. (The Indian names of the
chiefs are, as expected, not given.) *0.5 m.,* on L, Wheeler Rd. Parking at rd.
for Table Rock Trail. *(0.2 m.,* trailhead. *1 m.* steep trail to **Lower Table Rock
Preserve,** property of The Nature Conservancy, which thusly describes its
holding: "The isolation of the top of the rock has protected several rare and
unusual species, including the dwarf meadowfoam *Limnanthes flocossa,* a
variety which grows nowhere else. The western blue-gray gnatcatcher has
its most northerly known nesting site among the oaks on Table Rock. (The

preserve area served as a stronghold for the Takelma Indians during the Valley Wars of the 1850's.)"

* *2 m.*, jct., O 234. *8.3 m.*, Gold Hill.

From O 62 at Antelope Rd., White City: *4 m.*, Eagle Point Jct

* *0.1 m.*, **Eagle Point.** Take L. *1 block*, turn R. *0.3 m.*, turn L. *0.2 m.*, **Butte Creek Mill,** still functioning to capacity in charming 1872 structure. (See "Last of the Stone-Grind Millers" in author's *A Touch of Oregon.*) Close by are **Oregon General Store Museum** and **Eagle Point Museum** (in former country schoolhouse). E of Eagle Point are some intriguing rock formations and it was one of these, a cliff that was home to eagles, that inspired town name. PO est. 1872. In 1915 Eagle Point had pop. 200 and was shipping point on Butte Creek and Pacific & Eastern RR. Now Eagle Point is a full-grown entity of the Medford urban complex. Most distinguishing feature about the settlement: its highly efficient emergency ambulance service, which covers a big chunk of territory and charges very low fees. In late summer of 1987 **Antelope Creek CB** moved to Little Butte Creek.

3.6 m., jct., O 234. (See *O 234 under The Great Heartland, East Side Shunpiking, O 99, Gold Hill.*) *0.9 m.*, on S, Butte Falls Jct.

* *7.7 m.*, on R, Derby Rd., uphill.

* * On Derby Rd.: *1.7 m.*, gate. Beyond gate is all that is left of **Derby** — a collapsing homesteader's cabin, sagging corral, and bit of a RR trestle. (Obtain permission to go beyond gate.) PO 1892–1919. In 1982, Mrs. Lloyd Beers, Jackson County oldtimer, remembered that "around the early part of the 19 hundreds logging was heavy at and near Butte Falls and a railroad ran from Medford to Butte Falls with a rail switch at Derby Station." Another oldtimer, Alice Humphrey Carden, wrote: "My parents took up a homestead in that area in 1908 and I attended the Derby school from 1911 to 1919. The post office was just across the road until about 1912 or 1913 when it was moved a couple of miles to Derby station where my father had a little country store. Derby is just an 'area' now but when I was a small girl there was a post office and *two* stores."

* Return to Butte Falls Rd. Turn R. *0.5 m.*, on L, old **Derby School.** One-holer outhouse in back seems to indicate that students and faculty had to wait in line to relieve themselves. *5.6 m.*, on R, turnoff to **Butte Falls Cemetery.** (*0.5 m.*, on L, cemetery. Oldest marker is "Charles Arnold, First Grave, Died before 1868.") *2 m.*, **Butte Falls.**

The only settlement in Oregon to be enclosed by cattle guards, Butte Falls is distinctive in other ways too. It is far enough away from a city of size such as Medford to have its own individuality and distanced enough from a main pike to escape the whims of tourism. Few people go thru Butte Falls bound elsewhere; they go to Butte Falls, and not many do that. There is an insulated quality to the town, which gives it a tintype charm enjoyed by few other W Oregon villages. The single main street block faces the park, the fair

A relic of Derby

weather gathering place of the community. The school, on other side of park, is the indoor convening ground. Butte Falls in 1990 had 450 people, only half as much again as 1915 pop. But there is little optimism for even continuance of that slow growth. In 1915 Butte Falls was terminus of Pacific & Eastern RR, long gone. For most of its life the town has lived off logging, but with lumber depressed, vigor has been replaced by lethargy. A store-keeper said: "When the boys came out of high school, they went into logging. They've got nothing now. They go away, same as the girls." An unemployed logger said sadly: "I don't know how the town keeps going. In the last four or five years there's been only two houses built."

   * Beyond Butte Falls one road goes S to O 140 and another gallops 24 ranch m. to Prospect, on O 62.

O 62 from Butte Falls Jct.:

5.7 m., **Shady Cove,** named after cove 0.2 m. upstream on Rogue River. Deer are sometimes seen at edge of trees beyond E side of rd. in N part of spread-out town. Shady Cove is a rather recent settlement, with little history. But even if it had a lot of history, few people would know it. As with so many towns in Oregon, especially S Oregon, people who have been here less than 10 years seem to outnumber the others. Ask a resident, "Where did you come from?" and the invariable and laconic reply is "California." If all ex-Californians were to leave Oregon, the state would be considerably thinned. Throw in an exodus of New Yorker and a lot of Oregon settlements might become ghost towns.

Most people who drive O 62 are so bent on reaching Crater Lake that they fail to observe the hamlets and woods and fields along the hwy. (Which is a shame, because places like Shady Cove are worth a glimpse or two.)

2.3 m., **Trail.** Store. In 1915 Trail had sawmill, which is more than it has now. Jct., O 227. (See O 227, earlier.) *2.9 m.*, on L, or N, **Rogue Elk Inn,** built 1916 as stopover on way to Crater Lake. Among supposed guests — Herbert Hoover and Zane Grey. *0.2 m.*, on N, Elk Creek Rd.

* *0.5 m.*, **Elk Creek School.** *1.4 m.*, on R, viewpoint of Elk Creek Dam, controversial project based on differing long-range projections of water needs and availability. Reservoir (7 m.-long) will add abundantly to region's hefty water supply and add one more aquatic recreation area to recreation-rich S Oregon. *2.9 m.*, forks. Take R. *11.8 m.*, forks. Take L. First farm lane was site of **Persist.** Before county rd. was built, each homesteader scrounged out a private rd., extending halfway between neighbors. Longest stretch was supposedly built by William Willits, who with his wife settled here in 1884. In 1902 PO est. at the Willits home and Willits began carrying the mail to settlers. Even after county rd. was built he insisted upon using his own trace. Mail first came up from Trail, later from Prospect. Willits and some neighbors cut a crude road to Prospect, which the rare oldtimers hereabouts say was 3.5 m. "over the hill." That passage today is manageable, with difficulty, by jeep. Willits is remembered by the oldtimers as a secretive, cranky, dour fellow, but he did persist, and so he named the PO. Next to his home stood a dance hall to which folks from all parts of the Elk Creek valley and hills came for a night's fling.

A charming tale involving Persist was recalled in 1982 by Catherine Gribble Lynch of Medford:

"My mother was a 'Very proper Bostonian' lady who came 'out west' to visit her brother and his family. Her brother was Assistant U.S. Forest Service Supervisor, and through him my father met her. My father had been calling on mother for some time without too much encouragement. My mother had been raised to know that one did not put sentiment on public display, and in those days Medford was a small town and most every one, including the postal service 'knew each other'. Mother was quite upset one day to receive a postal card stating: 'I am going to Persist, love, John.' I guess mother's poise was shaken when she learned that Persist was the name of a town!"

0.,2 m., on S, **Rogue Elk CP.** CG, PA, BR. *1.8 m.*, on S, **Obstinate J Ranch** — many-sided stone and wood house and long barn with four doors and 17 windows at ground level. *1.3 m.*, **Casey SP,** on Rogue. PA, fishing, boating. *0.2 m.*, on N, Takelma Dr.

* *0.3 m.*, **McGregor Park and Information Center.** *0.2 m.*, turn R onto Cole Rivers Rd. *0.3 m.*, **Lost Creek Dam.** *0.3 m.*, **Cole Rivers Fish Hatchery.** Annual hatchery production includes 850,000 spring chinook, 225,000

coho, 225,000 summer steelhead, 225,000 winter steelhead, 215,000 rainbow legals and 500,000 rainbow fingerlings for total of approx. 2,240,000 fish weighing 350,000 lbs.

Start of Lost Creek Lake.

0.4 m., former site of **Leeds,** now under water. PO est. 1890 and named for W. H. Leeds, prominent newspaper publisher of Ashland and for a time state printer. In 1915, Leeds had PO, PS, stage to Eagle Point, fish hatchery, store.

3.9 m., on N, **Stewart SP.** Day use area, BR. *0.8 m.,* **Stewart SP.** CG, fishing, swimming, DS, boating, FHP. *11.1 m.,* **Rogue River.** Gorgeous views up and down stream. *0.7 m.,* leaving Lost Creek Lake. *5.7 m.,* turnoff S to Mill Creek Falls.

* *0.3 m.,* "T". Turn L. *0.2 m.,* parking area for Mill Creek Falls. *700 yd.* trail to 173-ft.-high **Mill Creek Falls.** *200 yds.* on, spot where both Mill Creek and Barr Creek Falls are clearly seen. Barr Creek is as high as Mill Creek but it is trickly compared to the thunder and fullness of Mill creek, which cascades thru a slot in a vertical cliff.

1 m., Rogue River crossing. *0.2 m.,* Prospect Jct.

* *0.7 m.,* **Prospect,** geographically divided village with colorful general store. Town started 1882 with name of Deskins, changed 1885 to Prospect. In 1915 it had pop. 25 and boasted that its PS was "heated by electricity."

0.1 m., **Prospect FS Ranger Station.** *1.9 m.,* turnoff S to **Mill Creek FS CG** *(0.9 m.)* 2 m., turnoff N to **River Bridge FS CG** *(1 m.)* 2.2 m., Abbot Camp Jct.

* *1.6 m.,* **Woodruff Bridge FS PA.** *1 m.,* forks. Take L. *0.9 m.,* **Abbot Creek FS CG.**

4.6 m., on N, **Union Creek FS CG,** near Rogue River Gorge, thru which the white water stream plunges in youthful exuberance. *0.2 m.,* **Union Creek.** Small resort village. People who can't find a place to stay at Diamond Lake (or Crater Lake) sometimes wind up here. *0.2 m.,* on N, Rogue River Gorge Viewpoint. Most striking view of the Rogue until it reaches Hellgate.

1 m., jct., O 230.

O 230

O 230 is an attractive road waltzing thru lordly stands of fir and absent of store or station. The road is basically a short cut between the Rogue River Valley and Diamond Lake.

From jct., O 62:

5.3 m., **Rogue River,** here a fine, stalwart course, but as the traveler follows the water upstream the Rogue diminishes in width and depth. Pursuing it toward its source, the Rogue is seen in reverse. For the unfolding drama of the river, it would be better to start in the E and motor W.

0.8 m., turnoff R, or E, to National Creek Falls Trailhead.

* *0.9 m.,* Rogue River. The stream is still broad and deep and moves with

Mill Creek Falls

authority. *0.3 m.*, forks. Take L. *2.5 m.*, turnoff for National Creek Falls. *0.1 m.*, trailhead for falls. Approx. *800 yds.* of moderate trail to bottom of falls.

   National Creek Falls is really a jumble of cascades — about six plummeting slices of stream, three on either side of a moss-shouldered separation. Descending about 150 ft., National is far more exciting to view than many "straight line" taller falls. National is showy, evocative, energetic, bouncing down to a big-timber choked creek. The streamlets tumble over each other, seem to gush out of boulders like water fountains, split on the sharp edges of rocks and fly off in all directions. No matter how hot it is at the trailhead it is always cool at the bottom and rare is it to find people here. In many another state this would be a paramount attraction. But in W Oregon, National Creek Falls is scarcely known and even less heralded.

6.2 m., jct., Hamaker FS CG — Buck Canyon Trail

  * To L, or W, 0.4 m., **Muir Creek,** reminding the voyager of the inspiring summons of John Muir: "Look up and down and all around you." 0.5 m., Buck Creek Trail. (0.5 m., Muir Creek Trail.)

  * To R, or E: 0.6 m., jct. Turn R. 0.8 m., **Hamaker FS CG,** which has vacancies when other FS CGs have long been filled. Those who come here seem to form a loose-knit, secret clan whose one mission is to hush all news of Hamaker's goodness. CG split by Rogue River, here a small but crackling stream, bravado in its announcement of bigger things to come. CG is in what is about as near to a 100% Douglas fir forest as there is in the state. Rogue River trail here.

National Creek Falls

Phantom Ship seems to float on the waters of Crater Lake   *Courtesy State of Oregon*

* Return to Hamaker FS CG jct. Turn R. *3.1 m.,* on L, spur rd., tough, narrow pike that can get wretched. Not for low cars. *2.6 m.,* Lake West, modest fishing hole near Upper Rogue River Trail. Below lake is roadless **Boundary Springs Scenic Area,** bordering Crater Lake National Park. Coming here without a camera or easel is a sin of omission.

6.4 m., on R, or E, **Crater Rim Viewpoint,** also called Mazama Viewpoint: a board map shows where Mt. Mazama stood about 6,600 years ago and points to the mtns. that survive it — Llano Rock (8,046 ft.), Red Cone (7,372 ft.), Hillman Peak (8,046 ft.) and The Watchman (8,025 ft.).

Upper Rogue River Trail leads 9 m. to Hamaker FS CG. *1 m.,* summit — 5,415 ft. *1.2 m.,* turnoff L, or N, onto FS Rd. 3703, Three Lakes Rd.

* *7.8 m.,* FS Rd. 3703-200. Turn R. *2.8 m.,* Skookum Lake Trailhead, at road's end. *0.6 m.,* on trail that ought to be breeze for physically fit, **Skookum Lake.** In rocky open areas between stands of fir, pikas scamper for food and sociability. In late spring and early summer, wildflowers are thick in wetlands of lakeshore. Fishers come here for brook trout, non-fishers for the peace and wilderness feeling.

1.7 m., **Mt. Thielsen Viewpoint.** *0.2 m.,* jct., *Diamond Lake S Shore. (See O 138, preceding.) 0.2 m.,* O 138.

On O 62 — at jct., O 230:

O 62 — Continued

5.8 m., turnoff to **Huckleberry FS CG** *(3.8 m.) 2.3 m.,* Crater Lake Nat'l Park boundary. *8 m.,* Crater Lake Jct.

* *8 m.,* **Crater Lake Lodge,** across road from Crater Lake rim and starting point of Ranger-guided and bus tours around lake.

From 1853, when the lake was first seen by a white, until 1869, when two daring travelers reached Wizard Island and bestowed the present name upon the waters, this faerie ultramarine bowl was known as Deep Blue Lake, Mysterious Lake and Lake Majestic, all appropriate.

The lake, chaliced in the caldera of an extinct volcano, Mt. Mazama, which may have reached a height of 15,000 ft. before its suicidal eruption about 4700 B.C., is walled by cliffs whose majestic proportions and configurations would anywhere else be objects of wonderment. Combined with the lake, one of the deepest (1,932 ft.), bluest and most beautiful in the work, the total is so devastating upon the senses as to render silence more credible than words.

It is believed that until 1888 the lake had no fish. In that year William Gladstone Steel gently slipped 37 fingerlings into the lake, survivors of the 600 he scooped from the Rogue River and hauled in a bucket the long and tormenting way, pausing at every stream to freshen the water. Over the roughest terrain, he carried the bucket in his hand. He regarded it as something of a miracle that the few survivors had sufficient life to swim away, even if feebly. Crater Lake now has fish pop. of thousands.

The Park is more than the lake: it comprises baroque volcanic formations, the richly tinted "Pinnacles," velvety meadows and dreamy marshes. More than 570 species of plants and 175 species of birds have been recorded here. Look for the red, yellow, and black flair of the western tanager; listen for the silvery tones of the hermit thrush. Look down from the 7,100-ft. elev. of the W rim to ponderosa and lodgepole pine; look up to mountain hemlock. Sharing the park with the ephemeral tourists are black bears, coyotes, red foxes, elk, mule deer, long-tailed weasels and a host of other mammals. John Muir wrote: "A thousand wonders are calling."

The most popular way to see the lake and the park is to take the 33 m. Rim Dr., which has wayside exhibits and overlooks. Next most popular: boat trips, which include talks by Park Rangers.

There are nature trails at Castle Crest Wildflower Garden and near Mazama CG as well as at Godfrey Glen. The park has 65 m. of trails, including 26 m. of Pacific Crest Trail, which crosses the park. A 1.7 m., trail leads

Pinnacles along Annie Creek near south entrance to Crater Lake National Park

Courtesy State of Oregon

along the rim wall to 8,060 ft. Garfield Peak; an 0.8 m. trail on the W side of the rim leads to 8,025 ft. The Watchman.

Although Rim Drive is closed from mid-October to about July, the park is open all year, with entrance being via O 62, W and S. Heavy snowfall (often upwards of 40 ft.) make for fine cross-country skiing. At the lodge, the cafeteria is open during the winter but from autumn on there is no tourist housing.

From Crater Lake Jct.:

1 m., on N, **Godfrey Glen Geological Marker.** Awesome view of canyon, looking down to Annie Creek, which has cut a gap thru volcanic materials deposited by Mt. Mazama. O 62 parallels a deep and richly-covered chasm as it moves E from the lodge jct. There are several viewpoints — and lots of informal overlooks. But be cautious.

8.7 m., leaving Crater Lake Nat'l Park. *3.7 m.*, on N, pictograph of Mt. Mazama and the mtns. around it. *0.5 m.*, forks.

* Straight off O 62: *1.6 m.*, "T". Turn L. *0.1 m.*, turn L. *0.2 m.*, **Kimball SP.** Primitive camp sites in pine and fir. Fishing. No water, though SP at headwater of deep blue, transparent Wood River.

2.2 m., **Ft. Klamath,** refreshing "cow town" with minimum but pleasant tourist facilities. **Ft. Klamath Community Methodist Church,** built 1912, only church in Wood River Valley, has the curious amalgam of Indian-Christian architecture. Not too many men are seen in Ft. Klamath come winter; they move with their stock to Calif., where the feeding is better. Last light in "business district" goes off at 10 p.m., when cafe closes. Until 6 a.m., Ft. Klamath seems deserted. But "downtown" is safe. No one here can remember the last time anyone was mugged on "main street", which is O 62. And all thru the night the sweet Wood River, Central Oregon's Afton, flows humming as in a dream.

* Turn R, or W, at gas station (Nicholson Rd.) *2.5 m.*, Hackler Rd. On SE corner, remains of 19th century schoolhouse, waiting to be preserved or decently buried.

* S on Weed Rd. to Seven Mile Rd. Turn toward Rocky Point and Lake of the Woods. Just beyond Forestry sign, at wide turnout on L side of road, park and take trail down bank to **Mares Egg Spring,** one of few places on Earth where are found the rare biological, botanic Nostoc Algae, or Mares Eggs. What looks like seaweed-colored cobblestones at bottom of spring are Mares Eggs. Please do not in any way disturb this fragile jewel. Vandalism anywhere is a crime; here it is an outrage screaming to the heavens.

0.5 m., crossing of Wood River. *0.7 m.*, **Ft. Klamath Cemetery.** First person buried here was soldier in 1863. *0.3 m.*, Ft. Klamath Historical Marker, stating fort est. 1863, abandoned 1889.

0.2 m., site of Ft. Klamath, now **Klamath CP.** Museum and old post jail. Here at the fort, on Oct. 3, 1873, were hanged Captain Jack and three other leaders of the besieged Indians in the so-called Modoc War. (For more on the Modoc War, the trial at the fort, the executions, and the disposal of Capt. Jack's body, see "Two Apart: Winema and Captain Jack" in author's *Tracking Down Oregon*.)

3.8 m., turnoff N to **Klamath Fish Hatchery.**

* *0.5 m.*, hatchery, on Crooked Creek, tributary of Wood River. Raise

Graves of executed Modocs at Ft. Klamath

mainly trout — cutthroat, brook and rainbow. Output is about 3 million fish a year.

1.9 m., on R, or E, **Klamath Agency.** Now privately owned, this site surely ought to be an historical SP. Most of the old bldgs. of the agency, HQ for Indian Reservation, stand, and seem in good condition. One of the finest "Old West" tintypes in state.

1.3 m., Chiloquin-Agency Lake Jct.

* Turn R, or E. *0.2 m.,* forks. Take L. *0.8 m.,* **Petric CP.** BL to channel leading to Agency Lake. *1.7 m.,* **Agency Lake,** the N arm of Upper Klamath Lake. A shallow lake, it is noted for its rainbow and brown trout and for its duck hunting. One would think the lake lonely but there are houses all along this shore.

* Turn L, or W. *4.6 m.,* **Chiloquin,** now HQ of the reborn Klamath tribe. A poor-looking, dismal town, Chiloquin, at elev. more than 4,000 ft., is bitter cold in winter, stultifying in summer.

From Chiloquin-Agency Lake Jct.:

5.5 m., jct., US 97.

(To N, *7.7 m.,* **Collier Memorial SP** — open air logging museum of early timber days.)

(To S, *6 m.,* **Modoc Point.** It was from here that the oppressed Modocs, consigned to land alien to them, began their return to Lost River, SE of Klamath Falls. This "insurrectionary" action brought on the "Modoc War" of 1872-78, fought in what is now Lava Beds Nat'l Mon. of N Calif. The leaders of the small band were hanged at Old Ft. Klamath.

(Just below Modoc Point, US 97 swings around E shore of **Upper Klamath**

Pelicans on Upper Klamath Lake   *Courtesy State of Oregon*

Lake, remnant of ancient inland sea and 2d largest body of fresh water W of the Rockies. Great flocks of geese and ducks made the lake home each autumn before continuing S on their annual migration. Among the many other species of waterfowl which frequent Upper Klamath are the huge-beaked, snow-white pelicans, protected by law.)

(*17 m., Klamath Falls.*)

O 140 — O 62 to Klamath Falls

This is the "scenic flyway" from Medford and much of the Rogue River Valley to Klamath Falls and Central Oregon. The route is swift, unhindered, and roads peeling off it lead to places of history, recreation, and enchantment.

From Medford, N on Crater Lake Hwy., O 62:

5.3 m., Central Point Jct.

    * *2.5 m.,* turn R. *1.2 m.,* city center **Central Point.**

2.4 m., jct., O 140.

Turn onto O 140.

3.2 m., Antelope Rd. At or near here was **Wellen,** homesteader settlement which in 1915 had pop of 150 and PS. No trace.

    * *0.8 m.,* turnoff to Agate Lake. *0.8 m.,* **Agate Lake,** shallow basin created by small dam. BL.

    * Return to turnoff to Agate Lake. Turn R. *0.7 m.,* forks. Straight on Yankee Creek Rd. *0.4 m.,* on L, site of **Antelope Creek CB,** spanning Antelope Creek: built 1922 at length of 58 ft. In late summer of 1987, it was moved to Little Butte Creek at Eagle Point.

    * Return to forks. Turn L onto Antelope Rd. This is a lonesome, true backcountry pike, immersed in silence and lost dreams. When the century was young, the land was more peopled. *9.7 m.,* on R, **Little Grizzly Peak.** To L, uphill, was first **Climax School.** At one time, its enrollment was more than 30. Site marked beginning of Climax area, which spread S to last place of settlement. Also L, uphill, **Climax Cemetery** (1890). Legend states that graves of three suicides are here. According to a local oldtimer and amateur historian, "John B. Wyland was in love with Dossie Worlow. John went east on a trip. When he returned, he found that his younger brother James had married — or was to marry — Dossie. There was a quarrel and James was to of hung himself in the barn. Then Dossie was to of hung herself. Then John took his life."

Another version of the grim tale was penned by Climax native Bill Holman on July 4, 1973, when he was in his 80s. Jim Wyland, he wrote, was a sheepherder, the best in the county. The Worlow girl, whose name Holman spelled as Jasckia, was Jim's lady friend. "He had been gone for a long time, shearing sheep. He came home, said to his dad, I am going to see my girl. His dad was worried as he knew the condition the girl was in. No one thought Jim had done it. He didn't stay long, came back home, said to his dad, there is some deer on the hill, I am going to take my gun, see if I can get one. He went up stairs, left his money and a note on the bureau what his intention was. First shot he grazed his head, next shot blowed his head off. The girl decided she had enough of it, so she goes out to the barn, stands on a box, ties a rope to a rafter, slips the end around her neck, kicks the box out, hung herself, the baby was never born."

    * *0.5 m.,* on R, site of 2d Climax School. *1.6 m.,* farmhouse; all that remains of **Climax** PO (1891–1933).

First settled in the early 1870s, about 20 homesteads rambled along upper Antelope Creek Valley when John Wyland, one of the cemetery suicides, circulated petition for PO. Every man and woman in the area signed, prompting Wyland to boast that his petition campaign had been a "tea-total landslide," in short, as he put it, "the climax" of his efforts. Hence the name. First PO held in home of Jacob and Mary Worlow, parents of the tragic Dossie. Climax PO was in at least six different locations but farmhouse, long known as the Wertz Place, is considered definitive. At least a sign, reading CLIMAX, is at the house. Which makes sense, since this is site of Worlow home.

What was Climax faces the back side of rugged 5,922-ft. Grizzly Peak. Into the present century, homesteaders traveled the rough 11 m. trace down the face of Grizzly Peak into Ashland, driving cattle and hauling farm produce, lumber, shakes and poles to the settlers below. That road has all but been obliterated.

Nevah Clifford, who "used to ride horseback from Eagle Point in my young teenage days," moved to the Climax area as a young bride in 1916 and lived there three years. She recalled "lot of rattlesnakes, deer, bobcats, and bear." Almost seven decades later, she returned and wrote: "But oh, it's so beautiful to go up in the mountains, so peaceful and all." Like many of the early Climax settlers, Nevah Clifford was proud of her pioneer heritage: "My grandparents came to the Oregon Territory in 1853 with a covered wagon

Site of Climax

train, 60 wagons. It was called the Preacher Wagon Train because there were so many preachers with this group."

*0.8 m., end of Antelope Rd., at cut-out-of-the-woods home of contemporary pioneer. Back in the trees, on overgrown lands of 19th century homesteaders, are trailer houses and cabins of the get-away-from-it-all comers. In 1966 Mabel Wertz, of the prominent pioneer Wertz family, told Ashland historian Marjorie O'Harra: "The cycle is almost complete. People are beginning once more to think of moving out where they can have the advantages of country living and recreation. They are beginning to realize what we have know all along, that this is God's Country:"

On O 140, at Antelope Rd.:

4.5 m., Eagle Point Jct. At corner is Brownsboro Tavern, at site of old **Brownsboro,** settled in early 1850s on Little Butte Creek. First PO, est. 1873, called Brownsborough; changed to Brownsboro in 1892. In 1915, settlement had pop. 50, PS, daily stage to Central Point, and was noted for breeding of high class stock, poultry raising, fruit growing.

* *4.7 m.,* historic **Butte Creek Mill.** Next to it, **Oregon General Store Museum;** next to that, old school bldg. *0.2 m.,* downtown Eagle Point.

4.7 m., Lake Creek Jct.

* Turn R. *0.1 m.,* forks. Take R. *1.4 m.,* **Lake Creek.** Store. PO est. 1886; name changed to Lakecreek in 1894; long gone. In 1915, burg had 30 pop., daily stage to Eagle Point. Across rd. is venerable community hall, type homesteaders built for varied get-togethers. Continue S. Pike passes several picturesque ranch houses, probably dating to 1890s. *3.5 m.,* Lost Creek Rd., jct. at bridge. Turn R. *0.5 m.,* **Lost Creek CB.** Locals say Lost Creek Bridge built about 1874, with covered part added in early 1900s. They assert it is the oldest CB in Oregon as well as having shortest span. CB researchers agree Lost Creek is shortest of all Oregon CBs but maintain that CB was built in 1919, at length of 39 ft. The 2nd Sat. of each May bridge lovers gather to repair CB and clean the area. At bridge is **Walch Memorial Wayside.**

* Return to jct. at uncovered bridge. Turn R. 8.7 m., fork. Take R. Cross bridge. *0.5 m.,* shallow turnout at L of curve going uphill. Unmarked trail curls *350 yds.* thru thick woods to small waterfall. **Dead Indian Soda Springs** emerges from rock sweet, pure and tingly, an elixir for the weary. Apart from the soda springs, S Fork of Little Butte Creek is delightful calendar art scene, narrowing into ripples and cascades and then compressing to squeeze thru stone trough. Bubbly spring rock is on other side of trough. Early homesteaders wagoned here on 4th of July to camp for week. Oldtimers still come here to collect water for arthritis and other ailments. One goes to Crater Lake or a state park or a well-trod hiking trail and then wonders, Where can I find solitude? Well, there are hundreds of such places in W Oregon; Dead Indian Soda Springs is only one of them.

15.9 m., turnoff to North Fork CG.

Lost Creek Bridge

     * 0.5 m., **North Fork FS CG,** on N Fork of Little Butte Creek. S of CG are high lava piles.

  0.2 m., turnoff to Willow Lake and Butte Falls.

     * 8.9 m., turn R onto FS Rd. (*10 m.,* **Parker Meadows CG,** in Medford Watershed.) *0.3 m.,* turnoff R onto Parker Meadows Rd. (*0.3 m.,* **Whisky Springs FS CG.** *1 m.,* marker dedicated to Old Military Road., Jacksonville to Ft. Klamath 1863–1909. *0.2 m.,* **Fourbit Ford FS CG.**) *1.7 m.,* turnoff to Willow Lake Rec. Area. (*1.5 m.,* **Willow Lake Resort,** CG, PA, beach, BL). *6.9 m.,* **Butte Falls Hatchery.** *0.9 m.,* **Butte Falls.** Only town in state enclosed by cattle guards. Statue of logger at entrance to city park defines economy of area.

0.6 m., turnoff to Rye Spring (*1.9 m.*). Another road sign that can be construed as deceptive. In the words of a logger, "There ain't a lot of nothin' there." Just a patch in the woods. Hunters know it best. Deer, beware!

  0.7 m., turnoff to Dee Springs CG and Fish Lake.

     * 0.4 m., jct. Turn R for Doe Point. *0.2 m.,* CG, PA. Return to jct. Turn R. *0.5 m.,* forks. To R, *0.1 m.,* **Fish Lake CG.** *0.1 m.,* boat launch on Fish Lake. To L, *0.1 m.,* Fish Lake Resort and Marina. **Fish Lake** is one more watery jewel in the Cascades, a zesty blue basin whose surface is constantly vacuumed by breeze. There are 10 lakes in Oregon called Fish and this one, at

elev. of almost 4,800 ft., is one of the prettiest. Not every Fish Lake deserves the appelation but this one lives up to its reputation.

0.6 m., Fish Lake jct.

* *0.1 m.,* jct. Turn R for Doe Point CG. *0.1 m.,* turn L. *0.1 m.,* **Doe Point CG,** PA. Return to jct. Turn R. *0.5 m.,* forks. To R, *0.1 m.,* **Fish Lake CG.** *0.1 m.,* Fish Lake BL. To L, Fish Lake Resort and Marina.

0.7 m., South Fish Lake Jct.

* That's what the hwy. marker reads. But road doesn't go to Fish Lake on public lane. However, 0.5 m. are lava outcropping which tell a little about formation of this land.

0.4 m., on S, minor lava beds which at first glance, at least, seem out of place in this drenched green landscape. *1 m.,* on N, Pacific Crest Trail. *0.7 m.,* summit — 5,105 ft. *2.4 m.,* turnoff to Fourmile Lake.

* *5.8 m., 5,444-elev.* **Fourmile** (aka Four Mile) Lake, 900-acre recreational gem created by dam. Resort, FS CG. Lake reflects dome of 9,495-ft. Mt. McLoughlin, the great beacon in these parts. Bill Hanley, the sage of Harney County, whose father had a cattle ranch up Butte Creek in the Cascades, described the mtn. as looking "like old John McLoughlin, always a white head, white hair streaming down his shoulders." No one has put it better. Fourmile Lake area is dotted by small lakes and ponds: Lilly, Badger, Woodpecker, Aphis, Clovis, Wolf, Malice, Bernice, Janice, Summit, Mirror,

Old Military Road Marker

Square, and Norris, to name some. And let there be no neglecting Bull Swamp. Some of the little lakes and ponds appear created by Paul Bunyan splitting out a wad of blue tobacco juice, but others are big enough to put a rowboat in and take a few tugs at the oars before reaching the opposite shore. Fourmile Lake is regarded as off-the-beaten-path by on-the-beaten-pathers but is in reality the jumpoff point to truer wilderness purity. FS twists thru saucy woods to Cold Springs, which is what name says.

0.6 m., jct., Lake of the Woods Resort.

   * *0.2 m.,* Rainbow Bay. Resort, PA, BL on **Lake of the Woods,** one of fairest of Oregon's Cascade lakes — 1,146 acres in size at elev. 4,949 ft., max, depth, 55 ft.; ave. depth, 27 ft. In background hovers Mt. McLoughlin looking down with concerned brow and long nose.

0.4 m., jct. Lake of the Woods.

   * *0.6 m.,* **Aspen Point Rec. Area,** CG, PA, water sports. At or near here was short-lived **Lake of the Woods** PO (1930–1931). Lake was named in 1870 by Capt. Oliver Cromwell Applegate of famous Applegate family. Oddly, utter banality of name has take on grace of Tennysonian poetry as trees have been felled and lake commercialized.

Mt. McLoughlin above Fish Lake   *Courtesy State of Oregon*

1.2 m., **Great Meadow Snowplay Area** — for winter sports. *0.2 m.,* jct., Dead Indian Rd. (See *Dead Indian Rd.,* immediately following.) *3.2 m.,* turnoff to Cold Springs.

* *10.8 m.,* **Cold Springs CG.** From here trails attuned to pace of moderate hikers poke into 20,000 acre Sky Lakes Area, undulating mile-high-plus plateau creviced with shower of lake and ponds bearing such folksy names as Trapper, Dwarf, Liza, Sonja, Puck, Mosquito, Natasha, and Heavenly. Lakes are as small as three acres and as large as 20 and almost all are fish-good. *2 m.,* on S, Varney Creek Trail. *0.4 m.,* jct. Ft. Klamath.

* *23.7 m.,* thru **Upper Klamath Natural Wildlife Refuge,** Ft. Klamath. (See O 62, immediately preceding.)

0.7 m., Rocky Point Jct. (on S is entrance to site of Tomahawk Ski Area.)

* N to resort area on Pelican Bay of Upper Klamath Lake. *2.5 m.,* **Harriman Springs Resort** (Marina). Built 1906 and long associated with RR tycoon E. H. Harriman. Lodge burned in 1942, present lodge put up 1953. Oldest cabin still called "Teddy's Cabin" because, says folklore, Theodore Roosevelt stayed in it. Among summers regulars at tavern are some of most outrageous and delightful tall story tellers in county. *0.8.,* **White Pelican Lodge,** built as Point Comfort early in century. Locals say inn was famous for its "galloping goats," euphemism for brothel. *0.4 m.,* **Rocky Point Resort,** on craggy Rocky Point of Pelican Bay. Pelican PO lasted from 1888 to 1907. Next PO here was Recreation, for Recreation Creek. It held out from 1913 to 1924, when name was changed to Pelican Bay, then Rocky Point. No more. *4.5 m.,* **Maline Springs FS CG.** *3.2 m.,* **Crystal Springs FS CG.**

From Rocky Point Jct. on O 140:

The road to Klamath Falls is swift and refreshing. It runs past cattle-filled meadowlands, thru pine woods, and often within sight of Upper Klamath Lake and its rich variety of waterfowl.

2 m., turnoff E to site of Odessa.

* *0.5 m.,* where, on Odessa Creek, **Odessa** stood. Started in 1890s as resort hotel and Indian trading post. Latter structure survives. PO 1902–19.

0.7 m., on E, turnoff for Odessa Creek FS CG.

* *0.9 m.,* CG. BL on Odessa Creek, which resembles a winding lake more than it does a creek. Rarely used and alive with birdlife, especially kingfishers. Deer often come close to CG.

0.5 m., turnoff to Varney Creek (4 m.) and **Mountain Lake Wilderness Area** (5 m.).

* Varney Creek Trail dips into the Wilderness, which is roadless. (This FS rd. crosses Varney Creek on its way toward Lake of the Woods.) The 7,000-ft. plus Wilderness has some lovely lakes, particularly Storm, Harriette, Mystic, Echo, and Avalanche. Mountain lakes are not recommended for those for whom roughing it is new, but to the initiated they are high romance.

3.9 m., on E, turnoff to Eagle Ridge CP.

  * This is quite a small adventure and should not be attempted in haste or on senile tires. *2 m.* turn L. *1. 3 m.,* forks. Take L. *2 m.,* **Eagle Ridge CP,** on Upper Klamath Lake. PA. Excellent view of lake enveloped by low, contouring pine hills. Continue *1.8 m.,* to end of trace, taking either fork. Walk past shell of bldg. and foundation that was **Eagle Ridge Hotel,** mineral spa early in century. Just L of foundation is outhouse that provided sanitary facilities for hotel. Continue to lake and follow edge of it 100 yds. to hot springs, now sedgy and dilapidated. In the resort's prime years, hundreds came in season. Today even the curious are rare. You can have the place all to yourself days at a time. But keep an eye on small children; the cliffs are steep. *19 m.,* downtown Klamath Falls.

Dead Indian Road
Ashland to O 140

  Despite the insensitivity of the name — one would think it had been changed by now — the road is invigorating, zooming thru green highlands still distant (or seemingly so) from urban touch. Prior to the construction of O 140 it was the most popular commercial road from the Rogue River Valley to Klamath Falls; today its primary use from late spring to mid-autumn is related to recreation.

  The road begins as a turnoff from O 66, *2 m.* of Ashland.

Remnant of Eagle Ridge Hot Springs

Howard Prairie Reservoir

Courtesy State of Oregon

6.8 m., on L, or N, Shale City Rd.

    * 4.8 m., site of **Shale City,** which was not by any stretch of the imagination ever a city. Southern Oregon historian Marjorie O'Harra described it as "an early 1900 project to refine oil from shale rock . . . At one time a black oil-like substance taken from this rock was bottled and distributed as a cure-all." Approx. 4 m. beyond this site is Climax, but the road is passable only for 4-wheel drives and motor bikes — and then with some difficulty.

10.4 m, Howard Prairie Rd.

    * 0.7 m., entrance to Lindsay Ranch — oldtime spread. *1.3 m.,* Grizzly CP. CG, PA, BR on **Howard Prairie Lake,** in park-like pine woods. The 6-m.-long, 4,500 ft. elev. lake is a sailboater's fancy; regattas held here in summer. Water skiers and swimmers find equal satisfaction with the water; fishers sing the praises of rainbow trout and catfish catches. *1.4 m.,* turnoff L *(0.4 m.,* Howard Prairie Resort & Howard Prairie Rec. Area.) *7.3 m.,* **Hyatt Lake BLM CG.**

1 m., site of **Lilyglen,** named for wild mtn. lilies that sunlit the meadows. PO 1904–1909. In 1915 Lilyglen was a stop on the tri-weekly stage to Ashland and was

Possible site of Swastika

recognized regionally for its sheep and goat raising. No more. Only old barn remains. Site now CP. CG, PA. Horse folks rendezvous to ride their mounts over trails here.

1.1 m., site of **Deadwood.** Log shack on N side of rd. is sole survivor of what may have been PO of **Swastika** from Oct. 10, 1911, to Sept. 15, 1912. When PO was moved here it could not be called Deadwood because there was PO with that name in Lane County. So settlers called the place Deadwood and got their mail at Swastika — same place.

2.2 m., possible site of first Swastika PO. It was given the name because cattle brand of postmaster Clayton E. Burton, native of Minnesota, was shape of swastika. When PO application was approved, a mail station had to be found. In 1969, Burton's sister, Luella Applegate, who lived in the Burton house, recalled: "We had a half dozen hens. We ate them in order to use the new henhouse for a post office." Swastika PO est. Dec. 11, 1909. Mail was brought up from Ashland, about 35 m. away, by local homesteaders, by semi-weekly mail stage, and, the 2d year, by a young man hired to make mail trip once a week. In summer of 1911 this PO was closed, moved W, and George W. Jones was named to take Burton's place as postmaster. A student of the area said of this Swastika, "There is a beautiful view of Mt. McLoughlin from the remaining shed down a long meadow." This site would fit the description. So here may have stood the now most unusually named PO in state. But back in the early 1900s nobody thought of it that way.

1.3 m., Forest Route 37.

    * (*7 m.*, O 140; *9 m.*, Fish Lake.)

6.8 m., Keno Access Rd.

21.6 m., thru lonely and rather mundane-looking 2d-growth pine, O 66.
5.5 m., turnoff to **Sunset FS CG.**

* *0.4 m.*, CG, BL on Lake of the Woods. One of the fairest bodies of water in the Cascades, Lake of the Woods, looking up to the always impressive Mt. McLoughlin, is a thing of beauty for all seasons. Recreationally, it is one of the most popular lakes in S Oregon, and for good reasons; it is reachable by excellent roads and, however many people are here, gives the feeling of being away from it all.

0.9 m., jct., Lake of the Woods.

* *0.3 m.*, turn L. *0.3 m.*, Lake of the Woods Resort.
1.5 m., O 140. (See *O 140*, immediately preceding.)

Oregon 66
Ashland to Klamath Falls

Oregon 66, traditionally known as the Green Springs Road, is the oldest, crookedest and least-used highway in Southern Oregon across the Cascades. Still, it has great beauty, particularly in its western half, where mountain vistas are enormously dazzling, and along its way are portals opening to recreational streams, lakes, and woods. There is no point using this road for speed, but for adventure and history, it is an excellent pike:

From Ashland:

2 m., jct., Dead Indian Road. (See immediately preceding.) *2.6 m.*, jct., Emigrant Lake.

* *0.5 m.*, **Emigrant Lake Rec. Area.** CG. Restful, but nothing spectacular.

1.9 m., jct., Old Siskiyou Hwy. (Old Hwy. 99).

* *0.4 m.*, on R, 2-story yellow house, built 1859; for many years was prominent stage coach stop, first stage coach inn this side of Siskiyous. **Barron PO** here 1875–1910. *0.5 m.*, on L, 1860-built 2-story house, constructed by brother of man who put up stage coach inn. *2.6 m.*, bridge. (*0.2 m.*, R, at siding, was **Steinman,** RR station with PO opened 3/2/1892, and of relatively short life. PO was only one in Oregon, and probably the nation, named for a pawnbroker.) *3.3 m.*, end of road at hwy. "T". Cross hwy. to dirt road. Park here. Walk *0.1 m.*, up dirt road to RR tracks. Turn L. Walk *0.1 m.* to RR tunnel. Here, on Oct. 11, 1923 took place only important train robbery attempt in Oregon history.

* From parking spot, turn R at "T". *0.7 m.*, Mt. Ashland-Colestin Jct., at 4,310-ft. Siskiyou Summit. Turn R. *1.3 m.*, turn L down Colestin Rd. *3.4 m.*, site of what was once spa of Colestin. Return to Colestin Jct. Turn W. *7.5 m.*, **Mt. Ashland Ski Lodge.**

(For details of attempted train robbery, naming of Siskiyou Mtns. and history of Colestin, see *The Great Heartland, 0 99, S of Ashland.*)

From jct., 0 66 and Siskiyou Hwy. (Old 99):

1.3 m., **Sanger Wayside,** on Emigrant Lake. *1.4 m.,* on S, Buckhorn Rd.

  * *0.7 m.,* on R, site of **Soda Springs,** also called Wagner Springs. An idyllic portrait of Wagner Soda Springs appeared in the Portland *World* of 7/2/1886: "There is a most fascinating charm about the spot — the gush of brawling waters — the sublime view of Ashland Butte rearing its snow covered head — the perfect seclusion of the place surrounded as it is by lofty mountains on all sides . . . A ride of two hours or less from Ashland bring us to the remote valley where the air is pure mountain, perfumed with the fragrance of variegated wild flowers and shrubs that grow in voluptuous profusion on the mountain sides. No harsher sound is heard than the coo of the turtle dove or the musical shrill of the lark piping its lilting notes to the bleating flocks that browse upon the mountain sides or rest under the shade of some ancient and expansive live oak tree. All render the springs a most delightful retreat to those in search of rest and recreation, or the recuperative powers of the water." The place was first a stage coach stop on the road between Ashland and Linkville (later Klamath Falls) and grew into a therapeutic spa, anchored by the 20-room Soda Springs House, described in travel literature as "a most delightful abode on the banks of Emigrant Creek." In addition, there was store, PO, dance hall, huge barns, a plant that bottled Siskiyou National Mineral Water and, of course, the soda springs, on Emigrant Creek, today across the road from where stood the resort hotel. In 1911, the hamlet folded and the property was turned to agriculture. A fire in Sept., 1926 destroyed all bldgs. except a barn. Today few people in the area know more than a few fragments about the history of this once-famous spa.

  7.1 m., summit, Green Springs Mtn. — 4,551 ft. *1.8 m.,* **Green Springs:** cafe, store.

Jct., Hyatt Res.

  * Turn L for Hyatt Lake. *3 m.,* forks. (L, Howard Prairie Lake, *6.2 m.;* Dead Indian Rd., *10.7 m.*) Go straight. *0.1 m.,* **Hyatt Lake Rec. Area.** CG, PA. *0.4 m.,* Hyatt Lake. BL. **Hyatt Lake** has distinction of looking far removed from urban centers, when it actually isn't, which is why it is patronized by so many people from the Rogue River Valley. Although only one peak, 6,113-ft. Table Mtn. nods down at it, and not a big nod, because the surface of the lake is 5,016 ft. above sea level, there is the illusion of many peaks facing it.

1.5 m., On L, or N, **Tub Springs SP** (aka Tubb Springs). PA Wayside. First whites may have been the Applegate Party, who passed this way in 1846, then built trail that was used as emigrant route to S Oregon in 1860s. Tubb Springs was named in 1868, same year wagon road was constructed by Jackson County. The road, which is reached by trail 150 yds. from hwy., was active until 1873. Many motorists pause here for cool, pure sip of drinking fountain water. Wayside smothered in pine scent, as is all this area.

2.1 m., **Lincoln,** which began life as tiny sawmill town and was named for Lincoln, N. H., where millowners had dwelled. In recent years, Lincoln has been the Oregon Extension of Trinity College of Deerfield, Ill., with fall classes. Part of its "campus" consists of bldgs. that had served as general store, offices, cookhouse and cabins of sawmill village in 1930s.

1 m., **Mountain View,** a casual spray of houses. A local resident said in 1985: "I was gone two years and when I came back there was lots of people here — maybe sixteen or twenty. Come back in a few years and you'll be surprised; we might even have a shopping center." Place has airport where light planes land when Rogue River Valley is fogged in. A lady said, "We had a pilot land and he was stuck here for two days. Of course, I fed him well." Plane landings average one per week.

1.1 m., **Pinehurst,** meaning pine woods, which describes location. As early as 1878 there was PO close by called Pioneer. It lasted until 1882, when homesteader who kept the mail in his cabin moved away. Next PO, opened 1886, moved here from Shake, and in 1911 had name changed to Pinehurst. The settlement has always looked big on maps of the area, simply because there was so much nothingness around it. In 1915, it had pop. 20 and PS. By 1940 the number was down to 10 — and no school. Today it may be zero, depending upon if anybody is occupying the lone house here. For some years, Pinehurst was known as the Greyhound bus supper stop on the Ashland-Klamath Falls run, but the inn, which was on N side of road, and where bus stopped, burned down quite a spell ago. All that remains today is rambling 2-story log house built about 1895, on S side of road.

The house was sometimes a hotel and restaurant but oldtimers in this neck of the woods remember it as a brothel. This may or may not be true. Folklore has often superseded reality as history and imagination that touches plausibility can take on the aura of fact. This much is certain: the brothel story is an integral part of backwood Oregon lore. From Curry County to the Wallowas and from Jordan Valley to Clatsop County, there are rumored — or sworn to have been — brothels in mining camps, logging camps, cow towns and in-betweens, particularly when picks, axes, and saddles were more numerous than men and men outnumbered women by a country mile.

1 m., purported site of **Shake,** originally a camping place on the S Oregon wagon road. The name comes from the hand-hewn pine "shakes", or shingles, used by early settlers to cover their homes. It is likely that a small mill for the manufacture of shakes existed here.

4.8 m., Parker Mtn. summit — 4,356 ft. *9.1 m.,* Hayden Mtn. summit — 4,695 ft. *4.8 m.,* approximate site of Wampus (PO 1908–11). **Wampus** has been described as a logger word to categorize a legendary monster of the woods or mtns., such as Sasquatch or Big Foot, but it is probably a fanciful interpretation of an Indian word. Pacific NW loggers had a penchant for taking Indian words and applying them to their own usage or lore. The white-bearded son of an early logger said of Wampus with a chuckle: "It was a good bunkhouse yarn, yes it was."

Still, is the "monster", known elsewhere as "The Abominable Snowman" or the "Yeti," completely concocted out of pure imagination? There is much international speculation and years of unrelenting research have gone into the quest. If the creature really exists, as logical a theory as any was advanced by Soviet scientist, Boris Porshnev. "It is not a 'snowman' at all, and not a 'man' in the traditional sense of the word either," he wrote. "Strictly speaking, the 'snowman' does not exist. It is a relict hominoid."

Explaining the concept, Prof. Porshnev declared in his monograph quoted in the book, *Enigma of Centuries.* "An anthropoid is so called because it looks like man. But what should we call creatures that have already 'separated themselves' from anthropoids? They are no longer apes, but not yet people: They are, so to speak, somewhere between the anthropoid apes and future man. I have in mind the early ape-men who walked on two legs and, in development terms, approached Stone Age man." (It must be added that his hypothesis touched off more heated debates.)

Turnoff S to John C. Boyle Dam.

   * *0.5 m.,* dam. Road leads one m. to **Topsy Rec. Site.** Good place to watch white pelicans, terns, and herons from May thru Aug.

1.2 m., Spencer Creek Jct.

   * *2.7 m.,* **Spencer Creek.** On E side of road was **Forest** (PO 1902-08), named for profuse and splendid stands of timber in area. They aren't that way any more. The road rivets thru cut-over and old-growth pine, with seldom a sound but nature. *12.1 m.,* **Surveyor BLM Rec. Site.** Few amenities but lots of clean air. *12.6 m.,* Dead Indian Rd.

0.5 m., turnoff to Topsy CG.

   * *0.8 m.,* **Topsy BLM CG.** on Klamath River.

At jct., 0 66 and turnoff to Topsy CG, historical marker tells of Applegate Trail, wagon roads and Pony Express trail in these parts. Klamath River first forded by whites 8 m. upstream on 10/4/1846. New fording found 0.5 m. N of historical marker on 10/11/1846. In 1868, Brown's Ferry est. here. River scene is one of singular beauty but rafters are not ecstatic about purity of the water.

5.4 m., **Keno Reservoir Rec. Area.** Here, too, white pelicans, terns and herons are seen from May thru Aug.

0.6 m., **Keno,** perhaps only PO in Oregon named for a bird-dog, which was, in turn, named for the card game. First PO (1876) here or near here called Whittle's Ferry. In 1878 name changed to Plevna. Keno PO born 1887. Keno is largest settlement between Ashland and Klamath Falls and makes Lincoln and Mountain View look like midgets. It actually has garage-station, store and cafe and is now treated as suburb of Klamath Falls, all the while maintaining its own craggy individuality that reflects its logging and farming heritage.

   Worden Jct.

* 0.5 m., on L, watercolor marsh that is artistically synonymous with dreamy plateau that extends into Calif. 7.2 m., US 97. N, 0.7 m., Worden, 24-hour cafe, truck stop, station.

12 m., downtown Klamath Falls.

If any city in Oregon typifies the imagery of the "Old West" as the center of wilderness violence, cattle rustling, vigilantes and Indian-white battles, it is surely **Klamath Falls,** traditionally called K Falls by its inhabitants. The camps of exploring parties were attacked by the Klamaths (Fremont lost three men in one such episode), immigrant trains were ambushed, cattle rustling was carried on as a wholesale business until the last of the outlaws was filled with lead, and the fiercely fought Modoc War was waged before there was a Klamath County. (See "Two Apart: Winema and Captain Jack" in author's *Tracking Down Oregon*.)

Klamath Falls was also a happy hunting ground for highwaymen. The most successful scored twice in one day. After holding up a N-bound stage he was about to take off when the S-bound stage came along. So he also robbed that before fleeing. (Tales of cached gold along Upper Klamath Lake were rife for the next two decades.)

Into the middle of the 20th century Klamath Falls maintained the image of a frontier town. The 1940-published *Oregon — End of the Trail* described the city then as a lot more exciting than it is now:

"The old West rubs elbows with the new in Klamath Falls. Typical survivors of the city's most colorful period, men and women who were a part of the pioneering and homesteading eras, linger here. Grizzled ranchers still sit at friendly poker games under the brighter lights of the new town. Sheepherders in from tending flocks on the lonely hills, Indians from the Klamath Reservation, and loggers from the deep woods, mingle freely, lending color to the modern business activity. Because of the many industrial establishments 'pay nights' (Saturday nights nearest the first and fifteenth of the month) are carnival-like periods. Great crowds of visitors, mill employees and townspeople, surge in and out of the stores spending the earnings of the previous fortnight. Stores and banks stay open until 10:30, and the moving-picture houses, dance halls and other recreational centers reap a large portion of the million-dollar pay roll before the night ends."

It was this nostalgia of the "Old West" that later elected and reelected as county sheriff Oregon's most colorful peace officer, Red Britton. (See "A Maverick Sheriff" in author's *A Touch of Oregon*.)

Although the atmosphere of Klamath Falls gives many visitors the feeling of being in an arid plateau town, the city is enveloped and pierced by water: Upper Klamath Lake, Link River (claimed by town boosters to be the shortest river in the world), Lake Ewauna and Klamath River. Upon all these except the Klamath River, and particularly Upper Klamath Lake, the huge-beaked, snow-white pelicans are numerous and formidable in spring and summer.

It was on the E bank of Link River, where that stream meets Lake Ewauna, that George Nurse, Ft. Klamath sutler, built a cabin in 1866, followed by a ferry (the strongest link between the rangelands of S-central Oregon and the Rogue River Valley) and a trading post. A year later about 100 immigrants joined Nurse in founding Linkville, which was changed to Klamath Falls in 1893.

Klamath Falls was late in developing. Not until the first decade of the 20th century did the RR come to town, to carry out the lumber and the crops produced thanks to the federal Klamath Basin Irrigation Project. By 1915 the city had a pop. of 4,200, 100 more than its elevation in ft., and it ran amuk in printer's ink, with 2 dailies and 2 weeklies.

From 1915 to 1940 the pop. increase was one long swell reaching more than 16,000 in 1940. Thereafter, despite annexation and the opening of Oregon Technical Institute, pop. slowed, and by 1980 was at approximately the same level as 1940. With lumber depressed, pop. further declined in the 1980s, with more people departing.

Long ago Klamath Falls became noted for its hot mineral springs, which have been used to heat public and private bldgs. But this geothermal bliss has not brightened the perception of the city held by many visitors, who see Klamath Falls as listless, dull, and, in general, about as uninviting as its climate most of the year.

Still, the city has far more to offer than many think. **Klamath County Museum,** 1451 Main, is well-stocked with memorabilia of area, including photos of

Val Brimmer Cabin

Western paintings in Favell Museum

Maude Baldwin, whose sharp eye and lens caught the early Klamath Falls vivid and unvarnished. One of the state's really creative photographers, she died at a relatively early age. Outside the old National Guard Armory where the museum has its home is the **Van Brimmer Cabin,** built 1864 on ranch W of Tulelake, Calif. and converted into fort during Modoc War of 1872–73. In 1880, window and fireplace were added and cabin served as residence until 1928. **Baldwin Hotel Museum,** 31 Main, turn-of-century inn, displays hollow Western brass beds, wood-burning stoves, early-day commodes, Quaker spinning wheel, 1820's mahogany sleigh bed, 17th-century cast-iron bed, cheval dressers, 1870s Alladin lamp — and more. (See "That Wonderful Baldwin Hotel" in *Tracking Down Oregon.*) Bldg. S of Baldwin and seemingly sharing common wall is narrowest bldg. in town, in county, maybe in state. Bldg. next S is, say oldtimers, oldest standing structure in KF. One block S, at Main and Conger, is site of first bldg. of Linkville, built by George Nurse, Linkville's first hotel keeper, postmaster and livery stable operator, in addition to ferryman and store keeper. Just S of plaque is bridge under which Link River flows into Lake Ewauna; platoons of pelicans are common sights here. (Across street, in Veterans Park, is old Southern Pacific engine.) A block S of bridge, and on same side, is **Favell Museum of Western Art and Artifacts,** the finest museum of its kind in the state and certainly one of the best of its kind in nation. Across street is **Klamath Art Museum,** where artists, who have studios in adjoining bldg., exhibit their paintings.

This Oregon, as we have said again and again, is a beautiful land, but it has suffered at the hands of the careless, callous and selfish, who in small or large ways have despoiled one square foot or many square miles. This we must never forget: the land is ours only temporarily: we keep it in trust for those who follow — if there is a time for following. To paraphrase Woody Guthrie:

> This land is your land, this land is my land;
> From the redwood forest to the Wallowa highland.
> From Jordan Valley to the Western Sea,
> This land belongs to you and me.

INDEX

Tillamook County), 170; Orth
(Jacksonville), 574; Palmateer (near
Currinsville), 355; Palmer (Dayton),
397; Palmer* (Portland), 264; Parrot
(Roseburg), 545; Peterson (near Mist),
137; Pittock* (Portland), 261, 279;
Porter (Shedd), 501; Rock Point (near
Rogue River), 565, 567; Rose Farm*
(Oregon City), 366, 446; Settlemier*
(Woodburn), 465; Shedden (near
McMinnville), 401; Smith Farm (near
Halsey), 502; Snipes (The Dalles), 602;
Stauffer-Will* (near Aurora), 299, 462;
Stevens (Springfield), 523; Straub (near
Salem), 484; Sweek (Tualatin), 383;
Tigard (Tigard), 385; Turner (Turner),
485, 638; Van Buren (Corvallis), 414;
Walker Hall (McMinnville), 155;
Waller Hall* (Salem), 477; Warren
(Warrenton), 11; Watson (Hoskins),
184; Whetstone (Medford), 573; White
(near Rogue River), 565, 567; Wilbur
(Wilbur), 541; William Case (near St.
Paul), 425; Winston (Winston), 547;
Woodward-Gellatley (Corvallis), 413;
Zorn (near St. Paul), 425
Hobsonville, 31
Hogem, 516
Hogg, T. Egonton, 57, 662, 664
Holladay, Ben, 17, 158, 456, 470, 525, 557
Holland, 237, 238
Holley, 511–512
Holman, Bill, 743
Holman, Frederick, 441
Holman, Joseph, 481
Hood, Admiral Samuel, 304
Hood Meadows, 331
Hood River, 325, 344, 592–594
Hooker, Joseph, 220, 557
Hoover, Herbert, 389, 390, 564, 733
Hopewell, 195, 396
Hopmere, 399, 433
Horsfall Dunes, 85–86
Horton, 212
Hoskins, 49, 184–185
Hot Springs:
    Austin, 340; Bagby, 339, 340; Belknap,
    691; Breitenbush, 341; Cougar, 690;
    Jackson, 579; Kah-nee-tah, 630;
    Umpqua, 725
Houlton, 133
Hubbard, 464
Hudson, 130
Hudson's Bay Company, 2, 57, 119, 134,
    196, 213, 221, 252, 267, 323, 406, 420,
    422, 423, 424, 436, 438, 450, 551, 582,
    600, 706
Hughes, Ellis, 296, 298, 449
Hugo, 561–562
Hullt, 380, 381
Hume, R.D., 108
Hunt, Wilson Price, 2, 119, 422, 469, 471
Hunter Creek, 109
Huntley, Carsena A., 542

Idanha, 643
Idleyld Park, 718
Inatuski, Shizue, 593
Independence, 187–188, 408
Indian Beach, 17, 19
Indian Chiefs:
    Billy Chinook, 632; Coboway, 16;
    Concomly, 1, 134; John, 102; Kaseneau,
    133; Paulina, 618, 670; Sam, 568, 730;
    Sochimo, 298; Wanaxha, 448
Indian Council Tree (Liberty), 652
Irvine, Margaret Hadley, 480
Irving, 518

Jacksonville, 92, 242, 251, 573–577
Jacoby, Andy, 545–546
Jacquith, W.W., 172
Jamestown, 211–212
Jasper, 683, 707
Jefferson, 488–490
Jennyopolis, 416
Jensen, Gertrude, 306
Jewell, 143, 149
Jewell Meadows Wildlife Area, 142
Jewett, Wilson, 79
John Day Fording, 611
John, James, 264
Johnson "Bohemia," 527
Johnson, William, 252, 293
Jones, Nathan B., 169–170
Jordan, 684
Junction City, 213, 516–517
June, 708

Kah-nee-ta, 627, 630
Kalmiopsis Wilderness, 114–116, 239, 240,
    262
Kansas City, 151, 154, 168, 292–293
Keasey, 137
Keil Family, 461, 462
Keil, Hugo, 461
Keil, Dr. Wilhelm, 299, 460–461
Keizer, 433, 474
Kelley, Hall Jackson, 162
Kellogg, 222
Kelso, 276, 621
Kelty, Oscar, 179, 400
Keno, 756
Kerby, 238–239
Kerns, S.F., 523
Kernville, 46, 47
Kesey, Ken, 213
King City, 388
King, Sid, 642
King Tuts Tomb, 347
Kings Valley, 47, 182, 184
Kingston, 639
Kinton, 386, 387
Kirk, Alexander, 506
Klamath Agency, 741
Klamath Falls, 756–759
Klondike, 608–609